Foundations and Functions of Theology as Universal Science

# European University Studies
Europäische Hochschulschriften
Publications Universitaires Européennes

**Series XXIII**
**Theology**
Reihe XXIII   Série XXIII
Theologie
Théologie

**Vol./Bd. 576**

**PETER LANG**
Frankfurt am Main · Berlin · Bern · New York · Paris · Wien

Mark William Worthing

# Foundations and Functions of Theology as Universal Science

## Theological Method and Apologetic Praxis in Wolfhart Pannenberg and Karl Rahner

PETER LANG
Europäischer Verlag der Wissenschaften

Die Deutsche Bibliothek - CIP-Einheitsaufnahme

Worthing, Mark William:

Foundations and functions of theology as universal science :
theological method and apologetic praxis in Wolfhart
Pannenberg and Karl Rahner / Mark William Worthing. -
Frankfurt am Main ; Berlin ; Bern ; New York ; Paris ; Wien :
Lang, 1996
   (European university studies : Series 23, Theology ;
   Vol. 576)
   Zugl.: München, Univ., Diss., 1994
   ISBN 3-631-30101-4

NE: Europäische Hochschulschriften / 23

BX
4827
.P3
W67
1996

D 19
ISSN 0721-3409
ISBN 3-631-30101-4
US-ISBN 0-8204-3177-X
© Peter Lang GmbH
Europäischer Verlag der Wissenschaften
Frankfurt am Main 1996
All rights reserved.

All parts of this publication are protected by copyright. Any
utilisation outside the strict limits of the copyright law, without
the permission of the publisher, is forbidden and liable to
prosecution. This applies in particular to reproductions,
translations, microfilming, and storage and processing in
electronic retrieval systems.

Printed in Germany 1 2 3  5 6 7

# Preface

In an age of information explosion, multi-culturalism, rapid technological advancement and global societies, the theological task of presenting the Christian faith in a manner that is both relevant and credible is more challenging than perhaps at any time since the pre-Constantinian era. A theology that claims to speak *about*, and in some real sense also *for* a God who is creator and sustainer of the world cannot afford to ignore the relevance of this God for any aspect of modern life and thought, nor, vice versa, of any aspects of modern life and thought for our understanding of this God. To do either would constitute an implicit denial of God as creator. Theology, as the 'science' of that God who created, sustains, and redeems the world, is therefore called to be a truly universal science in the sense that if it takes its own confession of God as creator seriously, then it must have the confidence to believe that it has something to say to all fields of scientific inquiry and religious thought and experience. It means as well, however, that it must also have the humility to recognise that all fields of scientific inquiry and all forms of religious thought and experience also have something to say to it.

In the later part of the 20th century no two Christian thinkers have done more to advance the case for theology's universality and to develop methodologies and an apologetic approach that take this universality into account than have Karl Rahner and Wolfhart Pannenberg. Both theologians, working respectively from the Roman Catholic and Lutheran theological traditions, have preformed an enormous service for a theology still coming to terms with the rapid intellectual, cultural, and religious changes of the modern world. The programs of both, which are examined in this present work, merit further study by anyone interested in the methodological foundations and apologetic praxis of Christian theology in the modern world.

This present work was submitted originally as a dissertation in summer semester 1994 to the Protestant faculty of theology at the University of Munich in partial fulfilment of the Doctor of Theology degree. The successful completion of the project was made possible by the assistance of several people. Many thanks are due first of all to my *Doktorvater*, Prof. Hans Schwarz, for much appreciated advice and guidance, not only with regard to my thesis project but in many other areas as well. Thanks also go to the second reader of my thesis, Prof. Jan Rohls, for several insightful suggestions which led to improvements in the text. I am also deeply indebted to Prof. Wolfhart Pannenberg for advice during various stages of the project and for the privilege of studying with him for two semesters prior to his retirement from the University of Munich. The chapters dealing with anthropology and the doctrine of God proved to be crucial for an understanding of the other parts of the work and were originally included as major chapters in their own right at the encouragement of Prof. Pannenberg. Frau Hildegaard Ferme, who assisted with various technical aspects of the production of the manuscript also deserves many thanks. Finally, Dr. Martin Rothgangel gave invaluable assistance and encouragement during the final stages of the completion of the thesis for which a mere word of thanks seems insufficient. I am additionally grateful to the staff of the Karl Rahner archive, Innsbruck, Austria, for access to their considerable collection and assistance in locating material, and to the Peter Lang Verlag for willingness to publish my work.

For the purposes of publication and on the advice of my thesis supervisor, all quotations from Pannenberg and Rahner within the main body of the text have been rendered into English, as well as most other foreign language quotations. It should be noted that throughout the thesis, unless otherwise noted, the translation of original German works are my own. In the case of the works of Pannenberg and Rahner, the location of quotations in the original German are indicated in each instance in brackets within the footnotes.

Finally, I wish to dedicate this book to my wife Kathaleen and my sons Geoffrey and Cedric. Their patience and support throughout the writing of the thesis have been constant and have contributed immeasurably to its completion.

Adelaide, South Australia                                      Lent, 1996

# Contents

Preface v
Abbreviations xiii

**Introduction** 3
0.1 Purpose and scope of study 3
0.2 Special problems in the comparison of Pannenberg and Rahner 4
0.3 Universality as unifying theme in thought of Pannenberg and Rahner 5
0.4 The organization of the study 7

## Part 1: Methodological Foundations of Theology as Universal Science

**Chapter 1:**
**W. Pannenberg: Concept and Method of Theology as Universal Science** 9

1.1 Question of the Scientific Nature of Theology in the History of Theology 9
    1.1.2 *Sapientia* or *scientia* 9
    1.1.3 Ernst Troeltsch and Adolf von Harnack 11
    1.1.4 Karl Barth and Heinrich Scholz 17
    1.1.5 Rudolf Bultmann 19
    1.1.6 T. F. Torrance and Gerhard Sauter 21
1.2 Pannenberg's Understanding of Science and the Criteria of a Science 25
    1.2.1 Theology as a human science 25
    1.2.2 Scholz's minimum requirements of a science 26
    1.2.2.1 The requirement of formal consistency 27
    1.2.2.2 The requirement of coherence 28
    1.2.2.3 The requirement of verifiability 29
    1.2.3 Preliminary evaluation of Pannenberg's conception of science 30
1.3 Theology as Universal Science 33
    1.3.1 The concept 'universal' 33
    1.3.2 Unitary knowledge, not unitary science 34
1.4 The Verifiability of Theological Statements 35
    1.4.1 Ludwig Wittgenstein and the demands of logical positivism 36
    1.4.2 Karl Popper and Thomas Kuhn 37
    1.4.3 Pannenberg's concept of 'verification' 39
    1.4.4 Verification and original or universal sin 42
    1.4.5 Verification and the resurrection of Jesus 43
    1.4.5.1 The resurrection appearances 45
    1.4.5.2 The empty tomb 47
1.5 Revelation as History and the Possibility of a Natural Knowledge of God 48
    1.5.1 Revelation as history as the indirect self-disclosure of God 48
    1.5.2 The universal character of history 51
    1.5.3 The Christ event as the proleptic end of history 53
    1.5.4 Implications for a natural knowledge of God 56

| | | |
|---|---|---|
| 1.6 | *Pannenberg and the Hermeneutical Task* | 57 |
| | 1.6.1 Foundations of Pannenberg's hermeneutics (Schleiermacher, Gadamer) | 57 |
| | 1.6.2 Hegel, hermeneutics, and universal history | 61 |
| | 1.6.3 Hermeneutics, relation of parts to the whole (Hegel, Dilthey, Habermas) | 62 |
| 1.7 | *Pannenberg's Theological Method: A Summary and Appraisal* | 66 |
| | 1.7.1 The classification of Pannenberg's theological method | 66 |
| | 1.7.2 The role of faith and the Holy Spirit (Paul Althaus' critique) | 68 |
| | 1.7.3 Pannenberg's method in the Protestant context: Innovation or synthesis? | 73 |

**Chapter 2:**
**K. Rahner: Transcendental Method and Intimations of a Philosophy of Science** 75

| | | |
|---|---|---|
| 2.1 | *Theology and Philosophy* | 75 |
| | 2.1.1 Unity of philosophy and theology | 76 |
| | 2.1.2 Philosophy as unthematic theology | 76 |
| | 2.1.3 Theology as thematic philosophy | 80 |
| | 2.1.4 Revelation as key to the distinction between theology and philosophy | 82 |
| 2.2 | *Transcendental Philosophy* | 85 |
| | 2.2.1 Immanuel Kant: Cognitive experience and the transcendental method | 85 |
| | 2.2.2 J. G. Fichte: Human knowing as striving toward the Infinite Absolute | 88 |
| | 2.2.3 Joseph Maréchal: God's existence as *a priori* condition of knowing | 89 |
| | 2.2.4 Martin Heidegger: Existential ontology | 91 |
| | 2.2.5 Rahner's estimation of transcendental philosophy | 92 |
| 2.3 | *Rahner and the Transcendental Method* | 93 |
| | 2.3.1 The transcendental anthropological method | 93 |
| | 2.3.1.1 *A priori* givenness and the pre-apprehension (*Vorgriff*) of being | 95 |
| | 2.3.1.2 The historical rootedness of transcendental experience | 97 |
| | 2.3.2 The transcendental method and the doctrine of the Trinity | 99 |
| | 2.3.3 The transcendental method as key to a unified science | 100 |
| | 2.3.4 "Transcendental" versus "metaphysical" | 102 |
| 2.4 | *The Concept of Revelation in Karl Rahner* | 104 |
| | 2.4.1 Universal revelation as transcendental determination of humanity | 104 |
| | 2.4.2 Revelation and transcendental experience | 105 |
| | 2.4.3 The self-revelation of God within history | 106 |
| 2.5 | *Karl Rahner's Hermeneutic* | 108 |
| | 2.5.1 Analogy and symbol | 108 |
| | 2.5.2 Eschatological hermeneutic | 111 |
| | 2.5.3 A transcendental hermeneutic | 114 |
| 2.6 | *Theology as Science and Theology among the Sciences* | 115 |
| | 2.6.1 Theology as a science in Roman Catholic theology | 115 |
| | 2.6.2 Intimations of a philosophy of science in Rahner | 117 |
| | 2.6.3 The problem of verification of theological statements | 122 |
| | 2.6.4 The ambivalence of the scientific character of theology | 126 |
| | 2.6.5 Theology as *reductio in mysterium* | 129 |
| | 2.6.6 Theology's place within the university | 130 |
| | 2.6.7 The universality of theology | 133 |

2.7  Rahner's Theological Method: A Summary and Appraisal                                136
   2.7.1 A summary of Rahner's method                                                       136
   2.7.2 Rahner's method in the context of Roman Catholic theology                          137
   2.7.3 Rahner and Pannenberg: A comparison of theological methods                         139

**Part 2: Theological Foundations of Theology as Universal Science**

**Chapter 3: The Anthropological Roots of Theology's Universality**                         141

3.1  Karl Rahner: The transcendence of finite humanity                                      141
   3.1.1 *Prolegomena to Rahner's theological anthropology*                                 141
      3.1.1.1 Theological anthropology and profane anthropologies                           141
      3.1.1.2 Locating theological anthropology within the theological enterprise           144
   3.1.2 *Humans as 'hearers of the word'*                                                  148
      3.1.2.1 The hearer as 'spirit in the world'                                            148
      3.1.2.2 Transcendentality of the hearers and the universal offer of grace             151
      3.1.2.3 The freedom of the hearer                                                     152
      3.1.2.4 The historicalness of the hearer and the unity of humanity                    155
      3.1.2.5 Creatureliness and the openness to God                                        157
   3.1.3 *Monogenism and original sin*                                                      158
      3.1.3.1 Monogenism and the unity of the human race                                    158
      3.1.3.2 The universality of freedom and of "original sin"                             162
   3.1.4 *Karl Rahner's anthropo-optimism: A Protestant critique*                           167

3.2. Wolfhart Pannenberg: The universality of human experience                              172
   3.2.1 *Prolegomena to Pannenberg's anthropology*                                         173
      3.2.1.1 History as the context of anthropology                                        173
      3.2.1.2 Theological anthropology and profane anthropologies                           174
   3.2.2 *Openness to the world and to God*                                                 178
      3.2.2.1 The human person as open to the world                                         178
         3.2.2.1.1 World-openness as *imago dei* (Herder)                                   180
         3.2.2.2 Openness to God as anthropological argument for God's existence?           184
   3.2.3 *The unity of humanity and universal experience*                                   189
      3.2.3.1 The universal experience of freedom                                           189
      3.2.3.2 Original sin and the universal experience of sin                              191
      3.2.3.3 The universal experience of death                                             193

3.3  *Excursus: Anthropology and Christology in Pannenberg and Rahner*                      195
   3.3.1 Rahner: Christology as beginning and end of anthropology                           196
   3.3.2 Pannenberg: Jesus Christ as founder of a 'new humanity'                            198
   3.3.3 The universal significance of Jesus Christ                                         199

3.4  *Summary and conclusions*                                                              203
   3.4.1 Pannenberg and Rahner: Starting with the human                                     203

## Chapter 4: God as Foundation of Theology's Universality 205

4.1 Wolfhart Pannenberg: God as All-Determining Reality 205
   4.1.1 *The unity of God* 206
      4.1.1.1 OT and Greek philosophical roots of Christian monotheism 206
      4.1.1.2 The internal unity of God and the doctrine of the Trinity 209
      4.1.1.3 The unity of God as foundation of theology's universality 214
   4.1.2 *The futurity of God* 215
      4.1.2.1 God as ontological primacy of the future: Critique of Ernst Bloch 216
      4.1.2.2 God as power of the future 220
      4.1.2.3 The futurity of God in relation to history and eternity 223
      4.1.2.4 God as power of future: contrast to Moltmann and process theology 229
   4.1.3 *God as all-determining reality* 233
      4.1.3.1 The shape of God as all-determining reality 233
      4.1.3.2 The all-determining God and determinism 235
      4.1.3.3 Is the all-determining God open to verification? 236

4.2 Karl Rahner: God as Absolute Mystery 239
   4.2.1 *'God': Preliminary considerations* 239
      4.2.1.1 Importance of the word 'God' 239
      4.2.1.2 The character of the Christian idea of 'God' 240
      4.2.1.3 God as person 242
      4.2.1.4 Identity of the economic and immanent Trinity 244
   4.2.2 *God as transcendent ground of all being* 246
      4.2.2.1 God as ground of all being (*alles Seienden*) 246
      4.2.2.2 "The God who dwells beyond the world" 247
      4.2.2.3 The transcendental argument for the existence of God 249
   4.2.3 *The knowledge of God* 252
      4.2.3.1 Is a direct, 'pre-revelatory' knowledge of God possible? 252
      4.2.3.2 The question of meaning as a question of God 254
      4.2.3.3 The universality of God and the unity of the ways of knowing God 256
   4.2.4 *God and the eschatological future* 257
      4.2.4.1 God, time, and eternity 257
      4.2.4.2 God and the consummation of the history of human freedom 259
      4.2.4.3 The eschatological integration of all reality into God 261
      4.2.4.4 Comparison to Pannenberg's concept of God as power of the future 262

4.3 *Summary and conclusions* 263
   4.3.1 God as foundation of theology's universality 263

## Part 3: The Apologetic Functions of Theology as Universal Science

### Chapter 5: Universality of Theology and the Non-Christian Religions  265

5.1 K. Rahner: Search for Anonymous Christianity in the World's Religions  265
5.1.1 *The theology of religions in Roman Catholic thought*  265
    5.1.1.1 Heritage of the Latin Fathers: *Extra ecclesiam nulla salus*  265
    5.1.1.2 The salvation-optimism of the Second Vatican Council
        (*Lumen gentium, Ad gentes, Nostra aetate*)  268
5.1.2 *The foundations of a philosophy of religion in Rahner*  272
    5.1.2.1 The essence of a philosophy of religion  272
    5.1.2.2 Relationship between the philosophy of religion and theology  275
    5.1.2.3 The world's religions as *praeparatio evangelica*  277
5.1.3 *The theory of an anonymous Christianity*  279
    5.1.3.1 The shape of an anonymous Christianity  279
    5.1.3.2 'Anonymous Christianity' and Judaism  283
    5.1.3.3 Responses to Rahner's theory of anonymous Christianity
        (Balthasar, Küng, Ratzinger, Lubac)  286

5.2 Wolfhart Pannenberg: Theology as the Science of Religion  290
5.2.1 *The theology of religions in Protestant thought*  290
    5.2.1.1 Liberal theology and the world's religions
        (Schleiermacher, Harnack, Troeltsch)  291
    5.2.1.2 Dialectical theology and religion (Barth)  296
    5.2.1.3 Attempt to overcome impasse of liberal and dialectical theology
        (Tillich)  300
5.2.2 *Toward a theology of the history of religions*  303
    5.2.2.1 The anthropological starting point of a theology of religion  303
    5.2.2.2 Pannenberg's proposal of a theology of the history of religions  307
    5.2.2.3 Non-Christian religions as witnesses to an all-determining reality  312
5.2.3 *Pannenberg's doctrine of election and non-Christian religions*  314
    5.2.3.1 The place of election in Pannenberg's theology  314
    5.2.3.2 Election, universality and non-Christian religions  317
    5.2.3.3 Israel, the Church, and the elect 'people of God'  320

5.3 *Excursus: The universality of God and the atheistic critique*  323
    5.3.1 Pannenberg: Atheism and the metaphysics of subjectivity
        (Feuerbach, Nietzsche, Bloch)  323
    5.3.2 Rahner: Atheism and implicit Christianity  328

5.4 *Summary and conclusions*  330
    5.4.1 Jesus as universal criterion of salvation  330
    5.4.2 Theology's claim to universality and the truth claims
        of the world's religions  333

## Chapter 6: Universality of Theological Science and the Natural Sciences 335

6.1 Rahner: Theology and the Regional Sciences 335
6.1.1 *Foundations of the dialogue between theology and the natural sciences* 335
    6.1.1.1 The historical context of the theology/science dialogue
    in Roman Catholic thought 335
    6.1.1.2 The regional character of the individual sciences 340
    6.1.1.3 Epistemological-theological foundations of the
    science/theology dialogue 342
6.1.2 *Rahner's evaluation and use of evolutionary theory* 346
    6.1.2.1 Rahner's assessment of evolutionary theory's meaning for theology 346
    6.1.2.2 Evolution and hominisation 348
    6.1.2.3 Christology within an evolutionary worldview (Teilhard de Chardin) 351

6.2 Pannenberg: Theology as "Queen of the Sciences" 356
6.2.1 *Foundations of the dialogue between theology and the natural sciences* 356
    6.2.1.1 The science/theology dialogue in the history of Protestant thought 356
    6.2.1.2 Implications of theology's universality for the natural sciences 367
    6.2.1.3 The possibility and need of a theology of nature 369
    6.2.1.4 The natural sciences and the primacy of history 373
6.2.2 *Pannenberg's appropriation of metaphors from physics* 377
    6.2.2.1 The concept of 'field' within philosophy, physics and theology 377
    6.2.2.2 Field theory and the Holy Spirit 380
    6.2.2.3 Contingency and natural law 385

6.3 *Summary and conclusions* 390
    6.3.1 Theology, natural science, and apologetic common ground 390

## Summary and Concluding Observations 393

7.1 Contrasting methodologies, converging apologetic 393
7.2 Theological method as foundation for apologetics 394
7.3 Universality as *Leitmotif* in the thought of Rahner and Pannenberg:
    Summary and Critique 396

## Bibliography 399

# Abbreviations

## Works of Wolfhart Pannenberg

| | |
|---|---|
| ATP | *Anthropology in Theological Perspective*, trans. Matthew J. O'Connell. Philadelphia: Westminster Press, 1985; and *Anthropologie in theologischer Perspektive*. Göttingen: Vandenhoeck & Ruprecht, 1983. |
| BQ | *Basic Questions in Theology*, 2 vols., trans. George Kehm. Philadelphia: Fortress Press, 1970/1971. |
| Grundfragen | *Grundfragen systematischer Theologie: Gesammelte Aufsätze.* Göttingen: Vandenhoeck & Ruprecht, 1967. |
| ST | *Systematic Theology*, vols. 1 and 2, trans. Geoffrey Bromiley. Grand Rapids: Eerdmans, 1991, 1994; and *Systematische Theologie*, vol. 3 Göttingen: Vandenhoeck & Ruprecht, 1993. |
| TKG | *Theology and the Kingdom of God*. Philadelphia: Westminster Press, 1969. |
| TPS | *Theology and the Philosophy of Science*, trans. Francis McDonagh. Philadelphia: Westminster Press, 1976. |
| TRG | *Theologie und Reich Gottes*. Gütersloh: Gerd Mohn, 1971. |
| WtT | *Wissenschaftstheorie und Theologie*. Frankfurt/M: Suhrkamp Verlag, 1973. |

## Works of Karl Rahner

| | |
|---|---|
| FCF | *Foundations of Christian Faith: An Introduction to the Idea of Christianity*, trans. Wm. Dych. New York: Seabury Press, 1978. |
| Grundkurs | *Grundkurs des Glaubens: Einführung in den Begriff des Christentums*. Freiburg: Herder, 1984. |
| GW | *Geist in Welt: Zur Metaphysik der endlichen Erkenntnis bei Thomas von Aquin*. Munich: Kösel-Verlag, 1964. |
| Hearers | *Hearers of the Word*, trans. Michael Richards. New York: Herder and Herder, 1968. |
| HdW | *Hörer des Wortes: Zur Grundlegung einer Religionsphilosophie*, ed. Johann Baptist Metz. Munich: Kösel-Verlag, 1963. |
| Schriften | *Schriften zur Theologie*, 16 vols. Einsiedeln: Benziger Verlag, 1954-1983. |
| SM | *Sacramentum Mundi*, 6 vols., ed. Karl Rahner et al. New York: Herder and Herder, 1968; and *Sacramentum Mundi*, 4 vols. Freiburg: Herder, 1969. |
| SW | *Spirit in the Word*. Sheed and Ward: London, 1968. |
| TI | *Theological Investigations*, 23 vols. New York: Crossroad, 1961-1992. |

*If the God of the Bible is the creator of the universe, then it is not possible to understand fully or even appropriately the processes of nature without any reference to that God. If, on the contrary, nature can be appropriately understood without reference to the God of the Bible, then that God cannot be the creator of the universe, and consequently he cannot be truly God and be trusted as a source of moral teaching either. To be sure, the reality of God is not incompatible with some form of abstract knowledge concerning the regularities of natural processes .... But such abstract knowledge of regularities should not claim full and exclusive competence regarding the explanation of nature; if it does so, the reality of God is denied by implication.*

- Wolfhart Pannenberg, "Theological Questions to Scientists" in: *Toward a Theology of Nature*, ed. Ted Peters, (Louisville: Westminster, 1993), 16.

*Theology deals with the one all-embracing and sustaining source of all reality and with the one all-integrating and reconciling goal of all history that we call God. But, insofar as theology acknowledges this God precisely as the incomprehensible mystery and declares man to be eternally distinct from this God of original unity, the singular uniqueness and dignity of theology in principle simply does not provide the means and the way to overcome th[e] pluralism of the sciences. Theology ... is not a kind of sovereign ruler reducing the other sciences to acting as instruments and carrying out its plans; it is one science among others, with the special task of providing a living example of the fact that the pluralism of the sciences does not permit any dominion that could be exercised by man in a kind of theological totalitarianism.*

- Karl Rahner, "Natural Science and Theology," in: *Theological Investigations*, vol.19 (New York: Crossroad, 1983), 19.

# INTRODUCTION

A high energy particle physicist was recently asked his opinion on the possible heat death of the universe. His answer was as enlightening as it was not. "I have no idea," he replied. "That's not my field. My specialty is theories dealing with the thousandth of a second before the Plank time." The incident illustrates the extent to which we are living in an age of "specialization," with scholars in all fields focusing their efforts on increasingly narrow fields. The increasing mass of knowledge has meant that not only do scholars often have little knowledge of fields other than their own but, even within their own fields there is growing specialization and isolation. Hence the high energy particle physicist often has no idea what his or her colleagues in astrophysics or solid-state physics are doing and the microbiologist may understand very little from biophysics or the biology of larger systems. In the human sciences the situation is not much different. Theology itself has not been immune from the trend toward specialization. In the department of systematics alone one speaks today of dogmatic theology, fundamental theology, philosophical theology, ethics (or moral theology), ecumenical theology, etc. - all with their respective "specialists" who are increasingly unaware or unconcerned with what is taking place outside their specific field.

Within this context of information explosion and specialization the radicality and necessity of theology's claim to universality becomes clear. Among contemporary theologians no one has made this claim more strongly, explored its methodological foundations more thoroughly, or pursued its implications more consistently than the German theologian Wolfhart Pannenberg. Next to Pannenberg few names come to mind. One that cannot be overlooked, however, is that of the Roman Catholic theologian Karl Rahner, who has pursued the theme of theology's universality with a nearly equal fervor and conviction. Together, these two theologians have not only done much to restore theology to its place within the academic world, but have also developed one of the boldest and most promising foundations for apologetics within modern theology.

0.1 *Purpose and scope of study*
In this work the methodological and theological foundations and the apologetic functions of theology's universality in the programs of Pannenberg and Rahner will be examined and compared. Our purpose thereby is threefold.

1. To describe the methodological and apologetical programs of both theologians in which the connection between the foundations and functions of theology's universality is emphasized.

2. To formally compare Pannenberg and Rahner's conceptions of theology's universality. As the nature of comparisons requires, the differences and similarities in the two theologians' programs will be indicated. Beyond this, however, we will ask what are the foundations of these differences and similarities, especially with reference to the distinct confessional and theological traditions as well as the seemingly opposing methodological commitments.

3. To explore the validity and value of theology's claim to universality as such within the context of the modern world.

The scope of this study is determined by the theme of universality. Rather than an examination generally of the theologies of Pannenberg and Rahner our interest here must necessarily be limited to those aspects of the two theologians' programs which deal either with the foundation of theology's claim to universality or with the function of this universality. Similarly, the breadth of the scope of this study requires as well that the philosophical and theological roots and context of the thought of the two theologians be restricted to that which contributes to or explains their programs of universality.

0.2 *Special problems in the comparison of Pannenberg and Rahner*

The fact that both Pannenberg and Rahner are German theologians who have responded to the intellectual challenge to theology in the German universities and whose careers overlap one another by three decades facilitates comparison of their thought. As one begins to read extensively in the writings of both theologians, however, the differences in language, style, documentation, philosophical and confessional background, etc. immediately present themselves and pose their own special problems of comparison. Whereas the sources of Pannenberg's thought are documented to the point that some may find tedious, footnotes are an infrequent aid to the researcher of the writings of Rahner. Similarly, whereas one must often read through countless pages of in-depth historical background before coming to Pannenberg's own contribution to a particular area of thought, one discovers more often than not in Rahner the presentation of his own unique perspective or solution to a problem with little or no discussion of the history of the problem in theological or philosophical thought or mention of other attempts at a solution. In this way the two authors could not have more divergent approaches to theological writing.

In language and style as well one encounters difficulties. Rahner's use and creation of terms and phrases is well-known, prompting his brother Hugo Rahner at one point to have jokingly considered translating his brother's works into German.[1] In Pannenberg one finds a specialized vocabulary reflecting the

---

[1] Cf. Franz Mayr, "Vermutungen zu Karl Rahners Sprachstil," in: *Wagnis Theologie: Erfahrungen mit der Theologie Karl Rahners*, ed. Herbert Vorgrimler (Freiburg: Herder, 1979), 143.

philosophical and theological roots of his thought which is often difficult for the uninitiated. When comparing the two thinkers the difficulty that presents itself is that the same terminology is seldom used to describe the same or similar phenomena. The extent to which both theologians actually mean the same thing or refer to the same phenomenon in many instances is not as clear-cut as one might like. Hence in a number of cases the conclusions drawn in comparing their thought are not as firm or definitive as one might wish.

Beyond these difficulties of style and language another, at least equally important, must be mentioned. Carl Braaten and Philip Clayton have noted with justification that "Pannenberg's thought has retained remarkable continuity with the core of his early writings."[2] There is very little in the later writings of Pannenberg which is not to be found, at least in seminal form, in his earliest writings. Major changes of direction or emphasis are also not to be found in his thought. Rahner, on the other hand, has been noted for a number of phases and turning points within his theological development. His so-called turn to anthropology and his increasing emphasis upon history are two cases in point. Hence while one can speak of an "early" and "later" Rahner this cannot be done with Pannenberg. The problem presented for a comparison of the two then becomes whether Pannenberg is to be compared to the early or later Rahner and how to avoid the danger of selectively citing Rahner according to the phase in his development that most lends itself to comparison with Pannenberg's program. The effort here will be made to take Rahner's thought into account within the context and scope of its own development, with preference being given to the thought of the later Rahner in most instances as representing a more mature and consistent presentation of his program.

0.3 *Universality as unifying theme in the thought of Pannenberg and Rahner*

The theme of universality, we will contend, is not a randomly chosen theme which both Rahner and Pannenberg happen to treat, but is rather a common thread which runs consistently through the programs of both theologians. Although one does not have to look long to become aware of the number of similarities in the themes and directions of the theologies of Pannenberg and Rahner there has been surprisingly little comparison done of the two theologians' thought.[3] Although the

---

[2] Carl Braaten and Philip Clayton, "Preface," *The Theology of Wolfhart Pannenberg*, ed. Braaten and Clayton (Minneapolis:Augsburg, 1988), 9.

[3] Exceptions are to be found, however, in the doctoral studies of John McCoy Jr., *Soteriology and the Doctrine of God: A Historical Typology and an Analysis of the Theologies of Karl Rahner and Wolfhart Pannenberg* (Princeton Seminary, 1979); James Bridges, *Human Destiny and Resurrection in Pannenberg and Rahner* (Rice University, 1986); and Matthew Vekathanam, *Christology in Indian Anthropological Context: An Evaluative Encounter with Karl Rahner and Wolfhart Pannenberg* (Frankfurt/M: Peter Lang, 1986), whose work is in many ways less a direct comparison of Rahner and Pannenberg's Christologies than a comparison of both authors to

shared theological context of the German intellectual environment facilitates comparison there are, as we have seen, a number of significant impediments to such comparison. Not only do the two theologians work out of two different confessional traditions with their own very different vocabularies and concerns, but they pursue what appear to be two very different and even incompatible theological methods. Whereas Pannenberg advocates an *a posteriori* pan-critical approach, Rahner employs an *a priori* transcendental method.

The unifying thread in both theologies which forms the focal point of our present study remains the bold and consistent claim of universality for the theological discipline. Briefly stated, the claim of theological universality has a twofold implication. First of all, theological knowledge is relevant to all other areas of knowledge. That is to say, if God is creator of all things and the transcendental ground of all being, then there is no aspect of the created world and consequently no branch of knowledge for which God and the knowledge of and from God is irrelevant. And second, theological universality implies not just that theological knowledge is relevant to all other branches of knowledge, but also that all other fields of knowledge and all the special sciences are relevant to theology. Hence theological universality, as understood in this study and as practiced by Pannenberg and Rahner, does not mean a pretentious reassertion of theology's old claim to be 'Queen of the Sciences' in the sense of a hierarchical domination, but rather much more it means a two-way dialogue between theology and all other branches of life and knowledge.

This concern for universality is at the fore of the theological programs of both Pannenberg and Rahner. As Robert Jenson has written, it has been Pannenberg's "overriding concern to assert the *universality* of the Christian claim, and indeed of any claim that speaks of God."[4] Similarly, one can say of Rahner that universality has been an abiding and central theme of his thought. Hence, given their methodological and confessional differences, this study adopts and seeks to demonstrate the view that the theme of universality is the most appropriate format for a comparison of the thought of the two theologians. Apart from the theme of universality the numerous common interests and similarities of their thinking tend to appear as merely coincidental and are not comprehensible within the overall structures and contexts of their thought.

---

specific streams of thought within Indian theology. Also to be noted here is the article by Yung-Han Kim, "Die universal-heilsgeschichtliche These der Rahnerschule und Pannenbergs universal-geschichtliche Konzeption," in: *Glaube und Geschichte: Heilsgeschichte als Thema der Theologie*, ed. Helge Stadelmann (Wuppertal: Brockhaus, 1986): 348-396.

[4] Robert Jenson, "Jesus in the Trinity: Wolfhart Pannenberg's Christology and Doctrine of the Trinity," in: *The Theology of Wolfhart Pannenberg*, ed. C. Braaten and P. Clayton, 188.

0.4 *Organization of study*

The present study is divided into three parts consisting of two chapters each. In part one we investigate the methodological foundations of theology's universality in the respective programs of Pannenberg and Rahner and inquire after the philosophical backgrounds of the two theologians' thought, their understanding(s) of the nature of theology (with specific attention to the conception of theology as a science), and the theological method(s) which characterize the work of each. With a view toward the apologetics of both authors the question of the relationship between theological method and apologetics is also taken into consideration. Given the claim that apologetics is grounded upon theological method[5] it must be asked to what extent the apologetics of Rahner and Pannenberg flow from their methodologies. Because Pannenberg has devoted more time to questions of theological method and to the implications of discussions in the contemporary philosophy of science for theology than has Rahner we begin our treatment of methodological foundations with his program in chapter one and turn our attention to Karl Rahner, with specific focus on his transcendental method, in chapter two.

Methodology alone, however, is not able to account for the claim and shape of theology's universality. Indeed, in many respects it is itself shaped by the presupposition of this universality. In order to complete the picture of the foundation of theology's universality we turn in part two to the theological basis for this universality. Given the anthropological starting points of both theologians the treatment of the doctrine of humanity is turned to first with special attention to the development of the concept of the solidarity of humanity in both theologians. The construction of common themes such as the universality of sin, death and freedom as well as the significance of anthropology for Christology is also considered. Finally, in chapter four we take up the doctrine of God in Pannenberg and Rahner. Here we argue that the key to the claim of theological universality in both theologians arises primarily out of their respective understandings of God.

In the final part of this study our focus shifts to the functions of theology's universality with regard to apologetics. The universality of theology cannot be simply grounded epistemologically and theologically. If it is more than mere theory then it must also be applied in regard to theology's dialogue with disciplines and worldviews outside the realm of Christian theology. In the present study the relationship of Christian theology to the world religions (chapter five) and to the natural sciences (chapter six) are examined as case studies in the

---

[5] Cf., for instance, Ted Peters, "Truth in History: Gadamer's Hermeneutics and Pannenberg's Apologetic Method," in: *Journal of Religion* 55 (1975), 56.

apologetic praxis of both theologians, in light of their contention of theology's universality. Both areas are not only increasingly important focuses for Christian apologetics today but have also been treated extensively by Pannenberg and Rahner in their own applications of their understanding of theology's universality.

# Chapter One

## WOLFHART PANNENBERG: CONCEPT AND METHOD OF THEOLOGY AS UNIVERSAL SCIENCE

### 1.1 Question of the Scientific Nature of Theology in the History of Theology

Before the issue of theology's universality as the science of God in the thought of Wolfhart Pannenberg can be properly taken up we must consider the history and significance of theology's designation as a science. The classification of theology as a science is crucial to Pannenberg's entire theological program. If theology is not a science (*Wissenschaft*)[1] in some meaningful sense, then its assertions are not open to verification and it is destined to become epistemologically isolated from the special sciences and can make no claims to universal relevance. Yet there has hardly been unanimity among theologians as to theology's scientific status. When Pannenberg published his in-depth study *Theology and the Philosophy of Science*[2] in 1973, the question of the scientific status of theology had long been a subject of debate among German Protestant theologians. In order to understand Pannenberg's conception of theology as a science it is necessary to examine the background of this discussion. Although we are specifically interested in the conceptualization of theology as a science among twentieth-century German Protestants, which provides the immediate contex for Pannenberg's own formulations, the roots of the question reach back much further.

#### 1.1.2 *Sapientia or scientia*

In the early centuries of the Christian church, and this was especially the case in the thought of St. Augustine, theology was generally understood as

---

[1] The German term *Wissenschaft* is generally translated as "science" although some distinction in the range of meaning is to be noted. Whereas *Wissenschaft* includes the natural and the human sciences the English "science" has increasingly been restricted to the natural sciences. We would therefore not agree with the characterization of *Wissenschaft* as "loose" (so David McKenzie, *Wolfhart Pannenberg's Religious Philosophy*, Washington, University of America Press, 1980, 55f.). Rather, the English term "science" has become too restricted. Since the Latin *scientia*, from which *science* derives, includes a broad range of quests for knowledge, and because neither German nor English have two separate words for science, we will here use "science" to refer to both the natural and human sciences, as in the broader sense of *Wissenschaft*, unless otherwise specified.

[2] Wolfhart Pannenberg, *Theology and the Philosophy of Science*, (*TPS*) trans. Francis McDonagh (Philadelphia: Westminster Press, 1976). [*Wissenschaftstheorie und Theologie* (*WtT*) (Frankfurt/M: Suhrkamp Verlag, 1973).]

*sapientia* (wisdom) in contrast to other forms of knowledge which were viewed as *scientia* (science). According to this schema theology was viewed as wisdom because it dealt with things eternal while the other disciplines were viewed as science because they dealt with things temporal. This distinction between theological and other types of knowledge, however, began to come to an end with the rise of the universities in Europe in the 12th century and the rediscovery of Aristotle in the West.[3] After this point theology was generally understood as a science in the Aristotelian sense, i.e., as a speculative science.

Not everyone, however, was content with such a conception of theology. Alexander of Hales argued that theology, unlike the other sciences, offered only a *certitudo adherentiae* and not a *certitudo evidentia*; and Roland of Cremona denied altogether that theology was a science in the Aristotelian sense.[4] William of Auxerre and St. Bonaventure, in the early part of the 13th century, were also not convinced that theology should be classified as a science in the Aristotelian sense.[5] It was, however, the view of Thomas Aquinas which prevailed in the medieval understanding of theology. As Lang observed: For Thomas the strict Aristotelian conception of science remained the ideal and the measure for the noetic evaluation of theology.[6]

Thomas not only held that theology was wisdom (*sapientia*) (*Summa Theologica* I.1.6), but he also argued that theology is a science (*scientia*), and more specifically, that it is a derived science. Thomas wrote:

> Sacred doctrine is a science. We must bear in mind that there are two kinds of sciences. There are some which proceed from principles known by the natural light of the intellect, such as arithmetic and geometry and the like. There are also some which proceed from principles known by the light of a higher science: thus the science of optics proceeds from the principles established by geometry, and music from principles established by arithmetic. So it is that sacred doctrine is a science because it proceeds from principles made known by the light of a higher science, namely, the science of God and the blessed.[7]

Although Thomas viewed theology as both wisdom and science, and as both a speculative and practical science, his emphasis was clearly upon the Aristotelian conception of theology as a speculative science. It was, then, this view which predominated through the remainder of the Middle Ages.[8]

---

[3] Cf. *ibid.*, 228. [226.]
[4] Cf. Albert Lang, *Die theologische Prinzipienlehre der mittelalterlichen Scholastik* (Freiburg: Herder, 1964), 159f.
[5] Cf. Pannenberg, *TPS*, 231. [*WtT*, 230.]
[6] Lang, 162.
[7] Thomas Aquinas, *Summa Theologica* (I.1.2), in: *Basic Writings of Thomas Aquinas*, vol. 1, ed. Anton C. Pegis (New York: Random House, 1945), 7.
[8] Pannenberg points out that two significant exceptions are Richard of Mediavilla and Duns Scotus, both of whom argued that theology was a *scientia practica*, the latter doing so ironically by means of an Aristotelian philosophy. Cf. Pannenberg, *TPS*, 232. [*WtT*, 230f.]

The intellectual turbulence of the Reformation period, not all of which can be attributed to the Reformation itself, did not bring into question the basic conception of theology as a science. Rather, the question at this point had become, 'What kind of a science is theology?' Within Protestant circles theology was seen more and more as a *practical* rather than a *speculative* science. This was perhaps at least partly in revolt against the dominant Thomistic theology of the day. Also, the independence of the other sciences from theology was beginning to be recognized in practice as well as in theory. Luther, with characteristic directness, let his opinion be known when he said in one of his table talks in 1531 that, "true theology is practical, ... speculative theology, therefore, belongs with the devil in hell."[9] According to Pannenberg, "theology became more existential and practical" with Luther's acceptance of it as a practical science.[10]

In the development of post-Reformation Protestant theology the emphasis upon theology as a speculative science in a Thomistic-Aristotelian sense began to re-emerge. Among Protestants J. W. Baier (*Compendium Theol. posit.* [1691] Prol. I.15) and J. F. Buddeus (*Instit. dogmat.* [1724] I.1.28) are credited with being the first to "emphatically ... call theology a *scientia*."[11] Although, as Johannes Gerhard's express rejection of the description of theology as a science indicates,[12] this was by no means a unified view even in the period of Lutheran orthodoxy. Yet the conception of theology as science became so prevalent that A. F. C. Vilmar found himself virtually alone among 19th century Protestants in rejecting the term "science" as applied to theology.[13]

### 1.1.3 *Ernst Troeltsch and Adolf von Harnack*

In the 20th century the question of the scientific status of theology, especially in Germany, has been shaped by movements for academic reform and the question of what relationship theology bears to the other academic disciplines. For German theologians, therefore, the way in which theology is understood and related to the other sciences became crucial for determining whether and in what form theology

---

[9] Martin Luther, *WA*, TR, no. 153, as recorded by Veit Dietrich: "Vera theologia est practica, ... speculativa igitur theologia, die gehort in die Hell zum Teuffel." Cf. Eng. trans in: *LW*, vol. 54, 22. It should be noted, however, that given the context and Luther's identification of Zwingli and Origen as speculative theologians, he was making polemic use of the distinction and may not have had in mind precisely the same definitions as did Thomas.

[10] *TPS*, 235. [*WtT*, 234.]

[11] Cf. Karl Barth, *Church Dogmatics*, trans. G.W. Bromiley (Edinburgh: T.& T.Clark, 1975), I.1,7.

[12] Johannes Gerhard, *Loci theol.* (1610), Prooem. 8. As Barth (*CD* I.1, 7) points out, both Gerhard and David Hollaz after him (*Ex. Theol. acroam.*, 1707, Prol., I.1) preferred the use of the term *sapientia* over that of *scientia*.

[13] So the assessment of Barth, *CD* I.1, 7. Cf. A. F. C. Vilmar, *Dogmatik*, 1874, I, 38; and Vilmar, *Die Theologie der Tatsachen wider die Theologie der Rhetorik: Bekenntnis und Abwehr* [1857], Darmstadt: Wissenschaftliche Buchgesellschaft, 1984), vif. In the foreword to the latter work Vilmar commented that unless the original sense of *Wissenschaft* as *episteme* or *doctrina* could be recovered, the word should be avoided in describing theology in order to avoid confusion (vif.).

would remain in the German universities.[14] Because of the urgency of the question of the scientific character of theology, therefore, it is difficult to find German theologians of the twentieth-century who have not addressed this question in some form. Yet we must limit ourselves here to a brief overview of the most significant contributions, especially those which have played a significant role in shaping the context for Pannenberg's own treatment of the question.

For modern German Protestant theology the treatment of the twofold question of the nature of theology and its place in the university system is usually traced back to Adolf von Harnack's famous speech, "Die Aufgabe der theologischen Facultäten und die allgemeine Religionsgeschichte" delivered on August 3, 1901 at the university of Berlin. The occasion for the topic of Harnack's inaugural address as university rector was the suggestion that the theology faculties be replaced on the universities with departments for the study of religion. This proposal was first put forward by Paul de Lagarde in 1873 who wrote that, "Theologians who enter into any obligations as far as their results and methods are concerned have no right to appear as servants of science."[15]

In the same year Franz Overbeck attacked the scientific character of theology in his writing *Über die Christlichkeit unserer heutigen Theologie*. Similar to Lagarde, Overbeck was of the opinion that theologians, because of their ecclesial commitments and obligations, have no right to appear as servants of science. He also proposed the elimination of theological faculties which were to be replaced by confessionally non-aligned faculties that would study religion in general.[16] For both Lagarde and Overbeck the critique of theology focused on the fact that it was not free of presuppositions (*Voraussetzungslos*). Their voices were soon joined by others such as that of theologian Ernst Troeltsch who, in a modification of these proposals, called for theology to broaden its base and build its science upon a general theory and history of religion. Troeltsch wrote: "Thereby theology is dependent upon the philosophy of religion. Only from this discipline will theology be able to contruct the essence and meaning of Christianity in such a way that the modern spirit of a freedom from presuppositions will be satisfied."[17] In his 1908 article "Rückblick auf ein halbes Jahrhundert der theologischen Wissenschaft" Troeltsch further wrote that: "Historical theology cannot be presuppositionless in the sense that it cannot hold the historical knowability of Jesus, ... the legitimacy

---

[14] Cf. Ernst-Lüder Solte, *Theologie an der Universität: Staats- und kirchenrechtliche Probleme der theologischen Fakultäten*, in: *Jus Ecclesiasticum*, vol. 13 (Munich: Claudius Verlag, 1971); and S. M. Daecke, "Soll die Theologie an der Universität bleiben? Zur Auseinandersetzung um eine Begründung der Theologie als Wissenschaft," in: W. Pannenberg, G. Sauter, S.M. Daecke and H.N. Janowski, *Grundlagen der Theologie - Ein Diskurs* (Stuttgart: Kohlhammer, 1974), 7ff.

[15] Paul de Lagarde, *Über das Verhältnis des deutschen Staates zu Theologie, Kirche und Religion*, in: *Deutsche Schriften* (1920), 40ff., cited by Ernst-Lüder Solte, 21.

[16] Franz Overbeck, *Über die Christlichkeit unserer heutigen Theologie* (1873), 2nd. ed. (1903), 121. Cf. also Solte, 21f.

[17] Ernst Troeltsch, "Voraussetzungslose Wissenschaft," [1897] in: Troeltsch, *Gesammelte Schriften*, vol. 2, *Zur religiösen Lage, Religionsphilosophie und Ethik* (Aalen: Scientia Verlag, 1962), 192.

and duration of Christianity in general, the non-Christian origin of the teachings of the Apostles, as eternally open questions ..."[18] But rather, Troeltsch proposes that:

> The possibility of a ... philosophy of religion, the fulfillment of its task in the sense of the recognition of the high value of Christianity, that is the common presupposition of pure scientific historical theology and the practically-mediated agnostic dogmatic. ... But both branches sprout from the common stem of a general religious-philosophical investigation, since the conclusion of the high value of Christianity does not need to be continually proven anew, but may rather be recognized as achieved. Only under this condition is the existence of theology and an innerly and not merely opportunistically grounded theological faculty possible.[19]

In all three critiques of academic theology a recurring theme is the question of the scientific (*wissenschaftlich*) nature of theology as a university discipline. Calls to remove theology from the university were (and continue to be) based upon the accusation that it does not qualify as a science and proposals for its reform (as Troeltsch's) have likewise been aimed to base theology on a general study of the philosophy and history of religion so that it might qualify as a science.

As the leading theologian of the time Adolf von Harnack, the newly elected rector of the University of Berlin, knew of no better topic for his inaugural address than that of the task of the theological faculties and the general history of religions, in which his argumentation was directed primarily against proposals to transform the entire theological faculty into a faculty for the general study of religions.[20] Harnack states the challenge to the theological faculties as follows:

> Is there not much [in the faculties of the modern university] ... that is outdated and backward? The theological faculty has reason to ask this question. Voices all around are declaring theology's program to be scientifically deficient: It only has a right to exist as a faculty for the general study of religion and the history of religion but not as a faculty for Christian theology. Only to the extent that it studies equally all religions can it really understand its own religion, and only in this way can it rid itself of prejudices which it otherwise could not; at the very least, however, it is demanded that in each theological faculty one or more chairs be established for the general study of religion.[21]

---

[18] Troeltsch, "Rückblick auf ein halbes Jahrhundert der theologischen Wissenschaft," [1908] in: *Gesammelte Schriften*, vol. 2, 222.
[19] *Ibid.*, 224f.
[20] So Carsten Colpe, "Bemerkungen zu Adolf von Harnacks Einschätzung der Disziplin 'Allgemeine Religionsgeschichte,'" in: *Neue Zeitschrift für systematische Theologie und Religionsphilosophie*, vol. 6 (Berlin: Verlag Alfred Töpelmann, 1964), 52.
[21] Adolf von Harnack, *Die Aufgabe der theologischen Facultäten* (Giessen: J. Ricker'sche Verlagsbuchhandlung, 1901), 6f.

For Harnack the essential question for the universities was whether those responsible for their organization had done the right thing by essentially restricting the theological faculties to the research and description of the Christian religion, or whether it would be better to enlarge them into faculties for the study of religion in general. Harnack admits, that from the perspective of abstract theory and from the experience of the praxis of the church in world missions, the study of only a single religion seems to be insufficient.[22] Harnack rejects this proposal, however, by arguing that the study of the Christian religion alone is sufficient to know the other religions, thereby rejecting not only the transformation of theological faculties into faculties of religion but even going so far as to deny the need for chairs for the study of religion in general. Harnack argued first of all that it would be an impossible task to study in sufficient depth each individual religion. It would then seem, he suggested, necessary to limit the theological enterprise to the study of one religion. Harnack argued:

> Certainly, seen from an ideal perspective, it remains a reduction for the theological faculty to fall back on one religion, but which religion is it? It is the religion which has as its own the Bible, whose history forms a recognized and never unbroken line going back almost three thousand years, and that can still today be studied as a living religion. In these three interrelated characteristics it rises so powerfully over other related manifestations that one might well venture to say: Whoever does not know this religion, knows no religion, and whoever knows this religion, including its history, knows all religions.[23]

On this basis Harnack could express his wish that the theological faculties "remain faculties for research into the Christian religion, since Christianity in its pure form is not just one religion alongside of others, but is the religion. It is the religion, however, because Jesus Christ is not one master alongside of others but is the Master, and because his gospel speaks to the inborn disposition of humanity that is revealed in history."[24] In this manner Harnack sought not only to preserve the traditional shape and function of the theological faculties but also to eliminate the apparent need for theology to become the "unprejudiced" study of all religions in order to meet the requirements of a presuppositionless science. Only in its present form as specifically Christian theology did Harnack believe that theology could take its "special place" among the other sciences. The special task, then, within the sciences, of an evangelical faculty of theology, is to preserve in its purity the Christian religion, protect it from misunderstandings, and to highlight its historically recognizable characteristics. Entrusted, therefore, with this great task, "it must decline to burden itself with responsibility for the religions of the whole earth." Harnack concluded his arguments with the warning that the battle is not

---

[22] *Ibid.*, 7ff.
[23] *Ibid.*, 11.
[24] *Ibid.*, 16.

yet over, although in ever wider circles within the church it is recognized that the same freedom needs to be preserved for theology as for every other science.[25]

Of course, there is a certain unmistakable Christian chauvinism inherent in Harnack's arguments. He could even write:

> Above all the fact comes into consideration that the Christian peoples are at the point of dividing up the earth between themselves, indeed, have nearly already divided it up. Whether a lasting and valuable civilization is possible without the preaching of the gospel is a question that could be affirmed or denied. What is certain is that the peoples who are now dividing up the earth among themselves stand or fall with the Christian civilization and that the future will tolerate beside it no other civilization.[26]

Thus it was in part through a minimalizing of the significance and worth of other cultures and religions that Harnack was able to make his claims for the sufficiency of the study of the Christian religion alone on the theological faculties. This point is also troubling to Pannenberg who, comparing the positions of Harnack and Troeltsch, wrote: "Harnack's arguments ... showed a Europe-centered outlook and a conviction of the superiority of Protestant culture. On the other hand, Troeltsch only a year later proclaimed the superiority of Christianity to other religions an open question, to settle which the comparative science-of-religion investigation was essential."[27] For Pannenberg, "the issue between Harnack and Troeltsch was simply the question whether theology could be a positive science restricted to the study of Christianity, or whether it needed a general base in comparative religion."[28] Interestingly, although Pannenberg would later take up the defense of the scientific character of theology and of its place on the university, in this way following Harnack, he demonstrates, as we shall see, in many regards more affinity to Troeltsch. Pannenberg, for instance, in order to uphold the scientific nature of theology, is not willing to proclaim the superiority of Christianity and the truth-value of its theological propositions as closed questions.[29] Also, similar to Troeltsch, albeit in regard to a different conception of science, Pannenberg is willing to adapt and open up theology in light of the criteria of scientific investigation.

Of course Harnack's controversial rectoral address did not put an end to the question of the scientific character of theology and its place on the university.[30] Ernst-Hermann Haenssler fought for 40 years for the removal of theology from the

---

[25] *Ibid.*, 17ff.
[26] *Ibid.*, 9.
[27] *TPS*, 317. [*WtT*, 319f.]
[28] *Ibid.*
[29] Cf. *ibid.*, 323. [326]
[30] For a discussion of the attacks against theology's place on the university and for the following information cf. Ernst-Lüder Solte, *Theologie an der Universität*, 21ff.

university on the basis of its failure to meet the criteria of a science.[31] Also to be mentioned are Jakob Farion (*Universitas und Universität*, 1954) who argued that theology can only be understood as a "science of a special kind" and that its methods do not allow it to claim a place on the university but that it belongs rather within the sphere of the church. To these names might also be added those of Gerhard Szczesny and Hans Albert, both of whom launched sharp and well publicized attacks against the scientific character of theology and its right to a place on the university in the 1960s which intensified the debate over the scientific character of theology leading up to Pannenberg's 1973 work.[32]

Harnack also lived to see the dawning of a new era in Protestant theology in which theology's scientific status came under attack from within the ranks of theology itself. We are speaking, of course, of the movement led by Karl Barth whose so-called revelation positivism drew early and strong criticism from Harnack. In 1923 Harnack published his famous "Fifteen Questions for the Despisers of scientific Theology among the Theologians" in which he directed his criticisms primarily against Barth. Despite the latter's own efforts at a response, Jürgen Moltmann has contended that Harnack's questions continue to remain without a satisfactory answer.[33] Harnack was especially critical of the rejection of historical-critical methodology evidenced in Barth's *Römerbrief* in regard to biblical interpretation and the understanding of the person of Jesus Christ who stands at the center of the gospel. In his final question Harnack asks whether there can in fact be any other theology than that which is "firmly bound to and blood relative of science in general?"[34]

Barth responded that perhaps the question should be turned around so as to inquire whether the other academic disciplines should not judge themselves by that which theologians ought to know. Additionally, Barth questioned whether theology should permit the current *opinio communis* to be the standard and measure against which theology is evaluated.[35] Yet Harnack found no satisfying answer in this response and wrote further, that he saw "in this scientific theology the only possible way to seize hold epistemologically of the object ... since there have existed thinking persons." Barth also claimed that the task of theology was one with that of the sermon. Harnack, however, countered that the task of theology was one with that of the tasks of science in general."[36] Here was the crux of the issue, and here was the point also at which the academic theology of

---

[31] Cf. Ernst-Hermann Haenssler, *Die Krisis der theologischen Fakultät* (1929); and, *Theologie - ein Fremdkörper in der Universität der Gegenwart* (1960).

[32] Cf. for example Gerhard Szczesny, Letter in the *Frankfurter Allgemeine Zeitung*, vol. 5.4 (1963), also in: Vorgänge (1963), 139f.; and Hans Albert, *Traktat über kritische Vernunft* (1968), 104ff.

[33] Jürgen Moltmann, ed. *Anfänge der dialektischen Theologie*, vol. 1 (Munich: Chr. Kaiser, 1966), 322.

[34] Harnack, "Fünfzehn Fragen an die Verächter der wissenschaftlichen Theologie unter den Theologen," [1923] in: *Anfänge der dialektischen Theologie*, 323ff.

[35] Barth, "Fünfzehn Antworten an Herrn Professor von Harnack," in: *Anfänge*, 325ff.

[36] Harnack, "Offener Brief an Herrn Professor K. Barth," in: *Anfänge*, 329ff.

Harnack and the new dialectical theology of Barth reached an impasse that was not able to be surmounted. In the following section we turn our attention to the thought of Karl Barth and the implications of his thought for the scientific status and character of theology.

### 1.1.4 Karl Barth and Heinrich Scholz

As can be seen from our discussion thus far, the question of the scientific character of theology among German theologians has been closely bound to the question of theology's place on the university. This close connection of the two questions explains at least in part the intensity of interest in the scientific character of theology among German theologians in this century. Even Karl Barth, well-known for his lack of interaction with the special sciences and his tendencies toward a fideistic basis for faith, maintained that "theology has no reason not to call itself a science" and suggested that "we should quietly insist on describing theology as a science" in order to make "a necessary point against a general concept of science which is admittedly pagan." Barth favored the designation of theology as a science, however, not in order to exalt it but to humble it and to remind it that it is just a science and to guard against what he called "an ontological exaltation" above the other sciences which he felt its classification as *doctrina* or even *sapientia* leads to.[37] Yet Barth also noted that "it would not make the slightest difference to its real business if [theology] ... had to rank as something other than science."[38]

In a 1931 article titled "Wie ist eine evangelische Theologie als Wissenschaft möglich?" which was directed particularly toward Karl Barth, the philosopher and theologian Heinrich Scholz listed six criteria for a science which he believed should be applicable to all disciplines, including theology, which aspire to consider themselves a science. These criteria can be roughly summarized as being those of (1) formal consistency, (2) internal coherence, (3) being subject to external controls and verification (4) impartiality, (5) consistency with the findings of other sciences and (6) formalisability. Of these Scholz gave special significance to the first three postulates, or requirements, which he considered undisputed.[39] Barth, while admitting that Scholz's conception of science "is still the proper concept of science in our time," rejected them nonetheless as not being applicable to theology. Barth wrote:

> Theology can only say point-blank that this concept is unacceptable to it. Even the minimum postulate of freedom from contradiction is acceptable to theology only when it is given a particular interpretation which the scientific theorist can hardly tolerate, namely, that theology does not affirm in principle that the

---

[37] Karl Barth, *Church Dogmatics*, I.1, 10f.
[38] *Ibid.*, I.1., 8.
[39] Cf. Heinrich Scholz, "Wie ist eine evangelische Theologie als Wissenschaft möglich?" [1931] in: Gerhard Sauter, ed., *Theologie als Wissenschaft* (Munich: Chr. Kaiser, 1971), 221ff.

'contradictions' which it makes cannot be resolved. ... The remaining sections of the law as stated by Scholz can only remind the theologian that he ought to know what he is about when he transgresses them, but also that as a theologian he cannot help transgressing them. Not an iota can be yielded here without betraying theology, for any concession at this point involves surrendering the theme of theology.[40]

Barth rejected the demands of Scholz because, as he made clear in a 1934 address at the Free Protestant Theological Faculty in Paris, he was convinced that subjecting theological statements to verification would betray and falsify theology's fundamental axiom, which is revelation. Barth contended that: "Theology's essential hypothesis, or axiom, is revelation, which is God's own act done in His Word and through His Spirit. How shall this axiom be exhibited or determined? It cannot be done directly, but indirectly. Not positively but negatively. Not by setting it a bound among other sciences. Theology would be falsified or misinterpreted, betrayed or given up, if it sought to make its fundamental assumption or axiom a direct and tangible exhibit. Theology would have ceased to be theology, if it sought to, or could, justify itself." Thus theology, for Barth, is "the freest and yet the most restricted of all sciences" since all questions of justification or verification are answered simply by "calling attention to the Church and the divine revelation upon which the Church was founded."[41]

Scholz contended that if theology rejected the minimum demands which he outlined the result would be that, "even if such a dogmatics could be constructed as a science, it would in any event at this decisive point exit the circle of sciences and must become something entirely different, namely a personal confession of faith, in the most decimated sense of the phrase, that has withdrawn itself from every earthly form of investigation."[42] Indeed, Barth's blanket rejection of Scholz's requirements confirmed, as van Huyssteen has poignantly observed, that "Barthian theology was not concerned with science and scientific reflection, but was much rather a personal religious credo expanded into a comprehensive doctrine and thereby placed beyond any form of control or testing."[43] Hence, as Rohls has summarized, Barth developed "a program of theological anti-

---

[40] Barth, I.1., 9.
[41] Karl Barth, "Theology" in: Karl Barth, *God in Action*, trans. E. Homrighausen and K. Ernst (New York: Round Table Press, 1936), 40f. Cf. also Jan Rohls, "*Credo ut intelligam*: Karl Barths theologisches Programm und sein Kontext," in: *Vernunft des Glaubens: Wissenschaftliche Theologie und kirchliche Lehre, Festschrift zum 60. Geburtstag von Wolfhart Pannenberg*, ed. Jan Rohls and Gunther Wenz (Göttingen: Vandenhoeck & Ruprecht, 1988), 422f. who notes that Barth sets himself decisively apart from Scholz in his contention that the self-examination of the Church in light of its speech about God "ist selbst Glaubensakt, der dogmatische Satz Glaubenssatz, und die Wissenschaftlichkeit der Dogmatik kann sich daher nicht an allgemeinen wissenschaftstheoretischen Kriterien bemessen."
[42] Scholz, 259.
[43] Wentzel van Huyssteen, *Theology and the Justification of Faith: Constructing Theories in Systematic Theology*, trans. H.F. Snijders (Grand Rapids: Eerdmans, 1989), 18

rationalism."⁴⁴ Similarly, Harnack commented already in the early days of dialectical theology regarding Barth's use of the concept of revelation that: "I have the impression that what Professor Barth is attempting with the help of the dialectic he employs leads us onto an invisible grate between absolute religious scepticism and naïve biblicism - the most agonizing interpretations of Christian experience and Christian faith!"⁴⁵ As we shall see, the impasse between Barth and Scholz over the requirements theology must meet to justify its claim to be a science becomes the starting point for Pannenberg's own entry into the discussion of the scientific status of theology.

### 1.1.5 *Rudolf Bultmann*

Rudolf Bultmann, representing the "left wing" of dialectical theology, shared many of Barth's assumptions, for instance that the resurrection is not subject to historical verification (although for very different reasons) and that revelation is to be located in word and not history. We read, for instance, in Bultmann's posthumously published *Theologische Enzyklopädie*, of his contention that "God's revelation as historical event is ... Jesus Chrsit as the Word of God."⁴⁶ Yet Bultmann did not understand "historical event" in this sense as something subject to historical investigation since "revelation is not a phenomenon of the world but is an event within existence ...."⁴⁷

Yet Bultmann, in contrast to Barth, attempted to develop a philosophy of science, albeit one that was more rooted in 19th than 20th century conceptions of science.⁴⁸ In a 1941 lecture titled *Theologie als Wissenschaft*⁴⁹ delivered at a theological conference in Alpirsbach he emphasized that each science has its own area of investigation (*Gegenstandsgebiet*) and its own corresponding methods. What is common to the methods of all sciences, however, is "speech in substantiated sentences that demonstrate the object and in which the part is understood on the bais of an understanding of the whole." Bultmann characterizes science more specifically as that which: (1) is an objectifying process or

---

[44] Rohls, "Credo ut intelligam," 434f.
[45] Harnack, "Nachwort zu meinem offenen Brief an Herrn Professor Karl Barth," in: *Anfänge der dialektischen Theologie*, 346f.
[46] Rudolf Bultmann, *Theologische Enzyklopädie*, ed. Eberhard Jüngel and Klaus Müller (Tübingen: J.C.B. Mohr, 1984), 95. The lectures contained in this volume were first delivered in 1926 and were revised several times until 1936, from which year the lectures in their current form arose.
[47] *Ibid.*, 159.
[48] This is to be seen, for example, in his attempt to rework the requirement of a "presuppositionless" science common in the last century and in his lack of interaction with current philosophers of science.
[49] Rudolf Bultmann, "Theologie als Wissenschaft" [first pub. 1947], in: *Zeitschrift für Theologie und Kirche*, ed. Eberhard Jüngel, vol. 81 (Tübingen: J.C.B. Mohr, 1984). This article has a very interesting history in that it was confiscated in the autumn of 1944 and used as evidence against Bultmann in a charge of high treason brought against him in April 1945 which, however, the end of the war prevented from ever coming to trial. Cf. Klaus W. Müller, "Zu Rudolf Bultmanns Alpirsbacher Vortrag über 'Theologie als Wissenshcaft'" *ibid.*, 470f.

procedure, (2) is objective in the sense of an uninterested and unprejudiced review of the object in its entirety and its inner connectedness, (3) uncovers the pre-scientific relationship to its object and methodically develops the understanding inherent in this relationship, and (4) has its own methods specific to its area of investigation.[50]

Given this conception of science, Bultmann asks whether and to what extent theology can be considered a science. Central to Bultmann's understanding of science is the concept of the object (*Gegenstand*) which a science investigates. The first and central question for Bultmann is what theology's "object" of investigation is. In answer to the question "What is theology as a science?" Bultmann writes that "its object is God, as he is seen in the only possible way of approach in faith. He shows himself in revelation and is seen in faith. Hence revelation and faith are the object of theology."[51] Although identifying God as the object of theology, he qualifies this through our existential encounter with God in faith. Therefore Bultmann, in contrast to many of his colleagues, could reject the notion that God, in an unqualified sense, is the object of theology since it is impossible to objectify God who is transcendent, unseeable, unfathomable, etc.

Bultmann similarly rejected either religion or faith alone as being the objects of theology since both lead to a generic science of religions which, in Bultmann's view, is not able to legitimize itself as Christian theology.[52] Bultmann opts instead for "God's eschatological activity" as the object of theology which he understands existentially as a unity of faith and God in which theology is seen as an encounter with faith, itself understood as eschatological phenomenon. The existential emphasis for Bultmann, however, removes the actual content of faith from the arena of scientific investigation and leaves in its place only the act of faith itself. According to Bultmann, therefore, "scientifically comprehensible is not that which is comprehended in faith, but rather the act of faith."[53]

Although the existential emphasis of Bultmann is not picked up by Pannenberg the key role of God's eschatological activity as object of theological science is important for Pannenberg. This is especially true inasmuch as for Bultmann this means that the very revelation of the essence of a historical phenomenon, and thereby also the possibility to verify truth claims based upon it or implicit in it, takes place only when history has reached its end. Speaking of the problem of hermeneutics in his 1955 Gifford Lectures titled "History and Eschatology" Bultmann contended:

> To each historical phenomenon belongs its future, a future in which alone it will appear as that which it really is. ... For ultimately it will show itself in its very essence only when history has reached its end. Therefore we can understand that

---

[50] "Theologie als Wissenschaft," 450.
[51] *Theologische Enzyklopädie*, 159.
[52] "Theologie als Wissenschaft," 452.
[53] *Theologische Enzyklopädie*, 162.

the question of meaning in history was raised and answered for the first time within an outlook which believed it knew the end of history. This occurred in the Jewish-Christian understanding of history which was dependent on eschatology.[54]

For Pannenberg, as we will see, this insight, taken together with his own unique view of the resurrection of Jesus, is decisive for his theological program.

### 1.1.6 T. F. Torrance and Gerhard Sauter

Among contemporary Protestant theologians of note only two, apart from Pannenberg himself, have dealt in depth with questions relating to the philosophy of science and the scientific character of theology. They are the Scottish theologian Thomas F. Torrance and Pannenberg's fellow German Lutheran Gerhard Sauter.

T. F. Torrance is a Reformed theologian who has pursued a decisively Barthian theology. Yet interestingly he departs from Barth in his estimation of natural theology and in his interest in the scientific character of theology. Torrance indicates something of the difference between himself and Barth in regard to natural theology when he writes:

> We cannot know God apart from the way in which he interacts with the world he has made or apart from the way in which we are constituted his creatures within that world. ... Since it is only within the ontological and referential relations of the universe to God that we may think and speak of God, there must be a close coordination between theological concepts and physical concepts: which is, after all, the inescapable implication of the Christian doctrines of creation and incarnation and the inseparable relation between logos and being which they establish. This being the case, an essential place must be found for so-called 'natural theology.'[55]

Torrance's commitment to a natural theology and interest in the relevance of the knowledge gained from the natural sciences for a knowledge of God led him to reflect upon the scientific nature of theology. Curiously, Torrance never takes up Scholz's challenge to Barth and the minimum requirements of a science which he formulated. Torrance produces instead his own 'minimum demands' for what he calls scientific questioning. Scientific questioning, including that of theological science, must meet the following requirements: (1) scientific questions must be

---

[54] Bultmann, *History and Eschatology* (Edinburgh: The University Press, 1957), 120. Pannenberg credits Dilthey with influencing this viewpoint of Bultmann (*TPS*, 166f. [*WtT*, 167.]). Cf. Wilhelm Dilthey, *Der Aufbau der geschichtlichen Welt in den Geisteswissenschaften*, in: *Gesammelte Schriften* vol. 7 (Göttingen: Vandenhoeck & Ruprecht, 1965), 233, where he writes concerning the relationship between the individual moment and the whole: "One must first await the end of history in order to have all the material needed for the determination of its meaning."

[55] Thomas F. Torrance, *Reality and Scientific Theology* (Edinburgh: Scottish Academic Press, 1985), 33.

genuine questions which are aimed at reality, (2) scientific questions must be appropriate to the nature of the object they aim to investigate, (3) scientific questions must group around and reflect the one supreme question that arises from the side of the object as it confronts us, i.e., the question as to its nature and ground, and (4) the "supreme formal requirement in scientific questioning is that we look for the central point of reference, and then in relation to it order all our questions."[56]

For Torrance the idea that scientific questions must be specific to their object has significant implications for theological science which leads him in a decisively different direction than Pannenberg and reflects his Barthian roots. Torrance writes, for instance, that "in theology the object is God, and the supreme question that is directed to us from the side of the object is in the form of a Person within our creaturely existence, the Lord Jesus Christ." This means, therefore, that "scientific questioning within theology is necessarily given a mode in accordance with the unique nature of its object, which differentiates it from the mode in which questioning arises in other fields of knowledge."[57] Thus Torrance develops a theo-centric and even Christo-centric scientific methodology which has little parallel with the other sciences. He also interacts very little with views arising out of the philosophy of science since the methodological requirements of theological science are in many ways very different from those dealing with the other sciences. The testing of the truth-claims of theological statements, therefore, bears little resemblance to the kind of verification that Scholz, for instance, called for.

For Torrance, theological propositions are to be tested in a twofold way: first in regard to their correspondence with the "Word and Truth of God," and here we see again hints of Barth; and second, in their coherence with one another.[58] Torrance maintains that theological statements are primarily of the type which he calls "existence statements" since they are arrived at through experimental or abstract reasoning. Such theological existence statements refer to the "Being and Existence of God as the given reality."[59] We can only convince others of the truth of such statements, however, "if we can get them to see or hear the reality they refer to as we see or hear it."[60]

Theological statements, then, seem to take on a subjectivity which makes it difficult if not impossible for them to be open to external corroborating verification from the other sciences. Perhaps this rather unique road between the Barthian positivism of revelation and his interest in the scientific and methodological rigor of theological propositions explains in part why surprisingly little attention has been given to his ideas from those involved in the discussion of

---

[56] Torrance, *Theological Science* (London: Oxford University Press, 1969), 123ff.
[57] Ibid., 125.
[58] Ibid., 164.
[59] Ibid., 164, 174.
[60] Ibid., 165.

the scientific status of theology within German theology.⁶¹ At least for Pannenberg, Torrance's program of theological science would seem to remain too dependent upon Barth to provide useful parallels to his own program. Similar to Pannenberg, Gerhard Sauter has actively defended not only theology's place in the universities but also the scientific status of theology. Wentzel van Huyssteen has identified five central areas of concern for Sauter in regard to his conception of a scientific theology.

1. The degree to which theologians can truly communicate the Reality on which they make their statements: the question of the rational limits of theology.
2. The describability of theology.
3. The relationship between history and the present: the hermeneutical problem.
4. Theology's capacity for truly creative, innovative thought and creditable [sic] problem solving.
5. The object of theology.⁶²

Although these points of concern reflect certain important parallels with Pannenberg's thought there are some decisive differences between the two.⁶³ Sauter wrote in a 1980 article outlining the differences that remained between him and Pannenberg that Pannenberg sees the basic difference between himself and Sauter in that he (Pannenberg) strives for "a scientific- theoretical (*wissenschaftstheoretische*) examination even of the emergence of faith" while Sauter limits himself to "an examination of theological propostions."⁶⁴ This difference, according to Sauter, expresses itself in three areas: in the valuation of

---

⁶¹ Torrance's significant contributions to this discussion, especially as one of the few English language theologians of note to take up in depth the question of the scientific nature of theology, is curiously overlooked by German theologians. S. M. Daecke in a dialogue in 1972 commented that Pannenberg and Sauter were the only contemporary Protestant theologians to have dealt with the question in detail (cf. Daecke et al., "Theologie als Wissenschaft: Ein Gespräch" in: *Grundlagen der Theologie - Ein Diskurs*, 58.) Similarly, Pannenberg only makes reference to his work once (and then only in a footnote) in his *Theology and the Philosophy of Science*, cf. 270, note 557. [*WtT*, 271, note 557.]

⁶² Wentzel van Huyssteen, *Theology and the Justification of Faith*, 106.

⁶³ For a comparison of Pannenberg and Sauter's theories of science as they relate to theology see Wolfgang Pfüller, *Zum Problem der Wissenschaftlichkeit der Theologie: Kritische Erörterung der theologisch-wissenschaftstheoretischen Positionen Gerhard Sauters und Wolfhart Pannenbergs* (Dissertation, Martin-Luther-Universität Halle-Wittenberg, 1979). Unfortunately, the generally critical view of theology's claim to be a science expressed in this dissertation hinders its usefulness in evaluating and appreciating the contributions of Sauter and Pannenberg in this area. One might ask whether the fact that the work was done in the former GDR, where theology's claim to any sort of scientific status would have run counter to officially held views, may have influenced this negative tone.

⁶⁴ Gerhard Sauter, "Überlegungen zu einem weiteren Gesprächsgang über 'Theologie und Wissenschaftstheorie'" in: *Evangelische Theologie* 40 (March/April 1980), 161.

hypotheses in theology, in the theological understanding of truth, and in the conception of what constitutes a science.[65]

Another significant and related difference between Sauter and Pannenberg on this point is to be found in Sauter's focus on the defense of the truth claims of Christianity within in the context of the praxis of the Church and 'churchly' discussion rather than upon the basis of an empirical verification. For Sauter, the foundation of theological statements should not be burdened with false demands such as the "claim of empirical verification."[66] Sauter focuses instead upon the 'verification' of universal theological statements such as "all persons are sinners." The key to the testing of this and similar statements is to be found in what Sauter calls a "language-logical reconstruction."[67] Such universal statements are difficult to falsify. Yet each universal statement stands within a foundational context of interconnectedness (*Begründungszusammenhang*). For Sauter this foundational context has a clearly recognizable empirical location, that is to say, it belongs to a practical sphere which appears by means of this foundational context and distinguishes it from others. In the case of theological statements this empirical location is the "Church," which determines not only where such speech takes place but also how such speech can and must be tested. Therefore, according to Sauter, "the question about the empirical content of theological statements has become the question about the communicative reliability of theological speech."[68] Pannenberg, for his part, has brought forth the criticism, founded in part upon disagreements with Sauter's understanding of history, that the justification of theological theories, when made to depend exclusively upon their function as 'regulators of the discourse of the church' (so Sauter), presuppose a topic of 'church discourse' and, according to Pannenberg, lead to "an extreme ecclesiastical conventionalism."[69]

Given the significant differences in agenda and approach between Pannenberg on the one hand and Torrance and Sauter on the other, it is not surprising that Pannenberg, rather than taking his starting point from an engaged dialogue with one of his contemporaries, returns instead strategically to the 1930s dispute between Karl Barth and Heinrich Scholz in the as the starting point for the development of his own conception of the scientific character of theology.

---

[65] *Ibid.*
[66] Sauter, "Grundzüge einer Wissenschaftstheorie der Theologie," in: *Wissenschaftstheoretische Kritik der Theologie*, ed. G. Sauter (Munich: Chr. Kaiser, 1973), 316.
[67] *Ibid.*, 318 and 271ff. In Sauter's terms, a "sprach-logische Rekonstruktion."
[68] *Ibid.*, 319ff.
[69] *TPS*, 292ff. [*WtT*, 294f.] Pannenberg's critique of Sauter, especially in regard to Sauter's concept of history, focuses on Sauter's *Vor einem neuen Methodenstreit in der Theologie?* (Munich: Chr. Kaiser, 1970).

## 1.2 Pannenberg's Understanding of Science and the Criteria of a Science

### 1.2.1 Theology as a human science

Pannenberg focuses his treatment of the question of the scientific status of theology upon the general concept of science. Pannenberg recognizes, of course, important divisions within the sciences, such as the basic division between the human sciences (*Geisteswissenschaften*)[70] and the natural sciences (*Naturwissenschaften*). If theology must be classified as belonging to a specific family of sciences this would certainly be to the human sciences, as Ernst Troeltsch first suggested.[71] For Pannenberg such a classification is based upon Christology. He writes:

> The connection of theology and the human sciences is established for Christian theology through the fact that God became man. This means that Christian theology conceives the reality of God as present for our world in a specific human history, namely, in the history of Jesus of Nazareth. Consequently, theology will of necessity occupy itself with the traditions stemming from this historical individual: with the process of their exposition, with the disparity of the times, yet also with the context of the Jewish religion and its authoritative documents, which in turn must be evaluated in connection with the history of human religions and of human history in *toto*. Not of least importance, Christian theology is concerned with the problems which these factors raise for the ques-tion of the present relevance and truth of the history and person of Jesus. Throughout, they are problems of the same kind as occur in the human sciences.[72]

Yet if too much emphasis is placed upon theology as a human science rather than upon its nature as a science in general there is a danger of thereby seeking to avoid the problem of a general philosophy of science and of the requirements which it would place upon any discipline, either among the human or natural sciences, which aspires to be a genuine science. Pannenberg therefore writes:

> There are good grounds to classify Christian theology with the humanities (*Geisteswissenschaften*) and the human sciences. In any event it belongs with the literary and linguistic sciences, with jurisprudence and the historical sciences, and with all sciences that have to do with the interpretation of texts, by means of which they acquire knowledge. One should not, in this regard, overstate the

---

[70] The term "Geisteswissenschaften," according to Pannenberg (*TPS*, 72f. [*WtT*, 74f.]), goes back to Wilhelm Dilthey's *Einleitung in die Geisteswissenschaften* (1883), *Gesammelte Schriften*, vol. 1 (Göttingen: Vandenhoeck & Ruprecht). For a more detailed treatment of the concept of human sciences and their relation to and distinction from the natural sciences see Dilthey, *Der Aufbau der geschichtlichen Welt in den Geisteswissenschaften, GS*, vol. 7.

[71] Cf. *TPS*, 103ff. [*WtT*, 105ff.] Pannenberg especially emphasizes the correlation of Troeltsch's classification with Dilthey's concept of human sciences as distinct from the natural sciences.

[72] Pannenberg, *Metaphysics and the Idea of God*, trans. Philip Clayton (Grand Rapids: Wm. Eerdmans, 1990), 139f. [The article "Theology and the Categories 'Part' and 'Whole'" from which this quote is taken, does not appear in *Metaphysik und Gottesgedanke*, Göttingen, 1988]

distinction between these disciplines and the natural sciences for there exist fundamental commonalities that unite all the scientific disciplines. Every science seeks to understand its object, and each develops models toward this end that describe the object and attempt to explain the connection between the various qualities that belong to the object.[73]

Pannenberg, therefore, rather than seeking refuge for theology in a special classification among the human or literary sciences, seeks to found theology's claim to be a science upon a general concept of science.

As we have already seen, however, definitions of what constitutes a science vary. Indeed, Wilfried Joest is right to describe science (*Wissenschaft*) as a collective name for a series of intellectual activities that vary greatly in their respective objects and methods.[74] Joest questions whether there is a generally accepted and concrete conception of what constitutes a science. According to Joest, various and even contradictory conceptions of what science is are to be found in contemporary discussions of the philosophy of science. So it is that "the theologian can be tempted to throw the question concerning the scientific character of his own discipline back onto the philosopher of science for the time being: Show me your concept of science and then I can attempt to say how theology relates to that which you understand by science."[75] The variety of definitions of science has in some circles led to a certain agnosticism concerning the question of the scientific character of theology. Horst Georg Pöhlmann has noted with justification that whether theology's claim to be a science is justified or not depends upon what one understands under the concept of science.[76] For Pannenberg, however, there exist minimum requirements of a science which are applicable to all disciplines aspiring to be termed a science, including theology.

### 1.2.2 Scholz's minimum requirements of a science

In his *Theology and the Philosophy of Science* Pannenberg takes up the question of the scientific status of theology beginning with Scholz's minimum requirements for a science. Pannenberg chose Scholz's demands as "a convenient starting point" for his discussion and maintained that, even though "after thirty years of intensive discussion in the philosophy of science" they are "in need of supplementation and refinement, as minimum requirements they remain valid."[77] Scholz attacked Barth's premise that questions of methodology are secondary to theology's relevance, defined as a commitment to God's self-disclosure - which constituted for Barth the primary criterion for theology's validity as a science.[78]

---

[73] Pannenberg, "Eine philosophisch-historische Hermeneutik des Christentums," in: *Theologie und Philosophie* 66:4 (1991), 481.
[74] Joest, *Fundamentaltheologie*, 251.
[75] *Ibid.*, 241.
[76] Horst Georg Pöhlmann, *Abriß der Dogmatik*, 5th ed. (Gütersloh: Gerd Mohn, 1990), 32.
[77] *TPS*, 326. [*WtT*, 329.]
[78] Cf., for instance, Barth, "Theology," in: *God in Action*, 39ff.; and Barth, *CD* I.1, 4ff.

Scholz, writing from the standpoint of the positivistic model of rationality then common in the philosophy of science, rejected Barth's subjection of methodology to theology's relevance. His three "undisputed minimum requirements" for a science which he put to Barth, again briefly stated, are: (1) The requirement of formal consistency of propositions, (2) the requirement of coherence, and (3) the requirement of testability or verifiability.[79] Pannenberg justifies the use of these seemingly dated requirements succinctly when he writes:

> Since [Scholz's requirements] ... are based on abstraction from all the material differences between particular sciences, they should not be regarded as an expression of the now superseded ideal of a 'unitary science'. The classical statement of this concept was made by logical positivism, which attempted to impose as a standard of scientific procedure an ideal of logical form and empirical control which it claimed to derive from the natural sciences. Scholz's minimum requirements, in contrast, ... call simply for the explicit formulation of the implications of statements. It is this which, in spite of advances in the philosophy of science, has prevented it from losing its relevance to all disciplines which try to formulate and test statements about states of affairs.[80]

Thus Pannenberg, by beginning his discussion with Scholz, commits himself to a defense of theology's scientific status which focuses on the nature of theological propositions and on verification.

### 1.2.2.1 *The requirement of formal consistency*

In contrast to Karl Barth, who rejected Scholz's requirements out of hand,[81] Pannenberg contended that theology indeed meets these requirements. Scholz's first requirement, the proposition postulate or requirement of formal consistency, according to Pannenberg, "is met if it can be assumed that theological propositions have a cognitive character." This means that theological propositions "are statements which typically say something about a state of affairs for which they claim truth, i.e. correspondence with the state of affairs which is the object of the statement."[82] For Pannenberg this is the most difficult of Scholz's three requirements for theology to meet. Because the positivist criterion of verifiability through sensory observations accessible to anyone at any time cannot be applied to religious language, some have attempted to portray religious language as purely expressive. Pannenberg, however, contends that religious language, even the language of devotion such as one finds in prayer or liturgical acts, at least implies "cognitive elements which, when considered in themselves, must be formulated into statements" since it contains assertions about the divine and about divinely instituted realities.

---

[79] Cf. Scholz, "Wie ist eine evangelische Theologie als Wissenschaft möglich?" 231ff.
[80] *TPS*, 326. [*WtT*, 329.]
[81] Cf. Barth, *CD* I.1, 9.
[82] *TPS*, 327. [*WtT*, 330.]

Similarly, Pannenberg has elsewhere written concerning the confessional statement "I believe in God the father almighty, creator of heaven and earth," that "this sentence contains no assertion regarding the existence of God and his attributes but is rather the completion of an encounter, namely faith. Yet upon closer examination it can be seen that the sense of this sentence does in fact contain a certain element of assertion, with which the encounter is originally connected."[83] So it is, therefore, that no essential difference exists between theological and devotional language since both have at least a cognitive intention. Yet although this cognitive *intention* is difficult to deny, it is not alone sufficient to show that religious and theological propositions have an *actual* cognitive character. The crux of the problem is that in order to be regarded as having a cognitive character the reality (God) which religious language asserts must be accessible independent of this language, i.e., it must be distinguishable from the assertions or propositions about it. This is difficult, however, since today, due to the disintegration of the traditional metaphysical doctrine of God, only "believers and theologians" seem to speak of God. For if the reality of God cannot be distinguished from the assertions of the faithful and of theologians about God, such assertions can no longer be taken seriously as assertions, but look instead like fictions created by believers and theologians.[84] Therefore the question of whether theological propositions qualify as assertions depends upon affirmative answers to Scholz's second and third criteria.

*1.2.2.2 The requirement of coherence*
Scholz's second requirement, the postulate of coherence, demands that theological statements relate to a single area of investigation. Pannenberg's emphasis upon the universal character of theology is key to theology's meeting of this demand. The single area to which theological statements relate is, according to Pannenberg, "the indirect self-communication of divine reality in the anticipatory experiences of the totality of meaning of reality with which the creedal traditions of the historical religions are concerned." This means, therefore, that "theology examines the historical religions to determine how far the all-determining reality of God makes itself known in them as the unifying unity of all reality distinct from itself. Christian theology devotes itself to a similar examination of Christianity, though it must always take into account Christianity's connection with other religions in the process of the history of religions."[85] Thus, as Wentzel van Huyssteen explains, "theology as the science of God is possible only as the science of historical religions. Christian theology becomes possible only in the next phase, as the science of the Christian religion."[86]

---
[83] Pannenberg, "Wie wahr ist das Reden von Gott? Die wissenschaftstheoretische Problematik theologischer Aussagen," in: *Grundlagen der Theologie - Ein Diskurs*, 31f.,
[84] *TPS*, 327ff. [*WtT*, 330ff.]
[85] *Ibid.*, 326f. [329f.]
[86] Wentzel van Huyssteen, *Theology and the Justification of Faith*, 89.

It is also necessary for this second requirement to be met for theology's object to be unitary, that is to say, "all propositions must be related to a single field of study." Pannenberg contends that Schleiermacher's conception of theology as a science fails precisely because in maintaining a plurality of objects it fails to meet this requirement.[87] Only God as the object of theology provides the necessary unitary field, and not the Word of or about God. So Pannenberg: "If, for instance, one characterizes the Word of God, which is commonly assumed by theology, as its real object, then this object does not appear to be clearly distinguishable from statements about it. ... But even when one does not understand the Word of God but God himself as the object of theology the difficulty arises as to how God is accessible as a reality distinct from among the assertions of the theologians." At this point, then, according to Pannenberg, the question of theology's object, or even the question of whether theology has an object at all, leads directly to the question of the controllability or verifiability of theological statements.[88] Thus, just as a final answer to theology's ability to meet Scholz's first requirement rests upon the second two requirements, so a conclusively affirmative response to Scholz's second requirement depends in turn ultimately upon theology's ability to meet Scholz's third requirement of verifiability. For Pannenberg, therefore, the scientific character of theology is made to rest ultimately upon its ability to meet the test of verifiability.

### 1.2.2.3 *The requirement of verifiability*

Concerning Scholz's third criterion, the requirement of verifiability, Pannenberg contends that it is impossible to evade since "verifiability is implicit in the logical structure of assertions."[89] This is the case since each assertion is subject to testing against the state of affairs which it describes and which must be accessible distinct from the assertion itself. Theological propositions or assertions cannot be verified directly against their object since God's reality is itself in dispute and also since such verification would contradict God's status as God. Yet Pannenberg maintains that an indirect verification is possible which is sufficient for satisfying Scholz's third requirement. As Pannenberg explains: "Assertions about a divine reality and divine actions can be tested by their implications for the understanding of finite reality, to the extent that the object of this assertion is God *as the all-determining reality*."[90] The structure and

---

[87] *TPS*, 270. [*WtT*, 272.]
[88] "Wie wahr ist das Reden von Gott?" 33f.,
[89] *TPS*, 331. [*WtT*, 334.] Although Pannenberg refers here to this requirement as one of verification, in another place he makes a distinction between verification and what he calls Scholz's postulate of control or testing. Pannenberg writes concerning Scholz's requirement that theology be subject to testing that, "this requirement is more general than the requirement of verification, which Scholz holds to be impossible in theology. His requirement is concerned only with intelligibility of formulation ..." *Ibid.*, 271. [272.]
[90] *Ibid.*, 332. [335.]

implications of this indirect verification as proposed by Pannenberg will be examined in detail later in this chapter.

### 1.2.3 Preliminary evaluation of Pannenberg's conception of science

A valid criticism of Pannenberg's conception of the scientific status of theology might be found in his use of Scholz's criteria since these might well be viewed as dated.[91] Since Pannenberg's express aim is to produce a defense of the scientific character of theology that is satisfactory in light of the criteria of contemporary philosophy of science his choice is at first somewhat surprising. Pannenberg himself seems to anticipate this charge when he goes to some length to defend his choice of Scholz's criteria of a science. One advantage of this choice, however, is that his defense of theology's status as science, by not simply building upon the latest propositions about the demands of a science from the philosophy of science, transcends to a certain extent the ever-changing formulations of what qualifies as scientific. Of course this advantage is only achieved when Scholz's requirements of a science prove modern and flexible enough to take into account recent developments within the philosophy of science. S. M. Daecke, writing at the about same time, confirms Pannenberg's estimation of the continuing relevance of Scholz's requirements when he noted that also for the 1970s they remained valid.[92] Also, as will be seen later in this chapter, Pannenberg adapts Scholz's third requirement significantly in light of advances in the philosophy of science brought about by Karl Popper and Thomas Kuhn, thereby minimizing the problem of interacting with a "dated" concept of science.

Another and perhaps even more significant reason for choosing to base the discussion upon Scholz's formulation of the requirements of a science is the significance of this particular formulation in the history of the discussion of the scientific nature of theology. Precisely because Barth could not or would not accept these requirements as applied to theology[93] Pannenberg is not only taking up a challenge from the philosophy of science which he believes has not been properly met, he is also decisively underlining his break with what he calls the revelation or scripture positivism of Barth.[94] Commenting on Barth's failure to continue the dialogue with Scholz after the latter contributed an article titled "Was ist unter einer theologischen Aussage zu verstehen?"[95] to a *Festschrift* for Barth's 50th birthday in 1936, Pannenberg wrote:

---

[91] William Bartley, a student of Karl Popper, in his 1962 book *Retreat to Commitment* showed amazement that even Karl Barth affirmed Scholz's criteria as being "the proper concept of a science" for the day since they were so enamored by positivism and were an "inadequate description of the discussion over the role of proofs in science." Cf. Wm. Bartley, *Flucht ins Engagement* (Tübingen: J.C.B. Mohr, 1987), 66.

[92] Daecke, "Soll die Theologie an der Universität bleiben?" 9.

[93] Cf. Barth, *CD* I.1., 9.

[94] Cf. *TPS*, 265ff. [*WtT*, 266ff.]

[95] For the text see Heinrich Scholz, "Was ist unter einer theologischen Aussage zu verstehen?" in: Gerhard Sauter, ed., *Theologie als Wissenschaft*, 265-278.

Karl Barth did not respond again to this argumentation from Heinrich Scholz. For Barth the irrational commitment of faith was indeed the risk, as he put it, of 'wholly uncertain obedience' toward the Word of God that only becomes recognizable as the Word of God through this obedience. All theological argumentation, according to Barth, presupposed this act. Not only did Barth think this way, but also Bultmann and ... the majority of prominent theologians of their time. Hence William Bartley can speak precisely of an 'escape into commitment' as characteristic of the whole of contemporary Protestant theology. To the extent that theological thought calls upon the commitment of faith it ultimately evades rational critique.[96]

It was precisely this tendency in theology which Pannenberg sought to break with by returning to and taking up Scholz's challenge to Barth.

Pannenberg's designation of theology as a science has not, however, been free of criticism. Most of this criticism has arisen out of philosophies of science at variance with that of Pannenberg's. We shall examine two such criticisms here which are typical of many others. One criticism which focuses on the minimum requirements of a science is that which has been leveled by David McKenzie. He argues that "the comparative aspect of Pannenberg's work on a testing procedure for theological claims is flawed" and that his procedure for testing truth claims "lacks the power to settle issues in the really crucial sense, and thus to establish theology as a science."[97] The "flaws" which McKenzie lists, however, would seem to concern difficulties that Pannenberg is aware of and deals with.[98] The heart of his criticism seems to rest upon theology's apparent inability to finally and conclusively settle or prove anything. McKenzie thus adds another requirement for science that would not appear to have good foundation in current philosophy of science discussions for he seems to be implying that to qualify as a science a discipline must be able to make assertions which can be absolutely and not merely provisionally or tentatively verified.[99] But can even the so-called "hard sciences" like physics meet such a requirement without closing a question to further discussion by denying the admission of new evidence or by denying that analytical mistakes may have been made? McKenzie's criticism would seem weak, therefore, inasmuch as it does not focus on the internal coherence of Pannenberg's

---

[96] "Wie wahr ist das Reden von Gott?" 30,

[97] David McKenzie, *Wolfhart Pannenberg's Religious Philosophy* (Washington, D.C.: University of America Press, 1980), 70f.

[98] McKenzie writes, for instance, that "Pannenberg's work on a testing procedure for theological claims is flawed in three respects. First, it requires a uniformity in the modern experience of reality which is simply absent. Second, it shows only that some ideas are historically more influential than others, not that they are true. And third, it cannot rank the monotheistic conceptions of God in terms of comprehensive and integrative power" (pp. 70f.).

[99] This would seem especially problematic in light of Popper, who against the view of logical positivism, whose influence is still to be felt in some quarters, maintained that absolute final verification of theories and assertions is impossible and that recognition of this is methodologically important. Cf. Karl Popper, *The Logic of Scientific Discovery*, 252ff.

own system but rather substitutes criteria for a science that are alien to Pannenberg's own conception of science and that are also problematic in light of current discussions within the philosophy of science.

A related but sharper criticism is that of the philosopher of religion Harvey White. Similar to McKenzie, White focuses his criticism of Pannenberg's conception of science upon the crucial concept of verification. White is especially critical of Pannenberg's making relevance a crucial aspect of verification.[100] That is to say, theological propositions must be relevant or correspond to our experience of reality. The problem for White arises in regard to religious pluralism. "Theology, whose scope is the total religious experience of mankind, must take into account faiths whose view of ... [the totality of meaning] is radically different from that ... of Christianity." Thus White concludes that:

> What a test of an hypothesis of the totality of meaning can establish ... is that it holds true in a particular historical context. But that is *all* that can be established. Insofar as providing a base for making choices between theological options (e.g., Christian or Buddhist), such a test will completely fail to do the job. If Buddhism is more 'meaningful' to me, then I will become a Buddhist. But that is not a test of Buddhism. It simply says something about me. ... The whole upshot of Pannenberg's thesis is that theological hypotheses must be relevant. This is a far cry from any sense of 'scientific' testing.[101]

This criticism, however, is directed only at a single aspect of Pannenberg's concept of verification, which has many components. It is true that theological propositions, according to Pannenberg, must correspond to our 'personal' experience of the totality of reality.[102] If they do not meet this requirement they are held by Pannenberg to be unsound. Meeting this requirement, however, does not constitute 'verification' but only an aspect of corroboration. In regard to making decisions between the truth claims of various religions I believe that Pannenberg's concept of verification does provide for the possibility of making such a decision and testing it against corroborating evidence which goes beyond a simple correspondence to personal experience. The question of the historicity of the resurrection of Jesus (which will be taken up more fully in our next section), is fundamental to the truth claims of Christianity. The resurrection, according to Pannenberg, is not only falsifiable, but precisely because it is, it is able to be provisionally "verified" through corroborating evidence.

Pannenberg's defense of theology as a science, I believe, is coherent and meets sufficiently the demands of at least one viable conception of science so that

---

[100] Harvey W. White, "A Critique of Pannenberg's *Theology and the Philosophy of Science*," in: *Studies in Religion/Sciences Religieuses* 11.4 (fall 1982), 433f., quote, 433.
[101] *Ibid.*, 436.
[102] *TPS*, 345. [*WtT*, 348.]

his claim to scientific status for theology is justified.[103] To demand that his program fulfill the requirements of each varying conception of science when there exists division among philosophers of science themselves in this area is unreasonable. If this were the case then the scientific status of every discipline would have to be suspended until all the philosophy of science issues could be settled. Whether one prefers the designation of theology as a science or not, Pannenberg has, I believe, sufficiently demonstrated that such a designation is possible.

## 1.3 Theology as Universal Science

The scientific status of theology is primarily of interest for our study inasmuch as theology is understood by Pannenberg as a universal science, which is crucial to his apologetic praxis. The mere status of theology as a science, however, does not constitute in itself a claim to universality. Theology's scientific status, rather, is significant in this regard only in that it could discredit theology's claim to universality if this claim could not be justified. This is the case since if theology does not possess a scientific character and its propositions are not open to some sort of verification, then it has no concrete epistemological links to the special sciences and becomes a discipline enclosed within itself.

### 1.3.1 *The concept of 'universal'*

Before proceeding to our discussion of Pannenberg's conception of theology as a universal science it is necessary to explain what is meant here by 'universal.' For Hegel, many of whose concepts have influenced Pannenberg, universality, or that which is "*allgemein*," as he preferred, is a central theme in his thought. Each part participates in and is defined by the whole, according to Hegel. Without the universal, the individual parts have no meaning. This is seen especially in his philosophy of history,[104] which he conceived of as a unified process, as well as in his view of the various scientific disciplines and their relationship to one another.[105] As Pannenberg has pointed out, Hegel, in his *Enzyklopädie der*

---

[103] Philip Hefner, "The Role of Science in Pannenberg's Theological Thinking," in: *The Theology of Wolfhart Pannenberg*, ed. Carl Braaten and Philip Clayton, 281ff., has suggested that Pannenberg's program can be understood as a science in terms of what the philosopher of science Imre Lakatos, *The Methodology of Scientific Research Programmes* (Cambridge: Cambridge University Press, 1978) has called a research programme in which a hard core of assertions is supported by a set of auxiliary hypotheses in which the hard core, in Pannenberg's case including God as all-determining reality and Jesus' resurrection as proleptic end of history, provides dramatic and unexpected interpretations of the world. The hard core itself is not subjected to the brunt of the falsification process but rather the supporting auxiliary hypotheses.

[104] Cf. Georg Wilhelm Friedrich Hegel, *The Philosophy of History*, trans. J. Sibree (New York: Dover Publications, 1956).

[105] Cf. Hegel, *Enzyklopädie der philosophischen Wissenschaften im Grundrisse* [1830], in: *Gesammelte Werke*, vol. 20 (Hamburg: Felix Meiner Verlag, 1992).

*philosophischen Wissenschaften im Grundrisse*, explored the totality of the subject matter of science in its organic unity.[106] For Pannenberg, this essential unity of knowledge has special significance for that science which has the one God and creator of all things as its object. There is no aspect of reality which lies beyond the scope or interest of theology and no part of this world or of human history which can be understood fully apart from the God who created all things and stands behind and reveals himself through universal history.

Pannenberg explained what he means by the term universality in relation to theology in his 1963 lecture "The Crisis of the Scripture Principle" delivered during a lecture tour in America. Pannenberg contended that: "The task of theology goes beyond its special theme and includes all truth whatever. This universality of theology is unavoidably bound up with the fact that it speaks of God. ... It belongs to the task of theology to understand all being [*alles Seienden*] in relation to God, so that without God they simply could not be understood. That is what constitutes theology's universality."[107] A fuller treatment of the role of God as foundation for theology's universality will be taken up in chapter four.

### 1.3.2 *Unitary knowledge, not unitary science*

Although theology's universality is not based upon its status as science, its scientific character does play an important role in Pannenberg's assessment of theology's universality - especially in regard to Scholz's requirement of coherence. In response to questions of clarification raised by Gerhard Sauter,[108] Pannenberg took up the question of the unity of knowledge implicit in the requirement of coherence, pointing out at the same time that neither the unity of knowledge nor the idea that theological science has universal character implies the controversial idea of a unitary science. Pannenberg wrote:

> The coherence of the truth implies the idea of a principal unity of all knowledge and of all science. It is not, however, to be taken in the controversial sense of a unitary science as this has been understood since logical positivism. ... Yet the concept of the unity of science can also be understood in the sense of the requirement for a coming together of all the individual sciences to form a whole. In this sense the unity of all knowledge and of all science - even if it cannot be formulated as a single picture - is the condition for the truth claims of each individual science in its theories, methods, and results. If Sauter calls my concept of science 'encyclopedic' in this context, then I have no defence, but can

---

[106] *TPS*, 17. [*WtT*, 21.]
[107] Pannenberg, "The Crisis of the Scripture Principle," in: Pannenberg, *Basic Questions in Theology* (*BQ*), vol. 1, trans. George Kehm (Philadelphia: Westminster Press, 1983), 1. ["Die Krise des Schriftprinzips," in: *Grundfragen*, 11.]
[108] Cf. Sauter, "Überlegungen zu einem weiteren Gesprächsgang über 'Theologie und Wissenschaft'" in: *Evangelische Theologie* 40 (March/April, 1980): 161-168.

only add that such a conception of science is necessarily derived from the concept of truth.[109]

In this way theology, as an individual science, is connected to the other individual sciences through the unitary character of all knowledge inasmuch as theology as a science meets the coherence test of truth, out of which arises necessarily the unity of knowledge as well as what Pannenberg refers to here as the encyclopedic character of science. Yet the concept of a universal science is not grounded upon a universal horizon of meaning (*Sinnhorizont*) arising out of the unity of "everyday" experience (implicitly) and religious experience (thematically) and the divine reality which constitutes these individual experiences, but rather upon the idea of God itself.[110] The implication of the reality of God which is understood as being in relationship with the entire living world is explained by Pannenberg as follows:

> If however there exists such a unity between the reality of God and the whole of human experience and life, then the reverse will also be true, namely, that everywhere, where the whole of reality is dealt with, the religious theme of the question of God is also touched upon. It will therefore then be possible to develop theological theories not only from firmly held (closed) propositions about God, but also from experiences of every kind in view of their implicit relationship to the reality of God. Only from this relationship is there an illumination of the inner consistency and coherence ... of the mutuality of the examination of those propositions which are to be tested and the universal statements upon which they are based.[111]

## 1.4 The Verifiability of Theological Statements

As we have already seen, the question of verification is the issue upon which theology's entire claim to be a science is dependent according to Pannenberg.[112] Heinrich Scholz's first requirement of a science, the proposition postulate which requires internal consistency, can only be met, according to Pannenberg, if

---

[109] Pannenberg, "Antwort auf G. Sauters Überlegungen," in: *Evangelische Theologie* 40 (March/April, 1980), 175.
[110] Cf. "Antwort auf Sauters Überlegungen," 180. Cf. also "The Crisis of the Scripture Principle," 11f. [The article originally appeared as, "Die Fragwürdigkeit der klassischen Universalwissenschaft," in: *Die Krise des Zeitalters des Wissenschaften* (Frankfurt/M, 1963) 173ff.]
[111] *Ibid.*, 180f.
[112] Pannenberg's position, at this point, is in marked contrast to that of many other contemporary Protestant theologians who have moved theological propositions outside the arena of factual, verifiable statements. Langdon Gilkey, *Religion and the Scientific Future* (London: SCM Press, 1970), 18ff., has written, for instance, that "theological truth no longer contains the sort of knowledge which entails particular factual propositions," and that the only legitimate aspects of theological language are "its transcending aspects pointing to ultimacy and sacrality" in which theology speaks rightly of "symbol" and "myth" and not of facts since the language of theology is symbolic and not "directly applicable to reality 'out there.'"

theology also meets Scholz's remaining two minimum requirements of a science. Similarly, the meeting of Scholz's second requirement, that of coherence which requires a single field or object, is contingent upon theology's ability to meet his third requirement, that of verification.

In Pannenberg's justification of making Scholz's formulation of the requirements of a science, already some forty years old at the time Pannenberg wrote his *Theology and the Philosophy of Science*, he suggested that, although still valid, they were "in need of supplication and refinement."[113] Pannenberg, indeed, makes some crucial and decisive "refinements" of Scholz's minimum requirements precisely at this point, especially in light of the work of Karl Popper and Thomas Kuhn.

Interestingly, even Scholz seemed to have had reservations about how and to what extent theological assertions could be verifiable. Concerning the truth claims inherent in theological statements he asked whether there is, in fact, any possibility to verify these claims. Scholz answers his own question by stating that, in his judgment, no such possibility exists. Instead, "all that can be attempted is this: that one look for reasons that are somehow suitable to support faith on the basis of truth."[114]

### 1.4.1 Ludwig Wittgenstein and the demands of logical positivism

As has been noted, Scholz's view of science and verification were set against the background of and greatly influenced by the philosophical movement known as logical positivism. Logical positivism, which arose out of the movement of analytical philosophy (including Frege, Russell, Ryle, Ayer, et al.)[115] and taken up and advocated by the 'Vienna circle' (especially Moritz Schlick and Rudolf Carnap), essentially put forward the epistemological view that there are only two kinds of meaningful statements: empirical statements, which can be verified through sense experience; and analytical statements, which are restricted to an analysis and definition of terms and are therefore either true or false by definition.

The "founder" of modern logical positivism, Ludwig Wittgenstein, contended in his "Tractatus logico-philosophicus" (1921) that "all philosophy is a 'critique of language'" (4.0031).[116] Wittgenstein was critical of previous philosophy, maintaining that most of the sentences and questions it has produced are only made possible by the fact that we do not understand our linguistic logic (*Sprachlogik*) and that for this reason the deepest problems of philosophy are in reality no problems at all (4.003). For Wittgenstein the only "strictly correct" philosophy can say nothing which is meaningful about "philosophy" and

---

[113] *TPS*, 326. [*WtT*, 329.]
[114] Scholz, "Wie ist eine evangelische Theologie als Wissenschaft möglich?" 259.
[115] On the rise of analytical philosophy and its basic shape see the description by the analytical philosopher Bertrand Russell in *History of Western Philosophy* (London: Routledge, 1991), 783ff.
[116] For this and the following see Ludwig Wittgenstein, *Tractatus logico-philosophicus*, trans. D. Pears and B. McGuinness (London: Routledge & Kegan Paul, 1961).

metaphysics. According to Wittgenstein: "The correct method of philosophy would really be the following: to say nothing except what can be said, i.e. propositions of natural science - i.e. something that has nothing to do with philosophy - and then, whenever someone else wanted to say something metaphysical, to demonstrate to him that he had failed to give a meaning to certain signs in his propositions." (6.53).

As Pannenberg notes, this meant that Wittgenstein "acknowledged only those statements to be meaningful which could be empirically verified or were of a purely logical-analytical nature." This meant, then, for the logical positivists, that "since statements about God are in principle not empirically verifiable ... they are not only false but are from the outset meaningless as assertions."[117]

Yet logical positivism, with its radical application of the criterion of meaningfulness, was not able to maintain its place as the dominant philosophy of science in large part because of its radical principle of verification which, as it turned out, could not itself be verified. The irony, of course, is that even Wittgenstein himself seemed to anticipate this, viewing it even as necessary: "My propositions serve as elucidations in the following way: anyone who understands me eventually recognizes them as nonsensical, when he has used them - as steps - to climb beyond them. (He must, so to speak, throw away the ladder after he has climbed up it.) He must transcend these propositions, and then he will see the world aright." (6.54).

In light of the criticism of Popper and others it was realized, as Pannenberg writes, "that the verification principle could only be defended in such a weak form that even metaphysical sentences could no longer be declared unworthy of rational discussion and hence excluded."[118]

*1.4.2 Karl Popper and Thomas Kuhn*

Pannenberg's own formulation and application of the verification principle is decisively shaped by the thought of philosopher of science Karl Popper. Popper, in his 1934 book *Logik der Forschung (The Logic of Scientific Discovery)*, rejected the rationality model of logical positivism. In doing so one important point in regard to our present discussion was that the logical positivist claim that metaphysical statements are meaningless was rejected. A move in the philosophy of science with great significance for theology. Popper also sought to find a criterion other than verification which would enable us to distinguish between the empirical sciences on the one hand and metaphysics, mathematics and logic on the other, since verification, in the strict sense of the logical positivists, was not suited to this task.[119] He suggested "that not the *verifiability* but the *falsifiability* of a system is to be taken as a criterion of demarcation."[120] Popper holds a theory to

---
[117] Pannenberg, *Metaphysics and the Idea of God*, 7. [*Metaphysik und Gottesgedanke*, 10.]
[118] Ibid.
[119] Karl Popper, *The Logic of Scientific Discovery* (London: Hutchenson, 1968), 34.
[120] Ibid., 40.

be falsified only if certain basic statements are accepted which contradict it. Crucial for Popper, however, is that a statement or theory be falsifiable, which means that it must "stand in a certain logical relationship to possible basic statements."[121] For Popper, falsifiability stands in close relationship to consistency, a further condition which an empirical system must meet. As he explains: "Statements which do not satisfy the condition of consistency fail to differentiate between any two statements within the totality of all possible statements. Statements which do not satisfy the condition of falsifiability fail to differentiate between any two statements within the totality of all possible empirical basic statements."[122]

Verification is rejected by Popper since empirical statements can only be tested by trying to falsify them, which includes checking their consistency. Yet although theories are not verifiable they can be "corroborated." Hence instead of discussing the probability of a theory or hypothesis Popper suggests that "we should try to assess what tests, what trials, it has withstood; that is, we should try to asses how far it has been able to prove its fitness to survive by standing up to tests. In brief, we should try to asses how far it has been 'corroborated.'"[123] Pannenberg, as we shall see, takes up not only Popper's emphasis upon falsification, but also contends that we should seek a provisional 'verification' or a 'corroboration' of theological statements. Hence he does not accept Popper's sharp distinction between verification and falsification, contending in agreement with Kuhn, that falsification is no more final than verification.

The American historian of science Thomas Kuhn broke through Popper's critical rationalism and proposed that scientific revolutions be seen as a process, a move which enabled him to point to the approximate character of both verification and falsification, which are necessary correlates. For Pannenberg, Kuhn's description of the processes involved in scientific revolutions "destroys the illusion that Popper's criterion of falsification can be clearly applied at any time." Rather, such questions are "the subject of an often lengthy process of scientific discussion."[124] Kuhn, in his groundbreaking book *The Structure of Scientific Revolutions*, summarized his critique of Popper's theory of falsification as follows:

---

[121] *Ibid.*, 86f.
[122] *Ibid.*, 92. With this also Popper arrived at an understanding of truth decisively different from that of logical positivism. As Jan Rohls, *Theologie und Metaphysik. Der Ontologische Gottesbeweis und seine Kritiker* (Gütersloh: Gerd Mohn, 1987), 619 writes: "Aufgrund seines Falsifizierbarkeitsprinzips gelangt Popper schließlich zum Verzicht auf den Begriff der Wahrheit und zu seiner Ersetzung durch den der Bewährung, wobei er sich vom Pragmatismus gerade dadurch unterscheidet, daß er die Wahrheit nicht durch den Begriff der Bewährung definiert. Das bedeutet zugleich, daß die Wissenschaft dem kritischen Rationalismus zufolge kein Wissen im strikten Sinne ist."
[123] *Ibid.*, 251.
[124] *TPS*, 57. [*WtT*, 59.]

The role ... attributed to falsification [by Popper] is much like the one this essay assigns to anomalous experiences, i.e., to experiences that, by evoking crisis, prepare the way for a new theory. Nevertheless, anomalous experiences may not be identified with falsifying ones. Indeed, I doubt that the latter exist. ... No theory ever solves all the puzzles with which it is confronted at a given time. ... If any and every failure to fit were ground for theory rejection, all theories ought to be rejected at all times. On the other hand, if only severe failure to fit justifies theory rejection, then the Popperians will require some criterion of 'improbability' or of 'degree of falsification.'[125]

For Pannenberg, however, this does not mean that the criterion of falsification is denied since "the process of scientific discussion makes sense only on the assumption that an anomaly could be shown to be a falsification of previous assumptions."[126] Instead, Pannenberg regards Kuhn's proposal as a contribution which redefines the scope and application of Popper's criterion of falsification.[127]

### 1.4.3 Pannenberg's concept of 'verification'

By following Popper and Kuhn Pannenberg does not weaken the requirements placed upon theology, nor are the risks that would be involved in the attempt of 'verification' minimized. Rather, quite the opposite is the case. As Pannenberg explains, the fact that "falsification and verification provide different types of certainty in the testing of hypothetical laws can be justified independently of the fact that the basic propositions on which the falsification is based themselves presuppose other, general, propositions. This relative character of basic propositions makes it more difficult to agree whether a particular observation falsifies a given hypothesis or not, but does not alter the fact that if agreement is reached on this point a single clear counterexample to a hypothetical law destroys that law's claim to validity, whereas in the converse procedure all positive confirmations can be no more than provisional."[128] Pannenberg here points to R. Carnap, *Philosophical Foundations of Physics* (New York, 1966) who puts the matter bluntly when he writes: "A million positive instances are insufficient to verify the law; one counterinstance is sufficient to falsify it."[129]

---

[125] Thomas S. Kuhn, *The Structure of Scientific Revolutions* (Chicago: University of Chicago Press, 1970), 146f.
[126] *TPS*, 57. [*WtT*, 59.]
[127] As Harvey White, "A Critique of Pannenberg's *Theology and the Philosophy of Science*," 420f., has written: "Thomas Kuhn's contribution to Pannenberg's argument is that scientific theories are never determinately falsified, but are replaced through an ill-defined process of judgment involving changes in world views of a scientific community. 'Truth' involves consensual agreement as to theoretical adequacy, which itself involves considerations of coherence, simplicity, scope, fruitfulness, etc."
[128] *TPS*, 54. [*WtT*, 55f.]
[129] Cited in *ibid.*, note 93. [56, note 93.]

The implications of such falsifiability for theology are enormous. If one says that a theological statement, such as "God exists" or "Jesus Christ has risen from the dead" can be verified this verification must always be seen as provisional. But more importantly, if the attempts at verification seem to fail, the truth claims of the statements must not be abandoned. One can always seek or hope for new verifying evidence or arguments. On the other hand, when one says that theological statements are open, at least in principle, to falsification, then one removes such assertions from the protective sphere of faith alone and admits that they are of such a nature that they could potentially be disproved by reason. For many theologians, including Karl Barth, this was too high a price to pay for theology's scientific status. For Pannenberg, however, there is much more at stake than merely the scientific status of theology. Indeed, theology has no choice but to open its statements, at least in principle, to the possibility of falsification if its truth claims are to retain any meaning whatsoever. Yet how verification and falsification are understood and applied must be specific to the science in question and its own specific subject matter.

Pannenberg, therefore, qualifies decisively what verification can mean for theological as well as philosophical statements since both of these have to do with the whole of reality which Pannenberg understands historically as a temporal process which is not yet complete. Thus Pannenberg can write:

> It is ... quite possible to verify theological statements, even in relation to their claim to truth. It is quite a different question, however, whether such verification can ever be brought to a final conclusion, negative or positive. ... The peculiar difficulty of making a final judgment in the case of philosophical and theological statements arises from the fact that such statements have to do with reality as a whole, and not just with its general structural features, but with the totality of its temporal process. Because of this a final judgment is impossible for someone who stands within this still open process, and not at its end.[130]

Pannenberg would agree, therefore, with John Hick and I. M. Crombie that only the eschatological future can ultimately verify theological statements.[131] Yet Pannenberg does not wish to use this important qualification as an escape from the requirements of verification. Thus he contends that since assumptions about reality as a whole are even now in our present lives unavoidable - and this includes theological assumptions - it is likewise necessary in the here and now to

---

[130] *TPS*, 343. [*WtT*, 346.]

[131] Cf. John Hick, *Faith and Knowledge* (Ithaca, NY: Cornell University Press, 1966), 169ff. and I.M. Crombie, "Theology and Falsification," in: A. Flew and A. MacIntyre, eds., *New Essays in Philosophical Theology* (New York: Macmillan, 1955), 109-130, both of whom are cited by Pannenberg. Hick writes: "the strength of the notion of eschatological verification is that it is not an *ad hoc* invention but is based upon an actually operative religious concept of God" (176). Yet he also qualifies: "the idea of an eschatological verification of theism can make sense, however, only if the logically prior idea of continued personal existence after death is intelligible" (178f.).

formulate criteria by which these assumptions or statements can be evaluated, at least provisionally, in relation to their truth claims.[132]

Theological statements are to be judged according to their ability to interpret convincingly our total experience of reality. In this sense the substantiation of our theological concept of God through insights which this concept provides into our experience of reality "must extend to all the dimensions of experience accessible at any particular time. It cannot be a mere existential certainty which is incapable of adducing any premises or arguments in its support." Neither, according to Pannenberg, can it compel anyone to assent to it through the force of logic. Thus "for these reasons the theological testing and reformulation of traditional religious statements can never attain theoretical certainty, but at most can form judgments only on their substantiation or non-substantiation and give reasons for saying how far a given religious assertion is to be regarded as substantiated or not."[133]

Pannenberg, therefore, suggests four specific criteria for verifying (or falsifying) theological propositions which he believes are proper to theology and its subject matter. According to Pannenberg theological hypotheses are to be judged not substantiated if:

1. they are intended as hypotheses about the implications of the Israelite-Christian faith but cannot be shown to express implications of biblical traditions;
2. they have no connection with reality as a whole which is cashable in terms of present experience and can be shown to be so by its relation to the current state of philosophical inquiry;
3. they are incapable of being integrated with the appropriate area of experience or no attempt is made to integrate them;
4. their explanatory force is inadequate to the stage reached in theological discussion, i.e. when it does not equal the interpretative force of existing hypotheses and does not overcome limitations of these which emerge in discussion.[134]

Wentzel van Huyssteen restates Pannenberg's four criteria for testing theological statements in positive form as follows:

1. Theological statements must demonstrably and testably express the essence of the biblical message.
2. Theological statements must emanate from a universally conceptualized theology, must examine the relationship between God and reality, and must therefore correlate closely with the level

---

[132] *TPS*, 343. [*WtT*, 347.]
[133] *Ibid.*, 344. [347.]
[134] *Ibid.*, 344f. [348.]

of problem-consciousness in modern philosophy and philosophy of science.
3. Theological statements must integrate human experiences as meaningfully as possible.
4. Theological statements must be fully cognitive of the status of problem-consciousness in modern theology.[135]

For Pannenberg, these criteria form the requirements by which theological statements can prove themselves provisionally. But in light of the fact that the eschaton has not yet come and the course of history continues to run we do not yet have access to the whole of reality in its completeness and are thus unable to form a final evaluation of the truth claims of theological statements.

### 1.4.4 *Verification and original or universal sin*

According to Pannenberg "provisional" testing or verification of theological statements is possible. How this verification is worked out in actual practice in the context of Pannenberg's theology can perhaps best be illustrated in the examples of the question of Jesus' resurrection from the dead and the Christian doctrine of original sin.

Pannenberg holds original sin to be a universal phenomenon which exhibits itself at the empirical level and is, therefore, subject to empirical verification. The universality of sin, according to Pannenberg, "must be verified anthropologically." Pannenberg further contends that the fact that the universality of sin is made known through revelation and is a presupposition of this revelation is justification for "looking for the root of human sin in the universal natural conditions of human existence"[136] Yet sin, in its form as opposition to God upon which the law and the cross shed light, is "obscure." That is to say, while "sin has an empirically verifiable universality and must be asserted as a universal presupposition for the Christian message of redemption, it also has a more hidden side." Thus sin, which is revealed first through the law and then in a more radical fashion through the cross, is "concealed in the immoderation of concupiscence." It is then only in this obscure form that "sin is universal by empirical standards." The material situation which is brought to light by the law and then decisively through the cross of Christ can, according to Pannenberg, "be shown to be universal at the empirical level, even if not under the name of sin."

Specifically, Pannenberg claims that, "the universality of sin is empirically verifiable in concupiscence and its implications."[137] For a "corroborating" verification of the theological doctrine of original (or universal) sin Pannenberg

---
[135] Huyssteen, 97.
[136] For this and the following see Pannenberg, *Anthropology in Theological Perspective*, trans. Matthew J. O'Connell (Philadelphia: The Westminster Press, 1985), 134f. [*Anthropologie in theologischer Perspektive*, Göttingen, 1983, 131f.]
[137] *Ibid.*, 138. [135.]

turns to the various special sciences which deal specifically with the phenomenon of human existence. In contrast to traditional dogmatic anthropology Pannenberg contends that his anthropology, including the doctrine of sin, "turns its attention directly to the phenomena of human existence as investigated in human biology, psychology, cultural anthropology, or sociology."[138] Of these non-theological disciplines Pannenberg gives the most weight to human biology, which he considers the "fundamental anthropological discipline." Pannenberg therefore begins his investigation with what biological research has to contribute and then moves on to human biology, especially to behavioral research, which in turn leads to the closely related fields of psychology and sociology.[139] In these fields Pannenberg finds wide-ranging corroborating evidence of the universal phenomenon of sin, albeit often not under that name. Of special significance are such findings as Freud's discovery of the "death drive" and Konrad Lorenz's treatment of the problem of aggression in humanity.[140]

Pannenberg, however, does not thereby relegate the biblical, revelatory witness to the universality of sin to a secondary status. Rather, it is the biblical revelation of sin's universality which is the basis for seeking verification of this phenomenon in the human structure of existence by means of the special sciences - yet precisely because the universality of sin is itself presupposition of the Christian message. Because of the importance of the phenomenon of the universality of sin for the Christian message and for Christian revelation, therefore, theology must examine, with the help of the special sciences, the phenomenon of sin as found in "the universal natural conditions of human existence." Hence for Pannenberg the assertion of the empirically verifiable universality of sin cannot be separated from the proclamation of the Christian message of redemption which presupposes sins empirical universality.[141]

### 1.4.5 Verification and the resurrection of Jesus

For Pannenberg "the resurrection of Jesus is the event which was, historically speaking, the point of departure for the history of Christendom. ... And this starting point is ... the permanent, substantial foundation for that faith. ... In the resurrection of Jesus we therefore have to do with the sustaining foundation of the Christian faith. If this collapses, so does everything else which the Christian faith

---

[138] *Ibid.*, 21. [21.]
[139] *Ibid.*, 22f. [22f.]
[140] *Ibid.*, 28ff., 142ff. [26ff., 139ff.] Cf. Konrad Lorenz, *On Aggression*, trans. M. Latzke (London: Methuen & Co., 1966); and Sigmund Freud, *Civilization and its Discontents* [1930], trans. Joan Riveriere, in: *The Standard Edition of the Complete Works*, vol. 21 (London: Hogarth, 1961), esp. 119ff. For a valuable study of the implications of Freud's work for the doctrine of original sin see also Sharon MacIsaac, *Freud and Original Sin* (New York: Paulist Press, 1974).
[141] Cf. *ATP*, 134, 137. [131, 134.]

acknowledges."[142] Thus we see the fundamental importance of the resurrection for Pannenberg. Yet because we ourselves have no experience of the reality of the resurrected Lord, as is implied in the story of Jesus' ascension in Luke, we must rely upon the accounts of those who claimed to have seen the risen Lord. These assertions of a resurrection, in turn, must be examined "solely and exclusively by the methods of historical research" since there is no other way of testing assertions about happenings supposed to have taken place in the past than by "the methods of historical research [which] have been developed precisely for the examination of assertions of this kind."[143] In making this claim that the resurrection is an actual event and is subject to verification (in the sense of approximation) through the methods of historical research Pannenberg parts company once again from dialectical theology, both as represented by Barth and by Bultmann. Whereas the former considered the event indeed historical but did not believe it was open to historical investigation, the latter agreed that the resurrection was not open to historical investigation, but precisely because it was not a historical event.[144]

In the second volume of Pannenberg's *Systematic Theology* seven theses concerning the resurrection of Jesus are presented. The last two of these theses deal with the verification of Jesus' resurrection as an historical occurrence. We will treat these here in reverse order. In thesis seven Pannenberg contends that: "The thesis that Jesus rose again, that the dead Jesus of Nazareth came to a new life, implies already a claim to historicity."[145] That is to say, the evangelists are speaking of an event which actually, physically occurred. Such a contention, according to Pannenberg, that an event actually took place in the past, implies not only a claim to historicity but presupposes as well the possibility of historical testability. Such historicity, however, does not necessarily mean that an event must be analogous or identical to other known events. Therefore a unique event such as the resurrection can also be historical.[146] Also, the claim to historicity in regard to the resurrection of Jesus, or any other event, does not mean that the discussion can be closed as to whether the event actually occurred or not. Finally,

---

[142] Pannenberg, *The Apostles' Creed in the Light of Today's Questions*, trans. Margaret Kohl (London: SCM Press, 1972), 96f. [*Das Glaubensbekenntnis: Ausgelegt und verantwortet vor den Fragen der Gegenwart*, Hamburg, 1972, 104f.]
[143] *Ibid.*, 107ff.
[144] Cf. Barth, *CD*, III/2, 446ff.; and Rudolf Bultmann, "New Testament and Mythology," in: *Kerygma and Myth*, trans. R. Fuller (London: SPCK, 1953), 41f. Carl Braaten, "The Current Controversy on Revelation: Pannenberg and his Critics," in: *Journal of Religion* 45 (1965), 226, wrote: "In the face of modern historical criticism which was unable to establish the historicity of the events of revelation, Barth together with the *Heilsgeschichte* theologians fled from history into the realm of suprahistory or prehistory, while Bultmann and the existentialist theologians dissolved the significance of all objective history into the inwardness of existential historicity. Negatively they are bound together by their refusal to verify the redemptive events by historical science and positively they agree in locating the event of revelation in the Word rather than in history."
[145] Pannenberg, *Systematic Theology* 2 (Göttingen: Vandenhoeck & Ruprecht, 1991), 359, [402.]
[146] *Ibid.*, 360f. [403.]

Pannenberg points out that the decision one reaches as to the historicity of the resurrection depends to a large extent upon one's understanding of reality and what one consequently considers to be within the realm of possibility.[147] As Pannenberg wrote in his commentary on the Apostles' Creed nearly two decades earlier:

> What this or that historian believes to be in any way possible depends on his own picture of reality and on the way in which he absorbs into this picture the points of view contributed by the various sciences, from physics to anthropology and sociology. The historian's judgment in a particular case is often determined and limited from the outset by his previous understanding as to the orbit of possibility. This is particularly clear in such an unusual problem as the question of Jesus' resurrection.[148]

The crucial question, then, is whether the historian is in a position to reckon with something like a resurrection. Pannenberg believes that a unique event like the resurrection of Jesus should be able to find a place within the historian's knowledge of reality just as much as the facts of physics or biology. Indeed, "the natural sciences cannot ... be the final court of appeal in the decision as to the possibility or impossibility of Jesus' resurrection. ... For the historian, this means that in forming a judgment about the past he must not from the outset permit only those possibilities which are in line with the normal and superficial course of events."[149] With this qualification, therefore, Pannenberg opens up the historicity of the resurrection of Jesus to historical investigation, which he takes up in his sixth thesis. Pannenberg maintains: "Decisive for confidence in the facticity of the resurrection of Jesus as the Christian message proclaims it are the primitive Christian testimonies to the appearances of the risen Lord to his disciples, along with the discovery of the empty tomb of Jesus in Jerusalem."[150] With this thesis Pannenberg focuses on a twofold verification of the historicity of the resurrection, first through the testimony of those who claimed to have seen the risen Jesus, and second, through the fact of the empty tomb.

### 1.4.5.1 *The resurrection appearances*

Concerning the witnesses to the resurrection appearances of Jesus Pannenberg insists that these cannot simply be accepted as authority but must first demonstrate their reliability by being subject to the same tests as the accounts of other historical occurrences.[151] For Pannenberg the question of the historicity of

---

[147] *Ibid.*, 361f., [404f.]
[148] *The Apostles' Creed*, 109 [*Glaubensbekenntnis*, 117.]; Cf. also Pannenberg, *Jesus - God and Man*, trans. L. Wilkens and D. Priebe (Philadelphia: Westminster, 1968), 98. [*Grundzüge der Christologie* [1964], (Gütersloh: Gerd Mohn, 1976), 95.]
[149] *Ibid.*, 110ff. [118ff.]
[150] *ST* 2:352f. [395.]
[151] *Ibid.*, 353.

the appearances of the Resurrected One is concentrated entirely upon the Pauline report in I Cor. 15:1-11, since the appearances reported in the Gospels which are not mentioned by Paul have such a strong legendary character that it is difficult to find the historical kernel within them.[152] Additionally, a reconstruction of the chronology of the resurrection appearances and Paul's meeting with many of the witnesses of these appearances in Jerusalem show that Paul's reception of these accounts lay very near to the events themselves, not to mention Paul's own firsthand encounter on the road to Damascus.[153] Of additional significance for Pannenberg is that Paul's listing of the appearances of the resurrected Jesus to Peter, then to the twelve, then before five hundred believers at one time, then to James the brother of Jesus, then to all the apostles and finally to Paul himself, especially in light of Paul's mention that some of these were still living and could verify the accounts, demonstrates that Paul intended to provide evidence for the factual resurrection of Jesus.[154]

Attempts to interpret the experiences of the disciples and other witnesses of the resurrected Jesus as products of enthusiastic imaginations or as parapsychological projections or visions are rejected by Pannenberg as insufficient explanations of these accounts. Pannenberg contends, rather, that "the Easter appearances are not to be explained from the Easter faith of the disciples; rather, conversely, the Easter faith of the disciples is to be explained from the appearances."[155]

Neither does Pannenberg accept the objection that a resurrection cannot be considered historical on grounds that it violates the laws of nature. In the light of developments in modern physics Pannenberg believes more caution needs to be exercised in making such judgments. "First, only a part of the laws of nature are ever known. Further, in a world that as a whole represents a singular, irreversible process, an individual event is never completely determined by natural laws. Conformity to law embraces only one aspect of what happens. ... The judgment about whether an event, however unfamiliar, has happened or not is in the final analysis a matter for the historian and cannot be prejudged by the knowledge of

---

[152] *Jesus - God and Man*, 89. [*Grundzüge*, 85.]

[153] The weight given Paul's "mystical" encounter of the risen Christ is somewhat surprising - even considering the probable, relatively early date of its written report. Given Pannenberg's stated goal of establishing the historicalness of the resurrection Paul's personal encounter of the blinding light on the road to Damascus some years after the events in Jerusalem would not seem, from the perspective of purely historical criteria, to be able to contribute much to the case for historicity. As an aside one is tempted to ask whether Pannenberg's own mystical and life-changing experience of light on the road home from school at the age of 16 (on the feast of Epiphany!) may establish a certain affinity with Paul's experience which could account, in part, for the weight he gives to this event. (Cf. Pannenberg, "An Autobiographical Sketch," in: *The Theology of Wolfhart Pannenberg*, ed. Braaten and Clayton, 12; and "Theta Phi Talkback Session with W. Pannenberg," in: *Asbury Theological Journal* 46:2 (fall 1991), 38f., for accounts of this incident.)

[154] *Jesus - God and Man*, 89. [*Grundzüge*, 86.]

[155] *Ibid.*, 96. [93.]

natural science."[156] And inasmuch as it is the historian's task to reconstruct the events which led to the rise of early Christianity and given the lack of any other credible explanation for the reports of the appearances of the resurrected Jesus, Pannenberg contends that the best and most acceptable explanation in the light of historical research is that the appearances actually occurred as reported.[157]

### 1.4.5.2 *The empty tomb*

Pannenberg notes that the report of the empty tomb, as found in its original form in Mark 16:1-8, was often criticized in earlier research as a late Hellenistic legend. Yet Pannenberg believes there are compelling grounds to doubt this judgment.[158] Despite all the historical criticisms directed against the account of the empty tomb and the fact that we are probably not dealing here with a purely historical report Pannenberg believes that individual data of historical significance have been preserved in the account. Pannenberg points out that both the early Christians and the Jews were agreed upon the basic fact of the empty tomb. What they disagreed about was *why* and not *whether* it was empty. If the tomb was not empty, given the fact that in Jewish thought a resurrection would necessarily imply an empty tomb, it is not conceivable that the resurrection accounts could have first been preached and believed in Jerusalem of all places where the tomb could be checked by anyone. Hence the dispute over why the tomb was empty and the fact that the opponents of the Easter message never claimed that the body of Jesus was still in his tomb are all significant witnesses to the historicity of the empty tomb.[159] Pannenberg concludes that the historicity of the empty tomb, which is falsifiable, has not been falsified and, even finds corroboration from historical investigation into the question. Pannenberg can write, therefore, that:

> Those who want to dispute the empty tomb of Jesus must show that contemporary Jewish witnesses to belief in the resurrection included some who did not think the resurrection of the dead need have anything at all to do with the body in the tomb. They must also assume that such views (not thus far attested) were sufficiently popular in Palestine, else the first Christians could not have successfully preached the resurrection of Jesus if his body had been intact in the tomb. Even then, an explanation would still be needed as to why the Gospels

---

[156] *Ibid.*, 98. [95f.]
[157] *Ibid.*, 98, 105f. [95, 103.]
[158] *Ibid.*, 101. [98.] Pannenberg refers here to the criticism of this view by his former teacher at Heidelberg, Hans von Campenhausen, *Der Ablauf der Osterereignisse und das leere Grab* [1952] (Heidelberg: Carl Winter, 1966). Campenhausen wrote his short study, as he reported, to show, "daß zu einer so weitgehenden Skepsis angesichts der wirklichen Überlieferungsverhältnisse, historisch geurteilt, kein Recht besteht" (54). Indeed, Pannenberg follows his former teacher in many respects in his own treatment of the resurrection appearances and the report of the empty tomb, as for instance in his concentration upon I Cor. 15 and estimation of its significance in his rejection of psychological explanations of the resurrection appearances as insufficient to explain the effect upon those present.
[159] *ST* 2:357ff. [399ff.]

present debates between Christians and their opponents regarding what happened to the body. So long as no proofs are offered on these points, we must assume that the tomb of Jesus was in fact empty.[160]

The combined impact of the accounts of the resurrection appearances and the report of the empty tomb, which Pannenberg sees as having arisen independently of one another and thus constituting two separate witnesses,[161] is held to be decisive for the question of the historicity of the resurrection. Thus he could conclude already in his 1964 work, *Grundzüge der Christologie* (*Jesus - God and Man*), that "if the appearance tradition and the grave tradition came into existence independently, then by their mutually complementing each other they let the assertion of the reality of Jesus' resurrection ... appear as historically very probable, and that always means in historical inquiry that it is to be presupposed until contrary evidence appears."[162]

## 1.5 Revelation as History and the Possibility of a Natural Knowledge of God

Although Pannenberg rejects the positivism of revelation found in Barth, revelation, understood as the self-disclosure of God, remains decisive for his theological program. Indeed, Pannenberg's understanding of revelation constitutes one of the most unique and one of the most crucial elements of his theological program.

### 1.5.1 *Revelation as history as the indirect self-disclosure of God*

Much of Pannenberg's early renown can be attributed to his short but incisive article, "Dogmatic Theses on the Doctrine of Revelation,"[163] which resulted from interdisciplinary discussions of a young group of theologians at Heidelberg. A collection of articles which arose out of this "working circle" appeared in 1961 as a supplemental volume to *Kerygma und Dogma* under the title *Offenbarung als Geschichte* (*Revelation as History*). Pannenberg's article provided the systematic, theological formulation of the group's groundbreaking conception of revelation.

Pannenberg presented the following seven theses regarding his proposal to understand revelation as history:

1. The self-revelation of God, according to the biblical witnesses, has not taken place directly, as in the manner of a theophany, but indirectly, through the actions of God in history.

---

[160] *Ibid.*, 358f. [401.]
[161] *Jesus - God and Man*, 105. [*Grundzüge*, 101f.]
[162] *Ibid.*, 105. [103.]
[163] Pannenberg, "Dogmatic Theses on the Doctrine of Revelation," in: *Revelation as History*, ed. W. Pannenberg, trans. David Granskou (New York: Macmillan, 1968. ["Dogmatische Thesen zur Lehre von der Offenbarung," in: *Offenbarung als Geschichte*, ed. W. Pannenberg (Göttingen: Vandenhoeck & Ruprecht, 1961.)]

2. Revelation does not take place at the beginning, but rather at the end of history.
3. In contrast to special manifestations of the Godhead historical revelation is open to all who have eyes to see. It has universal character.
4. The universal revelation of the divinity of God is not yet realized in the history of Israel but first in the destiny of Jesus of Nazareth inasmuch as the end of events has already taken place proleptically in him.
5. The Christ event does not reveal the divinity of the God of Israel as an isolated event but only insofar as it is a part of God's total history with Israel.
6. The universality of the eschatological self-disclosure of God in the destiny of Jesus is expressed in the development of non-Jewish concepts of revelation in the Gentile Christian churches.
7. The Word has to do with revelation as prediction, as instruction, and as report.[164]

The crucial point of these theses, which essentially outline Pannenberg's conception of revelation, is that revelation is understood as taking place in and through universal history which is accessible to all. He makes, therefore, a decisive and intentional break with the concept of revelation which dominated much of Protestant theology from the beginning of the dialectical theology up to the time of the publication of his theses on revelation.[165]

As the Roman Catholic theologian Avery Dulles has rightly noted, "at the heart of Pannenberg's proposal lies a crucial distinction between direct and indirect revelation."[166] For Pannenberg biblical revelation is indirect and not direct, as he clearly states in his first thesis. As he has elsewhere written, "we are given cause to think in terms of an indirectness of God's self-revelation by the finding that in the biblical texts themselves the direct content of the reception of revelation ... is not God himself but ourselves and our world."[167] This revelation, as we have seen, is also a self-revelation, meaning that God himself is the content of revelation.[168]

The concept of an indirect self-revelation of God through the history which he himself controls is, however, as Pannenberg himself pointed out, nothing new,

---

[164] Cf. *ibid.*, 125 - 152. [91-112],
[165] Cf. for instance Pannenberg's comments in the introduction to *Revelation as History, ibid.*, 3. [*Offenbarung als Geschichte*, 7.] For a detailed critique of Barth's concept of revelation see Pannenberg, *Systematic Theology (ST)* vol. 1, trans. Geoffrey Bromiley (Grand Rapids: Eerdmans, 1991), 235ff. [*Systematische Theologie* 1, Göttingen, 1988, 258ff.]
[166] Avery Dulles, "Pannenberg on Revelation and Faith," in: *The Theology of Wolfhart Pannenberg*, ed. Carl Braaten and Philip Clayton (Minneapolis: Augsburg, 1988), 171.
[167] *ST*, 1:244. [267.]
[168] *Ibid.*, 222ff. [243ff.]

for "it has its source in German idealism, as does the exclusive conception of revelation as self-revelation."[169] Pannenberg is especially indebted here, as in many other crucial aspects of his thought, to Hegel, who "gave systematic formulation to the conception of universal history as an indirect revelation of God in connection with his explication of the concept of self-revelation."[170]

The indirect character of revelation also has an important implication for our speech about God, namely, that we can only speak of God analogically, i.e., indirectly. As Pannenberg wrote in his article "Analogy and Doxology," "if the divine reality is not directly experienceable, then it can be spoken of only in an indirect manner." And also: "the indirectness of our speech about God already means that we can only speak of him analogically." Yet this does not mean that such speech of God is in any way deficient for it is, as in the classical analogy theory from the 13th century, grounded upon an analogy between God and the world which he created. Therefore, according to Pannenberg, "our knowledge is not simply inappropriate to the divine reality, for an analogy between God and the world does in fact exist."[171]

In the first volume of his *Systematic Theology* Pannenberg summarizes the significance of the distinction between direct and indirect revelation. He writes:

> If we had direct self-revelation, i.e., God's making himself known directly by special communication, in all these various forms and in association with all the various recipients and events, then inevitably their claims would be in competition with one another. The divine Self might be revealed in one special communication as distinct from another. But if the communications come directly from God, yet are indirectly communications about God himself which make known his nature and deity, i.e., to the degree that they have God as their Author, then we can view the various events of revelation as components [sic] parts of the one all-embracing event of self-revelation to which each of them makes its own specific contribution.[172]

---

[169] Pannenberg, "Introduction," in: *Revelation as History*, 19. ["Einführung," in: *Offenbarung als Geschichte*, 20.] Cf. also *ibid.*, 16 [18] where he notes that "when the totality of reality in its temporal development is thought of as history and as the self-communication of God, then we find ourselves on the road which German idealism has taken since the time of Lessing and Herder."

[170] *Ibid.*, 16. [18.]

[171] Pannenberg, "Analogy and Doxology," in *BQ* 1:212f. ["Analogie und Doxologie," in: *Dogma und Denkstrukturen*, ed. Wilfried Joest and Wolfhart Pannenberg (Göttingen: Vandenhoeck & Ruprecht, 1963), 96f.] Because the world falls short of the divine archetype, however, the transference back to God of that which "is read off of the world is no longer able to attain to the purity of the divine archetypes." Hence Pannenberg, although speaking of the analogical character of our language about God, is skeptical of the traditional doctrine of analogy and prefers instead to speak of doxological language. Cf. 213ff. [97ff.] Some, however, have seen in Pannenberg's emphasis upon doxology a shift away from analogy and a "loss of actual knowledge of the essence of God." So, for instance, Stanley Grenz, *Reason for Hope: The Systematic Theology of Wolfhart Pannenberg* (Oxford: Oxford University Press, 1990), 75.

[172] *ST* 1:243f. [266f.]

With this statement we come to the subject of our next two sections, which together make up the heart and essence of Pannenberg's concept of revelation and history, namely, the universal character of history and the central significance of the Christ event and the revelatory culmination of this universal history.

### 1.5.2 The universal character of history

As we have already seen, Pannenberg adopted from Hegel the crucial idea that the revelation which occurs as God's self-disclosure takes place in the context of universal history. Although the *Heilsgeschichte* school had emphasized the significance of history Pannenberg rejects this line of thought inasmuch as it separates redemptive history from profane history. Pannenberg opts instead for an approach which takes history as a whole into account, corresponding to God's own universality.[173] Only in the context of such a "universal historical horizon" can the question be raised whether God revealed himself at one place or another in history. Pannenberg's criticism of the *Heilsgeschichte* approach comes especially to light in his critique of Oscar Cullmann.

Inherent in the concept of a *Heilsgeschichte* as formulated by Cullmann, notes Pannenberg, is that a salvation history has to do with a special history (*Sondergeschichte*) within the general or universal history of humanity, which leads necessarily to a narrowing of its scope. Pannenberg points here specifically to Cullmann's claim that the New Testament history of salvation distinguishes itself radically from all other history.[174] Hence "the distinction between salvation history and general history is, according to Cullmann, grounded from the historical point of view in the willful choice of which events go into salvation history." Which means, as Pannenberg points out, that "salvation history, seen from this perspective, makes up 'a very small line' within general history." By separating salvation history from the rest of history in this way one seems to take salvation history outside of the scope of normal historical study - or that it must be protected from the critique of such study. Hence, according to Pannenberg:

> This thesis of the radical otherness of salvation history must lead to the suspicion that certain historical records, namely the biblical records, should be protected - through the subjectivity of the decision of faith which, for its part, is already based upon the claim of a revealed authority that evades rational insight - from the application of the general principles of historical criticism.[175]

Pannenberg finds Karl Rahner's conception of salvation history at this point more acceptable since it distinguishes itself from Cullmann's view inasmuch as its

---

[173] Pannenberg, "Redemptive Event and History," in: *BQ* 1:67. [*Grundfragen*, 67.]
[174] Pannenberg, "Weltgeschichte und Heilsgeschichte," in: *Probleme biblischer Theologie: Gerhard von Rad zum 70. Geburtstag*, ed. Hans Walter Wolff (Munich: Chr. Kaiser, 1971), 358. For Cullmann's view of *Heilsgeschichte* cf. Oscar Cullmann, *Salvation in History*, trans. S. G. Sowers (London: SCM, 1967). [*Heil als Geschichte*, 58f. for this reference]
[175] *Ibid.*, 359, 361.

uniqueness is not based upon the selection of a limited series of events but rather in view of the fact that it illumines the salvation-historical significance of history as a whole. Thereby also it is clear that for Rahner salvation has to do with the whole of humanity. Although this perspective is not entirely foreign to Cullmann, it is not, as it is for Rahner, constitutive of his conception of salvation history.[176]

For Pannenberg, therefore, a separation of a special salvation history from the rest of history is not acceptable. Hence he arrives at what he considers to be the central question for debate between history and theology, namely, "how is the conception of a unity of history possible?" Since "everything in history stands under over-arching continuities, no particular unitary event can be definitively understood from within itself." Therefore it is not a viable option "for historical thought to renounce the presupposition of a unity of history."[177] Pannenberg rejects both a teleological approach (Troeltsch) which necessarily neglects the contingency of events and a morphological approach (Toynbee, Jaspers) as insufficient for establishing the concept of the unity of history. More promising would seem to be the attempt to conceive the unity of history in such a way as to show that the contingency and continuity of events have a common root, namely in the unity of humanity. Yet even this approach proves unworkable since if one conceives of this unity of humanity as biological one does not yet have a historical unity, whereas if the unity of humanity is understood as the unity of a historical process one encounters the problem that the human spirit exists always and only as an individual and for the individual.[178]

For Pannenberg, it is precisely the futility of these attempts which indicate that the unity of history must be grounded in something which transcends history. Thus he concludes that "the God who by the transcendence of his freedom is the origin of contingency in the world, is also the ground of the unity which comprises the contingencies of history." Yet Pannenberg also notes that the unity of history "does not consist merely in its transcendent origin" since "events are not only contingent in relation to each other, but they also cohere among each other." Yet even this "indwelling connection between them is grounded in the transcendent unity of God."[179] Therefore, just as God is the foundation of the universal character of theological science, as we saw earlier, so it is that God is correspondingly and, within Pannenberg's system, necessarily the foundation of the universal or unitary character of history. Indeed, for Pannenberg, God is the foundation of all universality.

Similarly, just as Pannenberg concluded that if God is the creator then no part of the creation can be fully understood without taking him into account, so he contends that if God is the foundation of the unitary character of history, then the

---

[176] *Ibid.*, 361.
[177] "Redemptive Event and History," 68. [*Grundfragen*, 68.]
[178] *Ibid.*, 72ff. [73f.]
[179] *Ibid.*, 75. [74.]

concept of God is "indispensable for the historian."[180] Consistent with Pannenberg's philosophy of science and emphasis upon verification he reasons that the "exact form of the continuity of history grounded in the unity of God" can only be discovered through historical research. Such a theological approach, then, distinguishes itself from the usual sort of "redemptive-historical thinking by the fact that it wants to be in principle historically verifiable." Indeed, Pannenberg suggests that "a verification through subsequent testing by observation of the particulars may unreservedly be expected of a theological projection of history. Its ability to take into account all known historical details would be the positive criterion of its truth; the proof that without its specific assertions the accessible information would not be at all or would be only incompletely explicable, can be used as a negative criterion."[181]

As Avery Dulles has noted, "because of his universalistic approach to history, one might expect Pannenberg to look for revelation in the nonbiblical religions, but in fact he insists upon the uniqueness of biblical religion."[182] One might also expect that Pannenberg would insist upon concentrating upon the whole of history to discover God's self-revelation yet he focuses on one specific event, or event-sequence, as manifesting God's self-revelation. Hence Pannenberg, in reflecting upon a series of difficult problems which weighed down the concept of the self-revelation of God in history found in German idealism concluded:

> An individual act of God, a particular event, can indeed cast an indirect light on its originator, but cannot be the full and complete revelation of the one God. However, history as a totality is not open to us as a self-contained unit. Still, if this were the case, it would not seem possible for any single event to have absolute meaning analogous to that of Jesus Christ in Christian faith, for universal history is simply too boundless and unremitting in its progress.[183]

Pannenberg comes, therefore, to what is for him the decisive and culminating event in universal history, namely the death and resurrection of Jesus of Nazareth.

### 1.5.3 *The Christ event as the proleptic end of history*

History, according to Pannenberg, "is the most comprehensive horizon of Christian theology. All theological questions and answers are meaningful only within the framework of the history which God has with his whole creation - the history moving toward a future still hidden from the world but already revealed in Jesus Christ."[184] Central here is the fourth of Pannenberg's dogmatic theses which states: "The universal revelation of the divinity of God is not yet realized in the

---

[180] *Ibid.*, 76. [75.]
[181] *Ibid.*, 78. [76f.]
[182] Avery Dulles, Pannenberg on Revelation and Faith," 173.
[183] Pannenberg, "Introduction," in: *Revelation as History*, 19. [*Offenbarung als Geschichte*, 20.]
[184] "Redemptive Event and History," 15. [*Grundfragen*, 22.]

history of Israel but first in the destiny of Jesus of Nazareth inasmuch as the end of events has already taken place proleptically in him."

This thesis, however, is dependent upon the second: "Revelation does not take place at the beginning, but rather at the end of history." This is essentially a theological formulation of the philosophical thought found in Wilhelm Dilthey and first introduced into Christian theology in seminal form by Bultmann.[185] Dilthey maintained already at the turn of the century that we must wait until the end of history in order to have all the data necessary to determine its meaning.[186] Pannenberg's corrective to Dilthey is essentially that we do not have to withhold judgment on the meaning of history, which for Pannenberg is itself revelatory, since the end of history is already present to us proleptically in the Christ event.

Yet Pannenberg has encountered criticism at this point since his concept of history is universal and includes not just human history but all of creation. Ignace Berten, for instance, has criticized that it makes no sense from the standpoint of the physical sciences to speak of an end of all things and of all processes. He writes: "To arrive at a preceding or following matter from a matter present at hand is physically (always within the category of physics itself) unthinkable: the total state of the universe presupposes a state that can cause it, and the idea of the dissolution of matter into nothing is senseless."[187] In a response to Berten Pannenberg explained that he did not find this problem difficult since our present knowledge of natural laws is not complete. This means that the present hypotheses concerning natural laws "do not exclude the effectiveness of our current recognition of hidden parameters that could condition a future end of history that lays outside the horizon of our present knowledge of nature." Pannenberg also reiterates his conviction that the meaning structure of historical occurrences implies an end of history since only then will the totality of historical reality be complete and the meaning of individual events definitively known.[188] Thus on the basis of natural science's inability to rule out an end of history as well as the logical implication of such an end based on the meaning structure of historical events Pannenberg contends that he is standing on solid ground on this point.

A second point of difficulty Pannenberg has encountered involves the radical reconceptualizing of the Christ event as constituting the proleptic end rather than the center of history. Although Pannenberg first introduced the decisive term "proleptic" in his Dogmatic Theses to describe the significance of the Christ event, the concept itself was already laid forth two years earlier in his 1959 essay "Redemptive Event and History" where Pannenberg made the radical assertion that "Jesus is the anticipated end and not the middle of history."[189] Based upon

---

[185] Cf. Bultmann, *Geschichte und Eschatology*, 135.
[186] Cf. Dilthey, *Der Aufbau der geschichtlichen Welt in den Geisteswissenschaften*, in: *GW*, 7:233.
[187] Ignace Berten, *Geschichte, Offenbarung, Glaube: Eine Einleitung in die Theologie Wolfhart Pannenbergs*, trans. Sigrid Martin (Munich: Claudius, 1970), 77.
[188] Pannenberg, "Nachwort von Wolfhart Pannenberg," in: *ibid.*, 132.
[189] "Redemptive Event and History," 24. [*Grundfragen*, 29.]

philosophical considerations arising from Dilthey, Bultmann and ultimately Hegel this makes sense, but can this move be justified biblically and theologically? Pannenberg believes, indeed, that the biblical witness calls for such an interpretation.

Jewish expectation, as is seen for instance in Is. 40ff., was that in the consummation of history "God will be shown to be not simply the only God that Israel must worship but the only God of all peoples." Yet this is precisely an expectation for the consummation of history since "the basic history of Israel could show ... [Yahweh] to be the God of this people, but not yet the God of all peoples."[190] This expectation is closely connected to the fullness of God's self-disclosure, in which he will show himself to be the God of all peoples. Yet God's historical self-disclosure to Israel through his actions possesses only a "provisional character." These are "always surpassed with new events, new historical activity in which Jahweh presents himself in new ways. ... Only the end of all events ... [can] bring in the final self-manifestation of Jahweh, the perfection of his revelation."[191] The end of all historical events, according to Pannenberg, has already happened proleptically in the Christ event, especially in his resurrection. This event is of such a character that "the future of God is not merely disclosed in advance with the coming of Jesus; it is already an event, although without ceasing to be future."[192] Hence Pannenberg introduces a radical concept of the eschatological already/not yet tension and turns the traditional Christian conception of history on its head, viewing the Christ event as the proleptic end of history rather than the center of history. Pannenberg summarized his position concisely in his Dogmatic Theses when he wrote:

> Now the history of the whole is only visible when one stands at its end. Until then, the future always remains as something beyond calculation. And, only in the sense that the perfection of history has already been inaugurated in Jesus Christ is God finally and fully revealed in the fate of Jesus. With the resurrection of Jesus, the end of history has already occurred, although it does not strike us in this way. It is through the resurrection that the God of Israel has substantiated his deity in an ultimate way and is now manifest as the God of all men.[193]

And of significance for Pannenberg's contention that theological propositions must be open to verification, the proleptic nature of the Christ event means that, "as the revelation of God in his historical action moves toward the still outstanding future of the consummation of history, its claim to reveal the one God who is the world's Creator, Reconciler, and Redeemer is open to future verification in history, which is as yet incomplete, and which is still exposed,

---
[190] *ST* 1:246. [269f.]
[191] "Dogmatic Theses," 140f. ["Dogmatische Thesen," 103.]
[192] *ST* 1:247. [270.]
[193] "Dogmatic Theses," 142. ["Dogmatische Thesen," 104f.]

therefore, to the question of its truth."[194] The truth claims of the Christian religion, therefore, which are centered around the Christ event, can be neither conclusively verified nor falsified before the final eschaton.[195]

### 1.5.4 Implications for a natural knowledge of God

A final point which needs to be noted in regard to Pannenberg's concept of revelation as history is the implications of this view for a natural knowledge of God. Crucial here is his third dogmatic thesis which states: "In contrast to special manifestations of the Godhead historical revelation is open to all who have eyes to see. It has universal character." In explanation of this thesis Pannenberg wrote that we normally take care to understand revelation as something which is not accessible to the natural eye. "The revelation, however, of the biblical God in his activity is no secret or mysterious happening." Indeed, according to Pannenberg, an understanding of revelation which views it as something which stands in opposition to natural knowledge is in danger of confusing historical revelation with a gnostic secret knowledge.[196]

As Pannenberg elsewhere wrote: "One of the most hotly debated theses of *Revelation as History* was undoubtedly the statement that in the light of its historical effects the revelation of God 'is open to anyone who has eyes to see' and does not need any supplementary inspired interpretation."[197] Pannenberg directed this thesis against R. Rothe's view that "God's manifestation by historical facts stands in need of an inspired interpretation."[198] This is not to say, however, that because revealed knowledge is not supernatural, "that man is only confirming what he already knows through the force of his own intellect."[199] Indeed, Pannenberg maintains that this thesis "presupposes the relation of the Spirit to the Word in virtue of the latter's content."[200] Yet nevertheless, as Carl Braaten summarized Pannenberg's position, "in no sense does faith or the Holy Spirit enhance the revelatory content of the historical facts. The revelation is objectively there, even if no one sees it. In order to see it one has only to look in the right place and in the right way, but he does not need to wait for the lightning of the Holy Spirit to strike the fire of faith in him before he can lay hold of the revelation of God by historical reason."[201]

For Pannenberg a natural knowledge of God is possible, based upon the historical nature of revelation which is open to all who have eyes to see. Yet this does not mean that Pannenberg advocates a "natural theology" in the traditional

---

[194] *ST* 1:257. [281.]
[195] See chapter 4 of this study for a related discussion.
[196] "Dogmatic Theses," 135. ["Dogmatische Thesen," 98f.]
[197] *ST* 1:249. [272f.]
[198] Ibid. Cf. R. Rothe, *Offenbarung*, I, *Theologischen Studien und Kritiken* 31 [1858], repr. in *Zur Dogmatik* (Gotha, 1863).
[199] "Dogmatic Theses," 137. ["Dogmatische Thesen," 100.]
[200] *ST* 1:250. [273.]
[201] Carl Braaten, "The Current Controversy on Revelation: Pannenberg and his Critics," 229.

sense. Indeed, he distinguishes sharply between a natural knowledge of God and natural theology.[202] For Pannenberg the impossibility of a truly natural theology that is based upon pure reason "does not yet answer the question as to the possibility and actuality of a natural knowledge of God in the sense of a factual knowledge of the God whom the Christian message proclaims. ... What is at issue here is a *cognitio Dei naturalis insita* as distinct from a *cognitio Dei naturalis acquisita.*"[203] That is to say, we must distinguish between a natural knowledge of God which is innate (natural theology), and a natural knowledge of God which is acquired. For Pannenberg, the knowledge of God "is no constituent part of our natural endowment from birth."[204]

Pannenberg can affirm, therefore, that "there has not been a philosophical natural theology from the beginning of creation. But in the history of humanity there has always been in some form an explicit awareness of God which is linked to experience of the works of creation."[205] Pannenberg can thus confess that "by nature, i.e., from creation, God, the God of the apostolic gospel (Rom. 1:19-20), is known to all people," and in making this confession can also say that it is not "a statement of natural theology" but is rather "a statement made about us in the light of the revelation of God in Jesus Christ."[206] Hence a natural knowledge of God is indeed possible on the basis of the revelation of the Christ event which is "open to all who have eyes to see." Yet this knowledge does not arise out of a philosophical natural theology and it is always a knowledge of God as creator linked with our experience of his works of creation.

## 1.6 Pannenberg and the Hermeneutical Task

### 1.6.1 *Foundations of Pannenberg's hermeneutics (Schleiermacher, Gadamer)*

Although Pannenberg has been portrayed as rejecting the contemporary school of hermeneutical theology[207] he certainly does not reject the task and

---

[202] Wilhelm Weischedel, *Der Gott der Philosophen: Grundlegung einer Philosophischen Theologie im Zeitalter des Nihilismus*, vol. 2 (Darmstadt: Wissenschaftliche Buchgesellschaft, 1972), 75, 86, who does not seem to take note of the distinction Pannenberg makes between natural theology and a natural knowledge of God, contends that Pannenberg attempts unsuccessfully to ground a natural theology. Weischedel believes Pannenberg's attempt at a natural theology (or natural knowledge of God) fails because he must introduce trust that only the "believer" possesses in order to have certainty concerning the meaning of the historical Christ event since historical certainty is only possible at the distant end or culmination of history (84, 85). Yet Weischedel, in his criticism, seems to completely overlook Pannenberg's crucial concept of the proleptic occurrence of the end of history in the Christ event.

[203] *ST* 1:107. [121]

[204] Pannenberg, "How is God Revealed to Us?" in: W. Pannenberg, *Faith and Reality*, trans. John Maxwell (Philadelphia: Westminster Press, 1977), 50. [*Glaube und Wirklichkeit*, 71.]

[205] *ST* 1:117. [131.]

[206] *Ibid.*, 107f. [121.]

[207] Cf. Don Olive, *Wolfhart Pannenberg* (Waco, TX: Word Books, 1973), 66-75. Olive specifically lists the "hermeneutical theologies" of Barth, Bultmann and Cullmann, to all of which Pannenberg

theory of hermeneutics itself but makes it one of the building blocks of his theological method. Pannenberg is especially indebted to Friedrich Schleiermacher and Hans-Georg Gadamer for key elements of his own hermeneutics.

Hermeneutics has, since Schleiermacher, become an independent science or discipline concerned with the understanding of life and reality. Schleiermacher defined hermeneutics as the art of understanding[208] and, according to Gadamer, also as the art of avoiding misunderstanding.[209] Of course Schleiermacher's concerns were much broader than this. As Pannenberg explains, hermeneutics is for Schleiermacher "the theory of understanding in general in all forms of communication between people." And, Pannenberg adds, it is precisely this scope of his interest and this insight into the hermeneutic task which makes Schleiermacher so significant in the historical development of hermeneutics.[210] The great turn in the development of hermeneutics between Spinoza and Chladenius on the one side and Schleiermacher on the other is attributed to Schleiermacher's development of a universal hermeneutic. As Gadamer observed, "since Schleiermacher represents understanding as related ... to the problem of individuality, the task of hermeneutics presents itself to him as a universal one."[211] Or, as Pannenberg explains, "according to Schleiermacher, that people can understand one another results from the fact that individuals in their dealings with each other begin by assuming the unity of the human species. Individuals are linked by species consciousness in so far as each one of them is interested in what is human in general and in what is of significance for man."[212]

Schleiermacher's actual hermeneutic praxis, however, focused on the interpretation of texts or speech which could take place either grammatically or psychologically. Schleiermacher contended that "both are fully equal. ... The psychological is higher if one views language as only a means through which individuals communicate their thoughts. ... The grammatical is higher if one views language insofar as it conditions the thinking of all individuals."[213] Of these approaches, however, Schleiermacher actually favored the psychological[214] which had "the task of reconstructing the origin of the text in the author's thought with the implication that the interpreter could transpose himself into that thought."[215] And when Schleiermacher spoke of the interpretation of texts he had in mind

---

[208] takes exception, noting that "Pannenberg wants a unity to reality absent in Barth, a historicity of reality absent in Bultmann, and a philosophical awareness absent in Cullmann" (74).
Friedrich Schleiermacher, *Hermeneutik und Kritik* [1838], ed. Manfred Frank (Frankfurt/M: Suhrkamp, 1977), 75.
[209] Hans-Georg Gadamer, "Die Universalität des hermeneutischen Problems," in: H.-G. Gadamer, *Kleine Schriften*, vol. 1 (Tübingen: J.C.B. Mohr, 1967), 104.
[210] *TPS*, 159. [*WtT*, 159.]
[211] Gadamer, *Truth and Method* (London: Sheed and Ward, 1979), 162 and 167.
[212] *TPS*, 159. [*WtT*, 159f.]
[213] Schleiermacher, *Hermeneutik und Kritik*, 79.
[214] Cf. Gadamer, *Truth and Method*, 164; and Pannenberg, *TPS*, 160. [*WtT*, 160f.]
[215] *TPS*, 160. [*WtT*, 160f.]

primarily the exegesis of the biblical texts, which showed that his interest in hermeneutics was primarily theological. Although Pannenberg does not follow Schleiermacher in the praxis of his essential restriction of the hermeneutical task to the interpretation of texts or in his emphasis upon the psychological approach, Schleiermacher's emphasis upon a universal hermeneutic based upon the unity of humanity is an insight he incorporates into his own hermeneutic.

Of even greater significance than Schleiermacher to Pannenberg in the formulation of his own hermeneutic is the work of the German philosopher Hans-Georg Gadamer, in whose thought, according to Pannenberg "hermeneutical and historical motifs ... interpenetrate."[216] The importance of Gadamer for Pannenberg's program is especially important in regard to Pannenberg's attempt to develop the claim of the universality of theology. As Ted Peters has noted, because God can be no less universal than reality as a whole, "theological thinking ... requires a reflective framework that permits discourse about such a possibility of universality, and Pannenberg has found such a framework, or at least a foundation upon which such a framework might be constructed, in the postcritical hermeneutic of Hans-Georg Gadamer."[217]

Gadamer's view that interpretation is rooted in the complexity of history is of special significance for Pannenberg in the light of existentialist hermeneutical theology which tends to devaluate statements to having a meaning which is located only in personal experience. Important for Pannenberg is that,

> Gadamer's hermeneutical philosophy never loses sight of the complexity of historical tradition, even though its understanding appropriation is dominated by man's questions about himself and takes the form of an application of the text to be interpreted to the immediate situation of the interpreter. However, for Gadamer, the identity of the interpreter in his present can itself be acquired only in the complexity of historical tradition. Man's self has no prior basis in an ethical reflection which is independent of history.[218]

Indeed, for Gadamer humans possess an indelibly historical nature which leads him to conclude that humanity's way-of-being in the world can best be described as hermeneutical. In Gadamer's view, even the act of human understanding is seen as an historical event or a tradition-conveying event (*Überlieferungsgeschehen*). Hence, "understanding is not to be thought of so much as an action of one's subjectivity, but as the placing of oneself within a process of tradition, in which past and present are constantly fused."[219] As Peters observes, "Pannenberg argues that a further analysis of this conclusion would lead

---

[216] Pannenberg, "Hermeneutic and Universal History," in: *BQ* 1:116. ["Hermeneutik und Universalgeschichte," in: *Grundfragen*, 106.]
[217] Ted Peters, "Truth in History: Gadamer's Hermeneutics and Pannenberg's Apologetic Method," in: *Journal of Religion* 55 (1975), 45.
[218] *TPS*, 176f. [*WtT*, 176f.]
[219] *Truth and Method*, 258.

one back again to a fuller conception of history as the more comprehensive category for understanding reality."[220]

Gadamer rejects the so-called historicism which, in its confidence in its own methodology, overlooks the fact of its own historicity. That is to say, understanding or interpretation is also part of the historical process. Hence "true historical thinking must take account of its own historicality. Only then will it not chase the phantom of an historical object ..., but learn to see in the object the counterpart of itself and hence understand both." For Gadamer the true object of history is not an object at all but rather "the unity of the one and the other, a relationship in which exist both the reality of history and the reality of historical understanding. A proper hermeneutics would have to demonstrate the effectivity of history within understanding itself [i.e., im Verstehen selbst]."[221] Pannenberg, picking up on this theme, elucidates further the direction of Gadamer's thought:

> Gadamer excellently describes the way in which the past and the present are brought into relation to each other in the process of understanding as a 'fusion of horizons' [Horizontverschmelzung]. The horizons of the interpreter and of the text to be interpreted are different at first, but that is only their initial position, so to speak, in the process of interpretation. The interpreter's own horizon is not fixed, but capable of movement and expansion. In the process of understanding, the interpreter's horizon is widened in such a way that the initially strange matter along with its own horizon can be appropriated into the expanded horizon he attains as he understands.[222]

Therefore, as Gadamer writes, there is in actuality only a single horizon "that embraces everything contained in historical consciousness. Our own past, and that other past towards which our historical consciousness is directed, help us to shape this moving horizon out of which human life always lives, and which determines it as tradition."[223]

For Pannenberg, the practical application of this hermeneutic formation of a comprehensive horizon between text and interpreter has clear implications for the interpretation of the biblical texts. In the case of the New Testament, for instance, the interpreter must first of all become aware of the difference between his or her own intellectual context (or horizon) and that of the New Testament authors. Once this is done the interpreter will attempt "to achieve a synthesis, to formulate a comprehensive horizon of understanding within which both the intellectual world of the biblical texts as well as the differing intellectual world of modern man will each have their place and can thus be related to each other." In short, the interpreter carries on a conversation with the text, but a conversation that presupposes a methodical interpretation of the text based upon an explicitly formu-

---
[220] Peters, 38.
[221] Truth and Method, 267.
[222] "Hermeneutic and Universal History," 117. [Grundfragen, 107.]
[223] Truth and Method, 271.

lated comprehensive horizon so that both the adequateness of the common horizon and, ultimately, the 'correctness' of the interpretation itself can be tested.[224]

Yet despite Gadamer's focus upon history as a category of understanding he does not view history as universal history, as Pannenberg believes his system actually implies. Pannenberg writes: Gadamer seems to have his hands full "trying to keep his thoughts from going in the direction they inherently want to go," namely, in his efforts "to avoid the Hegelian total mediation of the truth of the present by means of history." But yet, "strangely enough, the phenomena which Gadamer describes move time and again in the direction of a universal conception of history."[225] It is at this point, then, that Pannenberg amends Gadamer's hermeneutic, returning precisely to a Hegelian concept of universal history.

### 1.6.2 Hegel, hermeneutics, and universal history

Pannenberg rejects the either/or choice between hermeneutic and universal history contending that "the competition between hermeneutic and universal-historical methods can ... also signify a convergence; for the correct resolution of both tasks must actually lead to the same results."[226] The problem with uniting the two concerns, however, lies with the problem that "the future could no longer be thought of as an open one, from Hegel's standpoint, insofar as its openness would consist in its continuously bringing forth surprising experiences." Also, according to Pannenberg, a related problem is Hegel's "failure to recognize the impossibility of taking account of the contingent and the individual by means of the universal. All these points indicate the limits of Hegel's philosophy and, thus, of his philosophy of history, too."[227]

For Pannenberg, however, "the task of a philosophy or a theology of world history dare not be sacrificed on account of the failure of the Hegelian solution" as Gadamer does. Instead, we must, according to Pannenberg, ask how it is possible, in contrast to Hegel, to develop a conception of universal history which "would preserve the finitude of human experience and thereby the openness of the future as well as the intrinsic claim of the individual."[228]

---

[224] "Hermeneutic and Universal History," 119f. [*Grundfragen*, 108f.] For Gadamer's own use of conversation [*Gespräch*] as a model for the hermeneutical process see *Truth and Method*, 345ff.
[225] "Hermeneutic and Universal History," 129. [*Grundfragen*, 116.]
[226] *Ibid.*, 99. [93.]
[227] *Ibid.*, 134. [120.] Precisely in regard to his understanding of history Pannenberg has been widely judged to represent a theological Hegelianism. Kurt Koch, however, has recently argued emphatically, and I believe correctly, that this is at best an oversimplification and more probably a misrepresentation of Pannenberg's own view of history. Koch points out that although Pannenberg's theology represents an interpretation of Hegels metaphysics of history, this is done under the presupposition of an anthropology of finiteness. *Der Gott der Geschichte: Theologie der Geschichte bei Wolfhart Pannenberg als Paradigma einer Philosophischen Theologie in ökumenischer Perspektive* (Mainz: Matthias-Grünewald-Verlag, 1988), 103f.
[228] *Ibid.*, 135.

The key to meeting this challenge, Pannenberg suggests, is to understand our knowledge of history as having provisional character. This in turn allows the horizon of the future to be held open and the finitude of human experience to be preserved since the end of history would not already be a decided, unchangeable outcome, but would be only provisionally known to us. In this way Pannenberg hopes also to keep the hermeneutical advantages of a universal history. For a universal history, according to Pannenberg, "enables us to span the distance of Jesus and our own time, and thus can furnish the basis for a solution to the hermeneutical problem."[229] Pannenberg believes that we can gather from the history of Jesus in relation to the Israelite-Jewish tradition the fact that "the end has become accessible in a provisional way." Hegel, however, was unable to see this because the eschatological character of Jesus' message remained obscured in the New Testament exegesis of his day.

Johann Baptist Metz, however, has asked whether Pannenberg's emphasis on a hermeneutic of universal history, especially in its anticipation of a unified meaning of history, "is not too little interrupted or irritated by what is described in the apocalyptic tradition as a universal catastrophe, in other words, as the reign of the Antichrist." For Metz, this leads to the impression that praxis remains secondary or becomes enslaved to a predetermined totality of meaning.[230] Pannenberg's insistence that a hermeneutic of universal history must take into account an open future and thus the possibility of action in the present would seem to answer this criticism. Pannenberg concludes his article on "Hermeneutic and Universal History" by writing:

> The possibility of taking a new look at the problem of universal history, on the basis of the original eschatological meaning of the history of Jesus as an anticipation of the end, is relevant ... because the hermeneutical theme itself leads back to the problem of universal history. This is so because it appears that an understanding of transmitted texts in their historical differentiation from the present cannot be adequately and methodically carried out apart from universal historical thought which ... must include the horizon of an open future and with this the possibilities of action in the present.[231]

1.6.3 *Hermeneutics and relation of parts to the whole (Hegel, Dilthey, Habermas)*

A final key component feature of Pannenberg's hermeneutic which we wish to examine here is the importance of the whole for understanding the parts, and vice versa. The categories of 'the part' and 'the whole' is of hermeneutical significance for Pannenberg on two levels. Pannenberg contends that first of all "the category 'part/whole' plays a similar role for theological hermeneutics in the matter of textual interpretation as it does for the literary-historical disciplines."

---
[229] "The Crisis of the Scripture Principle," 13.
[230] Johann Baptist Metz, *Faith in History and Society: Toward a Practical Fundamental Theology* (London: Burns & Oates, 1980), 55.
[231] "Hermeneutic and Universal History," 136. [*Grundfragen*, 121f.]

And secondly, "the category of the whole has another specific significance above and beyond this meaning" in its application to the interpretation of historical events and processes within universal history.[232]

The importance of the categories 'part' and 'whole' is an insight which goes back in modern thought to Hegel. In Hegel's *Wissenschaft der Logik* he deals with the classification of the part and the whole in which "the category of the whole appears as a step in the process of reflection, one which leads to the overcoming of the opposition of essence and mere being." Yet this "overcoming does not occur with the concept of the whole, because this concept has its truth in the parts out of which the whole is composed."[233] Pannenberg is critical, however, of Hegel inasmuch as he fails to recognize the logical imbalance of the parts and the whole even though he emphasizes that they mutually imply and condition one another. Because in Hegel's concept of the whole the parts are posited not as something other than the whole but rather as the whole's own moments the distinction between the whole and the parts is lost and one ceases "to look at the parts as parts." For Pannenberg, "such a way of viewing the problem has already lost the idea of the whole and is no longer able to describe the 'in itself manifold existence' as a plurality of parts whose concept already presupposes that of the whole." Thus Pannenberg, in opposition to the implications of Hegel's view, is able to say that "the difference of the world from God, ... as the condition of the unity of any creature with God, will not be transcended and eliminated even in the eschaton." Similarly, in opposition to Hegel's elimination of the difference between God (or 'the Idea') and the world, Pannenberg insists upon "the abstractness of every concept of the whole or of the totality, an abstractness that results from the anticipatory nature of all knowledge of the whole in a world which has not yet been completed and reconciled to the whole."[234]

For this critique of Hegel, which brings in the anticipatory nature of our knowledge of the whole since the world has not yet been completed, Pannenberg is indebted to the German Philosopher Wilhelm Dilthey. Dilthey used the categories of part and whole to describe the relation of historical events and the relation of the past to the future implied within them. For Dilthey, "the single moment has meaning through its connection with the whole, through the relationship between past and future, between individual existence and humanity." Yet Dilthey asks what kind of relationship can exist between the part (individual events) and the whole within an individual life - or even within history in general. This relationship, answers Dilthey, "is a relationship that is never completely finished. One must wait until the end of life and can only in the hour of death view the whole from which the relationship between all the parts of one's life will

---

[232] Pannenberg, *Metaphysics and the Idea of God*, 140f. For a discussion of the significance of the term 'category' cf. *ibid.*, 130ff. [The essay from which this and the following references are taken does not appear in *Metaphysik und Gottesgedanke*.]
[233] *Ibid.*, 147.
[234] *Ibid.*, 148f. and 152.

be able to be determined. One must first await the end of history in order to have all the material needed for the determination of its meaning."[235] According to Pannenberg, the consequence of this insight should have been a recognition of the "structural unity of life" which is dependent upon its eschatological future. Pannenberg charges Dilthey, however, with evading this implication "by claiming that the whole also became 'intelligible in its parts.'"[236]

Dilthey, therefore, did not believe we are not in a position to attach meaning to individual events since "the whole is indeed ... available to us insofar as the parts are comprehensible." In other words, the whole of history is present for us inasmuch as the whole is contained within the parts, that is, the individual events which have already taken place. But the ultimate meaning of events is not already determined since history remains open. Hence "the determination of the meaning of the past is conditioned by what we determine as the goal for our future."[237]

But this all presupposes that the events within an individual life or within history are all connected to one another. The question, then, for Dilthey is what connects these individual events or parts to the whole. His answer is that experience is a unity or a whole whose parts are bound together through a common meaning. He illustrates this with the example of a sentence whose individual words each have a meaning which connect them to the meaning of the sentence as a whole so that the meaning of the sentence depends upon the meaning of the individual words but yet the individual words also depend upon the sentence as a whole for their meaning in that specific sentence. Likewise, the common meaning of history as a whole, which cannot be known until history is complete, is that which binds the individual events of history together. The significance of this view for hermeneutics is made clear when Dilthey writes: "The parts of a life have a specific meaning for the whole of the same life: in short, the category of meaning clearly has an especially close connection to understanding."[238]

Another key contributor to the formation of Pannenberg's use of the categories 'part' and 'the whole' in his hermeneutic is the contemporary German philosopher Jürgen Habermas. Habermas expands hermeneutics to include criticism and rejects a hermeneutic which understands meaning subjectively. As Pannenberg explains, this "expansion of hermeneutic into criticism is brought about through the ... anticipation of the goal of history.... This means Habermas can describe his method of criticising present society in the light of an anticipated totality of human history as a dialectical one."[239] As Pannenberg explains,

> dialectic and hermeneutic share the fundamental feature of being concerned with the analysis of the interrelation of wholes and parts. However, whereas

---
[235] Wilhelm Dilthey, *Der Aufbau der geschichtlichen Welt in den Geisteswissenschaften*, 233.
[236] *TPS*, 162. [*WtT*, 162.]
[237] Dilthey, 233.
[238] *Ibid.*, 234f.
[239] *TPS*, 189. [*WtT*, 189.]

hermeneutic sees the whole only as a horizon which establishes the meaning of all the details and whose transformations initiate the continuing process of interpretation, and can therefore remain uncertain about the final form of the whole, dialectic considers the totality as such, without which the individual element could have no definitive meaning.[240]

Habermas has been criticized at this point, especially by Hans Albert, for suggesting that dialectic claims a totality which goes beyond the limitations of human experience and knowledge, or, in Habermas' words, "transcends .. the limits of formal logic."[241] Pannenberg agrees with Albert's assessment that this constitutes "an 'immunization strategy' by means of which 'Habermas tries to deny the possibility of giving a logical analysis of his concept of totality.'"[242] Pannenberg concludes from this discussion that "the dialectical concept of a whole as a social totality can perfectly well be represented theoretically with a hypothetical description. It is also describable as an individual system and is wholly susceptible to logical analysis; that is to say, it does not need to be removed, as it was by Habermas, from the competence of logic."[243] Thus Pannenberg accepts Habermas' concept of expanding hermeneutic to include a critical dialectic in regard to the analysis of the interrelation of the parts and the whole, yet he rejects Habermas's view that this dialectic be removed from the bounds of logic.

Pannenberg is similarly critical of Habermas' concept of a 'hermeneutical circle' in which "apprehension of the whole automatically presupposes knowledge of the parts, and conversely the parts cannot be apprehended without the whole" since a similar view of the circularity of hermeneutical procedures led Heidegger to deny hermeneutics, and particular historiological interpretation, scientific status. Indeed, Pannenberg admits that "if we accept the thesis of the circular character of all hermeneutic arguments, as Habermas does, it certainly makes no sense to continue to claim scientific status for hermeneutical procedures."[244] For Pannenberg, this is a further surrender of the ability to defend the concept of dialectical totality. Also, it would seem that the fact that, according to Habermas, "hermeneutisches Verstehen stets ad hoc verfahren muß und sich nicht zu einer wissenschaftlichen Methode ausbilden läßt," presents serious difficulties in maintaining hermeneutic's claim to universality, a claim which is vital to Pannenberg's own program.[245] But Pannenberg does not agree that "the

---

[240] *Ibid.*
[241] Cited by Pannenberg in *ibid.*, 191. [191.] Cf. Jürgen Habermas, "Analytische Wissenschaftstheorie und Dialektik," in: *Der Positivismusstreit in der deutschen Soziologie*, ed. Th. Adorno, J. Habermas, et al. (Darmstadt, 1980), 155.
[242] *Ibid.*, 191. [191.] Cf. H. Albert, "Der Mythos der totalen Vernunft," in: *Positivismusstreit*, 198f.
[243] *Ibid.*, 195. [195f.]
[244] *Ibid.*, 199. [199f.]
[245] Cf. Jürgen Habermas, *Zur Logik der Sozialwissenschaften*, 5th ed. (Frankfurt/M: Suhrkamp Verlag, 1982), 341ff.

perception of meaning is 'circular' in its intra-linguistic logic and therefore incapable of being scientific." Pannenberg presents the following argument for this contention:

> While all perception of the meaning of particulars always simultaneously presupposes an understanding of the whole, the implicit pre-understanding of this whole is not identical with an explicit and therefore more clearly defined preconcept of it, which has much more the status of a hypothesis about the whole implicitly presupposed by the particulars. Conversely, such a hypothesis presumes the particulars only in the way that any hypothesis relates to the material it has to interpret.[246]

Hence Pannenberg, consistent with his concern for a methodology thoroughly open to critical reason and 'scientific' investigation and verification, rejects moving hermeneutical procedures and arguments outside of the realm of logic and consequently outside the bounds of science. Therefore, just as theological propositions and revelation as history are open to critical reason so also is Pannenberg's hermeneutic, since the understanding of the whole contained in the parts is implicit and not explicit and therefore has the character of an hypothesis open to testing.

### 1.7 Pannenberg's Theological Method: A Summary and Appraisal

*1.7.1 The classification of Pannenberg's theological method*
In light of our examination of Pannenberg's distinctive view of the scientific status and nature of theology, including his emphasis upon a provisional verifiability of theological statements and his conception of revelation as history, we must inquire as to precisely what Pannenberg's theological method is, or at least what the essential characteristics of his method are. Pannenberg has focused more attention on questions of theological method than most contemporary theologians, having fully examined issues regarding revelation and history, the relationship of theology to philosophy and the scientific character of theology before writing his three volume dogmatics. Yet for all the material Pannenberg has produced which might rightly be classified as fundamental theology a simple classification or summary of his theological method is difficult, in part because of the amount and complexity of material and issues.

Hans Schwarz has called Pannenberg's theological method, along with that of Paul Tillich, dialogical, because he does not "retreat into a religious or Christian ghetto but engages in a dialogue with the whole of the created world" in such a way that nothing is exempt from his concern.[247] Similarly, it has been observed

---
[246] *TPS.*, 201. [*WtT*, 201.]
[247] Hans Schwarz, *Method and Context as Problems for Contemporary Theology: Doing Theology in an Alien World* (Lewiston, NY: Edwin Mellen Press, 1991), 14f.

that "Pannenberg's theological method involves the quest for points of contact in all religions and all academic disciplines."[248] Certainly this is descriptive of Pannenberg's approach, as well as of Tillich's. Yet methodologically speaking, there are significant differences between Pannenberg on the one hand and Tillich on the other. Philip Clayton, a former student of Pannenberg, has suggested that "pervasive criticizability is perhaps the central tenet of Pannenberg's theological method."[249] This description is also accurate, especially inasmuch as it takes into account his pervasive interest in the scientific nature of theology and the openness of theological statements to verification. Yet the idea of pervasive criticizability alone does not do justice to the full range and complexity of Pannenberg's method. Pannenberg's method has even been described as constituting a theology from below, yet he also makes use of elements of a theology "from above," as for instance in many of the more metaphysical and even speculative aspects of his doctrine of God.[250] Perhaps Frank Tupper best indicated the difficulty of describing Pannenberg's methodology when, writing of the "texture of Pannenberg's theological method" he dealt with theology as history, philosophy, God-talk, dogmatics, and anthropology, indicating something of the diversity of Pannenberg's approach.[251]

All this illustrates, of course, what anyone familiar with Pannenberg's thought is aware of, namely that his approach to and conception of the theological task is both comprehensive and complex. A single concept or term cannot do justice to its scope. Certain characteristics of his method can, however, be indicated. I would suggest that Pannenberg's essential method consists of a triad of closely related concerns, dealt with already in the context of this chapter; namely, the scientific character of theology and its openness to verification, the concept of revelation as history and the natural knowledge of God which it implies, and the task of a hermeneutic grounded upon a universal history along with the corresponding emphasis upon the relation of the parts to the whole. Several threads bind these concerns together, such as what has been called Pannenberg's "pan-critical rationalism," i.e., his concern to ground Christian faith solidly upon reason. The most important connecting thread in Pannenberg's method, however, is the underlying theme of universality.

Theology is universal science based upon the universality of its object, God the creator of all things. This God reveals himself within the context of universal history in such a manner that this revelation is also universal in that it is open to all who have eyes to see. Finally, the key to Pannenberg's hermeneutics is that it is based upon universal history and the relation of the parts to the whole. Upon

---

[248] Philip Clayton, "Anticipation and Theological Method," in: *The Theology of Wolfhart Pannenberg*, 127.
[249] *Ibid.*, 123.
[250] Cf., for instance, *Metaphysics and the Idea of God*; and *ST* 1:337ff. [*Metaphysik und Gottesgedanke* and *ST* 1:365ff.]
[251] Tupper, *The Theology of Wolfhart Pannenberg* (Philadelphia: Westminster Press, 1973), 45-76.

this basis Pannenberg has built a methodology which not only facilitates but leads inevitably to his specific approach to apologetics. One might, therefore, characterize Pannenberg's approach as a method of scientific, historical and hermeneutical universality, or perhaps, as a pan-critical-historico-hermeneutical method.

**1.7.2** *The role of faith and the Spirit in Pannenberg's program: Althaus' critique*

One of the most controversial and oft criticized aspects of Pannenberg's theological program concerns the place given to faith and the role of the Spirit of God in the epistemological process of understanding God's revelation. This critique, arising primarily but not exclusively out of "evangelical" circles is not surprising given the usual emphasis on faith over reason to be found there. D. Holwerda, for instance, has charged that "a basic problem in Pannenberg's theology is the transition from the probabilities of historical reason to the certainty of faith." According to Holwerda, "if faith requires certainty, Pannenberg must either assume an epistemology contrary to his dominant thesis that faith is not an avenue of knowledge but is dependent upon reason for its foundation, or acknowledge that he has not fully escaped the charge of subjectivism."[252]

In an even more radical critique Donald Bloesch, a leading contemporary "evangelical" theologian, characterizes Pannenberg as a modern representative of the "Christian rationalism of the enlightenment" and contends, over against Pannenberg, "that the revelation in Scripture is not open to general reasonableness but is disclosed only to the eyes and ears of faith."[253] Of course the problem rests in large part upon the fact that for Bloesch and other evangelicals revelation is "special revelation" and is to be found primarily, if not exclusively, in the scriptures, whereas for Pannenberg the scriptures are simply witnesses to that revelation which, as history, is open to all people who have eyes to see. For such evangelicals, therefore, it seems that Pannenberg is substituting reason for faith. Indeed, it has been rightly observed that "Pannenberg's emphasis on the universal character of revelation leaves little room for the traditional category of special revelation"[254] and along with it the role of faith given through the Holy Spirit.

Indeed, it is often precisely Pannenberg's commitment to the unitary character of knowledge and history and the universality of revelation, which are the keys to his methodological and apologetic programs, which provoke the most controversy. Pannenberg seeks to overcome the dichotomies of salvation history and profane history, of special revelation and general revelation, of faith and reason. Yet in his efforts to argue for the unitary and universal character of history, revelation and knowledge (which are all intricately related in the thought

---

[252] D. Holwerda, "Faith, Reason, and the Resurrection in the Theology of Wolfhart Pannenberg," in: *Faith and Rationality: Reason and Belief in God*, ed. Alvin Plantinga and Nicholas Wolterstorff (Notre Dame: University of Notre Dame Press, 1983), 306, 309.
[253] Donald Bloesch, *Essentials of Evangelical Theology*, v. 1 (New York: Harper & Row,1978), 54.
[254] Stanley J. Grenz, "The Appraisal of Pannenberg: A Survey of the Literature," in: *The Theology of Wolfhart Pannenberg*, ed. Carl Braaten and Philip Clayton, 25.

of Pannenberg), he is often accused of having collapsed or subsumed salvation history into profane history, special revelation into general revelation, and faith into reason.

The issue of the relationship between faith and reason and the role of faith and the work of the Holy Spirit in Pannenberg's theology can be seen already, and perhaps best, in the exchange between Pannenberg and Paul Althaus. In response to Pannenberg's conception of revelation as history formulated in his "Dogmatic Theses" Althaus responded the following year with an article in the *Theologische Literaturzeitung* titled "Offenbarung als Geschichte und Glaube."[255] Althaus, over against Pannenberg, maintained that: "The work of the Spirit is nothing other than that of the Word itself made effective. God did not delegate the power of the Spirit to the message itself. But he works through the message, inasmuch as he makes the Word powerful where and when he will. Only in this way can there be 'knowledge of God's revelation,' that is, through the Spirit of God, who through the Word gives faith. The Holy Spirit and faith belong to the essence of revelation." For Pannenberg, on the other hand, "the perception of revelation is not a matter of faith, but of reason. ... So then, not first faith, but reason that is come into its own recognizes revelation." Althaus charges, then, that this implies, "that he must understand the non-perception of revelation in the events of history as pure sinful reticence." Belief, according to Althaus, depends ultimately upon the grace of God given through his Spirit. Those who do not believe cannot simply be made to see by an appeal to reason. The tension, therefore, between belief and unbelief must remain. "It is not possible to deduce from the 'universal character' of revelatory history its natural unmistakableness and to solve the problem of non-perception purely anthropologically."[256] Althaus concedes that the emphasis upon revelation as history is a needed one, yet he believes the formula is incomplete as it stands since "the working of the Holy Spirit and the gift of faith belong to revelation as an indispensable moment." Althaus therefore suggests the formula be expanded to match the title of his own article: "Revelation as History *and Faith*."[257]

Pannenberg responded to Althaus' critique in the same journal the following year with his article "Einsicht und Glaube: Antwort auf Paul Althaus." Pannenberg credits Althaus with bringing to attention what is perhaps the most urgent theological problem arising out of the volume "Offenbarung und Geschichte" by focusing his critique upon the relationship between the knowledge of revelation and the Holy Spirit.[258] Pannenberg contends that many of the points raised by Althaus are only "apparent conflicts." Yet he also recognizes that "the

---

[255] Paul Althaus, "Offenbarung als Geschichte und Glaube: Bemerkungen zu Wolfhart Pannenbergs Begriff der Offenbarung," in: *Theologische Literaturzeitung* 87:5 (May 1962), 321-330.
[256] *Ibid.*, 327f.8.
[257] *Ibid.*, 329f.
[258] Pannenberg, "Einsicht und Glaube: Antwort an Paul Althaus," in: *Theologische Literaturzeitung* 88:2 (February 1963), 81f., for this and the following.

real point of contention, on the other hand, is to be found in the question of the relationship between faith and knowledgte." Pannenberg understands Althaus to be admitting that the faith which grounds and includes the knowledge of revelation presupposes a 'natural knowledge' in the impression that the reports contained in the proclamation are believable. But this is not yet the knowledge of God's revelation, according to Althaus, for this knowledge arises first with faith. Pannenberg contends that all the arguments of Althaus where legitimate disagreement with his own position exists are connected to this viewpoint.

In opposition to Althaus, Pannenberg contends that Althaus' exclusive characterization of faith as trust does not represent the Reformation understanding of faith. Yet whether one follows a Reformation understanding of faith or chooses to identify faith with an act of trust, in no case can one speak of "a founding of *fiducia* through *notitia* and *assensus*." Pannenberg maintains, rather, that if one identifies faith and *fiducia* as representing the same thing, then one will speak of a foundation of faith upon a presupposed knowledge as he himself has done. "In no case, however, may one eliminate from the beginning the question about such a founding relationship (*Begründungsverhältnis*) so that one formulates along with Althaus the proposition that faith itself founds this 'knowledge' or recogition and includes it within itself."[259]

Concerning the role of the Holy Spirit Pannenberg contends: "One cannot escape the dilemma between the truth question and the message of Christ simply by calling upon the Holy Spirit." Pannenberg does not intend to deny a role to the Holy Spirit in the understanding of revelation but wishes to guard against making the Spirit a criterion of truth in regard to revelation. Hence he writes:

> The fact that the one who is convinced by the proclamation confesses that this knowledge is effected in him or her through the Holy Spirit must not be misunderstood as if the Spirit were claimed as a truth criterion of the proclamation. Indeed, just the opposite. There is much more need for assurance when one speaks in the power of the Holy Spirit, which itself needs a criterion for credibility (1 Cor. 12:1f.), and this criterion is the confession of Jesus Christ as Lord (v. 3), that is to say, the content of the proclamation. The convincing power of the proclamation of Christ can only arise from its content. Where this is not the case, the preacher's calling upon the Holy Spirit achieves nothing.[260]

For Pannenberg, the question whether the message which is proclaimed is true or not can only be answered from its content through its pointing toward that from which it reports and the inherent meaning of the reported event. He contends that "this is the knowledge that faith must (logically) presuppose when it is not to become counterfeited as a self-empowering decision."[261]

---

[259] *Ibid.*, 83.
[260] *Ibid.*, 85f.
[261] *Ibid.*, 86.

Finally, concerning Althaus' suggestion that 'Revelation as History' be amended to 'Revelation as History *and Faith*,' Pannenberg concedes that "the revelation of God only achieves its goal when it produces faith and, therefore, is revealed to someone. Actually, however, it achieves its goal only with the glorification of the believer in the future of Jesus Christ." Therefore not only faith but also the glorification of the faithful is a part of revelatory history. Pannenberg thus returns to the crucial theme of eschatology whereby he again asserts that the eschatological end has already appeared proleptically in Jesus Christ. Since faith is included properly within the revelatory history which has already reached its end proleptically, Pannenberg suggests that faith also has a proleptic structure in relation to the future-orientation of trust. Hence Pannenberg concludes, that "for faith the trusting anticipation of the future is characteristic, but this anticipation if founded in an appropriately proleptic sense in the Christ event itself ..."[262] In this way Pannenberg attempts to make room for faith and the work of the Holy Spirit within his concept of revelation as history. In his recent *Systematic Theology* Pannenberg, speaking of the justification of a Christology from below, again has sought to make room for faith and the Holy Spirit without minimizing the role of reason. Pannenberg writes:

> We can believe without ... [a grounding argument for our faith]. But faith of that kind is not theology. Only arguments count in theology. Theology cannot ignore the question of the foundation of faith in Jesus Christ. It cannot ignore the underlying relation that leads to the rise of faith and the statements of the christological confession. The truth of Christian doctrine is at issue in theology. Of service in this regard is the discovery and reconstruction of the actual nature of the church's christological confession. Theological argument neither here nor elsewhere makes faith or the Holy Spirit superfluous. Nevertheless, it is also true that appeal to faith and the Holy Spirit is not itself an argument.[263]

In the end, however, as Pannenberg also recognized, the gulf between his own view and that of Althaus concerning the role of faith and the Holy Spirit in the cognition of revelation is not overcome. As Kurt Koch has also noted, by suggesting the addition of 'and faith' to 'revelation as history' Althaus "divides ... what for Pannenberg belongs indivisibly together, namely historical knowledge independent of faith and the criterion of credibility intrinsic to faith."[264] One cannot, therefore, simply call Pannenberg's view a corrective to the then common emphasis on an existentialist conception of faith which often tended to minimize if not to ignore its actual content. In this sense Pannenberg represents a genuine departure from traditional views of the relationship between faith and reason in understanding revelation. Whether in so doing he sacrifices too much of the role of faith and the Holy Spirit for the sake of offering a *reason*able foundation for

---
[262] Ibid., 90ff.
[263] *ST* 2:287 [326.]
[264] Koch, *Der Gott der Geschichte*, 102.

Christian belief remains to be seen. In any event, the suspicion lingers in some circles that Pannenberg has substituted proper methodology for the role of the Holy Spirit.[265]

A possible compromise between Pannenberg's position and that represented by Althaus, and in more radical forms by contemporary evangelicals, would be to suggest that for Pannenberg there exists a distinction between comprehension and commitment. Crucial is that comprehension of revelation is open to anyone who objectively examines this revelation through the eyes of reason, yet commitment to this revelation, which is what distinguishes one as a Christian, is only possible through the work of the Spirit of God. Another approach to moderating between these viewpoints is the suggestion that Pannenberg is not unaware of the role of faith but that he is simply trying to make clear that faith does not bring with it any kind of additional knowledge not already to be found in the content of revelatory history.[266]

Yet in the end it would seem that the probability involved in Pannenberg's concept of scientific verification is something qualitatively other than the believer's certainty of faith. Even Pannenberg would certainly agree that no theological method, including his own, is able to provide this certainty of faith. For the individual Christian, it would seem, the epistemological bottom line is that theological statements are ultimately subject to a verification of faith which comes through the testimony of the Holy Spirit. Thus Paul writes in Rom. 8:16 that "the Spirit itself bears witness with our spirit that we are the children of God" (Cf. also 1 John 5:6-9 and Heb. 10:15). Yet such a perspective must not necessarily come into conflict with Pannenberg's approach so long as we are clear that no new knowledge of revelation is added (in gnostic fashion) through such a verification through the Spirit. Neither is such verification capable of being passed on from one person to the next as in the case of scientific or rational verification. Indeed, it would seem that the verification of the Spirit, for the believer, might even be viewed as coming through the process of rational verification and not necessarily as a step extra to it. Hence correct knowledge of God leads into faith in God for Pannenberg so that, "right theological knowledge is drawn into the mystery of its

---

[265] So William Hamilton, "The Character of Pannenberg's Theology," in: *Theology as History*, ed. James M. Robinson and John B. Cobb Jr. (New York: Harper & Row, 1967), 188. Hamilton writes: "In Pannenberg it almost seems as if the proper methodology has been substituted for the Holy Spirit. History already contains God - 'history is reality in its total' and presumably divine reality is included in that total reality that is history - and man has in his hands the correct tool to dig into that reality and to discover God present there." Pannenberg, however, has responded that Hamilton's criticism is a crude caricature of his position which does not merit a detailed answer. He nonetheless notes, however, that "the difference between my conception and Hamilton's presentation of it is especially evident in my repeated indications that it is not theoretical knowledge which can create the fellowship with Jesus which alone assures salvation, and that such fellowship arises and lives only through trust in Jesus and his message." (Pannenberg, "Response to the Discussion," in: *Theology as History*, 268f.)

[266] So Thomas Parker, Faith and History: A Review of Wolfhart Pannenberg's *Jesus - God and Man*," in: *McCormick Theological Quarterly* 22 (1968), 74f.

object, and thus, as a reductio mysterium, it leads beyond itself into faith."[267] Yet despite this there remains an existential, even mystical element in such a role for the Holy Spirit as described above that has difficulty finding its proper place within the structure of Pannenberg's critical rationalism.

### 1.7.3 *Pannenberg's method in the Protestant context: Innovation or synthesis*

Pannenberg's break with the dominant streams of the Protestant theology of his generation can be most clearly seen in his very intentional distancing of his own position from that of the two main dialectical theologians of the twentieth century, Karl Barth and Rudolf Bultmann. Whereas the dialectical theologians laid great stress upon the existential nature of faith (going back to Kierkegaard in the case of Barth and to Heidegger in the case of Bultmann), Pannenberg rejects an existentialist understanding of faith as introducing a subjectivism which weakens or removes the rational basis for faith. Similarly, the historical investigation of events vital to faith such as the resurrection of Jesus was not of importance to either Barth or Bultmann, the former holding such events to be beyond the reach of historical investigation and the latter holding them to be simply non-historical. Pannenberg, of course, has sought to recover the historical rootedness of the Christian faith precisely by confessing events such as the resurrection to have taken place in history and thus as being subject to historical investigation.

In doing so, however, he has followed a rather unique path among theologians and has been one of the most discussed and least understood theological thinkers of our time. His contention that revelation is open to all who have eyes to see and that the Holy Spirit adds nothing to the content of revelation has provoked strong criticism from theologians ranging from Paul Althaus to American evangelicals such as Donald Bloesch and Carl Henry. His critical rationalism as applied to the openness of theological propositions to verification has also drawn criticism from a number of quarters. Indeed, in light of the triad of emphases composing the basic structure of his theological method which we have identified as the scientific nature of theology, revelation as history, and a hermeneutic built upon the relation of the parts to the whole within the context of universal history, Pannenberg would seem to stand alone among contemporary theologians. As with all original thinkers, his creativity has often made Pannenberg subject to the charge of innovation in the negative sense of creating a system of his own making simply for the sake of doing something new. Such a charge, however, would not seem justified in Pannenberg's case.

To be sure, there are many contrasts between Pannenberg and traditional Protestant thought. There are also, however, important points of continuity to be noted, not just with the Protestant theological tradition but also with the general philosophical tradition that has arisen within Protestantism. Pannenberg is not an

---

[267] "Response to the Discussion," in: *Theology as History*, 276.

innovator who suddenly decided to create an entirely new approach to theology. Rather, Pannenberg is much more a masterful systematizer and synthetizer of all that which he has found useful and which is consistent with the central concerns of his program. And thus neither can he be said to be eclectic.

The concept of theology as a science is and has been held by a number of theologians. The claim that theological science is universal not only lay at the heart of the medieval conception of theological science, which distorted this universality into a dominating view of theology as queen of the sciences, but it also continues to find contemporary supporters in various forms. Martin Kähler might be mentioned here as one theological predecessor to Pannenberg who held a similar view. The emphasis upon the universality of history of course goes back primarily to Hegel and both Schleiermacher and Hegel (as well as German idealism in general) held history to be the indirect self-revelation of God.[268] Additionally, the hermeneutical insight that it is only the end of history that will conclusively reveal the meaning of the individual events of history is to be found in Dilthey and Bultmann among others. That this has applicability for the ultimate verification of theological statements was noted by John Hick and, in less developed form, also by Bultmann and I. M. Crombie. Pannenberg's indebtedness to Karl Popper and Thomas Kuhn for his particular formulation of the concept of falsifiability of theological statements and upon the philosophers Hans-Georg Gadamer and Jürgen Habermas for many structures of his thought, especially in the area of hermeneutics, is also well-known.

The aspect that would appear most unique to Pannenberg's program is his seminal proposal that the end of history has already occurred proleptically in the Christ event, which provided a needed corrective to the Hegelian conception of universal history.[269] Yet even the concept of a proleptic end of history in the Christ event has important antecedents in the already/not yet tension of inaugurated eschatology and in some aspects of Bultmann's eschatological thought and also, if Pannenberg is correct, in scripture as well. Hence Pannenberg's originality lies not so much in his creation of a new system of theological thought as in his creative and original use and re-formulation, that is to say, in his innovative synthesis of insights drawn from a variety of sources encompassing especially the biblical witness, Protestant theology, and the Western philosophical tradition.

---

[268] We might note that the oft repeated attempt to dismiss Pannenberg's theology as Hegelian, however, does not do justice to the originality of Pannenberg's thought or his use of a variety of thinkers. Cf. also Grenz, *Reason for Hope*, 72.

[269] Cf. Braaten, "The Current Controversy on Revelation: Pannenberg and his Critics," 228.

# Chapter Two

## KARL RAHNER: TRANSCENDENTAL METHOD AND INTIMATIONS OF A PHILOSOPHY OF SCIENCE

In contrast to Wolfhart Pannenberg the Roman Catholic theologian and Jesuit priest Karl Rahner devoted very little of his writing specifically to questions of theological method or the scientific nature of theology. Although Rahner's interest in dialogue with the natural sciences was pronounced, neither a fully developed philosophy of science nor a clear statement of the scientific status of theology are to be found in his writings. The comparison of Pannenberg and Rahner at the point of theological method, therefore, presents some special difficulties. Yet if we are to gain an understanding of how and why their theological interests and insights so often overlap as well as an appreciation for the forms of their respective approaches to apologetics a comparison of their theological methods is essential. Although both theologians seem to begin from radically different points of departure, intriguing methodological parallels exist which are significant for understanding the many points of conjuncture in their theological and apologetic programs.

### 2.1 Theology and Philosophy

Similar to Pannenberg, Rahner has strong roots in the philosophical tradition. Reflecting his personal intellectual journey, therefore, the relationship between philosophy and theology is significant for Rahner's understanding of the role and function of theology, especially in relation to the other sciences. Louis Roberts, in fact, has claimed that for Rahner, "all sciences have the same relation to theology that philosophy has to theology, since all sciences deal ultimately with the same thing," namely humanity's total knowledge which is ultimately self-knowledge of our radical orientation to ineffable mystery.[1]

---

[1] Louis Roberts, *The Achievement of Karl Rahner* (New York: Herder and Herder, 1967), 162. Cf. also Karl Rahner, *Spirit in the World* (London: Sheed and Ward, 1968), 65ff. [*Geist in Welt* (Munich: Kösel-Verlag, 1964), 79ff.]

## 2.1.1 The unity of theology and philosophy

For Rahner the relationship between theology and philosophy is one that is both obvious and difficult.[2] In his 1969 response to the Vatican II proposal for the reform of theological studies Rahner noted that theology and philosophy must work more closely with one another and be better integrated. Yet whether philosophical studies should precede theological studies or should come at the end as a sort of culmination was not clear to him and remained an open question.[3] Similarly, in a 1971 speech marking the opening of the *Hochschule für Philosophie* in Munich Rahner conceded that "the relationship between philosophy and theology ... is in itself extremely obscure and complex."[4] Yet despite the difficulty of establishing the precise relationship between philosophy and theology, Rahner was convinced that an underlying unity between the two exists. And this underlying unity or synthesis must be maintained since there can be no proclamation of revelation without theology and no theology without philosophy since theology (including revelation) and philosophy are mutually dependent upon one another.[5]

## 2.1.2 Philosophy as unthematic theology

For Rahner, "a philosophy that is absolutely free of theology is not even possible in our historical situation."[6] But what kind of philosophy is it that cannot be absolutely free from theology? Philosophy, according to Rahner, is not simply an essentially alien instrument which theology makes use of but constitutes an "intrinsic element" or "*inneres Moment*" of theology itself.[7] Philosophy can only be an inner moment of theology because the reality of grace includes nature as an inner moment of its own reality.[8] Thus the relationship between philosophy and theology in the thought of Rahner parallels that between nature and grace.[9]

---

[2] Cf. Anne Carr, *The Theological Method of Karl Rahner* (Missoula, Montana: Scholars Press, 1977), 3f.

[3] Karl Rahner, *Zur Reform des Theologiestudiums* (Freiburg: Herder, 1969), 53f.

[4] Rahner, "On the Current Relationship between Philosophy and Theology," in: *TI* 13:66. ["Zum heutigen Verhältnis von Philosophie und Theologie," in: *Schriften* 10:74f.]

[5] Rahner, "Philosophy and Theology," in: *TI* 6:80. ["Philosophie und Theologie," in: *Schriften* 6:101.]

[6] Rahner, *Foundations of the Christian Faith: An Introduction to the Idea of Christianity* (hereafter *FCF*), trans. William Dych (New York: Seabury Press, 1978), 25. [*Grundkurs des Glaubens: Einführung in den Begriff des Christentums*, (Freiburg: Herder, 1984), 35]. Rahner indeed goes even further to claim not only that philosophy cannot be free of theology but also that "there can be no philosophy which could be simply a-Christian." Rahner, "Philosophy and Theology," 81. [*Schriften* 6:102.]

[7] Rahner, "Reflections on Methodology in Theology," in: *TI* 11:85. ["Überlegungen zur Methode der Theologie" in: *Schriften* 9:96.]

[8] Similarly, grace is not a particular, categorical ingredient of human nature but determines the very transcendentality of human freedom and knowing. So Karl Rahner, "Transcendental Theology," in: *Sacramentum Mundi*, ed. Karl Rahner, et al., 6:288. ["Transzendentaltheologie," in: *Sacramentum Mundi* 4:989f.]

[9] "Philosophy and Theology," 72f. [*Schriften* 6:93.]

Because the theological reflection on the *nature* of humans as the condition of *grace* belongs to the very nature of theology, Rahner arrives at a transcendental theology, "which looks like philosophy."[10] The fulfillment of grace, which is not a 'thing' but a certain condition within the person and which can only exist inasmuch as the natural person (i.e., nature) exists, is also at the same time the fulfillment of the natural person. In adopting this view of nature and grace Rahner goes against much of the grain of Neo-Scholastic theology which tended to emphasize the discontinuity between nature and grace.[11] For Rahner, however, nature, especially in the form of the natural person, becomes an inner moment of the concreteness of grace in that it is presupposed by grace.[12] Similarly, philosophy is presupposed by theology and participates in the concrete reality of the theological task.

Philosophy in this way, according to Rahner, is always and necessarily unthematic theology. As Rahner writes: "In every philosophy men already engage inevitably and unthematically in theology, since no one has any choice in the matter - even when he does not know it consciously - whether he wants to be pursued by God's revealing grace or not."[13] This is so, according to Rahner, because revelation is presupposed as a condition for the actual possibility of philosophy, even for those who do not consider themselves Christian. As Rahner explained in his *Foundations of Christian Faith*, "we can never philosophize as though man has not had that experience which is the experience of Christianity. This is true at least with regard to the experience of what we call grace, although this does not have to be reflexive and understood and objectified as an experience of grace."[14] That is to say, the experience of grace is a fundamental presupposition of any philosophy, even if this is not recognized, since all persons are enlightened by God's revelatory grace. Rahner explains in more detail:

> Where the official, explicit Christian revelation presupposes philosophy as the condition of its own possibility, and brings it into its freedom, this in no way takes the form of a positing of the *pure* possibility but inevitably takes place in the form of a philosophy already actuated to some extent by Christianity. This is so not only when men engage in philosophy who are explicitly conscious of being Christians but also when those men philosophize whom we might call

---

[10] Rahner, "Transcendental Theology," in: *Sacramentum Mundi* 6:287. [*Sacramentum Mundi*, 4:987.]

[11] Cf. J. A. DiNoia, "Karl Rahner," in: *The Modern Theologians: An Introduction to Christian Theology in the Twentieth Century*, vol. 1, ed. David Ford, 193f. For Rahner a parallel exists between grace-revelation-theology on the one hand, and nature-transcendence-philosophy on the other. (Cf. Rahner, *Hearers of the Word*, 173, note 8. [*Hörer des Wortes*, 213, note 8.]) On Rahner's rejection of Neo-Scholasticism see Gerald McCool, "Karl Rahner and the Christian Philosophy of Saint Thomas Aquinas," in: *Theology and Discovery: Essays in honor of Karl Rahner, S.J.*," ed. Wm. J. Kelly (Milwaukee: Marquette University Press, 1980).

[12] "Philosophy and Theology," 73. [*Schriften* 6:93.]

[13] *Ibid.*, 79. [100.]

[14] Rahner, *FCF*, 25. [*Grundkurs*, 35].

anonymous Christians (and this applies in principle to all men who do not explicitly call themselves Christians). The anonymous Christians - whether they know it or not, ... are enlightened by the light of God's grace which God denies to no man.[15]

Rahner's view that "true" philosophy is to a certain extent "Christian" on the basis of the possibility of divine revelation is already to be found explicitly and pointedly in his 1940 *Hearers of the Word*. Rahner concludes his book on revelation and the philosophy of religion with the bold statement that: "Philosophy, as genuine philosophy, is Christian when, as fundamental-theological anthropology, it loses itself in theology. Indeed, insofar as it is the constitution of man as a listener for a possible revelation from God, it always becomes merged with theology." So it is then that human philosophy, for Rahner, is seen as always being "constituted by its readiness to surrender its existential, basic character in favor of a theology, thus losing itself in the sense already explained. Philosophy, rightly understood, is always a *praeparatio evangelii* and is intrinsically Christian - not in the sense of a retrospective baptism, but because it forms a man who is able to hear God's message to the extent that he can do this for himself."[16]

If theology, on the basis of its own nature, presupposes philosophy as a condition of its own possibility, then philosophy, according to Rahner, is not only a preparatory forerunner of the message of the gospel (i.e., of the *logos* of God become flesh) but it also accomplishes this task as "unthematic" theology inasmuch as it addresses humans in the world on their own "ground" with the message of the incarnation.[17] This human "ground" upon which philosophy addresses the human person is understood by Rahner to be the transcendental determination (*transzendentale Bestimmung*) of humanity which is given through the self-revelation of God. When philosophy reflects necessarily upon this object, that is, humanity as it is transcendentally determined through and in the self-revelatory grace of God, then it is no longer philosophy but theology "inasmuch as in this process of reflection it becomes conscious of the fact that the initial process of reflection ... is called Christian revelation."[18] Thus Karl Rahner contends that an inevitable theological element is contained in every philosophy. As Rahner writes:

> For the theologian there lies concealed in every philosophy right from the first a theology which is either unreflectingly accepted or rejected in a manner which is ... culpable. Indeed theology is so present in every philosophy not merely in the

---

[15] "Philosophy and Theology," 78f. [*Schriften* 6:100.]
[16] Karl Rahner, *Hearers of the Word*, trans. Michael Richards (New York: Herder and Herder, 1969), 175f. [*Hörer des Wortes: Zur Grundlegung einer Religionsphilosophie*, ed. J. B. Metz (Munich: Kösel-Verlag, 1963), 215f.]
[17] *Ibid.*, 71. [91.]
[18] "On the Current Relationship between Philosophy and Theology," 64. [*Schriften* 10:72f.]

sense that the content of the philosophical propositions involve an objective reference to the realities of faith, or are open to them as that which ultimately fulfils and transcends these propositions, but rather in the sense that the very process of philosophizing, in the unity between *noesis* and *noema* inherent in it ..., involves, of its very nature, a hidden element of grace, and thereby of theology. The theologian, therefore, discerns in every philosopher a counterpart of himself; or better, he discerns his own theology in a situation involving either salvation or sin, present in that hidden manner in which God, the true God who is no mere 'this-worldly' idol, is present in the world as that which is most interior to it, most hidden within it, as its future.[19]

In Rahner one finds the tendency to collapse philosophy into theology, or more precisely, into natural theology. This is especially to be seen in Rahner's development of his philosophy of religion in *Hearers of the Word*. For Rahner the philosophy of religion is true philosophy and is representative of philosophy in general because it operates with the epistemological means common to all philosophy and approaches religion from the fundamentally accessible nature of humanity and from what one could call "the natural light of reason." On the basis of what Rahner designates a "metaphysical ontology" he contends that the philosophy of religion, and implicitly also philosophy in general, is *theologia naturalis* since anthropology, especially human self-knowledge, which Rahner by means of his transcendental philosophy identifies with philosophy itself, contains within it by nature a natural theology. As Rahner explains: "The philosophy of religion exists where it is [as] what it should be, namely, fundamental-theological anthropology. This fact expresses its true relation to theology. It is only philosophy; but it is *human* philosophy. Hence its original, interior, first and last act is the open readiness for theology."[20]

Rahner's view of philosophy as unthematic theology, however, has met with significant criticism precisely at this point. Leo Scheffczyk suggests that in Rahner's program "the independence of philosophy is reduced" since philosophy is "obliged to the knowledge of divine grace, which is not only counter to the self-understanding of modern philosophy, but which may also make the actual concerns of philosophy unfamiliar."[21] Wilhelm Weischedel has leveled a similar criticism against Rahner, contending that the supposedly pure, philosophical path of Rahner is debatable inasmuch as "he views his thought from the outset as being in the service of revealed theology and in this sense he also underlines the Christian character of his philosophical efforts. ... A philosophical theology, however, that from the very beginning is built upon the foundation of Christianity, does not allow its presuppositions seriously to be questioned and is therefore unphilosophical." Thus the type of philosophical theology advocated by Rahner

---
[19] Ibid., 64. [73.]
[20] *Hearers*, 170ff. [*HdW*., 208ff.]
[21] Leo Scheffczyk, *Die Theologie und die Wissenschaften* (Aschaffenburg: Paul Pattloch Verlag, 1979), 278f.

runs the risk of being accused of being unphilosophical precisely because it never earnestly questions the basic Christian presuppositions upon which it is built. As Weischedel concludes, Rahner has attempted to ground a philosophy of religion but the way is littered with unproved presuppositions which prevents him from being successful in his attempt to develop his position through "pure philosophical means."[22]

### 2.1.3 Theology as thematic philosophy

If philosophy can be understood as unthematic theology, then, according to Rahner, theology can also in a certain sense be understood as thematic philosophy. For Rahner, all theology is "necessarily and of its innermost nature in the truest sense also philosophical theology. For otherwise it would comprise faith and creed indeed, but no longer theology precisely as such. Indeed it would no longer even comprise faith and creed."[23] And again, Rahner contends that, "every theology which really involves conscious reflection and thought, and is intended to be something more than a mere record of saving history, ... is philosophical."[24] In this sense, then, philosophy and philosophizing become a necessity for theology for, "there must be philosophizing within theology if by 'philosophizing' here one understands the activity of thinking about the revelation of God in Christ."[25]

For Rahner, philosophy is not only a necessary pre-condition of revelation. The theoretical reflection upon the self-interpretation of human existence, which Rahner sees as the essence of philosophy, itself belongs "to the content of a revealed theology which announces Christianity to man so that this essential being of his ... does not remain hidden from him." Therefore anthropology becomes the presupposition from hearing the message of revelation and leads Rahner to the conclusion that "theology itself implies a philosophical anthropology which enables this message of grace to be accepted in a really philosophical and reasonable way."[26] According to Rahner, revelation that is heard and believed by

---

[22] Wilhelm Weischedel, *Der Gott der Philosophen: Grundlegung einer philosophischen Theologie im Zeitalter des Nihilismus*, vol. 2 (Darmstadt: Wissenschaftliche Buchgesellschaft, 1972), 74f.
[23] "Reflections on Methodology," 90. [*Schriften* 9:101.]
[24] *Ibid.*, 85. [96.]
[25] Rahner, "Philosophy and Philosophizing in Theology," in: *TI* 9:47. ["Philosophie und Philosophieren in der Theologie," in: *Schriften* 8:67.]
[26] *FCF*, 25. [*Grundkurs*, 36]. There is a significant parallel to be noted here between the thought of Rahner and that of Pannenberg for Pannenberg also contends that philosophy precedes and is presupposed by theology and that theology necessarily makes use of philosophical language since it takes part itself in the philosophical task of addressing the whole of reality. Pannenberg writes: "Christian preaching and theology are not the first to raise the question about the whole of reality. This question is not first envisaged from the side of Jesus Christ, but is always posed priorly and, indeed, methodically as the question of philosophy. Therefore Christian theology must avail itself of the language of philosophy ... if it intends to give expression to the whole of reality." Theology, however, distinguishes itself from philosophy inasmuch as it proceeds specifically from the Christ-event and understands the unity of reality only in its light. In so doing, according to Pannenberg,

human persons is already theology. "Such theology, however, being a necessary and unavoidable element of the hearing of revelation and hence of revelation itself, necessarily implies philosophy."[27]

What Rahner speaks of as theology as thematic philosophy is also sometimes designated by him as explicit philosophy. What in philosophy remains general becomes explicit and thematic in theology which addresses the fundamental questions of reality consciously in light of the Christ-event. Together with the concept of philosophy as unthematic/implicit theology, theology as thematic/explicit philosophy presents a parallel to what Rahner calls anonymous and explicit faith. According to Rahner, "by anonymous faith is meant a faith which on the one hand is necessary and effective for salvation ... and on the other hand occurs without an explicit and conscious relationship to the revelation of Jesus Christ contained in the Old and/or New Testament."[28] Therefore, when our reflection about God becomes thematic philosophy we move beyond the general context of philosophy as pre-condition for Christian revelation and reflect thematically (yet still in an important sense philosophically) upon this revelation in a manner that Rahner characterizes as constituting explicit (or thematic) rather than implicit (or unthematic) faith.[29]

Although Rahner's view of theology as thematic philosophy is not so extensively developed as his view of philosophy as unthematic theology and is in many places only implicit in his thought, it has nonetheless been subject to no less criticism. According to Scheffczyk "the true meaning of theology is abbreviated" in Rahner's program in which there seems to be no other function of theology other than as "the thematizing of philosophy ... or as the explication of the implicit Christianity of human thought."[30]

Similarly critical is Martin Tripole who suggests that Rahner "ultimately reduce[s] revelation and theology to philosophy." Tripole explains that "the problem with Rahner's position is that he would translate ... [the] order of grace and revelation into a philosophical-metaphysical system of knowledge of God and man" instead of remaining entirely within the order of knowledge only from grace and revelation. Tripole suggests that for Rahner the philosophical movement of

---

[27] theology "must use philosophical ideas and concepts which it finds on hand" but these "must be fundamentally transformed because and to the extent that the whole of reality appears in a new light from the standpoint of the Christ-event." Cf. Wolfhart Pannenberg, "What is a Dogmatic Statement?" 201.

[28] "Philosophy and Theology," 73. [*Schriften* 6:93f.]

Rahner, "Anonymous and Explicit Faith," in: *TI* 16:52. ["Anonymer und expliziter Glaube," in: *Schriften* 12:76.]

[29] "Reflections on Methodology," 91ff. [*Schriften* 9:102f.] Cf. also Scheffczyk, 243f., who contends that although Rahner is thus able to decrease the tension between natural and supernatural faith, the formulation of theology as a science is made more difficult "weil das Geheimnis der Offenbarung ... nicht auf die Philosophie zurückzuführen ist und keineswegs eine Explikation des Menschseins ist, das sich selbst nur thematisch und ausdrücklicher bewußt wird."

[30] Scheffczyk, 278.

his day, especially as it was influenced by Heideggerian existentialism, "seemed to provide a way to make Christianity palatable as a natural philosophy, turning it into a glorified form of philosophy of Being." Yet Tripole contends that Rahner's transcendental Thomism and all similar attempts "to reduce theology to philosophy have miserably failed" because they are ultimately unable to bring people to "a true appreciation of the revelation of God in Christ," which Tripole contends is the strongest test for any theology.[31]

For Rahner, however, it would seem that it is precisely his appreciation of the revelation of God which leads him to his view of the relationship between philosophy and theology. Indeed, the criticisms of Rahner's view of philosophy as unthematic theology and theology as thematic philosophy have focused upon the apparent reduction of theology and philosophy into one another. Typical of these criticisms is that advanced by Paul Molnar who contends that Rahner's thought "obviates God's freedom and any real distinction between philosophy and theology" because Rahner is unwilling to make a choice between being in general (the object of philosophical reflection) and the object of theological reflection, the triune God who transcends all philosophical reflection.[32] The question which must then be addressed in light of such criticism is whether Rahner clearly distinguishes between theology and philosophy and whether this distinction is sufficient to show the essential uniqueness and independence of each enterprise alongside of their mutual interdependence? Ironically, especially in light of Tripole's critique, it would seem that the key to this distinction between the nature and functions of theology and philosophy is provided precisely by their respective relationships to revelation.

2.1.4 *Revelation as key to the distinction between theology and philosophy*
While Rahner is convinced that theology and philosophy have a "common structure" and that "a really radical separation between pure theology and pure philosophy is presumably not at all possible," a distinction between the two is nevertheless to be made. For Rahner the decisive difference between theology and philosophy, both of which speak of God, centers around theology's responsibility to revelation. In contrast to philosophical discourse theological discourse is "God-talk [*Rede von Gott*], but God-talk understood insofar as God has revealed himself in a true sense extending beyond the created world; and in this sense we already have a linguistic peculiarity of theology in contrast to philosophy. Theology appeals to the speaking God, repeats his speech ... whereas

---

[31] Martin Tripole, "Philosophy and Theology - Are They Compatible? A Comparison of Barth, Moltmann, and Pannenberg with Rahner," in: *Thought* 53:208 (March 1978), 51ff.

[32] Paul Molnar, "Can We Know God Directly? Rahner's Solution from Experience," in: *Theological Studies* 46 (1985), 229.

philosophy once again, even though it be submitted to other conditions, speaks, as it were, the first sentence itself."[33]

Philosophy, specifically a philosophy of religion, is not the same as theology, only carried out on another level or with other means. Nor does it constitute a hypothetical order which would exist even if there were no theology. For although philosophy constitutes the readiness or preparedness for theology and as such is presupposed by theology as the *potentia oboedientialis* for revelation, it is not grounded in its own essence but is dependent upon the possibility of revelation.[34] Thus Rahner can claim, "the primary and most radical [*fundamentalste*] history of philosophy is the history of Old and New Testament revelation."[35] Expressed differently, the autonomy of the human person's freedom as hearer of God's Word (philosophy) is dependent upon the divine freedom of God's grace in revelation upon which theology if founded. Thus philosophy, when it reflects upon human beings (which is the true essence of its reflection)[36] as creatures determined transcendentally through God's grace in his universal self-revelation, is dependent upon this revelation for its very being. Philosophy, therefore, is not grounded in its own essence and, is this sense, according to Rahner, there is no "pure" philosophy. As Rahner explains: "In his thinking man as philosopher is in fact constantly subject to a theological *a priori*, namely that transcendental determination which orientates him towards the immediate presence of God. And this determination is something of which he is fully aware, even though it does not *ipso facto* follow from this that he can reflect upon it. There are, therefore, no pure philosophers - not even at the level of their conscious thinking."[37]

If, however, as already seen, revelation presupposes the temporal priority of philosophy as the condition of its own possibility does this not produce a contradiction when Rahner contends that no "pure" philosophy exists since it is dependent upon the grace-filled universal revelation of God? How can philosophy be determined by and grounded upon that which it temporally precedes? For Rahner this does not present a problem for he holds the temporal sequence of philosophy and revelation to be merely the historical form of their appearance and contends that the temporally prior, in this case philosophy, can only arise because it is the necessary pre-condition for the temporally later. Rahner writes that the dependence of philosophy upon revelation for its being can also be maintained

---

[33] Rahner, "The Language of Science and the Language of Theology," in: *Karl Rahner in Dialogue: Conversations and Interviews, 1965 - 1982*, ed. Paul Imhof and Hubert Biallowons, trans. Harvey Egan (New York: Crossroad, 1986), 303f. ["Die Sprache der Wissenschaft und die Sprache der Theologie," in: Imhof and Biallowons, eds., *Karl Rahner im Gespräch*, vol. 2: 1978-1982 (Munich: Kösel-Verlag, 1983), 221f.]
[34] *Hearers*, 173. [*HdW.*, 212f.]
[35] "On the Current Relationship between Philosophy and Theology," 63. [*Schriften* 10:72.]
[36] Rahner contends that "philosophy, when it is really true to its own nature, enquires into *all* and each within the totality; into man as such." (*Ibid.*)
[37] *Ibid.*, 63. [71f.]

"even though there is philosophy *before* revelation *in time*, for the temporal succession is precisely the historical manner of appearance of this essential relationship. Even what is earlier in time can be and can become precisely *because* it is the condition of the possibility of what comes later in time, for both come about because they are supported by the one God who simply wants one thing, viz., to communicate himself."[38]

Theology, in contrast to philosophy, is understood by Rahner as being grounded within its own self. Rahner explains that since hearing, from the perspective of human beings, must also take into account the silence of God, the self-manifestation of God remains unpredictable and unmerited grace.[39]

> Listening to God is the condition of hearing the word of God, and this listening is the free act of man in his true existential self-understanding. There is, first of all, no actual hearing that is necessarily linked with the listening. Perceiving the silence of God can also be an answer, made meaningful by listening. ... And further there remains the mystery of the actual self-constitution of the listener as the concrete act of man who is autonomous and free, even when subject to the free grace of God. Thus the actually accomplished constitution of the condition of the hearing of theology was itself a free act of God before it was man's. Because God himself thus produces the readiness to listen as condition of hearing his own word, theology is purely and simply founded upon itself. It is the word of the living God himself. The philosophy of religion preceded it only as condition that is itself created by God's speaking. It is a condition of theology which is heard by man and which itself is conditioned by the word of God.[40]

Philosophy, in Rahner's view, also has a certain responsibility to revelation. Philosophy, according to Rahner, is fundamentally the reflection upon and articulation of human self-understanding. Because the unity of the subject implies that every act of knowing is a function of every other act of knowing of the subject and because the hearing of the revelation is a part of the transcendental self-understanding of the person, Rahner concludes that "revealed knowledge [*Offenbarungserkenntnis*] is also the function of philosophy."[41] If philosophy neglects this function and sets itself up as the sole, unconditional foundation of human existence then it excludes revelation and salvation history from the start. This is not possible, however, because philosophy necessarily restricts itself to the presupposition of the possibility of revelation - a self-restriction which is also the work of theology as it constitutes an essential moment of philosophy.[42] Therefore the unity of philosophy and theology cannot be overlooked.

---

[38] "Philosophy and Theology," 76. [*Schriften* 6:97.]
[39] Paul Molnar, "Can We Know God Directly? 230, suggests that this so-called silence of God is not a true silence "since Rahner has already presupposed that his philosophy of religion, by which he knows this silence, is a 'condition that is itself created by God's speaking.'"
[40] *Hearers*, 174. [*HdW*, 213f.]
[41] "Philosophy and Theology," 74. [*Schriften* 6:94.]
[42] "Transzentaltheologie," 987f.

The distinction between theology and philosophy, however, though not so great as often supposed, is still to be maintained. Not only is theology grounded within its own self, but it has also to do not just with a general revelation but also specifically with the so-called special revelation of God whereas philosophy can only recognize that self-revelation of God which is known as general or natural revelation.[43] For Rahner, however, the precise relationship between philosophy and theology remains ambivalent, especially in drawing a distinct line between the two. Indeed, Rahner contends that "we do not have to be concerned about separating philosophy and theology methodologically in the sharpest way possible."[44] Yet if a clear distinction is not made it would seem both philosophy and a theology based upon revelation stand in danger of losing sight of their unique tasks and functions as well as their own limitations.

## 2.2 Transcendental Philosophy

Given the close interlocking of philosophy and theology in Rahner's program the importance of transcendental philosophy, the stream of philosophical thought most significant for Rahner, needs little explanation. For Rahner, "transcendental philosophy and transcendental theology are interconnected in terms of their subject-matter, and it is quite impossible for them to be separated one from another." Rahner holds that all philosophy and all metaphysics is to some extent transcendental philosophy inasmuch as these are truly worthy of the name philosophy or metaphysics.[45] Yet here we will restrict ourselves to a brief overview of some of the more significant philosophers who have understood themselves or have been understood by others as carrying out transcendental philosophy and who have had a direct influence upon Rahner's own concept of the nature and methods of a transcendental philosophy.

### 2.2.1 *Immanuel Kant: Cognitive experience and the transcendental method*

According to Rahner transcendental philosophy in the modern sense of the word first became possible after Descartes and can be traced back to him and to his emphasis upon the human person as the starting point for epistemology (*cogito, ergo sum*),[46] for it is with Descartes that the "turn to the subject" in modern philosophy begins. We will begin our overview, however, with Immanuel Kant who is usually seen as given rise to transcendental philosophy within German idealism and who is responsible for bringing to completion the "turn to the subject" begun by Decartes. Also, the thought of Kant has been much more influential upon Rahner, both directly and indirectly (especially through Joseph Maréchal and to a lesser extent Martin Heidegger) than that of Descartes. As Francis Fiorenza has rightly noted, "the influence of the interpretations of Kant's

---
[43] Cf. "Philosophy and Theology," 77. [*Schriften* 6:97f.]
[44] *FCF*, 25. [*Grundkurs*, 36].
[45] "Reflections on Methodology," 85. [*Schriften* 9:96.]
[46] Cf. *Ibid.*, 86. [97.]

philosophy by Maréchal and Heidegger form the inspiration and background" of much of Karl Rahner's thought - especially his first major work, *Spirit in the World*.[47]

Kant's *Critique of Pure Reason* (1781) has been characterized as "the point where the metaphysics of man takes a new and decisive turn in modern thought."[48] Kant contended that knowledge arises out of experience but, significantly, also raised the question whether an *a priori* knowledge arising from the faculty of cognition itself is possible. Kant summarizes the issue succinctly in the opening sentences of his *Critique of Pure Reason*. He writes:

> That all our knowledge begins with experience there can be no doubt. ... In respect of time ... no knowledge of ours is antecedent to experience but begins with it. But, though all our knowledge begins with experience, it by no means follows that all arises out of experience. For, on the contrary, it is quite possible that our empirical knowledge is a compound of that which we receive through impressions, and that which the faculty of cognition supplies from itself. ... It is, therefore, a question which requires close investigation ... whether there exists a knowledge altogether independent of experience, and even of all sensuous impressions? Knowledge of this kind is called *a priori*.[49]

Kant termed such an *a priori* knowledge independent of experience "transcendental knowledge." What Kant specifically understood under the concept transcendental knowledge was a knowledge not simply of objects to be known but of the way in which such knowledge could be *a priori* possible. Wrote Kant: "I apply the term *transcendental* to all knowledge which is not so much occupied with the objects as with the mode of our cognition of these objects, so far as this mode of cognition is possible *a priori*. A system of such conceptions would be called *transcendental philosophy*."[50]

The significance of Kant's *Critique of Pure Reason* for theology is to be seen in his contention that because of the limits of human cognitive ability, which needs sense experience in order to produce knowledge, that human reason cannot obtain a knowledge of God since God transcends human sense experience.[51] Essentially, Kant's critique demolished the viability of the traditional arguments for the existence and was seen as a repudiation of natural theology, all of which earned the *Critique of Pure Reason* a place on the Roman Catholic *Index* in 1827. It is therefore all the more surprising that the positive contribution to theology of Kant,

---

[47] Francis P. Fiorenza, "Karl Rahner and the Kantian Problematic," in: Rahner, *Spirit in the World*, xxi.
[48] So Thomas Sheehan, *Subjectivity and Transcendental Method as the Fundamental Groundwork of Karl Rahner's Theological Anthropology* (Ph.D. diss., Fordham University, 1971), 17.
[49] Immanuel Kant, *The Critique of Pure Reason* (Chicago: William Benton, 1952), 14.
[50] Ibid., 20.
[51] For this and the following see George Hendry, "Kant Anniversary," in: *Theology Today* 38 (1981), 365f.

who has been called "the philosopher of Protestantism," has been realized within the realm of Roman Catholic theology. This phenomenon is seen nowhere more clearly than in the adoption of Kant's transcendental method by modern Catholic theologians, especially Karl Rahner. Francis Fiorenza, noting the positive influence of Kant upon Rahner, wrote:

> The fruitful reception of Kant is indicated by Rahner's assumption of Kant's basic question: How is metaphysics possible if all human knowledge is necessarily referred to a sensible intuition? Rahner's answer to this question departs from the traditional scholastic and philosophical positions and offers a transcendental understanding of being. ... He denies explicitly that the absolute is known as some object or that the human mind could form an adequate objective concept of God. Instead he proposes a transcendental understanding of God, who is not known by man as an object of reality, but as the principle of human knowledge and reality. ... This transcendental orientation of man to God is the unifying principle of Rahner's theology. It is the result of his fruitful and serious dialogue with ... Immanuel Kant.[52]

Yet there are also decisive differences to be noted between Kant and Rahner. For Kant the transcendental method was a comprehensive system which he understood as "the determination of the formal conditions of a complete system of pure reason"[53] and which "denotes an investigation of our knowledge, which is directed, not to what actually happens when objects are presented to our cognitive faculties, but to the conditions which make it possible *a priori*, that is, prior to experience, for our cognitive faculties to produce knowledge."[54] Rahner, however, diverges significantly from Kant in this regard in that he removes natural theology from the inaccessible realm of the transcendent and locates it in the dimension of the transcendental where is becomes the precondition for the possibility of a knowledge of God. In doing so Rahner "seeks to resolve the apparent contradiction between Kant's denial of natural theology and the dogmatic affirmation of it by the first Vatican Council" by arguing "that the statement of the Council is not factual but transcendental."[55] Thus Rahner takes Kant's transcendental knowledge of "objects" which exists on a horizontal level and adds to it a vertical dimension, contending that a transcendental knowledge of God is also possible. But for this decisive move Rahner is dependent upon Maréchal and, before him, Fichte.

---

[52] Fiorenza, "Karl Rahner and the Kantian Problematic," xliif.
[53] *Critique of Pure Reason*, 210.
[54] Hendry, 366.
[55] *Ibid.*, 367.

## 2.2.2 Johann Gottlieb Fichte: Human knowing as striving toward the Infinite Absolute

G. W. F. Hegel contended that "Fichte's philosophy is the completion of Kantian philosophy."[56] This judgment applies especially to the specifically transcendental approach introduced by Kant. As Friedemann Greiner has noted: "The transcendental reflection developed by Kant is taken fundamentally further in the transcendental philosophy of Fichte. If its main concern is generally the demonstration of the subject-object connection of all knowing, then it leads in particular, on the basis of empirical experience, to an analysis of the *a priori* structure of the subject.."[57] Perhaps the most significant contribution of Fichte to the stream of transcendental philosophy which has been taken up by Karl Rahner is his idea that the human subject's act of knowing is at root a striving toward the "Infinite Absolute." In doing so he broke away from Kant in beginning with the absolute ego which posits its own existence and thus knows subjectively. As Roberts explains:

> While Kant had worked back from the manifold given in the content of consciousness to the all-embracing unity, Fichte adopted the converse order and started from the original activity of the ego and attempted to deduce from it the special forms of the manifold. ... Fichte was led to posit a dualism between infinite and finite. So the step from formal role to actual performance of the subject in the act was taken by Fichte, who thereby goes decisively beyond Kant and supplies the authoritative starting point for German idealism: the self-performing (actuating) and self-mediating spirit which experiences itself. ... Fichte then attained being subjectively in man's self-performance ... [which] meant that thought was wholly enclosed in subjectivity.[58]

For Fichte the system of transcendental philosophy meant that all reality is "ideal" and that the possibility of our own consciousness, of our own life, and of our own being is grounded in the ego as self-knowing subject.[59] This ego, or knowing subject, is conceived by Fichte as infinite, or as that which is determined by the predicate of infinity. The ego is active between the dualism or polarity of the finite and the infinite. The ego, however, determines its own self as infinite through its striving toward the Infinite Absolute.[60] The ego, therefore, is transcendent in that it possesses an "infinite activity that goes beyond ..." and which "goes beyond into infinity."[61] This transcendental starting point implies for

---

[56] G.W.F. Hegel, *Vorlesungen über die Geschichte der Philosophie*, vol 3, in: *Sämtliche Werke*, ed. H. Glockner (Stuttgart: Friedrich Frommann Verlag, 1965), 19:611.
[57] Friedemann Greiner, *Die Menschlichkeit der Offenbarung: Die transzendentale Grundlegung der Theologie bei Karl Rahner* (Munich: Chr. Kaiser, 1978), 60f.
[58] Roberts, *The Achievement of Karl Rahner*, 11f.
[59] J. G. Fichte, *Grundlage der gesamten Wissenschaftslehre* [1794] (Hamburg: Felix Meiner, 1970), 146 (I,227).
[60] *Ibid.*, 133ff. (I,214ff.).
[61] *Ibid.*, 134, 137 (I,214, I,227f.).

Fichte a necessary idealism - an idealism that Rahner himself, because of his commitment to the transcendental starting point, would seem unable to avoid. Fichte writes that when one views the sensual world "from the transcendental perspective, ... it is then not a world existing for itself: in all that we see, we glimpse merely the reflection of our own inner activity."[62]

### 2.2.3 *Joseph Maréchal: God's existence as a priori condition of knowing*

Joseph Maréchal (1878-1944), the Belgian Jesuit philosopher, is considered the founder of "transcendental Thomism"[63] on the basis of his seminal work, *Le point de départ de la métaphysique* (1922-1926).[64] Maréchal, who consciously took up the transcendental method of Kant, summarized his position as follows:

> La méthode transcendentale kantienne doit donc, selon nous, *être complétée*, non seulement pour expliquer rationellement l'object ontologique, cela va de soi, mais même pour expliquer rationellement l'object immanent. Dans celui-ci elle relève certaines conditions logiques assurément nécessaires, peut-être même prochainement suffisantes. Aussi croyons nous pouvoir affirmer que la méthode transcendentale, si l'on veut en développer complètement les virtualités et la fonder pleinement en raison, doit *s'achever* en une méthode métaphysique.[65]

Maréchal, however, was also critical of several deficiencies in Kant's transcendental method.[66] He believed that Kant did not succeed in solving the problem of the relation between the *a priori* of sense knowledge and the *a priori* of understanding nor did Kant succeed in an analysis of the transcendental act of affirmation. The reason that Kant was not successful in going further in his analysis, "according to Maréchal, lies in Kant's inconsistency. When he

---

[62] Fichte, "Über den Grund unsers Glaubens an eine göttliche Weltregierung," [1798] in: *Die Schriften zu J. G. Fichtes Atheismusstreit*, ed. Frank Böckelmann (Munich: Rogner & Bernhard, 1969), 29f.

[63] Cf. Harald Holz, *Transzendentalphilosophie und Metaphysik: Studie über Tendenzen in der heutigen philosophischen Grundlagenproblematik* (Mainz: Matthias-Grünewald-Verlag, 1966), 1ff. Cf. also Lourencino B. Puntel, *Analogie und Geschichtlichkeit* (Freiburg: Herder, 1969), 350, who writes that even though transcendental Thomism is a broad and diverse category, that all of its proponents have in common their use of the "sogenannte 'transzendentale Methode.'"

[64] Joseph Maréchal, *Le point de départ de la métaphysique, Lecons sur le developpement historique et théorique du problème de la connaissance*, vols. 1-5 (Louvain, 1922-26), especially book 3 of vol. 5, "La critique de la connaissance transposée sur la mode transcendantal," where he describes the transposition or translation of the metaphysical method of Kant into the transcendental method. For the influence of Maréchal work on the young Rahner and an account of Rahner's early exposure to Maréchal see Walter Kern, "Erste philosophische Studien 1924-1927," in: *Karl Rahner: Bilder eines Lebens*, ed. Paul Imhof and Hubert Biallowons (Zürich: Benziger, 1985), 20f. Rahner's indebtedness to Maréchal's interpretation of Thomas is acknowledged in the foreword his own book on Thomas' metaphysical epistemology, *Spirit in the World*, xlvii. [*Geist in Welt*, 9.]

[65] Maréchal, *Le point de départ de la métaphysique*, cahier 5, livre 3, 436.

[66] For this and the following, including quote, see Otto Muck, *The Transcendental Method*, trans. Wm. Seidensticker (New York: Herder and Herder, 1968), 118f.

introduces transcendental analysis, he conceives knowledge dynamically, but he does not take this dynamic aspect into account." In order to achieve a deeper analysis Maréchal turned to Fichte, who went beyond Kant "by making full use of the dynamic viewpoint for transcendental philosophy and by attempting to render Kant's dualisms meaningful."

From Fichte Maréchal picked up the concept that the very fact of the individual's act of knowing, which is a striving toward the Infinite Absolute, requires *a priori* the reality of its object as a condition of the possibility of this knowing. According to Maréchal an object is only metaphysical inasmuch as it is implicitly related to the absolute and all objects are thus already connected to the ultimate order through this implicit relationship with the absolute. Therefore for Maréchal, and for Rahner as well, as Anne Carr has pointed out, "the metaphysical order can never be reached unless the starting point is already in that order" and its relationship to the absolute already contained within it.[67] Gerald McCool wrote that Maréchal, building upon the foundations laid by Fichte and Kant, concluded that: "If the mind's real striving toward the Infinite Absolute is one of the a priori conditions of the speculative reason's objective judgments, God's real existence is an a priori condition of possibility for every categorical judgment of the speculative reason." And further, since God's real existence is "a necessary condition of possibility for any speculative judgment whatsoever, the judgments of speculative reason are *metaphysical affirmations*."[68]

Maréchal held that every statement contained within it an absolute which is to be seen in the law of contradiction which enables us to avoid inconsistent and contradictory statements. Maréchal, however, in the words of Louis Roberts, deduced from this fact that, "if every affirmation includes some absolute, then it can only be because there *is* an absolute Being. The intelligible world in its consistency and coherence necessarily implies the existence of a Being who *is* unconditionally. This is why every affirmation affirms implicitly that God is, so that by its inner dynamism, its 'natural appetite,' the human intellect drives toward God."[69] It is then this variation of the Thomistic cosmological argument (God being the first cause in the sense of the necessary and uncaused ground of knowing within each individual) that forms the basis of Rahner's own transcendental theory of knowledge and also lays behind his contention, which will be examined later in this chapter, that a direct knowledge of God is possible. Also, Maréchal, as McCool has pointed out, by assuming that the metaphysics of knowledge is an integral part of a metaphysics of reality in general, with the structures of each being mutually inter-dependent, was able through the application of his transcendental method to find "a remarkably similar dynamic

---

[67] Anne Carr, *The Theological Method of Karl Rahner*, 46.
[68] Gerald A. McCool, "Introduction: Rahner's Philosophical Theology," in: *A Rahner Reader*, ed. G. McCool (New York: Seabury, 1975), xivf.
[69] Louis Roberts, *The Achievement of Karl Rahner*, 14.

structure of human knowledge in both Kant and in St. Thomas,"[70] thereby building a bridge, we would suggest, between Thomas and the Protestant philosopher Kant that played a key conceptual role in helping Rahner to bring together strands from both thinkers in the formation of his own thought.

### 2.2.4 *Martin Heidegger: Existential ontology*

Although not usually thought of as a transcendental philosopher, important similarities exist between the thought of Heidegger and such existential philosophers as Maréchal,[71] a fact which did not go unnoticed by his student Karl Rahner. In 1934 Rahner was sent by his order to study philosophy in his hometown of Freiburg where Martin Heidegger was teaching.[72] Because this was already the beginning of the Nazi period and because of Heidegger's connections with the Nazis it was impossible for Rahner to study directly with Heidegger and instead he studied under the Neo-Scholastic philosopher Martin Honecker. Nevertheless, Rahner visited several of Heidegger's lectures and was very much influenced by his thought. Reflecting back upon his study with Heidegger and upon Heidegger's influence upon his own thought Rahner commented that Heidegger "taught how to read texts in a new way, ask questions, and see connecting lines between the individual texts and statements of a philosopher. ... He developed thereby a great philosophy of being. I am of the opinion that this philosophy of being always can and will have a fascinating significance for a Catholic theologian, for whom God is and will remain the unutterable mystery."[73]

Indeed, the influence of Heidegger, especially of the younger Heidegger, upon Rahner is pronounced - perhaps more so than Rahner himself recognized. Especially in Heidegger's existential approach to human *being* and his ontology of being. The incorporation of certain Heideggerian themes is also to be observed in Rahner's thought. As Roberts has noted, it is precisely in typically Heideggerian themes that the most influence upon Rahner is to be observed, especially in "themes of Being and Time, dread and fear, death and repetition, time and history."[74] In addition to this apparent borrowing of themes and terminology Thomas Sheehan has noted a similarity in the mutual starting point in metaphysics in both thinkers, although Rahner "does not analyse the question of Being in the same phenomenological way that Heidegger does," and in Rahner's view that than human persons need to ask the question of being within the world, though here

---

[70] McCool, "Rahner's Philosophical Theology," xvf.
[71] Cf. *Ibid.*, 15.
[72] For this and the following see "Philosophiestudium in Freiburg," in: *Karl Rahner: Erinnerungen im Gespräch mit Meinhold Krauss*, ed. Meinhold Krauss (Freiburg: Herder, 1984), 42ff.
[73] *Ibid.*, 47.
[74] Roberts, 16.

again Rahner would seem to understand world in a different sense than does Heidegger in *Being and Time*.[75]

Perhaps the single most important influence of Heidegger upon Rahner, however, is to be found in Heidegger's existential ontology. Heidegger's existential understanding of being, which he conceives of as an *a priori* being-in-the-world, illuminates being and makes it present to itself. In this way then the modern 'turn to the subject' manifests itself also in Heidegger. Heidegger has written: "*Dasein* is ... being, that indeed I myself am. ... This determination of the being of *Dasein* must, however, be seen and understood *a priori* on the basis of the constitution of being that we call *Being-in-the-world*." And for Heidegger, this Being-in-the-world is a necessary *a priori* description of being.[76] As Otto Muck has observed, "Rahner adopts Heidegger's fundamental-ontological approach, but he insists that temporality and historicity deal with the relation of man to being, not with being as such."[77] Similarities with Heidegger's existential ontology have been found in Rahner's anthropology in which he defines being as that which is illuminated of itself (*an sich selbst gelichtet*) and is also an *a priori* being in the world,[78] although, as previously noted, his understanding of the world within which this *a priori* being is located is decisively different from that of Heidegger for whom the world is an existential of the self and Being-in-the-world expresses itself through 'caring' (*Sorge*).[79] For Rahner the world's own reality is set within the framework of a universal history in and through which the self-revelatory grace of God manifests itself.

### 2.2.5 *Rahner's estimation of transcendental philosophy*

In the modern trend or turn toward transcendental philosophy Rahner sees more than a passing movement or phase in philosophy but rather, in a decisive sense, the Christianization of philosophy. Rahner contends, in fact, that "the turning from a cosmocentric objective philosophy of the Greeks to the anthropocentric transcendental philosophy of the moderns is perfectly Christian in principle."[80] Similarly, Rahner contended that when and to the extent supernatural grace, when it comes upon human transcendentality, is not handled as something which can only be grasped through external indoctrination but that humans must necessarily become aware of through their transcendentality, then "the totality of the message of the Christian faith is in a real sense already given in a transcendental experience."[81]

---

[75] So Thomas Sheehan, *Subjectivity and Transcendental Method as the Fundamental Groundwork of Karl Rahner's Theological Anthropology*, 162.
[76] Martin Heidegger, *Sein und Zeit* [1926], (Tübingen: Max Niemeyer, 1967), 53 (§12).
[77] Muck, *The Transcendental Method*, 185.
[78] Cf. Roberts, 16ff.; and Rahner, *Hearers*, 31ff. [*HdW*., 47ff.]
[79] Heidegger, *Sein und Zeit*, 52ff. and 316ff. (§12f. and §64ff.).
[80] "Philosophy and Theology," 79f. [*Schriften* 6:101.]
[81] "Reflections on Methodology," 109. [*Schriften* 9:122.]

For Rahner this inherent "Christianness" of transcendental philosophy can be postulated on the basis of his conviction that transcendental experience becomes necessarily the experience of God. He writes: "The experience of God ... is of transcendental necessity. It therefore exists always and everywhere, whenever man implements his spiritual knowledge and freedom, even if this is often not explicitly formulated. It exists even when he denies this transcendentally necessary relationship to God, explicitly and in objectively verbal form."[82]

Beyond a so-called inherent Christianness Rahner found also within transcendental philosophy an analogy to transcendental theology through which transcendental philosophy has been seen as being particularly well-suited to Roman Catholic theology. This is not to say, however, that transcendental theology within the Roman Catholic tradition is simply the application of transcendental philosophy to specifically theological concerns or questions.[83] Yet the insights of transcendental philosophy are essential to the establishment of a transcendental theology which, although not the whole of the theological enterprise, is an essential moment in this enterprise which seeks to deal with the concreteness of human history and of the fundamental existence and subjectivity of the individual.[84] In this way Rahner believes that transcendental philosophy finds a natural home within the context of Roman Catholic thought, especially in the analogy of the dual structure of *a priori* and *a posteriori*, which is to be found in both transcendental philosophy and Roman Catholic thought.[85]

## 2.3 Rahner and the Transcendental Method

### 2.3.1 *The transcendental anthropological method*

Paul Tillich's contention that "methodological awareness always follows the application of a method; it never precedes it,"[86] is certainly applicable in the case of Karl Rahner. The approach that Rahner came to identify more and more explicitly as the transcendental method is the method which he has been using, at least implicitly, from the time of his earliest theological writings.[87] Rahner's only major writing which deals specifically with theological method is his "Reflections on Methodology in Theology," composed of three lectures held at a theological conference in 1969 in Montreal. It is the second of these lectures, titled "Transcendental Theology," in which Rahner most clearly and thoroughly explains his concept and use of the transcendental method or, as he prefers, the transcendental anthropological method.

---

[82] Rahner, "Religious Feeling Inside and Outside the Church," in: *TI* 17:234. ["Kirchliche und außerkirchliche Religiosität," in: *Schriften* 12:589.]
[83] "Transcendental Theology," 287. [*SM* 4:986.]
[84] *Ibid.*, 288. [988f.]
[85] Cf. Anne Carr, *The Theological Method of Karl Rahner*, 262.
[86] Paul Tillich, *Systematic Theology*, 1:34.
[87] Cf. Carr, 4.

Rahner recognizes his own "unsystematic" approach to theology which makes it difficult to describe precisely his theological method.[88] He also is openly mistrustful of attempts to reduce theology to its methodology since theology is necessarily more than its hermeneutics.[89] Yet Rahner is very much concerned with hermeneutics, with the general problem of understanding. Indeed, it is out of Rahner's hermeneutics, or view of understanding, that his theological method arises. Specifically, his theological method is based upon the existential and transcendental structures of human existence and the epistemology which is derived from these. Rahner, therefore, despite wariness of methodology and his many claims to be an amateur and unsystematic theologian, makes very intentional and even systematic use of the so-called transcendental method which is decisive for his entire theological program.

Transcendental philosophy, which we have already examined, implies, according to Rahner, "a quite specific line of enquiry and methodology with which it approaches the material subjects of theology." In this sense, then, the term transcendental theology can be applied to a specific theological method.[90] It is a method, however, which does not provide answers (or even appropriate methodology) for every theological question. Rather, it inquires as to presuppositions and conditions that must exist in order for humans to know not only themselves but God. As Karl-Heinz Weger has rightly noted, "the transcendental method ... does not in the first place provide a content or make any statements. It is rather a certain way of asking."[91]

For Rahner, the specifically theological, transcendental method begins with the human subject, hence he prefers to call it the "anthropological transcendental method." Rahner begins with the assumption that humans are transcendental beings who reflect transcendentally upon their being.[92] For Rahner, this also means that the transcendental experience of our own humanness (or creatureliness) "necessarily and inescapably orients us towards the ineffable and holy mystery," i.e., God.[93] This starting point, however, has led to the accusation that Rahner's approach leads to a certain subjectivity since he does not start with theological or faith propositions but which humans themselves. Hans Urs von Balthasar has been especially critical of Rahner's method at this point contending that human beings become the ultimate standard by which the Word of God and even God is to be known and judged.[94]

---

[88] "Reflections on Methodology," 68ff. [*Schriften* 9:79ff.]
[89] *Ibid.*, 83. [94.]
[90] *Ibid.*, 84. [95.]
[91] Karl-Heinz Weger, *Karl Rahner: An Introduction to His Theology*, trans. David Smith (New York: Seabury, 1980), 21.
[92] "Transcendental Theology," 288. [*SM* 4:989.]
[93] *FCF*, 76. [*Grundkurs*, 84.]
[94] Cf. Hans Urs von Balthasar, *Cordula oder der Ernstfall* (Einsiedeln: Johannes Verlag, 1967), 64-112, esp. 102ff.

Rahner, conscious of his break with traditional theology in this regard and of the charges of subjectivism, contends that "in order to provide grounds for belief we can begin quite happily with man. There is no need to fear that this anthropological starting point necessarily leads to a subjective or reductionist version of Christian faith."[95] For Rahner, transcendental theological method, understood correctly, "simply means that, with reference to all statements of faith and theology (if they are to be justified) the question must be asked how and why man, in virtue of his own nature ..., is the one with whom these statements can and must actually be concerned. The description does not mean that in my theology man is a subject of faith and religion only in his abstract transcendentality and not in his historicity and history. For me, he is a subject of faith as a historical being in his concrete history."[96]

Rahner's anthropological transcendental method holds the *a priori* givenness of the human person's ability to know in balance with the *a posteriori* experiences of the concrete world and its history which enable the person to recognize his or her transcendentality. Rahner's understanding of humanity, therefore, confesses not only the *a priori* givenness of the individual's transcendence and the pre-apprehension of being which is the foundation of this transcendence but also the necessary historical and world rootedness of the individual and of his or her experience of transcendence.

### 2.3.1.1 *A priori givenness and the pre-apprehension (Vorgriff) of being*

Decisive for Rahner's method is not just that he begins with humans (a so-called theology from below), but also that he postulates an *a priori* givenness in human beings which exists apart from their experiences in the world. To be sure, the *a posteriori* experiences of the "real" world enable us to recognize the *a priori* givenness within us but it does not produce this givenness which, for Rahner, is the key to our transcendental knowledge. For Rahner, "man is transcendent being insofar as all of his knowledge and all of his conscious activity is grounded in a pre-apprehension (*Vorgriff*) of 'being' as such in an unthematic but ever-present knowledge of the infinity of reality."[97] The human subject, according to Rahner has already transcended sense experience inasmuch as "he experiences himself as conditioned and limited." In this sense, then, the individual has "posited himself as the subject of a pre-apprehension (*Vorgriff*) which has no intrinsic limit."[98]

This pre-apprehension has no intrinsic limit because it is a pre-apprehension of the unlimited. According to Rahner, "The pre-concept [*der Vorgriff*] that is the

---

[95] Rahner, "The Foundation of Belief Today," in: *TI* 16:9. ["Glaubensbegründung heute," *Schriften* 12:24.]
[96] Rahner, "Foundations of Christian Faith," in: *TI* 19:8. ["Grundkurs des Glaubens," in: *Schriften* 14:53f.]
[97] *FCF*, 33. [*Grundkurs*, 44.]
[98] *Ibid.*, 20. [31].

transcendental condition for the possibility of an objectively possessed object, and thus of the subsisting-in-himself of man, is a pre-concept relative to being that is unlimited in itself." This is only possible then because the pre-apprehension of being is ultimately a pre-apprehension of the absolute, unlimited Being, that is to say, God. Thus the pre-apprehension "is directed towards God." This does not occur directly, according to Rahner, but rather the pre-apprehension "aims at the absolute being of God in the sense that the *esse absolutum* is always fundamentally affirmed through the former's basic unlimited breadth."[99] This means, therefore, that the pre-apprehension of being (*Vorgriff auf esse*) in Rahner's thought, and revealed by transcendental analysis, points to the fact that human beings are structurally oriented to a horizon of being which is the omnipotent, omniscient, Absolute Being.[100] The implication of the pre-apprehension of being for human knowing, as pointed out by Weischedel, is that as condition for the possibility of knowledge on the part of finite humans, it (*der Vorgriff*) "sets no limit upon itself so that, from the perspective of its own viewpoint and intention, its goes into infinity."[101]

Human beings, according to Rahner, stand under a theological *a priori* of transcendental determination which orients them toward the immediateness of God.[102] A transcendental approach inquires about this *a priori* which is understood as the condition for the possibility of knowing, but such knowledge is itself only possible when the object of knowledge in question is already known *a priori*. The inquiry as to the *a priori* reference to the object of knowledge within the subject can then be understood already as transcendental theology.[103] This *a priori* knowledge, which can also be called "preconceptual knowledge," constitutes, according to Dych, "an intrinsic moment in theological method."[104] The precise implication of the *a priori* givenness within humans for Rahner's transcendental method has been summarized succinctly by Weger. He writes: "There is an *a priori* element in man that makes it possible for him to experience his existence in the way in which he in fact does experience it. It is the aim of Rahner's theological method to elaborate and clarify the meaning of this *a priori* element and to show that it exists. Part of this aim is also to point out precisely what it is in man and what its origin is."[105] Further, as concerns the specifically

---

[99] *Hearers*, 62ff. [*HdW.*, 81ff.]
[100] For a detailed analysis of Rahner's concept of the pre-apprehension of being see Anne Rogers Devereux, *Der Vorgriff (The Pre-Apprehension of Being) and the Religious Act in Karl Rahner* (Ph.D. diss., Georgetown University, 1973), esp. 32-99.
[101] Weischedel, *Der Gott der Philosophen*, 66. Cf also Puntel, *Analogie und Geschichtlichkeit*, vol. 1, 91.
[102] "On the Current Relationship between Philosophy and Theology," 63. [*Schriften* 10:71f.]
[103] "Reflections on Methodology," 90ff. [*Schriften* 9:102ff.]
[104] William Dych, "Method in Theology According to Karl Rahner," in: *Theology and Discovery: Essays in Honor of Karl Rahner, S.J.*, ed. William Kelly (Milwaukee: Marquette University Press, 1980), 44.
[105] Weger, *Karl Rahner: An Introduction to His Theology*, 20.

methodological foundation of Rahner's apologetic, it must be noted that his emphasis upon the *a priori* is crucial for the thematic of universality inasmuch as that which is *a priori* is not only necessary but is also universal and therefore accessible and applicable to all.[106]

2.3.1.2 *The historical rootedness of transcendental experience*

Rahner defines transcendental experience as "the subjective, unthematic, necessary and unfailing consciousness of the knowing subject that is co-present in every spiritual act of knowledge, and the subject's openness to the unlimited expanse of all possible reality."[107] The question which is raised in this admittedly subjective experience is whether the concrete reality of its historical context plays any role in determining this experience or whether it remains radically and a-historically 'subjective.' The radical *a priori* givenness of humans postulated by Rahner has led to the charge, especially from so-called political theology, that his approach leads to the loss of history. Among these critics is Johann Baptist Metz, a former student of Karl Rahner, who has charged Rahner with producing a "subjectless theology of subject" (*subjektlosen Subjekttheologie*) because it ignores the historicalness of human beings and the reality of their concrete historico-political situation. The result of this, according to Metz, is the suspicion that "the process of transcendentalization of the Christian subject may have been guided by a tendency to unburden and immunize." Metz also contends that through this same transcendentalizing of the Christian subject the danger arises of prematurely relaxing the tension of the historical-apocalyptic battle of Christianity.[108] Or put differently, Metz asks whether the process of transcendentalization in Rahner's thought does not "give Christianity a kind of omnipresence which would ultimately remove it from every radical threat in the sphere of history?"[109] The effort to overcome these tendencies in Rahner's theology has led Metz to develop the so-called political theology which seeks to take the historico-political situation of humanity more seriously.

Yet despite Rahner's emphasis upon the *a priori* givenness within humans and the pre-apprehension (*Vorgriff*) of being which accounts for humanity's openness to the world and essential transcendental character Rahner is not oblivious to humanity's historical context and rootedness. This is especially to be seen in his *Foundations* where Rahner states unequivocally that "man is a being whose origins lie within the world, that is, who has his roots in empirical realities."

---

[106] Cf., for instance, Michael Gelven, *A Commentary on Heidegger's Being and Time* (New York: Harper & Row, 1970), 49.
[107] *FCF*, 20. [*Grundkurs*, 31].
[108] Cf. Johann Baptist Metz, *Faith in History and Society: Toward a Practical Fundamental Theology*, trans. David Smith (London: Burns & Oates, 1980), 159ff. Cf. also Gerd Neuhaus, *Transzendentale Erfahrung als Geschichtsverlust?* (Düsseldorf: Patmos, 1982), esp. 17ff.
[109] Metz, "An Identity Crisis in Christianity? Transcendental and Political Responses," in: *Theology and Discovery: Essays in Honor of Karl Rahner, S.J.*, 175.

His being is such that these particular origins within the world always touch him as a single whole and in his entirety."[110] Human beings, in Rahner's theology, are seen as being conditioned not only by the world but by history. There is therefore not only a historical character to transcendental experience but the individual's transcendental nature and awareness is inseparable from his or her *a posteriori* experience of the concrete world. As Rahner explains:

> Man always experiences himself both in his activity in the world and also in his theoretical, objective reflection as one to whom an historical situation in a world of things and of persons has been given in advance, given without his having chosen it for himself, although it is in and through it that he discovers and is conscious of transcendence. ... It is in his infinite transcendence and in his freedom that man experiences himself as dependent and historically conditioned. Man never establishes his own freedom in some absolute sense, in the sense of a freedom which could make complete use of the material which is given to him in his freedom, or could cast it off in an absolute self-sufficiency. He never realizes completely his possibilities in the world and in history. Nor can he distance himself from them and withdraw into the pure essence of a pseudo-subjectivity or pseudo-interiority in such a way that he could honestly say that he had become independent of the world and the history that was given him.[111]

Indeed, Rahner is adamant in his contention that the transcendental approach does not "signify any devaluation of history or of the experience of that which is factual and irreducible to the transcendental. For when the subject turns in upon himself to recognize the transcendental conditions of the possibility of his own knowledge ... he apprehends himself as inescapably anchored in history, and realizes the *a posteriori* nature of his experience, something which precisely cannot be reduced to the transcendental dimension."[112] As Anne Carr has noted, for Rahner "the transcendental reality is never without historical mediation," the primary focus of this historical mediation being the appearance of Jesus Christ in history who united the divine and the human in his own person.[113]

Yet in the end the question remains whether Rahner's method is not more transcendental than historical so that the historical elements are overshadowed by the *a priori* transcendental elements? That Rahner is convinced of the importance of the historical and world-rootedness of humans and its implications for transcendental knowing is beyond question. Yet Rahner's doctrine of the *Vorgriff* and his assumption of an *a priori* given within humans that form the basis of the possibility of our transcendental knowledge of God seem nevertheless in the end to minimize the actual role of the historical and to leave Rahner open to the charge of a loss of history in the knowing subject.

---

[110] *FCF*, 28. [*Grundkurs*, 39].
[111] *Ibid.*, 42f. [52f.]
[112] "Reflections on Methodology," 88. [*Schriften* 9:99.]
[113] Anne Carr, 264.

## 2.3.2 *The transcendental method and the doctrine of the Trinity*

As an example of how the transcendental method functions in practice Rahner chooses the doctrine of the Trinity. He begins with five presuppositions which are drawn partly from a metaphysical anthropology and partly from an ultimate and irreducible experience of grace which makes itself known in the Christian revelation and in revelatory history. These are: 1. humans are in knowledge and freedom absolutely unlimited transcendentally. 2. This transcendentality has its own self-mediated history of interpretation in the entire history of humanity, a humanity which is historical precisely in its transcendentality. 3. In their transcendence humans are radically oriented toward the absolute mystery that one calls God and which freely makes possible and bears this transcendentality of humanity in creation. 4. For this transcendentality God is not only the horizon toward which (as the unmoved mover) the transcendental movement of human cognition and freedom leads but God also includes within himself the transcendental movement of humanity in the form of the offer of the miracle of ecstatic love in his self-communication to humans and bears this movement within this self-communication. 5. In accordance with the second point this self-communication of God to the transcendentality of humanity has its history in human history and as such becomes the history of the self-communication of God's own history of salvation and revelation in the unity of the offer of salvation and the revelation of the word.[114]

On the basis of these five presuppositions Rahner believes that a transcendental-theological understanding of the Trinity can be achieved. Rahner contends that from his starting point the reality of a threefold salvation economy becomes comprehensible. Rahner describes the economic Trinity as follows:

> In the self-communication of the one God this constitutes that incomprehensible mystery which never ceases to be such even in a really radical act of self-communication. To that extent the God who imparts himself in a (forgiving) love is called 'Father'. Now this God imparts himself in such a way as to be in himself in a state of absolute proximity to man, and as a sustaining principle of the transcendentality of man in his act of knowing and loving. To that extent he is called 'Holy Spirit'. Now this self-utterance of the one God to man is manifested in history as the irreversible faithfulness of God in Jesus Christ, and as such is called the incarnate Word of the Father.[115]

Rahner believes under these three aspects of the economic Trinity and these two ways of God's self-involvement in the world that the self-communication of God takes place without these three aspects being identified or understood as independent from one another. The next step, according to Rahner, is to move

---

[114] "Reflections on Methodology," 93f. [*Schriften* 9:105f.]
[115] *Ibid.*, 94f. [106.]

from the economic to the immanent Trinity, showing the identity between the two - a central and controversial point in Rahner's doctrine of the Trinity.[116]

This particular "method" for developing a doctrine of the Trinity would seem to many inherently circular since one appears to end up precisely where one started. Rahner himself admits that all of the arguments he employs in building his doctrine of the Trinity presuppose faith in the self-communication of God. Indeed, this is precisely the strength and the distinctiveness of the transcendental method, according to Rahner, and not a weakness since the faith in question is not simply something externally indoctrinated. This faith, then, is "an experience of a transcendental kind (called the grace of faith) such that the reality of it cannot be denied merely on the grounds that it is only through revelation *ab externo* that it is brought to its full self-realization and certainty at the level of conscious thought."[117]

### 2.3.3 *The transcendental method as key to a unified science*

The American Catholic theologian and Jesuit priest Bernard Lonergan has advocated strongly for the use of the transcendental method. In doing so Lonergan has pointed to a function of the transcendental method which has strong roots in transcendental philosophy and which, it would seem, is at least implicitly present in Karl Rahner's thought. Namely, Lonergan believes that the transcendental method is the key to a unified science - a concept long popular in many philosophical circles but which has come under much criticism from recent philosophers of science.[118] Lonergan writes:

> [The] transcendental method offers a key to unified science. The immobility of the Aristotelian ideal conflicts with developing natural science, developing human science, developing dogma, and developing theology. In harmony with all development is the human mind itself which effects the developments. In unity with all fields, however disparate, is again the human mind that operates in all fields and in radically the same fashion in each. Through the self-knowledge, the self-appropriation, the self-possession that result from making explicit the basic normative pattern of the recurrent and related operations of human cognitional process, it becomes possible to envisage a future in which all workers in all fields can find in transcendental method common norms,

---

[116] Cf. Bert van der Heijden, *Karl Rahner: Darstellung und Kritik seiner Grundpositionen* (Einsiedeln: Johannes Verlag, 1973), 436ff.; and Paul Molnar, "Can We Know God Directly?" 248ff. for criticisms of Rahner's identification of the economic and immanent Trinity.

[117] "Reflections on Methodology," 95. [*Schriften* 9:107.]

[118] The implications of transcendental philosophy and transcendental method for a so-called unified science would seem to be found already in J. G. Fichte's *Die Wissenschaftslehre* [1804] in which he argues that transcendental philosophy is the science of science and forms the foundation upon which all the individual sciences are founded. Cf. Greiner, *Die Menschlichkeit der Offenbarung*, 58ff.

foundations, systematics, and common critical, dialectical, and heuristic procedures.[119]

This concept is implicit in Rahner's own thought especially in his emphasis upon the anthropological starting point of all knowing, which parallels Lonergan's observation that it is the human mind which operates in all fields. For Rahner all philosophy, when it is truly philosophy, is transcendental philosophy, precisely because it begins with the presupposition of universal human transcendence.[120] Although Rahner does not speak of a unified science, a concept long abandoned by most philosophers of science, he does recognize a "unity of reality" which lays behind the experience of all the individual objects of scientific inquiry. Even if the individual sciences do not investigate or even recognize this original unity of reality it is implied in the very transcendental nature of human knowing which manifests itself in the experience/knowledge of all objects. Rahner contends that, "there is a transcendental experience to the extent that the experience of that prior awareness which comes before any individual object ... constitutes an inalienable *a priori* condition of the knowledge of objects assignable to particular categories, and to the extent that the knowledge of these involves, at least implicitly, this prior awareness."[121]

At the very beginning of *Hearers of the Word* Rahner takes up the question of the relationship between two different sciences. He contends that the various individual sciences stand in relationship to one another because each one brings with it something *a priori* which makes its very existence as a science possible and places it in relationship to the other sciences. As Rahner explains: "A particular science rests ultimately upon a foundation which it did not itself lay. Such a foundation is what makes it possible for that science to exist at all." Rahner then takes his argument further by suggesting that the ground laying behind each individual science must be the same, thus uniting the plurality of sciences in the unity of the thinking subject. Rahner concludes, therefore, "that the foundation of the sciences in the theory of science is *one*. ... There is, then, a unified fundamental science, which first of all gives to the particular sciences their various subject-matters in their several *a priori*, presupposed structures. ... It is this unified science which simultaneously must establish these sciences at their very origin as open to human understanding in its necessity and uniqueness."[122]

Therefore for Rahner, as Otto Muck has pointed out, "a transcendental metaphysics shows itself to be necessary with respect to the question concerning the relationship between the sciences arising from the diversity of the special

---

[119] Bernard Lonergan, *Method in Theology* (London: Darton, Longman & Todd, 1972), 24.
[120] Cf. "Reflections on Methodology," 85. [*Schriften* 9:96.]
[121] Rahner, "On the Relationship Between Theology and the Contemporary Sciences," in: *TI* 13:96. ["Zum Verhältnis zwischen Theologie und heutigen Wissenschaften," in: *Schriften* 10:106.]
[122] *Hearers*, 3ff. [*HdW*., 15ff.]

sciences in the unifying knowledge of man."[123] Roberts has similarly summarized the matter and pointed at the same time to the implications of the transcendental method as key to a 'unified science' well when he wrote: "Applying the transcendental method, Rahner ... argues that ... one must see that the *plurality* of sciences springs from *one* common ground. So a question about the relationship of any two sciences is not really a question about their own constitution, interrelations, and situation, but is really a question about their unity in the common metaphysical ground. And this is to reduce the problem to an existential question of man."[124]

### 2.3.4 "Transcendental" versus "metaphysical"

In many cases much of the apparent dissonance between the thought of Pannenberg and that of Rahner disappears when one realizes that the two theologians are often speaking of the same thing but from different contexts and with different terminology. A case in point would seem to be Rahner's use of the term transcendental and Pannenberg's emphasis upon the importance of metaphysics. As we have already seen, Rahner's conception not only of transcendental philosophy but his use of the concept "transcendental" itself is very broad.[125] David Tracy, an American advocate of transcendental philosophy, believes that the terms transcendental and metaphysical essentially point to the same thing, with "transcendental" being the modern formulation and "metaphysical" the more traditional. As Tracy explains: "Transcendental ... reflection attempts the explicit mediation of the basic presuppositions (or 'beliefs') that are the conditions of the possibility of our existing or understanding at all. Metaphysical reflection means essentially the same thing." The difference between the two, for Tracy, is essentially one of a "degree of adequacy to the task not a difference of kind."[126]

Indeed, Pannenberg himself suggests that much of what Rahner terms "transcendental" is what he himself chooses to call "metaphysical."[127] Considering the key roles played respectively by the concepts "transcendental" and "metaphysical" in the theologies and methodologies of Rahner and Pannenberg the suggestion deserves examination. Puntel, in his criticism of the

---

[123] Muck, *The Transcendental Method*, 203.
[124] Roberts, 38.
[125] Cf. Greiner, *Der Menschlichkeit der Offenbarung*, 15ff. Greiner speaks of a "gegenseitige Überschneidung und damit die Verdunklung der Begriffsnuancen des Transzendentalen" in Rahner and also writes that one can "schwerlich leugnen, daß es sich grundsätzlich um verschiedene und somit nicht ohne weiteres miteinander zu vermittelnde Reflexionsebenen handelt, die Rahner in dem Begriff des Transzendentalen vereint" (19).
[126] David Tracy, *Blessed Rage for Order: The New Pluralism in Theology* (New York: Seabury Press, 1978), 55f. and 63.
[127] Cf. Pannenberg, *ST*, 1:114f., note 166. [1:128f, note 177.]

transcendental philosophers, has claimed that the entire so-called transcendental method is another name for a new form of "the whole of classical metaphysics."[128]

Pannenberg notes that in Catholic thought metaphysics was "never really abandoned, only modernized," especially in the form of transcendental philosophy or transcendental Thomism.[129] Harald Holz has pointed out that Maréchal, upon whom Rahner is dependent for the form of much of his own transcendental philosophy, normally used the term "metaphysics" to speak of the transcendental realm of subjectivity upon which the meaning, methods and knowledge of philosophy is ultimately grounded.[130] Similarly, even though Maréchal distinguished between a metaphysical and transcendental critique of an object in which the former focused upon the object's ontological meaning while the latter dealt with the logical function of the constitution of the immanence of consciousness of the object, his analysis of the two is virtually identical and the critical methods of both lead ultimately to the same results.[131] Given Rahner's dependence upon Maréchal, therefore, there would seem to be additional grounds for suggesting that what he intends by the term transcendental may be largely what Pannenberg, following the classical use of terminology, means by metaphysical.

Yet the difference between Pannenberg and Rahner in this regard would seem to go beyond a mere semantic disagreement over the use of 'metaphysical' or 'transcendental' to describe the same reality - or, as Tracy suggests, a mere difference in the degree of adequacy to a particular task. Pannenberg contends that Rahner and other Catholic advocates of transcendental Thomism have attempted a rethinking of traditional metaphysics but, "with their assertions concerning the ontological state of humanity, world, and God, these Catholic thinkers certainly overstepped the boundaries of strict transcendental reflection in the Kantian sense, which is capable of speaking only of the conditions of possible experience as they are found within the experiencing subject." The implication, according to Pannenberg, is that either the results of such transcendental thought must be cast into doubt or the transcendental method itself "must be cast into another mode of reflection."[132]

Although holding Rahner and other transcendental theologians to the semantic parameters of the term transcendental as set by Kant would appear

---

[128] Puntel, *Analogie und Geschichtlichkeit*, 351. Puntel, in his critique of transcendental Thomism, writes: "Die [transzendentale] Methode dient ... zur Grundlegung des Gebäudes der klassischen Metaphysik. ... Auf *unreflektierte* Weise, sozusagen unter der Hand, entsteht durch die Übernahme der transzendentalen Methode eine andere, neue Gestalt des Ganzen der klassischen Metaphysik." Cf. also Puntel's extensive review of Holz' book, *Transzendentalphilosophie und Metaphysik*, in: *Philosophisches Jahrbuch* 75 (1967), 217-227.
[129] Pannenberg, *Metaphysics and the Idea of God*, 5. [*Metaphysik und Gottesgedanke*, 8.]
[130] Holz, *Transzendentalphilosophie und Metaphysik*, 4.
[131] So Puntel, *Analogie und Geschichte*, 63.
[132] *Metaphysics and the Idea of God*, 5. [*Metaphysik und Gottesgedanke*, 8.]

rigid,[133] the criticism would seem valid in that, especially in the case of Rahner, the breadth and diversity of what he includes under the category of transcendental may better be termed metaphysical. Yet to suggest that what Rahner understands as transcendental and what Pannenberg understands as metaphysical are largely identical would be misleading. Although definite and significant overlap is certainly present the radical "subjectivity," or centeredness upon the knowing subject which permeates Rahner's concept of transcendental theology and transcendental method would not seem ultimately simply reducible to the 'broader' or related category of metaphysics.

## 2.4 The Concept of Revelation in Karl Rahner

Avery Dulles has characterized Karl Rahner's perspective on revelation as "the most powerful restatement of the Catholic theology of revelation" in the post Vatican II period.[134] The powerfulness of Rahner's concept of Revelation is not only to be found in some of its unique features such as the integration of revelation into a system of transcendental theology but also and perhaps especially in its claim to universality.

2.4.1 *Universal revelation as transcendental determination of humanity*

The universality of revelation is understood by Rahner not just as that which, as the transcendental determination of humanity is accessible to and at work in all persons, but revelation is also universal in the sense that it has taken place at all times. The history of universal salvation, according to Rahner, is coexistent with the history of the world as "the categorical mediation of man's supernatural transcendentality, and is also at the same time the history of revelation which also "is coextensive with the whole history of the world." The radical implication of this view is that the history of revelation does not begin with Abraham or Moses but "takes place wherever the individual and collective history of the human race is taking place."[135] According to Rahner, this means that there exists a genuine universal revelation of God which is co-extensive with world history and thus cannot be simply identical with the categorical revelation of the Old and New Testaments since this revelation is limited in space and time.[136] In this sense, the universality of revelation determines not just modern humanity or those human

---

[133] Rahner himself was well aware of how far he had moved from a Kantian understanding of transcendental philosophy and transcendental method but saw this as a legitimate and necessary development. Cf. "Karl Rahner antwortet Eberhard Simons. Zur Lage der Theologie: Probleme nach dem Konzil," *Das theologische Interview* 1 (Düsseldorf, 1969), 29.

[134] Avery Dulles, *Revelation Theology: A History* (New York: Herder and Herder, 1969), 158f.

[135] *FCF*, 144f. [*Grundkurs*, 149].

[136] "On the Current Relationship between Philosophy and Theology," 61f. [*Schriften* 10:70f.] We might also note here that Rahner's division of revelation into categorical and transcendental/universal revelation finds no parallel in Pannenberg who emphasizes consistently the unitary character of revelation.

beings within the Church but the entirety of humanity - in all times and in all places. According to Rahner, such a universal, even if unreflected self-disclosure of God is to be understood "as a transcendental determination of man" in that the grace of God present in this universal self-revelation[137] determines all persons whether they consciously accept or reject it or even whether they are consciously aware of it. Hence the grace of God present *through, in* and *as* universal revelation is, in the form of the *offer* of grace, always given, not as an occasionally occurring categorical event, but as "a transcendental determination of human life, albeit one that is freely bestowed by God ... even when it is never objectified or conceived at the level of explicit consciousness." Rahner contends that "philosophical reflection ... will rarely if ever succeed in objectifying and reducing to human terms this gracious determination of man in his transcendentality which brings him into immediate contact with God." Yet this does not change the fact that humans are determined to the very ground of their existence by God's self-disclosure. Humans beings, therefore, as philosophically thinking beings, cannot dismiss the fact that the "transcendental determination of man is a factor present in virtue of the self-bestowal of God, and, moreover, present always and everywhere (at least in the sense of being offered)."[138]

### 2.4.2 *Revelation and transcendental experience*

One of the more difficult points in Karl Rahner's theology, and one that has inevitably led to misunderstanding, is the relationship between transcendental experience and revelation. On the surface the two appear to be contradictory propositions. On the one hand, Rahner stresses the self-revelation of God to created humanity. Yet Rahner's postulation of human self-transcendence and its implication for a theory of knowledge seems to suggest that the knowledge of God is already an *a priori* given within humans and that God's self-revelation becomes unnecessary. Rahner, however, vigorously rejects this implication and maintains that the transcendental experience of God's grace and the knowledge of God's grace obtained through his historical self-revelation are mutually conditioning moments of one and the same occurrence. Rahner explains:

> The history of revelation and the act of bearing witness to the faith, which comes from hearing, [are not] superfluous. It is precisely this history of revelation and history of faith at the social level that constitutes the historical process by which this grace-given transcendental experience, constituted and upheld as it is by the self-bestowal of God, is brought to the stage of self-realization. It is precisely in order to arrive at the most ultimate and transcendental dimension of his own

---

[137] For Rahner it is "free grace," which has its history within universal revelation, is that which transcendentally determines humanity rather than the bare fact of revelation. Cf. "Transcendental Theology," 288. [*SM* 4:989.]

[138] "On the Current Relationship between Philosophy and Theology," 62f. [*Schriften* 10:71f.]

nature that man is oriented towards his own history at both the individual and collective levels. But precisely as such this is the history of his own transcendental nature itself. Hence it is that revelation as the transcendental experience of grace and revelation as history do not mutually contradict one another but rather are the mutually conditioning elements in one and the same event.[139]

This contention of Rahner's is especially significant for a comparison of his theology with that of Pannenberg since precisely at this point the two seem to come into conflict. Pannenberg understands revelation as history and would seem to leave little room in his thought for what Rahner calls a transcendental experience of grace. At least on Rahner's part, however, such a transcendental experience of grace does not exclude an understanding of revelation in or as history but conditions such revelation and is conditioned by it. Indeed, for Rahner, the fact that transcendence is always mediated historically means that transcendence itself has a history which we call the history of revelation.[140] While this by no means harmonizes the positions of Rahner and Pannenberg it does point to the fact that their two approaches need not exclude one another. The question that remains, however, and that is decisive for determining to what extent common ground exists between Pannenberg and Rahner on this point, is to what extent God's self-revelation and the human transcendental experience of it are actually 'historical' in Rahner's thought. It is to this question which we now turn.

### 2.4.3 The self-revelation of God within history

A parallel to Pannenberg's theology of revelation is not only to be seen in the universality of revelation but also in Rahner's emphasis upon this revelation as a self-disclosure of God within history. Whereas for Pannenberg the self-revelation of God *is* history, Rahner might better be characterized as conceiving history as the concrete context within which the self-revelation of God takes place - particularly as this history is understood as the history of salvation which is coexistent but not identical with the whole of human history.[141] "Salvation-history and world-history are not ... absolutely identical but nevertheless coincide in space and in time."[142] Salvation history takes place within world history but this

---

[139] "Reflections on Methodology," 109f. [*Schriften* 9:122.]

[140] Rahner, "Observations on the Concept of Revelation," in: Karl Rahner and Joseph Ratzinger, *Revelation and Tradition*, *Quaestiones disputatae* 17, trans. W.J. O'Hara (London: Burns & Oats, 1966), 13. ["Bemerkungen zum Begriff der Offenbarung," in: K. Rahner and J. Ratzinger, *Offenbarung und Überlieferung*, *QD* 25 (Freiburg: Herder, 1965), 14.]

[141] On Pannenberg's evaluation of Rahner's concept of salvation history see "Weltgeschichte und Heilsgeschichte," 361ff., where he compares Rahner's formulation to that of Cullmann, arriving at a more positive assessment of the former.

[142] "Philosophy and Theology," 76. [*Schriften* 6:98.] Although not a recurring theme in Rahner's theology of revelation, Rahner seems to go beyond the idea that the history of revelation and human history are not identical when he writes elsewhere that revelation is "the innermost core of human history as such" and is "identical with the universal history of mankind" - a statement

does not mean that it is simply a piece or aspect of that history. Thus according to Rahner, "the completion of salvation is not a moment in history, but rather its abolution."[143] For Rahner God's self-disclosure (*Selbstmitteilung Gottes*) means that God himself can have a "history." Indeed, the self-disclosure of God is understood as the "source of the world, the ultimate ground of world-history, and its perfect culmination is the goal of world-history and the content of its final conclusion."[144]

Rahner elsewhere similarly contends that the "moment of God's self-communication ... belongs to this history [of salvation] and takes place within it. This self-communication is a moment in the history of salvation insofar as the self-communication and the freedom of its acceptance and rejection, which is really exercised in the concrete, historical corporeality of man and of mankind, come to appearance there." The historicalness of God's self-communication or self-disclosure does not stand in disjunction to the transcendental nature of revelation, "for this event of God's self-communication is indeed transcendental, but precisely *as transcendental* it is a real history."[145] Indeed, Rahner defines the Christian history of revelation (*Offenbarungsgeschichte*) as "nothing else than the developing process, taking place within history, by which man reflects upon this transcendental experience of the self-bestowal of God, a reflection which, of course, in its process of historical development, cannot be achieved by the individual as such taken in isolation, but is rather sustained by the history of reflexive thought discernible within the history of mankind as a whole right from its origins."[146]

For Rahner, the concrete self-disclosure of God in history takes place preeminently in Jesus Christ.[147] The mystery of God's self-revelation, according to Rahner, has a history because it has its origin in the free action of God and because humans are historical beings and our ultimate transcendentality must be brought to completion historically in space-time in a concrete encounter with the concrete world.[148] Where this appearance of divine self-disclosure achieves its

---

which would appear, if fully developed, to bring Rahner even closer to Pannenberg's concept of revelation. Cf. Rahner, "Observations on the Concept of Revelation," 11. ["Bemerkungen zum Begriff der Offenbarung," 13.]

[143] Rahner, *Zur Theologie der Zukunft* (Zürich: Benziger, 1971), 9.

[144] Rahner, "God's Self-Communication (Revelation II)" in: *Sacramentum Mundi* 5:354f. ["Selbstmitteilung Gottes," in: *SM* 4:522, 524.]

[145] *FCF*, 143. [*Grundkurs*, 148].

[146] "On the Relationship Between Theology and the Contemporary Sciences," 98. [*Schriften* 10:108.] See similarly Rahner's article "Transcendental Theology," 288. [*SM* 4:988], where he writes: "The self-communication of God in grace ... is undoubtedly a 'transcendental' existential of man."

[147] For a detailed discussion and critique of the role of christology in Rahner's efforts to ground transcendentality within history see F. Greiner's chapter titled "Transzendentalität und Geschichte: Die Christologie Rahners," in: *Die Menschlichkeit der Offenbarung*, 250ff.

[148] Rahner, "Intellectual Honesty and Christian Faith," in: *TI* 7:63. ["Intellektuelle Redlichkeit und christlicher Glaube," in: Karl Rahner and Wilhelm Dantine, *Intellektuelle Redlichkeit und*

highest pinnacle is where the dialogue between God and humanity becomes 'substantial' in that which theology calls the divine logos. It remains the irreducible fact of genuinely experienced history, according to Rahner, "that this takes place and is experienced precisely in Jesus of Nazareth. ... When we speak of the 'Church' ... [we] mean nothing else than that the historical facts are enduring and valid, that in Jesus of Nazareth the history of God's self-bestowal has manifested itself in an irrevocable form."[149] Therefore Rahner resolutely contends that the incarnation is the climax of the "self-communication of God to all spirit" and forms the "heights of the historical, irreversible (eschatological) manifestation of the victorious self-communication of God to the world."[150]

As Friedemann Greiner has observed, Rahner attempts to hold together the tension between transcendentality and history with the Christ event in which "the Christ event has the function of a self-fulfilling and exemplary manifestation and representation of that which, in its essence and entirety, even if only implicit, is already present." The question, however, as posed by Greiner, is whether ultimately Rahner attempts two combine two levels of reflection, the historical and the transcendental, which cannot be brought together. The result, as seen especially in the role of christology, is the danger that history is transformed into an epi-phenomenon of an original transcendental argumentation or experience.[151]

## 2.5 Karl Rahner's Hermeneutic

In treating Karl Rahner's theological method we have, at least implicitly, already dealt with his hermeneutic, especially as this is expressed in his distinctive transcendental approach to understanding and interpreting meaning and reality. The focus upon hermeneutic within contemporary philosophy and within Protestant theology, however, suggests that we explicitly summarize the specific contours of Rahner's transcendental hermeneutic. But before doing this, however, we must treat two significant aspects of Rahner's hermeneutic which we have not yet dealt with within the context of our discussion, namely his use of symbol and his hermeneutic of eschatological statements, which latter holds special significance for the comparison with the methodology of Pannenberg.

### 2.5.1 *Analogy and symbol*

Crucial to an understanding of Karl Rahner's hermeneutic is his theology of the symbol. Although Rahner himself admits that the concept of symbol is "much

---

*Christlicher Glaube*, and *Glaube und Wissenschaft: Ihre Kritische Funktion* (Freiburg: Herder, 1966), 24f.]

149 *Ibid.*, 64. [25.] Cf. also "On the Relationship Between Theology and the Contemporary Sciences," 98. [*Schriften* 10:108.] where Rahner writes that "this experience of the absolute self-utterance of God given in the transcendental experience of man achieves its supreme point in Jesus of Nazareth."

150 "Transcendental Theology," 289. [*SM* 4:991.]

151 Greiner, *Die Menschlichkeit der Offenbarung*, 289.

more obscure, difficult and ambiguous" than is usually assumed he holds certain aspects of the nature of symbol to be clear.[152] We are especially interested here in the role played by "symbol" in the process of knowing and understanding, especially in the self-understanding of the individual, and in the relationship between the whole and the parts in the symbol, a concept which finds clear parallel in Pannenberg's hermeneutic of the whole and the parts.[153]

In his important article, "The Theology of the Symbol," Rahner outlines his theology of the symbol in six propositions. 1. Being is of its very nature necessarily symbolic since it necessarily expresses itself in order to find its own nature. Thus, according to Rahner, the symbol "is the way of knowledge of self, possession of self, in general."[154] As DiNoia explained, Rahner's "'ontology of the symbol' takes self-involving performative utterances for its paradigm case of what constitutes a symbol. ... As in self-involving performances, an entity becomes itself in expressing itself."[155] 2. The actual or real symbol "is the self-realization of a being in the other, which is constitutive of its essence." With echoes of Tillich, Rahner explains that this means that the concept of being is analogous so that being in itself has inextricably to do with the concept and reality of the symbol which is part of the "uncovered" form of the original "truth" of being. Hence the symbol shares the *analogia entis* with that which is symbolized, namely being.[156] 3. The concept of the symbol "is an essential key-concept in all theological treatises, without which it is impossible to have a correct understanding of the subject-matter of the various treatises in themselves and in relation to other treatises." 4. "God's salvific action on man ... always takes place in such a way that God himself is the reality of salvation, because it is given to man and grasped by him in the symbol, which does not represent an absent and merely promised reality but exhibits this reality as something present, by means of the symbol formed by it." 5. The body is the symbol of the soul inasmuch as it is the self-realization of the soul and to the extent that the soul allows the body, which is distinct from it, to be present and appear. And inasmuch as Rahner feels that this last point must be completed by the insights of a Thomistic natural philosophy he concludes with a final proposition: 6. "In this unity of symbol and thing symbolized, constituted by soul and body, the individual parts of the body

---

[152] Rahner, "The Theology of the Symbol," in: *TI* 4:222. ["Zur Theologie des Symbols," in: *Schriften* 4:276.]

[153] Pannenberg, however, is apprehensive of the traditional doctrine of analogy itself, as we have already noted in chapter one, questioning whether it takes seriously enough God's transcendence and human finitude. He thus writes: "The transcendence of the infinite over against the finite forms the theme of my writings on the idea of the analogy between God and the world. The thesis of analogy appeared suspicious to me precisely as an infringement of God's transcendence." (Pannenberg, "Response to the Discussion," in: *Theology as History*, 251.)

[154] "The Theology of the Symbol," 224, 230. [*Schriften* 4:278, 285.]

[155] DiNoia, "Karl Rahner," 198.

[156] "The Theology of the Symbol," 234f. [*Schriften* 4:290f.] Cf. Paul Tillich, *Systematic Theology*, vol. 1 (Chicago: University of Chicago Press, 1951), 239ff.

are more than pieces put together quantitatively to form the whole body; they are rather parts in so special a way that they also comprise in themselves the whole."[157]

In an important sense Rahner begins his search for a foundational conception of the symbol with the recognition that that which is finite is characterized (or stigmatized) by the fact that it is not "simple" in the absolute sense but is intrinsically plural, that is, in the continuing and comprehensive unity of its reality. Such a plurality in an original (and originally "higher") unity can only be understood in that "the 'one' develops, the plural stems from an original 'one', in a relationship of origin and consequence; the original unity, which also forms the unity which unites the plural, maintains itself while resolving itself and 'disclosing' itself into a plurality in order to find itself precisely there."[158] Maria Motzko has indicated the significance of this point of Rahner's thought in her observation that, "the plural moments which are constituted within the dynamic unity of a being must be characterized by an inner agreement among themselves which cannot be one of simple juxtaposition. ... These plural moments in a unified being must be seen therefore as the unfolding of an original and superior unity. The original 'one' unfolds itself into plurality in order to reach its own full development."[159] The primary example of this original and superior unity which unfolds into plurality to achieve full development is to be found, according to Rahner, in the doctrine of the Trinity. The unity in plurality which is the Trinity constitutes a final ontological essence that cannot be reduced to a merely apparent higher unity. Indeed, "it would be theologically a heresy, and therefore ontologically an absurdity, to think that God would be really 'simpler' and hence more perfect, if there were no real distinction of persons in God."[160]

Rahner's theology of the symbol, however, provides not only a hermeneutic key to understanding the doctrine of the Trinity, but is also hermeneutically significant for an understanding of the human person. The plurality within original and superior unity is therefore also thematized by Rahner in his fifth and sixth propositions, in which he affirms the unity of the symbol with that which is symbolized, in the example of the body which serves as symbol of the soul. Each member of the body is a part which includes within it and participates in the original whole (i.e., the soul). As Roberts has noted, "Rahner thinks such considerations give a more clearly defined meaning to the teaching that the completely simple soul is given in each and every part of the body. The substantial and informative presence of the soul means that it forms the part precisely as part of a whole."[161]

---

[157] *Ibid.*, 245ff., [306ff.], for this and the preceding.
[158] *Ibid.*, 226f. [280ff.]
[159] Maria Motzko, *Karl Rahner's Theology: A Theology of the Symbol* (Ph.D. diss., Fordham University, 1976), 5f.
[160] "The Theology of the Symbol," 227f. [*Schriften* 4:282.]
[161] Roberts, 36.

It is precisely here that an important parallel with Pannenberg's hermeneutic arises. For Rahner, as for Pannenberg, there is an intricate connection between the parts and the whole. For both theologians the whole is included within the parts so that the whole is critical for an appropriate understanding of the parts. Pannenberg's reflections upon the whole and the parts is set primarily within the framework of history, i.e., individual events are only comprehensible in light of the whole of history which is only to be found or known at the end of history. Rahner, on the other hand, sets his reflections within the context of his theology of the symbol. The individual parts of a symbol allow an adequate understanding of reality because and to the extent that they participate in and include the whole. Thus while reflecting on two different conceptual levels both Pannenberg and Rahner express a hermeneutical concern for the whole which is consistent with both theologians' emphasis upon the universality of theology. For both there is a decisive rejection of a regional hermeneutics in which it is assumed that the parts can be understood on their own terms without reference to the whole, or that the whole is somehow an independent entity which does not in itself consist of and express itself in its various parts.

### 2.5.2 *Eschatological hermeneutic*

In Rahner's 1960 paper "The Hermeneutics of Eschatological Assertions" not only is a hermeneutic laid forth for the interpretation of specifically eschatological biblical and dogmatic statements but an "eschatological hermeneutic" itself, applicable to our present understanding of reality, is also to be detected.[162] We have already seen that in the thought of Pannenberg the final self-revelation of God takes place at the end of history, which he contends has already occurred proleptically in the Christ event. Thus the future is already radically and actively present. The question we wish to address here is whether in Rahner's hermeneutic anything similar to this central aspect of Pannenberg's program is to be found.

Of the seven theses Rahner presents in his essay we are particularly concerned with thesis four, which Rahner divides into two parts. In the first part Rahner states that the content of the knowledge of the genuine future, which co-forms the human present, is a knowledge of that which is still future and which is necessary for the understanding of present being [des *jetzigen* Daseins]. Thus according to Rahner the future co-constitutes the present just as our knowledge of the future is necessary for our present understanding of our existence. Rahner further explains that the knowledge of the future becomes the knowledge of the futureness of the present and eschatological knowledge is the knowledge of the eschatological present. Therefore, "an eschatological assertion is not an additional, supplementary statement appended to an assertion about the present

---

[162] Jon Sobrino, *Christology at the Crossroads*, trans. John Drury (New York: Orbis Books, 1978), 23, notes that the later Rahner "has been deeply influenced by the eschatological line of thought, which analyzes past and present reality in terms of the future."

and the past of the human person but an inner moment of this person's self-understanding."[163]

The second part of Rahner's thesis is itself divided into two parts. He emphasizes there that the future must already in a real sense be present. Rahner contends, first of all, that the future must already be present as hidden and inaccessible because only in this way does there remain room for creaturely freedom. And second "the future must really be present, that is, it must be already anticipated" so that its being present must in a real sense already exist in its hiddenness and genuine futurity; its presence, therefore, must constitute a real moment of our understanding of being.[164]

But what does this mean, that the future must already be present as a real moment of human self-understanding? For Rahner it is the present which seems to form the starting point of his hermeneutics of eschatological statements. The *knowledge* of the future more than the future itself is decisive for our present self-understanding. Peter Phan has summarized the intent of this thesis of Rahner's as pointing to the significance of our future fulfillment of salvation for our present understanding of ourselves. He writes: "Because man ex-sists into the future, the future in its hiddenness must be a real moment of the present self-understanding of the person. Indeed it can be known and understood *only out of the present*; it is the futurity of the present. Therefore the hermeneutics of eschatological assertions is ultimately the interpretation of the individual's present self-understanding in terms of his or her future fulfillment."[165]

As Rahner himself has explained in his *Foundations of Christian Faith*, eschatological statements, because of human nature, "are necessarily conclusions from the experience of the Christian *present*." And further, "what we know of Christian eschatology is what we know about man's present situation in the history of salvation. We do not project something from the future into the present, but rather in man's experience of himself and of God in grace we project our Christian present into the future."[166] Thus, Rahner, similar to Pannenberg, contends that the future (or at least our understanding of the future) is already present and as such is hermeneutically significant as a real moment in our present self-understanding. Yet this understanding of the future is a projection into the future from our existential present, and not a reading of the present from the vantage point of the future - otherwise it would be apocalyptic and not eschatology.[167] Eschatology, according to Rahner, "is man's view from the perspective of his experience of

---

[163] Rahner, "The Hermeneutics of Eschatological Assertions," in: *TI* 4:332. ["Theologische Prinzipien der Hermeneutik eschatologischer Aussagen," in: *Schriften* 4:412.]

[164] *Ibid.*, 333. [413.]

[165] Peter C. Phan, *Eternity in Time: A Study of Karl Rahner's Eschatology* (London: Associated University Press, 1988), 70.

[166] *FCF*, 432. [*Grundkurs*, 415].

[167] Cf. Rahner, "Hermeneutics of Eschatological Assertions," 337. ["Hermeneutik eschatologischer Aussagen," 318f.]

salvation, the experience which he now has in grace and in Christ."[168] Similarly, Rahner has elsewhere written that "the eschatological statements of scripture and tradition certainly do not constitute any anticipated descriptions, as though by an inspired journalist, of God and in the light of that which will one day come to pass. Rather they are anticipations of [the] final consummation based upon that which, considered as God's deed of salvation, is already present."[169]

For Rahner, as for Pannenberg, the future element of salvation with its focus on present of the future finds its pinnacle in the Christ event.[170] Hence for Rahner, Jesus Christ is "the eschatologically definitive and historically manifested self-communication of this mystery," i.e., God.[171] Rahner elsewhere states that Jesus of Nazareth is "the eschatological climax of the self-utterance of God to mankind, and of the primary history of reflection upon this self-utterance." Jesus is then this eschatological high point inasmuch as in him "this offering of God's self-bestowal becomes something more than a sheer offering. Rather, through the deed of God, it takes place and is revealed as *de facto* victorious and irreversible." The Christ event, then, in this sense, can be called by Rahner the "historical manifestation of the eschatological victoriousness and irreversibility of the self-utterance of God."[172]

Pannenberg, in a recent assessment of Rahner's paper on the hermeneutic of eschatological statements, has affirmed the constitutive role of the knowledge of the future for the present which bears certain similarities to his own thought. Pannenberg writes:

> The most important contribution of contemporary theology to an anthropological foundation and interpretation of eschatological statements was made in 1960 by Karl Rahner. According to Rahner, foundational for eschatology is the hiddenness of the future of eschatological consummation on the one hand, and the orientation of human beings as historical creatures toward this future on the other. When the future has here to do with the future of salvation as 'the completion of the *whole* person,' then the knowledge of this future - irrespective of its hiddenness - is already constitutive for the present of human life. This present can be understood precisely as fragmentary reality only in light of a knowledge of its possible wholeness. The eschatological content,

---

[168] *FCF*, 433. [*Grundkurs*, 416].
[169] "Reflections on Methodology," 98. [*Schriften* 9:110.]
[170] Pannenberg, in a treatment of the foundation of eschatological statements in his *Systematic Theology*, vol. 3, notes the parallel with Rahner's thought when he writes: "Vom Wissen um die Zukunft, vor allem um die (mögliche) Heilsgegenwart geht der Gedankengang Rahners über zu der tatsächlichen Gegenwart dieser Heilszukunft in Jesus Christus, von dem aus wiederum der Glaubende den 'Vorblick *aus* seiner durch das Ereignis Christi bestimmten heilsgeschichtlichen Stiuation *heraus* ... auf die endgültige Vollendung' gewinnt." Pannenberg, however, though affirming the role of Christ in the presence of the future of our salvation in Rahner's thought, believes that in Rahner's argumentation from general anthropological considerations to the person of Christ "Zwischenglieder" or links between the two are overlooked. (*ST* 3:586).
[171] "Reflections on Methodology," 82. [*Schriften* 9:93.]
[172] "On the Relationship Between Theology and the Contemporary Sciences," 98. [*Schriften* 10:108f.]

therefore, is not something additional to the self-understanding of human beings in their present and in their relation to the past, but rather 'an inner moment in the self-understanding of the human being.'[173]

Ultimately, therefore, Rahner arrives at a perspective similar to that of Pannenberg. Yet the manner in which this is achieved is decidedly different from that of Pannenberg. For both theologians the future (or end of history) is vital for knowledge in the present since history, for both, is a universal history consisting of a unity of past, present and future.[174] For Pannenberg this is based upon his philosophical, epistemological assumption that only at the end of history can anything be definitely known and verified whereas for Rahner the crucial point is his existential understanding of human beings who are not just composed of their present but are inseparable from their past and their future - with their ultimate future resting in Christ. Thus for both theologians the Christ event is key to understanding the impact of the future upon the present. In Rahner's thought this leads to an emphasis upon the *knowledge* of our salvific future and its constitutiveness for the present. In Pannenberg, however, the Christ event, especially the resurrection, points to the impact of the future *as such* upon the present.

### 2.5.3 *A transcendental hermeneutic*

For Karl Rahner, the decisive factor in his approach to hermeneutics is the turn to the human subject, and especially to human experience. As Peter Phan has noted, "Rahner, in his hermeneutics ... turns from the objective content of the experience to the subjective human consciousness. This center of consciousness is the locus of the divine self-manifestations." Therefore, in an important sense Rahner can be said to recast "Schleiermacher's 'feeling of absolute dependence' in terms of the experience of 'creatureliness.' Creatureliness, for Rahner, is an experience of radical difference from and radical dependence on God and is available only in the transcendental experience."[175]

For Rahner this means that humans, as transcendent beings, implicitly affirm absolute being as the ground of all knowing. "This absolute, incomprehensible reality, which is always the ontologically silent horizon of every intellectual and spiritual encounter with realities, is therefore always infinitely different from the knowing subject. It is also different from the individual, finite things known. It is present as such in every assertion, in all knowledge, and in every action." The implications for Rahner's transcendental hermeneutic of this starting point is that it allows him to establish the "relationship between both the knower and the known as finite existents, and the absolutely infinite," that is, God. As the absolutely infinite God is necessarily absolutely different and thus cannot be the object of our

---

[173] *ST* 3:585,
[174] Cf. "Transcendental Theology," 289. [*SM* 4:992.]
[175] Phan, 66.

knowledge and comprehension but rather the ground thereof.[176] This insight, however, is only possible on the basis of our subjective, transcendental experience of creatureliness in which the knowing subject experiences him or herself "as being borne by an incomprehensible ground." The transcendentally achieved experience of creatureliness, therefore "always means both the grace and the mandate to preserve and to accept that tension of analogy which the finite subject is; to reflect upon and understand and accept himself as what is truly real," a reality which consists not only of human responsibility but of absolute dependence upon God.[177]

But the experience of creatureliness has not just hermeneutical significance for human self-understanding but also for our understanding of the world. Our transcendental experience of creatureliness, according to Rahner, demythologizes and denuminizes the world, an insight which is "decisive for the Christian understanding of existence and of the world, and not only for the modern feeling about existence." Therefore, human beings experience their creatureliness and encounter God within this creatureliness, "not so much in nature, in its stolid and unfeeling finiteness, but in [God] himself and in the world only as known by him and as freely administered in the unlimited openness of his own spirit."[178] In this way transcendental theology, according to Rahner, becomes hermeneutically necessary in order to understand the meaning of historical events, especially as these concern the whole person in the existential reality of his or her salvation. And beyond this, the transcendental method is vital to an understanding of God in his relationship to the world in which God is not simply a part of the world nor a purely external factor to the world. Thus only the knowledge of God gained by the transcendental method "prevents God from being regarded as a part [of the world] within the all, or a dimiurge whose action on the world is merely 'from without.'"[179]

## 2.6 Theology as a Science and Theology among the Sciences

### 2.6.1 *The scientific status of theology in Roman Catholic theology*

We have already treated the history of the understanding of theology as a science with particular attention given to the Protestant tradition. Although the scientific status of theology does not play as important a role in the thought of Rahner as in Pannenberg a comparison of the two suggests a brief look at Rahner's own approach to the question as well as at the Roman Catholic context from within which he reflected.

Unlike the Protestant context from within which Pannenberg has approached the question there has been comparatively little discussion of the scientific

---
[176] *FCF*, 77f. [*Grundkurs*, 85].
[177] *Ibid.*, 80. [87].
[178] *Ibid.*, 80f. [88].
[179] "Transcendental Theology," 288. [*SM* 4:989.]

character of theology up until about the middle of the twentieth century within Roman Catholic theology.[180] This is due largely to the fact that the Aristotelian, Thomistic conception of science and the scientific character of theology has remained largely unchanged in Catholic theology since the late Middle Ages.[181] Thomas sought to establish the place and niche of *sacra doctrina*, or a theology based upon revelation among the sciences. This was accomplished by designating theology as a derived science since it "proceeds from principles made known by the light of a higher science, namely, the science of God and the blessed," that is, the *scientia Dei et beatorum* (*Summa Theologica* I.1.2). The significance of this move is that it provides a solution to the dilemma of verification since a discipline claiming to be a science and founded upon faith propositions which is not subject to rational proof is a contradiction. Thomas suggested, however, that it was only in our human situation that theological or faith statements could not be proven or known with certainty.[182] In the realm of God and the angels these things could be known with certainty and thus theology (as human words about God) qualifies as a derived science just as the science of optics is derived from geometry or the science of music from arithmetic and do not have to prove the principles upon which they are founded but simply assume them (*Summa Theologica* I.1.2). [183]

Human knowledge and human knowing in the Thomistic system is the starting point for a knowledge of God just as much as it is the starting point for the knowledge of temporal objects and realities. Theology is scientific in the sense that it knows just as other sciences know, with the qualification that the manner and content of its knowing are distinct from those of the other sciences in that theology's own uniqueness is grounded in the uniqueness of its axioms and ultimately in the uniqueness of God. The Thomistic emphasis upon the human starting point and the relatedness of the knowledge of God to other kinds of knowledge underlies and in an important sense is confirmed by the Vatican I

---

[180] Rahner himself has admitted that "*Catholic Theology* to the present day has developed only preliminarily and hesitantly a theological epistemology and methodology [*theologische Erkenntniss- und Methodenlehre*]" which has "not yet been thematically constructed within a Catholic theology." Rahner, "Theologische Erkenntniss- und Methodenlehre," in: *Herders Theologisches Taschenlexikon* 7:257f.

[181] Cf. Leo Scheffczyk, *Die Theologie und die Wissenschaften*, 203.

[182] Cf. Martin Schmidt, "Die Zeit der Scholastik," in: Carl Andresen, ed., *Handbuch der Dogmen- und Theologiegeschichte*, vol. 1 (Göttingen: Vandenhoeck & Ruprecht, 1988), 652.

[183] Therefore, as Martin Schmidt concludes concerning scholastic theology in general and the theology of Thomas Aquinas in particular: "Die Besonderheit der Offenbarungstheologie beruht, wie das bei jeder Wissenschaft im Vergleich zu anderen Wissenschaften der Fall ist, auf der Besonderheit ihrer Axiome, nicht auf einem besonderen Erkenntnisverfahren. Eine scholastische Theologie, die ihre Wissenschaftlichkeit mit dem Gebrauch aristotelischer Begriffe und Beweismethoden ausweist, macht damit nicht eine Konzession an ihre Zeit, benutzt die Wissenschaftlichkeit nicht lediglich als äußeres Gewand, während sie im Innern eine höhere Art von Erkenntnis darstellt. Sie versteht sich vielmehr als Wissenschaft (*scientia*) im gewöhnlichen Sinn des Wortes, weil sie anders sich nicht als Mittlerin einer den Menschen wirklich dienlichen Wahrheit verstehen kann." (In *ibid.*, 652f.)

affirmation of the possibility of a natural knowledge of God based upon (ordinary) human reason.[184]

Leo Scheffczyk notes that the dependence upon the modern *scientia* oriented scientific ideal in Catholic theology has forced the question of the uniqueness of the object of theology somewhat into the background while at the same time raising the interest in the question of methodology. Yet these new directions in the Catholic discussion of the scientific character of theology have led in very few cases to "coherent and comprehensive new proposals ... intended as a direct answer to the challenge posed by the modern philosophy of science. In most cases theology was indeed developed and oriented from a new starting point but the scientific-theoretical (*wissenschaftstheoretische*) foundation was seldom built."[185] Thus even today the discussion of the scientific character of theology on the Catholic side remains much less intensive than that on the Protestant side in large part because the essential Thomistic understanding of theology as a positive and derived science remains largely unquestioned despite the many changes and reformulations of the conception of science which have come out of recent developments in the philosophy of science.

### 2.6.2 *Intimations of a philosophy of science in Rahner*

The question that confronts anyone examining Rahner's view of the relationship between theology and the sciences and his approach to theological method is why it is that no clear formulation of a philosophy of science is to be found in Rahner. At least part of the answer to this question would seem to be found in Rahner's rootedness in and continuing acceptance of the Thomistic tradition.[186] In regard to the general trend among Catholic theologians to adapt but not disgard an essentially Thomistic epistemology and conception of science Karl Rahner proves no exception. In one sense, Rahner's apparent lack of his own philosophy of science is in part to be accounted by his acceptance of a basically Thomistic conception of science and of theological science which he has adapted with certain insights from existential (Heidegger) and transcendental philosophy. Indeed, Martin Tripole has suggested that Rahner's entire "philosophical anthropology appears to be nothing more than a global acceptance of ...

---

[184] Cf. the Dogmatic Constitution "*De Filius*" (April 24, 1870) where it is confessed that, "*eadem sancta mater Ecclesia tenet et docet, Deum, rerum omnium principium et finem, naturali humanae rationis lumine e rebus creatis certo cognosci posse.*" H. Denzinger and A. Schönmetzer, *Enchiridion Symbolorum* (Freiburg: Herder, 1976), 3004.

[185] Scheffczyk, 205.

[186] *Ibid.*, 243. Scheffczyk suggests that Rahner's transcendental method which posits an *a priori* of belief in every individual (anonymous Christians), in regard to a philosophy of science, "erbringt ... eine große Erleichterung für den Nachweis, daß auch die Offenbarungstheologie eine Wissenschaft ist. Die Begründung ist hier so selbstverständlich, daß eigentlich ein Nachweis des eigenen Wissenschaftscharakters der Theologie unnötig wird."

Transcendental Thomism touched up and modernized by Heideggerian perspectives and terminology."[187]

Rahner's relationship to a Thomistic theory of knowledge and of science is to be seen already in his first book, *Spirit in the World* (*Geist in Welt: Zur Metaphysik der endlichen Erkenntnis bei Thomas von Aquin*), published in 1939. First of all, as Anne Carr has pointed out, "Rahner begins from the Aristotelian-Thomistic a posteriori starting point that all knowledge comes through the senses."[188] Thus Rahner, in agreement with Thomas, argues that the human subject cannot know anything without a "phantasm."[189] Also, in agreement with Thomas, Rahner proposes that knowledge, especially human knowledge, be understood as a unity. But what is it that is unified in this unity of human knowledge? Rahner writes that it is "Knowledge of an existent in the world in its here and now and knowledge of being in its totality. If we say that sensation is being with a thing in the here and now of the world, and that intellect is the knowledge of being in its totality, we can also say that it is a question of understanding the intrinsic possibility of the unity of sensation and intellect, the fact of which unity forms the point of departure for all our considerations."[190]

Already here, however, one can detect the stamp of Rahner's own transcendental and existential perspective upon his interpretation of Thomas inasmuch as the unity of human knowledge arises already out of the human situation in the here and now in a self-transcending self-knowledge - a knowledge which arises out of human experience and cannot be separated from it. Thus Rahner, commenting further on what precisely is united in the unity of human knowledge and knowing, writes that the being (*Sein*) in the here and now of the individual things of the world through sense experience is of such a nature that "in its concrete possibility it is already and always being with being in its totality through intellect, and vice versa. But from this it follows that neither sensibility nor thought as such can be met with in the concrete by itself; where they are found they are already always one."

The significance of this view of the unity of intellect and experience, of thinking and sensing, for the nature of speech and statements about things is that it is not possible to make statements about sense experience (*Sinnlichkeit*) which do justice to the totality of what it encompasses without also expressing that which rational reflection and thought entails at the same time. "And since, nevertheless, statements about sensibility and thought must be made one after the other, each further statement affects and modifies the sense of the previous statements. And

---

[187] Tripole, "Philosophy and Theology - Are They Compatible?" 40.
[188] Anne Carr, 83.
[189] Cf. Rahner, *Spirit in the World* (London: Sheed and Ward, 1968), 28ff. [*Geist in Welt: Zur Metaphysik der endlichen Erkenntnis bei Thomas von Aquin*, 32ff.]; and Thomas Aquinas, *Summa Theologica*, 808f. (I.84.7).
[190] *Spirit in the World*, 66. [*Geist in Welt*, 79.]

all of them have their ultimate meaning only in the totality."[191] Here then is to be found the epistemological foundation for Rahner's view of the individual sciences as regional sciences which, from the side of experience, address only an aspect of the totality of reality. And here also is the foundation for theology's claim to universality, which we will later take up, which, addressing the unity of reality and of human existence and experience has something concrete to say and contribute to the various regional sciences.

Fundamental for Rahner's use of the transcendental method is the fact that this view implies an "original unity of being and knowing" which means that human existence already implies a "knowing."[192] This fundamental point, according to Puntel, is the foundation of the metaphysical structure of human knowing - a structure which points clearly back to humans themselves.[193] As Rahner more fully elaborates:

> Being and knowing exist in an original unity. Knowing does not come upon its object by chance. Thomas explicitly rejects the common conception of knowing as a coming upon something. ... Being is the one ground which lets knowing and being-known spring out of itself as its own characteristics, and thus grounds the intrinsic possibility of an antecedent, essential, intrinsic relation of both of them to each other. Knowing is the subjectivity of being itself. Being itself is the original, *unifying* unity of being and knowing in their *unification* in being-known. In this latter the two of them are not brought together accidentally, purely factually and extrinsically, but are actualized in their original relatedness to each other. The transcendental intelligibility of being cannot be conceived in any other way: 'for a plurality is not unified of itself' [*non enim plura secundum se uniuntur*].[194]

Rahner contends, then, that knowledge, or knowing, is to be understood as the subjectivity of being itself, as a "Bei-sich-sein des Seins." In Thomas' epistemology, as understood by Rahner, it is being itself which is the original, *onto-logical* unifying unity of being and knowing. And every actual unity of being and knowing "in the actualization of knowledge is only raising to a higher power that transcendental synthesis which being is 'in itself.'" In Thomas, therefore, it is to be observed that the "knowability of a being varies according to what it is."[195] As he explained in *Hearers of the Word*, Thomas emphasizes "the original unity of the knowable and its cognition, and this signifies more than a mere reciprocity between the two. *Intellectum et intelligible oportet proportionata esse et unius generis*: they must derive from a single origin." This leads then necessary to the *Bei-sich-sein* of being, according to Rahner. Hence he can conclude that

---
[191] *Ibid.*, 66f. [80.]
[192] *Ibid.*, 68. [81.]
[193] Cf. Puntel, *Analogie und Geschichtlichkeit*, vol. 1, 88.
[194] *Spirit in the World*, 69. [*Geist in Welt*, 82.]
[195] *Ibid.*, 70f. [83f.]

"knowledge in its original essence is the being-present-to-itself, or the 'subjectivity' of the being of the thing which is, [for which] we find a clear parallel in St. Thomas. What we have called 'being-present-to-itself' corresponds to St. Thomas's *reductio subjecti in seipsum*. For St. Thomas, knowledge is a coming-into-itself of the knowing subject, that is, a being-present-to-itself."[196] This perspective forms not only the crux of Rahner's own transcendental theory of knowledge but also the fundament of the functional, albeit not fully developed philosophy of science with which Rahner seems to operate.

Yet Rahner, by retaining basic Thomistic epistemological structures, is by no means oblivious to the problems confronting modern theology. Indeed his task has been characterized as that of making "theology intellectually respectable in the modern world by honestly confronting the difficulties posed by modern philosophy and science."[197] In order to accomplish this Rahner needs to find a starting point for theology which is open to critical examination. The presupposition of God, of course, is unverifiable and is rejected out of hand by many potential dialogue partners from the start. Rahner starts instead with the presupposition of a common human existence and experience, that is to say, Rahner begins with anthropology.[198] As William Dych has written: "If human existence and our experience of it can be analyzed to discover categories in which God can be spoken of intelligently by the strictest canons of knowledge and truth, then theology has at least a starting point to begin speaking of God in the contemporary world."[199] Yet the knowledge gained from human experience is not the same as the knowledge gained, say, from physics or biology. The knowledge we gain from human experience is an experiential knowledge which comes from within and is called by Rahner "unthematic" knowledge in contrast to the "thematic" knowledge of the special sciences.[200] The point of contact comes, however, as a second level is reached and this experiential, unthematic knowledge is objectified and becomes explicit and thematic as we seek to reflect upon it and express it.[201]

If, however, there is a fundamental original unity of being and knowing and a point of contact with the other sciences which comes when theology reflects upon and objectifies the knowledge gained through the transcendental experience of

---

[196] *Hearers*, 41, 43. [*HdW*., 59, 61.]

[197] William V. Dych, "Theology in a New Key," in: Leo J. O'Donovan, ed., *A World of Grace: An Introduction to the Themes and Foundations of Karl Rahner's Theology* (New York: Crossroad, 1981), 2.

[198] Cf. Rahner, "Theology as Engaged in an Interdisciplinary Dialogue with the Sciences," in: *TI*, 13:92. ["Die Theologie im interdisziplinaren Gespräch," in: *Schriften*: 10:101f.]; and "The Foundation of Faith Today," 9ff. [*Schriften* 12:24ff.] Cf. also Anne Carr, "Starting with the Human," in: *A World of Grace: An Introduction to the Themes and Foundations of Karl Rahner's Theology*, ed. Leo O'Donovan, 17ff.

[199] Dych, 3.

[200] Cf. *FCF*, 21ff. [*Grundkurs*, 32ff.]

[201] Cf. Dych, 4f.

human beings, why could not theology also consider itself a science since it too deals with knowledge and with a "knowing" which are not unrelated to that in the special sciences? The answer for Rahner would seem to be found in the distinction he makes between categorical and transcendental experience. While theology reflects also upon historical occurrences, especially upon the Christ event, the experiences of these occurrences which form the basis of theological reflection are transcendental and not categorical. They are indeed truly historical and therefore also contingent, but when made the object of historical, categorically objectifying science their decisive, "transcendentally experienced" character disappears. Rahner writes:

> The Christian experience of the victory of transcendentality leading to the mystery of God achieves its full realization precisely in the experience of Jesus. Now this statement obviously involves a fundamental trust in the powers and significance of unique historical events which, in this unaccountable uniqueness of theirs, do not as such constitute subjects falling within the purview of the sciences as understood today, not even that of the historical sciences. For even historical events, considered as subject-matter for the historical sciences, are viewed by these, certainly in their *de facto* contingency, but not in their character as absolute and as posited 'once and for all.' ... Nevertheless historical events as such, and as freely posited, have the character of being absolute and posited 'once and for all' in this sense, even though this cannot ever be authenticated by science, concerned as it is with objectifying concrete 'this-worldly' [*kategorial*] realities. Rather this character inherent in historical events vanishes the moment we seek to make it a subject for investigation by such sciences.[202]

The distinction drawn by Rahner between categorical and transcendental experience implies an original and legitimate distinction between the ultimate object(s) of theology and the sciences. Yet, according to Rahner, this does not mean that an absolute disparity exists between theology and the other sciences. "Theology has ... a concrete 'this-worldly' [*kategoriale*] history of its own, in which it can be made the subject of historical science in the secular sense. ... But ... in its assertion that an event of absolute transcendence has taken place, theology postulates the historicity of Jesus and of his interpretation of himself, and thereby achieves an established point of contact with the historical sciences."[203]

Yet despite this point of contact with the historical sciences a fundamental, epistemological distinction remains between theology and the "other sciences" in Rahner's thought. As Kuno Füssel has argued, however, this does not mean a rejection of or lack of understanding of modern philosophies of science on the part of Rahner. In fact, Füssel suggests that Rahner and Wittgenstein are in fundamental agreement with one another in that "logic and mysticism are not actually contradictory, but only point under different circumstances to the fact that

---
[202] "On the Relationship Between Theology and the Contemporary Sciences," 99f. [*Schriften* 10:110.]
[203] *Ibid.*, 100f. [111..]

the questions about God, meaning, death, etc. mark the limits of scientfic explanation."[204] Indeed, Rahner has written that a possibility within the philosophy of science must be sought by which theology and its methodology can be grounded in a way that is not unscientific. Rahner contends: "I can examine three of ten thousand stones that make of the structure of an objective fundamental theology, but even then the other stones remain scientifically ... unexamined. In other words: there must be a scientific-theoretical possibility for the foundation of faith that forms the basis for the legitimate and ongoing task and method of contemporary theological disciplines. ... Such a different foundation for faith ... must not and dare not ... be unscientific."[205] The search for such a foundation for the theological enterprise, we would contend, played at central role (even if often only in an 'unthematic' way) in Karl Rahner's theological efforts.

### 2.6.3 The problem of verification of theological statements

The problem of the verification of theological statements, especially in light of the demands for empirical verification to come out of the logical positivism of the Vienna circle or Popper's requirement of falsifiability, is a subject not dealt with in depth by Rahner. When Joachim Schickel pressed Rahner on the matter in a 1981 interview Rahner responded that he felt that the idea of verification could be so modified as to allow for the verification of theological statements. Yet Rahner does not choose this path although he recognizes it as a possibility. Instead, Rahner questions whether the whole concept of verification and falsifiability are appropriate to the kind of language necessarily engaged in by theology. Rahner explains:

> My opinion is that it goes without saying that to begin with I can propose the sentence: Meaningful sentences should be verifiable. ... But ... can this sentence, which I do not now want to call into question, be verified or falsified in the manner required? And then I would say that it would not be possible. In other words, the thinking of thought has other laws and other legitimations than purely empirical verification or falsification, which is what is demanded by ... positivism. ... The natural scientist can speak about empirical objects with this method of verification, but about the essence of natural science, about the meaningfulness of carrying on science, about himself or herself as the responsible human being carrying on science he or she is unable to speak in the manner of natural science. At that point this language simply comes to an end, and it is revealed to be a regional language.[206]

---

[204] Kuno Füssel, "Der Wahrheitsanspruch dogmatischer Aussagen: Ein Beitrag Karl Rahners zur theologischen Wissenschaftstheorie," in: *Wagnis Theologie: Erfahrungen mit der Theologie Karl Rahners*, ed. Herbert Vorgrimler (Freiburg: Herder, 1979), 212.
[205] *Zur Reform des Theologiestudiums*, 73.
[206] Rahner, "The Language of Science and the Language of Theology," in: *Karl Rahner in Dialogue*, 306f. ["Die Sprache der Wissenschaft und die Sprache der Theologie," 226ff.]

Are theological statements, then, in any sense open to verification from the other sciences? Rahner contends that theology and the special sciences cannot be so understood from the beginning that "cases of conflict between it and the historical sciences are totally inconceivable. It belongs to the very nature of theology to accept that such cases of conflict are possible."[207] If this indeed is the case, then one would think that some form of verification and in principle falsifiability would be possible in regard to theological statements. Yet Rahner recognizes this potential for conflict only in the context of the "eschatological hope" that no such conflict will prove so radical as to be recognized as being insurmountable. And, at least in the case of the natural sciences, Rahner seems to adopt a stance near that of Barth in which he posits such a distinction between theology and the natural sciences and their respective objects and methods that potential conflict as well as verification or falsification would seem to be definitively ruled out. Rahner writes:

> Theology and natural science cannot in principle contradict one another since both *right from the outset* are distinct from one another in their area of investigation and in their methodology. ... Natural science investigates in a posteriori experience individual phenomena which human beings (ultimately through the experience of their senses) encounter in their world, and the relationship of these phenomena to one another. Theology has to do with the totality of reality as such, and with the ground of this reality, and its method is ultimately one of a priori questioning.[208]

The apparent contradiction between Rahner's claim that theology cannot rule out the possibility of potential conflict with the sciences (since this belongs to the nature of theology) and the assertion that conflict between theology and the natural sciences is not possible, cannot be entirely resolved. A step toward resolution of this problem, however, (at least within Rahner's own thought) is provided by his contention that although primary conflict between the natural sciences (which study *a posteriori* particulars) and theology (which deals with the *a priori* whole of reality) is not possible, secondary instances of conflict can and do occur.[209] Also, it would seem that Rahner, who in the earlier cited context was speaking about the human sciences and especially the historical sciences may have these especially if not exclusively in mind in regard to their ability to potentially come into real conflict with theology. The latter cited comment, however, would seem to apply specifically and in a more restricted sense to the natural sciences. Indeed, Rahner makes an important distinction between the natural and the human sciences in regard to their relationship to theology,

---

[207] "On the Relationship Between Theology and the Contemporary Sciences," 101. [*Schriften* 10:111.]

[208] Rahner, "Natural Science and Reasonable Faith," in: *TI* 21:19. ["Wissenschaft und christlicher Glaube," in: *Schriften* 15:26.]

[209] *Ibid.*, 24ff. [31ff.]

suggesting that "the dialogue between theology and the natural sciences ... will be possible, but will differ, in certain notable respects, from the dialogue between theology and the intellectual disciplines [*Geisteswissenschaften*]."[210]

Yet if this is the solution to the apparent contradiction, the problem remains whether and on what basis one can so radically separate the human sciences from the natural sciences. Are historical occurrences and social structure so different from physical processes (which are also in a sense historical occurrences) and substances that the two stand in an entirely different epistemological relationship to theology? Rahner's own philosophy of science, unfortunately, is not sufficiently developed in relation to modern philosophies of science to answer definitively these questions within the context of his own theology and epistemology. The possibility of verification or openness to falsification from the human sciences does not seem to be absolutely excluded by Rahner, though such verification plays no significant role in his valuation of theological assertions.

Rahner is aware that we live in an age when it is common for an educated person "to receive the impression that theology is a mere interweaving of ideas which are, of their nature, incapable of any verification."[211] Yet if theology is to be open to any sort of verification this must be understood within the context of Rahner's transcendental method. Instances of God's grace, for instance, through their transcendental derivation and interpretation, have a contact point to human, transcendental experience which allows them to be "verified" because and inasmuch as "what they express is neither more nor less than the absolute radicalization of the transcendentality of the human spirit in knowledge and freedom." Indeed, Rahner contends that the original, transcendental experience of grace is "the ultimate verification" for all dogmatic statements.[212] Yet such a verification of theological statements (or experiences) is quite different from the kind of verification spoken of within philosophy of science discussions.

Indeed, Rahner's own understanding of the nature of theological statements would seem to require some form of concrete and accessible "verification" since Rahner believes that theological or dogmatic statements inherently contain truth claims which are also comprehensible in the context of secular language. Rahner contends that "a dogmatic statement is one which claims to be true even in that formal sense which we are familiar with from ordinary everyday language and knowledge. Even a dogmatic statement should fulfil all those inner structures and laws which do or can belong to an ordinary statement [*profanen Aussage*]."[213] Indeed, Rahner maintains that a dogmatic statement itself implies the claim, "that not all dogmatic statements can be equally true or false. In other words, it

---

[210] Rahner, "Theology as Engaged in an Interdisciplinary Dialogue with the Sciences," 91f. [*Schriften* 10:101.]

[211] "Reflections on Methodology," 101. [*Schriften* 9:114.]

[212] *Ibid.*, 92 and 110. [104 and 122.]

[213] Rahner, "What is a Dogmatic Statement," in: *TI* 5:43f. ["Was ist eine dogmatische Aussage?" in: *Schriften* 5:56.]

involves the recognition that it is completely possible to pose the question of truth in this objective sense with regard to such statements and that not all statements are equally true or false simply because they refer to what is beyond sense experience."[214]

The critical question, however, is how the truthfulness (or falseness) of a theological or faith statement is to be evaluated. In place of verification or falsifiability as criteria by which theological statements are to be judged Rahner prefers much more to evaluate theological propositions by their intellectual "honesty" (*Redlichkeit*). Similar to Pannenberg, Rahner does not believe an ultimate distinction can be made between statements of faith and theological statements.[215] Both types of statements ultimately make assertions which theology seeks to justify as intellectually honest. Yet Rahner contends that the complexity of the situation today, including the pluralism of the various sciences and within theology itself in addition to the variety of scientific methods in the various disciplines, makes a direct justification of the faith as a whole and of the individual assertions of faith as intellectually honest impossible. Yet in order to achieve an intellectually honest faith Rahner contends that it is not necessary "to have thought out in a 'scientifically' adequate way all the presuppositions" objectively implied in the content of faith.[216] To suggest otherwise, according to Rahner, would bring faith and intellectual honesty into inevitable conflict.

Rahner maintains that it is necessary for theology in the "contemporary situation in which it stands and which it can no longer control, to develop *indirect* methods of achieving a justification of faith such as will satisfy the demands of the individual conscience on the question of intellectual truth."[217] Rahner believes that these indirect methods for establishing the intellectually honesty of the Christian faith and of its individual statements will first of all vary according to the nature of the concrete material with which they deal and, second, constitute no additional and secondary method but are integral to theological method in general. As a concrete example of the application of such an indirect method for the justification a faith Rahner brings up the question of the legitimacy of belonging to the Roman Catholic Church rather than to the churches of the Reformation. This example is chosen by Rahner precisely because of its apparent subjectivity. In essence, Rahner suggests that because of the better historical continuity with the early church found in the Roman church and because the three *sola*s of the Reformation are today also affirmed within the Roman church, that there is no

---

[214] "What is a Dogmatic Statement?" 47. [*Schriften* 5:59f.] Cf. also 48ff. [61ff.]
[215] See Rahner, "Reflections on Methodology," 75. [*Schriften* 9:86.], where he writes that "it is quite impossible to arrive at any completely clear dividing line between the propositions of faith and the propositions of theology." Cf. Pannenberg, *TPS*, 327f. [*WtT*, 330f.], and "Wie wahr ist das Reden von Gott?", 31f.
[216] Rahner, "Intellectual Honesty and Christian Faith," 50. ["Intellektuelle Redlichkeit und christlicher Glaube," 11.]
[217] "Reflections on Methodology," 75. [*Schriften* 9:86.]

legitimate ground for leaving the Roman church to join one of the churches of the Reformation.[218]

But it is precisely at this point that we see how far Rahner's concept of the justification of the intellectual honesty of theological or faith statements is from the modern conception of verification and falsifiability. First of all, Rahner's "indirect method" works only for those who already believe the statement, that is (in this case), those already in the Roman church, and is not testable outside of this context. Protestants could of course argue similarly in order to justify their remaining within Protestantism.

Yet all this seems to amount to little more than the contention that certain beliefs or faith statements are justifiable as long as there are no good reasons to believe otherwise. What Rahner does not answer in his example (and this is a fundamental weakness of his whole indirect method), is what might constitute a good reason to leave the Roman church. That is to say, to put the matter in Popperian terms, there would seem to be no equivalent to anything resembling falsifiability - even in principle - thus the verification (or justification of intellectual honesty) of a belief or theological statement would seem meaningless. While the basic concept of the justification of the intellectual honesty of theological or faith statements appears to parallel to a certain extent what Pannenberg seeks to achieve with his concept of verification, the end result in the actual praxis of Rahner's indirect method for this justification would seem to be that everyone is able to justify continuing to believe what they already believe since there are no concrete possibilities provided for the "falsification" of faith statements.

### 2.6.4 *The ambivalence of the scientific character of theology*

Karl Rahner once gave a detailed outline of what he felt should be included in a comprehensive dogmatics text. Included within his proposal was a chapter to be titled "The Idea of Theology as Science" which was to follow a lengthy, opening treatment of revelation and precede the discussion of fundamental theology.[219] Unfortunately, the dogmatics text and the chapter on the idea of theology as a science were never written. Therefore Rahner's conception of theology as a science (or non-science) must be gathered from statements and comments scattered throughout his writings. The following is an attempt, based upon such scattered and necessarily unsystematic comments, to determine Rahner's view of the status of theology as a science.

Rahner refers frequently to his discipline as a science and to the undertaking of the theological task, even on the so-called "first level of reflection" found in his introductory *Foundations of Christian Faith*, as scientific.[220] Rahner even goes

---

[218] *Ibid.*, 76ff. [87ff.]
[219] Rahner, "A Scheme for a Treatise of Dogmatic Theology" in: *TI* 1:22. ["Aufriss einer Dogmatik," *Schriften* 1:32.]
[220] Cf. *FCF*, 3ff. [13f.]

so far as to contend that "theology already exists as a science at that stage at which, prior to any explicit transcendental reflection, it records saving history and considers its significance." He also contends that theology is not a mere mythological and unscientific prefiguration of science which the modern sciences more and more are eliminating. Rahner instead suggests that theology, if it is not to forget its true identity, understand itself "as the 'science' of mystery as such ... which we call God."[221] Similarly, Rahner has also suggested that theology "is a *faith* science [*Glaubens*wissenschaft], *science* of faith [Glaubens*wissenschaft*], *churchly* science, and *historical* science."[222] And Kuno Füssel, writing about Rahner's contribution to a theological philosophy of science, has boldly claimed that "Rahner's theology deserves more than any other Catholic theology of his time to be called 'scientific.'"[223]

Yet Rahner is by no means convinced that theology *must* be designated as a science. He suggests that in the interdisciplinary dialogue between the sciences and theology we can leave the question aside "whether theology can or should regard itself as a science which can take its place in the interdisciplinary dialogue as one particular science, or alternatively whether, even if it is something quite different, it should nevertheless hold firmly that it has a right to intervene at least at specific points in this dialogue, even though it is not intended to be a science."[224] Rahner's contention that theology must not necessarily be designated as a science does not stem from the fact that he doubts whether it could be claimed with good reason to be a science. Rahner writes that "using today's methods of the philosophy of science a plan could be drawn up containing the whole spectrum of all possible human sciences and then the question could be asked whether in the purpose of this general plan there would be any place for something like theology. One could continue the almost two-centuries-old debate by asking if theology can lay claim to being a science and what its justification is for this claim."[225] Such an attempt to classify theology among the sciences and justify its status as a science, as we have seen in Pannenberg, is indeed possible. Rahner, however, in all his many articles on the relationship between theology and

---

[221] "Reflections on Methodology," 90 and 102. [*Schriften* 9:101 and 114.]
[222] "Theologische Erkenntnis- und Methodenlehre," 259f.
[223] Füssel, "Der Wahrheitsanspruch dogmatischer Aussagen: Ein Beitrag Karl Rahners zur theologischen Wissenschaftstheorie," 200. Füssel supports this claim by the criteria that Rahner's theology is "argumentative," which Füssel sees as necessary if theology is to sustain a claim to be a science. Füssel contends that Rahner's theology is argumentative in a threefold way. "a) Sie erläutert Sinn und Funktion der von ihr benutzten oder eingeführten Grundbegriffe unter Angabe des konstitutiven Interpretationsrahmens bzw. durch Klärung des Rückbezugs auf normierende Traditionen; b) sie anerkennt die Verpflichtung zur Verteidigung der mit dem Aufstellen der theologischen Sätze verbundenen Geltungsansprüche durch Beibringung überprüfbarer und vernünftiger Gründe; c) sie ist bestrebt, die in der Theologie üblichen Verwendungsweisen grundlegender Denkkategorien in möglichst hohe Verträglichkeit mit ihrem Gebrauch in anderen Wissenschaften zu bringen" (200).
[224] "Theology as Engaged in an Interdisciplinary Dialogue with the Sciences," 86. [*Schriften* 10:95.]
[225] Rahner, "Theology Today," in: *TI* 21:56. ["Theologie Heute," in: *Schriften* 15:63.]

philosophy and between theology and the natural and human sciences makes no clear effort either to say what kind of a science theology is or why it could lay claim at all to being a science.[226] Similarly, Rahner stresses that the question of the scientific status of theology can be left open,

> even though in doing so we are in no sense questioning the fact that from the practical and technical point of view theology cannot renounce its task of organizing something which at first sight appears like the systematic investigation of a science in the true sense, and even if we are convinced that this scientific or quasi-scientific enquiry on the part of theology (whatever interpretation may be placed upon it either by theologians themselves or by others) both can and should be engaged in within the framework of a university.[227]

For Rahner, therefore, the ambivalence of theology's status as a science is not the result of any internal deficiency or lack of scientific rigor on the part of theology. Rahner has indeed written that he presupposes the 'unscientific' character of theology but that the "'unscientific character' of this unique discipline lies in its object and not in its subject and its methods."[228] Theology has a status and stature that is not dependent upon its designation as scientific or its acceptance as a science by the other disciplines. If theology allows its self-understanding to become dependent upon this designation, as Rahner feared some younger theologians have done, then, according to him, "theology would already have given up its true role, and would also have to be silent in the interdisciplinary dialogue, because it would then have nothing to say."[229]

Similarly, Rahner suggests that making theology a science in the sense of the other sciences implies the vulgarization of theology as science,[230] a concept which seems to echo Barth's protest against an idea of science which he felt to be pagan.[231] If theology chooses this path and tries to simply adapt itself to the other sciences and their conception of science then Rahner's criticism would seem valid that theology, in such a case, abandons its independent status and seeks to gain a

---

[226] Rahner does, however, seem to recognize an especially close affinity between theology and the human sciences, specifically the social and historical sciences, without actually classifying theology as belonging to one of these categories as such. Cf. Rahner "Theology as Engaged in an Interdisciplinary Dialogue with the Sciences," 91f. [*Schriften* 10:101.]

[227] *Ibid.*, 86. [95.]

[228] Rahner, *Zur Reform des Theologiestudiums*, 73f.

[229] "Theology as Engaged in an Interdisciplinary Dialogue with the Sciences," 86. [*Schriften* 10:95.]

[230] Cf. Rahner, "Some Clarifying Remarks about My Own Work," in *TI* 17:244. ["Einfache Klarstellung zum eigenen Werk," in: *Schriften* 12:600.] Yet for an apparent justification of a certain vulgarization of theology see his "foreword" to Peter Eicher's *Die anthropologische Wende* (Freiburg: Universitätsverlag, 1970), xiif., where he writes: "Die 'haute vulgarisation' von früher ist nicht mehr das sekundäre Nebenprodukt *aus* der Wissenschaft in Theologie ..., sondern mehr oder weniger die einzige Weise, in der einer, der über Wichtiges auf diesem Gebiet schreiben will, schreiben kann, unabhängig von der Genauigkeit der Wissenschaft."

[231] Cf. Karl Barth, *CD* I.1, 11.

new self-understanding on the basis of its acceptance as a science by the other sciences. Even if such acceptance is well justified, in Rahner's view, theology no longer has anything to say to the other sciences in interdisciplinary dialogue since it comes into this dialogue not with the intention of saying what theology should but rather with the intention of demonstrating merely that it "belongs." In conclusion, we might suggest that Rahner, while in many places and in many ways *assuming* the scientific *character* of theology, never *asserts* its scientific *status*, especially not in the sense of the special or "vulgar" sciences. And when Rahner occasionally speaks of the "unscientific" character of theology this must be understood in a qualified sense as "pre-scientific."[232]

2.6.5 *Theology as reductio in mysterium*

The discussion of Rahner's ambivalent view of theology as science has not yet answered the question, what precisely theology is according to Karl Rahner. Rahner himself, in his only major work on theological method, chose to describe theology as *reductio in mysterium*. The *reductio in mysterium*, or the "reduction or 'tracing back' to the mystery" would seem to be Rahner's counter to the model of theology as a science whose statements are subject to the positivistic requirements of verification.[233] Instead, Rahner understands theological statements as radical *reductio in mysterium* so that each "theological statement is only truly and authentically such at that point at which man willingly suffers it to extend beyond his comprehension into the silent mystery of God."[234] This does not mean, however, that theology and theological statements bear no relation to concrete experience. Instead, "Rahner conceives of foundational theology as '*reductio in mysterium*': not in the sense of some ... impersonal contemplation of a far-away divine mystery, but rather as a manner of reflection that *begins from* religious experience."[235] The experience of God as mystery does not imply a dead end or a limit to knowledge, but is rather its deepest content. In this way theology as *reductio in mysterium* does not make the experience of God as mystery into an experience of meaninglessness or absurdity.[236]

---

[232] Cf. Klaus Fischer, *Der Mensch als Geheimnis: Die Anthropologie Karl Rahners* (Freiburg: Herder, 1974), 232f., who observes that: "Kierkegaards Adjektiv 'unwissenschaftlich' war bekanntlich ironisch gemeint und sollte die völlige Andersartigkeit der 'Glaubenswissenschaft' bezeichnen. So wäre auch Rahners Intention verfehlt, wollte man glauben, ihm sei daran gelegen, seine subjekt-orientierte transzendentale Methode als in sich unwissenschaftlich abzuqualifizieren."

[233] Cf. Fischer, 232ff., for a convincing argument that Rahner's model of theology as *reductio in mysterium* is not meant as a counter to the scientific character of theology in the broader sense.

[234] "Reflections on Methodology," 103. [*Schriften* 9:115.]

[235] Michael O'Callaghan, "Rahner and Lonergan on Foundational Theology," in: *Creativity and Method: Essays in Honor of Bernard Lonergan, S.J.* ed. Matthew Lamb (Milwaukee: Marquette University Press, 1981), 130.

[236] So Dych, "Method in Theology According to Karl Rahner," 51.

Theology has, it would appear, to do with mysteries (in the plural), according to Rahner, yet ultimately, "there is, and there can be, only one single absolute mystery in the strictest sense of the term, namely God himself." Apart from its reference to God every temporal "Seiende" is in its positivity without mystery (*geheimnislos*) and is as such a mere object of science. Hence, "just as all worldly realities are withdrawn from the sphere of the numinous through recognition of the fact that they have been created and are different from God, so too they must in themselves also be removed from the sphere of any ideologizing, i.e. they must be radically submitted to the control of the sciences in the knowledge that no being accessible to the categories of human cognition can be mysterious, unfathomable or obscure."[237] All the mysteries with which theology has therefore to deal with are, according to Rahner, to be reduced to the unity of mystery found in God himself. Thus the "mystery which Christian faith acknowledges consists in the sheer fact that the absolute reality of God himself ... cannot only achieve a creative confrontation with that which is other to itself, but actually wills to commit itself to and bestow itself upon this." For Rahner, therefore, is it on this basis clear "that theology cannot contain as many mysteries as one wishes to ascribe to it. Basically ... there can only be *one* mystery: God as he is in himself." It is then the task of theology to relate all the apparent mysteries which it encounters back to this one mystery, God, who is not delivered over to "science" as an object of empirical inquiry.[238]

Yet it is also the understanding of theology as *reductio in mysterium* which provides theology with the possibility of an ultimate "verification" of dogmatic statements that empirical inquiry, which cannot reach the divine mystery, is incapable of. Rahner explains that if "theology constitutes the *reductio in mysterium* and in fact *in unum mysterium* ... this does not mean that what we are treating of here is merely a process of unifying and systematizing ... the various dogmatic statements in which revelation is expressed. Equally, and in a more basic sense, we are concerned with the attempt to interpret all these various statements as a summons to that ultimate and transcendental experience of grace which is implicit in all these statements and which signifies the ultimate verification of them all."[239] In this context Anne Carr's contention that Rahner's method, which moves from particular mysteries to their unity in the reduction in mysterium, "results in a theology which is essentially the science of mystery" would seem justifiable.[240]

2.6.6 *Theology's place within the university*
Similar to Pannenberg, much of the attention given by Rahner to questions concurring the scientific nature of theology and theology's relationship to the other

---
[237] "Reflections on Methodology," 105f. [*Schriften* 9:117f.]
[238] *Ibid.*, 106ff. [119f.]
[239] *Ibid.*, 110. [122.]
[240] Anne Carr, 268.

sciences arose in response to the discussion among German academics concerning whether theology belongs on the university.²⁴¹ Like Pannenberg, Rahner answered the question strongly in the affirmative, yet his defense of theology's place on the university is not bound to the question of theology's scientific character.

Rahner summed up not only the position of theology on the university but also something of the atmosphere surrounding it when he wrote:

> A crucifix might just about be tolerated in a room of a university clinic, but certainly not in a lecture hall. They [the exponents of the other sciences] consider it to be a sign of benign tolerance when the individual sciences do not involve themselves in matters theological, but beyond this nothing at all is owed to theology, except of course to treat it as a cultural phenomenon or as an element of human consciousness which remains a factor to be reckoned with in psychology or psychoanalysis. But conversely, theology today vis-à-vis the other sciences has become cautious and reserved even to the point of timidity. It is glad that it is even tolerated. And when its representatives discourse with other scientists, it is a distinct rarity that theology itself is the principal partner in the dialogue. This timidity on the part of theology is, in the last analysis, not engendered by the external situation in which it has to live in today's world, but is rather a consequence of its own history. It is theology itself which prompted and affirmed the idea of today's secular world, and then issued a declaration of its own incompetence in this world. The God of theology seems today to be shrouded in silence; the Christ of theology can no longer be found in the uppermost sphere of the *caelum empyreum*.²⁴²

Or similarly, Rahner suggests that theology is only tolerated on the university today because many view it as not being worth the effort to try to remove. Asks Rahner: "Do they not tolerate us simply because the other faculties have problems enough of their own without wrangling with theology, which, after all, does not do anybody any harm?"²⁴³

The question in light of these circumstances, then, according to Rahner, is: "Should not theology withdraw from the university?" For Rahner the answer is and must be a definitive "no," since despite all these difficulties theology today still has something to say to the other sciences because theology speaks of God and therefore opens a dimension "which human beings in their autocratic autonomy cannot be the custodians of, because this dimension of God's incomprehensibility is something which does not belong to human beings, but rather human beings belong to it. And for this very reason human beings must be ultimately understood as creatures who are always and fundamentally

---

²⁴¹ For an incisive description of the debate within and outside of the Roman Catholic Church in the last two centuries over the place and role of theology on the university see Wolfhart Beinert, "Universitätstheologie und Kirche," in: *Stimmen der Zeit* 211:11 (November 1993), 723-740.
²⁴² "Theology Today," 62f. ["Theologie Heute," 69.]
²⁴³ *Ibid.*, 56. [63.]

incomprehensible, creatures whose definition cannot be circumscribed by any limits. For this reason theology stands as the official representative of a radical opposition to any attempt to absolutize any reality which can be experienced immanently and any immanent value, and the servants of these realities and values are also the natural sciences."[244] Theology, therefore, should not remain on the university primarily for its own sake but for the sake of the other disciplines since (and here Rahner and Pannenberg stand near to one another) theology speaks of the all-encompassing God. That is to say, theology possesses universal relevance on the basis of the nature of God who is ultimately the object of its inquiry and speech.

Rahner also doubts whether theology could be removed from the university on the basis of any claim that it is not a science since, as Rahner asks, "Does anyone really know for sure just what a science is in a university today?" In recognition of the discussions in contemporary philosophy of science over the precise nature and qualifications of a science Rahner suggests that the charge that theology is not a science is not only difficult to prove but may not be all that relevant to the question of whether theology belongs in the university. Neither is it adequate, according to Rahner, to suggest that theology does not represent the entire population but only the interests of that part of the population that considers itself Christian. Rahner again asks, holding up the same requirements to the other sciences that theology's critics raise against it: "Must an area of learning which has its proper place in a university be sustained by the interest of the public as a whole? If this were the case, then quite a few university subjects would have to be dropped due to lack of interest on the part of the public at large." Indeed theology has the same right as other disciplines to be on the university if nothing else, according to Rahner, because theology belongs to the intellectual and cultural inheritance of the people and if it were expelled would certainly out of necessity come back in through the "back door" in such disciplines as philosophy, cultural history and others. Rahner also argues that theology, perhaps to a greater extent than the other sciences, opens up doors of communication to other world religions and world views, thus serving "cultural cooperation on a global level."[245] Finally, Rahner criticizes the modern tendency to evaluate everything on the university in terms of its economic worth.

> A university science would demean itself if it were to measure its ultimate value by the yardstick of commercial utility. Truth is under no obligation to vindicate itself to purely pragmatic or financial interests. My teacher Heidegger once said in a lecture that metaphysics was a subject that had no practical value, something that housemaids made fun of. Well, that is precisely its dignity. And that goes for theology as well.[246]

---

[244] *Ibid.*, 63. [69f.]
[245] *Ibid.*, 57ff. [63ff.]
[246] *Ibid.*, 57f. [63f.], for this and the following.

If the enemies of a university theology are successful in excluding it then theology will certainly continue to exist but, Rahner warns, considerable damage will be done to the spirit of objectivity, to tolerance, and to sober reflection which are precisely the things that the opponents of theology in the university claim to value. Theology should indeed remain in the university, and precisely as theology and not as the generic study of religions. Theology should remain within the university, according to Rahner, because it has something to say. It speaks about God, whose relevance is universal. Yet when theology speaks only about the speech about God and not about God himself, although in so doing it may win for itself greater acceptance within the university, it is no longer theology. As Rahner writes: "Theologians must speak of God and not only of the words used in speaking about God. They would make their task easier for themselves and more acceptable if they would only speak about the words used in speaking of God. But if they did this, they would betray their true and ultimate task. Then they would be no more than philosophers of religion or scientists of religion. But in the university God himself must be spoken of."[247]

Therefore rather than build the case for a university theology based upon the criteria of a particular philosophy of science Rahner chooses another, twofold approach - without suggesting that theology is not a science or that a case for its scientific status could not be made. First, Rahner takes up the various criticisms of and objections to a university theology suggesting that none of these are adequate grounds to remove theology from the university and that if they were, then many other disciplines would also have to be excluded. Even the question of the scientific nature of theology, if one could show that theology is not a science, is not adequate if, for no other reason, because the conception of precisely what constitutes a science today is itself not clear. But more significantly, Rahner argues that theology should remain within the university not just because there is no good reason to remove it. Rather, theology should remain because it has something to say to the other disciplines based upon a correct understanding of its true nature and task.

### 2.6.7 *The universality of theology*

Theology has scientific characteristics but is yet "something entirely different" from the other sciences, indeed, it is something more than a mere science. According to Rahner, "if a science always presupposes an object which can be palpably grasped and classified, then theology may not presume to be a science given this presupposition." This is so since Rahner defines theology as "the discourse over the incomprehensible mystery that we call God." If science is to be understood, therefore, in this restrictive sense, then theology cannot and dare not, according to Rahner, consider itself a science. Instead, theology

---

[247] *Ibid.*, 69. [74f.]

must aspire to something beyond this. It must break through the borders which are imposed upon an individual science by its very nature. It must extend its interest to everything if it is required to speak of the unfathomable primordial ground of all reality. The object of its interest can be nothing but God, if this true God is exalted in a way that no words can express above all that exists or can be conceived outside of himself. It must address itself to everyone since God is the concern of every human being whether he or she wants this or not, and because every form of indifference to the all-encompassing mystery of his existence has as its result the most frightening relationship to this God, and does not really bring about his absence.[248]

The universality of God is relevant for theology's claim to universality in regard to questions of epistemology because the individual objects of the individual sciences, according to Rahner, reflect an original "unity of reality" and this unity of reality not only finds its foundation in God but will again be achieved at the "eschatological integration of all reality in God," that is, into a point where God alone stands.[249]

The universality of theology, however, is not only grounded upon the universality of God, the object of theology, but also upon the universality of human existence. As Dych has pointed out, theology for Rahner is "universally valid" precisely because "it claims to be an interpretation of *all* human existence."[250] Rahner writes that theology, which speaks of the all-encompassing mystery of God's existence, must speak in such a way "as to be always aware that it is only repeating in feeble and inadequate words what the existence of every human being, who is constantly being pursued by God, bears testimony to - and it must continue to do this whether people listen or not"[251] Therefore Rahner can also write that,

> Theology proceeds from the assumption that basically speaking it is quite impossible for any individual to escape from being a theologian, at least implicitly, provided that by theology we understand the consideration of human life as a whole and in itself, over and above all the more restricted outlooks of science, and in its orientation towards the absolute Mystery. But precisely on this account the theologian will say that it is both good and necessary to have, among the participants in the interdisciplinary dialogue, one who has not any other part to play in it than to draw attention to that factor which all the participants have a duty to pay heed to, one who has no special interest in

---

[248] *Ibid.*, 60f. [67.]
[249] "On the Relationship Between Theology and the Contemporary Sciences," 96 and 102. [*Schriften* 10:106 and 112.] An important comparison is to be made here between Rahner's concept of an original unity of reality and Pannenberg's concept of a "unitary knowledge" or a "unity of knowledge." Cf. Pannenberg, "Antwort auf G. Sauters Überlegungen," 180f.
[250] Dych, "Theology in a New Key," 6.
[251] "Theology Today," 61. ["Theologie Heute," 67.]

upholding any particular science, but rather has a responsibility to all in common.[252]

Precisely here one sees what Rahner means when he claims that theology must be more than a science since it transcends the limits of a "regional" science interested only in its specialized field and instead concerns itself with everything and therefore with questions that all regional sciences are also to some extent concerned with since theology presupposes the unity and universality of God and of human existence and experience.[253] Similarly, the universality of theology implies a certain responsibility of theology to the other sciences. As philosophy loses its position over the other sciences the danger arises that some of the individual sciences seek to dominate or reign over the others. The unique task of theology in this situation, according to Rahner, is to serve as mediator between the various special sciences and to point to those things which its dialogue partners, as regional sciences, may be blind to. Thus theology "will gently and modestly put the question to the other partner, whether there is not here and there a blind spot in the eye of this particular science or this particular scientist, which needs to be taken into account." Theology must be

> the upholder of self-criticism on the part of the sciences. It must persuade them to be modest in outlook, to be aware of their provisional nature and their limited perspective, which they can never wholly overcome. ... It will ward off the temptation to which every science is liable of setting itself up as wholly autonomous and totalitarian in character, and to subsume all other sciences as subordinate to itself and to submit them to its yoke. It is theology which defends a pluralism among the sciences which is wholly incalculable and incapable of systematization, against a danger which even today, in the age of the so-called end of metaphysics, has still not been banished. For in the place of philosophy other individual sciences are beginning to claim a monopoly of authority over the rest.[254]

Theology, according to Rahner, can no longer simply relate to philosophy - and to the other disciplines as they are mediated and interpreted by philosophy. Theology must enter into direct "dialogue with the pluralistic historical, sociological and natural sciences which no longer allow themselves to be mediated or interpreted philosophically." For Rahner, it is this situation which "sheds light upon the difficulty of a scientific theology: ... It must be in contact with so many philosophies in order to be a science in this direct sense. Theology must have contact with the pluralistic sciences which no longer let themselves be interpreted by philosophy and finally with the host of non-scientific manifestations of the life of the mind which are to be found in art, in literature and in society

---

[252] "Theology as Engaged in an Interdisciplinary Dialogue with the Sciences," 88. [*Schriften* 10:97.]
[253] Cf. *Spirit in the World*, 67ff. [*Geist in Welt*, 80ff.]
[254] "Theology as Engaged in an Interdisciplinary Dialogue with the Sciences," 89f. [*Schriften* 10:98f.]

which are so numerous that everything that enters into view can neither be mediated by philosophy nor by the pluralistic sciences but yet forms a field of the mind and represents a human self-understanding that theology must relate to."[255]

Rahner's nearness to Pannenberg is especially to be seen in theology's claim to be universal. Not only is this claim founded upon the universality of God and of humanity in Rahner's thought, as in Pannenberg's program, but Rahner also bases the universality of theology upon the universality of revelation. Despite the fact that Rahner puts much less weight on the question of the scientific status of theology than does Pannenberg this does not weaken theology's claim to universality within Rahner's thought. Whereas for Pannenberg the scientific character of theology is crucial in his case for the universality of theological science, Rahner arrives at the same goal by insisting that too much concern over whether theology is designated a science or not risks making it just another "regional" science and clouds the fact that it must be "more than a science," concerning itself with everything since God himself encompasses all things. Only with this qualification of Rahner's understanding of science and of theology as a science can one say that, in light of the universality of the theological enterprise, that theology, for Rahner, is a universal science.

## 2.7 Rahner's Theological Method: A Summary and Appraisal

### 2.7.1 *A summary of Rahner's method*

Given the fact that Rahner himself had difficulty answering the question what precisely his theological method was and spoke of his "non-system system,"[256] a succinct summary or characterization of Rahner's method is no easy task. The normal characterization of Rahner's approach to doing theology as transcendental method certainly holds merit, especially as the designation Rahner himself used to describe his method. Within the context of the Roman Catholic theological tradition and with a view to the apologetic demands of modern, scientific, pluralistic societies Rahner approaches the theological task with the transcendental reflection which is possible because of the *a priori* pre-apprehension of being within the human 'knower.' In doing so Rahner has sought to adapt the Thomistic theological tradition to the 'turn to the subject' in modern philosophical thought. The transcendental method, especially as developed and understood by Maréchal, is the key to the synthesis which he attempts between modern transcendental and existential philosophy and traditional Roman Catholic theology.

Although the transcendental method, especially in Rahner, constitutes more of an approach to the theological task than a concrete methodology it has, as we

---

[255] Rahner, *Zur Reform des Theologiestudiums*, 70.
[256] "Reflections on Methodology," 68f. [*Schriften* 9:79.]; and P. Imhof and H. Biallowons, eds., *Karl Rahner in Dialogue*, 196f.

have seen, implications for Rahner's actual 'method' of doing theology. Rahner's understanding of revelation and its universality, crucial to so many of his distinctive theological insights, such as his theology of 'anonymous Christians,' is only possible in Rahner's thought when the transcendentality of all persons is presupposed. Rahner's so-called 'indirect method' is also dependent upon his transcendental starting point in that the individual human knower rather than any concrete method of external verification ultimately becomes the criterion by which the truthfulness of a theological or faith statement is evaluated. Sobrino perhaps summed up Rahner's methodological approach best when he wrote: "It seems clear that Rahner's hermeneutic [i.e., theological method] is eclectic. He does not want any specific methodology to place obstacles in the way of the theological object we are trying to comprehend. But within this basically eclectical approach Rahner shows a preference for a transcendental hermeneutics."[257]

The turn toward the subject in Rahner's own methodology has led inevitably to charges of subjectivism and a loss of historical context. Rahner's theological method, however, goes beyond its mere transcendental starting point. Leo O'Donovan is correct in his assessment when he writes that Rahner's method "was neither simply transcendental nor, still less, dogmatically positivist. With growing insistence it centered instead on the concrete dialectic of historical transcendence."[258] It is especially in this growing concern for history as the concrete context of God's self-revelation and the human person's experience of it that the gulf between Rahner and Pannenberg is narrowed and their common emphasis upon the universal relevance of theology finds a point of contact in their respective methodological foundations.

Even though Rahner never dealt thoroughly or particularly systematically with questions of theological method he has exercised a great deal of influence in this area, sparking a number of reviews and discussions of his method. As Bernard Lonergan has written: "If Fr. Rahner has not tackled the problem of method in a general fashion, he has given us an extremely penetrating account of the difficulties of that task at the present time. ... In brief, ... Rahner has laid down the conditions and expounded the need for a radical development in theological method."[259]

### 2.7.2 *Rahner's method in the context of Roman Catholic theology*

Rahner's theological method strikes one as being both typical and atypical of contemporary Roman Catholic theology. Depending upon which elements are emphasized, Rahner has either been lauded or sharply criticized by his fellow Catholic theologians. Rahner himself felt that there was not necessarily anything

---
[257] Jon Sobrino, *Christology at the Crossroads*, 24.
[258] Leo O'Donovan, "Karl Rahner, S.J., 1904-1984," in: *Journal of the American Academy of Religion* 53:1 (March 1985), 130.
[259] Bernard Lonergan, "Response to Fr. Dych," in: *Theology and Discovery: Essays in Honor of Karl Rahner, S.J.*, ed. Wm. Kelly, 54f.

particularly unique about his method which would distinguish him from any other "Catholic theologian conditioned by tradition."[260] Both the teaching office of the Church and papal authority are supported by Rahner, even if he was often critical of specific teachings.[261]

Even the transcendental method, which has led to many criticisms, is well represented within contemporary Catholic theology. Yet one might rightly ask whether the transcendental method is more specifically Jesuit than broadly Roman Catholic. One cannot help but note that the two principal founders of so-called transcendental Thomism, Joseph Maréchal and Pierre Rousselot, two of the most prominent philosophical advocates, Johann Baptist Lotz and Emerich Coreth, and the two most prominent theologians who have advocated the transcendental method, Karl Rahner and Bernard Lonergan, are all Jesuits. Indeed, Rahner himself has suggested that a fundamentally existential, transcendental approach is to be found in the exercises Ignatius Loyola, the founder of the Jesuit order.[262] Such a tendency within Ignatius could, in part, explain the positive reception the transcendental method has found among so many Jesuit thinkers.

Nevertheless, as Rahner has rightly noted, transcendental philosophy, upon which the transcendental method is grounded, has had a great impact upon the entire Catholic theological tradition through a broad reception of transcendental theology. Rahner has maintained that there is an essential analogy between Roman Catholic thought in general and transcendental theology.[263] Anne Carr has observed that transcendental theology, for Rahner, is more than simply the application of transcendental thinking to particular theological data. Rather, transcendental theology is "the elucidation of a particular analogy between transcendental thought and Roman Catholic theology, an analogy brought to light ... in the present historical period."[264]

Rahner's distinctive understanding of transcendental theology and its implications, however, have led him in directions which some critics believe push against the very boundaries of what can still be accepted as Roman Catholic

---

[260] "Reflections on Methodology," 68. [*Schriften* 9:79.] DiNoia, "Karl Rahner," 188, has written that "Rahner's approach to methodological issues shares in common with classical Catholic theology a set of basic convictions about the nature and method of theology" so that "his work stands firmly within the Catholic theological tradition."

[261] Cf. Manuel Alcalá, "Das Spannungsverhältnis von Theologie und kirchlichem Lehramt im Leben und im Werk Karl Rahners," 355ff. in: *Wagnis Theologie: Erfahrungen mit der Theologie Karl Rahners*, ed. Herbert Vorgrimler (Freiburg: Herder, 1979). As Altmann has noted concerning Rahner's view of the teaching office of the Roman church, "er kann die formale Autorität in der Kirche von der Erfassung des Menschen als je einmaliges Subjekt sowie von der Geschichtlichkeit ... stark relativieren, niemals aber von der Sache, vom Kerygma her grundsätzlich in Frage stellen. Walter Altmann, *Der Begriff der Tradition bei Karl Rahner* (Frankfurt: Peter Lang, 1974), 262.

[262] Cf. Rahner, "Die Logik der existentiellen Erkenntnis bei Ignatius v. Loyola," in: Rahner, *Das Dynamische in der Kirche, Quaestiones disputatae*, vol. 5, 74-148.

[263] "Transcendental Theology," 287. [*SM* 4:986.]

[264] Anne Carr, *The Theological Method of Karl Rahner*, 262.

theology.[265] In many cases Rahner's critics have seemed to be more acutely aware of the conflict, either real or potential, inherent in Rahner's theological method than Rahner himself. Although Rahner entertained no doubt of the binding nature of church dogma, his methodology, as Anne Carr has pointed out, raises unavoidably the question "of the authentic meaning of dogma in a cultural situation in which dogma ... has become largely impossible" - a question which remained unresolved in Rahner's own thought.[266]

### 2.7.3 Rahner and Pannenberg: A comparison of theological methods

In many regards two more differing approaches to theological method could not be found than those of Karl Rahner and Wolfhart Pannenberg. Whereas Rahner begins with the *a priori* givenness within human beings which makes possible a transcendental knowledge and has been criticized as leading to a radical subjectivism, Pannenberg's approach can be characterized as that of a critical rationalism which is radically *a posteriori* and which seeks to avoid any appearance of subjectivism. Likewise, while Rahner has been accused (justly or unjustly) of a loss of history and a non-historical subject-oriented method, Pannenberg takes history with such radical seriousness that it becomes the center point of his methodology and is integrally connected to revelation, which is thus open to all who have eyes to see and to the methods of the science of history to such an extent that he has been accused of leaving no room for the role of the Holy Spirit and of faith in the knowledge of God.

Yet despite the many obvious differences in the theological methods of Karl Rahner and Wolfhart Pannenberg there are several important similarities to be noted which point to common concerns, points of departure, and presuppositions - albeit not to a common 'method.' Human experience plays an important role for both Rahner and Pannenberg so that both can be said to make anthropology a key starting point for their theologies - though this anthropological starting point, as we shall see in our next chapter, is understood and applied differently in both.

Similarly, both theologians accept the possibility of a natural knowledge of God; Rahner on the basis of human transcendental experience, and Pannenberg on the basis of a 'general revelation' in history. For both, a natural knowledge of God would not be possible were it not for the universality of revelation which for Rahner takes place within the concrete context of human history and which for Pannenberg *is* human history. Likewise, for both theologians revelation is God's self-disclosure in history which reaches its pinnacle in Jesus of Nazareth.

Metaphysics plays an important role in the theology of both theologians, though much of what Pannenberg would consider metaphysics is called by Rahner transcendental philosophy or theology. Therefore the transcendental method, one of the unique features of Rahner's theology, is not entirely without parallel in

---

[265] Eugen Drewermann, who himself has been the center of controversy within the Roman Catholic Church, has somewhat irreverently suggested that Rahner's theological positions were certainly ripe for excommunication, had he written in such a manner that the Roman hierarchy were able to understand him! Cf. Drewermann, *Glauben in Freiheit oder Tiefenpsychologie und Dogmatik: Dogma, Angst und Symbolismus* (Düsseldorf: Walter-Verlag, 1993), 219.
[266] *Ibid.*, 267.

Pannenberg. Similarly, Pannenberg's distinctive emphasis upon the proleptic nature of the Christ event in which the end is already present also finds some parallel, as we have seen, in Rahner's hermeneutical insight that the future is already present in Christ inasmuch as our awareness of this future which has been won for us by Christ shapes our understanding of the present.

Though Pannenberg and Rahner understand theology differently, for both there exists a close relationship between philosophy and theology. As we have seen, both contend that theology necessarily presupposes philosophy as condition and context for explicitly *Christ*ian reflection. And both theologians stress as well that God himself is the unifying and universal subject matter (or object) of theology. For both theologians this leads inevitably to the universality of theology. The universality of theology in both Rahner and Pannenberg is supported by an epistemology which contends that there exists an ultimate or original unity of reality and knowledge. Hence knowledge gained from the special sciences is relevant for theology just as theological knowledge is relevant for the special sciences.

That two theologians with such very different methodologies should have so many points of contact is initially surprising. Yet common, underlying methodological concerns are to be found in both Pannenberg and Rahner which to a great extent account for the similarities amidst so much diversity. Pannenberg's focus upon the ability of natural reason, the possibility of a natural knowledge of God, and his conception of theology as a science, even though on this latter point there is some significant discontinuity with Rahner, all correlate well with the basic concerns and approach of the Roman Catholic theological tradition within which Rahner is firmly rooted. As Heinrich Petri has noted, "the theology of Wolfhart Pannenberg has from its beginning the orientation of a fundamental theology, and that, in such a way, that it thoroughly corresponds with the formulation of questions of Catholic fundamental theology."[267]

Additionally, Pannenberg emphasizes the role of human experience, which, although very distinct from Rahner's transcendental approach, provides an important point of common concern. On Rahner's part, his concern to ground his transcendental theology and human transcendental experience in the context of universal history - and this is especially true of the later Rahner - provides a significant, if often subtle bridge to Pannenberg's theological approach. But perhaps even more significant in both theologians is their underlying belief in the universality of God's self-revelation and the universality of any theology based upon this revelation. This concern for and awareness of universality is already to be seen, albeit in often very different ways, in their respective theological methods. It is also, as will be seen later in our study, essential to the apologetic approach of both theologians to non-Christian worldviews. As we turn next in our study to the theological foundations of the universality of theological science, particularly as seen in theological anthropology and the doctrine of God, the theme of universality becomes even more explicit.

---

[267] Heinrich Petri, "Die Entdeckung der Fundamentaltheologie in der evangelischen Theologie," in: *Catholica* 33:4 (1979), 254.

# Chapter Three

## THE ANTHROPOLOGICAL ROOTS OF THEOLOGY'S UNIVERSALITY

Anthropology, or the question of humanity, is the area of theological inquiry that shares a common object of investigation with more special sciences than any other department of theology. Anthropology has been viewed as a bridge between theology and the other sciences and as a key to apologetics. Since Pannenberg and Rahner have both developed theologies which begin with the human, the significance of the anthropological foundations of their respective apologetics is all the more highlighted. The underlying concern for apologetics may even account in part for the extensive attention both theologians have given to developing theological anthropologies. The theme of anthropology is indeed of such centrality in the thought of both Pannenberg and Rahner that several volumes have been written exploring the anthropologies of each. In this chapter, however, we are not able to examine all of the aspects of the theological anthropologies of either theologian.

To some extent, especially in the case of Rahner and his concept of human transcendentality, we have already treated some of the anthropological foundations of the universality of theology in the preceding two chapters on methodology. In this chapter, therefore, we limit our focus to a necessarily selective examination of the foundations of Pannenberg and Rahner's anthropologies and especially to those elements which point specifically to the unity of humanity and the universality of human experience, which are vital to the apologetic approaches of both theologians. We will also seek to examine the fundamental differences between the anthropologies of the two theologians with special attention given to the question of whether Rahner, in Thomistic fashion, has a too optimistic view of humanity and Pannenberg, in characteristic Protestant tones, perhaps a too pessimistic view.

### 3.1 Karl Rahner: The Transcendence of Finite Humanity

#### 3.1.1 Prolegomena to Rahner's Theological Anthropology

3.1.1.1 *Theological anthropology and profane anthropologies*

Although anthropology suggests a natural point of contact between theology and the special sciences Rahner is careful to distinguish theological anthropology from what he calls "profane" anthropologies. For Rahner a specifically theological anthropology does not, in the strictest sense, include a "reflection upon the profane sciences which treat humanity, each in its own manner, aposteriorically and not from the perspective of the revelatory word of God." If theological anthropology, according to Rahner, begins with the profane sciences then it becomes dependent upon other, non-theological anthropologies, that is to say, upon "what the human person knows 'naturally', ... apart from the historical revelatory word."[1] Rahner concedes that there are many sciences which have something to say about humanity, including ethnology, sociology and psychology, but these all have the tendency to formalize everything in humans and to lead back to abstract structures so that the individual, concrete human person disappears.[2]

Such statements, however, do not mean that Rahner rejects the profane anthropologies or believes that they have nothing to do with theological anthropology. He is also convinced that theological anthropology is obligated to continually reevaluate and reexamine its statements in order to better understand the human person in the light of contributions from the ongoing historical experience of humans, which includes also "the profane anthropological sciences as a moment of the history of the human person."[3] In his article, "The Theological Dimension of the Question about Man," Rahner addresses the relationship between theological and profane anthropologies and seeks to show the connection which exists between the two. The plurality of sciences, according to Rahner, demonstrates "that man is a being with many dimensions, and that these dimensions cannot adequately be traced back to one another, or to a single starting point, which could be arrived at by means of scientific and empirical reflection." When a Christian anthropology based upon revelation sets itself alongside of these partial and regional anthropologies from the human sciences it too often becomes a naive and harmless additional perspective. Yet Christian anthropology "if it interprets itself properly, is not one 'limited' human science among others."[4]

The fact that Christian or theological anthropology is not simply another regional anthropology can, according to Rahner, be seen already from its content

---

[1] Rahner, "Theologische Anthropologie," in: *Lexikon für Theologie und Kirche*, ed. Josef Höfer and Karl Rahner (Freiburg: Herder, 1957), 1:618f. and 623. Cf. also Ignacy Bokwa, *Christologie als Anfang und Ende der Anthropologie: Über das gegenseitige Verhältnis zwischen Christologie und Anthropologie bei Karl Rahner* (Frankfurt/M: Peter Lang, 1990), 140f.

[2] Rahner, "The Theological Dimension of the Question about Man," in: *TI* 17:53f. ["Die theologische Dimension der Frage nach dem Menschen," in: *Schriften* 12:387.] Indeed, for Rahner, "directly or indirectly, all natural sciences involve anthropology; they all say something about man." Rahner, "On the Relationship between Natural Science and Theology," in: *TI* 19:16. ["Zum Verhältnis von Naturwissenschaft und Theologie," in: *Schriften* 14:63."]

[3] Rahner, "Zum theologischen Begriff des Menschen," (Mensch III) in: *Herders theologisches Taschenlexikon*, ed. Karl Rahner (Freiburg: Herder, 1973), 5:31f.

[4] "The Theological Dimension of the Question about Man," 56f. ["Die theologische Dimension," 390f.]

which adds nothing additional or new to the profane anthropologies. Rather, "it actually bursts these secular anthropologies radically apart, thereby making access possible, for the first time and finally, to the one mystery which we call God." When theological anthropology, however, understands itself simply as another regional anthropology, then a false conception of God is unavoidably conveyed.[5] According to Rahner, "all the sciences except theology are in a real sense anthropology. ... Theology exists solely because there is a word from God to man."[6] It is therefore God, as pointed to by a true theological anthropology, who is the key not only to the distinction between theology and the special sciences but also to the relationship between theological anthropology and the profane anthropologies.

A similar connection, as Rahner pointed out in *Hearers of the Word*, is to be found between a philosophical anthropology and theological anthropology, based upon the relationship between God and the human person as hearer of a possible revelation. Rahner explained: "Philosophy, as genuine philosophy, is Christian when, as fundamental-theological anthropology, it loses itself in theology. Indeed, insofar as it is the constitution of man as a listener for possible revelation from God, it always becomes merged with theology."[7] If the whole person points to a relationship with God when the dimensions of humanity explored by the special sciences are "radicalized" and "thematized," then all questions concerning humanity arising from the profane anthropologies are transformed into "*the one theological question*." Hence Rahner can claim that the theological dimension of the question about humanity is identical with all the various dimensions of humanity which come into view in the profane anthropologies to the extent that these various dimensions are viewed in their radical depth and are as such thematized.

Theological anthropology, therefore, as that which radicalizes and thematizes the statements of the profane anthropologies so that they too point to the human person's relationship with God, is seen to be more than a regional anthropology. Rahner writes: "This thematisation of the question about man in its ultimate, radical form - the question which is ultimately man himself ... - is not limited or an additional anthropology, if only because this radical form of the question is nothing other than man's initiation into the incomprehensible mystery which we call 'God'."[8] Indeed, a theological anthropology itself is first only possible when one is able to say "that the human person is that being which has to do with

---

[5] *Ibid.*, 57, 59. [392, 394.] Rahner contends, therefore, that no contradiction ultimately exists between a theocentric and an anthropocentric theology since the latter points necessarily to God (56, [389]).

[6] *Hearers*, 167. [*HdW*., 205.]

[7] *Ibid.*, 175. [215.] and for the following.

[8] "The Theological Dimension of the Question about Man," 60f. ["Die theologische Dimension," 394f.]

God."[9] Therefore, rather than rejecting the profane anthropologies, Rahner concludes that "the theological dimension of the question about man is nothing more than the radical depth of all other, seemingly merely secular dimensions of anthropology."[10] Yet Rahner, in contrast, as we will see, to Pannenberg, clearly makes theological presuppositions, if not theological anthropology itself, his starting point rather than the profane anthropologies with which he enters into dialogue.[11]

The apologetic significance of this approach is to be found precisely in the realization of the unifying function of theological anthropology which enters into dialogue with the various profane anthropologies and thematizes and radicalizes their findings about human beings, showing in what ways they too point to God as the ground of their being. In Karl Rahner's theological anthropology the function of theology as "universal science" is therefore exemplified.[12] Not only does theology have something to learn from the various dimensions of humanity uncovered by the special sciences but it fulfills these by unifying them and pointing them to the *one* reality that stands behind their diverse findings.

3.1.1.2 *Locating theological anthropology within the theological enterprise*

The place Rahner gives to anthropology within the total theological enterprise is characterized by two thoughts which are woven through his theological reflections on the topic. First, "it is fundamentally possible to read all theological statements as anthropology," that is to say, all theology is really anthropology. Second, and what serves as a qualification to the first thought, it is not desirable in practice to push this anthropological starting point of theology so far as to draw all of theology into anthropology.[13] That is to say, the theological enterprise, seen in its totality, is more than simply anthropology. Rahner cautions that if "the whole of dogmatics were drawn into theological anthropology" then

---

[9] "Zum theologischen Begriff des Menschen," 32.
[10] "The Theological Dimension of the Question about Man," 68f. ["Die theologische Dimension," 404.]
[11] Otto Hermann Pesch, *Frei sein aus Glaube: Theologische Anthropologie* (Freiburg: Herder, 1983), 34, writes that Rahner's approach to anthropology in regard to the profane anthropologies is paradigmatic for a group of approaches (including that of Albrecht Peters, for instance) which begin with fundamentally theological statements which concern "the human being a a *creature* called to receive the self-revelation of God." Thus for Rahner, according to Pesch, "the location of theological anthropology within systematic theology is the doctrine of creation."
[12] Despite Rahner's intention to integrate the results of profane anthropologies within his own 'turn to anthropology,' the controversial priest and psychologist Eugen Drewermann has accused Rahner of failing in his program precisely because he remained too bound to traditional teaching and failed to take adequate account of the secular anthropologies of the twentieth century. Drewermann is especially critical of Rahner's failure to take account of the "unconscious dynamic of the human psyche" which psychology has uncovered in the drives, dreams and emotions of human beings. Cf. Eugen Drewermann, *Glauben in Freiheit oder Tiefenpsychologie und Dogmatik*, vol. 1 (Düsseldorf: Walter-Verlag, 1993), 213f. and 224.
[13] "Theologische Anthropologie," 624.

we would run the risk of establishing an "inescapable dualism of the spiritual creature between 'essentials' and 'existentials.'"[14] Thus Rahner, as Otto Hermann Pesch has noted, while advocating the turn to anthropology, assured at the same time that it would not come to contraction or abbreviation of theology in the broader sense.[15]

The reason that it is possible to read all theological statements as anthropology is because Rahner understands "Anthropologie als dem Ort der Theologie."[16] Indeed, Rahner goes so far as to contend that dogmatic theology today must be theological anthropology.[17] Just as theological anthropology must not be viewed as just another regional anthropology alongside of the profane anthropologies, neither can it be an isolated and regional department within dogmatics. According to Rahner, "the question of man, and the answer to this question, should not be considered a separate area, distinct from the other areas of theological inquiry. It must be looked upon, rather, as the whole of dogmatic theology." Yet for Rahner this in no way implies an anthropocentric theology which stands in contradiction to a theocentric theology.[18] As Heinrich Fries explained, in Rahner's thought, "God and God's revelation are the answer to the question that is the human being. Therefore theology is to be conveyed as anthropology. Theology will not thereby disappear, but will be fixed as presupposition and goal."[19] Indeed, already in *Hearers of the Word* Rahner contended that there can only exist a positive theology because God speaks, not because the human being thinks. Yet despite this qualification Rahner also stressed that even in such a science as theology the human person,

---

[14] *Ibid.*, 625.

[15] So Otto Hermann Pesch, "'Frei sein aus Gnade:' Hinweise zu einer theologischen Anthropologie," in: *Sind wir von Natur aus religiös?*, ed. W. Pannenberg, 108.

[16] Rahner, "Grundsätzliche Überlegungen zur Anthropologie und Protologie im Rahmen der Theologie," in: *Mysterium Salutis: Grundriss Heilsgeschichtlicher Dogmatik*, ed. Johannes Feiner and Magnus Löhrer (Zürich: Benziger, 1967), 406.

[17] Anton Losinger, *Der anthropologische Ansatz in der Theologie Karl Rahners* (Ottilien: Erzabtei St. Ottilien, 1991), 45f., has suggested that theology expresses itself as anthropology in Rahner's thought in three ways: (1) The philosophical self-experience of humans necessarily presupposes the possibility of experiencing God. (2) In the context of the dogmatic question of nature and grace human nature is conceptualized in its centeredness in the 'supernatural existential' of the divine self-communication which essentially leads to the immediacy of God. (3) The salvation-historical fact of the incarnation of the Logos in Jesus Christ achieved a communion between God and humanity and made it possible to approach the central content of Christianity anthropologically.

[18] Rahner, "Theology and Anthropology," in: T. Patrick Burke, ed., *The Word in History: The St. Xavier Symposium* (New York: Sheed and Ward, 1966), 1. ["Theologie und Anthropologie," in: *Schriften* 8:43].

[19] Heinrich Fries, "Fides quaerens intellectum," in: *Vernunft des Glaubens: Wissenschaftliche Theologie und kirchliche Lehre - Festschrift zum 60. Geburtstag von Wolfhart Pannenberg*, ed. Jan Rohls and Gunther Wenz (Göttingen: Vandenhoeck & Ruprecht, 1988), 102.

cannot be completely overlooked and excluded, because there would be no word of God were there no one who was at least intrinsically capable of hearing it. Thus there is a theological anthropology, not just in the specific or strict sense that God himself in his *Logos* reveals to man the ultimate structure of his own human essence, so that a theological anthropology is a part of the *content* of theology; but in the sense that an unreflective, perhaps naive, self-understanding by man is the condition of the possibility of theology at all.[20]

Hans Urs von Balthasar, however, has been especially critical of Rahner at this point, suggesting that theology becomes anthropology to such an extent in his theology that the priority (if not the necessity) of God is in danger of being overlooked. In an obvious play on Rahner's own terminology Balthasar suggests that atheists might view such an anthropocentric Christianity as anonymous atheism and its proponents as anonymous atheists. Concerning the dialogue with atheists he writes: "But while we can address our partners very sincerely as anonymous Christians, ... they will certainly reciprocate by greeting us as anonymous atheists, since our entire alleged Dogmatic is only a roof over a field, forest, and meadow humanism and its anthropology."[21] This accusation is at least partly justifiable, Balthasar contends, in light of the overly anthropological emphasis in Rahner's thought. Without mentioning Rahner by name Balthasar summarizes his criticisms against Rahner's anthropocentric theology:

> Whoever claims to do 'theology as anthropology' claims, at the very least, that every sentence spoken about God in this science is somehow also spoken about humanity. Such a theologian, however, leaves silenced in the shadows the presupposition of all theology, that it is namely the Logos of the God who speaks and who encounters the listening but not the already speaking human being. Hence the '-logy' in its illusory univocity is an obscuration. Whoever speaks of 'anonymous Christians' cannot ... prevent a final univocity between Christians with the Name and Christians without the Name. Consequently, it cannot, despite all belated protests, be that serious a matter whether one confesses the Name or not. And whoever proclaims the identification of the love of God with the love of neighbor, and who sets up the love of neighbor as the primary act of the love of God,[22] should not be surprised ... when it becomes unimportant whether a person believes in God.[23]

In this manner Balthasar criticizes the anthropocentric theology of Rahner as essentially leaving no room for a theo-centric emphasis. Rahner, however, argues

---

[20] *Hearers*, 168. [*HdW*., 206f.]

[21] Hans Urs von Balthasar, *Cordula oder der Ernstfall* (Einsiedeln: Johannes Verlag, 1967), 104.

[22] Cf. Rahner, "Reflections on the Unity of the Love of Neighbor and the Love of God," in: *TI* 6:247 ["Über die Einheit von Nächsten- und Gottesliebe," in: *Schriften* 6:295.] where he writes: "The categorized explicit love of neighbor is the primary act of the love of God. The love of God unreflectedly [*unthematisch*] but really and always intends God in supernatural transcendentality in the love of neighbor as such."

[23] Balthasar, *Cordula oder der Ernstfall*, 102f. Cf. also 84ff.

that a theocentric theology cannot be contradicted by an anthropocentric theology since 'theocentric,' correctly understood, transforms itself into 'anthropocentric' through God's self-disclosing grace. And likewise, "man can find himself only when he gives himself up in adoration and love into the free incomprehensibility of God, i.e. when he himself transforms his anthropocentrism into theocentrism."[24] For Rahner anthropology and *theo*-logy belong together inasmuch as a proper anthropology is a pre-condition of speaking about God theologically and a proper anthropology is itself only possible when theology makes God its primary focus. Hence Rahner has contended that we can ultimately only speak about God "by engaging even in the midst of all this (in the midst of theology) in anthropology; and ultimately any information about anthropology, about the nature and dignity of man, can be given only when we engage in theology about God and from God."[25] The point Rahner wishes to make is not only that "anthropocentricity and theocentricity in theology are not contradictories" but also that anthropocentricity opposes the view that humanity is merely a particular, regional topic within theology alongside of other topics.[26]

According to Rahner an anthropological statement is only theological when it points either explicitly or implicitly to God "and is not understood simply as a specialized, regional statement about some aspect of humanity." Hence, while it is possible, though according to Rahner not desirable, to read all theological statements as anthropology, all anthropological statements are not automatically to be understood as theology - even when they pass themselves off as *theological anthropology*. The crucial test of the theologicalness of anthropological statements, whether they come originally from the so-called profane anthropologies or from theological anthropology, is whether they point back to God as the absolute reality who stands behind all human experience and all persons. In this light, then, Rahner is able to contend that "theology (in the strict sense) and anthropology mutually condition one another."[27]

Beyond the realm of dogmatics Rahner suggests that anthropology, in an age when dogmatics has become increasingly diverse and complex, could be the key to unifying the broader array of theological disciplines including biblical, historical, and practical theology. Thus the significance of theological anthropology is understood as having not just a unifying function within the more restricted category of theology as dogmatics but is seen by Rahner as providing the key to unifying the entire theological encyclopedia.[28]

---

[24] "The Theological Dimension of the Question about Man," 56. ["Die theologische Dimension," 389f.]
[25] Rahner, "The Dignity and Freedom of Man," in: *TI* 2:241. ["Würde und Freiheit des Menschen," in: *Schriften* 2:253.]
[26] "Theology and Anthropology," 1. [*Schriften* 8:43].
[27] "Zum theologischen Begriff des Menschen," 32.
[28] Cf. Rahner, "Reflections on the Contemporary Intellectual Formation of Future Priests," in: *TI* 6:133f.

### 3.1.2 Humans as 'Hearers of the Word'

For Rahner the most distinctive and decisive characteristic of human beings is that they are hearers of the word of God.[29] This aspect is not only developed in his 1941 book of the same title but has appeared consistently in Rahner's theology as the primary category under which he explicates his understanding of humanity.[30] Not only is the concept of humans as hearers of the word key to his understanding of human beings, it is also the starting point for his entire theological program. As has been quite accurately observed, Rahner "begins, not with God, nor with Scripture, nor with the teachings of the Church, but with the person who is presupposed by Christianity as the hearer of its gospel."[31] And, as Rahner himself states, theology is grounded not upon the word of God, but upon "the hearing of the word of God by man," and more specifically, upon "the *a priori* possibility of the capacity to hear a revelation which might conceivably proceed from God."[32] Or, in Rahner's own terminology, he starts with the human being as *potentia oboedientialis* (obediential potency) for a possible revelatory word of God.[33] In what follows we examine some of the most important and interrelated themes which Rahner has taken up under the category of humans as hearers of the word.

#### 3.1.2.1 *The hearer as 'spirit in the world'*

Fundamental to Rahner's understanding of humans as hearers of a potential word of God is his concept of humans as spirit in the world, that is, as simultaneously spiritual and material beings, which he developed in his first book, *Spirit in the World*. Here, picking up on Thomas' concept of humans as *convertendo se ad phantasma*, Rahner argued that the "world" is a complementary concept to humanity since humans are spiritual beings who exist in the concrete context of the world. The human, according to Rahner, has an ambivalent, double orientation. "He is always exiled in the world and is always already beyond it." Or, expressed differently, "man is the mid-point suspended

---

[29] Peter Eicher, *Die Anthropologische Wende: Karl Rahners philosophischer Weg vom Wesen des Menschen zur personalen Existenz* (Freiburg, Switzerland: Universitätsverlag Freiburg, 1970), 140f., observes that for Rahner the very being (*Dasein*) of the human person as well as the person's relation to the divine is grounded upon an inner-worldly, historical word.

[30] Cf. Ignacy Bokwa, 49, who observes that: "Die Erkenntnisfähigkeiten des Menschen ermöglichen es ihm, das Wort Gottes zu vernehmen: der 'Geist in Welt' ist 'Hörer des Wortes'. Dieser Ansatz wird im Lauf der theologischen Arbeit Rahners unverändert bleiben."

[31] Anne Carr, "Starting with the Human," in: *A World of Grace*, 17.

[32] *Hearers*, 9. [*HdW*, 22.]

[33] The *potentia oboedientialis*, a term taken from Thomas Aquinas, means for Rahner "the capacity of the creature, obediently accepting the disposition and action of God, to receive a determination for which the creature is not 'in potency' in such a way that this determination is 'due' to it. The potency is not such that if not actualized by the determination in question it would be frustrated, and hence could not have been constituted by a wise creator unless this determination were to be added." Rahner, "Potentia oboedientialis," in: *SM* 5:65. [*SM* 3:1245.]

between the world and God, between time and eternity."[34] For Rahner two crucial propositions are contained within his contention that the human person is spirit in the world. First, human beings are spiritual, transcendent beings. For Rahner, this means the *spirit*ualness of human beings points to their experience of relatedness and orientation to God. Hence, "man is spirit because he finds himself situated before being in its totality which is finite. ... He knows of absolute *esse* in that he experiences his movement towards *esse*. Therefore he is spirit."[35] And for Rahner, the human person is spirit in the primary instance. Hence, "man is spirit. This is the first ... proposition of a metaphysical anthropology."[36] Rahner begins with the spirit as that which is primary in humans so that for him human beings are embodied spirit, that is to say, a spirit with a body, and not primarily a physical, biological organism which has achieved intelligence. And second, the concrete context of their transcendent being is a being in the material world. Hence humans are not just spiritual but material - not just soul but also body. As Rahner unequivocally wrote:

> The human being is a unity. And this unity of the human person is a dogma of faith. But this defined unity is not guarded when one simply allows for two neighboring things (soul and body) to come into contact with each other and declares them to be united, whereby one, even if unwilling to admit it, doesn't describe anything more than an 'interaction' (*Wechselwirkung*) - a mutual influencing of the two. The unity is as original as the coming into being of both parts, the mutual influencing is the completion of the *being* of both 'parts': they are moments of the one reality that we call a human person. In our inner and outer experience we always encounter only the whole: a souled body and a corporeal spirit.[37]

Rahner, in one of his many encyclopedia articles, stated that the spiritualness of the human person includes transcendence, freedom, immortality, and personality.[38] The most crucial of these concepts for Rahner's anthropology, transcendence and freedom, will be dealt with in the following two sections. Here, we will concern ourselves specifically with what it means to "be in the world." Rahner, in terminology reminiscent of Heidegger's *Being and Time*,[39] describes what it means for the human to be in the world.

---

[34] Rahner, *Spirit in the World*, 406f. [*Geist in Welt*, 405f.]
[35] *Ibid.*, 186. [195.]
[36] *Hearers*, 37. [*HdW.*, 55.]
[37] Rahner, "Die Frage nach dem Erscheinungsbild des Menschen als Quaestio disputata der Theologie," Introduction to Paul Overhage, *Um das Erscheinungsbild der ersten Menschen*, QD 7 (Freiburg: Herder, 1959), 11f.
[38] "Theologische Anthropologie," 625.
[39] Rahner's reliance upon Heideggerian categories in his description of humans' being in the world is also pointed out by Anne Carr, *The Theological Method of Karl Rahner*, 185. Carr writes: "Rahner adopts Heidegger's method in pointing to the circular structure of human knowing and

Man lives within a world of existent things which are the objects of his activity. Man is not simply one of the goods and chattels at the disposal of his environment, but lives in a world over against which he takes up his stance and from which he differentiates himself in thought and deed. ... He does not simply come into some sort of cognitive contact with the things of his world, as it may be supposed the animals do. But in judgment, he distinguishes himself from the thing he knows. He turns the environment of his physical-biological life into the object of his activity, into his world. He not only knows and feels his environment, but judges it, thus constituting it for the first time as a *world*. He is the subject that stands over against an object.[40]

The philosopher Peter Eicher notes that the relationship of human beings to the world in Rahner's thought falls into four main categories through which humans constitute their world, namely, (1) through their free actions, (2) through their objective knowing, (3) through their linguistic behavior, and (4) through their living in a historically constituted world.[41]

For Rahner, spirit and matter, also within human beings, form a unity because both that which is spiritual and that which is material have their origin in the one God who created both. Additionally, it is through our experience of the spiritual and material realities that we know God. Thus God stands as the "ground and all-embracing, pre-given unity of the experience of the spirit and the material world in their unity." This is not to say that God is simply the creator of two disparate realities, but rather, "because we have already discovered an original reference of both realities to each other as something given in our experience, we call him one and the same cause of matter and spirit." And, according to Rahner, it is only through the experience of the unity of spirit and material in the person as knowing subject that we can recognize that these two seemingly opposite realities point to and have their origin in the one God.[42] In Rahner's thought it is constitutive of being human that the person as spirit, in the act of knowing that which is in space-time, is "always dependent on the total unity of reality, i.e. on God, who existed before the multiplicity of his immediately-given objects."[43] Thus the human hearer as spiritual subject living in a material world (and not just an environment in which he or she comes into contact with 'things') is a necessary condition for the knowledge of God as the one creator of both the spiritual and material realities. It is thus of fundamental importance for

---

being in the world, as already and always historically conditioned when human reflection attempts to grasp it."

[40] *Hearers*, 54. [*HdW*, 72.] Cf. also *Spirit in the World*, 397. [*GW*, 396]; and Neuhaus, *Transzendentale Erfahrung als Geschichtsverlust?*, 73.

[41] Peter Eicher, 121.

[42] Rahner, "The Unity of Spirit and Matter in the Christian Understanding of Faith," in: *TI* 6:155. ["Die Einheit von Geist und Materie im christlichen Glaubensverständnis," in: *Schriften*: 6:187f.]

[43] "The Dignity and Freedom of Man," 239. ["Würde und Freiheit des Menschen," 251.]

Rahner's thought that the human person as hearer of the word be understood as spirit in the world.

### 3.1.2.2 Transcendentality of the hearers and the universal offer of grace

For Rahner the spiritual character of human beings is seen primarily in their transcendence, a transcendence which Rahner, in strongly Heideggerian terminology, defined as an absolute openness to being in *Hearers of the Word*. Wrote Rahner: "Man is absolute openness to being in general, or, in a word, ... man is spirit. Transcendentality with regard to being in general is the basic constitution of man. And so we enunciate the first proposition of our metaphysical anthropology."[44] In the later Rahner the Heideggerian language has largely faded but the basic emphasis remains. In *Foundations of Christian Faith*, for instance, we read: "Man is always present to himself in his entirety. ... In his openness to everything and anything, whatever can come to expression can be at least a question for him. ... In the fact that he experiences his finiteness radically, he reaches beyond this finiteness and experiences himself as a transcendent being, as spirit."[45] We have already dealt in detail, however, in the preceding chapter with human transcendentality and transcendental experience. Here our focus will be upon the connection Rahner has drawn between human transcendentality and the universal offer of grace.

In his 1977 article, "Experience of Transcendence from the Standpoint of Christian Dogmatics," Rahner brings forth the following thesis: "Whenever there is a final radical self-realization of man in mind and freedom and the person thus commits himself to finality, it may be assumed that such a self-realization (which can also ... take place in a mystical experience of transcendence) in practice is always sustained and radicalized by what is known in Christian theology as Holy Spirit, supernatural grace, self-communication of God." On the basis of this thesis Rahner draws the connection between human transcendentality and the universal offer of grace. If, according to Rahner, we begin with the assumption of a universal salvific will of God which is present always and in every place in human history, even outside of the verbalized preaching of the gospel and the context of the Church, then we must also assume certain things about human transcendentality. Namely, we can (and indeed must) conclude that what we call the Holy Spirit and supernatural grace - at the very least "in the mode of a real offer to man's freedom as radicalizing existential of man's transcendentality - exists as such always and everywhere and therefore also outside institutionalized Christianity."[46]

For Rahner, therefore, the universal grace (or at least the offer of grace) manifests itself originally in the radicalizing self-disclosure of God to the

---

[44] *Hearers*, 53. [*HdW*, 71.]
[45] *FCF*, 31f. [*Grundkurs*, 42f.]
[46] Rahner, "Experience of Transcendence from the Standpoint of Christian Dogmatics" in: *TI* 18:181. ["Transzendenzerfahrung aus katholisch-dogmatischer Sicht," in: *Schriften* 13:216f.]

transcendentality of human beings. And when this offer of grace is truly universal, then human transcendentality must also be universal. So then, according to Rahner, the possibility of faith is always and everywhere present, even among those who find themselves in non-Christian religious traditions or who consider themselves atheists.[47] The implication of the connection between the universality of the offer of grace and the universality of human transcendentality for Rahner is clear when he writes:

> If we presuppose this thesis of the universal reality of the offer of grace always and everywhere and primarily to the transcendentality of man as such and if we consider the fact that this grace is present as accepted and sustained by man's freedom, if moreover we start out from the assumption that such an unconditional acceptance by man's freedom of his own transcendentality can exist also ... with a special intensity in mystical experiences of transcendence, then it follows that the mysticism rightly interpreted by Christian theology as a real experience of grace can and must be found even outside institutional Christianity.[48]

This insight into the connection between human transcendentality and the universal offer of grace is foundational for Rahner's apologetic directed toward atheistic and non-Christian religious worldviews. It forms a bridge between Rahner's methodology and his apologetics which we explore more fully in chapter five. For Rahner the connection between a universal offer of grace and the universality of human transcendental experience, or at least the potential for such experience, leads him to his radical and uniquely apologetical suggestion of an "anonymous" Christianity. Rahner contends: If one holds fast to the "universality of the factuality of grace from the outset as an existential of man's transcendentality as such, then the possibility of a supernatural, grace-inspired anonymously Christian mysticism outside verbalized and institutionalized Christianity cannot be denied." The apologetically significant theory of an anonymous Christianity (which will be taken up in detail in chapter five of our study) is therefore seen to be grounded in Rahner's anthropology, namely, in the insight that all transcendental experience points to a single, "original mystical phenomenon" which is grounded upon the universal self-disclosure of God to human beings in and through their transcendentality.[49]

### 3.1.2.3 *The freedom of the hearer*

Freedom, for Rahner, is an indispensable quality of humanity. In a 1969 article he wrote that where freedom, understood as the possibility of absolute and definitive self-determination, exists, there is also the human person; "if it is not

---

[47] *Ibid.*, 181f. [217.]
[48] *Ibid.*, 182. [217f.]
[49] Cf. *ibid.*, 182f. [218f.]

present, then one cannot speak of a human being, however complex its other psychic mechanisms, behavioral patterns, etc. might be."[50] It is therefore understandable that the freedom of the hearer has been called "*the* central datum of theological anthropology" in the thought of Rahner.[51] Freedom, in Rahner's thought, constitutes a necessary parallel to human transcendentality since only in freedom is it possible to 'know' transcendentally and to be able to hear and respond to the message of grace directed toward human transcendentality in God's self-disclosing 'transcendental' communication. Freedom is therefore understood by Rahner precisely as a "transcendental freedom" which is present in the whole range of human experience and which points to the person as a unified whole.[52] According to Rahner the real freedom of human persons is "one freedom because it is a transcendental characteristic of the one subject as such." Hence, inasmuch as "I experience myself as person and as subject, I also experience myself as free, as free in a freedom which does not refer primarily to an individual, isolated psychic occurrence, but in a freedom which refers to the subject as one and as a whole in the unity of its entire actualization of existence."[53]

Upon this basis Rahner attempts a definition of freedom in reference to the human subject as a whole. Freedom, in Rahner's thought, is above all related "to the single whole of human existence" even though the existence of this whole is not restricted to a single spatial or temporal point but is spread over time and space. Freedom is additionally the responsibility of this unified subject for him or herself. Rahner defines freedom, therefore, as "the capacity of the one subject to decide about himself in his single totality."[54] Freedom must always concern the person "as such and as a whole" since the object of freedom is "the subject himself, and all decisions about objects in his experience of the world around him are objects of freedom only insofar as they mediate this finite subject in time and space to himself." Therefore freedom, properly understood, is seen not as the power or ability to decide to do one thing or anther but rather as "the power to decide about oneself and to actualize oneself."[55]

Rahner wishes to avoid a Gnostic understanding of freedom by grounding this freedom of the subject toward his or her own self in its historical

---

[50] Rahner, "Exkurs: Erbsünde und Monogenismus," in: Karl-Heinz Weger, *Theologie der Erbsünde*, QD 44 (Freiburg: Herder, 1969), 221.
[51] Roberts, *The Achievement of Karl Rahner*, 195.
[52] In relation to this point Klaus Fischer, *Der Mensch als Geheimnis: Die Anthropologie Karl Rahners* (Freiburg: Herder, 1974), 150, has pointed out the integral connection that exists within the framework of Rahner's epistemological metaphysics (*Erkenntnismetaphysik*) between freedom and unity of the spirit so that the two concepts can even be viewed as interchangeable.
[53] *FCF*, 37f. [*Grundkurs*, 48f.]
[54] *Ibid.*, 94. [101.]
[55] *Ibid.*, 38. [49.] Pannenberg, *Anthropology in Theological Perspective*, 115, has pointed out that this connection which Rahner draws between freedom and selfhood means that the so-called 'freedom of indifference' which is neutral in regard to the various possible objects of choice is rejected by Rahner.

concreteness. Hence, "freedom is freedom in and through history and in time and space" and only in this way is it "the freedom of the subject in relation to himself."[56] Indeed, the historicalness of the human person, as Rahner claimed in *Hearers of the Word*, is dependent upon the freedom of the person. The human person is historical, Rahner contended, to the extent that he or she is free to act, a freedom rooted ultimately in the person's original transcendence toward God, that is to say, in his or her relation to the Absolute. Hence this moment of freedom "belongs essentially to the historicity of man. Genuine historicity is there only where we find the uniqueness and unpredictability of freedom."[57]

Yet even though freedom exists in time and history it has, according to Rahner, a single, unique function, namely, "the self-actualization of the single subject himself."[58] Freedom, therefore, in Rahner's thought is essential to being human, or, in Rahner's terms, it is an existential of the person.[59] Freedom and its concrete actualization are integral components of the person's "absolute dignity before God and in the community of other persons." As such freedom, which is actualized in the concrete ability to decide, has a higher value to the person as person than any material security that determines the physical existence as such.[60]

Freedom, in Rahner's thought, appears to begin and end with the human. Its foundation is human transcendence and its goal is human self-actualization, hence human freedom has the appearance of an absolute autonomy. Yet this fundamental freedom of the hearer is not absolutely autonomous for it itself presupposes the ontologically and temporally prior being and the freedom of God. Klaus Fischer has therefore correctly noted in regard to Rahner's anthropology, "that the spirit of human beings can only exist in pre-apprehension of their absolute ground, and hence their freedom cannot be original, but can only 'in comprehension' arise from this source."[61] For Rahner, the circle of grace is complete since the freedom of the hearer, which is a necessary pre-condition for hearing or experiencing the grace of God, is itself only possible because of the preceding grace of God. Hence Rahner contends that the self-constitution of the hearer as the concretely free act of humans in all their autonomy remains "subject to the free grace of God. Thus the actually accomplished constitution of the condition of the hearing of theology was itself a free act of God before it was man's."[62]

This human freedom, even though it is a freedom dependent upon the prior freedom of God, implies necessarily and inescapably human responsibility.[63]

---

[56] *Ibid.*, 95. [102.]
[57] *Hearers*, 133. [*HdW*, 165.]
[58] *FCF*, 95. [*Grundkurs*, 102.]
[59] Cf. also in this regard Ignacy Bokwa, 83f.
[60] "The Dignity and Freedom of Man," 247, 249. ["Würde und Freiheit des Menschen," 261,263.]
[61] Fischer, 164.; Cf. also Bokwa, 84ff.
[62] *Hearers*, 174. [*HdW*, 214.]
[63] Cf. Brian McDermott, "The Bonds of Freedom," in: *A World of Grace*, 52f., who characterizes Rahner's view as being primarily that of "responsible freedom."

Hence Rahner seldom discusses human freedom without at the same time treating human responsibility, both of which, according to Rahner, "belong to the existentials of human existence."[64] Human responsibility is ultimately manifested in human freedom as it is actualized in a free and absolute 'yes' or 'no' to God.[65] Human freedom, if it is real freedom, must be "a freedom which decides about God and with respect to God himself." Already in a 1952 lecture Rahner emphasized that to the extent that, on the basis of the "necessary relation of the spirit to the absolute which supports freedom, freedom is in the last analysis the possibility, through and beyond the finite, of taking up a position towards God himself."[66] For Rahner, therefore, the ultimate responsibility and risk of human freedom is to be found in the ability to say an absolute 'yes' or 'no' to the transcendent ground of our being, and thereby also and at the same time a 'yes' or 'no' to our own self. Freedom, according to Rahner, is the freedom to say 'yes' or 'no' to God, "and therein and thereby is it freedom in relation to oneself. ... As a being of freedom, therefore, man can deny himself in such a way that he really and truly says 'no' to God himself."[67] Thus there is a "dark possibility" inherent within human freedom that a person says an absolute final 'no' to his or her own self and, unavoidably and at the same time, to God as the transcendental ground of human *being*.[68]

### 3.1.2.4 *The historicalness of the hearer and the unity of humanity*

As we have seen above, the freedom of the human subject is only possible within the concrete reality of history. Despite, therefore, the strong existential, transcendental orientation of Rahner's anthropology, the historicalness of humans as hearers of the word, especially in the later Rahner, is also emphasized.[69] As Rahner himself has written, "man as a personal being of transcendence and of freedom is also and at the same time a being in the world, in time and in history."[70] Even in Rahner's earlier work the historicalness of the hearer of the

---

[64] *FCF*, 93 [*Grundkurs*, 101], and for the following quote, 98 [105].
[65] Cf. also in this regard Rahner, "Sündenlehre," in: *Herders theologisches Taschenlexikon*, 7:168f.
[66] "The Dignity and Freedom of Man," 246. ["Würde und Freiheit des Menschen," 259.]
[67] *FCF*., 100f. [*Grundkurs*, 107f.]
[68] Cf. McDermott, 54ff.
[69] Johann Baptist Metz, *Faith in History and Society*, 65, summarizes Rahner's transcendental theology as follows: "Man exists as an anticipation of God and this anticipation conditions the possibility of his knowledge and his behaviour." Metz asks, then, whether "this anticipation itself has anything to do with history, in other words, whether the anticipation has temporal structures." For Metz the answer to this question is clearly 'no' since the concept of experience as found in transcendental anthropology does not have the structure of historical experience - at least as judged by the criteria of Metz's own political-theological conception of history. Similarly, Pannenberg contends that "Rahners 'transzendentale' Anthropologie [überspringt] die konkrete Geschichte des Menschen, um unmittelbar das Resultat dieser Geschichte als Bestandteil einer zeitlos allgemein zu denkenden Struktur des Menschseins zu verankern." (Pannenberg, "Weltgeschichte und Heilsgeschichte," 357, note 18.)
[70] *FCF*, 40. [*Grundkurs*, 51.]

word plays an important role in his understanding of the human person. In *Hearers of the Word* Rahner grounds the spatiality and temporality of humans upon their materialness. Thus the "concept of *materia* ... is the cause of *space* and *time*" ... of an existent being. He concludes, therefore, that "in terms of his nature a man exists is time and space."[71]

From this historical being in space-time which is based upon the material nature of humans Rahner draws an important point concerning the unity of humans within their historicalness. The *materia* of humans "is the cause of the actual repeatability of the same thing." The human person in "repeatable" or "reproducible" so that the individual person must be understood as one among many, as fundamentally one member of an entire race. Rahner does not attempt to demonstrate this point biologically but metaphysically on the basis of the *a priori* and metaphysical insight, that "man, in virtue of his essential constitution as a material essence in its '*quidditas*,' is repeatable" and that there can therefore be a plurality of persons.[72] In examining the temporality of a material being, Rahner contends, it is to be seen that a single material being "is never able all at once to realize the never-ending extent of the possibilities which lie enclosed within its materiality." This leads him to conclude that a single individual "is never able, totally, to realize the possibilities that are proper to him by reason of his material essence as a particular individual." This means, then, that the individual can only realize his or her possibilities as a material being as part of a total humanity, and only when the individual's possibilities are realizable is the individual real. The dependence of the individual upon the entire race of humans points, according to Rahner, not to the insignificance of the individual, but rather to "the existence of a human race which can manifest only in its totality the essence that is granted to each individual man in the foundation of his potentialities as such." Hence, the individual person "is real only as a part of humanity." What does it mean, then, for the human person to be a historical being in time and space? Rahner writes:

> Man is not merely set within a space-time world as an adjunct to his essential constitution, ... [rather,] space-time is his interior specific constitution. Because *materia* is his essential element, space and time arise out of himself as interior factors of his existence. If we say that man is essentially one of many of the same kind with whom he is thrown together in time and space by reason of his interior essence, then we are saying only that he is historical in the concrete sense of *human* history.[73]

---

[71] *Hearers*, 130, 132. [*HdW*, 161, 163.] It should be noted, however, that Rahner, at the same time, also founded human historicalness upon the spiritual essence of the human. Thus he writes: "Man is an historical being precisely as spirit, so that he is obliged to depend upon his history not only by virtue of his biological existence, but also as the foundation of his spiritual existence." (*Ibid.* 16. [30]).

[72] *Ibid.* 132. [163.]

[73] *Ibid.*, 132f. [164f.]

From the historicalness of the "hearing of the Word" Rahner is able to point to "the historicalness of persons themselves ... their belonging to an environment, their corporeal nature, and the race of a single humanity in which they stand" as a necessary aspect of the person's being in history.[74] Once again, therefore, Rahner's analysis of the essential qualities of the human being as hearer of the word of God point not to isolated, individual hearers but to the unity of humanity which as a unified whole constitutes the *potentia oboedientialis* for God's self-revelation.

### 3.1.2.5 *Creatureliness and the openness to God*

The hearer of the word of God must stand in relationship to this God in order to be in a position to hear the message of his self-revelation. Rahner chooses human creatureliness as the main model for comprehending this relationship of the human hearer of the word to God. Bound with his emphasis upon human transcendentality Rahner contends that the individual only recognizes his or her relationship to God through the transcendental experience of his or her own creatureliness. Thus to understand what is meant by "creatureliness as a person's fundamental relationship to God" Rahner begins with the transcendental experience of creatureliness, which is "the place where we have the basic and original experience of creatureliness ... in which the subject along with his time itself is experienced as being borne by an incomprehensible ground."[75] The human person, according to Rahner, as a spiritual person "implicitly affirms absolute being as the real ground of every act of knowledge and of every action, and affirms it as mystery. This absolute, incomprehensible reality, which is always the ontologically silent horizon of every intellectual and spiritual encounter with realities, is therefore always infinitely different from the knowing subject."[76] That is to say, it is in the transcendental experience of our own creatureliness and finiteness that we recognize God in his infinity and wholly otherness.

Our creatureliness, however, points not only to God's infinity and wholly otherness but also to our radical dependence upon God. As human beings we are part of the created world and are therefore creatures because our being is dependent upon God's free act of creation and continuing sustenance. Our very difference from God points to our dependence upon God, which may seem unusual to us since in our human experience the more something is dependent upon us the more it resembles us. But the inverse is true in regard to God and his creatures. Therefore we and the other existents of our world not only exist in reality but "are different from God not in spite of, but because we are established in being by God." In God's act of creation the other is created precisely as other

---

[74] "Theologische Anthropologie," 625.
[75] *FCF.*, 79f. [*Grundkurs*, 87.]
[76] *Ibid.*, 77. [85.]

and thus remains created being while at the same time also being set free in its own autonomy - but always an autonomy which is dependent and not absolute.[77]

A further point drawn by Rahner from the fact of human creatureliness concerns the nature of the world in which human hearers find themselves. This world, according to Rahner, is a world that is demythologized and denuminized in Christian thought precisely because it, like the hearers of the word, is created being. This insight is decisive for Rahner's understanding of existence in the world. Inasmuch as the world, created by God in freedom, has its origin in God, it is not itself God. "It is seen correctly, therefore, not as 'holy nature,' but as the material for the creative power of man." Therefore human persons experience their creatureliness and encounter God with this creatureliness within their own selves and within the world as they know it and in "the unlimited openness" of their own spirit.[78] An openness which orients the human subject ultimately toward God and is thus also and especially an openness to God.

Openness to God has been called "the key concept of Rahner's anthropology."[79] It is to be seen not just in human creatureliness but perhaps most clearly here through the help of the transcendental experience of this creatureliness which points us ultimately toward God as the ground of our being. As we shall see later in this chapter an important parallel is to be seen here with the thought of Pannenberg, who holds that world openness (cf. 'creatureliness') points to human self-transcendence that reveals an openness to God.

Louis Roberts, in summarizing what the person is in Rahner's thought, reiterates not only many of the essential points which we have covered in the preceding sections but also points to the inherent openness of humans as creatures to God and to God in Christ. In Rahner's anthropology the human being, as the creature of God, is spirit. This means that "he is freedom; he is individual; he is dependent on a community; he is a person in the world. Man is a corporeal-material living being, a spiritual, personal, religious, God- and Christ-centered being. He is God-centered by nature and grace and he is Christ-centered because his being has an ontic and spiritual-personal capacity for communicating with Christ."[80] In Rahner's thought, the God-openness of humanity is at the same time a Christ-openness.

### 3.1.3 Monogenism and original sin

*3.1.3.1 Monogenism and the unity of the human race*
Monogenism, as Rahner straightforwardly defines it, "is the doctrine which affirms that the whole of mankind, at least those who lived after original sin, stem

---
[77] *Ibid.*, 78f. [86f.]
[78] *Ibid.*, 80f. [88.]
[79] So Bokwa, 353.
[80] Roberts, 185f.

biologically from one single pair of ancestors."[81] The defense of monogenism, overlooked by most dogmaticians today, has been taken up by Rahner. At stake for Rahner is not simply the rejection of a polygenism in which humanity is viewed to have several biological "parents," but more importantly the unity of the human race. One theological problem at stake is whether "the dogma of original sin necessarily implies monogenism." The answer for Rahner is "no," for humanity would be a unity even without the doctrine of monogenism. The unity of humanity, according to Rahner, would be maintained even without a doctrine of monogenism since this unity is also and more fundamentally grounded upon [1] humanity's origin in the one God with his one plan for the history of humanity and his universal offer of salvation through which all individual humans are already members of a humanity before God; [2] through the common essence or being; [3] through the factual interdependence of all individuals in the one space-time history; [4] through the real relationship of all persons to the one Christ; [5] through the common goal in the kingdom of God.[82]

Yet despite this multifaceted foundation of human corporeal unity Rahner does not abandon the question of monogenism as irrelevant. The actual context in which Rahner worked out his views on monogenism was that provided by the papal encyclical *Humani Generis* which seems to rule out the defense of polygenism even as a scientific hypothesis. Yet *Humani Generis* does not give a theological definition of monogenism, but instead claims only that it is theologically certain.[83] Rahner, then, takes up the task of a theological definition of monogenism, seeking to describe both what the doctrine does and does not teach.

The doctrine of monogenism, as we have already seen and as Rahner himself often reiterates, is not necessitated by the doctrine of original sin. Neither does monogenism rule out the possibility of a moderate theory of evolution within the human species since both theories (monogenism and anthropological evolution) are grounded in the single common principle of the transcendent, divine causality.[84] Monogenism, however, is necessary in Rahner's view for a conception of the unity of humanity both in perdition and in salvation. A universal perdition, according to Rahner, is only possible when it is based upon the unity of the human race and has its foundation at the very beginning of humanity, "for a

---

[81] Rahner, "Monogenism," in: *Sacramentum Mundi*, 4:105. [*SM* 3:594.] For a discussion of monogenism from a biological and theological perspective and with reference to Rahner's position see Paul Overhage, *Das Problem der Hominisation*, *QD* 13: 179ff.

[82] Ibid., 106. [596f].

[83] Cf. Roberts, 200f.; and Rahner, "Theological Reflections on Monogenism," in: *TI* 1:231ff. ["Theologisches zum Monogenismus," in: *Schriften* 1:255ff.] Cf. *Humani generis* (1950), in: Denzinger 3897, where we read: "*Cum vero de alia coniecturali opinione agitur, videlicet de polygenismo, quem vocant, tum Ecclesiae filii eiusmodi libertate minime fruuntur. Non enim christifideles eam sententiam amplecti possunt, ...*"

[84] Cf. Theological Reflections on Monogenism," 296. [*Schriften*, 1:322]. Cf. also Rahner, *Die Hominisation als theologische Frage*, *QD* 12.

situation of *damnation* can only be brought about by one who himself belongs totally to this temporal history."[85] The situation is similar regarding the solidarity of humanity in salvation which is based upon Christ as head of this humanity. Rahner writes:

> The fact of the redemption of *all* men by the *one* Christ from whom we are not physically descended in no way shows that an individual and his action for others can be morally significant before God independently of whether he stands with regard to the others in an ontologically real relationship of membership or not. For the question is precisely whether Christ can only be Head and Mediator of humanity because and only because he is a member of a humanity monogenistically one from its origin.[86]

The biblical evidence, according to Rahner, shows that the unity of the community of the redeemed is not simply a juridical or factual coming together of isolated individuals of various origins but is rather a racial community of a single humanity. "Because and in so far as Christ entered into this community by being 'born of woman' (Gal. 4:4) he is solidary with men and they with him." Even the geneological list of Luke 3 which traces Jesus' geneology back to Adam is brought forward by Rahner as testimony to the significance of Jesus' entering into the one human race.[87]

Rahner concludes his treatment of monogenism with the presentation of a possible metaphysical proof. Rahner assumes first of all that neither monogenism nor polygenism can be empirically proven. At the same time, however, he does not wish to rely only on a few Bible texts for the support of monogenism since this would seem to take the question completely out of the realm of natural knowledge and lead to a theological positivism which Rahner holds to be dangerous. The question is therefore asked whether and to what extent monogenism is philosophically demonstrable.[88]

Rahner develops a metaphysic of generation along the following lines: The human person is inseparable spirit and body so that the person's spiritual being can only be realized through his or her corporeality.[89] The personal spirit which is dependent upon body cannot exist by itself as absolute "alone" spirit since such aloneness, if it were possible, would be "hell." When, therefore, the assumption is correct that humans are bound to the world in that their spirit can exist only as personal spirit when they are also corporeal beings, then Rahner argues that the human person as corporeal spirit exists necessarily in dependence upon a relationship with another "you" which is also present in its own boundness to space-time. Thus "it is not only as an isolated person but also as isolated *man* that

---

[85] *Ibid.*, 281. [307.]
[86] *Ibid.*, 274. [299f.]
[87] *Ibid.*, 276f. [302f.]
[88] *Ibid.*, 286. [311f.]
[89] On the spirit/matter unity in the human cf. also *Die Hominisation als theologische Frage*, 49ff.

an individual man is incapable of perfection - or is Hell." That this is the case, he contends, is supported even by the tendency of modern physics which shows that every material being is co-determined through the whole of material reality.[90]

The concrete possibility of the individual as living, personal spirit occurs with the first living being of its kind. Yet "this is not merely the first instance of a purely ideal multitude which arises by the emergence ... of the individuals; it is the institution of the totality in its origin." Thus according to Rahner, "the real dependence of the individual spatio-temporal living thing upon the totality of its form of life reaches its real completion and concrete manifestation in generation." Generation must then be understood transcendentally as the only possible origin of the individual within its kind. The implication of this line of argumentation for the monogenism/polygenism question is drawn clearly by Rahner. He writes:

> Generation is the one necessary way of forming community; where the human species has already been instituted in its origin, no other way of man's spatio-temporal extension in community than that of generation is possible. The institution of a new origin would be the institution of another species. Monogenism and the unity of species allow of being distinguished conceptually but not of being separated in reality. Conversely, wherever 'polygenistic' phenomena are really to be found, what we are in presence of is the genesis of a metaphysically new species, not the multiple original coming to be of the same one; or (if this is not the case) not the genesis of a new species in the metaphysical sense but merely accidental spatio-temporal variations of the same species.[91]

One might expect here the objection that a single procreating pair would be required every time a new species appeared in the plant or animal world. As Paul Overhage points out, however, one cannot object to Rahner's metaphysical argument for monogenism, "that, if it is true, then also in the plant and animal world the first appearance of a new species must occur in a single, procreating pair. Where a new species appears in several specimens that are independent of one another, then it is not a genuinely metaphysical new species."[92] This is the case, as Rahner himself has explained, because

> a new 'entelechy' or 'form' of an essentially diverse species ... does not arise in several mutually independent instances. ... But in regard to the animal kingdom man is a metaphysically new, essentially diverse species. ... Thus while it is entirely conceivable that biological development in the animal kingdom reached so advanced a stage of development in a number of exemplars that the transcendent miracle of 'becoming man' could take place in them, this miracle took place only once, because it should and could unfold itself by self-

---

[90] "Theological Reflections on Monogenism," 287f. [*Schriften* 1:312f.]
[91] *Ibid.*, 288f. [314f.]
[92] Paul Overhage, *Das Problem der Hominisation*, 187.

multiplication, did not come to pass more than once, if indeed genuine creation was not to become a cosmic spectacle.[93]

The logical assumptions necessitated by Rahner's argumentation, especially concerning the corporeal dependence of personal spirit and consequent dependence upon others of its kind make Rahner's metaphysical argument for monogenism less than compelling. Indeed, Rahner himself noted some 15 years after publication of his article that his attempted metaphysical proof of monogenism "has found little acceptance."[94] It should be pointed out, however, that Rahner intended only to demonstrate the possibility of such an argument. His thoughts on the metaphysical necessity of monogenistic generation do indeed point to the importance of the doctrine for his anthropology.

Monogenism is more than a convenient illustration of the unity of humanity, rather, it is necessitated metaphysically by the nature of human spirit itself. Monogenism, therefore, points not only to the solidarity of the human race, but the very experience of this solidarity (or unity) as detected by Rahner in his philosophical-anthropological inquiry into the nature of human spirit points back to a metaphysically necessary common origin of the human species. Rahner's arguments regarding monogenism and the unity of humanity, therefore, may not be apologetically compelling to all but they do point to a consistency within his anthropology which itself strengthens the appeal of his position.

### 3.1.3.2 *The universality of freedom and "original sin"*

The doctrine of monogenism, although accepted by Rahner, is not bound inextricably with the doctrine of original sin in his thought.[95] Rahner is not willing to stake the doctrine of original sin and what is therewith implied upon a doctrine of monogenism, especially in a day when evolutionary views have led many to advocate a doctrine of polygenism.[96] As far as the doctrine of original sin is concerned, it is not of decisive importance whether humanity arises from a single original pair, or out of a "'population' more widely extended in terms of space and

---

[93] "Theological Reflections on Monogenism," 294f. [*Schriften* 1:320f.]

[94] "Exkurs: Erbsünde und Monogenismus," 182f. Rahner further wrote: "Mein Versuch kommt mir auch heute noch nicht dumm vor. Aber er leidet an der Problematik, daß man nur dann *sicher* sagen könnte, die schöpferische Tätigkeit Gottes bei der Hominisation werde im Polygenismus aus einer transzendentalen zu einer kategorialen und so falsch mirakulösen Tätigkeit, wenn bewiesen ist, daß ein einziges Menschenpaar am Anfang nicht nur abstrakt, sondern konkret für Erhaltung und Wachstum der Menschheit ausreicht, Gott also nicht durch sich selbst tun müsse, was der Mensch selbst tun kann. Der polygenistische Evolutionist, der diese konkrete Möglichkeit bestreitet, wird also durch mein Argument von Monogenismus nicht überzeugt sein."

[95] This is in apparent contradiction to the position stated in *Humani generis*, Denzinger 3897, which contends that the view that humanity arose from a multiplicity of parents (polygenism) is irreconcilable with biblical statements and official teaching of the Roman Church on original sin.

[96] Cf., for example, Piet Schoonenberg, "Der Mensch in der Sünde," in: *Mysterium Salutis* II, ed. J. Feiner and M. Lohrer, 931; and Schoonenberg, *Original Sin*, trans. J. Donceel (Notre Dame: University of Notre Dame Press, 1965), 150ff.

time which emerged from the animal kingdom and in which the historical origins of the human race as a single entity are to be located."[97] More important for Rahner as fundament for an understanding of original sin than a strict doctrine of monogenism is what he calls a "formal philosophy and formal theology of the *beginning.*" In Rahner's version of a formal theology of the beginning protology and eschatology (especially that of the beginning and end of humanity) are seen as belonging together and influencing/determining the present which is the context of human freedom.

For Rahner, then, it is freedom, caught up in the tension between protology and eschatology, which is the decisive characteristic of humanity and of the origin of humanity. He contends that the beginning is constituted "as now in force in virtue of that original stage which is prior to our own freedom and hidden from us, *and at the same time* in virtue of the event in which freedom was first exercised." This freedom is different in kind from the creaturely freedom which we now experience which handles situations co-determined by that which is original so that we can no longer act according to its luminous essence but must seek this essence in the future - thus "pursuing protology in eschatology." What this formal theology of the beginning means in concrete terms for Rahner is that:

> For an anthropology that is existential-ontological in character, and especially one that is theological, 'beginning' is from the outset not the first moment in a whole series of moments following one upon another, but rather the basis, of its very nature unique, on which the whole of history rests, a basis which, in virtue of the fact that it has been posited by God himself, and of the uniqueness of the free act which educed it from sheer ultimacy, is itself *sui generis.*[98]

The beginning of humanity is therefore not understood as the first in a series of sequential events (as implied by a strict doctrine of monogenism), but rather as the single and unique foundation of the whole of human history which Rahner locates primarily within the absolute originalness of the act of freedom. Or, put differently, the beginning of humanity is characterized by an original freedom which was given in humanity and which was not yet co-determined through a human decision of freedom.[99] When this point is not taken note of, according to Rahner, the doctrine of original sin becomes either a bare mythology or it is rationalized and equated with some "first sin" in a sequence of similar sins. Original sin in reality, however, belongs in Rahner's view "to the initial constitution of that ultimate beginning which is withdrawn from us and never recurs, and the true nature of which is only gradually revealed in the light of the future which is Christ."[100] Original sin, in Christ's concrete order of salvation, is

---
[97] Rahner, "The Sin of Adam," in: *TI* 11:252f. ["Die Sünde Adams," in: *Schriften* 9:264.]
[98] *Ibid.*, 254. [265f.]
[99] *Ibid.*, 260f. [273.]
[100] *Ibid.*, 254. [266.]

always a dialectical moment of the effective salvific will of God who always mediates through Christ the grace that was not mediated through Adam. Therefore original sin and grace, to the extent that each precedes the personal decision of the human person, do not stand in chronological relationship to one another but form together the dialectical situation of humanity to the extent that we are determined not only from the beginning (original sin) but also from Christ as our end and goal.[101]

Concerning the solidarity and unity of humanity usually seen in a doctrine of original sin Rahner focuses not so much on a solidarity in sin or guilt (especially not the early Rahner) but rather on a solidarity in receptivity for God's grace. The crucial point he takes from Romans 5 is not the focus upon the universality of perdition wrought through Adam and original sin but the fact that original sin must not be understood as being more universal than the redemption wrought through Christ. For Rahner, original sin finds its primary significance in the role it plays in God's plan of salvation. Original sin and redemption, according to Rahner, are two existentials of the human salvific situation which always determine our human *Dasein*. Original sin, therefore, "was only permitted by God within the domain of his unconditional and stronger salvific will, which from the very beginning was directed towards God's self-communication in Christ."[102]

Although Rahner stresses the unity and solidarity of humanity he does not view the biological/genetic solidarity of humanity as ground for the grace of God directed toward the individual. "For the individual man his derivation from, and thereby his union with the single human race is neither the basis nor, in any direct sense, the medium of his justification and sanctification." On the other hand, Rahner contends that, according to God's will, "the descent of the individual man from the single human race and its divinely ordained beginning *had* to be if not the basis, then at least the direct medium, in which that justifying holiness of man was communicated to him ... and therefore has the force of an existential modality ... because this holiness was intended as a gift to, and claim upon, humanity as a whole by the Creator of mankind."[103]

For Rahner, therefore, our common 'origin' in Adam means that the salvation-historical solidarity of humanity is the fundamental presupposition for the doctrine of the "universality of salvation as one and the same for all" and for "the doctrine of the redemption of all through Christ" so that already a solidarity in salvation and salvation history implies that one is intended to receive salvation, "in virtue of the fact that [one] ... is a member of this human race." Only secondarily does Rahner also refer to the sinfulness of humanity implied in our origin in Adam which is also a presupposition of God's grace which is shown to sinners and not to those who have no guilt before God.[104] We detect then here already a tendency in

---
[101] *Ibid.*, 258f. [270f.]
[102] Rahner, "Original Sin," in: *Sacramentum Mundi* 4:330. ["Erbsünde," in: *SM*, 1:1109.]
[103] "The Sin of Adam," 255f. [*Schriften* 9:267f.]
[104] *Ibid.*, 259. [271f.]

Rahner toward an anthropo-optimism in which the solidarity of humanity is not seen primarily (and in a strict sense perhaps not at all) in original sin but rather in God's grace, which for Rahner is the fundamental point to be taken from Adam's sin.

The question that remains, then, is what precisely Rahner understands, in this light, under the concept of original sin. The suspicion that Rahner has difficulty with the traditional understanding of original sin[105] would seem to be confirmed when he moves on from the conclusions to be drawn about the receptiveness of humans to God's grace to the actual substance and meaning of original sin.[106] Original sin, in Rahner's thought, has a merely analogical character in comparison to the guilt that comes from individual sins. According to Rahner, "that state of analogous guilt which is called original sin is not a projection of the personal state of guilt 'of Adam' to us, but is constituted by the absence of the holy Pneuma, ... the absence of which correspondingly, prior to any personal decision, constitutes an analogous state of guilt, seeing that this deficiency consists not merely in the fact that the holy Pneuma is not present, but implies a deficiency which is the opposite of the situation which *ought* to exist."[107] As Roberts has explained, this view implies that for Rahner "original sin is the absence of that supernatural elevation planned originally for man" which produces a situation of incompleteness dividing God and humanity. Yet because this situation does not constitute real, actual sin, it can only be understood analogously as original sin.[108]

Rahner delineates at least three differences between the analogical character of original sin and the personal guilt of actual sins.[109] (1) The personal guilt (of Adam) which stands at the beginning of human history does not constitute the condition of guilt of original sin as if the guilt of the first actual sin were passed on through successive generations. As Rahner elsewhere explained, "the notion that the personal deed of 'Adam' or of the first group of people is imputed to us in such a way that it has been transmitted on to us biologically, as it were, has absolutely nothing to do with the Christian dogma of original sin."[110] (2) "The deficiency [of

---

[105] Johann Adam Möhler, *Symbolism or the Exposition of Doctrinal Differences between Catholics and Protestants as Evidenced by their Symbolical Writings*, trans. James Robertson (London: Gibbings & Co., 1894), 47, summarizes the Roman Catholic doctrine of original sin, as found in the symbolic statements of the Roman church, as follows: "Adam, by sin, lost his original justice and holiness, drew down on himself by his disobedience the displeasure and the judgments of the Almighty, incurred the penalty of death, and thus, in all his parts, in his body as well as soul, became strangely deteriorated. This ... condition is transmitted to all his posterity, ... entailing the consequence that man is of himself incapable ... to act in a manner agreeable to God, or in any other way to be justified before him ..."

[106] Indeed, Pannenberg comments that Rahner (along with the Roman Catholic theologian Piet Schoonenberg) is looking "for something to replace the idea of 'original sin'" in his theology. (Cf. Pannenberg, *ATP*, 281, note 111. [273, note 111.])

[107] "The Sin of Adam," 257. [*Schriften* 9:269.]

[108] Roberts, 207.

[109] For this and the following see "The Sin of Adam," 258. [*Schriften* 9:270.]

[110] *FCF*, 110. [*Grundkurs*, 116f.]

grace] which inhibits a state which 'ought to exist' inhibits ... not that which, in accordance with the moral demands of God, should be brought about by the individual as such in his own capacity for free decision. ... Rather this state which ought to be, and to which the deficiency of which we are speaking is opposed, is that which is constituted by the will of the Creator as such in his will to endow humanity with grace." (3) The idea of original sin, because it is to be understood analogically, has nothing to do with a so-called collective guilt which assumes that the personal guilt of an individual or individuals is passed on to others.

Less than ten years later, however, there is no mention of the analogical character of original sin in his treatment of the doctrine in *Foundations of Christian Faith*. Here Rahner unfolds instead a doctrine of original sin which sounds very much like a theory of social influence in which original sin is located in the shared sinful context of humanity.[111] Human freedom in the world means that individuals exercise their freedom in a situation which they find prior to themselves and which is imposed upon them. For the individual it means that "he actualizes himself as a free subject in a situation which itself is always determined by history and by other persons. ... Consequently, the guilt of others is a permanent factor in the situation and realm of the individual's freedom."[112] Rahner connects this idea to the doctrine of original sin by pointing out that such a "universal, permanent and ineradicable co-determination of the situation of every individual's freedom by guilt ... is conceivable only if this ineradicable co-determination of the situation of freedom by guilt is also *original*," that is, is already imbedded in the origin of human history. Since this, according to Rahner, is the case, then one can conclude that the universal and ineradicable nature of the co-determination of the human context of freedom by guilt in the single (universal) history of humanity "implies an original determination of this human situation by guilt already present at the beginning." That is to say, "it implies an 'original sin.'" This original sin, however, is not something which is either transmitted or transmittable to successive generations. Original sin, in Rahner's view, is much more "the stamp of guilt of others" which our own freedom bears and cannot eradicate since it has been present ever since the very beginning of the history of our freedom. Thus original sin is viewed by Rahner primarily as a context of guilt which co-determines the freedom of each individual person and which is embedded in universal human history at its very point of origin.[113]

Because 'original sin' is embedded at the very beginning of the single history of humanity it has universal implications for Rahner's anthropology, even if its hardness would seem somewhat softened by Rahner's understanding of it as analogical or as a mere context of guilt in comparison to the more traditional 'traducian' theory of biological/genetic transmission of actual guilt. First of all,

---

[111] Cf. Pannenberg, *ATP*, 127 [124], who makes a similar assessment of Rahner's view, comparing it with the social context character of original sin found within Ritschl's concept of a kingdom of sin.
[112] *FCF*, 107. [*Grundkurs*, 113.]
[113] *Ibid.*, 110f. [116f.]

original sin is understood universally in that it means that every person's situation is determined by the guilt which is embedded in the history of the human race. Hence all persons share a common context of sin and guilt. Second, sin, which Rahner defines as the "actualization of transcendental freedom in rejection of God," is unavoidably actualized, i.e., committed by all persons because of our common context of freedom co-determined by guilt. The experience of actual sin and personal guilt, therefore, is universal. Third, and most important, because of the universality of 'original sin' God's self-communication comes to all persons in their context of guilt but not through 'Adam,' who stands at the beginning of human history, but through Jesus Christ, who is the goal of human history.[114]

The circle of human unity is thus complete, having begun in the protology of the human race, and in a qualified sense witnessed to by monogenism, then manifesting itself in the universal context of guilt we call original sin, and finally expressing itself in God's salvific will directed to all persons through Jesus Christ. As Rahner himself summarized in an earlier work, the unity of humanity, which is not merely a collection of the many individual humans but a genuine and real unity, "is manifested in the monogenetic descent of all men from the one Adam, is raised to a supernatural destiny, and unfolds in original sin and the one history of the human race in salvation and perdition." This unity is then elevated and confirmed once and for all in the incarnation of the divine Logos.[115]

### 3.1.4 Karl Rahner's Anthropo-optimism: A Protestant Critique

The most fundamental presupposition upon which the theology of Rahner is built is that human beings are hearers of a potential word of God who are capable, in their freedom, to hear and respond to the grace-bearing, revelatory word of God.[116] This emphasis upon human freedom and ability to hear and choose on the basis of the light within each person in his or her own transcendentality expresses an optimism about humanity that has stronger roots in philosophical anthropology than in the biblical and theological (especially Augustinian) theological tradition. Indeed, Rahner's anthropology, which goes beyond Thomas on this point, has even been called semi-Pelagian.[117] Is such a label, or accusation, however, just?

---

[114] Cf. *ibid.*, 113ff. [119ff.]
[115] Rahner, *The Church and the Sacraments* (New York, 1963), 12. [*Kirche und Sakramente*, QD 10 (Freiburg: Herder, 1960), 12.]
[116] Cf. Carr, "Starting with the Human," 19.
[117] Cf., for instance, George Lindbeck, "The Thought of Karl Rahner, S.J.," in: *Christianity and Crisis* 25 (18 October 1965), 211. Eugen Drewermann has even put forward the radical theis that Rahner's anthropology is at root gnostic. He sees this especially in the idea that humans, through their transcendental awareness of their finiteness, can know the infinite God who thereby appears to become a mere function of the human intellect. This in turn would seem to point toward an anthropo-optimism that is implicitly gnostic. Drewermann, who feels the gnostic element inherent in Rahner's theology should be recovered for modern Christianity, has written of Rahner's epistemological metaphysics, which is built upon a specific, existential anthropology: "Der Mensch ist das Wesen, dem es in allem Erkennen des Endlichen letztlich um das Erkennen Gottes geht, da er, als selber Unendlicher, nur von Gott, dem Unendlichen, her wahrhaftig zu sich

The label of semi-Pelagianism must be understood (at least inasmuch as it has come from the Protestant side), from the perspective of Protestant theology whose view of humanity is strongly rooted in the biblical and Augustinian theological tradition as opposed to Rahner's rootedness within the Aristotelian and Thomistic philosophical tradition and the existential thought of Martin Heidegger. Indeed, since Trent the suspicion of semi-Pelagian tendencies in Roman Catholic theology has often been voiced on the part of Protestants.[118] Rahner's specific views on original sin, the connection between sin and death, and his emphasis upon human freedom as the determinative factor in being human, however, would seem to go clearly beyond the role attributed to human freedom and the conception of sin found in the Tridentine documents. In addition to these areas, Rahner's optimistic view of humanity is also to be seen in his ontological anthropology, the transcendentality of humans which enables them to know God apart from the grace of revelation (together with his theory of anonymous Christians), and in his thoughts in regard to the possibility of universal salvation. We would suggest, however, that it is more fruitful to speak of Rahner's position as 'anthropo-optimistic' since it identifies more clearly the character of his anthropology while avoiding the rhetoric of accusation.

Rahner's anthropo-optimism comes perhaps no place more clearly to the fore than in his interpretation of original sin as the ineradicable and universal context of humans in which their situation of freedom is co-determined by guilt. Pannenberg objects to Rahner's view of original sin as not taking seriously enough human perdition and our bondage to evil which is not social but has to do with our very nature as human beings. Pannenberg believes the same criticisms can be leveled against Rahner's view as against Albrecht Ritschl's on the Protestant side, who took sins and actions rather than sin and the *being* of the person as his starting point. Pannenberg, citing Paul Althaus, contends:

> The whole point of original sin is that 'we become subject to the power of evil in the heart not simply as a result of the laws governing the ongoing historical influence of evil, for example enticement, tradition, environment, and the atmosphere in which we grew up; we are subject to it "before" any of those things enter the picture, and "by nature," that is, simply by our humanity, no matter at what point in human history we are located.' Precisely at this level,

---

selbst kommt. Alle menschliche Kultur- und Geistesgeschichte ist deswegen faktisch immer schon auch Offenbarungs- und Heilsgeschichte Gottes. Schon diese These ... von Rahner ... mußte im folgenden doch provozierend genug wirken: war nicht hier schon die Gefahr aller 'Gnosis' sichtbar, Gott selbst mit dem Menschen zu identifizieren beziehungsweise ihn in eine Funktion des menschlichen Intellekts selbst zu verwandeln?" (Drewermann, *Glauben in Freiheit*, 214). Drewermann further contends that in order to achieve what Rahner ultimately intends with his turn toward anthropology, namely a 'reconciliation' between our speaking about God and our speaking about humans, the apprehension against Gnosis must be overcome (226). But given Drewermann's propensity for idiosyncratic interpretations, we must ask whether Rahner's high estimation of the human ability to know God directly can in any real sense be said to be gnostic.

[118] Cf. Möhler, *Symbolik*, 88f.

antecedently to any and all actions of any individual, there is a corporate will, a 'unity of the human race in its willing,' that precedes the reciprocal historical relationships of individuals. The same point is being made in the Augustinian formula taken over by the Council of Trent, namely, that Adam's sin was transmitted 'by propagation, not by imitation' (*propagatione, non imitatione*).[119]

In rejecting the "Augustinian" conception of the dogma of original sin and adopting a social context approach not dissimilar to that of Ritschl, Rahner seems indeed to have adopted a view in which the radical seriousness of the sinfulness of human nature is replaced by a "context of guilt" which corrupts and leads astray human freedom.[120]

Rahner's anthropo-optimism also shows itself in his approach to death. Rahner rejects the Augustinian view, which has been by and large adopted by Protestant theology, that death is something negative or evil and which is brought about by sin.[121] Instead, Rahner turns to philosophy for the foundation of his theology of death. Following Heidegger he understands death not as the result of sin but as the fulfillment of life.[122] As Pannenberg has noted, "Rahner is of the opinion that because life comes to an end in death, it attains its fulfillment through death."[123] Rahner, in Heideggerian language, speaks of human life as "an existence unto death" which is distinct from the death of an animal because the human "exists always and inescapably confronted with his end, with the totality of his existence, with its temporal end." But death is not just the temporal end of human beings but is their fulfillment since a never ending temporal life would become "madness if it cannot reach fulfillment" in death. Therefore, although such things as love and faithfulness come into being in space and time, they "do not reach fulfillment there" but only in the death of the individual.[124] Rahner even compares his view with that of Buddhism, noting that "Death for the Christian is the event in which his or her one and only life is completed. ... All serious and reasonable persons - even Far Eastern adherents of a belief in the transmigration

---

[119] *ATP*, 127f. [124f.] For Althaus' comments see Althaus, *Die christliche Wahrheit* (1952), 371ff.
[120] For a description of Ritschl's conception of original sin and the 'Pelagian' element inherent within it see Hans Schwarz, *Evil: A Historical and Theological Perspective*, tr. Mark Worthing (Minneapolis: Fortress Press, 1994), 149ff. Schwarz points out that the chief distinction that Ritschl saw between himself and Pelagius is that whereas Pelagius made the individual human will responsible for sin Ritschl makes the corporate human will responsible.
[121] Rahner contends, however, that not even the Christian should deny or conceal "the comfortless absurdity of death." (Rahner, "Ideas for a Theology of Death," in: *TI* 13:179. ["Zu einer Theologie des Todes," in: *Schriften* 10:191.]
[122] Cf. Neuhaus, 83, who observes that the language used by Rahner already in *Hearers of the Word* to speak of the nature of human *Dasein* is terminology which "für Heidegger unlösbar mit der Bestimmung des Daseins als Sein zum Tode verknüpft sind." Drewermann, *Glauben in Freiheit*, 221, similarly notes that Rahner is reliant upon his teacher Heidegger for the equation of finiteness, end, and fulfillment.
[123] *ATP*, 139. [136.]
[124] *FCF*, 270f. [*Grundkurs*, 265f.]

of souls - will hold that one's task is to escape the cycle of birth and death and to complete one's own history of freedom in an ultimate and eternal fulfillment."[125]

In a 1968 speech before a conference of medical doctors who confront on a regular basis the biological death of human beings Rahner put forward a similarly optimistic view of death as the fulfillment of the history of freedom of the individual which brings the individual not into nothingness but before God. Rahner contended that "the death of man consists in the immediate confrontation of man, together with the whole of his history as a free person now consummated and complete, with the absolute mystery, with God." And similarly, that death is the arrival of the human person's "existence as consummated and complete with God." Rahner argues that since death is the culmination or fulfillment of the individual's history of freedom, then death is that "towards which the will of the free person tends at its deepest and most ultimate, because this free person must seek the end of that which merely prolongs itself in time in order to achieve his consummation."[126]

Pannenberg, for good reason, finds Rahner's view that life finds its fulfillment in death dubious, commenting that "death does not bring life to its fulfillment but terminates it and prevents its fulfillment."[127] Indeed, Rahner's view is rooted neither in the biblical nor the theological tradition but would rather seem to find its primary support in the 'pagan' philosophy of Heidegger. The idea that death is in any sense the radical consequence of sin is almost entirely missing from Rahner's later theology. In his 1958 booklet, *On the Theology of Death*, which John Macquarrie has called "a Christian and theological answer to Martin Heidegger's study of death and its significance for human existence,"[128] Rahner emphasized the connection between sin and death, noting that humans die as a consequence of sin and do not just reach fulfilment. He concluded at that time that the human person "dies a death which is obscure and hidden in character, which overwhelms him from without and dispossesses him utterly, ... a death which even now really ought not to be. He is experiencing a death, the darkness of which is an expression and consequence and punishment of the perdition which ensues for him from Adam's sin." And similarly, he maintained that "death is primarily an expression and manifestation of the essence of sin in the bodily constitution of

---

[125] Rahner, "Death as Fulfillment," in: *Karl Rahner in Dialogue*," 238. ["Der Tod als Vollendung: Ostergespräch mit Gerhard Ruis," in: *Karl Rahner im Gespräch*, 122.]

[126] Rahner, "Theological Considerations on the Moment of Death," in: *TI* 11:319. ["Theologische Erwägungen über den Eintritt des Todes," in: *Schriften* 9:333f.] Cf. Peter Fischer, *Die Anthropological Wende*, 367ff., for an analysis of the philosophical implications Rahner's view of dying as a human act of freedom in regard to our finiteness.

[127] *ATP*, 139. [136.]

[128] John Macquarrie, "Theologians of our Time V. Karl Rahner, S.J.," in: *The Expository Times* 74 (April 1963), 195.

man, and as such, is a consequence, a punishment of sin."¹²⁹ In the later Rahner, however, sin and death are seldom discussed as having anything to do with one another.

On one of the infrequent occasions when the topic was broached by the later Rahner he admitted that a connection between guilt and death exists in the Bible and that the darkness of death is "a sign of the person's sinful condition." Yet Rahner questions the meaning of this connection for modern persons since "we have recognized biological death as a phenomenon that existed long before the history of human sin and since ... we cannot imagine that the person was supposed to have lived continuously and forever without sin." Thus Rahner concludes that death "as the coming to an end of the history of freedom is an event that has always existed even prior to sin."¹³⁰

Even beyond the question of death Rahner's tendency toward an anthropo-optimism can be detected in his inclination toward a theory of universal salvation which, although he does not subscribe to it in its most radical form, would seem to be the logical conclusion of his optimistic view of humanity and his seeming 'minimizing' of the effects of sin.¹³¹ Rahner is optimistic in his evaluation of the human will's ability to ultimately say yes to God. It is this optimism which led him to look positively upon a doctrine of apocatastasis.¹³² Yet it is also his very high assessment of human freedom which prevented him from a positive affirmation of such a doctrine of universal salvation. Rahner is thus hopeful that perhaps all persons will say an ultimate yes to God but at the same time he recognizes that an affirmation of this position would imply a certain bondage of

---

[129] Rahner, *On the Theology of Death, Quaestiones disputatae* 2, trans. C.H. Henkey (New York: Herder and Herder, 1965), 48f. [*Zur Theologie des Todes, mit einem Exkurs über das Martyrium, QD* 2 (Freiburg: Herder, 1958), 50ff.]

[130] "Death as Fulfillment," 239. ["Der Tod als Vollendung," 123f.] In *On the Theology of Death*, 34f. *Zur Theologie des Todes*, 33, Rahner also contends that Adam would not have lived indefinitely even if he had not sinned, but had this been the case, Rahner suggests that his earthly life would have encountered its fulfillment in a "death without death" that Rahner compares to a resurrection of the body without first experiencing of death, which entered the world with sin.

[131] The tendency toward a doctrine of universal salvation has been difficult to avoid for theologians focusing upon the universality of theology and of the God of whom theology speaks. Hence even Pannenberg has been accused of tending toward a theology of universal salvation even though he himself explicitly rejects such an outcome. Cf. Daniel Williams, "Response to Pannenberg," in: *Hope and the Future of Man*, ed. Evert Cousins (Philadelphia: Fortress, 1972), 86f.; and Carl Braaten, "Christianity among the World Religions," in: *The Theology of Wolfhart Pannenberg*, ed. Braaten and Clayton, 311. Braaten writes: "There is a slender line in the history of theology that holds out hope for universal salvation. Those who have held the belief in a universal consummation of the totality of reality ... in the final future of God have done so as a function of their 'high' Christology. ... Pannenberg's theology of universal history would seem to lead to the same conclusion." For Pannenberg's rejection of the necessity of such an outcome of history see *ST* 3:500f.

[132] Cf. Peter Phan, *Eternity in Time*, 152ff.

the will (though in a very different sense than as found in Luther) which he is not willing to accept.[133]

In conclusion, therefore, it would certainly seem that from a Protestant perspective, which is heavily influenced by the biblical view of humanity and by the Augustinian and related Lutheran and Calvinist theological traditions, that Rahner's "optimistic" view of humanity comes in many ways at least very near to what has historically been identified as semi-Pelagianism (to an even greater extent than that of Thomas who faced the same accusation). Yet the term semi-Pelagian, with all its historical baggage and undertones of heresy, is misleading when applied to Rahner. Protestant theology, however, although it can find much of value in Rahner's anthropology, and perhaps even also a corrective to its own often too pessimistic view of humanity, must view his essential anthropo-optimism with caution in light of its overly optimistic view of human nature and the human condition and its over-reliance upon philosophical traditions rooted outside of the Christian tradition. It is here also that a difference is to be detected between Rahner and Pannenberg, for whereas anthropology is the foundation of Rahner's theological program, which at least in part accounts for his apparent anthropo-optimism, anthropology for Pannenberg, while also a major emphasis of his theology, is more of a methodological starting-point.

### 3.2 Wolfhart Pannenberg: The Universality of Human Experience

From the very beginning of his theological career Wolfhart Pannenberg has made anthropology a center point of his theological enterprise. His concept of revelation as history, which we have examined in detail in chapter one, revealed an approach to God's self-disclosure which was inextricably intertwined with human history. In 1962 Pannenberg turned his attention specifically to anthropology with his short book, *What is Man?* in which such themes as world-openness, God-openness, and the 'I' centeredness of humans came to the fore. In his 1964 treatment of Christology, *Jesus - God and Man*, Pannenberg developed a Christology "from below" in which the humanity of Jesus, and thus also anthropology, becomes the starting point for Christology. Pannenberg's definitive treatment of anthropology, *Anthropology in Theological Perspective*, appeared in 1983 and is divided into three parts. In part 1, "The Person in Nature" he sketches the major developments in recent philosophical anthropology. In part 2, "The Human Person as a Social Being," Pannenberg examines the various aspects of human identity dealing especially with the ego and the nature of sin and alienation. In the final part of his work, "The Shared World," he takes up inter-personal aspects of human beings such as culture, institutions, family, etc. Finally, in the second volume of his recently completed *Systematic Theology*

---

[133] Cf. *ibid.*, 153.

Pannenberg once again has taken up the subjects of anthropology and of a Christology from below.

As was also the case with Rahner, a comprehensive summary of even the most significant aspects of Pannenberg's anthropology is not possible within the framework of our present study. Instead we will focus on those aspects of Pannenberg's understanding of humanity which are pertinent to his conception of theology as universal science, with particular attention given to the significance and shape of the universality of human experience which runs throughout his thought. Indeed, Pannenberg recognizes that the foundation of theology's claim to universal validity cannot be laid if proper attention is not paid by theologians to anthropology. As Pannenberg explains: "If theologians are not to succumb to self-deception regarding their proper activity [i.e., their concern with God], they must begin their reflection with a recognition of the fundamental importance of anthropology for all modern thought and for any present-day claim of universal validity for religious statements." And also, "in the modern age anthropology has become not only in fact but also with objective necessity the terrain on which theologians must base their claim of universal validity for what they say."[134]

We will take up our treatment of Pannenberg's anthropology in three parts. First, by way of prolegomena, we will inquire as to the relationship between theological anthropology and the special sciences - especially history - in the formulation of Pannenberg's concept of humanity. The rest of our treatment will follow Pannenberg's own suggestion that there are essentially two poles to theological anthropology: the image of God and human sinfulness.[135] Thus we will treat under the general category of openness to the world and to God those elements which are for Pannenberg decisive for an understanding of the image of God, and under the category of universal experience we will look at the range of human experiences, including freedom and death, related to human sinfulness.

### 3.2.1 Prolegomena to Pannenberg's Anthropology

#### 3.2.1.1 *History as the context of anthropology*

Fundamental for Pannenberg's anthropology, as for his theology in general, is the importance of history,[136] especially as it is understood as universal history. Thus anthropology, while taken up into history in Pannenberg's program, does not provide the foundation of this program, as in Rahner, but rather history itself is

---

[134] *ATP*, 16. [16.]

[135] Cf. for instance, Pannenberg, "Anthropologie in theologischer Perspektive: Philosophisch-theologische Grundlinien," in: *Sind wir von Natur aus religiös?*, ed. W. Pannenberg (Düsseldorf: Patmos, 1986), 95, and *ATP*, 20 [20], where Pannenberg writes: "Dogmatic anthropology has had two central themes: the image of God in human beings, and human sin."

[136] For a brief, but unfortunately not fully developed critique of the relation of history to Pannenberg's anthropology see Johann Baptist Metz, *Faith in History and Society*, 65 and n. 21, p. 80, who, in the context of a critique of Rahner's transcendental anthropology, asks whether even Pannenberg's 'anthropology of anticipation' "has anything to do with history?"

this foundation.[137] Human life, Pannenberg emphasizes, "whether it is the life span of the individual or the larger story of peoples and states, takes concrete form in history."[138] This is the case, as Pannenberg pointed out already in *What is Man?*, since humans are by nature historical creatures. This does not simply mean that humans live within the context of a series of successive decisions, as emphasized by existential philosophy, but much more that "each man also lives in an interconnected series of events, which involves both his own decisions and also the things that happen to him. Together these things constitute his history, which is entirely particular and unique."[139]

Significant for Pannenberg's conception of the universality of human experience is his view of the universality of history, within which all human experience occurs. History cannot simply be divided, according to Pannenberg, into the history of individuals and the history of peoples and states. This is the case since the history of individuals is interwoven into the history of the world in which they live. Likewise, "the history of institutions and communities shows that these do not exist independently of their members but are determined by the experiences and activities of individuals." Thus even through conflicts between individuals and peoples all persons are "drawn into the process of a single all-embracing history." In this sense Pannenberg understands history as "ecumenical." Human life, therefore, takes its concrete form within a history that must be understood as the history of the human race." The basis for the universality of human experience is therefore already to be found in Pannenberg's conception of the universality of history within which human life takes place. History, according to Pannenberg, is "an all-embracing web into which everything is woven" and which "transcends the shared world of each particular community and culture."[140] It is not surprising, therefore, as we will see in the following section, that Pannenberg attributes the most weight to the science of history and historiography, among the 'secular' sciences, in regard to the question of humanity.

### 3.2.1.2 *Theological anthropologies and profane anthropologies*

As in many other aspects of his thought Pannenberg makes a deliberate and clear break with Karl Barth who, as Macquarrie has noted, he criticizes "as 'arbitrary' and 'subjectivist' because he rejected secular anthropologies and tried to build a theological anthropology on a purely biblical and Christocentric basis."[141]

---

[137] One cannot make anthropology the foundation of a theological system, in Pannenberg's view, because anthropological statements are by nature abstract. At the same time, however, one must begin with the abstract and thus anthropology is an appropriate starting-point.
[138] *ATP*, 485. [472.]
[139] Pannenberg, *What is Man? Contemporary Anthropology in Theological Perspective*, trans. Duane Priebe (Philadelphia: Fortress Press, 1970), 139. [English translation of *Was ist der Mensch?* (Göttingen: Vandenhoeck & Ruprecht, 1962), 96.]
[140] *ATP*, 485f. [472f.]
[141] John Macquarrie, "What Is a Human Being?" in: *The Expository Times* 97 (April 1986), 202. Cf. *ATP*, 16, 18f. [16, 18f.]

Pannenberg contends that since the 19th century there has been no choice for theologians but to begin with and base their argumentation upon anthropology, which in our age has characterized the general intellectual environment to which theologians must address themselves. Pannenberg contends that Karl Barth's rejection of the so-called priority of humanity in 19th century theology and his deliberate effort to begin with God has not successfully avoided what is essentially unavoidable. Pannenberg asks: "How does Barth actually arrive at the notion of beginning with God? One can then say that the anthropological foundation of theology is carried to an extreme, namely to the pure and simple decision to begin with God."[142]

Pannenberg, in contrast to Barth, makes the secular or profane anthropologies the deliberate starting point for his theological anthropology. From his time in Wuppertal (1958-1961) Pannenberg was convinced that it was not his task as a theologian to develop his own anthropology based upon selected texts from the Bible with little or no regard for what other disciplines were saying about humanity.[143] For Pannenberg the so-called anthropolization of the concept of God, brought about through and in conjunction with modern atheistic argumentation,[144] has meant that theological anthropology has taken on the role and rank of a fundamental theology.[145] In order for theological anthropology to accomplish its task, according to Pannenberg, it is therefore imperative,

> that the various disciplines of an empirically orientated anthropology - human biology, sociology, psychology - along with their methods and themes, be thoroughly taken into account. A thesis that relies only upon the experience of humans as it is accessible apart from scientific investigation, as is the case with Tillich's thesis concerning an ultimate concern in every human life, is no longer sufficient in its general applicability, regardless of how insightful it might otherwise be.[146]

Not surprisingly, of all the profane anthropologies Pannenberg attributes the most importance to the historical approach to humanity. He contends that human biology, sociology, and psychology, in comparison to the historical concreteness of humanity, are only "abstract approximations to human reality." Pannenberg

---

[142] Pannenberg, "Anthropologie in theologischer Perspektive: Philosophisch-theologische Grundlinien," 89.
[143] Ibid., 90.
[144] Pannenberg sees this already with Feuerbach who based his atheistic thought upon anthropology and contented that religion, and with it the idea of a God, is the result of a misunderstanding of humanity. Cf. ibid., 88.
[145] This fundamental anthropology is located in his own thought between dogmatic and metaphysical anthropology, as Alfred Gläßer, *Verweigerte Partnerschaft? Anthropologische, konfessionelle und ökumenische Aspekte der Theologie Wolfhart Pannenbergs* (Regensburg: Verlag Friedrich Pustet, 1991), 14, has pointed out.
[146] Pannenberg, *Gottesgedanke und menschliche Freiheit* (Göttingen: Vandenhoeck & Ruprecht, 1972), 20f.

maintains that, "of all the disciplines that have the human being for their subject, the science of history and historiography come closest to grasping human reality as it is experienced."[147] Already in *What is Man?* Pannenberg wrote:

> The anthropological sciences with their pictures of man never arrive at man in his concreteness. Neither biology nor cultural anthropology, neither sociology nor the anthropology of rights, and certainly not existential ontology arrives at man in his concreteness. Their pictures of man are abstractions. [Yet] ... abstract consideration is the condition without which a person can say nothing at all about man.[148]

Pannenberg contends that, in order to develop a concrete picture of humanity from all of these various abstractions, they must be brought together and examined not just in their individual contexts or in the context of the individual but from the perspective of communities. Thus sociology, which presupposes the results of the study of humans as individuals, would seem to be in the best position to bring together these various aspects. Yet, according to Pannenberg, "the approach of sociology must also be superseded to make room for a more comprehensive science that would pursue the concrete change in the life of individuals and of groups of men. That is historical science. Presupposing all other anthropological investigations, it arrives at the closest approximation to concrete human life."[149]

The science of history is, therefore, according to Pannenberg, "the crown of all anthropological sciences." The question of the relation of theological anthropology to the profane anthropologies then becomes largely a question of the relationship of theology to history in the thought of Pannenberg. The historical situation of humans in which they encounter the self-revelation of God is, according to Pannenberg, the only legitimate starting point for theology.[150] As we have already seen, the historical situation of which Pannenberg speaks is a part of a larger, unified history, a history which finds its culmination and its unity in Jesus of Nazareth. Thus he contends that the unifying conceptualization of world history which has arisen in Western society has its "ultimate root in Christianity's universal historical consciousness." Pannenberg writes:

> Today also the unity of history is still accessible only from the God of Israel. That means, however, that men's destiny is also determined by their relationship to the God of Israel and his revelation in Jesus of Nazareth. The unity of history is established by the appearance of the end of all events through God's revelation in Jesus. In this unity of history, man's destiny attains its unified configuration,

---

[147] *ATP*, 485. [472.]
[148] *What is Man?*, 137, [95.]
[149] *Ibid.*, 138. [95f.], and for the following quote.
[150] Cf. Pannenberg, "Christliche Glaube und menschliche Freiheit," in: *Kerygma und Dogma*, vol. 4 (1958), 274f.

which incorporates each individual man with his uniqueness and his particular path.[151]

Theology is that science which examines the ultimate foundation of universal history, namely the self-revelation of God in the person of Jesus Christ. In this way Pannenberg views history as the "most comprehensive horizon of Christian theology," since "all theological questions and answers are meaningful only within the framework of the history which God has with humanity ... - the history moving toward a future ... already revealed in Jesus Christ."[152] Through the theological investigation of the Christ event theology is not only rooted in the context of the universal history of humanity but it provides a necessary service in uncovering the roots and, indeed, the "end" of this universal history. Theology, in this manner, must be concerned with the results of all the various special sciences devoted to the study of humanity. The fulfillment of this task has been, in a certain sense, one of the primary goals of Pannenberg's theological program.

What Pannenberg hopes to accomplish is a unified and comprehensive view of humanity which brings together the various specialized methodologies and insights. Pannenberg observes that we live in an age of anthropology in which "a comprehensive science of humanity is a primary goal of the intellectual efforts of the present," including those of the theological discipline. Pannenberg further believes that: "the sciences that concern themselves with the study of human beings are tody well on their way to taking the place in general consciousness that metaphysics held in previous centuries."[153] What role, however, can or should theological anthropology play within this process? Pannenberg contends that theology's goal must be a critical appropriation of the results of secular anthropologies. The aim of this task, according to Pannenberg, "is to lay theological claim to the human phenomena described in the anthropological disciplines. To this end, the secular description is accepted as simply a provisional version of the objective reality, a version that needs to be expanded and deepened by showing that the anthropological datum itself contains a further and theologically relevant dimension."[154]

The question which needs to be critically asked, however, is whether Pannenberg subjects theological anthropological insights too much to those of the profane anthropologies, especially in his *Anthropology in Theological Perspective*. Otto Hermann Pesch has characterized Pannenberg's anthropology as that which "proceeds on the basis of the investigations of the human sciences, questions them methodically in light of their concealed openness for Christian faith-statements about humanity, and evaluates them theologically. ... But does it produce a *theological* anthropology when the anthropologies of the human

---
[151] *What is Man?*, 148, [102f.]
[152] Pannenberg, "*Redemptive Event and History*", 2. [*Grundfragen*," 22.]
[153] Was ist der Mensch., 5.
[154] *ATP*, 20. [19.]

sciences are measured against theological propositions and are questioned about theological implications? ... Should the matter, however, not be understood differently, should not proposals like Pannenberg's seek to be more than theological re-action to the action of the human sciences?"[155]

Pannenberg's truly broad and in-depth dialogue with the secular anthropologies is an undeniable achievement. The question is whether theological anthropology plays in Pannenberg's approach merely a secondary role to secular anthropologies and does not emerge as a full dialogue partner. Granted, it was not Pannenberg's intention in his major work on anthropology to write a dogmatic anthropology but rather a "fundamental-theological anthropology" which does not argue from dogmatic data and presuppositions but rather "turns its attention directly to the phenomena of human existence as investigated in human biology, psychology, cultural anthropology, or sociology and examines the findings of these disciplines with an eye to implications that may be relevant to religion and theology."[156] Yet given Pannenberg's conviction concerning the mutuality of the dialogue between theology and the special sciences, as examined in chapter one of our study, one might have expected that the implications of theological insights into humanity for the secular anthropologies would have received more attention.

### 3.2.2 Openness to the World and to God

#### 3.2.2.1 *The human person as open to the world*

As with the other main lines of Pannenberg's anthropology the world openness of humans is already to be found in *What is Man?* One of the most significant developments to come out of the profane anthropologies in the modern era, according to Pannenberg, is the discovery of the human openness to the world[157] which is found in the freedom of the person "to enquire and to move beyond every given regulation" of human existence. In short, world openness is that which "makes man to be man, ... distinguishes him from animals, and ... lifts him out above nonhuman nature in general."[158] The world openness of humans does not have the same function as the environment for animals. As Pannenberg explains: "Man is not bound to an environment, but is open to the world. That means that he can always have new experiences that are different in kind, and his possibilities for responding to the reality perceived can vary almost without limit."

---

[155] Pesch, *Frei sein aus Gnade: Theologische Anthropologie*, 34. Gläßer, *Verweigerte Partnerschaft?*, 14f., in a related vein has suggested that Pannenberg's anthropological method enters into a grey area in that it seeks both a critical incorporation of the non-theological anthropologies and at the same time seeks to contribute to the foundation of theology in general.

[156] *ATP*, 21. [21.]

[157] The term "world-openness" it would seem first entered the anthropological discussion through Max Scheler's 1928 work, *Die Stellung des Menschen im Kosmos*. Scheler, in turn, seems to have relied for some of the key elements of this concept upon the thought of Jacob von Uexküll. Cf. Koch, *Der Gott der Geschichte*, 137.

[158] For this and the following quotation, *What is Man?* 3ff, [ 6ff.]

Whereas animals have an environment, human beings have a world, which means that humans are not limited to a specific environment but are open to the world. For Pannenberg, therefore, the concept of 'openness to the world' "serves as a collective term for a great number of specifically human behavioral characteristics, which in turn are related to corresponding unique features of the physical nature of humans. Openness to the world, therefore, is a broad expression denoting the uniqueness of human beings."[159]

To or for what, however, is the human person open, that is to say, open in such a way that this openness signifies more than simply the relationship of the human person to his or her 'environment'? Pannenberg answers that the human being:

> is open to constantly new things and fresh experiences, while animals are open only to a limited, fixed number of environmental features that are typical of the species. ... The openness to the world that modern anthropology has in view differs not only in degree but also in kind from the animal's bondage to its environment. Therefore, this expression cannot involve only an openness to the 'world.' Rather, openness to the world must mean that man is completely directed into the 'open.' He is always open further, beyond every experience and beyond every situation. He is also open beyond the world.[160]

Already in the basic form of Pannenberg's concept of openness to the world an unmistakable parallel is to be seen to Rahner's emphasis upon humans as "spirit *in the world*." In both models humans are distinguished from animals precisely in their relationship to the world, namely, in the fact that humans have a world which they relate to or are open to and not just an environment.[161] Both theologians also distinguish themselves sharply from Heidegger at this point. Humans interact with, rule over, and indeed create their 'world.' As Pannenberg notes: "For man the things are not, as Heidegger thought, primordially ready-to-hand."[162] Additionally, this openness to the world or being in the world, for both theologians, points ultimately to an openness which transcends the world, namely, to an openness toward God.

In his *Anthropology in Theological Perspective* the theme of openness to the world is developed further. Especially decisive for Pannenberg here is the concept of exocentricity developed by the philosopher Helmuth Plessner in *Die Stufen des Organischen und der Mensch* which appeared in 1928. According to Plessner, "the limits of animal organization are to be found in the fact that the individual's own self ... is hidden, because it does not stand in relationship to the positional center, while the medium and its love of its own body are present and exist in the positional center, which is oriented to the absolute here and now. ...

---

[159] "Anthropologie in theologischer Perspektive: Philosophisch-theologische Grundlinien," 96.
[160] *What is Man?*, 7f., [9f.]
[161] Cf. Rahner, *Hearers*, 54, [*HdW*, 72], and *Spirit in the World*, 397. [*GW*, 396.]
[162] *What is Man?*, 6, [8.] Pannenberg's reference is to Heidegger, *Sein und Zeit*, 54f., 68f., and 73ff.

The animal lives from its center and toward its center. ..."[163] Like the higher animals, according to Plessner, human beings too have the center of their vital manifestations within themselves, yet transcend this center. He explains: "Human beings, as living things that are positioned in the center of their existence, know this center, experience it, and therefore transcend it. They experience the binding to the absolute here and now, the total convergence of the environment and their own bodies against the center of their position and are therefore no longer bound by it." In distinction to the higher animals, therefore, humans are also exocentric. Plessner writes: "If the life of the animal is centered, then the life of the human being, without being able to break the centricity, is at the same time exocentric. Exocentricity is the form of frontal positioning characteristic for humans over against their environment."[164] This means, as Pannenberg explains, that humans "have their center not only within themselves but at the same time outside themselves." With the term exocentricity Plessner sought to replace Max Scheler's concept of openness to the world and point to "the ability of human beings to adopt an attitude toward themselves, a capacity for self-reflection, which at the same time is the basis for the human ability to stand back from things and treat them as objects, *as* things."[165]

Already in *What is Man?* Pannenberg pointed to the significance of Plessner's designation of humans as exocentric although he did not yet develop the implications of the concept for a theological understanding of humanity. Pannenberg noted that Plessner's concept of exocentricity does not contradict the concept of openness to the world, "but in substance presupposes it. Only because man in open objectivity can linger with the 'other,' which he finds before himself, is he able to come back to himself from that other."[166] Although Plessner's terminology of "exocentricity" has not generally been followed in modern discussions of anthropology, in part at least because of the vagueness of many of his explanations of what precisely he meant by the term, Pannenberg has taken up the concept, viewing it as complementary to that of world openness. Pannenberg makes use of the concept of exocentricity to underline the fact that human beings are not just ego-centered but also are by nature open to the world and to God.

### 3.2.2.1.1 *World-openness as imago dei (Herder)*

Although Pannenberg is indebted to Plessner for his concept of exocentricity which points to the openness of humans to the world, it is the thought of Johann Gottfried Herder upon which he draws most heavily for the form which his

---

[163] Helmuth Plessner, *Die Stufen des Organischen und der Mensch: Einleitung in die philosophische Anthropologie* [1928] (Berlin: Walter de Gruyter, 1965), 288.
[164] Ibid., 291f.
[165] *ATP*, 36f. [34f.] Cf. also 80ff. [77ff.] As Pannenberg notes, Plessner pointed out that human beings are not unrestrictedly open to the reality of things outside them. A capacity and readiness for objectivity are indeed present in principle, but are in practice always limited (*ATP*, 60 [57]).
[166] *What is Man?* 3, note 1, [104.]

concept of world openness takes as an expression of the *imago dei*.[167] In *What is Man?* Pannenberg contended that it is "no accident that modern anthropology, which is oriented to man's openness to the world, has its historical roots in biblical thought. The biblical story of creation declared man to be loved over the world. To be sure, he was to exercise dominion for God as his representative, as his image."[168] In *Anthropology in Theological Perspective* Pannenberg turns to the thought of Herder in developing further this connection between the *imago dei* and the openness to the world. He contends that if Herder is correct in linking the concepts of God's image with the anthropological data that is often summed up under the category of openness to the world, then there is a "connection between the image of God and the call to rule the world" (Gen. 1:26f.) which represents "an objective connection that can be recognized in the phenomenon called 'openness to the world.'"[169]

Herder, the 18th century philosopher and theologian who Pannenberg takes as the point of departure for modern philosophical anthropology, believed that animal instincts were replaced in humans by a divinely given direction for human life in the form of the image of God. As Pannenberg quotes Herder: "God, ... to the brute thou gavest instinct; and on the mind of man thou didst impress thy image."[170] The essential points of Herder's concept of the image of God which Pannenberg draws upon are as follows: 1. The image of God guides humans in a manner analogous to the function of instinct in animals so that humans are not simply left to chance. 2. The image of God functions teleologically and as standard for human behavior because the *imago dei* represents the goal of human existence so that the image of God and the humanness of the human person belong together. 3. The image of God means that humans initially possess only a disposition to reason, humanity and religion. The full stature of their humanity is reached, according to Herder, not through action but through education in which three factors play a role: tradition and learning through which others influence us, reason and experience which are the organic powers within us that contribute to our education, and divine providence which, mediated through other persons,

---

[167] Indeed, Pannenberg has identified Herder as the "father of modern anthropology with its statements concerning the characteristic of humans as beings open to the world." Pannenberg, "Anthropologie in theologischer Perspektive: Philosophisch-theologische Grundlinien," 96.

[168] *What is Man?*, 11, [12.] That modern science and technology, and not only the anthropological sciences, can point to the biblical understanding of the image of God as ruler of the world is indicated when Pannenberg elsewhere notes that, "the breath-taking advances of modern science and technology have created the impression that man has dislodged God by hoisting himself into mastery of the world. In this connexion, strange to say, it is often overlooked that man's actual mastery over the world is part of the biblical idea of his being made to the image of God." Pannenberg, "Man - the image of God?" in: *Faith and Reality*, 39f. [*Glaube und Wirklichkeit*, 58.]

[169] *ATP*, 76. [73.]

[170] Cf. J. G. Herder, *Outlines of a Philosophy of the History of Man*, trans. T. Churchhill (New York, 1966), 256 (IX, 5).

leads us toward the goal which God has for humans and humanity in collaboration with the first two factors.[171]

For Pannenberg the continuing significance of Herder's view is to be found in the fact that his concept of the image of God "has for its function to describe the unfinished humanity of human beings in such a way as simultaneously to counter the difficulty that the fulfillment of human destiny cannot be thought of as the accomplishment of the very ones in whose lives that destiny is to become a reality." If humans were able to accomplish their own destiny then they would have to already be what they must still become. Yet at the same time humans' future destination of humanness is seen as already playing a role in their natural being. Without this latter condition the future could not be understood as the fulfillment of human destiny. Pannenberg contends that "both of these conditions are fulfilled in the idea of the image of God, because it makes it possible to think of the goal of essential human realization as at the same time constitutive of the initial human state."[172]

The idea of an 'eschatological fulfillment of the image of God at the end of history as a culmination of humanity fits well with Pannenberg's own view of history and eschatology, explored in chapter one, in which it is precisely the end of history in which its ultimate meaning will be revealed and the completion of God's plan for his creation realized. Thus Pannenberg is uncomfortable with the view that humans originally possessed the fullness of the image of God and then lost it in the fall.[173] Rather, he agrees with Herder that "the *imago dei* of human beings is originally found only in the purpose of humans directed toward that which they shall become, and not in what they already are from the beginning. Hence the concept of an *imago dei* shifts from an original given to a God-determined purpose for the human person that will only first be fully realised in the perfection of the person at the end of his or her history, in the eschatology ..."[174] When one remembers that Pannenberg affirms that the end of history has already proleptically occurred in the person of Jesus Christ it is quite understandable, as we will later see, that the *imago dei* finds its culmination in Jesus Christ as the representative of all humanity.

Pannenberg takes exception with Herder's conception of the image of God, however, at a point crucial for his apologetic approach. Herder contended that the image of God is not mediated through the biological situation inherent to human beings but is introduced from outside. Pannenberg notes, however, that "on this

---

[171] *ATP*, 45f. [42f.]
[172] *Ibid.*, 60. [57.]
[173] At this point Pesch has argued, contra Pannenberg, that scholastic theology did not hold this view but rather one much closer to that which Pannenberg, following Herder, pursues. Writes Pesch: "In Wahrheit steht die genau gelesene scholastische Lehre (ich denke besonders an Thomas von Aquin) näher bei Pannenbergs Konzeption von der 'werdenden' Gottebenbildlichkeit als manche nachtridentische *und* nachlutherische Auffassung." Pesch, "'Frei sein aus Gnade:' Hinweise zu einer theologischen Anthropologie," 130.
[174] "Anthropologie in theologischer Perspektive: Philosophisch-theologische Grundlinien," 97.

point Herder's line of thought can no longer satisfy present-day requirements for rendering plausible the introduction of theological concepts into the description of empirical anthropological matters." For Pannenberg, therefore, if Herder's approach is to have any continuing validity in the modern discussion then "it must be shown that the religious and theological concepts are not extrinsic to the phenomena but correspond to a dimension exhibited by the latter." Thus Pannenberg agrees with Scheler and Plessner, both of whom have argued that the "essential structure of the human form of life" belongs to the essence of humanity, that is to say, is intrinsic to human beings.[175]

After establishing the foundational points of a Herderian conception of the *imago dei* and adapting these to modern thought Pannenberg seeks to demonstrate in what manner the human relation to the world is an expression of this image. Pannenberg contends that not only does the concept of *imago dei* point to the human destination to communion with God but also to an openness to the world. Here we return to Pannenberg's concept of the image of God as world-openness, namely, the idea that the openness to the world expressed in the *imago dei* is closely connected to the destiny of humans to rule the earth as expressed in Gen. 1:26f. In explaining this concept Pannenberg draws again upon the concept of exocentricity. He writes:

> Only because in their exocentric self-transcendence they [humans] reach beyond the immediately given to the broadest possible horizon of meaning that embraces all finite things ... is it possible for them to grasp an individual object in its determinateness that distinguishes it from other objects. ... This process of defining the individuality of things has become the basis for all human mastery of nature. Precisely because human beings reach beyond the given, and therefore ultimately because human exocentricity is characterized by an impulse, inconceivable except in religious terms, to the unconditioned do they have the ability to rule over the objects of their natural world.[176]

This dominion of the world, however, only finds its full expression in Jesus Christ. Hence for Pannenberg the *imago dei*, as it reached its fulfillment in the resurrected Christ, is the key to the humanity of all persons, whether they know of Jesus or not. Pannenberg, in a 1977 lecture, summarized the significance of the *imago dei*, as fully realized in Christ, for the humanity of each person. He wrote: "The image of God, which is realized in the resurrected Christ, is the destiny of every person, and this destiny which transcends the human being and leads to a communion with God that is made manifest in Christ, constitutes the humanity and human dignity of every person, even if that person knows nothing of Jesus."[177]

---

[175] *ATP*, 66. [63.]
[176] *Ibid.*, 76. [73.]
[177] Pannenberg, *Die Auferstehung Jesu und die Zukunft des Menschen*, Eichstätter Hochschulreden, vol. 10 (Munich: Minerva Publikation, 1978), 10.

That Pannenberg, as seen above, makes use of the concept of human self-transcendence in relation to exocentricity provides a certain point of contact to Rahner's transcendental anthropology. Indeed, Pannenberg himself has seen this similarity and notes his agreement with Rahner's development of humans' relationship to God out of their structure as 'question' of existence and the contingence of their existence upon God out of which they are able to affirm their being/existence, despite its contingence, as absolute. Pannenberg, however, contends that Rahner's transcendental anthropology leads to a leap which passes over the concrete history of humans in the contention that the understanding of the establishment of human existence through the 'absolute being' has to do with God as a free person. This is the case since the experience of a "preceding fixed state of being finds its concrete form in the whole diverse religious experience [and] ... does not appear immediately in the particular historical expression of faith in only a single God and in this God as a free person."[178] Pannenberg, in contrast, understands human self-transcendence as taking place concretely only in the process of human history. Pannenberg, in a critical passage, explains the significance of concrete human history for his understanding of self-transcendence, in contrast to Rahner's usage. He writes:

> The fact that the humans exist as their question about their own selves, about their salvation, and about God, from whom alone their salvation comes, cannot, admittedly, be sufficiently founded upon a general anthropology. This fact arises instead first out of the historical experience that humans have had with the question about their own selves, their salvation and peace, and with the divine reality made known through these. The self-transcendence of human beings, without which no wholeness of human life could be thought of, is concretely completed only in the process of a history. Without this process of history there remains only an abstract structural moment lacking any concrete content.[179]

3.2.2.2 *Openness to God as anthropological argument for God's existence?*

It has been rightly observed that in the theology of Pannenberg the tension between ego-centricity and openness to the world is only resolved when it is realized that at its core, openness to the world means openness to God.[180] Indeed, for Pannenberg, true human openness toward the world implies as an openness which necessarily points beyond the world - an openness which ultimately is directed toward God.[181] Openness toward the world means that the human person "is open beyond the world." Indeed, "openness beyond the world is even the

---

[178] Pannenberg, "Weltgeschichte und Heilsgeschichte," in: *Probleme biblischer Theologie*, ed. Hans Walter Wolff (Munich: Chr. Kaiser, 1971), 357, note 18.
[179] *Ibid.*, 357f.
[180] So Ringeling, *Christliche Ethik im Dialog*, 65f., and Tupper, 71. Also, *What is Man?* 14, [13.]
[181] This is necessitated, in Pannenberg's thought, by his belief, "daß die Wirklichkeit des Menschen mit Recht als durch sich selbst schon auf Gott bezogen in Anspruch genommen werden kann." Pannenberg, "Anthropologie in theologischer Perspektive," 92.

condition for man's experience of the world."[182] Therefore, Pannenberg postulates, there is a directedness toward an unknown opposite being (unbekanntes Gegenüber) which is at the heart of human openness to the world. Although this directedness to something beyond the world does not constitute a 'proof for God's existence' it does point to the fact that human beings cannot be explained solely in terms of reference to their own selves and their "environment." Pannenberg writes:

> Man's infinite dependence on an unknown being before whom he stands has turned out to be the core of the somewhat vague expression 'open to the world.' To be sure, this does not result in any theoretical proof for the existence of God. However, we have shown that simply by living his life man presupposes a vis-`a-vis upon which he is infinitely dependent, whether he knows it or not. It has been further shown that this presupposition is unavoidable for understanding the basic biological structure of human existence, as long as a person refuses to be satisfied with the vague designation 'openness to the world' and wants to know what this expression can mean. [But] ... nothing has yet been determined about who or what that entity upon which man is infinitely dependent really is. Men's dependence upon God is infinite precisely because they never possess this destiny of theirs but must search for it.[183]

For Pannenberg the openness of humans to the world presupposes a God-relatedness and points to the core distinction between humans and animals. Thus, "what the environment is for animals, God is for man. God is the goal in which alone his striving can find rest and his destiny be fulfilled."[184] For Pannenberg, however, this does not constitute an anthropological argument for the existence of God. He made this emphatically clear, for instance, in a 1984 lecture delivered to a meeting of the *Katholische Akademie* of Bavaria held in Regensburg in which he summarized the main arguments of his then recently published anthropology. Pannenberg, in light of his deduction of an openness toward God based upon the basic anthropological data of human openness to the world asks whether such an investigation leads inevitably to a natural theology of sorts in that it attempts to demonstrate the existence of God through the available knowledge concerning human beings - as Eberhard Jüngel had understood him to imply? Pannenberg insists that this was not his intention. He explains:

> It is indeed correct that only Got can demonstrate God's existence. If humans would prove God, then the result of this proof would no longer be God. The essence of God does not depend upon our ability to prove his existence on the basis of one or another given reality that is distinct from God. It belongs to the divinity of God that only God can demonstrate his existence. Yet I am of the opinion that one can show that ... religion belongs to the humanity of human

---
[182] *What is Man?* 8, [10.]
[183] *Ibid.*, 10f., [11f.]
[184] *Ibid.*, 13, [13.]

beings. This, however, is a controversial point. ... But even the fact of Atheism and the muffled, unsatisfied and the still clouded yearning after meaning of humans in secular societies, the public consciousness of which already dispute in principle the general truth and reliability of the answers of religion, are able to be taken as evidence that the category of religion belongs to the humanity of human beings. When I say that this can be demonstrated, then I do not mean thereby that an uncontroverted unity either exists or is even achievable among all those interested in this question. I am only claiming that one can with good grounds and with arguments show that the reality of human beings in the most varied areas of their phenomenological existence has just such a religious dimension.[185]

The distinction which Pannenberg makes, however, between his demonstration of the inherent religiousness of humanity and a demonstration of the existence of God has not been obvious to all. Hermann Fischer, for instance, has questioned whether Pannenberg has not in fact produced a sort of anthropological argument for the existence of God. He writes: "When the analysis of anthropological findings shows that not only the *question* about God is, as a problem, inalienable to humans, but also that humans implicitly *co-affirm* the divine reality, then such argumentation is no longer clearly distinguishable from an anthropological argument for the existence of God. Then also is factually more said than - according to Pannenberg - fundamentally can be said." Thus Fischer concludes that "although an anthropological proof for the existence of God is not intended, the world-openness of human beings appears to necessarily include their God-relatedness and to lead to an argument for the existence of God."[186]

Wilhelm Weischedel has similarly seen in Pannenberg's concept of openness a proof for the existence of God. Pannenberg, according to Weischedel, "ascribes ... to much to philosophical anthropology." In Pannenberg's thought "the reality of God is established from the fact of the world-openness of human beings. If this is an essential element of the human being, then the reality of God must necessarily also be accepted." Weischedel, however, suggests that Pannenberg's deduction of a directness or openness toward God from the data of our world openness only works when the existence of God is already presupposed on the basis of a preceding faith. Hence Weischedel concludes that the argumentation of Pannenberg is not a necessary conclusion, but rather the stuff of a preceding faith in an infinite Being who brings ultimate satisfaction to human striving.[187]

Weischedel, in fact, sees in Pannenberg's apparent anthropological argument for the existence of God an attempted new grounding of a natural theology on the basis of anthropology. An attempt which Weischedel believes fails precisely because the presumed anthropological argument for the existence of God fails.[188] A similar accusation of an attempted re-establishment of a natural theology in

---

[185] "Anthropologie in theologischer Perspektive: Philosophisch-theologische Grundlinien," 93f.
[186] Hermann Fischer, 49.
[187] Weischedel, *Der Gott der Philosophen*, vol. 2, 76f.
[188] *Ibid.*, 77.

connection with an anthropological proof for the existence of God has been leveled by William Hamilton. Hamilton wrote:

> There is, in Pannenberg's work, a presupposition concerning the natural religiousness of man. ... Pannenberg's is a theology of the religious *a priori*, though in a form more ontological than epistemological. ... Man's specific human structure, his openness to the world, requires resurrection for his own unique self-understanding. ... Man can find fulfillment, true self-understanding, true meaning, only in God. But what kind of a statement is this? ... What kind of evidence does one cite for the truth of such a statement? If there are men who declare that their fulfillment is not in God, does this invalidate the statement? This presupposition that man can find his fulfillment only in God is, at the very least, not a self-evident truth. It seems to proceed more from some other world rather than from the real world of the twentieth century with its genuine and painful unbelief.[189]

Pannenberg's response to Hamilton serves as an answer to the whole field of criticisms concerning his alleged introduction of an anthropological argument for the existence of God and of a natural theology or religion in connection with it. Pannenberg responds that he knows as good as Hamilton or anyone else, "that talk about God no longer is - or is not yet once again - taken by modern man to be self-evident truth."[190] But how then does Pannenberg clarify the misunderstanding that seems to have arisen with so many in regard to what he is saying with the concept of openness to the world and to God? Pannenberg responds that he has sought to demonstrate that the human being becomes a *question* about God. "But one cannot simply deduce from the openness of the question that God exists. Indeed, even the claim that by his questioning concerning himself and the meaning of his existence and of everything that has being, man is questioning concerning God, can, strictly speaking, only be justified if the reality on which man turns out to be dependent in the openness of his questioning meets him personally and hence as 'God.'" Pannenberg further explains:

> That man is a 'question' that finds its answer in the encountering reality of God does not signify a 'theology of the religious *a priori*,' as Hamilton claims. The truth of religious experience - especially as experience of God - is not to be derived from man's structure as question, but from his *being met by* the reality that is experienced as the answer to the open question of his existence, and thus claims his ultimate confidence as the ground of his existence. That a *recognition* of the reality presupposed in man's self-transcending personal dependency comes to pass only through the *experience* of this reality itself as concrete meeting, I

---

[189] William Hamilton, "The Character of Pannenberg's Theology," in: *New Frontiers in Theology: Discussions among Continental and American Theologians*, vol. 3, *Theology as History*, ed. James Robinson and John Cobb (New York: Harper & Row, 1967), 178f.

[190] Pannenberg, "Response to the Discussion," in: Theology as History, ed. Robinson and Cobb, 226. ["Stellungnahme zur Diskussion," in: *Theologie als Geschichte*, ed. Robinson and Cobb (Stuttgart: Zwingli Verlag, 1967), 290.]

emphasized in *Was ist der Mensch?* ... I also called attention in that essay to the character of personhood connected with such meeting that first makes it possible to call the reality thus experienced 'God.' ...

Of course, it is here that the question of human existence first finds its proper answer, since it is through the personality of the divine power encountering him that man is himself awakened to personhood. I have certainly not held it to be a 'self-evident truth.'... Rather I have established my claim ... through considerations of the structure of the so-called 'world-openness' of man, in which, along with anthropologists like M. Scheler, A. Gehlen, A. Portmann, M. Landmann, and others, I see the specific structure of human behavior summarized[191]

In light of Pannenberg's emphasis upon human beings as 'question' (within the structure of their openness to the world) which points to God as the 'answer' he would seem to be correct that this does not imply the necessary existence of God or constitute an anthropological argument for God's existence in the strict sense. Kurt Koch, in this light, would seem correct when he contends that the question of whether an anthropological proof for the existence of God is to be found in Pannenberg "must be clearly answered in the negative, as Pannenberg himself has frequently stressed." Koch explains that it is precisely the kind of 'natural theology,' in the negative sense of the term, which seeks to deduce the existence of God from the religious experience of human beings which Pannenberg's theology guards against. Hence in Pannenberg's thought, "the anthropological argument can ... only show that humans are religious by nature and that religion represents a continuing constant of human reality. It cannot, however, give a theoretical guarantee of the existence of God."[192]

Otto Pesch, on the other hand, while agreeing that Pannenberg has not presented an anthropological argument for the existence of God, feels that his thought leads in this direction and that the elucidation of such an argument would even be appropriate. In a poignant comment on Pannenberg's anthropology Pesch asks: "Why does Pannenberg not have the courage to argue for the existence of God? ... If the natural *asking after* God is not a proof, then does the certainty about the reality of God still proceed from an act of decision about God's reality, which is exactly what Pannenberg wishes to avoid?"[193] The line between openness toward God and an anthropological argument for the existence of God in Pannenberg's thought, therefore, is seen to be a fine one which Pannenberg avoids crossing only with careful reasoning. Indeed, one is tempted to ask with Pesch whether the tension in this area of Pannenberg's thought might be better overcome

---

[191] *Ibid.*, 225 [289f.]
[192] Kurt Koch, *Der Gott der Geschichte: Theologie der Geschichte bei Wolfhart Pannenberg als Paradigma einer philosophischen Theologie in ökumenischer Perspektive* (Mainz: Matthias-Grünewald Verlag, 1988), 199f.
[193] Pesch, "'Frei sein aus Gnade:' Hinweise zu einer theologischen Anthropologie," 132.

if he crossed that line and elucidated formally the anthropological argument that so many believe to have discovered within his concept of human openness to the world and to God.

Would this, however, be possible, in at least some limited but still coherent fashion without entailing the kind of 'natural theology' which Pannenberg so fervently wishes to avoid. To do so would seem to necessarily entail a role for faith in the process of recognizing the reality of the 'indications' of God's existence - a role which Pannenberg has consistently sought to minimize. Hans Schwarz has rightly observed that "Pannenberg recognizes ... that man's striving for an infinite does not prove the reality of God, but the reality of man's finitude." Therefore, his "intriguing analysis leaves us only with the phenomenal possibility but not with the phenomenal actuality of God's existence. Similar to the traditional 'proofs' of God's existence, the transition from the possibility to the actuality of God's existence would require a decision of faith."[194]

We would suggest that some if not much of the apparent confusion and misunderstanding over Pannenberg's supposed anthropological argument might be explained as follows. If the role of faith or of a faith decision in connection with the anthropological 'pointers' toward the existence of God is minimized or left out altogether, then one is left with Pannenberg's dilemma: On the one hand he has developed a series of 'arguments' based upon human openness to the world which point to the possible if not probable existence of a higher being; but because, on the other hand, these arguments are not and cannot be empirically compelling, he cannot formulate them as arguments for the existence of God without either accepting the premises of a natural theology or conceding an important place to the role of faith in the 'knowing' process for the believer. Because neither of these options are acceptable to Pannenberg we should suggest that he is thus unable to take what would seem to many to be the logical step of formulating his analysis of human openness to the world and to God into an anthropological 'argument' for God's existence. Rather, he is left with the task of strenuously denying that he has actually produced such an argument over against the many critics who believe to have detected precisely that in his analysis of human openness to the world and beyond the world.

### 3.2.3 The Unity of Humanity and Universal Experience

*3.2.3.1 The universal experience of freedom*
In one of Pannenberg's first published writings, "Christliche Glaube und menschliche Freiheit" (1957), he takes up the question of human freedom. Although Pannenberg concerns himself here primarily with the freedom of the Christian we also find some indications of his view of human freedom in general.

---

[194] Hans Schwarz, *The Search for God: Christianity - Atheism - Secularism - World Religions* (Minneapolis: Augsburg, 1975), 72.

This is especially the case inasmuch as, in Pannenberg's view, "the proclamation of the freedom of the Christian does not speak of some special, additional freedom that is distinct from the freedom of the person as a human being and that must be added to this freedom."[195] Similar to Rahner human freedom is seen as a gift of God and is therefore dependent upon divine freedom which precedes all human freedom. Pannenberg, in his 1972 work, *Gottesgedanke und menschliche Freiheit*, makes this point in his response to the atheistic charge, as developed by Nietzsche, Hartmann and Sartre, that the idea of God and human freedom are mutually exclusive. Pannenberg, instead, argues that it is precisely God who is the ground of human freedom. He writes:

> The question in only whether it [i.e., the atheistic critique] deals with a problem that every conception of God encounters, or whether the understanding of the reality of God could be developed in such a way that God could be thought of a the ground of human freedom and would no longer appear as a negation of this freedom. ... God, conceived of as an existing being according to the analogy of things present at hand, even if such a God existed, could belong only to the totality of everything that is transcended by freedom. No present at hand Being can be the ground of freedom but rather only a reality that discloses the freedom of its future, the coming God.[196]

Also similar to Rahner, human freedom, for Pannenberg, carries with it responsibility, specifically a universal responsibility for the world, especially as this freedom is expressed most fully in the freedom of the Christian.[197] Yet the extent of the responsibility inherent in human freedom is much more restricted in Pannenberg than in Rahner who, as we have already seen, extended the responsibility inherent in human freedom to include the freedom to say either a yes or no to God. Pannenberg, however, in his *Anthropology in Theological Perspective*, contends that humans are not essentially free to say no to God. According to Pannenberg, when God is rejected, "he is rejected because of the view that the idea of God is merely a human construct." And when God is believed to be a living reality yet his will is rejected, "this is due to doubt about whether this or that is in fact God's will."

Thus, although maintaining that humans are responsible for their sins against God, Pannenberg believes that we do not actually say no to God but to false conceptions of what God is or what he wills based upon faulty or incomplete understanding. Therefore, according to Pannenberg, "the idea of a choice *against* the good or *against* God is a contradiction in terms" since persons must regard their choices as good or as 'for God' otherwise they would not make these choices. It is here that Pannenberg locates the characteristically Lutheran emphasis on the

---

[195] "Christlicher Glaube und menschliche Freiheit," 251.
[196] *Gottesgedanke und menschliche Freiheit*, 23.
[197] "Christlicher Glaube und menschliche Freiheit," 255 and 257.

bondage of the human will. "The bondage of the will consists in that human beings regard as good what is objectively bad for them and therefore choose it."[198] Hence we see that Pannenberg has a less optimistic view of human freedom than does Rahner, attributing to it far less freedom over against God. As Schwarz has written: "Pannenberg speaks of a bondage of the will that ... rules out the possibility that humans can find their own way back to the original balance of tension between exocentricity and ego-determination. ... The bondage of the will, according to Pannenberg, has left intact the ability to choose, but it has reduced the scope of this ability and points toward a structure of motivation which precedes the decisions and the actions of the individual and that is the cause of the failure of the human self."[199]

Although differing with Rahner over the extent of human freedom there is unanimity between the two theologians in regard to the universality of human freedom. Freedom, as an essential quality of being human, is to be found in and is experienced by all persons. For Pannenberg this means not only that all persons are able to choose between alternatives, since freedom is more than this, but also that all persons have the potential to follow or choose the good, when they are really free.[200] But this means they are also able, in the weakness of their 'freedom' to reject the good. In this sense the universality of human freedom is the presupposition for the universality of human sinfulness.

### 3.2.3.2 Original sin and the universal experience of sin

For Pannenberg the essence of human sin is located in human self-centeredness. Already in *What is Man?* Pannenberg contends that at that point where the ego comes into contrast with openness to the world the ego comes to be closed off toward God and thereby also toward its own human destiny. This state of being closed up within itself, according to Pannenberg, is the essence of sin.[201] This ego-centeredness is universal in that it is already present in all persons as sinfulness before they commit a single actual sin. Human beings, therefore, "do not first become sinners through their own actions and by imitating the bad example of others; they are already sinners before any action of theirs. This, then, is the first and fundamental element in the concept of original sin."[202] Thus Pannenberg accepts the doctrine of original sin. Yet, like Rahner, he is critical of

---

[198] *ATP*, 116ff. [113ff.]
[199] Schwarz, *Evil: A Historical and Theological Perspective*, 174f.
[200] Pannenberg, in an unpublished series of theses on freedom distributed to his seminar on freedom at the University of Munich, 29 July 1993, writes: "Die menschliche Fähigkeit zur Wahl zwischen Alternativen, die mit der Unausweichlichkeit der Selbstbestimmung verbunden ist, ist noch nicht Freiheit. Sie ist aber eine Bedingung der Freiheit, die sich darin äußert, daß wir dem Anruf des Guten folgen" [thesis 12]. "Die Wahl zu haben, dem Anruf des Guten zu folgen oder sich ihm zu versagen, ist Ausdruck der Schwäche der Freiheit, die noch nicht gefestigt ist in der Verbundenheit mit dem Guten" [thesis 13].
[201] *What is Man?* 68, [49.]
[202] *ATP*, 119f. [116f.]

traditional formulations of the doctrine. Unlike Rahner, however, Pannenberg does not assume a doctrine of monogenism. He writes: "Adam is seen ... as the prototype of all human beings, as their embodiment, as the Human Being pure and simple." And also, the rooting of universal human responsibility for our sinfulness in Adam,

> can be regarded as plausible to the extent that Adam is regarded not as the historical ancestor of the race but as a mythical prototype and embodiment of the entire race. ... If Adam is understood as the historical ancestor, his situation necessarily ceases to be a paradigm for the human situation as such, since prior to the fall he was in a situation that differed in principle from that of all his descendants, whose history has been decided in advance by his, and this in a negative way. How, then, can the individual fault of Adam be imputed to his descendants ...?[203]

Pannenberg thus rejects the 'traducian' theory of the transmission of original sin from generation to generation as developed by Augustine. He rejects as well the imputation theory developed in later Protestant theology in which the guilt of Adam's sin is simply imputed to his descendants, a theory which Pannenberg judges to "represent no advance at all" to the problem of original sin. Neither does a combination of the concupiscential and imputation theories found in early Lutheran dogmatics provide help since the theory shares the defect common to both parent theories, namely, that it is "unable to explain the co-responsibility of Adam's descendants for the sin of their ancestor." All these problems, however, do not imply for Pannenberg "that the object which the doctrine of original sin was intended to explain, namely, the radicalness and universality of sin, must be abandoned." Only that the universality of sin, and original sin, must be explained in new ways. For Pannenberg the concept of original sin designates that structure which lays behind and precedes all human decisions. It is not transmitted through concupiscence from generation to generation nor is it imputed to all Adam's descendants but is already seen to be universal inasmuch as it is rooted within the very structure of human behavior.[204] In this sense sin is common to all persons (*allgemeinmenschlich*). As Koch observes, the universal character of sin for Pannenberg is to be found in the "truth element (*Wahrheitsmoment*) of the traditional doctrine of original sin."[205]

The ultimate significance of the universality of sin for Pannenberg, and the reason that he seeks new ways of conceptualizing original sin to the extent that it

---

[203] *Ibid.*, 122, 124. [119, 121.]
[204] Cf. *ibid.*, 124ff. [121ff.]
[205] Koch, *Der Gott der Geschichte*, 155. Therefore sin, and original sin, in Pannenberg's thought, "[liegt] in der Wurzel des Menschseins des Menschen ... und all sein Tun zu durchdringen vermag. Indem die Erbsündenlehre damit in besonderer Weise die Radikalität und Universalität der Sünde des Menschen zum Ausdruck zu bringen fähig ist, zeigt sie, wie sehr die Sündhaftigkeit des Menschen bis in die Naturbedingungen des menschlichen Daseins hinein verwurzelt ist."

would seem necessitated by this universality, is that it points beyond the phenomenon of human self-centeredness and to the universality of the salvation provided by Christ. Pannenberg writes: "The universality of sin, which is ... [a] decisive element in the concept of original sin, is a presupposition for the universality of the redemption wrought by Jesus Christ." And similarly, "the universality of redemption *presupposes* the universality of sin."[206] This emphasis upon the relation between the universality of sin and the universality of redemption is also found already in *Human Nature, Election, and History*, where Pannenberg wrote: "The message that man has been reconciled to God in Christ would lack universal significance if all men, without Christ, were not actually constrained by the bondage of sin. The manifestation of the universality of sin in the cross of Jesus is presupposed by the universal salvation achieved by that event."[207] Therefore the universal experience of sin finds its ultimate significance in that it points to the solidarity of humans in our bondage to sin which is a necessary corollary of the universality of Christ's redemptive death on the cross.

### 3.2.3.3 *The universal experience of death*

As we have already briefly touched upon in our discussion of sin, death, as the result of sin, is conceptually closely bound to the concept of sin. And because all persons are sinners all persons ultimately face physical death, a death which, apart from God's intervention through Christ, would be the final destiny of all persons. Pannenberg writes: "Death is the future of every individual human being, and without the hope of the resurrection death would be the ultimate future of humanity. This would be the last word about human beings were God not their future."[208]

In regard to the relationship between sin and death Pannenberg consciously distances his position from that of Rahner who, as we have seen, views death as the fulfillment of life rather than as the inevitable result of sin. Death, in Pannenberg's view, does not bring life to its fulfillment but terminates it. Thus "there is little reason to doubt the hostility to life that is the predominant characteristic of death in the Bible."[209] In order to maintain a relevance of the biblical characterization of death as the consequence of sin in our modern understanding of life we must continue to affirm the Pauline view of the connection between sin and death. Thus, according to Pannenberg, "sin in particular must have death for its natural consequence, inasmuch as the opposition to God contained in sin reaches its logical term in a complete separation from God that is sealed in death." It is for this reason, as Pannenberg points out, that for

---

[206] *ATP*, 120, 134. [117, 131.]
[207] Pannenberg, *Human Nature, Election, and History* (Philadelphia: The Westminster Press, 1977), 13. [*Die Bestimmung des Menschen. Menschen, Erwählung und Geschichte* (Göttingen: Vandenhoeck & Ruprecht, 1978), 7.]
[208] *Die Auferstehung Jesu und die Zukunft des Menschen*, 12.
[209] *ATP*, 139. [136.]

Paul, "the decisive proof of the universal spread of sin is the fact of death and its dominion over all life (Rom. 5:12)."[210]

Pannenberg admits, however, that this connection between sin and death is difficult to establish in the present age in which the "understanding of life as found in biology no longer assumes that life comes from God; therefore it is no longer obvious that separation from God has death as its natural consequence." For help in establishing the connection between sin and death within the modern context Pannenberg turns to help from unexpected quarters, namely, the thought of Paul Tillich. Although Tillich considered sin the sting of death but not its physical cause, Pannenberg notes that he also "developed a set of concepts that connect sin and death much more closely than might have been expected in view of ... [Tillich's belief that sin is not the cause of death], and that enable us to relate biblical statements on the subject to the modern understanding of life and death."[211]

Tillich's view is that sin leads to self-destruction inasmuch as it consists of unbelief, which he characterizes as the individual's "estrangement from God in the center of his being." For Tillich, this constitutes "the religious understanding of sin as rediscovered by the Reformers and as lost again in most Protestant life and thought." Hence sin, in Tillich's view, leads a person outside of the divine center to which the human's own center belongs in such a way that sinners become the centers of their own selves and their own worlds.[212] This understanding of sin as a centeredness in the self without the balancing exocentricity in which the self is also centered in God parallels Pannenberg's own conception of sin. Tillich is able, based upon this conception of sin, to interpret sickness as a dissolution of the self-integration found in a 'healthy' life since the centeredness in the self, according to Tillich, leads to exactly the opposite effect, producing a disintegration of the self as a result of estrangement. Hence sin, or evil, for Tillich is "the structure of self-destruction which is implicit in the nature of universal estrangement."[213]

Pannenberg concludes that Tillich's thought at this point is able to explain more than he thought it could since "by its inner logic his thought clearly leads to the conclusion that physical death, which is the final outcome of the dissolution of the organism, is a consequence of sin and not simply that sin is the sting of death." Although Pannenberg suggests that Tillich's view would have to be studied in detail and "tested against empirical data of the most varied kinds" in order to in any sense 'verify' it, he is inclined to accept it provisionally on the basis of its agreement with key aspects of his own anthropology, especially of his understanding of the *imago dei*. Pannenberg writes: "The viewpoint of self-integration and its dissolution fits into the argument of the present book inasmuch as the image of God, conceived as the destiny of human beings, is to be

---
[210] *Ibid.*, 140 and 138. [137 and 135.]
[211] *Ibid.*, 140f. [137f.]
[212] Paul Tillich, *Systematic Theology*, vol. 2, 48f.
[213] *Ibid.*, 61.

understood as providing direction for the process of self-integration in the living of human life, while sin, being the failure to achieve this destiny, destroys human identity."[214]

### 3.3 *Excursus*: Anthropology and Christology in Pannenberg and Rahner

Both Rahner and Pannenberg have developed what have been called Christologies "from below,"[215] an approach Rahner fully adopted only in his last years.[216] As Pannenberg himself has noted, Rahner's approach to Christology from below (what Rahner has called an "ascendance Christology") resembles in many ways his own approach, "even though ...[Rahner's] basis in transcendental anthropology points in another direction."[217] For both theologians the so-called approach to Christology "from below" has meant an integral connection between anthropology and Christology, between humanity and the God who became human. For Rahner, this expresses itself quite understandably in his emphasis upon incarnation. Pannenberg, however, somewhat unusually develops his Christology from below from the perspective of the resurrection of Christ.[218]

Christology, which stands alongside of anthropology and the doctrine of God in the thought of Pannenberg and Rahner as a theological foundation of theology's

---

[214] *ATP*, 142. [139.]

[215] Cf. Frank Tupper, *The Theology of Wolfhart Pannenberg*, 129ff.; and Ignacy Bokwa, *Christologie als Anfang und Ende der Anthropologie*, 41, 135ff. For Pannenberg's justification of opting for a methodological approach to Christology from below see *Jesus - God and Man*, 33f. [*Grundzüge*, 26ff.] For a criticism of Rahner's formulation of a Christology from below as too tied to anthropology see Walter Kasper, "Christologie von unten? Kritik und Neuansatz gegenwärtiger Christologie," in: *Grundfragen der Christologie heute*, ed. Leo Scheffczyk (Freiburg: Herder, 1975), esp. 153ff.

[216] In an interview on the occasion of his 70th birthday Rahner commented: "Ich glaube, man könnte meiner Christologie tatsächlich ... die Frage stellen, ... ob ich nicht von einer, wie ich es nenne, Deszendenzchristologie in den letzten Jahren mehr und mehr zu einer bescheideneren, nüchterneren, weniger spekulativen Aszendenzchristologie übergegangen bin." Rahner, *Gnade als Mitte menschlicher Existenz: Ein Gespräch mit und über Karl Rahner aus Anlaß seines 70. Geburtstages* (Freiburg: Herder, 1974), 87.

[217] *ST* 2:287, note 47 [326, note 47.]

[218] Peter Hodgson, "Pannenberg on Jesus," in: *Journal of the American Academy of Religion* 36 (1968), 373ff., criticizes Pannenberg's Christology from below suggesting that by his stress upon the resurrection the historical Jesus is overlooked, i.e., not taken with "radical seriousness," thus raising the question whether Pannenberg has indeed followed the path of a Christology from below. As Tupper, 274, notes, Pannenberg responded to this criticism contending that a correspondence exists between the Jesus traditions and the resurrection tradition. Cf. Pannenberg, "A Theological Conversation with Wolfhart Pannenberg," in: *Dialog* 11 (1972), 286ff. Yet this development is entirely consistent with Pannenberg's Christological thought in which the resurrection holds the central role. John Cobb, in describing the importance of the resurrection for Pannenberg's Christology, has quite aptly observed that "nowhere in the whole history of theology has the historical resurrection of Jesus been treated as more determinative of every christological problem" than in Pannenberg's thought. (Cobb, "Wolfhart Pannenberg's 'Jesus: God and Man,'" in: *Journal of Religion* 49 (1969), 201.

universality, will be dealt with here as an excursus under the category of anthropology. This excursus, together with the discussions of Jesus Christ as pinnacle of God's self-revelation found in chapters one and two, must for reasons of space suffice for our treatment of the Christological foundation of the universality of theology in Pannenberg and Rahner. Hence no attempt will be made here to present a comprehensive review of the Christologies of either Rahner or Pannenberg. We will instead focus on the connections between anthropology and Christology in both theologians and on the universal significance of Jesus Christ as representative member of the one humanity.

### 3.3.1 *Rahner: Christology as beginning and end of anthropology*

In Rahner's view, anthropology and Christology, when properly understood, mutually condition one another within dogmatics. Christian anthropology, according to Rahner, "only attains its full meaning when it conceives of man as the obediential potency for the hypostatic union." And similarly, Rahner contends that "we can develop a Christology today only from the standpoint of such a transcendental anthropology."[219] This presupposes that in Rahner's view Christ took on truly human form and being, that is to say, that our human reality was/is united with the Word of God in Jesus Christ so that he was/is human in every sense of the word. Hence for Rahner, "the doctrine of the unconfused [*unvermischten*] and unchanged real human nature implies, ... that the 'human nature' of the Logos possesses a genuine, spontaneous, free, spiritual active center, a human self-consciousness, which as creaturely faces the eternal Word in a genuinely human attitude of adoration, obedience, a most radical sense of creaturehood."[220] Christology, therefore, according to Rahner, is "the radical and unsurpassable repetition of anthropology so that post-incarnational anthropology must be read as deficient Christology and Christology must be read as the goal and source of anthropology."[221]

In what sense, however, can Christology be seen not just as the goal or end but also as the source or beginning of anthropology? This is the case, according to Rahner, because *what* humans really are has been revealed historically and unsurpassably in Jesus Christ. Therefore an adequate protology or theology of human origins is only possibly eschatologically, that is to say, as seen from the perspective of the incarnation of the divine Logos in the person of Jesus Christ.[222]

---

[219] "Theology and Anthropology," 2. [*Schriften* 8:43].
[220] Rahner, "Current Problems in Christology," in: *TI* 1:176f and 157f. ["Probleme der Christologie von heute," in: *Schriften* 1:197 and 178.] Cf. Bert van der Heijden, *Karl Rahner: Darstellung und Kritik seiner Grundpositionen*, 399ff. for a discussion and critique of Rahner's conception of the humanity of Jesus Christ.
[221] "Grundsätzliche Überlegungen zur Anthropologie und Protologie im Rahmen der Theologie," 417.
[222] At this point a comparison can be seen between Teilhard de Chardin's evolutionary understanding of the incarnation in light of the eschatological, teleological manifestation of the Omega Point, and Rahner's own view. A connection to Teilhard can also be seen in Rahner's attempt to reconcile the

Ontologically, Rahner maintains that "the possibility that there be men is grounded in the greater, more comprehensive and more radical possibility of God to express himself in the Logos which becomes a creature."[223] As Rahner has also contended:

> Protology and eschatology are innerly connected to one another to the extent that the beginning is a beginning open toward its end and the beginning is only fulfilled in its end. The growing presence of the eschaton which was given in Christ, albeit in obscured form, in the increasing self-fulfilment of humans, is at the same time the growing presence of the beginning. As a consequence the beginning as continuing destiny of the human being is only achievable in a retrospective etiology of the salvational situation of the human being at any given time.[224]

In Rahner's view, therefore, one cannot speak of human origins until one knows what the human really is, and this is only possible in and through Jesus Christ. A retrospective etiology is possible only from the perspective of the salvational situation of humans, which for Rahner is inextricably bound to the fact that humanity, in the whole of its history, is the subject of God's salvific self-disclosure which finds its culmination in the God-person Jesus Christ. Therefore Rahner concludes:

> Since only in Jesus Christ and in his Pneuma does a person know reflexively and in official openness that he can be the subject of the absolute self-manifestation of God and that it runs de facto through the entire history of humanity, and since this experience principally is only surpassed by the direct contemplation of God, an unsurpassable protology is therefore only possible through Christ and only from this perspective is it able to be reflected upon in its own formal essence.[225]

At the same time Rahner understands Christ as the end or goal of the human person, and indeed of all humanity, precisely because the divine Logos, in the incarnation (or more specifically in the hypostatic union) became a human being in the person of Jesus of Nazareth. In this sense he is the ideal or the model for humanity (and for anthropology), but he is also the goal of the very humanity of which he became a part.[226] And not only of humanity, for Christ is also the goal of the whole creation as the high point of God's self-disclosure - a creation of which human beings are an integral part.[227]

---

[223] incarnation with an evolutionary view of the world which he accepts as a given. See, for instance, *FCF*, 178ff. [*Grundkurs*, 180ff.]
[224] *FCF*, 223. [*Grundkurs*, 221.]
"Grundsätzliche Überlegungen zur Anthropologie," 417f.
[225] *Ibid.*, 420.
[226] *Ibid.*, 416; and "Theologische Anthropologie," 625f.
[227] Rahner, "Die Christologie innerhalb einer evolutiven Weltanschauung," in: *Schriften* 5:201f.

Christology, as the source and goal, the beginning and end of anthropology, is the key to anthropology's connection to the total theological enterprise, thus making Rahner's argumentation complete. Anthropology is theology but only because its beginning and its end are to be found in Christology, especially in incarnational Christology. As Rahner writes, because the union of the real essence of God and of humanity expresses itself in God's eternal Logos, "Christology is the beginning and the end of anthropology, and this anthropology in its most radical actualization [namely, as Christology] is for all eternity theology. It is ... the theology which God himself has spoken by uttering his Word as our flesh."[228]

### 3.3.2 Pannenberg: Jesus Christ as founder of a 'new humanity'

Pannenberg has noted that traditionally the two central ideas associated with the Christian concept of humanity have been the *imago dei* and the notion of sin originating in the 'fall.' Both of these concepts, however, are firmly rooted in the Old Testament. Pannenberg suggests that the most significant and distinctively *Christian* contribution to the understanding of humanity "is to be found in the Christian assertion that man has been reconciled to God in Christ," which has led to "the modification of the other two concepts [*imago dei* and sin] in Christian thought."[229] It is the concept of reconciliation through Christ, therefore, which provides the structural center for Pannenberg's emphasis upon Jesus Christ as the founder of a new humanity.[230]

Jesus Christ, however, can only be the founder of a new humanity when he is also connected to the old humanity. For Pannenberg the Pauline image of Christ as the second or last Adam points to the significance of the human person Jesus for all humanity as he in whom humanity is fulfilled.

> The fulfillment of human destiny has been revealed in Jesus through his resurrection from the dead. Jesus did not experience this event only for himself but for all men; Jesus' resurrection allowed the destiny of all men to a life in nearness to God, as Jesus had proclaimed it, to appear in him. ... Jesus is the New Adam, the second heavenly man, the life-giving Spirit in contrast to the first, earthly man. ... As death came through the first man, so the grace of God, life, and righteousness (Rm. 5:15ff) has come through the second true man. Jesus ... [as] man's representative before God, bring[s] ... the destiny of men to fulfillment in his own person.[231]

---

[228] *FCF*, 225. [*Grundkurs*, 223.] Cf. also, Rahner, "Zur Theologie der Menschwerdung," in: *Schriften* 4:151.

[229] *Human Nature, Election, and History*, 13. [*Die Bestimmung des Menschen*, 7.]

[230] A new humanity, according to Pannenberg, is necessary if sin and death are to be overcome. Jesus as the model of a new humanity shows us that humans must be changed. Cf. Pannenberg's sermon from Easter Sunday, 1970, "Der neue Mensch," in: *Gegenwart Gottes: Predigten* (Munich: Claudius Verlag, 1973), 135.

[231] *Jesus - God and Man*, 196f. [*Grundzüge*, 200ff.]

Similarly, Pannenberg has elsewhere written concerning Jesus as the eschatological new person that, "this function of Christ for Christians ... has significance for all humanity. For this reason Paul can speak of Christ, that is, the second and last Adam, the founder of a new humanity. ... What has taken place through Jesus Christ is therefore not only important for Christians and their future but is significant for the future of all humanity."[232]

Jesus is understood to be the highest completion or perfection of humanity by Pannenberg, who points to Rahner's view of Christology as the beginning and end of anthropology as essentially testifying to the same thing. In his concept of Christ as the fulfillment of all humanity Pannenberg believes that the insights of modern anthropology into the openness of humans for the world are made fruitful for Christology and point beyond a mere openness to the world but more importantly to an openness toward God. Writes Pannenberg: "In fact one must understand Jesus' unity with God as the fulfillment of the openness to the world that is constitutive for man as such, if this openness has its real meaning in an openness extending beyond the world to God."[233]

In his *Systematic Theology*, Pannenberg develops further the implications of Jesus as the second or last Adam for the whole of humanity. He writes: "Paul's view of Christ as the new eschatological or last Adam has a social reference oriented to human community. It tells us that 'we' all shall 'bear' the image of the new and heavenly man (1 Cor. 15:49) and shall be changed into his likeness (2 Cor. 3:18)."[234] Jesus, however, is only the second Adam who founds a new humanity inasmuch as this role is realized concretely in his own human history. Therefore "in the case of Jesus ... the particular identity of his person is related to the course of his history, and especially to its outcome in the passion and the Easter."[235] Pannenberg can thus conclude in regard to Jesus that "only as the crucified and risen Lord is he the new and eschatologically definitive man."[236] In this way the importance of history, and consequently also of a Christology from below for the understanding Jesus as the fulfillment of humanity is made clear.

### 3.3.3 *The universal significance of Jesus Christ*

For Karl Rahner the unity of humanity and Jesus Christ's participation in this unity through his incarnation points unmistakably to the universal relevance of the redemption provided through his death.[237] Indeed, Rahner maintained that the

---

[232] Pannenberg, "Auferstehung Jesu und Zukunft des Menschen," in: Rudolf Schnackenburg and W. Pannenberg, *Ostern und der neue Mensch* (Freiburg: Herder, 1981), 54f.
[233] *Jesus - God and Man*, 199f. [*Grundzüge*, 204.]
[234] *ST* 2:304 [344.]
[235] *Ibid.*, 303 [342.]
[236] *Ibid.*, 312 [352.] Cf. also Pannenberg's sermon, "Der neue Mensch," 136, where he notes that the "Schatten des Todes auf unserm Leben ist überwunden durch die Auferstehung Jesu. Darin ist er der neue und wahre Mensch, daß an ihm das unvergängliche Leben erschienen ist."
[237] Cf., for instance, *The Church and the Sacraments*, 12f. [*Kirche und Sakramente*, 12f.], where Rahner contends that Jesus, in his sacrificial death, is a member of the one humanity. Hence

universality of redemption could theoretically be derived alone from the fact of the incarnation and the unity of humanity. Thus he could contend that "humanity is one and is saved as a single whole through the incarnation of the eternal Logos in this unity." The salvation wrought by Christ must necessarily be shared with all humanity, according to Rahner, "otherwise the unity of human history would be destroyed, if the necessary salvation of one of its members were irrelevant to the destiny and possibility of salvation of the whole of mankind."[238] Yet for Rahner the Logos' participation in the universality of the human race and human history is by itself insufficient for pointing to the salvific significance of the death and resurrection of Jesus. "The death and resurrection of Jesus must possess universal importance in themselves for salvation and cannot merely be regarded as isolated events, of no significance in themselves, in a life which only has universal relevance for salvation in being the life of the eternal Logos ... which entered the unity of humankind and took on a human nature." Yet at the same time Rahner cautions that the cross itself cannot be thought of alone as the ground for salvation, otherwise we would have to abandon any idea of the universality of salvation "since the majority of mankind have no explicit knowledge of the cross." It is better, according to Rahner, to say that the cross (together with the resurrection) of Jesus has a proto-sacramental causality (*ursacramentale Ursächlichkeit*) for all humanity.[239] Or, in the words of the Second Vatican Council, which Rahner quotes with approval, Jesus Christ as proto-sacrament is the original "sign and instrument of the innermost union with God and of the unity of the whole of mankind."[240]

For Rahner the universal significance of Jesus Christ for the salvation of human beings is tied to anthropology in a twofold manner. First, a relationship between Jesus and the rest of humanity is assumed. This relationship, as we have already seen, is built upon the fact of the incarnation of the divine Logos. Jesus has salvific significance for all humanity precisely as a member of this same human race. Secondly, Rahner assumes that the relationship between Jesus and humanity is mutual. That is to say, the cross of Jesus has universal salvific significance for humanity only when the relationship between Jesus and humanity is mutual, "if, that is, not only is Jesus related to mankind but also mankind is related to him." For Rahner this means concretely that all persons "who reach salvation must have a relationship to *Jesus Christ* in their saving faith [for] ... the

---

[238] through the incarnation of the divine Logos, argues Rahner, the one humanity, in its geneological (racial) unity and in its one history, is a "consecrated humanity," that is to say, this one humanity has "become the people of God."
Rahner, "The One Christ and the Universality of Salvation," in: *TI* 16:211. ["Der eine Jesus Christus und die Universalität des Heils," in: *Schriften* 12:265.]

[239] *Ibid.*, 211. [266f.]

[240] *Ibid.*, 214f. [270.] Cf. "*Lumen gentium*" 1, in: Denzinger 4101. The Dogmatic Constitution itself states actually that the church *in Christ* is this sacrament. "*Cum autem Ecclesia sit in Christo veluti sacramentum seu signum et instrumentum intimae cum Deo unionis totiusque generis humani unitatis.*"

fact that Jesus is the universal cause of salvation implies that all men are related to Jesus by means of the faith that is necessary for salvation."[241] The universality of salvation thus presupposes a universality of the relationship to Jesus, which in the case of those persons who lived before Christ and those from other religions who have not heard or have not heard clearly the gospel of Jesus Christ this produces a problem.

It is at this point that Rahner suggests that a relational faith in the self-disclosing God is possible even where the Word-revelation of the Old and New Testaments has not reached. We come here to the heart of Rahner's theory of anonymous Christians, which will be taken up in more detail in chapter five. At this point suffice it to say that for Rahner the postulate of an unthematic and implicit givenness of God beyond the space-time boundaries of the Word-revelation makes it possible for all persons to have an implicit relationship to Jesus Christ. So also the possibility of a universal salvation through Christ is seen to be a real one.[242]

For Pannenberg the universal significance of Jesus has already been noted in his emphasis upon Jesus as founder of a new humanity. That this is "not just of significance for Christians but for the future of humanity in general"[243] is to be seen most clearly in Christ's substitutionary death for all persons. As Tupper notes: "Pannenberg seeks to establish the justification for assigning universal significance to Christ's death on other grounds [than the scriptures alone], namely, in the course of Jesus' historical activity which led to the cross as well as in the validity of the category of 'representation' or 'substitution' ... as a universal aspect of human experience."[244]

For Pannenberg this comes especially to expression in the account of Christ's descent into hell, in which he pursues a line of thought very much parallel to that of Rahner in regard to the significance of Christ for those who have not heard clearly or have not heard at all the message of his redemptive death and victorious resurrection. Pannenberg writes:

> The symbolic language of Jesus' descent into hell expresses the extent to which those men who lived before Jesus' activity and those who did not know him have a share in the salvation that has appeared in him. That is an extremely important question for all Christian missions and for the self-understanding of Christianity in the midst of humanity: Does only the person who believes in Jesus with a conscious decision have a share in the nearness of God that he has opened? Or must account be made for an unconscious participation in salvation by men who never or only superficially came into contact with the message of Christ? The concept of Jesus' descent into hell, of his preaching in the realm of the dead, affirms the latter. It asserts that men outside the visible church are not

---

[241] Ibid., 216f. [272f.]
[242] Ibid., 218ff. [274ff.]
[243] "Auferstehung Jesu und Zukunft des Menschen," 54f.
[244] Tupper, The Theology of Wolfhart Pannenberg, 160.

automatically excluded from salvation. Who participates in salvation and who does not remains, to be sure, open. ... By considering Jesus' death within the whole context of his activity and fate, the universal understanding of Jesus' substitution expressed in the concept of the preaching in Hades may be correct, in contrast to the occasionally defended restriction of the preaching in Hades to the fathers of Israel.[245]

A so-called 'universalism' is therefore witnessed to in Christ's descent into hell and preaching to the dead, not in that it points necessarily to the salvation of all persons, i.e., an *apocatastasis panton*, but rather in that it shows the 'openness' of salvation to all, not just to those within the Church or who have come into contact with the gospel message. Christ's substitutionary death, therefore, transcends all boundaries of time, distance or circumstance in its ramifications and is this sense, according to Pannenberg, is universal.

Pannenberg additionally reinforces his emphasis upon the universal nature of the substitutionary or vicarious death of Jesus in regard to the representative role of the Jewish judges and of Pilate. Pannenberg contends that the "efficacy of the vicarious significance of Jesus' death, not only for his judges but for the whole Jewish people, and beyond them for all mankind," depends upon the involvement of those who judged Jesus as representatives of the Jewish and Roman peoples as well as of law and humanity in general. That is to say, it is important that those involved in Jesus' death acted as representatives and not simply as individuals. And, according to Pannenberg, even though the resurrection of Jesus showed these judges to be false judges and in the wrong, this does not overturn or undo in any way the representative nature of Jesus' death for the Jewish people and beyond them for all humanity. Jesus therefore died in the stead of his judges, and, "through the very fact that these judges did not only act as isolated individuals but as the office-bearers of their people, the vicarious power of Jesus' death on the cross also extends beyond their sphere to the whole people, and indeed to the whole of mankind, since the Jewish nation, as God's chosen people, stands before God for the whole of mankind."[246] Thus just as sin and death are seen to be universal among human beings so also is Jesus's vicarious death universal inasmuch as all persons, as sinners, and indeed as blasphemers, were represented in putting him on the cross and are beneficiaries of his defeat of death, as illustrated at least symbolically in Jesus' descent into hell.[247]

---

[245] *Jesus - God and Man*, 272f. [*Grundzüge*, 280f.]
[246] *The Apostles' Creed*, 83ff. [*Das Glaubensbekenntnis*, 90ff.]
[247] Cf. *Jesus - God and Man*, 260 [*Grundzüge*, 267], where Pannenberg writes: "Does Jesus' death have vicarious significance for all humanity beyond Israel? This is possible only under the presupposition that not only the Jews but with them all men are disclosed as blasphemers by Jesus' cross."

## 3.4 Summary and conclusions

### 3.4.1 Pannenberg and Rahner: Starting with the human

Pannenberg, relying upon the insights of secular anthropologies, sees humanity as characterized by openness and self-transcendence - a self-transcendence which points ultimately beyond the world to the reality of God.[248] Similarly, although using different terminology, humans, as potential hearers of the word, are characterized by Rahner as spirits in the world - by which he understands "in the world," as we have seen, in a way parallel to Pannenberg's world-openness - and as transcendental, a transcendentality which points to God and allows the human person to be *potentia oboedientialis*. Pannenberg, along with Rahner, also affirms that 'spirit,' even with specific reference to the corporeal aspect of human beings, is the fundamental or primary concept descriptive of the human reality. Pannenberg writes: "Human beings are not 'spirit' in contrast to their bodily nature. All human expressions of life, even their bodiliness, are encompassed within the life of the spirit. Spirit is the most comprehensive term possible for the description of human reality."[249] In fundamental points, therefore, the anthropologies of Pannenberg and Rahner resemble one another in several significant ways.

Both theologians, in their own way, also make room for the insights of secular anthropologies within their own theological anthropologies. Although Rahner takes as his starting point theological anthropology whereas Pannenberg begins with the human sciences, both achieve a similar result, namely, the integration of theological and profane anthropologies through interdisciplinary dialogue aimed at producing a more comprehensive picture of humanity.

Also, as has been observed, "Wolfhart Pannenberg carries out the dialogue between theology and anthropology similar to Rahner, on the basis of the theme of the religious meaning of humans and their historical form within Christianity."[250] In this connection the emphasis upon the rootedness of human beings within history has been seen to be decisive for both theologians. Pannenberg and the later Rahner also both adopt an approach to Christology "from below," thus making the humanity of Jesus Christ, and along with it anthropology, the starting point for their reflections upon the person and work of Jesus Christ. Whereas Pannenberg's Christology from below was seen to be present in his earliest Christological reflections, Rahner adopted this approach decisively only in his later writings. The difference in approach between the early Rahner and

---

[248] For Pannenberg, self-transcendence, a term reflective of Rahner's anthropological emphasis, is essentially the same thing as world-openness. Writes Pannenberg: "Weltoffenheit - es wird gelegentlich auch der Ausdruck 'Selbsttranszendenz für dasselbe Phänomen gebraucht - besteht darin, daß der Mensch sich von den Eindrücken, die auf ihn einstürmen, distanzieren kann." Pannenberg, "Anthropologie in theologischer Perspektive," 96.
[249] *Ibid.*, 105.
[250] Ringeling, *Christliche Ethik im Dialog*, 62.

Pannenberg, however, would not seem to point to a fundamental difference in this regard between the anthropologies of the two theologians so much as it points, as we earlier suggested, to an inconsistency between the anthropology and Christology of the early Rahner. In the later Rahner the anthropological starting point prevails also in his Christological reflections, making the underlying similarity between his own approach and Pannenberg's more visible. The distinction between the two theologians in regard to their formulations of Christologies from below, as we have already indicated above, is rather to be seen in Rahner's emphasis upon incarnational Christology whereas Pannenberg's approach leads him to focus his Christological reflections upon the resurrection.

While differences in the two theologians' emphases upon human transcendentality and historicalness are evident in their writings, these, upon closer examination, have been seen too be not as great as they might initially appear. The most fundamental difference we uncovered had instead to do with original sin and the relationship between sin and death. While Rahner, as we saw, advanced views that can be labeled as 'anthropo-optimistic,' (or as some would have it, even 'semi-Pelagian'), Pannenberg remains firmly rooted in the Augustinian tradition. The shape of human freedom and the place he gives to it in his thought, however, along with the form of his concept of the *imago dei*, would seem to prevent his view of man from degenerating into an anthropo-pessimism, even though his views on sin and death might with some justification appear to tend in this direction to those coming from a Rahnerian perspective.[251] With the significant exception of the doctrines of original sin and death, therefore, we would conclude that even though the emphases often differ, nearly every critical point in the anthropological thought of either theologian finds its parallel in the thought of the other - even if it is often clothed in different terminology arising out of their varied confessional and philosophical contexts.

Significantly, the themes of the unity of humanity and the universality of human experience, developed in both the anthropologies of Rahner and Pannenberg, become the pre-condition for their apologetic approach. For both Pannenberg and Rahner the common ground between the Christian and the non-Christian which, as we will see in our final two chapters, becomes the starting point for their dialogue with modern science and with non-Christian worldviews, is the data of a shared humanity. Only on the basis of the unity of humanity and the universality of human experience is an apologetic approach to the non-Christian religions, atheism, and modern scientific worldviews possible. And only when universality is found to exist at the level of the shared human experiences of freedom, sin and death and in the unity of the human race can theology's reflections upon the Word of God spoken to humanity claim universal relevance.

---

[251] Brian Walsh, for instance, though not himself a "Rahnerian," has argued that Pannenberg exhibits a pessimistic view of humanity in that he is not able to affirm the goodness of all being because he makes fallenness constitutive of creatureliness. Walsh, "A Critical Review of Pannenberg's Anthropology in Theological Perspective," in: *Christian Scholars Review* 15:3 (1986): 258-259.

# Chapter Four

## GOD AS FOUNDATION OF THEOLOGY'S UNIVERSALITY

For Pannenberg as for Rahner the second decisive pole of the theological foundation of universality is to be found in the doctrine of God. We take up the discussion of God at this point not because the doctrine of God is secondary to anthropology for either Pannenberg or Rahner but rather because of the anthropological starting points of both theologians mandated the treatment of humanity first. In many ways we have already ventured unavoidably into the proper domain of the doctrine of God in the preceding three chapters. Here the doctrine will be taken up in a more systematic way with particular focus upon its implications for theology's claim to universality. In this regard, it will be seen that the doctrine of God is of even greater significance for the establishment of Christian theology's claim to universality than anthropology.

### 4.1 Wolfhart Pannenberg: God as All-Determining Reality

It has been noted that "perhaps the truly novel, radical dimension of Pannenberg's theology is his doctrine of God."[1] Amidst so much fanfare and discussion surrounding Pannenberg's concept of revelation as history, the verifiability, or better, falsifiability of theological statements, and his wide-ranging investigations in anthropology, his doctrine of God is sometimes either overlooked or given too little attention.[2] It is, however, as we shall see, precisely Pannenberg's understanding of God which stands at the center not only of his theological system, but also of his claim of theology's universality. Hence for Pannenberg, "the concept of God can never be simply one issue among others. It is the central issue, around which everything else is organized. If you take away that one issue nothing would be left to justify the continuation of that special effort that we call 'theology.'"[3]

---

[1] Tupper, *The Theology of Wolfhart Pannenberg*, 285.
[2] Although many have commented, usually negatively, on his conception of God as the power of the future, there has been comparatively little *extensive* analysis of Pannenberg's doctrine of God as such. So also Marc Kolden, *Pannenberg's Attempt to Base Theology on History* (Ph.D. dissertation, University of Chicago, 1976), 263.
[3] Pannenberg, "Problems of a Christian Doctrine of God," in: Pannenberg, *An Introduction to Systematic Theology* (Grand Rapids: Eerdmans, 1991), 21.

## 4.1.1 The Unity of God

### 4.1.1.1 *Old Testament and Greek philosophical roots of Christian monotheism*

Pannenberg, consistent not only with convention but with the importance of God in his thought, begins his three volume *Systematic Theology*, following a chapter devoted to prolegomena, with his treatment of the doctrine of God. He begins with his concern for the content of the word 'God.' A fruitful discussion of God, he maintains, is only possible when we are clear what we mean by 'God.' For Pannenberg 'God' has to do with the totality of reality and the word is rejected today only at the peril of losing all ability to speak meaningfully of the totality of reality. Pannenberg finds himself here in agreement with Rahner, who he says is correct in his contention that if the word 'God' is dropped from our vocabulary "we would no longer be confronted by the one totality of reality or the one totality of our existence. The word 'God,' and that word alone, does this."[4] Our contemporary situation of doing theology, however, is characterized, according to Pannenberg "by the fact that in the world of secular culture the word 'God' is not taken for granted, or if so, it is taken as a token of religious language, valid only within the enclave of religious discourse. The word is not self-evident as pointing to the ultimate reality that embraces, governs, judges, and explains everything else."[5] Hence a first task of the theologian who wishes to (indeed must) speak of 'God' today is to establish the content of this word as having to do with all reality.

To establish his conception of God as having to do with the totality of reality and the totality of all human existence Pannenberg turns not to religious experience but to the Old Testament conception of Yahweh and to the 'Greek' philosophical tradition.[6] Already in the Old Testament conception of Yahweh Pannenberg finds the thesis that this God is *the* God. Here, contends Pannenberg, we have the instance of the restriction of a general category, namely the category 'god' or 'divinity,' to a single instance, namely Yahweh. Only on the condition of the uniqueness of the term 'God' can we talk intelligibly about God. It is significant, therefore, that the restriction of God to a single instance has been taken up in Christian theology. Pannenberg writes:

---
[4] *ST* 1:71. [81.] Cf. also "Problems of a Christian Doctrine of God," 21f., where Pannenberg contends that "the concept of God cannot be exchanged for other concepts" and that "an entire dimension of what it means to be human falls into oblivion where the word 'God' disappears."

[5] "Problems of a Christian Doctrine of God," 22.

[6] Pannenberg would seem to have in mind especially the Platonic tradition. Hence already in his 1959 article, "The Appropriation of the Philosophical Concept of God as a Dogmatic Problem of Early Christian Theology", in: *BQ* 2:122 ["Die Aufnahme des philosophischen Gottesbegriffs als dogmatisches Problem der frühchristlichen Theologie," in: *Zeitschrift für Kirchengeschichte* 70 (1959), 3], he wrote: "It was from Platonism, above all, that early Christian theology borrowed the conceptual tools for its reflection upon the nature of God. In so doing, it did not so much fasten on Plato himself as on the so-called Middle Platonism." The question about God as the origin of present things and processes in Middle Platonism led, according to Pannenberg, quite naturally and even stringently to the idea of the unity of God - an idea taken over from Middle Platonism especially in the arguments of the apologist Justin Martyr (126f. [6]).

The concept of the 'divine' as a general designation of 'gods' has been taken over in Christian theology by the metaphysical concept of God which already embraces the unity of the divine as the one origin of the cosmos. This concept, having the form of a general description, could play the part in Christian theology that the general term 'God' (Elohim) had in the early biblical understanding of God, especially in making intelligible the assertion of the sole deity of Yahweh.[7]

Therefore whereas the Old Testament worshippers of Yahweh had to distinguish their God sharply from the plurality of gods of the Gentiles Pannenberg contends that philosophy already thought of God as one and that this God can thus be identified with "the one God of the Bible, the Father of Jesus Christ."[8] It is therefore a regression, argues Pannenberg, if Christian theology rejects the one God spoken of by the philosophers claiming that theology deals only with the 'Christian' God and no other since this implies a plurality of gods among whom the Christian God is simply one among others. At stake is the claim to universality. Christian theology has therefore traditionally recognized the metaphysical implications of such a restriction of the term 'God' and has not so restricted it "because in so doing it could [not] maintain the universality of what the Bible says about the one God in opposition to popular polytheism and state-protected cults."[9] This stance, however, while arrived at by Christian theology in contact with the Greek philosophical tradition, is grounded not in that tradition but in the biblical witness to the universality of God.[10] As Pannenberg noted already

---

[7] *ST* 1:68f. [78f.], for this and the following quote.

[8] Pannenberg does not, however, hold that Greek philosophical theology and its emphasis on the one God can be identified without qualification as monotheistic, which remained the unique contribution of the Old Testament religion to Christian theology. Thus Pannenberg wrote already in "The Appropriation of the Philosophical Concept of God," 127f. ["Die Aufnahme des philosophischen Gottesbegriffs," 7]: "Since Parmenides ... contrasted the One, as the truly imperishable being, to the transitory Many, the theme of the unity of the divine no longer faded away. In the final draft of his doctrine of ideas, Plato set forth the One as identical with the Good in being the ontological ground of the ideas. Aristotle and the Stoics also maintained the unity of the divine. One sees, particularly in these two lines of development, however, that such a unity of the divine may not be claimed as 'monotheistic' without qualification. It can be combined with polytheistic popular religion in many ways."

[9] *ST* 1:69. [79.] For Pannenberg's analysis of the reception of the philosophical concept of God in early Christian theology see his article, "The Appropriation of the Philosophical Concept of God," especially the summary of his arguments, 140ff. [41ff.]

[10] Yet Greek thought was also a source of the concern for universality. This, according to Pannenberg, becomes especially clear in the mission to the Gentiles, in which aspects of the Greek philosophical tradition's idea of God is seen within the Christian church. As Pannenberg explains: "The link with Greek thought, essentially universal in orientation, was part of the inner logic of the mission to the pagans. ... That was how the Greek philosophical tradition, especially of the philosophical question of the true God, came to be accepted. We should not be misled into thinking that the ancient Hellenistic heritage was thrust on the early Church as something alien, still less as a falsification of the Gospel. Its appropriation followed necessarily from the universal nature of the Christian message and is not to be separated from the foundation of the Church." Pannenberg, "He will be our God," in: *Faith and Reality*, 82, [*Glaube und Wirklichkeit*, 108.]

in one of his earliest writings: "The debate with the philosophical question about the true form of the divine was indeed occasioned by encounter with the Hellenistic intellectual world, but it is also grounded in the biblical witness to God as the universal God, pertinent not only to Israel but to all peoples."[11]

Pannenberg, therefore, in clarifying what is meant by the term 'God,' does not turn to religious experience since the word 'God,' at least in a general sense, is itself one of the most important keys to religious experience and presupposes the clarification of such experiences. Pannenberg instead turns to philosophy, or better, to philosophical theology which "has viewed the one God as the origin of the unity of the cosmos." In this sense philosophy has opposed the various religious traditions which gave the gods spheres of operation within the cosmic order and even roles in establishing this order but without recognizing that the unity of the cosmos finally demands the unity of its divine origin. Pannenberg thus contends that, "in no way is it opposed to what the Bible says about God that philosophical theology made the relation to the world, to the world as a whole, the criterion of its concept of God." Early Christian theology, therefore, was correct to maintain that "the God manifest in Jesus Christ is none other than the Creator of the world and therefore the one and only God."[12] This confession, therefore, finds its roots not in religious experience but in concerns that can be best categorized as belonging to philosophical theology and its concern for the unity of the cosmos - a concern which, according to Pannenberg, leads necessarily to the unity of God.

In a polytheistic context, admits Pannenberg, the concern was not always (nor could it really be) for the totality and unity of existence, neither did the word 'god' symbolize such concerns. Yet, as Pannenberg contends, "once the plurality of the gods was reduced to the concept of the one God as the origin of the one world, the word 'God' did in fact become a key word for awareness of the totality of the world and of human life." Pannenberg credits this decisive move to two sources. First of all, to Israel's crucial transition from the worship of only one God (monolatry) to the belief that only one God exits (monotheism). And second, Pannenberg credits the "pioneering" thought of the philosophical theology of the Greeks which "helped to make the Christian message of the revelation of the one God to all people in Jesus Christ intelligible and plausible to non-Jews."[13]

Pannenberg, therefore, finds the roots of the understanding of the unity of God which underlies the unity of all reality not only in the monotheism of the Old Testament but also, and significantly for Pannenberg, in the tradition of philosophical theology dating back to the Greeks. This insight into the origin of the 'unity of God' leads Pannenberg at the same time to make the plea that Christian theology neither forget nor disown this philosophical legacy, something

---

[11] "The Appropriation of the Philosophical Concept of God," 134. [12.]
[12] *ST* 1:70. [80.]
[13] *Ibid.*, 71f. [82.]

Protestant theology, according to Pannenberg, has been in danger of doing from Ritschl to Barth. The philosophical theology of the Greeks, warns Pannenberg, is "not to be summarily expelled from our Christian understanding as an alien factor which falsifies the supposedly purely moral message of the gospel." To do so would have far-reaching and momentous consequences for our understanding of God and his universality. Indeed, for Gentile Christians such a rejection of the philosophical foundations of our understanding of God would destroy "the presuppositions of their own turning to the God of the Jews as the one God of all peoples."[14]

### 4.1.1.2 *The internal unity of God and the doctrine of the Trinity*

An additional aspect of the unity of God in Pannenberg's thought is his concern for the internal unity of God as expressed in his formulation of the doctrine of the trinity and of his proposal to understand God (as Spirit) in terms of a field. As Pannenberg writes: "In the discussion of the unity of divine 'nature' in the three 'persons' of the Father, Son, and Spirit in my ... *Systematic Theology* [it is proposed] ... that we should conceive of the 'spiritual' nature of the one God in Father, Son, and Spirit in terms of a field of power rather than in terms of a single divine subject or person."[15]

For Pannenberg the doctrine of the Trinity has taken on an increasingly important role within his theology and thereby has likewise taken on increasing importance as well for the emphasis upon unity and universality found throughout his theological program.[16] Indeed, his development of the doctrine of the Trinity has been recognized as one of the most innovative aspects of his dogmatics with his moving from the threeness of the trinitarian persons to the unity of God standing "against the bulk of the Western theological tradition."[17]

Philip Clayton has summarized the foundation of Pannenberg's doctrine of the Trinity and its focus on God's unity. He observes that for Pannenberg, for each distinct person of the Trinity, "the other two represent 'the one God,' and each has his full divinity only through the other two persons. Hence, in the resurrection of the Son through the Spirit, the Father's Godhood is confirmed; in his self-differentiation from the Father, the Son's full Godhood appears through the Spirit; in his glorification (*Verherrlichung*) of the Father and Son, the Spirit's

---

[14] *Ibid.*, 72. [82.]
[15] Pannenberg, "A Response to My American Friends," in: *The Theology of Wolfhart Pannenberg*, ed. Carl Braaten and Philip Clayton, 327. Pannenberg additionally contends that his proposal would not only help to restore a sense of mystery to Christian talk about God but would also have significant apologetic consequences in that it would "improve the Christian position in the upcoming period of dialogue and contest with other world religions."
[16] Philip Clayton, "The God of History and the Presence of the Future," in: *Journal of Religion* 65 (January 1985), 98, has identified Pannenberg's "new emphasis upon the Trinity as the unifying principle for systematic theology ... [as] a shift which began to emerge in his work in the 1970s."
[17] Grenz, 69.

equal Godhood is established."[18]

Pannenberg's emphasis upon the unity of God in the Trinity has led several critics to conclude that Pannenberg emphasizes the unity of God to so great an extent that God's tri-unity is not taken seriously. Jürgen Moltmann, for instance, has even linked Pannenberg's doctrine of God with Sabellian Modalism which he believes is to be found among certain contemporary theologians, particularly Barth and Pannenberg, when an idealistic modalism (taken over from Hegel) makes its way into the Christian doctrine of the Trinity and threatens to disregard the three distinct persons of the Trinity in favor of the one God. Moltmann sees this tendency, which leads to what he calls a "Christian monotheism," when one makes the reign of God the starting point for Trinitarian reflection, as does Pannenberg. Moltmann writes: "If one begins with the reign of God, then God is thereby presupposed as the identical subject of his reign. The doctrine of the Trinity can then only be portrayed as 'Christian monotheism.'"[19] This tendency in Pannenberg, which Moltmann points to, can be seen, for instance, in Pannenberg's understanding of the Trinity from the perspective of the reign of God and the difference between God's future and present. The reality of God is to be found in the arrival of the creating, saving power of the future whose reign is constituted through its coming. For Pannenberg, this is expressed in the trinitarian language of the Christian faith. He writes:

> God is not an existing entity but is the future of his coming Kingdom. As this future, he was and is present through that man, Jesus, who testified to the coming Kingdom of God. Through this man God is present to the world as the spirit who gives freedom and life by creating faith. ... The trinitarian distinctions [between Father, Son and Spirit] are based on the difference between future and present. As we have seen, future and present - and consequently the 'persons' of the Trinity -are comprehended in the unity of God [and express God's eternal presence, which is the Spirit.] In this light, we see the contrast between the trinitarian concept of God and the idea of God as taught by philosophical monotheism in classical antiquity. The trinitarian concept describes the particular unity of the living God, while philosophical monotheism concieved of the dead or static unity of a supreme being. ... The trinitarian idea of God is congrous with historical process.[20]

---

[18] Clayton, "The God of History and the Presence of the Future," 104.

[19] Jürgen Moltmann, *Trinität und Reich Gottes: Zur Gotteslehre* (Munich: Chr. Kaiser, 1980), 155f. Pannenberg has been similarly critical of Moltmann's doctrine of the Trinity, suggesting that the charge of tri-theism against his doctrine of God is at the very least understandable. Pannenberg further rejects Moltmann's stance against "monotheism" contending that "die Trinitätslehre ist gerade im Sinne der altkirchlichen Theologie als die christliche Form des Monotheismus zu verstehen. Sie muß geradezu als Bedingung eines konsequenten Monotheismus interpretiert werden." Hence, "die Trinitätslehre ist konsequent monotheistisch." Pannenberg, "Die Subjektivität Gottes und die Trinitätslehre," in: *Kerygma und Dogma* 23 (1977), 39.

[20] *Theology and the Kingdom of God (TKG)*, (Philadelphia: Westminster Press, 1969), 70f. [Cf. *Theologie und Reich Gottes (TRG)*, (Gütersloh: Gerd Mohn, 1971), 28f.] The first three chapters of this book were originally present in English during a lecture series in the United States in

The American theologian William Hill has found similar difficulty with Pannenberg's doctrine of the Trinity. Though also locating part of the problem on a reliance upon Hegel his criticism focuses not on God's reign as starting point but on the problem of the distinct personhood of the Spirit which Hill contends Pannenberg does not distinguish from the person of the Father, thus leading to a sort of "dyadic concept of God" - relying instead upon Hegel's understanding of God as Spirit and as Subject. The end result, according to Hill, is that in Pannenberg's thought the threeness of God collapses "dialectically into a unity that either is abstract and impersonal in kind, or reduces to the moral unity of a divine *koinonia.*" Hence, in Hill's view, "Pannenberg's trinitarianism does not allow that God is Three Persons. He is rather one Person, who posits historically a human person (the man Jesus) as his other, who belongs nonetheless to the essence of his divinity. He then acts personally through the human history of that other upon others (believers) as Spirit, bringing them to full personhood."[21]

Still others, however, picking up on a different stream within Pannenberg's trinitarian reflections, have noted the danger in Pannenberg's thought that he actually stresses too much the individual persons of the Trinity so that his theology is open to the charge of tri-theism.[22] This tendency, it is alleged, is especially to be seen in his frequent trinitarian reflections in his recently completed *Systematic Theology.*[23] His efforts to overcome this danger, one might suggest, could account in part for his simultaneous emphasis upon the oneness of God which has led to the suspicion of many critics that there are not three persons but only one in Pannenberg's conception of God.[24]

For Pannenberg the unity of God is to be seen precisely in his trinitarian actions in creation and history. As Clayton has rightly noted, Pannenberg's "Trinitarian formulation ties God indissolubly with creation and history. Clearly, for Pannenberg God's unity is bound with his acts in history."[25] God, according to Pannenberg, acts in history in love which reaches beyond Israel to all people. Indeed, the unity of God finds concrete form and expression in history "in the work of divine love" which is grounded in the relationship between the persons of the Trinity. Love, then, is for Pannenberg the "unity of the divine being of Father,

---

21 1966/67. Additions to quotation in brackets here and in following citations of this work represent additions or alterations made in the German text of 1971. In the German the last sentence quoted has been sharpened to read: "Der trinitarische Gott ist in sich selbst ein geschichtlicher Prozeß."
William Hill, *The Three-Personed God: The Trinity as a Mystery of Salvation* (Washington, D.C.: Catholic University of America Press, 1982), 164ff.

22 Cf., for instance, Falk Wagner, in: *Die Flucht in den Begriff: Materialien zu Hegels Religionsphilosophie,* ed. F. Wagner and F. Graf (Stuttgart, 1982): 196-227 (especially 204 and 210-18). Cf. also Grenz, 70, who writes that Pannenberg, "in emphasizing the threeness of God his conception is open to the charge of being tritheistic."

23 Cf., for instance, his discussions in 1: 300ff.; 2:34ff.; 483ff.; 3:217ff.

24 Grenz, 70, is quite correct to assert that Pannenberg's attempt to overcome this danger is centered in "his innovative development of the unity of the divine being."

25 Clayton, 104f.

Son, and Spirit" who love in the unity of free persons that cannot be separated.[26] Already prior to the appearance of the first volume of his *Systematic Theology* Pannenberg had made love a key to his understanding of the Trinity and the unity of God. Pannenberg, who considers love to be "identical with the divine essence" contended that: "The unity of the three persons is expressed by referring both to love as the essence of the trinitarian God and to the attributes comprehended in this love."[27]

The work of God's love not only arises out of and points to the unity of God but also to God's universality inasmuch as it is foundational for the connection - and distinction - between the transcendent God and his immanence in all creation. Hence Pannenberg contends: "Only the doctrine of the Trinity permits us so to unite God's transcendence as Father and his immanence in and with his creatures through Son and Spirit that the permanent distinction between God and creature is upheld." And additionally, "it is the unity of God with his creature which is grounded in the fact that the divine love eternally affirms the creature in its distinctiveness and thus sets aside its separation from God but not its difference from him."[28] On the basis of this distinction between God and the creature which allows God to be both transcendent and immanent and in light of the Christian contention that the three persons of the Trinity are only one essence, Pannenberg contends that "Christian theology can even maintain, in response to Judaism and Islam, that only the trinitarian God, who, in his infiniteness, not only transcends the world but is also immanent in it, can be conceived in a consistently monotheistic fashion." According to Pannenberg, then, it is finally only the God conceived of in trinitarian terms who "can truly be all in all." It follows for Pannenberg that "the doctrine of the unity of the divine essence" is indispensable precisely within and through the doctrine of the Trinity which he regards as the "culmination of monotheism."[29]

God's love as grounded in the doctrine of the Trinity, according to Pannenberg, only reaches its goal with the "consummation of the world in the kingdom of God" and only then does the doctrine of God reach its conclusion.[30]

---

[26] *ST* 1:445 and 422ff. [480 and 456ff.]

[27] Pannenberg, "Father, Son, Spirit: Problems of a Trinitarian Doctrine of God," in: *Dialog* 26:4 (fall 1987), 256. [Probleme einer trinitarischen Gotteslehre," in: *Weisheit Gottes - Weisheit der Welt*, W. Baier and S. Horn, et al. (1987), 40f.]

[28] *ST* 1:445f. [480f.] The concept of love, according to Pannenberg, also makes it possible to link together conceptually "the unity of the divine essence with God's existence and qualities and hence to link the immanent Trinity and the economic Trinity in the distinctiveness of their structure and basis" (447, [482]). Thereby Pannenberg, while stressing an essential unity between the immanent and economic Trinity, sees this unity in light of their distinctiveness in contrast to Rahner who identifies the two. The distinction between the immanent and economic Trinity also allows Pannenberg to admit to change within the economic Trinity while at the same time holding to the immutability of the Godhead in the immanent Trinity.

[29] "Father, Son, Spirit," 256f. ["Probleme einer trinitarischen Gotteslehre," 40f.]

[30] *ST* 1:447. [482.] Cf. also Grenz, *Reason for Hope*, 55f. who observes that "the deity of the one God, that is, God's unity, is bound to the work of the three persons in the world (the economic

Ultimately, therefore, Pannenberg's conception of the Trinity points to the futurity of God since the unity of Jesus with the Father is communicated 'negatively' in Jesus' self-surrender to God which pointed to the difference between himself and the Father. Thus, according to Pannenberg, "the difference between what is presently extant, and the future of God and his lordship, shows up in the personal relationship of Jesus to the Father. Only in that he acknowledges this difference, by placing himself completely in the service of the coming reign of God, and does not serve himself, is he one with God." Christians also, through the '*Spirit* of Christ' serve God's future and his coming kingdom which is already among us. In this way, according to Pannenberg, "the doctrine of the Trinity is the seal of the pure futurity of God"[31] - a topic of consideration which we will take up a little later in this chapter.

Within Pannenberg's trinitarian thought the Spirit has taken on an increasingly important role since he began to connect the concept of divine Spirit to the idea of 'field.' This application of the concept of field to the Spirit of God has been called a "revolutionary move" foundational to the task of demonstrating the unity of God.[32] Grenz has summarized Pannenberg's use of the concept of the Spirit as field in pointing to the unity of the divine essence as follows:

> Pannenberg mines from the field theory insight into the two uses of *Spirit* in the biblical materials - *Spirit* as the divine essence as such and as the third person of the Trinity - both of which are theologically important. If Spirit were solely the impersonal divine field ... the divine essence, which is Spirit, would be impersonal. ... However, the Spirit is not only the common life of the Father and the Son but also appears as a personal center of activity. The ... argument he offers here draws on the dialectic of self-differentiation. Although both the Father and the Son are differentiated from the essence of the Godhead that is Spirit, they are bound together through the Spirit, the third person of the Trinity.[33]

Pannenberg, in his move toward a conception of the Spirit as field, has accorded a greater role to the Spirit than is to be found in much traditional trinitarian theology. The turn in his own thought toward pneumatology, as already mentioned, would seem to be traceable to his adoption of the 'field' concept from physics - a topic which we will more fully examine in chapter 6. At this point in our discussion it must suffice to note that Pannenberg finds the idea that the divine Spirit might be understood in a manner similar to the idea of a unified field of force (Michael Faraday) to be consistent with the biblical statements about the Spirit of God. When he applies this model to the relations between the trinitarian persons and the divine essence which they hold in common the problem of an

---

[31] Trinity), which itself is completed only eschatologically." Pannenberg, "The God of Hope," in: *BQ* 2:249. ["Der Gott der Hoffnung," *Grundfragen* 1:398]
[32] Grenz, 54.
[33] *Ibid.*, 61.

ordering to a subject, as is necessitated by an understanding of Spirit as *nous*, is avoided. Instead, "the deity as field can find equal manifestation in all three persons." Hence, "the trinitarian persons ... are not independent of the Spirit of love that binds them. They are simply manifestations and forms - eternal forms - of the one divine essence."

In order to avoid a form of modalism, which some (including Moltmann), as we have seen, have detected in his thought, Pannenberg seeks to formulate his concept of Spirit as unifying field in the context of traditional trinitarian language. He writes: "The idea of the divine life as a dynamic field sees the divine Spirit who unites the three persons as proceeding from the Father, received by the Son, and common to both, so that precisely in this way he is the force field of their fellowship that is distinct from them both."[34] To what extent this formulation actually solves the problem and whether Pannenberg does justice to the concept of field as understood within physics are questions which we must return to in the final chapter of this study.

### 4.1.1.3 *The unity of God as foundation of theology's universality*

The foundation of theology's universality, as discussed already in chapter one, is rooted decisively in the nature of theology's object. Here we see a deliberate move away from the position of Barth. Pannenberg, commenting upon Barth's doctrine of the sovereignty of God during a 1991 visit to America said:

> I was especially impressed by Barth's emphasis on the sovereignty of God ... but I drew different conclusions than Karl Barth did. I concluded that if God is sovereign as the Almighty Creator of everything, there should be no animal, no human being, and certainly not human nature, there should be no stone on this earth that could be adequately understood without this God. In other words, we don't need some prior decision of faith, we only need to remove our prejudices and look on reality as it presents itself. If God exists, that will be enough. Therefore, I follow another theological method than Karl Barth followed. ... If we really believe in God, we may ask for His truth in the reality of the history that we believe is the history of His manifesting Himself.[35]

Similarly, Pannenberg wrote in his 1981 article, "Theological Questions to Scientists," that: "If the God of the Bible is the creator of the universe, then it is not possible to understand fully or even appropriately the processes of nature without reference to that God. If on the contrary, nature can be appropriately understood without reference to the God of the Bible, then that God cannot be the creator of the universe."[36] Thus it is not merely the doctrine of God but the

---

[34] *ST* 1:382f. [414f.]
[35] Pannenberg, "Theta Phi Discussion with Wolfhart Pannenberg," in: *The Asbury Theological Journal*, 46:2 (Fall 1991), 24f.
[36] Pannenberg, "Theological Questions to Scientists," in A.R. Peacocke, ed. *The Sciences and Theology in the 20th Century* (Notre Dame, IN: University of Notre Dame Press, 1981), 4.

doctrine of God as creator upon which theology's claim to universality rests. For Pannenberg the status of the world as "created" implies that the world as a whole and in all its parts is contingent in its existence. That is to say, the world need not exist at all, but owes its existence entirely to the "free activity of divine creation."[37] This likewise means, for Pannenberg, that theological propositions, inasmuch as they are statements about God, also possess a universal character. Thus Pannenberg can contend that, "statements about God refer essentially to the totality of reality and imply an understanding of this whole insofar as we can speak meaningfully about God only by speaking of him as the creator of the universe."[38]

It is clear that for Pannenberg, theology's claim to universality rests neither upon its methodology nor upon the nature of religious truth in general but rather upon a radical taking seriously of the doctrine of God as creator. That is to say, theological science derives its unity and universal relevance from its object: God, the creator of heaven and earth and all that is in them. And specifically, theology derives its unity and universality from the oneness of God. Hence, according to Pannenberg, even when the implications of theology's universality have not been fully realizied by theologians theology has reasserted its claim to universality again and again precisely because its universality is "rooted in the monotheistic idea of God."[39] And this leads necessarily to a connection to all other ways of relating to truth. Not only does this, in Pannenberg's view, justify the possibility of a natural knowledge of God (as distinct from a natural theology),[40] but it also has implications for the other sciences. As we have seen, Pannenberg is clear in his view that no part of this physical world which God created can be adequately understood apart from God. That is not to say that physics, for example, cannot know anything with certainty without reference to God, only that this knowledge remains necessarily incomplete and in some sense deficient if God is not taken into account.

### 4.1.2 The futurity of God

Pannenberg's doctrine of God and his emphasis upon the significance of the end of history which is already in and through Christ proleptically present come to together in his thought to form one of the most thought-provoking and

---

[37] Pannenberg, "The Doctrine of Creation and Modern Science," in: *Zygon* 23:1 (March 1988), 8.
[38] "What is a Dogmatic Statement?" in: *BQ* 1:200. ["Was ist eine dogmatische Aussage?" in: *Grundfragen* 1:172.] Cf. also *TPS*, 297 [*WtT*, 299.] where he contends also that "theology as the science of God ... derives its unity from its object."
[39] "The Crisis of the Scripture Principle," in: *BQ* 1:3. ["Die Krise des Schriftprinzips," in: *Grundfragen* 1:12.]
[40] For Pannenberg's defense of the validity of natural knowledge of God (or what he calls a "theology of nature") see Pannenberg, "Kontingenz und Naturgesetz," in: A.M. Klaus Müller and W. Pannenberg, *Erwägungen zu einer Theologie der Natur* (Gütersloh: Gerd Mohn, 1970), 34ff. Cf. also *ST* 1:73-118. [83-132.]

controversial aspects of his theology, namely, his conception of God as future. Indeed, as will become apparent in the following discussion, Pannenberg's eschatology is largely developed out of his doctrine of God. Hence he contends that the treatment of eschatology within systematic theology always takes place "upon the foundation of the science of God, for God is the object of theology."[41] Or, as he earlier stated, pointing to the reason for a theo-logical foundation: "For Christian theology the concept of God is intimately connected with the contingent nature of new occurrences and thus with the future."[42] For Pannenberg, therefore, the discussion of last things begins with God and, as we will see, a God who is himself to be understood as future.[43]

### 4.1.2.1 *God as ontological primacy of the future: Pannenberg's critique of Ernst Bloch*

It seems to have been Pannenberg's encounter with the thought of Ernst Bloch which gave him the impetus to go beyond speaking of the future of God to an affirmation of the futurity of God as what has been called an "ontological primacy of the future itself as the ... locus of the fullness of divine being."[44] In his 1965 article "The God of Hope," which originally appeared in a *Festschrift* for Ernst Bloch,[45] he interacts with Bloch's concepts of the kingdom and of 'God' as found in his magnum opus, *Das Prinzip Hoffnung*.[46] Bloch's atheistic critique contends that the 'God-hypostasis' has become untenable since the messianic axis

---

[41] *ST* 3:582.

[42] Pannenberg, "The Future and the Unity of Mankind," in: *Ethics*, trans. Keith Crim (Philadelphia: Westminster Press, 1981), 177. [*Ethik und Ekklesiologie* (Göttingen: Vandenhoeck & Ruprecht, 1977), 168.] Pannenberg further explains that the "theological assumption that the future is not simply an extrapolation from and a continuation of past and present but a reality in its own right is based on the concept of God." And, for Pannenberg, this is true even if one does not accept the idea of God as power of the future but retains a more traditional concept. Hence, for all Christian theology "the idea of God as the future of the world gives expression ... to the theological understanding of the future as an independent reality that confronts the present" (178).

[43] David Polk, "The All-Determining God and the Peril of Determinism," in: *The Theology of Wolfhart Pannenberg*, ed. C. Braaten and P. Clayton, 153, has suggested a trio of overlapping concerns which have led Pannenberg to his understanding of God as essentially futural: "(1) If God is indeed the guarantor of the unity of universal history, can one properly speak of the full reality of God *within* the context of ongoing, unfinished, nonunified history? (2) If Jesus' teaching and activity are oriented toward an essentially *futural* reign of God, in what sense can one refer to God in the present? Would not a God whose power is not yet consummated be less than God? (3) Since it is the case that in our human questioning we are open beyond everything extant in our world, must God not be conceived ... in a manner that transcends everything presently real?"

[44] So Polk, 153.

[45] Cf. Pannenberg, "Der Gott der Hoffnung," in: *Ernst Bloch zu ehren*, ed. Siegfried Unseld (Frankfurt/M: Suhrkamp, 1965).

[46] Polk, 154, has noted that Pannenberg's reading of Bloch seems to have opened him up to what he was seeking, namely, "a notion of the ontological primacy of the future in terms of which he could bring to verbal expression and provisional completion his insights into the futurity of God." From this point on, notes Polk, "Pannenberg has consistently pursued a 'thoroughgoing eschatological' transformation of the doctrine of God."

of the history of religions was progressively humanized and then ultimately neutralized in the consubstantiality of Jesus Christ with God. As Bloch explains, with the death of Jesus on the cross "a new God appears, a previously unheard of God who sheds his blood for his children, and who as the word that has become flesh is capable of an entirely earthly ... fate of death. Hence a human being has here through the complete abandonment of hubris surpassed every previous concept of God."[47] Without the God-hypostasis, which had been presupposed as the 'projection of space,' no religious hypostatizations, including the idea of the kingdom, would seem possible. For Bloch, however, the true content of the kingdom is its utopia so that, as Pannenberg explains, "the hope of the kingdom transcends every one of its particular but again surpassable realizations." Thus "the idea of the kingdom does not completely coincide with any social utopia and remains 'in itself a still to be attained classless society.'"[48] The idea of the kingdom, therefore, remains, even when the idea of God is rejected. Bloch, then, in agreement with Joachim of Fiore, can contend that social utopia "is itself an achieved classless society distinguished from the summum bonum of the religious-utopian kingdom through that leap that is itself set in place by the explosive intention (*Sprengintention*) of rebirth and transfiguration. *The kingdom remains the core religious idea ...* "[49]

Pannenberg rejects Bloch's concept of the kingdom as being in itself inconsistent and lacking satisfactory basis.[50] As Pannenberg writes in a penetrating critique of Bloch's concept of the kingdom:

> Bloch's appeal to the potencies and latent aspects of the process are difficult to reconcile with his emphasis on the factor of novelty in the coming future. If the future is already laid out in these potencies and latent aspects of the historical process - in our case, in the wishes and hopes of man - then it cannot arrive with the suddenness and underivability of something whose novelty essentially transcends everything that was or is. Yet how would things stand if the hope of the kingdom were only the symbolic expression of the demonstrable psychological strivings of man? Obviously, it could then also be demolished by the fact that men had become satisfied and content with themselves and their present circumstances. If it were established only as an expression of human wishing, the hope of the kingdom could easily collapse into the triviality of a self-satisfied present.[51]

---

[47] Ernst Bloch, *Das Prinzip Hoffnung*, vol. 2 (Frankfurt/M: Suhrkamp, 1959), 1494f. Cf. also 2:413 where Bloch contends that "der echte Materialismus, der dialektische, hebt eben die Transzendenz und Realität jeder Gott-Hypostase auf."
[48] Pannenberg, "The God of Hope," 238f. [*Grundfragen*, 390f.]
[49] Bloch, 2:1411.
[50] For an analysis of Pannenberg's own view of the kingdom with particular reference to Ritschl's view of the kingdom and Heidegger's structure of Dasein and the priority of the category of futurity see Philip Hefner, "The Concreteness of God's Kingdom: A Problem for Christian Life," in: *Journal of Religion* 51 (1971), especially 193-199.
[51] "The God of Hope," 239. [*Grundfragen*, 391.]

Although Pannenberg rejects Bloch's atheistic analysis as well as his view of the utopia of the kingdom and can in this way be said not to have been directly influenced by Bloch in a positive sense,[52] his critique of Bloch brought him to a conclusion decisive for his own conception not only of the kingdom but also of God. Indeed, Pannenberg admits that "perhaps Christian theology will one day have to thank Ernst Bloch's philosophy of hope for giving it the courage to recover in the full sense its central category of eschatology."[53]

The primacy of the future and its novelty, Pannenberg concluded, "are guaranteed only when the coming kingdom is ontologically grounded in itself and does not owe its future merely to the present wishes and strivings of man." And, according to Pannenberg, when the kingdom is conceived of biblically as the kingdom of God "out of concern for the primacy of the future of the kingdom over all present realities, including ... psychological states," then the kingdom of God and the being of God are identical with one another since the being of God is located in his lordship. As Pannenberg explains: God is only God "in the execution of this lordship, and the full accomplishment of his lordship is determined as something future. To this extent, the God to whom the hope of the kingdom refers is characterized in a radical and exclusive sense by 'futurity as a quality of being.'"[54] Hence, with this identification of the kingdom with the being of God, what is true of the kingdom is also true of God, namely, that his futurity and novelty (i.e., God's performing of new, unpredictable and contingent acts within history such as the resurrection of Jesus) are guaranteed only when God is grounded ontologically in his own self - a self which is realized in its fullness only in the future.

This connection between God and the future kingdom is grounded by Pannenberg upon his understanding of the world as God's creation - what is not possible within Bloch's thought. Pannenberg argues that if there is a world, then God must reign over it in such a way that God's creation of the world is an indispensable presupposition of the future of the kingdom in the world. Given this connection between the world as God's creation and the future of the kingdom Pannenberg is able to contend that, in the light of biblical revelation, God's reality is "inseparably connected with the future of God's kingdom within this world."[55] This does not mean, however, that the reality of God is ultimately and ontologically contingent upon a reality outside of God. God's reality is contingent

---

[52] The degree of influence that Bloch had upon Pannenberg in this regard is an open question. Polk has agreed with Pannenberg that the influence is minimal since Pannenberg has interacted with only a limited section of Bloch's major work and is not discernibly indebtedness to Bloch in his theology as a whole. Rather, Polk explains, "what appears to be the case is that he [Pannenberg] was already moving in the direction of his ideas of God's futurity on the basis of the implications arising within his own work, independently of any influence from Bloch's eschatological philosophy, so that what emerged was a confluence of similar modes of reflection." Polk, 154.
[53] "The God of Hope," 237f. [*Grundfragen*, 390.]
[54] *Ibid.*, 239f. [391.]
[55] *ST* 3:583,

upon the future of the kingdom only because and to the extent that the kingdom itself is contingent upon the reality of the world understood as God's creation. Not only has Bloch's concept of the kingdom influenced Pannenberg but also his conception of God. Although Pannenberg notes that the idea of God has been explored neither conclusively nor convincingly by Bloch he nevertheless finds his conception of God fruitful. In a crucial passage in which Bloch affirms the kingdom without God he not only rejects the idea of God but in so doing defines the kind of god he is rejecting. The God he rejects, Pannenberg contends, is very different from God as the power of the future. Bloch writes:

> The kingdom, even is secularized form, ... *remains as messianic front-space* (Front-Raum) *also apart from all theism*. ... The utopia of the kingdom annihilates the fiction of a creator God and the hypostasis of a God of heaven, but not the end-space (End-Raum), where the *ens perfectissimum* has the abyss of its still unthwarted potentiality. The being of God, indeed God in general as its own essence, is superstition; faith is only in a messianic kingdom of God - without God. Atheism is therefore so little the enemy of religious utopia that it is its presupposition: *without atheism messianism has no place*. ... Not-present-at-hand, not-having-become is the real fundamental determination of the *ens perfectissimum*, and had it become, it would have been nothing so distinct from his kingdom, as that which is God hypostatized.[56]

The key for Pannenberg in his analysis and response to Bloch's form of atheism is not so much Bloch's view of God but his view of humanity. As Pannenberg notes, Bloch approached the human situation from a very different viewpoint than that of his fellow atheist Feuerbach who clothed humanity "with all the predicates of the infinite," thereby obscuring "the real situation of every human present, which is filled with conflict" and suffering. As Pannenberg explains:

> In contrast to Feuerbach, Bloch has gone through the experience of the finitude of everything present, and therefore can find relief not in some fictitious idea of the species but only in the hope of a fulfillment that comes from the direction of an unheard of, victorious future. This newly emerged difference raises again the question of the ontological priority of the future over the present, and thereby reopens the theme of some kind of divine being transcending the present human race and the world: 'Only in relation to the "hidden God" [Deus absconditus] is the *problem* of what is at stake in the legitimate mystery of the "hidden man" [homo absconditus] kept open' [Bloch, 2:1406]. The primacy of the future, and therewith of the "hidden God" who is its ground, is necessary in order that man's humanity be protected against trivialization and continue to be summoned to its future possibilities.[57]

In a manner reminiscent of his own argument from world-openness to

---

[56] Bloch, 2:1413.
[57] "The God of Hope," 240f. [*Grundfragen*, 392.]

openness toward God Pannenberg detects in Bloch's analysis of the human situation and the hope that comes from a victorious future the importance of the ontological priority of the future and with it the implication of "some kind of being transcending the present human race and the world." In this way Pannenberg identifies the primacy of the future with the primacy of the *Deus absconditus*. The question which he must and does ask, however, is what meaning the term 'God' can still have within this context. What is clear for Pannenberg is that within the context of Bloch's thought the idea of God as an absolute in the mode of being present (in contrast to a not-yet-being) is not possible or is no longer possible. Thus Pannenberg concludes that "we must agree with Bloch that he has transposed the question of the most perfect being into a temporal mode, and turned it into 'the highest utopian problem, that of the end' [Bloch, 2:1412]. In this sense his atheism is to be accepted." The question of God, however, arises once again according to Pannenberg in that the end of which Bloch speaks must be conceived of as itself being numinous, which leaves only the possibility of a God with futurity as a quality of his being, which rules out a return to theism - at least traditional theism - in which "the idea of the future as a mode of God's being is still undeveloped ... despite the intimate connection between God and the coming reign of God in the eschatological message of Jesus."[58]

*4.1.2.2 God as the power of the future*
Pannenberg, taking up the challenge of sketching out the kind of God that would be acceptable within Bloch's system, makes the radical proposal of considering God as the power of the future. The God of the Bible, according to Pannenberg, is only God inasmuch as he proves himself to be God and is only the God of the world inasmuch as he proves himself to be lord of the world - but this proof, Pannenberg contends, "is still a matter of the future, according to the expectations of Israel and the New Testament." On this basis Pannenberg concludes that God "exists only in the way in which the future is powerful over the present" since it is the future which decides what will come (or become) out of what exists in the present. Pannenberg provides the following description of God as power of the future, a God whom he believes escapes the most serious criticisms of Bloch:

> As the power of the future, God is no thing, no object presently at hand, which man could detach himself from and pass over. He appears neither as one being among others, nor as the quiescent background of all beings, the timeless being underlying all objects. ... As the power of the future, the God of the Bible always remains ahead of all speech about him, and has already outdistanced every concept of God. ... The power of the future and it alone can be the object of hope and trust. For the future is powerful in the present.[59]

---

[58] *Ibid.*, 241f. [392.]
[59] *Ibid.*, 242f. [392f.]

The power of the future, as not an "object presently at hand," is not ruled out by Bloch's analysis which does not allow for an absolute which is present at hand. It is especially through his conception of the power of the future as essentially ontological that Pannenberg is able to avoid the idea of God as an object presently at hand.[60] Even the concept of God as creator, which Bloch rejected in favor of the idea of the kingdom (understood as the still unrealized consummation) since the idea of a creator-God appeared to him to be an expression of "a mythology of an opulent past" (Bloch 2:1500), is made acceptable, according to Pannenberg, when God is thought of as the power of the future. This is the case since, as Pannenberg contends, the "reflection upon the power of the future over the present leads to a new idea of creation, oriented not toward a primeval event in the past but toward the eschatological future." The God of the coming kingdom became "the occasion for an eschatological reversal of the idea of creation" as soon as he was recognized in the message of Jesus, in which "the eschatological future and creation belong together most intimately" - a fact which theology has not yet recognized because its reflection upon creation remains oriented toward a mythical, primordial origin.[61] What a "reversal" of the idea of creation in light of the ontological primacy of the future means has been recently clearly stated by Pannenberg in his contention that the future of God "is the creative origin of all things in the contingency of their existence and at the same time the final horizon for the definitive meaning and essence of all things and events. On their historical way through time people and things exist only through anticipation of that which they will become in light of their ultimate future, the advent of God."[62]

What such a reversal of the idea of creation does not imply, however, is a conflict with the traditional, scientific understanding of causality. In the first place, Pannenberg contends that his claim that God's love is the cause of all occurrences "does not violate scientific descriptions of natural processes [through natural law]." Likewise, the ontological reversal which this thought leads to when applied to God as power of the future who is powerful in the present also produces no conflict. It is necessary, according to Pannenberg, to rethink the idea of creation from the perspective of the future instead of from a beginning which is the foundation of all things. In making this move he seeks to understand all being and all events as originating out of the absolute future. Yet, as he explains,

> this conception of divine power does not violate or compete with the physicist's quest for natural causes. Our considerations are based on a reversal of the time

---

[60] Cf. Philip Hefner, "The Concreteness of God's Kingdom," 194, who writes concerning Pannenberg's position: "This power of the future is ontological in scope and character, so that Pannenberg escapes the restrictiveness that might ensue if he located the Kingdom of God in the ethical functions of man or in some other functions, such as feeling. As an ontological reality, the power of the future and the kingdom ... encompasses the whole man and all of his activities."

[61] "The God of Hope," 243. [*Grundfragen*, 393f.]

[62] *ST* 3:573, God, as the power of the future, therefore, is also to be seen as God who is active in our present. So Pannenberg, *TRG*, 39, 70.

sequence usually presupposed in notions of causality. In contrast to formulations about natural order, which describe the impact of past conditions on present and future, we have suggested an idea of creation which understands the present - and each present now past - as resulting from its future.[63]

Perhaps more significant for our purposes, however, than the apologetic ramifications of the concept of God as the power of the future for the dialogue with Bloch's form of atheism is the question of the implications of this view for God's universality. As we saw already at the beginning of this chapter, God is only God when he is *the* God, that is, when he is the being behind the totality and unity of all reality, and when he is personal. The difficult question which then needs to be asked, according to Pannenberg, is: "To what extent are we justified in calling the power of the future, through which the coming kingdom has its ontological priority over the wishes of men, 'God'?"

Crucial for Pannenberg are two questions regarding the personal character of God as the power of the future.[64] First, asks Pannenberg; "Does the power of the future have any more personal character than the concept of a timeless ground of being in the depths of reality, in the background of the realm of being?" And second, if the first question can be answered in the affirmative; "Would such a divine personality be defensible against the criticism ... that it is an anthropomorphic hypostatization?" Crucial is whether the concept of person is, as Fichte and Feuerbach both maintained, derived from the human ego and then transposed unto God as the object of our religious experience, or whether instead the reverse is the case, that is to say, the phenomenon of the personal has its origin in the appearance of a numinous object and is transferred from there to humans through their religious experience.

By opting for this latter view Pannenberg is able to overcome the arguments of Fichte and Feuerbach and argues that since personality expresses itself in a freedom which is open to the future, that "futurity as a condition of freedom constitutes the very core of the personal."[65] Hence God as the power of the future can truly be called 'God,' and as God has universal relevance since he is the power of the future over every present and over every person. Or, as Pannenberg puts it: God's future has "ontological primacy ... over every presently existing form of human realization."[66] Hence God, as power of the future, is also powerful in the present. As John Cobb has explained Pannenberg's position: "God's present

---

[63] *TKG*, 67, 70. [Cf. *TRG*, 24, 28.]
[64] Robert Jenson, *God after God: The God of the Past and the God of the Future, Seen in the Work of Karl Barth* (Indianapolis: Bobbs-Merrill, 1969), 175, has rightly noted that for Pannenberg "a 'God' who lacked universality, or who lacked individual personality, would not be God. Only if we can find a new way to think of God as at once universal and individually personal can the crisis of western religion be overcome."
[65] "The God of Hope," 244ff. [*Grundfragen*, 394ff.] Cf. *The Apostles' Creed*, 27ff. [*Glaubensbekenntnis*, 35ff.] for a discussion of God as person in light of the atheistic critique of Fichte.
[66] *Ibid.*, 248.

reality is as the Power of the Future. Since what we really are is not determined until the end, since all meaning and being are grounded in anticipation which is finally directed to that end, God is the all-determining power in the present even though he is not now extant."[67]

### 4.1.2.3 The futurity of God in relation to history and eternity

The relationship between time and eternity has recently been identified by Pannenberg as the key problem confronting eschatology - a problem whose solution has ramifications for all areas of Christian doctrine.[68] This is certainly seen to be true for Pannenberg's doctrine of God. For Pannenberg the futurity of God does not exclude God's eternity for God is the future not only of our present but of every previous age. Hence, "with the eschatological future God's eternity enters into time, and from this point is creatively present to all finite things that have preceded it."[69] God is not, in this way, a remote being who distances himself ever further from the historical process. For Pannenberg, the God who reveals himself in history must be integrally connected to this history.[70] God is the power of the future active in the present in such as way "that he has allowed every event and age to participate in his immediate historical future, which through its realization has ceased to be future. If God is to be thought of in this way as the future of even the most distant past, then he existed before our present and before every present." Hence Pannenberg concludes that because God's existence as the future is powerful in every present, "the futurity of God implies his eternity."[71]

From this view of eternity we can begin to understand the relationship between God and history since God's eternity encompasses all history and every event within history. Already in his "Dogmatic Theses" Pannenberg suggested that history belongs to the very essence of God. Here Pannenberg brought history and the universality of God together when he contended that "the history that demonstrates the deity of God [and] is broadened to include the totality of all events ... corresponds ... to the universality of Israel's God." Yet it is only the whole of history which can conclusively demonstrate that the God of Israel is *the*

---

[67] Cobb, "Wolfhart Pannenberg's 'Jesus: God and Man," 201.

[68] *ST* 3:641 and 572f. In *ST* 1:445f. [480f.] Pannenberg points to the resolution of the problem of time and eternity and its implications for the reconciliation of God with his creatures in the doctrine of the incarnation and its connection also to the doctrine of the Trinity. He writes: "The incarnation of the Son sets aside the antithesis of eternity and time as the present of the Father and his kingdom is present to us through the Son. This present not only contains all the past within it, ... but it also invades our present in such a way that this becomes the past and needs to be made present and glorified by the work of the Spirit. The removal of the antithesis of eternity and time in the economy of God's saving action according to the wisdom of his love is the reconciliation of the antithesis between Creator and creature."

[69] *ST* 3:573,

[70] As Grenz, 76, has rightly observed, "Pannenberg delineates an understanding of God's relationship to time that seeks to do justice to God's eternal being apart from the world while avoiding the distancing of God from the temporal world found in much of traditional theology."

[71] "The God of Hope," 244. [*Grundfragen*, 394.]

God and this can take place only at the end of history. Hence the end of history as the ultimate revelation of God belongs itself to the essence of God along with the entire course of history that it presupposes. As Pannenberg explained:

> Placing the manifestation of God at the end of history means that the biblical God has, so to speak, his own history. ... It is not so much the course of history as it is the end of history that is at one with the essence of God. But insofar as the end presupposes the course of history, because it is the perfection of it, then also the course of history belongs in essence to the revelation of God, for history receives its unity from its goal. Although the essence of God is from everlasting to everlasting the same, it does have a history in time. Thus it is that Jahweh first becomes the God of all mankind in the course of the history that he has brought to be.[72]

We see therefore that in Pannenberg's thought God's universality depends upon the identification of history, especially the end of history, as essential to his own being. This concept from the early Pannenberg is then fleshed out, so to speak, through the emphasis upon God as the power of the future in the later Pannenberg. Indeed, the characterization of God as the power of the future would appear, in many ways, the logical conclusion of the line of thought Pannenberg began to develop already in his dogmatic theses on the doctrine of revelation.[73]

Also, history is not unimportant to the being of God himself since "the eternity of God is itself still dependent on the future of the world."[74] Yet Pannenberg, however, does not follow Hegel at this point in identifying completely God and history. As Grenz has written: "Pannenberg criticizes his forebear for what he sees as the shortcomings of the Hegelian solution to the traditional theological problem. God and history are to be linked but not fused. God is to be thought of as fulfilled through the relationship to the world but not restricted by it."[75] This is accomplished in Pannenberg's thought by his introduction of the idea of a mutual self-differentiation of history and the world from God.[76] Additionally, Pannenberg's contention that "the eternity of God is dependent on the future of the world" does not imply an idea similar to that found within process thought in which God "becomes" along with history or that God depends upon history for his being. Rather, it is the consummation of history which is the locus for the recognition that the biblical God is *the* God who exists from eternity to eternity. Pannenberg explains:

---

[72] "Dogmatic Theses," 133f. ["Dogmatische Thesen," 97.]
[73] Polk, 154, seems to suggest also that this is the case when he contended that Pannenberg's thoughts were already moving in the direction of a concept of God as power of the future "on the basis of implications arising from his own [earlier] work" before his interaction with Bloch.
[74] *The Apostles' Creed*, 174. [*Glaubensbekenntnis*, 181.]
[75] Grenz, 72.
[76] Cf. Pannenberg, "The God of History," *Cumberland Seminarian* 19 (winter/spring 1981), 34ff. ["Der Gott der Geschichte," in: *Kerygma und Dogma* 23 (1977)]

Refuted ... is the idea of a divine becoming in history, as though the trinitarian God were the result of history and achieved reality only with its eschatological consummation. In our historical experience it might seem as if the deity of the God whom Jesus proclaimed is definitively demonstrated only with the eschatological consummation. It might also seem that as if materially the deity of God is inconceivable without the consummation of his kingdom, and that it is thus dependent upon the eschatological coming of the kingdom. But the eschatological consummation is only the locus of the decision that the trinitarian God is always the true God from eternity to eternity. The dependence of his existence on the eschatological consummation of the kingdom changes nothing in this regard. It is simply necessary to take into account the constitutive significance of this consummation for the eternity of God.[77]

A criticism which has been raised especially by American theologians against Pannenberg's general view of God as the power of the future in relation to his conception of time is that Pannenberg appears to conceive of God as exclusively future, which, given the assumption of an absolute end of history, would seem impossible since at the end of history we could no longer conceive of God as future.[78] Robert Jenson has raised the question in regard to Pannenberg's fundamental and overriding concern for wholeness and universality. He asks whether this concern has not lead Pannenberg to a concept regarding the futurity of God too dependent upon his postulate of the totality of history so that God becomes necessarily bound to the end of this history, i.e., the point at which its wholeness becomes apparent or reaches fulfillment. Jenson's criticism is then that "if God is God in that history stops and becomes a completed entity, this God is the God of *past* history after all; and what we are bidden to await is the transformation of the God who is the power of the future into the God who *was* the power of the future."[79]

In a similar vein John McCoy, in his 1979 Princeton dissertation, has also asked whether "something crucial has not been sacrificed in establishing the being of God in terms of futurity." In selecting futurity as an essential category for establishing the essence of God McCoy wonders whether Pannenberg has not "rendered God the *creature* of history rather than its creator" since, while rejecting the idea of development in God he "still maintains the idea of *time* as foundational to the very essence of God" - an essence (including the unity and fullness of God) which "waits upon the future to the extent that that unity can only

---

[77] *ST* 1:331. [359.]
[78] In addition to the two critiques examined here, American evangelical theologian Donald Bloesch, *Essentials of Evangelical Theology* (San Francisco: Harper & Row, 1987), 1:31, contends that Pannenberg's view of God as power of the future (which he equates with Moltmann's position) precludes God as an "existent being who lives and moves among his children here and now." Langdon Gilkey, *Reaping the Whirlwind* (New York: Seabury, 1976), 234ff., has similarly criticized that Pannenberg's view not only eliminates the theological basis for political action but means that our present experience has no relation to the divine.
[79] Jenson, *God after God*, 178.

be perceived and grasped in 'anticipation.'"⁸⁰ In this light McCoy asks of Pannenberg's conception of God as the power of the future:

> How is it that God can be the power of the future *in* the consummation? Is this not a contradiction in terms? If the consummation is understood as above time, will not a temporal category as definition for God 'run out' precisely in the consummation? God at the end of *all* future is no longer the power of the future for this would point to a beyond transcendent of the consummation of history, and this is a contradiction. This does not preclude a *partial* definition of God as power of the future, but it does preclude allowing a temporal category to be *exhaustive* of that definition.⁸¹

McCoy doubts, however, that Pannenberg could adopt such a proposed modified view of God as power of the future without abandoning his entire approach to history. In the view of Jenson and McCoy, therefore, we would seem left with what is essentially a self-contradictory position. Namely, for God to be the power of the future as conceptualized by Pannenberg, all history must realize its wholeness and universality in a single end of history, a so-called consummation. But, if as Pannenberg also contends, futurity belongs to the essence of God, what becomes of futurity (and of God) when history is consummated and there is no more 'future' in the sense of a continuation of history?

The keys to understanding this apparent contradiction are elucidated by Pannenberg in his *Theology and the Kingdom of God* - a work which had not yet appeared when Jenson expressed his criticism and which McCoy seems not to have fully taken into account - and in his 1983 "Ingersoll Lecture" at Harvard, which, of course, neither had access too, although the essentials of its most relevant points were already to be found, albeit in less poignant form, in earlier writings. Pannenberg's concept of God as all-determining power of the future includes at its heart the postulate of the priority of the eschatological future as that which "determines our present." For Pannenberg, this unavoidably implies "a reversal in our ontological conceptions."⁸² As Philip Clayton has rightly observed: "When Pannenberg writes of the 'coming God' who has broken proleptically into history from the end of history, he is calling into question a classical ontology that works with static categories of being rather than time-dependent ones."⁸³

This brings us to the first key to overcoming the difficulty. Jenson, and more particularly McCoy, do not seem to have taken this 'reversal' of ontological thinking into account in its full radicalness in their critique of Pannenberg. That is

---

⁸⁰ John McCoy Jr., *Soteriology and the Doctrine of God: A Historical Typology and an Analysis of the Theologies of Karl Rahner and Wolfhart Pannenberg* (Ph.D. dissertation, Princeton Seminary, 1979), 236.
⁸¹ *Ibid.*, 239.
⁸² TKG, 54. [Cf. TRG, 12.]
⁸³ Clayton, "The God of History and the Presence of the Future," 106.

to say, they have thought about the specific proposals of Pannenberg's system still assuming an ontological priority of the past which works with static categories of being and have quite understandably reached the conclusion that Pannenberg's thought on this point is contradictory. McCoy, for instance, finds that Pannenberg makes God captive to history since if there is an ontological priority of the past then the God who will first be revealed in his fullness at the end of history is dependent upon that history for his being. The ontological priority of the future, however, means that God already is (and always has been) what he will be revealed to be at the end of history. The identification of time, particularly as its reaches its culmination in the end of history, with God implies then the reverse, namely, that history is dependent upon God as the power of the future. As Pannenberg writes:

> The very essence of God implies time [*Zeit [gehört] zum Wesen Gottes*]. Only in the future of his Kingdom come will the statement 'God exists' prove to be difinitely true. But then it will be clear that the statement was always true. In this impending power the coming God was already the future of the remotest past. He was the future also of that 'nothing' which preceded Creation. ... Therefore, the movement of time contributes to deciding what the definite truth is going to be, also with regard to the essence of God. But ... what turns out to be true in the future will then be evident as having been true all along. This applies to God as well as to every finite reality. God was present in every past moment as the one who he is in his futurity. He was in the past the same one whom he will manifest himself to be in the future.[84]

Hence there indeed comes a point for Pannenberg in which history reaches its culmination and there is no more future in the sense in which we understand it. Because God is the foundation of all universality the end of history, as understood by Pannenberg, must be a part of the essence of God. From our present perspective - and every imaginable human present - the end of history is necessarily future, thus futurity is an integral part of God's essence.

The question as to where things stand with God's futurity at the end of history within Pannenberg's system - and here we come to the second key to overcoming the apparent contradiction in Pannenberg's thought - would therefore not seem so difficult. The end of history (and in this sense of time)[85] remains

---

[84] *TKG*, 62f. [Cf. *TRG*, 20f.]

[85] Pannenberg, "Constructive and Critical Functions of Christian Eschatology," (Ingersoll Lecture) *Harvard Theological Review* 77:2 (1984), 137, makes clear that he does maintain that there will be an end of time - a point he had made also in earlier writings. He writes: "Historical experience involves the idea of a universal history and ... this in turn implies the notion of an end, because there is no historical process without an end." [Jenson, curiously, expressed that it was not clear to him "whether Pannenberg expects ... a stop of history or whether the process of new interpretations of the wholeness of history is itself expected to go on indefinitely" (p. 178) - a difficulty arising probably from the fact that in his critique of Pannenberg Jenson relies on only two articles of Pannenberg's.] Cf. also Pannenberg, *ST* 3:632f., where he contends that the

integral to God's being - and in some sense the end of history remains eternally the future of all human history. Yet at the end of history we see that the God who is there revealed in his fullness (along with history which is revealed in the fullness of its meaning) is the same God that stood at the 'beginning' of human history, there being no development within God. Hence we have now more than a mere 'anticipation' of God. To speak, however, as Jenson does, of God who is the power of the future being transformed into the God who *was* the power of the future does not make sense within Pannenberg's system.

This is made especially clear in Pannenberg's 1983 Ingersoll Lecture, "Constructive and Critical Functions of Christian Eschatology." There he observed that in light of Kant's view (as expressed in the antithesis to his first antinomy in the *Critique of Pure Reason*) that an end is only conceivable within time and within the course of continuing processes that "it is considered inevitable to raise the question of what will happen after the supposed end." Or, put differently, what will become of God as the power of the future after the end. Pannenberg argues, however, that "if such an end is conceived as the end of time and not as the end of a temporal process within time, then it would be contradictory to ask what will happen *after* that end. The end of time does not border on some other time, but the notion of an end of time expresses the finite character of time as such. The end of time borders on eternity where the finitude of time, the separation of its succeeding instants from its predecessors and successors will be removed."

This end of time, however, is not some bleak, eternal death, as would be the case "if there were nothing on the other side of such an end." Rather, as Pannenberg explains: "The end of time borders on eternity: God himself is the end of time, and as the end of time he is the final future of his creation. This does not entail the annihilation of time, but the lifting up of temporal histories into the form of an eternal presence."[86] Hence God remains what he always was, namely, the power of every human future. When these human futures reach their culmination in the eschatological end of history we remain with God's infinity and the categories of past and future are no longer intelligible. Hence the problem of how to designate God, the power of the future, when there is no more 'future,' loses its pertinency.[87]

---

[86] biblical concept of a fulfillment of history necessarily implies as end of history. *Ibid.*, 137f.

[87] Stanley Grenz, *Reason for Hope*, 74, has characterized the related criticisms of several other American theologians as missing the point. He writes: "Gilkey ... seems to overstate his case in claiming that the trend to move God to the future divests present experience of any relation to the divine [Gilkey, *Reaping the Whirlwind*, 234ff.]. The same is the case with Hill's claim that Pannenberg equates God with history, insofar as history is the unfolding of the being of God [Hill, *Three-personed God*, 298ff.]. Even Cobb seems now to have missed the point. He declares that Pannenberg's viewpoint is non-theistic in that God becomes but another name for the end of history itself [Cobb, review of *Jesus-God and Man*, in: *Journal of Religion* 49, 200f.]"

### 4.1.2.4 *God as power of the future in contrast to Moltmann and process theology*

Pannenberg's emphasis upon the futurity of God has led often to comparison - and sometimes confusion - with two other movements within contemporary Protestant theology. First, with Jürgen Moltmann's theology of hope, and second with process theology based upon the thought of Alfred North Whitehead. In both instances important distinctions, despite often overlapping emphases, are to be made between Pannenberg's doctrine of God and those of Moltmann and process thought, respectively.

Pannenberg has often been categorized along with Jürgen Moltmann as an eschatological theologian or even a theologian of hope.[88] Moltmann, like Pannenberg, has distanced himself from process thought, stressing that God's being is in 'coming' and not in 'becoming' and that God's being is to be conceived eschatologically.[89] Moltmann also follows Bloch in conceiving of God as a "God with 'future as his essential nature'" and contends also that "a proper theology would therefore have to be constructed in the light of its future goal."[90] He also has stressed his agreement with Pannenberg that "just as the kingdom of God is not a mere 'accident' of his divinity ... so the future too is the mode of his being that is dominant in history."[91] There is, however, a decisive difference between the two theologians which reveals itself precisely in regard to Bloch. As Don Olive has noted: "Moltmann, following Bloch, makes 'not-yet-being' the basic reality of this world, whereas Pannenberg does not. The 'not-yet' in Pannenberg's thought is a function and characteristic of historical reality, but it is not that reality itself. The 'not-yet' is not completely future, having already arrived in the appearance of Jesus."

Thus, "the basic difference between Pannenberg and Moltmann lies in their views of reality and the theologian's task in relation to it. For Pannenberg it is the theologian's task to interpret reality as made known in the fate of Jesus. ... For Moltmann, on the other hand, the only reality available is the reality of 'not-yet-being.'"[92] Moltmann himself, in a critique of Pannenberg's program of revelation as history, contends that if this school of thought were to accept the so-called 'cross of the present' (Hegel) in all the godlessness of the modern world, then "revelation would not manifest and verify itself *as* history of our present society, but would disclose to this society and this age for the very first time the eschatological process of history." Therefore, concludes Moltmann, "the theologian is not concerned merely to supply a different *interpretation* of the

---

[88] Cf., for example, Carl Braaten, "Toward a Theology of Hope," *Theology Today* 24 (July 1967): 208-226; and Robert Jenson, *God After God*, 175.

[89] Jürgen Moltmann, "Der 'eschatologische Augenblick': Gedanken zu Zeit und Ewigkeit in eschatologischer Hinsicht," in: *Vernunft des Glaubens*, 581.

[90] Moltmann, *Theology of Hope*, trans. James Leitch (New York: Harper & Row, 1975), 16.

[91] Moltmann, "Trends in Eschatology," in: *The Future of Creation: Collected Essays*, trans. Margaret Kohl (Philadelphia: Fortress, 1979), 27 and 179, note 40.

[92] Don Olive, *Wolfhart Pannenberg*, 81.

world, of history and of human nature, but to *transform* them in expectation of a divine transformation."[93] Pannenberg has been critical of Moltmann on similar grounds, commenting that "Moltmann's own work turned out to focus more on certain political consequences, which he and his followers derived from the eschatological hope, than on the transcendent content of the biblical hope itself."[94]

Pannenberg, therefore, cannot simply be viewed or categorized together with Moltmann as a "theologian of hope." The contrast between the theologian's task as transformation or interpretation leads back inevitably to Pannenberg's rejection and Moltmann's acceptance of Bloch's concept of 'not-yet-being' as the basic reality in the world. At heart is a different view of history and a different conception of the futurity of God. For Pannenberg the end of history, and with it the fullness of God's reality - also and even precisely in his futurity - are already proleptically present in Jesus Christ. The God who is future is therefore in a decisive and real sense already a part of our present reality, that is to say, God, as the future, is powerful in the present.

The similarities between Pannenberg's thought and process theology have also lead to many comparisons between the two.[95] Process thinkers have appeared especially interested in drawing out what they consider ideas in Pannenberg's doctrine of God which resemble those in process thought.[96] Indeed, Pannenberg has written that he agrees with process thought "that the traditional concept of Substance is problematic, because it is separated from existence and development in time." Pannenberg, however, has stressed that he is not convinced "that it is possible to dispense altogether with the concept of essence. ... Then it is the ultimate future that will have to make the final decision as to what the essence of things is. That future then becomes the substance of the things about which it decides."[97] Similarly, like Whitehead, Pannenberg also accepts the idea that time

---

[93] Moltmann, *Theology of Hope*, 84.

[94] "Constructive and Critical Functions of Christian Eschatology," 120. Philip Hefner, "The Concreteness of God's Kingdom," 195ff., has criticized Pannenberg precisely at this point from a point-of-view nearer to Moltmann's for not giving sufficient attention to the concrete political structures of life in relation to the kingdom of God even though he admits that according to Pannenberg, there must be "a meaningful conjunction between the power and the content of God's kingdom and the concrete structures of the present situation of human life."

[95] A brief but broad-ranging critique by Pannenberg of Whitehead's thought is to be found in his article "Atomism, Duration, Form: Difficulties with Proceßphilosophy," in: *Metaphysics and the Idea of God*, 113ff. ["Atom, Dauer, Gestalt. Schwierigkeiten mit der Prozess Philosophie," in: *Metaphysik und Gottesgedanke*, 80ff.] Pannenberg expresses in this article the criticism of American process theologians that they tend to read Whitehead dogmatically, taking him "to be an entirely self-sufficient systematic thinker and, as such, authoritative" (113f. [80]).

[96] Cf., for example, W. Pannenberg and Ford Lewis, "A Dialog about Process Philosophy," *Encounter* 38 (1977); John Cobb Jr., "Pannenberg and Process Theology;" and Lewis Ford, "The Nature of the Power of the Future," both in: *The Theology of Wolfhart Pannenberg*, ed. C. Braaten and P. Clayton.

[97] Pannenberg, "The Future of God and the Unity of Mankind," 191. ["Zukunft und Einheit der Menschheit," 180f.]

belongs to the essence of God's being. Pannenberg, however, contends that God has priority over the world and time as power of the future - thus taking a traditional view of God's immutability as opposed to Whitehead's concept of change within God.[98] Pannenberg, in a key passage in which he distinguishes his view from that of Whitehead and process thought, writes:

> The process philosophy of Whitehead and Hartshorne made the contribution of incorporating time into the idea of God. Theirs was an enormous achievement. But we cannot agree when Whitehead suggests that the futurity of God's Kingdom implies a development in God. It is true that, from the viewpoint of our finite present, the future is not yet decided. Therefore, the movement of time contributes to deciding what the definite truth is going to be, also with regard to the essence of God. But - and here is the difference from Whitehead - what turns out to be true in the future will then be evident as having been true all along. ... What distinguishes the present argument from Whitehead's philosophy is the ontological priority of the future as this priority is evident in the idea of God as the one who is coming.[99]

It is also to be noted that a significant difference between Pannenberg and process thought in the conception of time itself impacts their respective ideas of God. For Pannenberg, time itself comes to an end. For process thought, however, the world, and time along with it remain ever in progress and God, therefore, remains eternally future in the literal sense and cannot be identified with the absolute future of the world. Hence John Cobb, distinguishing the process view from that of Pannenberg, writes: "God as future exists for the world as its lure and creative empowerment. But on our Whiteheadian perspective, God cannot be simply identified with the absolute future of the world. God is forever future, no matter what the present might be."[100]

The process theologian David Polk notes that "Pannenberg wants to affirm the process contribution of 'incorporating time into the idea of God' but precisely without allowing for the seemingly incumbent consequence of acknowledging development within God."[101] The decisive difference is that Pannenberg's God is not a God in process of becoming in his own being but is in the process of being fully revealed within a still incomplete history. This does not mean that there is no room for 'becoming' in Pannenberg's concept of God, only that this is not an ontological becoming of being or a development within God. As Lewis Ford writes: "Pannenberg recognizes that 'God's being is still in the process of coming to be' [TKG, 56], but not that there is any development."[102] It is the fullness of

---

[98] Cf. also Greiner, *Die Theologie Wolfhart Pannenbergs*, 85.
[99] TKG, [Cf. TRG, 20f.] Cf. the subsequent German text where the argument at this point has been even further sharpened.
[100] Cobb, "Pannenberg and Process Theology," 89.
[101] Polk, 166.
[102] Lewis Ford, "The Nature of the Power of the Future," 85. Indeed, Pannenberg specifically rejects

the knowledge of God and the revelation of God rather than the ontological fullness of God which, in Pannenberg's thought, can be said to be futural.[103]

Thus, although striking similarities between Pannenberg's concept of God and that of process thought are unmistakable, Pannenberg's God is not a God in process of becoming, in an ontological sense, but rather a God in process of being revealed - a revelation whose fullness will come only at the end of history. This also allows, as we will see in our next section, Pannenberg to understand God as all-determining reality since the fullness of God as the power of the future is active in the present. Process thought, on the other hand, must reject this conception of God since a God in process of becoming with the world cannot be the all-determining power over all reality. In process thought God is seen simply as "that factor in the universe which ... lures the world toward new forms of realization." Process theology, according to two of its leading figures, John Cobb and David Griffin, rejects the existence the God who is viewed as "controlling power" and replaces him with the God of creative love who persuades. Hence "persuasion and not control is the divine way of doing things."[104] That strong criticisms of Pannenberg's idea of God as *power* of the future and all-determining reality should arise from process thinkers is thus by no means surprising. That so many process theologians, however, continue to establish dialogue with Pannenberg's doctrine of God or even to give it a process reading witnesses to an affinity with certain aspects of Pannenberg's thought. Pannenberg, however, pursues a markedly different path than process thinkers; hence attempts at co-called process readings of his thought prove ultimately unsatisfying.

In the end, the uniqueness of Pannenberg's emphasis on the futurity of God over against other contemporary theological streams which emphasize eschatological elements is clear.[105] While Pannenberg interacts with these other

---

[103] process theology's dismissal of God's immutability. So Pannenberg, "Der Gott der Geschichte: Der trinitarische Gott und die Wahrheit der Geschichte," in: *Kerygma und Dogma* 23 (1977), 83. Pannenberg, *ST* 1:331, [359.], explains in connection with the economic and immanent Trinity that God is the same in his eternal essence as he reveals himself to be historically. With this point Pannenberg contends that "the idea of a divine becoming in history" is refuted, "as though the trinitarian God were the result of history and achieved reality only with its eschatological consummation."

[104] John Cobb and David Griffin, *Process Theology: An Introductory Exposition* (Philadelphia: Westminster Press, 1976), 43 and 52ff. Process thought is critical of any idea of God as controlling power or as cause of all things. Thus Cobb and Griffin have written: "In traditional theological thought, all events were understood to be totally caused by God. ... However, there are two major problems with this notion. First, it raises serious doubt that the creative activity of God can be understood as *love*. ... Second, since the Renaissance and Enlightenment, the belief has grown that there are no events which happen without natural causes. Accordingly, the notion of 'acts of God' has lost all unambiguous referents" (49f.).

[105] Cf. Clayton "The God of History and the Presence of the Future," 106, who writes regarding the uniqueness of Pannenberg's view of the coming God: "Similarities with the positions of Hegel, Heidegger, Ernst Bloch, Moltmann and others can be shown, though in no case strongly enough that Pannenberg could be subsumed under their ontological positions."

streams of thought he seems neither dependent upon nor indebted to them. The reason for this, it would seem, is not an aloofness on the part of Pannenberg, but rather a radically different starting point and orientation for his reflections. In an insightful observation Robert Jenson has written: "Unlike with some of the others now developing eschatological theologies, a passion for the future as such does not seem to be Pannenberg's original concern. Rather, his thinking starts with a concern for wholeness."[106] This concern of Pannenberg's for wholeness (especially of history) and for universality, which is decisive for his approach to God as the power of the future, will be examined more fully in the following section as we turn our attention to Pannenberg's view of God as all determining reality and the power which determines all reality.

### 4.1.3 God as all-determining reality

#### 4.1.3.1 *The shape of God as all-determining reality*

In his *Theology and the Philosophy of Science* Pannenberg contended that the Christian claim that God is all-determining reality - an idea which arises from a combination of Hebrew monotheism and the critique of polytheism in Greek philosophy - "must be taken as a linguistic convention" which, as a nominal definition of the concept of God is pre-given in Western philosophy and theology.[107] For Pannenberg's thought, however, the importance of God as all-determining reality has taken on an importance which transcends that of a mere 'linguistic convention.' Indeed, it has been rightly observed that no one advocates among contemporary theologians more emphatically for a concept of God as universal, all-determining reality as Pannenberg.[108] Neither, especially in light of the critique of process philosophy and theology - not to mention all those who recoil today from anything even resembling determinism -, does it seem possible any longer to treat the definition of God as all-determining reality as a 'given.' Pannenberg, however, who has expended much effort in defending and exploring its ramifications, certainly does not treat the concept as a given. The question which then confronts us is, what is the content that stands behind this concept of God as all-determining reality which is so fundamental to Pannenberg's thought that he can classify it as a linguistic convention and a pre-given?

For Pannenberg the reign or power over all-reality belongs fundamentally to God's being as God. God's existence as God, according to Pannenberg, does not depend upon there being finite reality over which God is the all-determining power since "the independence from the existence of finite being certainly belongs to the Godhood of God."[109] Yet the very divinity of God requires that "if there are finite beings, then to have power over them is intrinsic to God's nature" since they

---
[106] Jenson, *God after God*, 175.
[107] *TPS*, 302f. [*WtT*, 304f.]
[108] So Kurt Koch, *Der Gott der Geschichte*, 25f.
[109] Cf. *TRG*, 13. This sentence does not appear in the English original.

belong then also to 'all reality.' Hence Pannenberg concludes that the idea of God's reign cannot, therefore, be separated from his nature as God.[110] That is to say, Pannenberg makes the power of God over all reality just as much an essential attribute of God's being as his futurity.

The significance of the concept for Pannenberg is further to be seen in that his entire program of the universality of theology is grounded fundamentally in the understanding of God as all-determining reality. Already in a 1962 paper Pannenberg made this connection clear, setting the tone for much of his thought on the universality of theology and the doctrine of God which he would later develop more fully. He wrote:

> The task of theology goes beyond its special theme and includes all truth whatsoever. This universality of theology is unavoidably bound up with the fact that it speaks of God. The word 'God' is used meaningfully only if one means by it the power that determines everything that exists. Anyone who does not want to revert to a polytheistic or polydaemonistic stage of the phenomenology of religion must think of God as the creator of all things. It belongs to the task of theology to understand all being [*alles Seiende*] in relation to God, so that without God they simply could not be understood. That is what constitutes theology's universality.[111]

The emphasis Pannenberg places here and elsewhere (especially in his conception of God as power of the future) upon the reign [*Herrschaft*] of God, rests upon the integral connection Pannenberg draws between God's reign (or power) and his being. Hence Pannenberg writes that "God's being and existence cannot be conceived apart from his rule. Or, to put it in the language of the philosophy of religion, the being of the gods is their power. To believe in one god means to believe that one power dominates all."[112] Hence we see that at stake for Pannenberg is not only the universality of theology but the foundation of monotheism itself. If God is the all-determining reality then he can neither be one object among many nor one god among many. As Peters has noted, if Pannenberg is correct, then "God can be no less universal than reality itself, or reality as a whole" since "to speak of God as the all-determining power of all things ... requires that we speak about the totality of reality."[113]

Because God is all-determining reality, according to Pannenberg, "things as a

---

[110] *TKG*, 55. [Cf. *TRG*, 13f.]
[111] Pannenberg, "The Crisis of the Scripture Principle," *BQ* 1:1. The article originally appeared as, "Die Fragwürdigkeit der klassischen Universalwissenschaft," in: *Die Krise des Zeitalters des Wissenschaften* (Frankfurt, 1963), 173ff. ["Die Krise des Schriftprinzips," in: *Grundfragen* 1:11.]
[112] *TKG*, 55. [Cf. *TRG*, 13.]
[113] Ted Peters, "Truth in History: Gadamer's Hermeneutics and Pannenberg's Apologetic Method," 44. Peters has also pointed to the similarity here with Tillich who pointed out that "if God is brought into the subject-object structure of being, he ceases to be the ground of being and becomes one being among others. He ceases to be God who is really God." (Tillich, *Systematic Theology* 1:172.).

whole are the object of study" for theology. But for theology the further question must be asked: "Given ... reality as a whole, what can we say about God as the all-determining reality?" At this point Pannenberg suggests that we cannot conceive of reality as a whole without at the same time conceiving of something outside this reality which gives all reality its unity. In a sense then, the totality of reality is not really the totality of reality since "the totality which has its unifying unity outside itself cannot be the totality of everything that exists." For Pannenberg, following the insight of Greek philosophy, God is the unifying reality demanded by the so-called totality of all reality since the concept of a totality of all reality, or even of all finite reality, is in itself deficient and in need of a unifying unity outside itself, namely God as the all-determining reality.[114]

4.1.3.2 *The all-determining God and determinism*

John Cobb has rightly noted that Pannenberg opposes all "traditional forms of causal determinism." He contends, however, that precisely with respect to his conception of God as power of the future - a view designed to safeguard the idea of human freedom - that Pannenberg advocates a "determinism based on the causal efficacy of the future."[115] David Polk, significantly also a process theologian, has similarly seen in Pannenberg's God as the all-determining power of the future a so-called 'soft determinism' since God is seen to be "willing to share decisions of causal efficacy with other centers of power *that God godself creates*."[116] Both Cobb and Polk concede that Pannenberg's view allows more freedom to human beings than so-called classical forms of determinism. At heart, however, both consider Pannenberg's God deterministic. Cobb, while God determines out of the causal efficacy of the future rather than the past; and Polk, while God wills human beings' freedom on the basis of his own nature as the power of the future - thus we are free only because God as the power of the future has so willed (or determined) that we should be free. Do such criticisms do justice to Pannenberg?

When Pannenberg describes God as the power of the future which determines all reality, or as the all-determining power of the future, the charge of determinism comes as no surprise. At issue, however, is whether Pannenberg's decisive provisio that God is the all-determining power, but *of the future* - his major contribution to the modern theological understanding of God - is sufficient to avoid the charge of determinism. Cobb and Polk are certainly correct that Pannenberg's view does not represent a *classical* deterministic position. Is it, however, in any real sense, still deterministic?

Significantly, many of the loudest charges of determinism have come from process theologians. In the view of process theology, however, nearly every

---

[114] *TPS*, 305ff. [*WtT*, 307ff.]
[115] Cobb, "Pannenberg and Process Theology," 68.
[116] Polk, 165.

conception of God diverging from their own - especially those associated with traditional theism - is judged to be deterministic. Hence process theologians, for example, reject the doctrine of a *creatio ex nihilo* since it implies a 'controlling' God.[117] Lewis Ford provides us a key to why this is so. There is a necessary inverse connection, he contends, between the idea of development in God (the crucial thought being that of process theism) and determinism. In his critique of Pannenberg's doctrine of God he contends that while there is no development within God in Pannenberg's view "it is difficult to see how our actions can constitute God's inner nature, since our actions are radically contingent and might not have been. If God's nature comes into being as that which it is, without any inner change, then that nature is the constitutive and all-determining factor of our activity in the present." When this is the case, according to Ford, then there is no room for human freedom and we are left with a divine determinism.[118]

Despite the criticisms of process thinkers, however, Pannenberg believes himself to have avoided the problem of determinism and to have allowed room for a real expression of human free will. The key to avoiding a deterministic God, for Pannenberg, is to be found in his conception of God as the power of the future, within which context Pannenberg understands God as all-determining reality. As the power of the future God "does not rob man of his freedom to transcend every present state of affairs. A being presently at hand, and equipped with omnipotence, would destroy such freedom by virtue of his overpowering might. But the power of the future is distinguished by the fact that it frees man from his ties to what presently exists in order to liberate him for *his* future, to give him his freedom."[119]

### 4.1.3.3 *Is the all-determining God open to verification?*

In a 1964 lecture on "The Question of God" Pannenberg noted that theological use of the word God remains meaningful over against atheistic criticism only "if the claim of Christian proclamation to derive from an experience of God does not remain a mere assertion but is capable of verification." Such verification would not, according to Pannenberg, need to involve a so-called pre-

---

[117] Cf., for instance, John Cobb and D. Griffin, *Process Theology*, 65; and Lewis Ford, "An Alternative to *creatio ex nihilo*," *Religious Studies* 19 (1983), 205ff. Cobb and Griffin write: "Process theology rejects the notion of *creatio ex nihilo*. ... That doctrine is part and parcel of the doctrine of God as absolute controller. Process theology affirms instead a doctrine of creation out of chaos ... in which there is nothing but very lowgrade actual occasions happening at random, i.e., without being ordered into ... a series of occasions." Pannenberg, "Atom, Duration, Form: Difficulties with Process Philosophy," 28, has noted in this regard that "the idea of radical self-creation of each actual occasion is the reason why Whitehead's metaphysics cannot be reconciled with the Biblical idea of creation nor, therefore, with the Biblical idea of God."

[118] Ford, "The Nature of the Power of the Future," 85ff. Ford adds that Whitehead's solution to the problem "is to reconceive the eschaton in terms of divine experience, whereby our (present) free acts are included in the (future) divine experience. ... This is possible only if God is in becoming, capable of being enriched, rather than in being, whether present or future" (87).

[119] "The God of Hope," 242f. [*Grundfragen*, 393.]

revelatory court of appeal before which God would have to legitimate himself since this would be incompatible with "the majesty of divine revelation." Rather, "Christian speech about God can be verified only in such a way that it is the revelation of God itself which discloses that about man and his world in relation to which its truth is proved." Pannenberg believes that in this way theological statements about God would rise above the level of mere assertion and that they could "lay claim to the existence of man and of the world ... as witnesses for the reality of the biblical God."[120]

Does this mean then that a sort of anthropological verification of God is to be sought? Although the question of God is not unconnected to anthropology in Pannenberg's thought he clearly rejects this route, as one might suspect from our discussion of an anthropological argument for God's existence in the preceding chapter. In his 1986 article, "Religion und menschliche Natur," Pannenberg contends that "human beings are from their beginning, by their very nature." Yet he is adamant that "the foundation for the knowledge of God's reality can only come from God himself, and that that takes place through God's self revelation to us."[121] This then brings us again to Pannenberg's understanding of revelation as history. Hence already in his Dogmatic Theses on the Doctrine of Revelation Pannenberg states that only the entirety of historical occurrences can finally demonstrate the Godhood of Yahweh, and this can only take place at the end of history when it will be seen that Yahweh is the one and only God of all reality.[122]

The verification, to the extent that this then is actually possible, of God, or of our experience of God, is thus seen to be tied to Pannenberg's conception of the unity of all reality. This has not just to do with his theory of history, but also with human experience. Hence Pannenberg has recently contended that "Christian truth claims about God must ... face [the] ... question of a confirmation through the human experience of meaning and its implications for the understanding of reality as a whole." That is to say, our truth claims about God must prove themselves by their ability "to integrate the relations implicit in everyday experiences of meaning within an encompassing context of meaning that grounds all individual meaning" so that these claims function as a "comprehensive interpretation of the experience of the world's reality." Although this kind of "verification" by no means offers (nor does it pretend to offer) empirical proof of the existence of God, it does seek to point out that our conception of God must be able to serve as a comprehensive interpretation of human experience if the God proclaimed by the Christian tradition is to "be understood as and believed to be the creator and perfecter of the world as actually experienced by humans."[123] Hence, although Pannenberg

---

[120] Pannenberg, "The Question of God," in: *BQ* 2:206f. ["Die Frage nach Gott," *Grundfragen* 365.]
[121] Pannenberg, "Religion und menschliche Natur," in: *Sind wir von Natur aus religiös?*, ed. W. Pannenberg, 24.
[122] "Dogmatic Theses," 133f. ["Dogmatische Thesen," 97.]
[123] Pannenberg, *Metaphysics and the Idea of God*, 168. [The source of this reference, "Meaning, Religion, and the Question of God," does not appear in *Metaphysik und Gottesgedanke*.]

stresses the role of our personal experience of reality and existence in the "verification" of our talk about God this must rise above the individual experiences of our own limited lives and point to the totality of experience and existence. In his 1972 exposition of the Apostles' Creed Pannenberg makes this point clear. He writes:

> God proves himself to be God in our experience of existence, undoubtedly in our highly personal experience. ... But when we limit ourselves to this very narrow, personal sphere of living, no generally applicable and tenable reason can be found why it should have to be particularly the God of the Bible who is the true God. ... It is the breadth of total experience of every and all reality which provides the field where we have to inquire whether the divine nature of the God of the Bible can stand up to verification; it is not the narrow bounds of an entirely personal experience of life, taken in isolation.[124]

Van Huyssteen summarized Pannenberg's position well when he explained that for Pannenberg, "if God is real, He must be the all-determinant reality. And although the concept of God can in itself not be tested or verified directly against its object, it is in fact possible to assess that concept in terms of its own implications. Thus the concept of God ... becomes testable by its implications for our experience of reality."[125] The existence of God, however, is not in this way made to be dependent upon human experience. But rather, because Pannenberg conceives God as the all-determining reality human experience is dependent (contingent) upon God. This requires, therefore, an understanding of God which is universal, that is, which explains the entirety of our experience of the reality over which God is powerful. Yet at the same time because all reality is not accessible to us and because our experience of reality, occurring as it does before the end of history, is necessarily tentative, God cannot be finally verified by human experience in the present.[126] As Pannenberg explained in the first volume of his *Systematic Theology*:

> As the revelation of God in his historical action moves towards the still outstanding future of the consummation of history, its claim to reveal the one God who is the world's Creator, Reconciler, and Redeemer is open to future verification in history, which is as yet incomplete, and which is still exposed, therefore, to the question of its truth. This question is given an ongoing answer in the life of believers by the power of revelation to shed light on their life experiences. In theological thinking, then, the question finds a provisional answer in the assurance that our own reality and that of our world are seen as determined by the God of revelation.[127]

---

[124] *Apostles' Creed*, 35. [*Glaubensbekenntnis*, 42f.]
[125] Van Huyssteen, *Theology and the Justification of Faith*, 86.
[126] Cf. van Huyssteen, 87, who draws a similar conclusion.
[127] *ST* 1:257 [281.] for this and the following quote.

Pannenberg has similarly observed that final 'verification' of God in his capacity as creator must also wait upon the future consummation of creation when we will see that God is creator of all things precisely in that he will be revealed to be the final future of all things. As Pannenberg has explained: "In the consummation of creation all doubt that the world is the creation of God will be laid to rest. As the future and the completion of this world, God will also be conclusively shown to be the world's creator. Therefore God is the author of the existence and being of all things inasmuch as God is their final future."[128] Similarly, Pannenberg has argued that the question whether God can be understood as the origin of all reality will remain a matter of dispute until human history reaches its consummation in the kingdom of God. "Until then there can be no final and indisputable answer to the question about the reality of God. The incompleteness of history and the incompletableness of individual experience make no other solution possible."[129]

In this light Christian theology is called to continue to test and verify the truth claims of Christian revelation and especially of God through a "systematic reconstruction of Christian doctrine." God as all-determining reality remains necessarily an hypothesis in process of verification through our experience of his revelatory word (especially in Christ) and of reality. Only at the eschatological end of history will this process of verification be complete, until that time verification of God and our speech about God remains necessarily provisional. Hence Pannenberg, as we have already seen, can contend that: "Only in the future of his Kingdom come will the statement 'God exists' prove to be definitely true. But then it will be clear that the statement was always true."[130]

## 4.2 Karl Rahner: God as Absolute Mystery

### 4.2.1 'God': Preliminary Considerations

#### 4.2.1.1 Importance of the word 'God'

For Rahner as for Pannenberg the word 'God' describes something essential in our experience of reality and without it this would be lost. Hence he contends that the word 'God' itself witnesses to a genuine reality - at the very least in the form of asking the question about this reality. In this manner even the atheist, according to Rahner, asks implicitly this question when he or she invokes the word 'God' in an attempt to deny the reality that it represents.[131] According to

---

[128] *ST* 3:583.
[129] *Apostles' Creed*, 36. [*Glaubensbekenntnis*, 44.]
[130] *TKG*, 62. [Cf. *TRG*, 20.]
[131] Rahner, "The Question of Meaning as a Question of God," in: *TI* 21:206 ["Die Sinnfrage als Gottesfrage," in: *Schriften* 15:204], contends that "a knowledge of God is ... already present when the question of meaning as a question that is meaningful and that answers itself is accepted in the concrete actualization of human life with its decisions of conscience, even when some people have

Rahner: "The word 'God' is not just any word, but is the word in which language ... grasps itself in its ground. This word *exists*, it belongs in a special and unique way to our world of language and thus to our world. It is itself a reality, and indeed one that we cannot avoid. This reality might be present speaking clearly or obscurely, softly or loudly. But it is there at least as a question."

Hence in Rahner's view the "absolute death of the word 'God' ... would be the signal, no longer heard by anyone, that man himself had died."[132] This is the case because, in Rahner's view, the word 'God' is not a foreign word to humans but rather a given which goes hand in hand with our own existence.[133] As DiNoia notes, "the experience of God [is] at the very center of human existence."[134]

The fact, however, that the word 'God' does exist, and whether the precise form that it takes be *Gott* or *deus* or *theos* or *El* or even perhaps the old Mexican *teotl*, its existence points to the reality, or at the very least the question about the reality, which it represents. Even Wittgenstein's protest that we must remain silent about things which we cannot clearly speak of does not forbid the word 'God.' Rather, if Wittgenstein's maxim is properly understood, then the word 'God' as the final word before "wordless and worshipful silence" points precisely to God as absolute mystery. The word 'God' points to God as absolute, ineffable mystery as that within which our being and indeed all being is grounded. Therefore the real word 'God,' according to Rahner, in distinction to the combination of letters g-o-d that one finds in a dictionary among so many other words, "confronts us with ourselves and with reality as a whole, at least as a question."[135] Hence already when one considers the very word 'God' we have to do, in Rahner's view, with not only our own reality but with all reality. We might conclude, then, from a Rahnerian perspective, that any discussion of 'God,' even when the intention is to deny his existence, presupposes at least implicitly God's universality. [136]

### 4.2.1.2 *The character of the Christian idea of 'God'*

In a 1981 lecture in which Rahner sought to delineate what features a specifically Christian concept of God should have he focused on two points. First

---

[132] the impression that they can make nothing out of the word *God*."
*FCF*, 49f. [*Grundkurs*, 59.]

[133] Cf. Karl-Heinz Weger, *Karl Rahner: An Introduction to His Theology*, 55, who writes that when Rahner speaks of God and of the human experience of God he is "concerned to show that 'God' is not a foreign term for man, but is rather simply the name given to a reality that always accompanies man's expression of his own life and has to be revealed to man and made explicitly conscious by an appeal to his own experience."

[134] J. DiNoia, "Karl Rahner," in: Ford, *The Modern Theologians*, vol. 2:190.

[135] *Ibid.*, 45 and 51.

[136] Michael Buckley, "Within the Holy Mystery," in: *A World of Grace*, ed. L. O'Donovan, 32, summarized what for Rahner is implied in the word 'God': "'God' must make sense of everything else, must draw it into a unity. In this pervasive dependence upon Him ... all things come into a community among themselves and the meaning of 'God' is experienced. Thus the word names the One who mysteriously unifies everything and so is always present. 'God' can summon up all of reality as its correlative. ... The word names that which alone calls reality into a whole."

of all, contended Rahner, a Christian concept of God will distinguish itself from all others, e.g., atheistic, pantheistic, deistic, etc., in that it "lets God really be God." For Rahner this means that a Christian doctrine of God should not box God in but must confess him as the one creator of the world who is almighty, infinite, eternal, etc. and who, moreover, is different and distinct from the world in his essence. Yet as Rahner admits, although letting God be God in this manner is fundamental to a Christian understanding of God, it is not yet a *specifically* Christian concept of God.[137]

The second and decisive step in the attainment of a specifically Christian idea of God is the recognition that such a concept of God can only be derived from revelation as opposed to what Rahner calls a metaphysical knowledge of God accessible from the creaturely world itself. The knowledge which revelation provides about God that cannot be obtained from the world as such, according to Rahner, points to the otherness of the world which itself is the very foundation of God's self-communication to his creatures. Rahner writes:

> This God, whom Christianity radically distinguishes from the world as free creator, is the God who has in his most proper reality, and not merely by the mediation of created realities, as inmost dynamism and definitive goal offered and communicated himself to the world in its spiritual creatures so that the otherness of the world can be understood as the condition of the possibility of this self-communication of God; creation exists as the presupposition of grace, and creaturely history actually takes place as an element of the history of God himself. And God's revelation says further that this history of God in his world in the dialogue of human and divine freedom in Jesus Christ has already attained the phase of the irrevocability of an actually blessed conclusion.[138]

The specifically Christian concept of God, however, does not mean that it is inconceivable that these concepts be found outside the Christian religion. The universality of God, and more specifically his universal salvific will, leaves open the possibility "in the history of religion to discover both of these characteristics of the Christian concept of God in non-Christian ideas of God as well, at least in traces and in the vaguest of notions." If such concepts are then in fact discovered in non-Christian religions then Rahner contends that Christian theology should attribute this to the "self-revelation of God which ... must always and everywhere be present in history, because owing to God's universal salvific will salvation and faith must always and everywhere be possible."[139]

---

[137] Rahner, "The Specific Character of the Christian Concept of God," in: *TI* 21:194. ["Über die Eigenart des christlichen Gottesbegriffs," in: *Schriften* 15:193.]

[138] *Ibid.*, 194f. [193f.]

[139] *Ibid.*, 195. [194.] Rahner, in fact, in the same article (188f.), contends that Christian theology can even learn about God from non-Christian religions. He asks: "Is it unthinkable that we might learn something from the monotheism of Islam? Why should it not be possible to come to an even clearer realization of a Christian personalism contained in the Christian concept of God by bringing in elements of truth contained in the religions and philosophies of the East in respect to a

### 4.2.1.3 *God as person*

The two characteristics of letting God be God and of God's otherness to the world which makes possible his self-disclosure do not exhaust, in Rahner's thought, all that is characteristic of the Christian concept of God. As Rahner contended in his *Foundations of Christian Faith*, "the statement that God is a person, that he is a personal God, is one of the fundamental Christian assertions about God."[140] In this regard there is a close convergence with Pannenberg who also maintains the essentialness of God's *person*alness.[141]

For Rahner the question of the personhood of God does not in the first instance have to do with the three persons of the Trinity. Rather, the question about God's personal character which must first be asked is whether God is person only in relation to us or whether he is also a person in his own self, that is, in his own inmost being. God, according to Rahner, is person in his inmost being and not just in relation to us. Indeed, God is absolute person. In contrast to much contemporary thought which tends to view the attribute person as applied to God as an anthropocentric projection[142] on the deity Rahner argues that it is we ourselves who are dependent upon God as absolute person for our personhood. God as absolute person is the ground of all being and the ground of all personhood. If God were not in himself person then he could not be the ground for our personhood. As Rahner explains:

> The assertion that God ... is the absolute person who stands in absolute freedom vis-à-vis everything which he establishes as different from himself ... is really self-evident, just as much as when we say that God is the absolute being, the absolute ground. ... It is self-evident first of all that the ground of a reality which exists must possess in itself beforehand and in absolute fullness and purity this reality which is grounded by it, because otherwise this ground could not be the ground of what is grounded, and because otherwise the ground would ultimately be empty nothingness which, if the term is really taken seriously, would say nothing and could ground nothing.[143]

Rahner is aware of the objections and problems associated with attributing personhood to God. Yet Rahner believes that if we are able to predicate anything at all of God, "then the concept of 'personhood' has to be predicated of him." But when we do this it must be in such a way that we are open to the 'darkness' of holy mystery which means that we must let God be a person in the way in which he chooses to encounter us within our human history. Our experience then points back to God as ground of our own personhood and to God as absolute person in

---

[140] seemingly non-personal nature of absolute being?"
*FCF*, 73. [*Grundkurs*, 81.]
[141] Cf. "The God of Hope," 244ff. [*Grundfragen*, 394ff.] and *Apostles' Creed*, 27ff. [*Glaubensbekenntnis*, 35ff.]
[142] Rahner has especially in mind the atheistic critique stemming from Fichte. So Buckley, 44.
[143] *FCF*, 73f. [*Grundkurs*, 81f.]

himself and not as some impersonal cosmic ground of being.[144] In this sense, Rahner has essentially built upon the foundation already established in *Hearers of the Word* where God's personhood is arrived at from the starting point of human transcendental experience. He wrote:

> As a spirit, and as such a knowing absolute being, man stands distinct from this absolute being who is a free autonomous powerful *person*. This personal countenance of God is not an attribute resulting from the retrospective fitting out of absolute being with human features. The personality of God is displayed in the self-disclosure of absolute being before human transcendence, for this appears through man in the question mark associated with all being, which at the same time is problematicality.[145]

Hence, arguing from the human, Rahner seeks to demonstrate the validity of attributing personhood to God. Therefore he can contend: "In its very constitution a finite spirit always experiences itself as having its origins in another and as being given to itself from another - from another, therefore, which it cannot misinterpret as an impersonal principle."[146]

What is initially somewhat surprising is Rahner's hesitancy to speak of the threefold manifestation of God's being in the Trinity as "persons." In regard to the Trinity Rahner prefers rather to speak of three distinct "Subsistenzweisen" (subsistent 'beings' or "ways of existing"), instead of three persons which has become increasingly open to misunderstanding.[147] Rahner's suggestion, however, that we replace the term 'person' in relation to the Three of the Trinity[148] does not, when seen in context, minimize the importance of the 'personhood' as attributed to God as such. Hill, for instance, suggests that one of the reasons for this move is an attempt to avoid the tendency toward subordinationism arising out of his representation of the Father as the *Fons Divinitatis* and of the *Logos* and *Pneuma*, respectively, as his auto-expression and self-repossession.[149] Bert van der Heijden has similarly, and it would seem correctly, pointed out that Rahner's concern is to avoid a tri-theism that the use of the term 'person' for the individual 'ways of being' of the Trinity might lead to.[150] Rahner's suggestion to understand

---

[144] Buckley, 44, explains that in Rahner's thought "God is the ground of all personal reality and ... this reality is realized in God as its transcendent source. ... That personal reality which in us is limited and defined by another, is found in God without limitation and in its radical originality."
[145] *Hearers*, 89. [*HdW*, 111f.]
[146] *FCF.*, 74f. [*Grundkurs*, 82f.]
[147] Cf. Rahner, "Der dreifaltige Gott als transzendenter Urgrund der Heilsgeschichte," in: *Mysterium salutis* II, 389ff. For a discussion of Rahner's concept of person in relation to the Trinity cf. F. Bantle, "Person und Personbegriff in der Trinitätslehre Karl Rahners," in: *Münchner Theologische Zeitschrift* 30 (1979):11-24; and Walter Kasper, *Der Gott Jesu Christi* (Mainz: Matthias-Grünewald, 1982), 349ff.
[148] Cf. Rahner, *The Trinity*, trans. J. Donceel (New York: Herder and Herder, 1970), 101.
[149] Hill, 144f.
[150] Cf. Bert van der Heijden, *Karl Rahner: Darstellung und Kritik seiner Grundpositionen* (Einsiedeln: Johannes Verlag, 1973), 440f.

the Three of the Trinity as 'ways of existing' rather than as 'persons,' therefore, does not imply that personhood is not rightly and necessarily attributed to God as such.

### 4.2.1.4 Identity of the economic and immanent Trinity

Although the doctrine of the Trinity does not play as decisive a role in Rahner's theology with regard to God's universality and unity as in Pannenberg it is nevertheless an important component of his doctrine of God. Like Pannenberg, Rahner also is part of the resurgence of trinitarian theology in contemporary theology. Rather than attempt a full treatment of Rahner's doctrine of the Trinity we shall treat here briefly only two aspects of his trinitarian understanding that are typical of his doctrine of the Trinity and which allow comparison with Pannenberg's trinitarian formulations. Specifically, we will concern ourselves with his identification of the economic and immanent Trinity and with his understanding of the problem of God's immutability in relation to his trinitarian understanding.

A somewhat controversial aspect of Rahner's doctrine of God has been his identification of the immanent and economic Trinity, that is to say, of the way God is *for us* with God as he is *within himself*.[151] At stake for Rahner is the knowledge of God. He wishes to emphasize that the God who we come to know through his actions *for us* in history is identical with God as he is *in himself*. Hence for Rahner it is clear that "the economic Trinity is the immanent Trinity, and the immanent Trinity is the economic Trinity."[152] As Hill correctly explains, in Rahner's thought, "the Trinity that becomes manifest in time, in sacred history, is not otherwise than the Trinity which eternally is the deity itself. What the believer experiences in God's dealing with man within history is not merely an analogue of the inner-divine Trinity, a replica reflected within the creaturely sphere that only conveys the truth that God is in himself three-personal."[153]

If the economic and immanent Trinity were not identical then the self-communication of God would come into question since we experience God through the economic Trinity and assume that the God we learn to know, or who reveals himself to us in this way, is indeed God as he is. Rahner explains that if the economic Trinity were not the Trinity of and for itself (the immanent Trinity), then we could not speak of a real self-communication of God. This is the case, according to Rahner, since "any distinction in this act of self-communication such that it was not attributed to God in and for himself would appear as merely

---

[151] Cf. Bert van der Heijden, 435ff.; Paul Molnar, "Can We Know God Directly?" 248ff.; and Wm. Hill, *The Three-Personed God*, 140ff., for criticisms of Rahner's identification of the economic and immanent Trinity. Walter Kasper, *Der Gott Jesu Christi*, 333ff., however, offers a qualified dedence of Rahner's identification of the economic and immanent Trinity and speaks of Rahner's view as having found a broad consensus among contemporary theologians.

[152] Rahner, *The Trinity*, 25.

[153] Hill, *The Three-Personed God*, 140.

creaturely. The 'self-communication of God' would be mediated through a creaturely act. We would have God not in himself and for himself, but merely as he is reflected in creaturely reality."[154] Or, as Rahner has elsewhere argued, the fact that the economic and immanent Trinity are identical becomes comprehensible through that which is implicit in the self-revelation of God and which is deducible on the basis of transcendental theology which shows us that "this self-communication of God necessarily comes to man as transcendence and as history, in a unity and distinction of both elements" of the Trinity.[155]

The criticism is not easy to avoid that Rahner's identification of the economic and immanent Trinity takes on the form of necessity so that the incarnation and hypostatic union become not only possible but ontologically necessary. Molnar, for instance, has noted that because Rahner identifies the inner-trinitarian relations "with the 'being' of his symbolic ontology, he cannot describe the inner relations of the Godhead as free but as necessary occurrences conforming absolutely to 'symbolic reality'" as recognized by metaphysics.[156] Hill similarly suggests that an overemphasis upon the continuity between the eternal processions and the temporal mission lays at the heart of Rahner's thought at this point so that the explanation for creation and redemption are to be sought in God's very being as Trinity. Hence, rather than locate the possibility of creation and redemption in God's own being as Trinity and leaving the actualization to the mystery of God's love these become necessitated by the immanent Trinity in a way that, in Hill's view, threatens the freedom of God's transcendence. Hill contends that the identification of the economic and immanent Trinity compromises "the utter transcendence of God's *creative* love" and that Rahner's trinitarian thought "stresses self-communication so far that *creatio ex nihilo* loses its full ontological density."[157]

Another problem, which would seem also connected at least indirectly to Rahner's identification of the economic and immanent Trinity is that of God's immutability. Pannenberg, by distinguishing between the economic and immanent Trinity, was able to allow for change within the economic Trinity while remaining firmly committed to God's immutability.[158] Rahner, however, is forced by his identification of the economic and immanent Trinity to either maintain the immutability of the economic Trinity (which he does not wish to do - especially with reference to the incarnation and its implications[159]) or question the

---
[154] "Reflections on Methodology," 95. [*Schriften* 9:107.]
[155] "Transcendental Theology," 288. [*SM* 4:990.]
[156] Molnar, "Can We Know God Directly? Rahner's Solution from Experience," 251.
[157] Hill, 141.
[158] Cf. Polk, "The All-Determining God," 165ff.; and Lewis Ford, "The Nature of the Power of the Future," 85ff. Yet Pannenberg, however, also showed an openness to Rahner's program of identifying the economic and immanent Trinity, especially inasmuch as such a view must "constantly link the Trinity in the eternal essence of God to his historical revelation, since revelation cannot be viewed as extraneous to his deity." (*ST* 1:327ff. [355ff.])
[159] Cf. Rahner, "On the Theology of the Incarnation," *TI* 4:113f. ["Zur Theologie der

immutability of the immanent Trinity and thereby of the divine essence (which the Roman magisterium does not permit).[160] The question which must be raised, therefore, is whether perhaps in his attempt to preserve the unity of God's being *in himself* with God as he reveals himself *for us* Rahner has brought into question God's immutability.

### 4.2.2 God as Transcendent Ground of All Being

#### 4.2.2.1 *God as ground of all being (alles Seienden)*

Foundational to the claim of God's universality is his relatedness to all things, which are namely contingent upon him. For Pannenberg, this universality of God was demonstrated primarily through his doctrine of creation in which God is seen to be creator of all reality. Rahner draws a similar theological conclusion based upon the doctrine of creation. The Christian, according to Rahner, confesses that all things, both spiritual and material, are the creation of one and the same God and that all things thus have their origin in this one God. As Rahner explains: "This means not only that all things in their variety proceed from *one* cause which, because it is infinite and all-powerful, can create the most varied things. It also means that this variety manifests an inner similarity and commonality, and that this variety of differentiation forms a unity of origin ... - that is, it forms a *single* world."[161] In one of his later writings Rahner made similarly clear his conviction that God's universality and the unity of all things is grounded in the doctrine of creation. He wrote:

> Theologians proceed from the assumption that absolutely everything that is not God is created by one and the same God. ... Everything that is, therefore, must bear the stamp of origin of this one primordial ground of being; everything must have an ultimate unity and community. The postulate of an ultimate unity of the whole world which cannot be resolved into a definitive, ultimately unthinkable disparity of several worlds ... is implicit in the belief in creation.[162]

Yet for Rahner, God's universality is even more fundamentally arrived at metaphysically. Although arguing from a theological doctrine of creation as does Pannenberg he also, and this is especially the case in his earlier writings, pursues a philosophically oriented argumentation for the universality of God, namely, his metaphysical conception of God as the ground of all being (*alles Seienden*). The

---

Menschwerdung," in: *Schriften* 4:145f.] Rahner, therefore, proposes to understand the immutability of God as a 'dialectical' truth.

[160] As McCoy, 145, writes, on the issue of the concept of the immutability of God "it appears that Rahner becomes caught between his loyalty to the "*magisterium*" and his profound conception of the dynamics in the life of God himself."

[161] *FCF*, 181f. [*Grundkurs*, 183f.]

[162] Rahner, "Natural Science and Reasonable Faith," *TI* 21:34. ["Naturwissenschaft und vernünftiger Glaube," in: *Schriften* 15:42.]

question about the absolute ground of all being, consistent especially with developments in the thought of the later Rahner, takes as its starting point already the human questioning after being which leads to metaphysics. Rahner contended that the human being can never stop at this point in either thought or action. Instead, "he wants to know what every thing is, especially in the unity in which all is always present to him. He enquires into the ultimate reasons, into the final cause of all reality, and to the extent that he recognizes each separate thing as existing, and ever being brought face to face with himself in such knowledge, he enquires into the being of all that exists. He practices metaphysics."[163]

To this human questioning after the ground of our being - indeed, the ground of all being - there can be only one answer, namely, God. Yet precisely as the ground of all being God cannot be grasped as a tangible object. Wrote Rahner: "God is not a datum which can be directly grasped in his true self by man and his experience. For metaphysical perception, God is seen as the absolute cause of existent things [*absoluten Grund der Seienden*] and of the knowledge of being. He is revealed every time man enquires into anything which exists, but who remains knowable only as the remote cause of all that which is."[164] God as the ground of all being, therefore, is the ground of all knowing and of all human science but is not himself the object of any human science.

For Rahner, God's universality is not only grounded theologically upon the doctrine of creation, but fundamentally and metaphysically upon the ontological contingence of all being upon the absolute ground of all being which he names God.[165] On this basis Rahner can confess that the God who is experienced as present is "the transcendental ground and horizon of everything which exists and everything which knows."[166]

### 4.2.2.2 "The God who dwells beyond the world"

Rahner, whose theological method we have characterized as transcendental, makes his starting point the nature of human persons who through the experience of their creatureliness 'transcend' their worldly context in their relationship to and knowledge of God. Such a methodological approach presupposes that the God who is to be known and experienced by his creatures is himself transcendent since transcendental experience points necessarily to a ground that transcends our created sphere.[167] Hence for Rahner all statements about God arise out of our human experience of transcendence.[168] Already in *Hearers of the Word* Rahner

---

[163] *Hearers*, 33. [*HdW*, 50.]
[164] *Ibid.*, 7f. [20.]
[165] Cf. *ibid.*, 86ff. [108ff.]
[166] *FCF*, 83. [*Grundkurs*, 91.]
[167] Molnar, 236f., draws the opposite conclusion as Rahner, suggesting that because God is transcendent his creatures cannot know him directly and by suggesting otherwise Rahner is "theoretically calling God's transcendence into question."
[168] Cf. Rahner, "The Concept of Mystery in Catholic Theology," in: *TI* 4:50f. ["Über den Begriff des Geheimnisses in der katholischen Theologie," *Schriften* 4:70.]

stressed this point when he wrote:

> God is the objective reaching out [*das Woraufhin*] of the human spirit, but he is that precisely because he appears as the free power which stands in contradistinction from the finite. Thus when finite intellect knows him, such knowledge is based upon his own free delimiting of the finite ... [and] is already always an answer to a free world that the Absolute has spoken. This is implicitly affirmed as just such a free act, if the finite spirit in virtue of his transcendence feels himself to be founded upon reference to the Absolute.[169]

And again elsewhere he wrote that "the Wither of transcendental experience is always there as the nameless, the indefinable, the unattainable. ... All conceptual expressions about God, necessary though they are, always stem from the unobjectivated experience of transcendence as such: the concept from the preconception, the name from the experience of the nameless. The preconception given in transcendence is directed to the nameless."[170] And yet this nameless one is also the one we 'name' God - the one in whom this 'unobjective' transcendental experience finds is true 'object.' Hence transcendental experience is directed toward that absolute "which we call 'God', and which constitutes the true 'subject' of theological statements."[171]

As Peter Eicher has rightly noted with reference to Rahner's theology, "the Wither of transcendental experience of the boundaries is itself not an object, but rather the infinite horizon of all appearing objects," whereby "horizon," in Rahnerian terminology,[172] indicates that which stands behind all observable or experiencable phenomena, namely, God.[173] Or, as Manuel Cabada-Castro has pointed out, Rahner locates God philosophically in the dimension of the transcendental "in which and from which humans, in their knowledge, ... live." Hence "this transcendental experience is most essential for humans, moreover it makes every empirical experience possible."[174] Therefore, as Rahner writes: "'God' is known through and in the transcendence previous to ... [objectiving

---

[169] *Hearers*, 89. [*HdW*, 111.]
[170] "The Concept of Mystery in Catholic Theology," 50f. [*Schriften* 4:70.]
[171] "On the Relationship Between Theology and the Contempory Sciences," 96. [*Schriften* 10:106.]
[172] Eicher, *Die anthropologische Wende*, 281f. "Horizon," in Rahner's usage, has been defined as "the co-presence in all human experience of the fullness of being - God - as the source and goal of human knowledge and freedom, the unlimited context of all limited human experience" ("Glossary," in: *A World of Grace*, ed. L. O'Donovan, 192.)
[173] Cf. *ibid.*, 114. Hill, *The Three-Personed God*, 136f., has, however, questioned whether Rahner can make this 'leap' required to call the horizon of our transcendental human knowing God. Hill contends that even if our experience of this horizon "(understood by way of the transcendental method of reduction) testifies both to this primordial, anticipatory 'knowing' and to a certain positivity on the part of what is thereby 'known,' this still leaves unexplained how it can be called God."
[174] Manuel Cabada-Castro, "Ort und Bedeutung des philosophischen Gottesbegriffs in Denken Karl Rahners," trans. Evelin Höhne, in: *Wagnis Theologie*, 164.

conceptions of him], even where the object of knowledge is something finite."[175]

Of special importance to Rahner is the relationship between God as the primordial ground of being and that which has been grounded in existence, namely, everything other than God. In other words, the relationship between God and that which has been created. God, as the one who is other than and transcends the created realm, because of his otherness, always relates to his creatures in a mediated way. In all God's relationships to the created realm, contends Rahner,

> God remains strictly speaking the one who dwells beyond the world, the one who is related to this world by what he creates and effects different from himself. His intervention in this world takes place always through something different from himself. ... At least where the difference between an absolute God and a relative world is clearly maintained in contrast to pantheism or panentheism, the relationship between God and the world must be conceived as mediated always by something that is different from God even though it has an orientation to him. Regardless of whether this mediation is conceived as a gift, as a word that represents God, as a sacrament, ... or what you will, God is always related to us ... by means of something he establishes different from himself.[176]

For Rahner human transcendence points ultimately to its "Woraufhin" - the transcendent God. God as transcendent ground of being remains beyond our human grasp. The God who dwells beyond the world, i.e., the God who is transcendent, remains finally for Rahner - precisely as the transcendent ground of all knowing and all being - the Absolute Mystery.[177]

### 4.2.2.3 The transcendental argument for the existence of God

Many have detected in Rahner's thought a transcendental argument for the existence of God.[178] The question of whether Rahner has actually produced such an argument for the existence of God and whether, if so, it is to be understood as an *a priori* argument for God's existence, will be the focus of this section. Such

---

[175] "The Concept of Mystery in Catholic Theology," 50. [*Schriften* 4:69.] Eicher, then, has rightly summarized that our transcendental, 'subjective' experience points inevitably in Rahner's thought to a transcendent God. "Gott ist uns nur in der Vermittlung des Urteils über das endliche Seiende gegeben und explizit nur im transzendentalen Rückgriff auf diese Urteilsbedingung faßbar; kann immer nur als das Woraufhin unserer unendlichen erkennenden und strebenden Transzendentalität erfaßt werden. Gott steht also mitten in unserer Subjektivität, welche ohne die Bejahung Gottes gar nicht möglich wäre, so daß das Wissen von Gott eine strenge Funktion der eigenen Subjektivität und der Erkenntnis von Welt darstellt." (Eicher, *Die anthropologische Wende*, 281f.)

[176] "The Specific Character of the Christian Concept of God," 189f. [*Schriften* 15:189.] Rahner adds that this cannot be otherwise since a radical conception of God's transcendence does not permit the human beings as creature to presume identity with God since we are ultimately *non capax infiniti*. Yet, as Rahner also notes, it is the very recognition of our distance from God which makes our salvation possible.

[177] Cf. Cabada-Castro, 165.

[178] Cf., for instance, Eicher, 280f.

an argument, it would seem, is already to be found in Rahner's first book, *Spirit in the World*, where he argues from the pre-apprehension of being (*Vorgriff auf esse*) which is the basis of transcendental knowledge. Rahner contends:

> In ... pre-apprehension as the necessary and always already realized condition of knowledge ... the existence of an Absolute Being is also affirmed simultaneously. For any possible object which can come to exist in the breadth of the pre-apprehension is simultaneously affirmed. An Absolute Being would completely fill up the breadth of this pre-apprehension. Hence it is simultaneously affirmed as real. ... In this sense, but only in this sense, it can be said: the pre-apprehension attains to God.[179]

Yet for Rahner this does not constitute an *a priori* argument for God's existence since the pre-apprehension can be shown to be necessary for knowledge (a vital step in the 'proof') "only in the *a posteriori* apprehension of a real existent and as the necessary condition of the latter."[180] For Rahner, therefore, the proofs of Thomas are merely an application of this situation to his "ontology of the real." Rahner contends, then, that he is not offering an *a priori* proof of God's existence but has simply said that "the *affirmation* of the real limitation of an existent has as its condition the pre-apprehension of *esse*, which implicitly and simultaneously affirms an absolute *esse*." On the other hand, Rahner does not believe that a proof of God's existence per se is somehow irrelevant or that the *a priori* knowledge of God does not play an important role in such a proof. Thus, according to Rahner, a proof of God's existence "does not become superfluous at all, but is first made possible and also ... is demanded by the peculiar nature of ... *a priori* knowledge."[181]

In *Hearers of the Word* Rahner again took up the topic of a 'transcendental' argument for the existence of God in which he essentially remained by the position staked out earlier. Rahner formulated the argument here as follows:

> God is posited, too, with the same necessity as this pre-concept [*Vorgriff*]. He is the thing of which is affirmed absolute 'having existence.' ... In the pre-concept the cause of his specific possibility is unknowingly [*unthematisch*] affirmed. ... The pre-concept is directed towards God. It does not aim directly at God, so as to prevent absolute being in its specific self, immediately and objectively. It does not make itself specifically an immediate datum. The pre-concept aims at the absolute being of God in the sense that the *esse absolutum* is always

---

[179] *SW*, 181. [*GW*, 190.]

[180] Paul Wess, *Wie von Gott sprechen?* (Vienna: Verlag Styria, 1970), 64ff., has been critical of Rahner on this point, contending that even though Rahner admits the necessity of *a posteriori* knowledge he nevertheless argues that the reality of God, on the basis of human *a priori* experience of transcendence, is to be implicitly affirmed, thus minimalizing the place of *a posteriori* knowledge. In doing this, although not in so radical a manner as Anselm, Wess contends that Rahner has equated thought with being.

[181] *Spirit in the World*, 181f. [*GW*, 190f.]

fundamentally affirmed through the former's basic unlimited breadth. This is no purely *a priori* proof of the existence of God, for the pre-concept and its breadth declare itself as an actual and necessary condition for all knowledge only through the *a posteriori* perception of a real existent thing.[182]

Peter Eicher believes that Rahner has here in fact offered a transcendental proof of God's existence. This differs from the traditional Thomistic type argument from causation, according to Eicher, in that the transcendental proof of God's existence "does not proceed causally from the real existence-constitution of the finite being to an infinite God." Rather, the transcendental argument, as formulated by Rahner, "judges the affirmation of the one existing as a finite being in order, as the condition of the possibility of such affirmation, to demonstrate the pre-apprehension of the Infintie which exists from itself." Hence, the fact that God in fact exists is experienced as primal evidence (*Urevidenz*) in the pre-apprehension of being so that God's existence cannot, in an intelligible manner, be denied: *ergo Deus est*.[183]

Rahner, however, does not believe that he has offered here an argument for the existence of God in the strict sense. Rather, he has merely made epistemological use of the real-ontological formulation of the traditional proofs as found in Thomas. The difference, for Rahner, is that instead of claiming that the affirmation of factually existing finite being demands as its condition the existence of the infinite being of God (which would constitute a 'proof' of God's existence), he contends only that the affirmation of the actual finitude of a 'being' (*Seienden*) requires as the condition of its possibility the affirmation of the existence of an *esse absolutum*, or infinite being. Yet as Rahner himself admits the intention is essentially the same, only in the latter formulation he believes he has technically avoided a proof of God's existence in the technical sense.[184] In this manner Rahner, reminiscent of Pannenberg's so-called anthropological proof, would seem to construct an argument for God's existence which, for reasons arising at least in part out of the context of the Kantian critique of all such arguments, he himself seeks to disqualify as an actual 'proof' in the traditional sense on largely technical grounds.

It would also seem clear that Rahner, like Pannenberg, however, does not believe that God's existence can be proven or verified in anything other than a preliminary fashion. The key insight for Pannenberg in this regard, as we have seen, is tied to his idea that only at the end of history will God be shown absolutely to be real and to be the one creator of the world. Thus because history

---

[182] *Hearers*, 64. [*HdW*., 83f.]
[183] Eicher, 281. DiNoia, 191, on the other hand, contends that Rahner has not offered a new argument for the existence of God but rather "advances a transcendental argument" for the possibility of the traditional arguments which itself takes as its starting point the structure of human knowledge. Rahner, therefore, does not intend to demonstrate God's existence but rather that that toward which our "knowledge is oriented is the Absolute Mystery which we call God."
[184] *Hearers*, 64f. [*HdW*, 84.]

is still in progress any 'verification' of our speech about God can be necessarily only preliminary. For Rahner the focus is upon the continuing history of our human *conception* of God. When we do not lose sight of God's mystery and incomprehensibility then we will realize that our speech about God is always in progress, having its own history, and an absolute proof or final definition of God is beyond our reach. As Rahner explained: "When we conceive a specific element in the Christian concept of God we must not lose sight of the fact that this concept of God has not yet finished its own historical course, and that if this concept confesses the infinity and the incomprehensibility of God, then it actually postulates thereby a history of our own concept of God that can never be concluded."[185]

### 4.2.3 The Knowledge of God

#### 4.2.3.1 *Is a direct, 'pre-revelatory' knowledge of God possible?*

One of the most controversial aspects of Karl Rahner's thought has been his views on the role of revelation (or lack thereof) in the knowledge of God. Rahner contends that there is always present in transcendental experience "an unthematic and anonymous, as it were, knowledge of God. Hence the original knowledge of God ... has ... the character of a transcendental experience."[186] Rahner indeed insists that this transcendental knowledge of God is *a posteriori* inasmuch as it "comes from and through encountering the world."[187] Yet he also contends that "the knowledge of God is ... a *transcendental* knowledge because man's basic and original orientation towards absolute mystery, which constitutes his fundamental experience of God, is a permanent existential of man as a spiritual subject." We become aware of these transcendental structures which are given in our subjectivity through the concrete and definite presentation of the world to us. Therefore the knowledge of God is not grounded entirely in itself. But neither, insists Rahner, "is it simply a mystical process within our own personal interiority." What Rahner understands by the *a posteriori* aspect of our transcendental knowledge of God can be seen when he writes:

> The a posteriori character of the knowledge of God would be misunderstood if we were to overlook the transcendental element in it and understand the knowledge of God after the model of an a posteriori knowledge whose object comes entirely from without and appears in a neutral faculty of knowledge. In the knowledge of God a posteriority does not mean that we look out into the world with a neutral faculty of knowledge and then think that we can discover God there directly or indirectly among the realities that present themselves to us objectively, or that we can prove his existence indirectly. We are oriented toward God. This original experience is always present. ... This does not

---

[185] "The Specific Character of the Christian Concept of God," 189. [*Schriften* 15:188.]
[186] *FCF*, 21. [*Grundkurs*, 32].
[187] *Ibid.*, 51f. [61].

destroy the a posteriori character of the knowledge of God, but neither should this a posteriority be misunderstood in the sense that God could simply be indoctrinated from without as an object of our knowledge.[188]

Thus Rahner, unwilling to completely abandon the Neo-Scholastic emphasis upon the *a posteriori* character of the knowledge of God nevertheless understands this *a posteriori* in such a way that it includes and is even determined by its transcendental element so that ultimately the knowledge of God does not come entirely from without but also from within. Rahner contends that revelation is necessarily "heard" by a person "who already knows other things besides this revelation. ... But the hearing of a message by someone who already has other knowledge can only be possible - since it takes place in the unity of this one person - in confrontation with this other knowledge." Therefore the hearing of the revelatory message is possible only by means of "categories already possessed from elsewhere."[189]

For Rahner, we all possess an implicit knowledge of God which precedes and makes possible the explicit knowledge of God which expresses itself in religious and philosophical thought. According to Rahner, the unthematic and ever-present knowledge of God which we have even when we are thinking of things far from God "is the permanent ground from out of which that thematic knowledge emerges which we have explicitly" in theological and philosophical reflection. In such reflection and in prayer, Rahner contends, "we are only making explicit for ourselves what we already know ourselves." Therefore all "explicit knowledge of God in religion and in metaphysics is intelligible and can really be understood only when all the words we use point to the unthematic experience of our orientation towards the ineffable mystery."[190]

Such comments have led to the accusation that Rahner maintains the possibility of a direct knowledge of God independent of and preceding revelation. Paul Molnar has suggested that Rahner's position constitutes a denial of God's transcendence. Molnar contends that Rahner confuses revelation with human self-knowledge and that his methodological assumptions "that knowledge of God's revelation cannot contradict knowledge gained from one's metaphysical reflections about God and the world, actually makes human experience the determining factor in his theology."[191] For Molnar, the transcendence of God excludes the possibility that God's creatures might know him directly. Yet Molnar contends that Rahner's method leads him "to confuse the movement of the world with God's free movement" so that "man's experiences are in fact indistinguishable from God himself." If God is transcendent, according to Molnar, there can be no direct knowledge of God on the part of his creature who cannot know God (as He

---
[188] *Ibid.*, 52f. [61f.].
[189] "Philosophy and Theology," 73. [*Schriften* 6:93.]
[190] *FCF*, 53. [*Grundkurs*, 63].
[191] Paul Molnar, "Can We Know God Directly? 230, note 12, and 232.

expresses himself in trinitarian form) "without first acknowledging the priority of God's free self-revelation."[192] Thus it follows in Molnar's critique that Rahner's view leaves no room for God's transcendence. But does this criticism do justice to Rahner's position?

Rahner himself would certainly not agree that his theology leaves no room for God's transcendence. He writes:

> God is something quite different from any of the individual realities which appear within the realm of our experience or which are inferred from it, and ... the knowledge of God has a quite definite and unique character and is not just an instance of knowing in general. ... Since the original experience of God is not an encounter with an individual object *alongside of* other objects, and since in the human subject's transcendental experience God is absolutely beyond us in his transcendence, we can speak of God and the experience of God, and of creatureliness and the experience of creatureliness only *together*, in spite of the difference of what is meant in each instance.[193]

Similarly, Molnar's criticism that Rahner's view fails to recognize the priority of God's self-revelation over human, transcendental knowing also does not do justice to Rahner's position. As we saw in chapter 2, human knowing (or philosophy) indeed exercises a *temporal* priority over revelation in Rahner's theology, which gives rise to Molnar's criticism. Rahner's contention, however, that revelation is *ontologically* prior to the possibility of human knowing (an aspect of Rahner's thought which Molnar does not deal with) would seem to effectively counter Molnar's criticism. And even if, in a qualified sense, one could maintain that Rahner advocates a direct, pre-revelatory knowledge of God that this could only possibly be a knowledge of God's existence and not of his relation to his creatures for this latter knowledge, according to Rahner, is only available through revelation. As Rahner explained in one of his last writings:

> If the ultimate answer attainable by human beings to the universal question of meaning contains an ultimate affirmation of the reality of the infinite God ... this does not mean that it is possible on the part of human beings alone and of the freedom and spiritual nature proper to them to attain an ultimate and definitive determination of the exact relationship of human beings to this absolute meaning of their existence called God. ... On this point it is only Christian revelation that provides a precise and radical answer.[194]

### 4.2.3.2 *The question of meaning as a question of God*

In a 1982 lecture Rahner took up the idea that the question of meaning is in actuality a question of God. His argumentation here bears stark resemblance to

---
[192] *Ibid.*, 236 and 260f.
[193] *FCF*, 54. [*Grundkurs*, 63f.]
[194] "The Question of Meaning as a Question of God," 21:206. [*Schriften* 15:204.]

Pannenberg's deduction of openness to God from the phenomenon of world-openness as well as his 'verification' of speech about God by reference to the totality of the human experience of reality. Similar to Pannenberg, when Rahner speaks of meaning he is speaking of "the one total, universal and definitive meaning of the whole of human existence" which humans experience. Rahner's express aim is to demonstrate that "the question of meaning understood in this sense is to be considered as identical with God." For Rahner, "meaning" and "God" mutually explain one another so that "what absolute meaning is can be understood by the word *God* and vice versa."[195] To achieve this, however, Rahner must first demonstrate, over against skeptics and agnostics, that the question of meaning itself is actually meaningful. He wrote:

> If we want to explain the question of meaning as a question of God, we presume the existence of such a universal and absolute question of meaning and the possibility of meaningful inquiry into such meaning, indeed that the very assertion that a question of meaning is really meaningful and not meaningless from the very outset already includes in itself the reality of such meaning. ... But skeptics and agnostics will say that a total and definitive meaning of existence cannot be found. Life ultimately fades away into a void; the question of and the demand for a definitive, all-embracing meaning of existence are meaningless from the very outset.[196]

Rahner, over against such skepticism, contends that an absolute and universal meaning of human existence can be maintained in light of and because of our human reason and freedom since the totality of the real meaning of the whole of existence can only be attained by a complete commitment to this existence with all its dimensions - including reason and freedom. For those who cannot or will not see the wholeness of the meaning of human existence this is to be attributed to a failure to make full use of their own reason and freedom because they have become too entangled in the details of their own existence. Hence the "total question of meaning must be asked, and mind and freedom must say that they must have a fulfillment by a meaning that is one and infinite."[197] The human being, therefore, cannot escape the question of the total meaning of existence - but neither can humans penetrate and manipulate this meaning which remains mystery precisely because it is rooted in God.[198]

At this point, Rahner's argumentation becomes reminiscent of Pannenberg's 'verification' of God through the total human experience of reality, discussed previously in this chapter. Our observations about the absolute and total meaning of human life must, according to Rahner, be brought into a "direct relationship with a statement about God. Indeed, the question of meaning must be understood

---
[195] *Ibid.*, 196f. [195f.]
[196] *Ibid.*, 197. [196.]
[197] *Ibid.*, 198ff. [197ff.]
[198] For this and the following quote cf. *ibid.*, 203. [201f.]

as being explicitly a question of God. The "total, comprehensive, and definitive meaning of our life" is itself a reality and not merely a mental construct. And for Rahner this reality can be none other than 'God.' He writes: "We consider the existence of this universal meaning toward which we are tending without creating it ourselves to be present as an absolute reality, and we call this reality God. Thus for us the question of meaning and the question of God are identical. The reality of an absolute meaning and the reality of God are identical." This implies as well, for Rahner as for Pannenberg, that God is not known apart from human experience and the totality of human existence so that, as Rahner puts it, "all genuine ways to the knowledge of God ... must always lead over the totality of human existence with its limitless transcendentality and freedom."[199] The universality of God in Rahner's thought, therefore, is seen to extend to all questions of meaning since these are ultimately questions of God who is identical with the absolute reality of the totality of meaning.

### 4.2.3.3 *The universality of God and the unity of the ways of knowing God*

In Rahner's view the three different ways of knowing God in scholastic theology constitute an intrinsic unity. The first of the three ways is a natural knowledge of God which occurs without revelation and which was confirmed by the First Vatican Council.[200] Here we find a knowledge of God based upon the light of natural reason, that is, a knowledge which is essentially *a posteriori*. The second form of knowledge of God is spoken of by scholastic theology and comes through revelation in word, that is to say, it is a knowledge of God which comes through his own revelation. Rahner lists also a third way of knowing God. This knowledge of God comes through God's self-revelatory salvific activity in human history. "In this knowledge," according to Rahner, "God's action and his existence are known together through the effective witness he gives to himself." This knowledge, then, is an *a priori* knowledge of God "from and in man's individual and collective personal experience of existence."

What is important in Rahner's thought is that he recognizes a unity of this one natural and two self-revelatory ways of knowing God. This means that "in the concrete actualization of existence ... there is no knowledge of God which is purely natural, since even theological knowledge is an activity of man which takes place in freedom" - freedom which comes from God. As Rahner explains further: "The *concrete* process of the so-called natural knowledge of God in either its acceptance or its rejection is always more than a merely natural knowledge of God. ... It is at once both natural knowledge and knowledge in grace, it is at once both knowledge and revelation-faith."[201]

---

[199] *Ibid.*, 205. [203f.]
[200] Cf. the Dogmatic Constitution "*Dei Filius*" (1870), in: Denzinger 3004.
[201] *FCF*, 55ff. [*Grundkurs*, 64ff.].

Hence the natural and 'supernatural' knowledge of God, although Rahner distinguishes between them, form a unity.[202] The ways of knowing God form a unity because, first of all they all lead to the same result. Thus, "ultimately all the ways of leading to the knowledge of God will be identical when viewed" form the perspective of their "final exactness" which, whether labeled "ways" or "proofs" point ultimately to the same reality.[203] Additionally, and more significantly, the unity of the ways of knowing God points to and is founded upon the very unity of God who makes himself known in both natural and 'supernatural' knowledge and who is the foundation of all being and of all knowing.[204]

### 4.2.4 God and the Eschatological Future

Karl Rahner concluded his *Foundations of Christian Faith* with a three-part creed, in the final section of which he makes a "futurological" confession. Rahner writes: "Christianity is the religion which keeps open the question about the absolute future which wills to give itself in its own reality by self-communication, and which has established this will as eschatologically irreversible in Jesus Christ, and this future is called God."[205] In the following discussion we shall seek to elucidate Rahner's conception of God and the future - indeed, of God as the future - within the broader framework of his eschatology.[206]

#### 4.2.4.1 *God, time, and eternity*

Like Pannenberg, Rahner does not understand eternity as unending history. But neither does he view eternity as something entirely unconnected to time as we now experience it. He conceptualizes eternity instead as the "mature fruit" of time - especially of time as understood as the histories of human freedom. In a critical passage Rahner explains the relationship between time and eternity as follows:

> Eternity comes to be in time as time's own mature fruit, an eternity which does not really continue on beyond experienced time. Rather eternity subsumes time by being liberated from the time which came to be temporarily so that freedom and something of final and definitive validity can be achieved. Eternity is not an infinitely long mode of pure time, but rather it is a mode of the spiritual freedom which has been exercised in time. ... The achieved final validity of human existence which has grown to maturity in freedom comes to be *through* death, not *after* it. What has come to be is the liberated, final validity of something which was once temporal, and which came to be in spirit and in freedom, and which therefore formed time in order to be, and not really in order to continue on in time. For otherwise it would exist precisely in a mode which would not be final and definitive, but rather it would have before it an open future of a

---
[202] So Manuel Cabada-Castro, 161.
[203] "The Question of Meaning as a Question of God," 205. [*Schriften* 15:203.]
[204] Cf. *FCF*, 83. [90f.]
[205] *Ibid.*, 457. [439.]
[206] For a full discussion of Rahner's eschatology see the detailed study by Peter C. Phan, *Eternity in Time: A Study of Karl Rahner's Eschatology* (London: Associated University Presses, 1988).

temporal nature in which everything could once again go on becoming different indefinitely.[207]

Rahner, in contrast to Pannenberg, approaches the question of time and eternity primarily from the perspective of human experience. Hence in his 1979 article, "Eternity from Time," he concerns himself with the human experience of eternity. Rahner suggests that there is a tyranny of our conception of time which makes it difficult to conceptualize eternity as anything other than an unending sequence of moments, that is to say, as never-ending time rather than a true eternity which is fundamentally different from time. "If eternity is conceived ... as time open to infinity," asks Rahner, "have not the world, man and history always ahead of them that which is not yet?" But if this is eternity, Rahner, suggests, it sounds more like the damnation of Ahasuerus, the Jew condemned to wander eternally without ever arriving anywhere. "Under the tyranny of this concept of time," questions Rahner, "is not the eternal heaven dissolved into an eternal hell?"[208]

To get beyond this sort of conception of eternity as never-ending time Rahner suggests that we seek a concept of eternity which has the character of being 'permanent' and is not subject to endless succession. Surprisingly, to accomplish this, Rahner turns to time itself to seek that within time which is eternal and which does not simply exist in the now and then give way to something new and perishing. Rahner believes to find this "permanency" in time at three levels. First, we find a hint of eternity in the totality of history in which even though individual occurrences fad away they also are brought together into a totality or history which "does not disintegrate or crumble into a dust of pure individual moments." There must be something within time itself, Rahner contends, which is more than time - something which gives time its unity. As second Rahner brings forward the way in which time is unified and shaped in our mental process of experiencing it, especially in the way in which past, present and future are mentally brought together by us to form a unity (or continuity) in our experience. And finally, Rahner suggests that eternity is experienced in time most clearly "when the intellectual subject in man makes a free decision" which involves the whole person.[209] With these arguments Rahner wishes to point to the wholeness and unity of time and to our experience of time as "evidence" of an eternity which goes beyond the merely temporal and which awaits the individual after death.

Rahner approaches the question of God in relation to time and eternity primarily as it relates to our human experience. Therefore, whereas Pannenberg makes God his starting point for his understanding of eternity Rahner begins with the human and with human experience. Yet at the end he confesses that when we

---
[207] *FCF.*, 437. [420.]
[208] Rahner, "Eternity from Time," *TI* 19:169ff. ["Ewigkeit aus Zeit," in: *Schriften* 14:422ff.]
[209] *Ibid.*, 172ff. [425ff.]

look into eternity we are looking into the unknown which is ultimately found in God. As we approach eternity as Christians "we are actually going into the unknown, the unimaginable, and, properly speaking, know only that it is filled with the incomprehensibility of God and his love and that it is final." Eternity, for Rahner, is thus the victory of God's love. Indeed, "this love is the cause and guarantee that our brief time, which passes away, creates an eternity which is not made up of time."[210]

A formal agreement is therefore to be found with Pannenberg inasmuch as eternity is not viewed as an unending succession of time and is something God brings about. However, in contrast to Pannenberg, Rahner approaches the question decisively from the perspective of human experience. This is to be seen, for example, in Rahner's contention that hope is "the basic modality of the very *attitude to the eternal* which precisely as such sets the true advance towards eternity 'in train'." Whereas by Pannenberg it is God as the absolute future and as the content of eternity which sets 'in train' the advance toward its/his own self, Rahner approaches the question from the perspective of the individual and his or her 'attitude' of hope. The conclusion is therefore justified that for Rahner, the future "is both humanity's achievement and God's gift."[211]

### 4.2.4.2 *God and the consummation of the history of human freedom*

Because the idea of the consummation, and indeed the end of history plays such a central role in Pannenberg's understanding of God we turn here briefly and by way of comparison to Rahner's conception of the consummation of history and its significance for his doctrine of God. Similar to Pannenberg, Rahner contends that the very nature of history, especially as the history of personal freedom, demands a consummation - a consummation which Rahner understands as taking place 'within' history. Rahner contended that history, properly understood and as is occurs through the exercise of human freedom, "demands of its very nature to be brought to a definitive consummation. ... [This] consummation is not something that is located 'beyond' history, as it were, seeing that it is in history that that takes place for which we are responsible even though it may not appear on the surface of any reality that we know ..."[212]

Rahner elsewhere similar contended that: "With regard to the question about the end of ... history, we have to repeat the reservation here that we may not allow the spiritual and collective history of the world to come to an end within a world-time which continues on. ... The history of the human race as a whole is moving in its history towards a fulfillment of the human race which will end history." At this end of history all things and all individual histories of freedom will find their end in God. Rahner, indeed, goes beyond Pannenberg even in underlining the

---

[210] *Ibid.*, 176f. [430ff.]
[211] Phan, 183.
[212] Rahner, "The Theological Problems Entailed in the Idea of the 'New Earth,'" in: *TI* 10:270. ["Über die theologische Problematik der 'Neuen Erde,'" in: *Schriften* 8:590.]

universality of this end which, he suggests, will subsume even all possible extraterrestrial histories into the fullness of God![213]

In Rahner's significant 1966 lecture on the nature of the consummation of history delivered to the *Görres Society for Achieving an Encounter Between Natural Science and Theology* he listed five instances (or things) to which the word 'consummation' can potentially be applied. These are (1) a particular material event, (2) the sum total of all such events, i.e., the material world as a whole, (3) the spiritual and personal history of an individual, (4) the unity of all such personal histories, and (5) "the real unity of the material world together with the history of the spirit at both the individual and the collective levels, in other words to the real unity and totality of the temporal creation, of the 'world' in the widest sense."[214]

Consummation cannot be applied simply to the world and its history as 'physical' world and 'physical' history for these are incapable of consummation since the material world possesses "no will to achieve its own consummation, but rather tends to continue as that which is abidingly unconsummated." Rahner contends, rather, that consummation is a concept which "can meaningfully be applied only in that kind of history which is worked out in personal freedom."[215] In regard to the consummation of the individual's history of freedom God is the *consummation* and goal, and not only this but he is also the spiritual creature's ultimate and innermost principle. Hence, "God in his absolute immediacy is, in the concrete order of reality, not only the consummation, the goal (*beatitudo objectiva*) of the spiritual creature, but the principle in the movement which is most proper and necessary to it, the sole really connatural principle by which it is impelled towards the consummation of this goal." God is therefore the goal and consummation of the spiritual creature as well as the innermost principle which impels it toward its consummation in God. As Rahner explains: "God is the absolutely incomprehensible who constitutes this future and maintains the movements towards it." Although this sounds like a God who controls the consummation of the individual and the process leading toward it the future of the creature remains open since God, who is the creature's future, is its future "because he is that love which is absolutely free."[216] Hence Rahner, in a manner not unsimilar to Pannenberg, understands God not only as the future but as 'controlling' the present which leads to this future. Yet God as that love which is free works in such a way with his creatures that they also remain free and the future, in a genuine sense, remains open.

To this point in his argument, however, Rahner has concerned himself

---

[213] *FCF*, 445f. [*Grundkurs*, 427f.]
[214] Rahner, "Immanent and Transcendent Consummation of the World," in: *TI* 10:273f. ["Immanente und transzendente Vollendung der Welt," in: *Schriften* 8:593f.]
[215] *Ibid.*, 274, 276. [594, 596.] Phan, 194f., observes that on this basis "the material world can be said to be 'consummated' only to the extent that it has an intrinsic reference to the free spirit."
[216] *Ibid.*, 282. [601f.] Cf. also Phan, 183.

primarily with the consummation of the individual. The question which remains is what conclusions are to be drawn from these arguments for the consummation of the world as a whole. Since the world, in Rahner's thought, is a unity of spirit and matter in which matter is an essential element the consummation of the world as a whole, for which God is also the goal, must include the entirety of the world as spirit and matter. The material world, according to Rahner, transcends itself on the basis of its essential orientation toward spirit which is implanted in it by God and by which it tends toward spirit as the goal of its self-transcendence. In this way the material world achieves through the goal of its self-transcendence its own consummation. And this "movement towards its consummation is, right from the outset, sustained by divine power, which consists in the love which bestows itself absolutely in freedom."[217] Rahner arrives at the conclusion that there will be a consummation of history[218] which God not only brings about but also of which he himself is its content - the absolute future and the single goal of all reality. Rahner writes:

> The innermost principle of this self-movement of the sun and the other planets towards their consummation which lies concealed in the incomprehensibility of God as the absolute future is God himself. He is the 'transcendent' consummation, and therefore can and will, precisely as *God*, himself be the 'immanent' consummation and the 'immanent' principle of the movement towards this single real and uniquely fulfilling consummation that is the *fulness* of finality: God - all in all.[219]

### 4.2.4.3 *The eschatological integration of all reality into God*

Rahner's concept of the consummation of the world leads to the question of how radically Rahner understands God as the one goal and absolute future of all reality. For Rahner, like Pannenberg, the world has one future and that is God. Not only is God the future of the world, but it is God who acts to bring about this future. In a decisive statement, Rahner, at the conclusion of a paper on the relationship between theology and modern sciences, wrote: "The eschatological integration of all reality in God, and in his knowledge and love, is the deed of God himself, a deed which takes place precisely at the point at which, and in virtue of the fact that, man endures the pluralism of his world, and so too of his knowledge, and does not suppose that he is standing at a point at which all reality, and the knowledge of it, is one. For at this point stands only God himself."[220]

The eschatological integration of all reality into God, for Rahner as for Pannenberg, is at the same time the eschatological verification of God's

---

[217] *Ibid.*, 284, 288f. [604, 608f.]
[218] Significantly, Rahner understands the connection between God and history in such a way that he can even say that "history itself passes into the definitive consummation of God." Cf. "The Idea of the 'New Earth,'" 270. [*Schriften* 8:590.]
[219] "Immanent and Transcendent Consummation of the World," 289. [*Schriften* 8:609.]
[220] "On the Relationship Between Theology and the Contempory Sciences," 102. [*Schriften* 10:112.]

universality and of his role as creator of all things. The consummation of the world, therefore, as was also seen to be the case with Pannenberg, does not mean the destruction of the world (either material or spiritual) but rather its fulfillment in God, whose universality as all-encompassing and absolute mystery, even prior to any theological word about God, is to be seen in the knowledge of God's creation and in the relationship of his spiritual creatures to him.[221]

### 4.2.4.4 Comparison to Pannenberg's concept of God as power of the future

For Rahner, as for Pannenberg, God not only has to do with the future but he *is* the future. For Pannenberg, as we have seen, this means that God as all-encompassing reality is the goal of history. That is to say, as history reaches its consummation it finds its final end in God's eternity.

Rahner comes to a very similar set of conclusions concerning the eschatological future. Indeed, Peter Phan has observed that "Rahner's use of the category of the future to reconceptualize God" implies, similar to Pannenberg, that God is the "'power of the future' effecting and transforming the present *from* the future in a kind of 'reverse causality.'"[222] Specifically, and at the very least, we can say that Rahner agrees, at least in broad essentials, with Pannenberg that (1) history will come to an absolute end, (2) this end or consummation will be universal, including all individual histories, and (3) God himself is identified with this end, as the goal and absolute future. An important difference between the two theologians arises when one asks how this end of history is brought about.

For Pannenberg God himself as the power of the future brings all things to their culmination in him and his eternity. Rahner, while not denying God's efficacy in bringing about the eschatological future, lays much more emphasis upon the human role than does Pannenberg. As we have previously seen, the individual histories which come together collectively to form the end of history are histories of freedom. Consistent with his 'turn to anthropology' in his theology as a whole Rahner begins his eschatology from an anthropological starting point - even though its culmination is found in God. He writes:

> [Eschatology] is the doctrine about man insofar as he is a being who is open to the absolute future of God himself. ... Christian eschatology is nothing else but a repetition of everything we have said so far about man insofar as he is a free and created spirit who has been given God's self-communication in grace. Eschatology is not really an addition, but rather it gives expression once again to man as ... a being who ex-ists from out of his present 'now' towards his future. Man can say what he is only by saying what he wants and what he can become. ... Because of man's very nature, therefore, Christian anthropology is Christian futurology and Christian eschatology.[223]

---

[221] Cf. *ibid.*
[222] Peter Phan, 199.
[223] *Ibid.*, 431.

These words, with which he opens his discussion of eschatology in *Foundations of Christian Faith*, set the tone for the development of his eschatology. Rahner does not shy away from speaking of God and the future and indeed of God as the future but it is only via the history of human freedom that this future is arrived at.

## 4.3 Summary and conclusions

### 4.3.1 God as foundation of theology's universality

Comparing Pannenberg and Rahner's respective concepts of God presents some special difficulties which must be noted. The underlying concerns and structures of their doctrines of God are in many respects very different from one another. In order to facilitate comparison, therefore, it will was beneficial to emphasize the issues and structure of one presentation as a 'standard model' against which the other could be analyzed. Pannenberg's concept of God fulfilled this function in our treatment for three reasons. First, his concept of God is the more original and has received more attention in theological discussion. Second, it more intentionally focuses and builds upon the idea of God's unity and universality which is the overriding theme of our entire study. And finally, it is more concrete in its language and specific in its proposals than is Rahner's concept of God, which tends to be somewhat vague.[224] The unavoidable result of this approach is that full justice was not able to be done to Rahner's treatment of God within the context and structures of his own thought. Nevertheless, enough points of contact were found to facilitate a fruitful comparison.

In contrast to the area of anthropology there has been relatively little comparison drawn between the respective doctrines of God of Pannenberg and Rahner. A notable exception is the 1979 Princeton doctoral study of John McCoy, *Soteriology and the Doctrine of God: A Historical Typology and Analysis of the Theologies of Karl Rahner and Wolfhart Pannenberg*. McCoy contends that the most significant difference between the two theologian's doctrines of God does not appear in their thoughts on anthropology nor does it arise out of their differing philosophical orientations since, "both wish to stress the chief factor in the experience of man as his transcendence over the established and the finite and his infinite drive or openness to ever new possibility." The difference, according to McCoy, comes in regard to the manner in which this orientation of the human being is linked with the reality of God. The difference is that while "Pannenberg posits the futuristic referent of the eschatological horizon as determinative for God's involvement in history, ... Rahner ... proceeds to his doctrine of God, not with a temporal category, but with the dialectic of grace."[225] It is not, however, the case that there is absolutely no temporal aspect of Rahner's

---

[224] Weger, *Karl Rahner: An Introduction*, 68, is quite correct when he observes that "Rahner's way of speaking about God is marked by a certain vagueness," especially when it moves on the philosophical level.

[225] John McCoy, Jr., *Soteriology and the Doctrine of God*, 241f.

concept of God nor that there is no 'dialectic of grace' or aspect of love in Pannenberg's.[226]

Important similarities, however, are also to be noted between the two theologians' conception of God. God as foundation of universality in the thought of Pannenberg and Rahner, developed multifariously by both theologians, is ultimately founded upon their conception of God as creator of all things - or in Rahner's case the creator of all things as derived from an understanding of God as ground of all being. Their respective understandings of creation and of God as creator points both to the unity of all things created and to God's universal lordship.

Although a concept of God as the one creator of all things can no longer be assumed to be part and parcel of every Christian doctrine of God there is nothing particularly unique in itself in this common aspect of the thought of Pannenberg and Rahner. What distinguishes both theologians at this point is not so much the formal content of their respective doctrines of God as creator but their radical application of this concept to their understanding of the world. Pannenberg, for instance, has stressed on several occasions that "if the God of the Bible is creator of the universe, then it is not possible to understand fully or even appropriately the processes of nature without reference to that God."[227] The same holds true in regard to the whole of history.[228]

Therefore more than the mere contention of God's universality alone Pannenberg and Rahner distinguish themselves by their application of this universality in their approach to apologetics. As we will examine in detail in the following two chapters, this is especially to be seen in their respective applications of universality in their approach to world religions as well as in their dialogue with the natural sciences.

---

[226] Cf. *ST* 1:442ff. [477f.], and McCoy, 242f.

[227] Pannenberg, "Theological Questions to Scientists," in: *The Sciences and Theology in the 20th Century*, ed. A. R. Peacocke (Notre Dame, IN: University of Notre Dame Press, 1981), p. 4. Cf. also Pannenberg, "Theta Phi Discussion with Wolfhart Pannenberg," 24f.

[228] Cf., for instance, *The Apostles' Creed*, 38ff. [*Glaubensbekenntnis*, 46ff.] Pannenberg writes: "Historical unity is not inherent in nature. It is only recognized in retrospect, viewed from the aspect of man. But it is not based on man, either. This suggests the question of whether it is not the God of history, the God of the Bible, who is the basis of the historical unity of natural events as well" (42f., [50f.]).

# Chapter Five

## THE UNIVERSALITY OF THEOLOGY AND THE NON-CHRISTIAN RELIGIONS

### 5.1 Karl Rahner: The Search for Anonymous Christianity in the World's Religions

#### 5.1.1 The theology of religions in Roman Catholic thought

Karl Rahner characterized the view of non-Christian religions in the patristic period and the period following as a salvation-pessimism (*Heilspessimismus*) which focused on the masses of damned and the exclusion of those outside of the church from salvation. In contrast to this view he saw the documents arising out of the Second Vatican Council as representing a salvation-optimism (*Heilsoptimismus*).[1] In order to understand the context and intent of Rahner's own view of non-Christian religions we will look first at these two poles within the history of Roman Catholic thought. We do this in full awareness, however, that as we examine the salvation-optimism of the Second Vatican Council we are already moving beyond the mere context of Rahner's thought and are already in very significant ways seeing its impact.[2]

##### 5.1.1.1 *Heritage of the Latin Fathers: Extra ecclesiam nulla salus*

The well-known axiom, "*Extra ecclesiam nulla salus*" ("no salvation outside the church"), which dates back to Cyprian (c. 200-258), characterized for centuries the Roman Church's view of non-Christian religions. The axiom has especially come to be associated with the thought of Augustine who, echoing Cyprian, asked: "*Salus extra ecclesiam non est, quis negat?*"[3] The axiom, which arose out of the conviction of the church's universality and uniqueness, was gradually radicalized over the centuries to the point that more and more it came to

---

[1] Cf. Rahner, "The Abiding Significance of the Second Vatican Council," in: *TI* 20:99ff. ["Die bleibende Bedeutung des II. Vatikanischen Konzils," in: *Schriften* 14:314ff.]

[2] Cf., for instance, George Augustin, *Gott eint - trennt Christus? Die Einmaligkeit und Universalität Jesu Christi als Grundlage einer christlichen Theologie der Religionen* (Paderborn: Bonifatius, 1993), 31, who has contended that "die neue Anerkennung und positive Beurteilung der nichtchristlichen Religionen durch das II. Vaticanum ist der Pionierarbeit Karl Rahners zu verdanken."

[3] So Augustine, *De bapt.*, IV 17, 24. Bonifac Willems, *Erlösung in Kirche und Welt*, QD 35 (Freiburg: Herder, 1968), 97f., has suggested that Augustine did not hold to this axiom so firmly as did Cyprian and even made a point to find exceptions to it. Willems, however, seems to be alone in this assessment of Augustine

emphasize exclusiveness. Yet even in the Fathers themselves, as Rahner has admitted, there is little doubt that the idea that "divine grace can lead man to his final salvation without leading him first into the visible Church ... met with very little approval in the ancient Church."[4] In the Bull *Cantate Domino*, issued in 1442 by the Council of Florenz, the axiom took on formally - or better, was seen to have taken on - the radical meaning of exclusivity associated with it to the present. There we read that the church firmly believes, confesses and preaches that *"'nullos extra catholicam Ecclesiam exsistentes, non solum paganos', sed nec Iudaeos aut haereticos atque schismaticos, aeternae vitae fieri posse participes, sed in ignem aeternum ituros."* That is, no one who exists outside the catholic church, not just the pagans, but also Jews or heretics and schismatics, is able to participate in eternal life but will wander in eternal fire. The Bull goes on to affirm that no one, regardless of how many alms given or even if they die for the name of Christ can be saved if they are not within or have not remained within the unity of the catholic church.[5] Especially after the schism of the Western Church in the period of the Protestant Reformation, the *extra ecclesiam* formula was understood more and more to mean no salvation outside the structure of the Roman Catholic Church.[6]

A step toward moderation of this approach is to be seen in Pius IX's Allocutio *"Singulari quadam"* from 1854 in which he writes: "We must hold fast in the Faith that nobody outside the Apostolic Roman Church can be saved; she is the only ark of salvation and everyone who does not enter it must perish in the flood. But we must hold fast just as firmly to the truth that in the eyes of the Lord no one who lives in invincible ignorance of the true religion is stricken with this guilt."[7] This moderation was further strengthened in the First Vatican Council's admission of the possibility of an *in voto* membership in the church,[8] that is, a

---

[4] Rahner, "Membership of the Church According to the Teaching of Pius XII's Encyclical *'Mystici corporis Christi*,'" in: *TI* 2:40f. [Die Gliedschaft in der Kirche nach der Lehre Pius' XII. 'Mystici Corporis,'" in: *Schriften* 2: 47.]

[5] *Cantate Domino*, in: Denzinger, 1351.

[6] The statement of Pius IX in his Encyclical "*Quanto conficiamur moerore*" of 1863 (Denzinger, 2867), despite the interpretative flexibility of the *extra ecclesiam* axiom which reveals itself in this same document, nonetheless typifies the restriction of the formula to the institution of the Roman Church. He wrote: "*Sed notissimum quoque est catholicum dogma, neminem scilicet extra catholicam Ecclesiam posse salvari, et contumaces adversus eiusdem Ecclesiae auctoritatem, definitiones, et ab ipsius Ecclesiae unitate atque a Petri successore Romano Pontifice, cui vineae custodia a Salvatore est commissa, pertinaciter divisos aeternam non posse obtinere salutem.*"

[7] For original text see the early editions of Denzinger's *Enchiridion Symbolorum*, 1647 (1504). The citation used here is taken from Rahner, "Membership of the Church According to the Teaching of Pius XII's Encyclical *'Mystici corporis Christi*,'" 38f. [*Schriften* 2:45.] Cf. also similarly Pius IX's Encyclical "*Quanto conficiamur moerore*" of 1863 (Denzinger, 2866).

[8] For an account of the development of the transition from the Roman Church's approach to those "outside the church" between the First and Second Vatican Councils see Peter Schreiner, "Roman Catholic Theology and Non-Christian Religion," in: *Journal of Ecumenical Studies* 6 (1969),

membership by desire, which was again underscored in Pius XII's encyclical *Mystici Corporis Christi*.[9] Developed to allow those who out of ignorance do not belong to the church to be seen as belonging to it by desire, the move signaled a significant loosening of the *Extra ecclesiam nulla salus* axiom. That the *in voto* teaching "did not imply the severe and narrow interpretation" which some gave it can be seen in a 1949 explanatory letter of the Holy Office to the Archbishop of Boston.[10] While on the one hand the *Extra ecclesiam nulla salus* axiom is said to be an infallible pronouncement of the church, the letter also states that as far as eternal salvation is concerned it cannot always be demanded that one is incorporated into the church as member but only that he or she must be a member through their desire - a desire which must not always be explicit but can be implicit.[11] From such thoughts the step to the suggestion of the implicit faith of "anonymous Christians" in Rahner's thought becomes comprehensible. Yet in the pre-Vatican II era Rahner's view was still radical in comparison to the official pronouncements of the magisterium of the time.

The tendency of pre-Vatican II thought was to speak of pagans, or lost souls, or those outside the church but not to examine their religions as such. The comment of Arnulf Camps about Benedict XV's comments on those "outside the church" in his 1919 letter "*Rerum ecclesiae*" holds true for most pre-Vatican II thought. Notes Camps: "It is here only talk about an innumerable number of souls, not about their religion."[12] In the period immediately preceding Vatican II, especially in the pronouncements of Pius XII and John XXIII, there was a tendency to begin to recognize the significance of the traditions, customs, convictions, art, etc. of other peoples. What was not yet present, however, were any statements on the theological significance of non-Christian religions as such. Hence even with Pius XII and John XXIII, despite much progress in their recognition of the value of other cultures and peoples, "the other religions are not viewed as a social and religious entity that somehow could be the means of salvation."[13]

The somewhat ironic conclusion, then, of the *Extra ecclesiam nulla salus* discussion in recent times, according to Schreiner, is that "all authors and all

---

[9] 376ff. Additionally, for a discussion of the origin of the *in voto* clause in the baptismal theology of the Middle Ages see Rahner, "Membership of the Church," 40ff. [*Schriften* 2:46ff.]
Cf. *Mystici corporis*, Denzinger, 3821 and 3822 on the salvation of those outside the visible church. Rahner's evaluation of this document, according to Ratzinger, provided the starting point or origin of his own idea of an "anonymous Christianity." So Ratzinger, *Das neue Volk Gottes: Entwürfe zur Ekklesiologie* (Düsseldorf: Patmos-Verlag, 1969), 340, note 1.

[10] So Schreiner, 378. Those alluded to were certain members the St. Benedict's Center and Boston College who offered a rigorous interpretation of "outside the church no salvation" (Cf. Denzinger, introduction to 3866ff.)

[11] Cf. the letter of Pius XII, "*Extra Ecclesiam nulla salus*," Denzinger, 3866 and 3870.

[12] Camps, "Die heutige Stellung der Römisch-Katholischen Kirche zu den nichtchristlichen Religionen," in: *Jesus Christus und die Religionen*, ed. A. Paus (Vienna: Verlag Styria, 1980), 234.

[13] *Ibid.*, 239.

solutions, in one way or the other, agree that there is salvation outside the church, i.e., God does not exclude those outside the church from salvation; he grants salvation, however, through the church as the proper mediator; and in this sense those people do belong to the church."[14] With this emerging theological consensus the way was pathed for the Second Vatican Council to move beyond a mere "view" of those outside of the church and to develop a theology of religions in the fullest sense.

### 5.1.1.2 The salvation-optimism of the Second Vatican Council
### (Lumen gentium, Ad gentes, Nostra aetate)

Regardless of how one evaluates the "traditional" Roman Catholic approach to non-Christian religions, it is beyond question that the Second Vatican Council produced a wide-ranging new orientation toward the religions of the world.[15] Rahner, in reflecting upon the lasting significance of the recently concluded Council over whose theology he himself had much influence, focused his attention on the Council's confirmation and affirmation of the long process from a salvation-pessimism to a salvation-optimism, which we have briefly looked at in the preceding section. According to Rahner:

> The pessimism of Augustine in regard to salvation was reconstructed and slowly transformed in an inexpressibly wearisome process in the Church's theoretical and existential consciousness. From the assumption that unbaptized children are tormented by the fires of hell to the abolition by modern theologians of limbo ... was a very long way. But all these insights, acquired bit by bit, leading to an optimistic view of the prospect of salvation ... the Church had not ratified and taught absolutely firmly before the Council. The Council however says that even someone who regards himself as an atheist, if only he follows his conscience, is united to the paschal mystery of Christ.[16]

In what follows we will sketch briefly the most important doctrinal pronouncements of the Second Vatican Council which reflect this salvation-optimism and form the foundation stone of a new approach to non-Christian religions in contemporary Roman Catholic theology. We concern ourselves here especially which the Constitution of the Church, "*Lumen gentium*" (1964), the

---

[14] Schreiner, 379. Rahner, "Membership of the Church Acc. to the Teaching of Pius XII's Encyclical '*Mystici corporis Christi*,'" 24, [*Schriften* 2:30] contends that when the Church prior to *Mystici corporis* taught "that only baptized Catholics belong to the Church, it is not thereby maintained that there is nothing Christian *outside the Catholic Church*." Thus the question is left open, concerning "the possibility of grace for those who do not belong in the full sense to the Church."

[15] So for example George Augustin, *Gott eint - trennt Christus?* 29; Camps, 242ff.; and Hans Waldenfels, *Begegnung der Religionen* (Bonn: Norbert Borengässer, 1990), 46ff.

[16] "The Abiding Significance of the Second Vatican Council," 100. ["Die bleibende Bedeutung des II. Vatikanischen Konzils," 315.] For the Council's statements on atheism see the Pastoral Constitution, "*Gaudium et spes*," Denzinger, 4319 - 4321.

mission decree "*Ad gentes*" (1965) and the document explaining the church's relationship to other religions, "*Nostra aetate*" (1965).

Before looking at the texts of the Council itself, however, note must be taken of the papal encyclical of Paul VI "*Ecclesiam suam*" (1964), credited with being the first official document of the Roman Catholic Church to address the subject of the dialogue with the world's religions.[17] The encyclical is of especial importance in that its proposal of a tri-level classification of the Roman Church's dialogue outside its own borders, especially as concerns the non-Christian religions, was taken over by the Council documents themselves. Here three concentric circles of dialogue are recognized. First, the dialogue with other Christians; second, the dialogue with the non-Christian religions; and third, the dialogue with the entire world - including atheism.[18] The tone set in the encyclical was also groundbreaking in that one speaks here not of pagans but of religions and not of confrontation of the true religion with false religions but of dialogue - even if this dialogue in the end proves to be an imbalanced dialogue between the center (Christian faith in God) and the periphery (the non-Christian religions).[19]

In *Lumen gentium* one finds the fundamental dogmatic statements concerning God's universal salvific will which form the cornerstone of the Council's view of the non-Christian religions.[20] The tone of *Lumen gentium*, which speaks more of the recognition of the unity of humanity in salvation than of other religions per se, is set in its opening sentence and runs throughout the document. Because "Christ is the light of the nations" the Council desires that his glory, as reflected in the Church, "shine upon all persons through the Church's proclamation to the whole creation."[21] Hence the universal salvific will of God is to be reflected as well by Christ's church. This is more explicitly expressed as the document turns to the topic of the people of God in which it is declared that it has pleased God not to save humans as individuals but to make them one people and as such provide them salvation, whereby the unity of humanity, which we have also seen to be a major theme in the anthropology of Rahner, becomes the starting point for the Council's understanding of God's salvific will toward humans.[22] And still more clearly all persons are called to participate in the new people of God, which is based upon the model of and stands in continuity with God's covenant with the people of Israel.[23]

---

[17] So Camps, 242.
[18] For Rahner's own theology of this tri-level view of religion see "Church, Churches and Religions," in: *TI* 10:30ff. ["Kirche, Kirchen und Religionen," in: *Schriften* 8:355ff.]
[19] So the criticism of Schreiner, 396.
[20] So Camps, 243.
[21] *Lumen gentium* 1, Denzinger, 4101.
[22] Ibid., 9, Denzinger, 4122. "*Placuit tamen Deo homines non singulatim, quavis mutua connexione seclusa, sanctificare et salvare, sed eos in populum constituere, qui in veritate Ipsum agnosceret Ipsique sancte serviret.*"
[23] For Pannenberg's treatment of the question of the people of God in relation to and in continuity with Israel see our discussion in section 5.2.3.3.

This new people of God is and must remain one and is found over the whole earth and at all times. This is to be seen in the universal character of the people of God which, in the form of the church catholic, strives to bring together all people under the headship of Christ in the unity of the Spirit. It is to this catholic unity of the people of God, the Council boldly proclaims, that all are called and in various ways already belong; in the first place Catholic believers, then those of other Christian traditions, and finally all people - who are all called to salvation through the grace of God.[24] Yet, as Camps reminds us, this membership in the people of God is something that all are called to and thereby remains potential so that the church continues to be viewed as necessary for salvation.[25] Hence a formal contradiction with the axiom of the Latin fathers is avoided and the teaching continuity of the church maintained.

The second document which demands attention is the mission decree *Ad gentes* in which the specific problems of Christian mission in face of the non-Christian religions is dealt with. Unfortunately, owing to the fact that *Ad gentes* and *Nostra aetate* were produced simultaneously and by different committees, the problems presented on the one hand by the desire to affirm that which is salvific within the non-Christian religions and to recognize thereby their legitimacy, and on the other hand the necessity of missionary evangelization of these same religions, is neither overcome nor dealt with thoroughly.[26] Nevertheless, the recognition that a hidden presence of God is to be found among all persons in all religions (*Ad gentes* 9) is a significant step beyond previous mission theologies. Also, rather than a rejection of non-Christian religions *Ad gentes* speaks of the possibility of their being enlightened and healed through God's grace. In light of the recognition of salvific elements within other religions, therefore, the question which necessarily arises is, what is the motivation for mission? As Camps writes: "The Council answered simply, that persons who without guilt do not know the gospel, can achieve salvation, and that the necessity and right of the proclamation of the gospel by the Church is still maintained."[27]

In *Nostra aetate*, the most significant document as far as concerns the question of non-Christian religions, the Council recognizes the situation and challenge of the plurality of religions made unavoidable with increasing contacts between various nations and peoples.[28] Starting from the perspective of the unity

---

[24] For this and the above see *Lumen gentium* 13, Denzinger, 4134f., especially the crucial declaration: "*Ad hanc igitur catholicam Populi Dei unitatem, quae pacem universalem praesignat et promovet, omnes vocantur homines, ad eamque variis modis pertinent vel ordinantur sive fideles catholici, sive alii credentes in Christo, sive denique omnes universaliter homines, gratia Dei ad salutem vocati.*"
[25] Camps, 244.
[26] Cf. *ibid.*, 245.
[27] *Ibid.*, 246.
[28] Cf. *Nostra aetate* 1, which opens with the recognition: "*Nostra aetate, in qua genus humanum in dies arctius unitur et necessitudines inter varios populos augentur, Ecclesia attentius considerat quae sit sua habitudo ad religiones non-christianas.*"

of humanity through our common origin *Nostra aetate*, which deals specifically with the question of the relationship of the church to the non-Christian religions, contends that God is the final goal of all humans and extends his providence and salvific councils over the whole of humanity.[29] Upon this basis it is clear that an absolute rejection of the non-Christian religions or their value is no longer possible - if it ever truly were within Roman Catholic thought. It is therefore explicitly recognized that from earliest times a certain perception of a higher reality or even of a highest 'divinity' (*Summi Numinis*) or of a "Father" is to be found among the various peoples and religions. Also in the religions of the modern world such as Hinduism and Buddhism there is a pursuit of these questions which seeks answers to the restlessness of the human heart in which many things are correctly perceived.

Thus, although the Roman Catholic Church does and must preach Christ as "the way, the truth and the life" (John 14:6) it does not reject that which is sacred and true within other religions and recognizes even in them often a ray of truth which shines upon all persons.[30] The relationship of the church to Islam, which also confesses one almighty God who created all things and honors Jesus, though only as a prophet, and to Judaism, in whose roots we recognize the inception of our own faith and election, are given special attention and the history of failures and misunderstandings on the part of the church over against both these faith communities is recognized.[31] Hence the Council rejects all hatreds and prejudices against those of different races or of different religions since it is recognized as fundamentally inconsistent to call upon God the father of all when we reject others who are also created in God's image.[32]

Although the line of argumentation in *Nostra aetate* leads primarily to a rejection of persecution or discrimination based upon ethnicity or religion the document also has implications for a theology of religions, revealing a markedly new direction in the view of non-Christian religions as having salvific elements of sacrality and truth within them which can illumine all peoples and which must not be rejected by Christians. Hence Rahner, commenting on the Vatican Council's statements as a whole concerning other religions shortly after the Council's close, affirmed the presence of genuinely salvific elements in the non-Christian religions and attributed this view to the Council as well. Wrote Rahner: "Even today, and

---

[29] Cf. *ibid.*, where we read "*Una enim communitas sunt omnes gentes, unam habent originem, cum Deus omne genus hominum inhabitare fecerit super universam faciem terrae, unum etiam habent finem ultimum, Deum, cuius providentia ac bonitatis testimonium et consilia salutis ad omnes se extendunt ...* "

[30] So *ibid.*, 2. "*Ecclesia catholica nihil eorum, quae in his religionibus vera et sancta sunt, reicit. Sincera cum observantia considerat illos modos agendi et vivendi, illa praecepta et doctrinas, quae, quamvis ab iis quae ipsa tenet et proponit in multis discrepent, haud raro referunt tamen radium illius Veritatis, quae illuminat omnes homines.*"

[31] *Ibid.*, 3 and 4.

[32] *Ibid.*, 5.

*after* the coming of Christ, it is still perfectly conceivable that a non-Christian religion still exercises a positively saving function for the individual."[33]

Arnulf Camps has identified in *Nostra aetate* four important advances in the Roman Catholic approach to non-Christian religions. First, for the first time in the history of the councils of the church is a statement of such importance made in regard to the non-Christian religions. Second, the other religions are recognized as socially composed givens in which supernatural sacrality and truth are to be found. Third, dialogue with the non-Christian religions and cooperation with them for the benefit of humanity as a whole has unavoidable implications for missionary methods. Specifically, Christian mission must take as its starting point the positive aspects within the other religions and seek to be incarnated or born anew within them, i.e., a stress on continuity rather than rejection and replacement. Here we see a parallel with what Rahner had meant already in his pre-Vatican II *Hearers of the Word* with his conception of the world's religions as *praeparatio evangelica*. And fourth, according to Camps, the document, as well as the Council as a whole, left many questions open in regard to the non-Christian religions pointing repeatedly to issues which must be further examined or thought out, leaving room for continuing dialogue and growth in understanding.[34]

The Second Vatican Council, therefore, implementing as we shall see many elements advocated by Rahner, expressed the church's and Christianity's historic claims to uniqueness and universality over against the world's religions in a way that sought to recognize that God, on the basis of his universal salvific will, is already at work and present to varying degrees within them. To what extent the documents of the Council correspond to the approach of Rahner as one of the most influential Council theologians and to what extent Rahner's own theology of religions went beyond and continued to go beyond the stance of the Council will be the focus of the following sections.

### 5.1.2 The foundations of a philosophy of religion in Rahner

#### 5.1.2.1 *The essence of a philosophy of religion*

In Rahner's 1940 work *Hearers of the Word* he expressly sought to ground a philosophy of religion. Philosophy of religion, according to Rahner, is to be understood as the philosophical determination of what religion is and should be. He contended that the philosophy of religion is philosophy because "it works with the means of cognition which are proper to philosophy in general. It defines religion in terms of a position that is antecedently and always fundamentally accessible to it. It defines it by reason of the unalterable essence of man, of the world that is of necessity presented along with man, and by reason of the clear

---

[33] "Church, Churches and Religions," 48. [*Schriften* 8:372.]

[34] Camps, 249f. Rahner, "Church, Churches and Religions," 32, [*Schriften* 8:357], also points to the ambiguity of the Council's statements on non-Christian religions in general as a positive feature which leaves the doors to debate and dialogue open.

and necessary formal basic laws of thought, all of which we are accustomed to describe as 'the natural light of reason.'"[35]

In this definition two significant points are to be noticed. In the first place, the philosophy of religion is philosophy as seen from its epistemology. The knowledge of the nature and form of religious experience and practice does not call for a special kind of knowledge or a rejection of the 'ordinary' way of knowing. Second, it is to be noted that Rahner already here begins with human beings in that the philosophy of religion determines what religion is or ought to be from the perspective of the nature of the human person. Hence he can write that "fundamental-theological anthropology is the philosophy of religion proper," and that, vice versa, "genuine philosophy of religion is a fundamental-theological anthropology of the kind we have tried to pursue in its external outlines."[36] Religion, then, and the knowledge of religion has fundamentally to do with human beings, and the philosophy of religion, according to Rahner, is to be understood as "the knowledge which man *on his own* is able to acquire of the correct relation of man to God as the Absolute."[37] And it is in this manner that the fundamental, theological anthropology is to be understood which Rahner identifies with the philosophy of religion. The philosophy of religion, according to Rahner, begins with a theological anthropology whose first and fundamental task is to deal with humans as potential hearers of God's revelation. He explains:

> The hearing of a revelation presupposes a definite basic constitution of man and must consciously affirm this revelation as free hearing. The word of God, in order to be audible from its past, must itself go forth as human speech, and once again this presupposes this definite constitution of man. And so it appears that theology has to presuppose for itself a *theological* anthropology which we might call 'fundamental-theological anthropology,' and which can appear materially as of the substance of *theo*logical anthropology.[38]

From this basis Rahner establishes that true philosophy of religion is to be understood as natural theology when understood as one with a metaphysical anthropology. A true philosophy of religion, according to Rahner, must do more than simply describe religious phenomena as found in different cultures. It must ask the question of truth and ask about the being and necessity of religion in general. Or, as Rahner states, at the very least it must come to a knowledge of the "absolute and personal God who is above this world" and thus recognize religion

---
[35] *Hearers*, 170. [*HdW*, 208f.]
[36] *Ibid.*, 169f. [208.]
[37] *Ibid.*, 7. [19f.] In contrast to scholastic theology which understood philosophy of religion as the foundation of 'natural religion' on the basis of a 'natural theology' Rahner accepts the more prevalent, modern understanding of the philosophy of religion as being primarily "philosophical reflection of the historically, psychologically, and phenomenologically exalted fact of concrete religions," that is to say, an understanding of the philosophy of religion which takes fully into account the concrete human and historical nature of religion (*ibid*, 7, note 4, [20, note 4]).
[38] *Ibid.*, 169. [207.]

as the "existential bond of the whole man to this God." Based upon this presupposition Rahner concludes that the philosophy of religion includes within it a metaphysical anthropology - not in such a way that the two cannot be distinguished from another but that both presuppose the propositions of the other as essential and necessary.[39]

Rahner grounds this connection between the philosophy of religion and metaphysical anthropology in a twofold manner. First, the philosophical knowledge of God, which he identifies as the core of a normative philosophy of religion, is only possible within metaphysics since natural theology is not a science grounded within itself but is an inner moment of a general ontology - or of metaphysics. And a general ontology, in turn, is also already metaphysical anthropology. Hence Rahner concludes that "a general anthropology and thus a *theologia naturalis* are always already inherent in anthropology - in man's knowledge of himself. The philosophy of religion is *theologia naturalis*, but this is possible only in a more original and permanent unity with metaphysical anthropology." And second, Rahner believes that the connection between the philosophy of religion and metaphysical anthropology can be even more clearly seen in that "the philosophy of religion, as the systematic interpretation of the existential bond between man and God, must know not merely about God, but also about man who is supposed to be bound to God." Hence, in Rahner's view, "all philosophy of religion is ... necessarily an affirmation also concerning the nature of man and is implicitly metaphysical anthropology."[40]

At this point Rahner's argumentation runs full circle and he concludes that such a metaphysical anthropology, understood as an inner moment of the philosophy of religion, necessarily becomes a fundamental, theological anthropology in the sense earlier defined. The conclusion of the matter, therefore, is that a philosophy of religion, as a sort of fundamental, theological anthropology, presupposes and is presupposed by revelation - that is, by the fact that God has spoken. He summarizes the point as follows:

> Whatever else it might be in itself the philosophy of religion will always be a fundamental-theological anthropology, the final word of which is the systematization of the necessity which directs us to listen for the word of God. And because such a word has in fact been spoken, philosophy of religion is not required to do more than to sketch out this sort of fundamental-theological anthropology. For whatever it might make of man's religion by the rational light of reason [German text: *natürlichen Licht der Vernunft*], the philosophy of religion would always be surpassed by revelation.[41]

Given this understanding of the philosophy of religion in light of God's self-revelation we must ask about the relationship between theology, which is based

---
[39] *Ibid.*, 170. [208f.]
[40] *Ibid.*, 171f. [ 210.]
[41] *Ibid.*, 172. [211.]

upon this revelation, and a philosophy of religion which exists in awareness of the fact that God has spoken.

### 5.1.2.2 Relationship between the philosophy of religion and theology

Theology, unlike the philosophy of religion, is, in its original form, not a science constituted by human beings for it is originally the hearing of the revealed word of God which proceeds from God's own free council. Hence theology is not in the first instance a system constructed from human propositions, "but the totality of divine speech addressed by God himself to man." This word of God, however must be heard and grasped in "an original unity of *auditus* and *intellectus.*" This means, in turn, that the word of God thus heard "can and should ... be made by man the object of his enquiring, systematizing thought" and should be "fitted into the whole complex of human science."[42] However, since Rahner contends that the simple hearing and accepting of a message from God seems to be "beyond the reach of scientific-theoretical foundation" - and precisely here one must also find a place for the philosophy of religion - such a foundation "can *cover* not the word of God, but the hearing of the word of God by man, and this only with regard to the a priori possibility of the capacity to hear a revelation."[43] If we are to enquire further, however, about the relationship between theology and the philosophy of religion, then a common ground between the two must be sought. For Rahner this is to be found in metaphysics, specifically in a metaphysical anthropology - as was discussed in the preceding section.[44] For Rahner the problem poses itself as follows:

> The fundamental difficulty of defining ... [the relationship between theology and the philosophy of religion] is underlined precisely when we bring together our provisional knowledge of these two sciences. We are to enquire after a single metaphysical foundation upon which both sciences are primarily constituted; and the relationship between the two is to be conceived by enquiring into their common root. But what can this common root be? The constitution of the philosophy of religion takes place in metaphysics - correctly regarded: *is* metaphysics itself. But can theology, too, be founded only upon metaphysics?[45]

This would seem difficult, however, for then theology appears to emerge too late on the playing field. Hence, the philosophy of religion would seem to have "a metaphysical foundation such that, *a priori*, it takes up the place which theology might possibly fill." Thus the one science, the philosophy of religion, would seem to have abrogated the other, theology, "rendering it intrinsically impossible."

---

[42] Precisely here Rahner finds a so-called second form of theological science. Theology in the first sense (God's divine speech), and theology in the second sense (human systematized thought) can be distinguished using the scholastic categories of positive and scholastic theology.
[43] *Ibid.*, 8f. [21f.]
[44] *Ibid.*, 14ff. [28ff.]
[45] For this and the following quote see *ibid*, 12. [25f.]

"What, then," asks Rahner, "have the philosophy of religion and theology to do with each other? How can they, in their duality, together and simultaneously be concerned and derived from a unified, common foundation, in a scientific-theoretical study? Our demand to have both initially constituted from one foundation within a single metaphysical problem seems from the outset to be absurd." A solution, suggests Rahner, starts with a correct understanding of the philosophy of religion and its task. He writes:

> The philosophy of religion, if it is to leave inviolate the interior autonomy and historicity of theology, ... cannot be allowed to trace lines that theology merely follows up and fills out more fully. The philosophy of religion must of itself point man to some possibility of revelation proceeding from God ... which occurs in history. ... In terms of its own essence it must leave to the God who may conceivably reveal himself in history the institution and definition of religion. ... This, however, is equivalent to saying that metaphysics which is already the philosophy of religion must be of such a kind as to recognize God as the free and the unknown. ... To the extent that such a metaphysics conceives God precisely as the absolute Unknown ... it does not presume to be able to make any *a priori* pre-judgment concerning the way in which this absolute, personal Unknown proposes to deal with men. ... If, as genuine 'natural' metaphysics, it does all this, then it automatically concedes first place to a possible theology.[46]

When the philosophy of religion, as metaphysics, is understood in this manner, and when it defines humans as essentially historical beings who are obligated to listen to any possible revelation from God, then, according to Rahner, "the philosophy of religion becomes the sole possible man-centered foundation of theology." This means, therefore, that theology and the philosophy of religion "actually find a single metaphysical basis in one scientific-theoretical question; and so their mutual relationship is defined in this sense."[47]

Hence Rahner is able, at the end of his study, to conclude that theology is grounded in itself in that God works the readiness to hear in humans as a condition of the hearing of his word - and only in this manner is theology in its original sense or form possible. "The philosophy of religion precedes it only as condition that is itself created by God's speaking. It is a condition of theology which is heard by man and which itself is conditioned by the word of God."[48] So characterizes Rahner the relationship between the humanly constructed science of the philosophy of religion and theology which through God's free act of self-revelation is grounded in its own self. Both find their common ground in a metaphysical anthropology which in turn is based upon the fact that God has spoken to his creatures which are capable of hearing his word. When the

---

[46] *Ibid.*, 13f. [27f.]
[47] *Ibid.*, 14f. [28f.]
[48] *Ibid.*, 174. [214.]

phenomena of religion in various cultures are observed this is done in light of God's revelation. This approach to the phenomenon of non-Christian religions, as we shall see later in this chapter, plays a decisive role in Rahner's development of his theory of anonymous Christianity inasmuch as Rahner begins with the fact of God's speaking to humans which are capable of hearing his word as the fundamental building block and conclusion of his metaphysical anthropology.

### 5.1.2.3 *The world's religions as praeparatio evangelica*

In a short 1973 encyclopedia article on the theological concept of religion Rahner contends that God's revelatory presence has been available at all times but that human beings cannot realize their transcendental orientation toward God apart from the context of a historical, objective and social religion which in this way can be said to be legitimate. Inasmuch as the Old Testament religion and its salvation history meets these requirements Rahner understands it to be paradigmatic for the pre-Christian history of religions in general - without thereby eliminating its superiority over the other religions.[49] In this sense then the world's religions, which remain today in many regards pre-Christian, can legitimately be viewed as preparatory for the gospel in a manner at least analogical to that of the ancient Hebrew religion, even if not on the same level or with the same clarity.[50] As such, non-Christian religions viewed in this manner as pre-Christian have elements of grace and can prepare one for a full knowledge of the gospel, hence they can be characterized as legitimate. Thus Rahner writes,

> that a non-Christian religion - also apart from the Mosaic religion - does not only just have elements of a natural knowledge of God, mixed with human original sin and the depravation that it produces. It also has a supernatural moment of grace which human beings are given by God on account of Christ. On this basis non-Christian religions can, without denying their error and depravation, be recogized, even if in varying degrees, as *legitimate* religion.[51]

---

[49] Rahner, "Der theologische (-normative) Begriff der Religion," in: *HtT* 6:213. For Rahner not only the superiority but also the absoluteness of Christianity over against other religions is not questioned in light of the recognition of salvific elements in other religions. Christianity is not reduced to one option among others. Rahner and K. Weger, *Was sollen wir noch glauben? Theologen stellen sich den Glaubensfragen einer neuen Generation* (Freiburg: Herder, 1979), 29.

[50] Cf. also *FCF*, 156f. [*Grundkurs*, 160f.], where Rahner writes that "the Christian historian of religion does not have to understand the non-Christian history of religion outside the Old and New Testaments merely as a history of man's religious activity. ... He can observe and describe and analyze the phenomena in the history of non-Christian religions without reservations, and interpret them with regard to their ultimate intentions. If he sees the God of the Old and New Testament revelation also at work there, however primitive they might be or however depraved ..., he is in no way prejudicing Christianity's absolute claims."

[51] Rahner, "Grundzüge einer katholisch-dogmatischen Interpretation der nichtchristlichen Religionen," in: *Pluralismus, Toleranz und Christenheit* (Nuremberg, 1961), 61f.

Or similarly, Rahner contends that a theology of salvation history which takes God's universal salvific will seriously cannot overlook the enormous temporal interval separating Adam from the Old Testament revelation of Moses. Not considering the idea of a transmission of a 'primordial revelation' adequate in light of the fact that concretely only the historically and socially constituted (pre-Mosaic) religions could be considered to have been the transmitters of such a tradition, Rahner concludes that "these religions had the possibility and the obligation to awaken and to keep alive man's relationship to the mystery of existence which lays claim upon him, however the individual religions might interpret this primordial mystery of existence and concretize man's relationship to it, and perhaps even do so in a depraved way." And this argument applies also to modern, non-Christian religions which, to the extent their adherents have not yet heard or rightly understood the gospel, may also be considered pre-Christian. Hence, according to Rahner, we cannot "deny a priori and in principle at least a partial positive function to non-Christian religions for people who have not yet been reached by the Christian message in a way which would constitute an immediate obligation for them."[52]

For Rahner, everything which looks beyond itself, which prepares people to hear the word of God, is preparatory for the gospel. Also philosophy, in Rahner's view, fulfills this function. Philosophy, correctly understood, according to Rahner, "is always a *praeparatio evangelii* and is intrinsically Christian - not in the sense of a retrospective baptism, but because it forms a man who is able to hear God's message to the extent that he can do this for himself."[53] In this sense even the philosophical traditions arising out of non-Christian cultures and religions cannot simply be a-Christian but are also preparatory for the gospel to the extent that they already represent an anonymous Christianness which contact with the Christian philosophies of the West can bring more fully to light. Explains Rahner:

> As we have said already, there can be no philosophy which could be simply a-Christian. The Western message of Christianity, even by means of the philosophy which precedes and accompanies it, has also undoubtedly the task of furthering the philosophical self-understanding of the non-Western world and of helping it to become more conscious of itself and free itself both from error and the abbreviation of its self-interpretation. Yet, since the Western world, during its wanderings into strange lands while carrying Christ's message, always encounters a world in which Christ's grace has long been at work even though not called by its own name, the reverse must necessarily also happen if everything runs its proper course: the anonymous Christianity ... of non-Western philosophy can bring to light and eradicate abbreviations of its Christian nature in the explicitly Christian philosophy of the West.[54]

---

[52] *FCF*, 315. [*Grundkurs*, 307.]
[53] *Hearers*, 175f. [*HdW.*, 215f.]
[54] "Philosophy and Theology," 81. [*Schriften* 6:102.]

## 5.1.3 The theory of an anonymous Christianity

More than perhaps anything else Karl Rahner is known for his theory of an anonymous Christianity.[55] Although he contends that the question of the terminology itself is a secondary issue - and indeed used this terminology less frequently himself in his latter years - he remained convinced that the phenomenon which he sought thereby to describe was undoubted, that is, that there are beyond question people who fall into the category that he chose to call "anonymous Christianity."[56] Anonymous Christianity, as defined by Rahner, "is what we call the condition of a man who lives on the one hand in a state of grace and justification, and yet on the other hand has not come into contact with the explicit preaching of the Gospel and is consequently not in a position to call himself a 'Christian.'"[57] It is a theory, according to Rahner, which arose from two facts: "first, the possibility of supernatural salvation and of a corresponding faith which must be granted to non-Christians, even if they never become Christian; and secondly, that salvation cannot be gained without reference to God and Christ, since it must in its origin, history and fulfilment be a theistic and Christian salvation."[58] In the following sections we will focus on the shape and structure of Rahner's proposal of a theory of anonymous Christianity within the context of Vatican II Catholic thought[59] as well as upon the responses it has drawn from fellow Roman Catholic theologians.

### 5.1.3.1 *The shape of an anonymous Christianity*

One of the earliest as well as one of the clearest and most fundamental statements of Rahner's concept of an anonymous Christianity is to be found in his 1961 lecture "Christianity and the Non-Christian Religions," delivered on the eve of the Second Vatican Council. In this lecture he set forth four theses concerning non-Christian religions, the first two laying the foundation for his theory and the second two dealing directly with the idea of an anonymous Christianity. Rahner's first thesis is that "Christianity understands itself as the absolute religion, intended

---

[55] Eamonn Conway, *The Anonymous Christian - A Realitivised Christianity? An Evaluation of Hans Urs von Balthasar's Criticisms of Karl Rahner's Theory of the Anonymous Christian* (Frankfurt/M: Peter Lang, 1993), 5, traces the concept of anonymous Christianity suggesting that the essence of the idea can already be found in certain statements of Justin (*Apologia* I, 46) and Augustine, *Retractationes* I, 13, 3) and that the term anonymous itself was first used in this sense by Pierre-Lambert Goosens (1827-1883) and Auguste Dechamps (1810-1883), and in more recent times by the French philosopher Maurice Blondel (1861-1949).

[56] Rahner, "Foundations of Christian Faith," in: *TI* 19:10, contends that "the term as such is not important. Anyone who thinks it implies a depreciation of explicit and institutionalized Christianity need not use it. The thing itself, however, cannot be disputed, at least after Vatican II."

[57] Rahner, "Atheism ans Implicit Christianity," in: *TI* 9:145. ["Atheismus und implizites Christentum," in: *Schriften* 8:187.]

[58] "The One Christ and the Universality of Salvation," 218. [*Schriften* 12:275.]

[59] Rahner himself has declared that the essence of the theory of anonymous Christianity is completely consistent with the teaching of the Council which "explicitly" says the same thing. So Rahner, "Anonymous Christians," in: *TI* 6:398. ["Die anonymen Christen," in: *Schriften* 6:554.]

for all men, which cannot recognize any other religion beside itself as of equal right."[60] This self-evident aspect of Christianity's self-understanding connects Rahner to the tradition of the church and to that aspect of theology's universality which demands that the Christian faith cannot be simply one religion among others and still be universal. Yet the fact that Christianity was not always present but itself has a beginning in human history means that it was not always the way of salvation for all persons and thus necessarily encounters human beings historically as a socially constituted religion. The implication of this first thesis that is of special significance for his theory of anonymous Christians is that Rahner can affirm "that Christianity is truly the religion of all mankind, but he leaves the question open as to the exact temporal moment that this obligation becomes real for an individual."[61]

Rahner's second thesis affirms the grace of God and elements of truth in non-Christian religions in language similar to that used later by the Council.[62] He contended: "Until the moment when the gospel really enters into the historical situation of an individual, a non-Christian religion ... does not merely contain elements of a natural knowledge of God, elements, however, mixed up with human depravity which is the result of original sin and later aberrations. It contains also supernatural elements arising out of the grace which is given to men as a gratuitous gift on account of Christ."[63] Rahner further divides this thesis into two parts. In the first place, it means that it is possible *a priori* to assume the presence of supernatural, grace-filled elements within non-Christian religions. That is not to say that all elements of non-Christian religions are either good or harmless. Rather, the legitimacy of non-Christian religions is recognized without disallowing the recognition of their errors and failings. Rahner intends to point out here, on the basis of God's universal salvific will, what he believes to be the necessary conclusion that "every human being is really and truly exposed to the influence of divine, supernatural grace" by means of which God communicates himself even in cases where the individual takes up an attitude of refusal toward this grace. And secondly, this thesis means that "the actual religions of 'pre-Christian' humanity too must not be regarded as simply illegitimate from the very start, but must be seen as quite capable of having a positive significance." To this extent Rahner's first two theses are in essential agreement with the view of non-Christian religions coming out of the Second Vatican Council. Where Rahner diverges from the Council's theology of religions - or better, where the Council could not follow Rahner - is in the radicalness of his application of this

---

[60] Rahner, "Christianity and the Non-Christian Religions," *TI* 5:118. ["Das Christentum und die nichtchristlichen Religionen," in: *Schriften* 5:139.]
[61] Roberts, *The Achievements of Karl Rahner*, 276.
[62] Cf., for instance, *Nostra aetate* 2 (Denzinger, 4196).
[63] For this and the following see "Christianity and the Non-Christian Religions," 121ff. [Das Christentum und die nichtchristlichen Religionen," 143ff.]

fundamental recognition of God's grace at work even among members of non-Christian religions, namely, in Rahner's theory of an anonymous Christianity.

In Rahner's final two theses his theory of anonymous Christianity is stated in brief form as follows. First, assuming the correctness of his second thesis, "Christianity does not simply confront the member of an extra-Christian religion as a mere non-Christian but as someone who can and must already be regarded ... as an anonymous Christian." If, as Rahner argues, it is wrong to regard "pagans" as not having been touched in any way by God's grace - understood as the a priori horizon of all their spiritual acts -, then it must be conceded that these may have already accepted this grace as ultimate entelechy of their existence by accepting their mortality as opening up to infinity and that they have thus "already been given revelation in a true sense even before" they encounter any missionary preaching.[64]

And finally, Rahner contends that, in the face of a religious pluralism which is not likely to disappear in the near future, it is "absolutely permissible for the Christian ... to interpret this non-Christianity as Christianity of an anonymous kind which he does always still go out to meet as a missionary, seeing it as a world which is to be brought to the explicit consciousness of what already belongs to it as a divine offer or already pertains to it also over and above this as a divine gift of grace accepted unreflectedly and implicitly."[65] Here Rahner does what *Ad gentes* did not do in seeking to provide a solution to the tension between the recognition of salvific elements in non-Christian religions and the necessity of mission.[66] As has been rightly pointed out, the statements of the Council in regard to respecting decisions of conscience of those of other religions essentially raises the same question as Rahner's theologoumenon of anonymous Christianity, namely, why should an implicit Christianity that makes salvation possible be converted into an explicit Christianity? That is to say, why the need for evangelization and mission at all?[67] Rahner responds to this question by contending that rather than being content with the existence of anonymous Christians the motivation of Christian mission should be to encounter these with

---

[64] *Ibid.*, 131. [154f.]
[65] *Ibid.*, 133. [156.]
[66] In his 1970 article "Anonymous Christianity and the Missionary Task of the Church," in: *TI* 12:161. ["Anonymes Christentum und Missionsauftrag der Kirche," in: *Schriften* 9:498ff.], Rahner treats this point more thoroughly. Here Rahner, as response to the criticism that the theory of anonymous Christians is inconsistent with the church's task of universal mission, contends that: "In speaking of the universal missionary task of the Church as a right and duty of the Church herself this is taken to include the basic duty of every man to become a Christian in an explicitly ecclesiastical form of Christianity, because it is quite impossible to separate these two entities from one another."
[67] So Karl-Heinz Weger, "Überlegungen zum 'anonymen Christentum,'" 506f. Weger cautions that in Rahner's view it would be a mistake to fall prey to a cheap salvation-optimism in light of the recognition of the existence of an anonymous Christianity.

the gospel so that their implicit faith become explicit.[68] The church, in turn, is no longer understood as the communion of those who possess God's grace as opposed to those who do not, but as "the communion of those who can explicitly confess what they *and* the others hope to be."[69] Or, as Roberts explains, the fact that the covenant of universal salvation history is valid for all persons means for Rahner that "the church will better recognize itself as the historical expression of what exists outside the visible church also."[70]

On the basis of this approach, Rahner suggests that, "one can be tolerant, humble and yet firm towards all non-Christian religions." And, as far as the proclamation of the gospel is concerned, in another 1961 article, Rahner specifically contended, "that the proclamation of the gospel in the final analysis does not make one absolutely abandoned by God and Christ into a Christian, but rather makes an anonymous Christian into a human being, since this one now knows his Christianity in the depths of his pardoned being."[71] Precisely the optimistic conception of the natural person which this perspective presupposes, however, as we shall see in the following section, has lead to severe criticism from a number of fellow Catholic theologians.

At this point, in light of numerous potential misunderstandings, we must comment briefly on what the theory of an anonymous Christianity, in Rahner's thought, is not. In the first place it is not an appeal for the particular label "anonymous Christians" or "anonymous Christianity" but rather an attempt to describe a phenomenon which in one form or another Rahner holds to be theologically unavoidable. Hence, as Rahner has contended in many places: "The issue at stake does not have to do so much with the particular term 'anonymous Christianity' itself, yet the situation which is thereby described is undeniably central for the relationship of modern Christians to the world around them."[72] Rahner's apparent "backing off" from the theme of anonymous Christians in his later years, seen in this light, reflects more a recognition of the difficulties created by the terminology than any substantive change in his theological position. Secondly, despite the fact that Rahner is to many best known for his theory of an anonymous Christianity, he contends it is not the (nor even a) central theme of his theological thought. Concerning the location of the teaching about anonymous

---

[68] Yet it must be noted that while still leaving a legitimate place for mission and evangelization, Rahner's theory would seem to imply a significant shift in the way the task and goal of these endeavors be understood. Hans Schwarz, *The Search for God*, 143, has rightly pointed out that Rahner's position would seem to exclude "a conversion in the traditional sense as the goal of missionary activity. In most cases the goal would rather be an explicit self-realization of one's hitherto anonymous Christian existence and an ever growing awareness of God's grace and truth."

[69] For this and the following quote from Rahner see "Christianity and the Non-Christian Religions," 134. [Das Christentum und die nichtchristlichen Religionen," 157f.]

[70] Roberts, 278.

[71] "Grundzüge einer katholisch-dogmatischen Interpretationen der nichtchristlichen Religionen," 72.

[72] "Anonymous Christians," 396, translation my own. ["Die anonyme Christen," 552.] Cf. also "Atheism and Implicit Christianity," 145. [*Schriften* 8:187.]

Christians within the theological corpus he contends that it is not "a hermeneutical *principle* by which the whole corpus of conventional theology and dogmatics is to be critically reduced ... in order to make Christianity in this form more acceptable." Rather, the teaching of an anonymous Christianity could perhaps be much better described, according to Rahner, as a fringe phenomenon (*Grenzphänomen*), the necessity, possibility and expressibility of which is derived from many other individual doctrines of the Christian faith.[73]

Hence Rahner contends over against numerous critics who he believes have misunderstood the implications of the teaching, that it would be foolish to think that the theory of an anonymous Christianity means a minimalizing or slighting of the significance of the church's mission or preaching or of the meaning of baptism or the word of God.[74] Finally, it must be pointed out that Rahner's theory of an anonymous Christianity is not a "many paths leading to salvation" theory which essentially denies the Christian claims to absoluteness and universality, but rather a radicalizing of these claims and the theology of religions implicit in them. For Rahner, his concept of an anonymous Christianity is nothing less than a taking seriously of God's universal salvific will - long an established aspect of Roman Catholic thought.

### 5.1.3.2 *'Anonymous Christianity' and Judaism*

The possibility of anonymous Christianity within the non-Christian religions is conceded, as we have seen, only on the condition that a legitimate and sufficient encounter with Christianity has not yet taken place, a qualification which would seem to apply, in Rahner's thought, to all non-Christian religions. The question which arises in the context of the contemporary religious situation is what, if any, distinctive place does or could Judaism hold within Rahner's thesis of anonymous Christianity?[75] In regard to Judaism Rahner's thought presents special difficulties for although a unique place is given to the Jewish people (especially in the form of Old Testament Israel) in salvation history, Rahner's theory of an anonymous Christianity does not seem to allow for any special or distinctive conception of Israel in regard to salvation in comparison to the other non-Christian religions.[76]

---

[73] *Ibid.* Georg Evers, "Die 'anonymen Christen' und der Dialog mit den Juden," in: *Wagnis Theologie*, ed. Herbert Vorgrimler, 524, however, contends that the theme of anonymous Christianity in not a secondary concern in Rahner's theology but is a central and even necessary consequence of his fundamental theological assumptions.

[74] "Anonymous Christians," 396f. ["Die anonyme Christen," 552f.] Rahner sees the concept of an anonymous Christianity as a deduction from traditional (often sterile) theological concerns and an honest viewing of the present day situation of human beings.

[75] Of course, it is not an *a priori* necessity that Judaism be regarded fundamentally differently than other non-Christian religions in a Christian theology of religions. Whether this ought to be the case indeed remains an open question. Yet in light of current trends in Christian-Jewish dialogue and in recent theologies of religion, the question poses itself quite naturally and earnestly.

[76] Evers, "Die 'anonymen Christen' und der Dialog mit den Juden," 534f., puts the problem succinctly when he points out, "daß nach der These vom 'anonymen Christentum' die Heilsmöglichkeit innerhalb eines religiösen Systems grundsätzlich vorläufig zu einer existentiellen

Evers attempts to rescue this situation by stressing the role of eschatology within Rahner's thought and proposing that "precisely in dialogue with the Jews the Christian should know that the 'incompleteness of the existential, historical realisation' of the Christian expectation of salvation and its orientation toward its future completion, allows a broad basis for dialogue that does not have as its goal the premature removal of the dialogue situation, speak conversion, but has the patience to wait until the fullness of time."[77] Yet Evers' proposed solution remains unconvincing. In the first place, it still fails to make any real distinction between Judaism and other non-Christian religions (apart from the fact that we have more common ground upon which to base a dialogue), for the proposed 'eschatological' solution would apply equally to all other religions and seems ultimately to suggest that mission be replaced by or reduced to encounter-oriented dialogue. Additionally, the solution does not seem to arise out of Rahner's thought itself, that is to say, it bears the appearance of being imposed upon his system. In the Rahner passage cited by Evers, for instance, the point behind the recognition of the incompleteness of our present historical situation is not to eliminate 'conversion' as an ultimate goal of 'dialogue' with non-Christians but is to point out that this recognition not only does not undermine Christianity's claim to absoluteness and universality but is essential to it. Rahner writes: "Only by the recognition of its historical origins out of a particular, finite past and its directedness toward a still future self-realization can Christianity make the claim to universal validity. Indeed, this recognition anticipates its validity and justifies its universality."[78]

That Rahner himself was unwilling in the light of the eschatological fulfillment and coming together of all peoples to discontinue a 'mission to the Jews' is made clear in his dialogue with Jewish theologian Pinchas Lapide, who, similar to Evers, suggested that Rahner's eschatological perspective eliminated the need for any evangelistic efforts toward the Jews. Lapide contended: If you believe that the church awaits the eschatological day in which all peoples, including Israel, will worship the Lord with one voice, "then the Christian mission to the Jews is unnecessary, for if one places the day of future religious concord in God's hands, what is the point still of human proselytizing?"[79] Rahner responded:

---

Begegnung mit dem Christentum, das heißt in einem gewissen Sinn 'nur auf Zeit' gegeben ist. Mit dieser theologischen Aussage läßt sich für das Judentum sagen, daß es auch nach dem Kommen Jesu Christi als der Selbstmitteilung Gottes seine Heilsbedeutung behält, solange es nicht zu einer wirklichen Begegnung mit dem Christentum gekommen ist. ... Kommt es aber zu einem wirklichen Dialog, so bringt diese ... Begegnung ... die 'bona fides' letztlich in Gefahr. Es wäre dies eine etwas seltsame Konsequenz, wenn man wirklich sagen müßte: Durch einen existentiellen 'gelungenen' Dialog entfällt die relative Heilsbedeutung des Judentums."

[77] *Ibid.*, 536.
[78] Rahner, "Über den Dialog in der pluralistischen Gesellschaft," in: *Schriften* 6:52. (trans. my own)
[79] Pinchas Lapide and Karl Rahner, *Encountering Jesus - Encountering Judaism: A Dialogue*, trans. Davis Perkins (New York: Crossroads, 1987), 6. [*Heil von den Juden? Ein Gespräch* (Mainz: Matthias-Grünewald-Verlag, 1983), 12.]

> It is not quite so simple. The relationship of the Church to Israel may be essentially different from the relation of the Church to the Gentile peoples, but I cannot therefore simply interpret the Christian mission to the Jews as superfluous. This is because it must, in its essence, be different from the mission to the Gentiles and because we do not know the day of the unity between Israel and the Gentile Church. We also certainly don't know the day on which Japan as a people will actually enter the Church, and so the Church still works for the conversion of the Japanese.[80]

We see in Rahner's words indeed a recognition that the relationship between the church and Judaism may very well be different from that to other peoples and that the mission to the Jews would also take on a distinctive form.[81] Yet in relation to our contention that his thesis of anonymous Christianity does not allow for an essential differentiation between Judaism and other religions two things are to be noted. First of all, this special or unique relationship and mission are nowhere in Rahner's writings grounded upon his understanding of anonymous Christians, which thesis itself treats all persons outside the church essentially on the same basis. And second, Rahner does not explicitly explain upon what basis this unique relationship between Judaism and the church is to be based. From the context of Rahner's thought it would seem that this basis is to be found in Israel's special role in the history of salvation and upon the recognition of a continuity between ancient Israel and modern Judaism. As regards salvation, however, and this is also to be glimpsed in Rahner's final comment comparing mission to the Jews and mission to the Japanese, there is no fundamental distinction made between a Jew and a member of another non-Christian religion.[82] Nor would it seem possible to make such a distinction on the basis of Rahner's thesis of an anonymous Christianity.

In conclusion it would seem that although Rahner's thesis of an anonymous Christianity opens the possibility for recognizing a continuing salvific working of God in present-day Judaism it is not capable of attributing permanence to this salvific element (for it remains conditional upon the lack of an adequate encounter with Christianity) and it further is not able to make any fundamental distinction between Judaism and other non-Christian religions apart from the recognition of common historical roots which it shares with Christianity and the special role it played (with emphasis upon the past tense) in the history of salvation.

---

[80] *Ibid.*

[81] That Rahner saw a special relationship existing between Christianity and Judaism on the basis of much common history and belief and that this relationship must be nurtured and preserved is discussed by Roberts, *The Achievement of Karl Rahner*, 280f.

[82] For Rahner Jesus Christ remains the unsurpassable and only Messiah for all people, including the Jewish people, not just in the future - as some have suggested - but also in the present. So Rahner, *Encountering Jesus - Encountering Judaism*, 109f. [*Heil von den Juden?* 121f.]

### 5.1.3.3 Responses to Rahner's theory of an anonymous Christianity (Balthasar, Küng, Ratzinger, Lubac)

Although Rahner's theory of an anonymous Christianity has found widespread popular acceptance it has been heavily criticized by many his theological colleagues.[83] Among fellow German-speaking Roman Catholic theologians alone Hans Urs von Balthasar, Hans Küng, Walter Kasper, and Joseph Ratzinger have all, albeit for differing reasons, sharply criticized Rahner's theory of an anonymous Christianity. Balthasar has asked whether, if so much is possible for and through an anonymous Christianity, one might begin to ask what the sense is in becoming or remaining a Christian by name. He writes:

> Finally, after centuries of being frozen solid, the confessional differences ... are melting together. ... Christians and Christians, Christians and Jews, Christians and non-Christians ... are finally communicating together in the great space of God's creation, which as a whole is provided with an exponent of grace. ... But there is a catch. One can no longer see clearly, when things are going so well with the anonymity, why one should still be a Christian that bears the name. And one has the feeling that the *polloi* already are taking up this new theological vogue ... to dispense with the burdensome externality of the name.[84]

Also, as we have earlier seen, Balthasar felt that Rahner's theory was not able ultimately to maintain the distinction between Christians who call themselves and know themselves to be such and those who are "anonymous." He finds the term also belittling of those of different faiths or who claim to be atheists suggesting that atheists could just as well insist that Christians are all anonymous atheists, thereby not taking our confession to be Christians seriously.[85]

Hans Küng, in a similar vein, criticized Rahner's theory of anonymous Christians asking rhetorically whether the application of the label anonymous Christians to those outside the church solves the problem of the traditional formula, *extra ecclesiam nulla salus*, by extending the concept or reign of the (Roman) church to include the sum total of humanity. Writes Küng:

> Are the masses of the non-Christian religions really marching into the holy Roman Church? Or is this going on only in the theologian's head? Anyway, in reality, they - Jews, Muslims, Hindus, Buddhists and all the others, who know

---

[83] Weger, *Karl Rahner: An Introduction to His Theology*, 115, believes the objections to Rahner's concept of anonymous Christianity can be reduced to three points. "The first is that the name does not really suit the matter covered. The second is that the doctrine of anonymous Christianity is an offensive taking over of non-Christians. The third is that it is a relativization of Christianity." It might be added that a fourth and more serious point, which Weger does not take into account, is that Rahner's theory presupposes an overly optimistic view of natural, unregenerate humanity.

[84] Hans Urs von Balthasar, *Rechtenschaft 1965* (Einsiedeln: Johannes Verlag, 1965), 12.

[85] So Balthasar, *Cordula oder der Ernstfall*, 102ff. For a detailed analysis of Balthasar's critique of Rahner's theory see Conway, *The Anonymous Christian - A Relativised Christianity?* Conway suggests that Balthasar's own position is not so far away from Rahner's as his rhetoric implies.

quite well that they are completely 'unanonymous' - remain outside. Nor have they any wish to be inside.... The will of those who are outside is not to be 'interpreted' in the light of our own interests, but quite simply respected. And it would be impossible to find anywhere in the world a sincere Jew, Muslim or atheist who would not regard the assertion that he is an 'anonymous Christian' as presumptuous. To bring the partner to the discussion into our own circle in this way closes the dialog before it has ever begun. ... A pseudo-orthodox stretching of the meaning of Christian concepts like 'Church' and 'salvation' is no answer to the challenge of the world religions.[86]

Küng's criticisms, however, - though more than a simple semantic difference - do not reflect a fundamental disagreement with Rahner over the possibility of the salvation of those outside the Church. Küng's own salvation-optimism can be seen in his contention that, rather than labeling non-Christians as 'anonymous Christians,' they should be taken seriously by Christians precisely as non-Christians "and nevertheless granted the possibility of salvation outside the Church."[87] Hence the heart of the disagreement with Küng and others who tend to share Rahner's salvation-optimism lies with the understanding of the Church and the problems associated with making people members of it who, as Küng puts it, quite *un*anonymously do not wish to be a part of it.

In Joseph Ratzinger we find a criticism of Rahner's position arising from other grounds. Ratzinger contended that in Rahner, "the problem of the concept 'anonymous Christians is found above all else ... in the fact that in its curtailed form it fixes the problem in the wrong direction."[88] This false direction of Rahner's thought on anonymous Christians arises primarily from his anthropology. Ratzinger, questioning the foundation of Rahner's theory of an anonymous Christianity which he rightly detects already in *Hearers of the Word* focuses on Rahner's relating of salvation history not to a particular people or group of people but in a radical sense to humanity in general so that the human person as such is 'Christian' to the extent that he or she accepts his or her humanness - a position which Ratzinger maintains comes to full and consistent expression in the idea of anonymous Christians. In the end, Ratzinger suggests that what Rahner has accomplished is a "melting together of the general and the particular, of history and essence, of being a Christian and being a human 'as it is' on the basis of a self-affirmation of the human person beyond him or herself: being a Christian is acceptance of one's self." Over against Rahner, Ratzinger directs the following series of questions:

> Is it true that Christianity doesn't contribute anything to that which is common to humanity, but only makes it aware? Is the Christian really only the human

---

[86] Hans Küng, *On Being a Christian*, tr. Edward Quinn (New York: Doubleday, 1984), 98.
[87] Küng, "Anonyme Christen - wozu?" in: *Orientierung* 39 (1975), 215.
[88] Joseph Ratzinger, *Das Neue Volk Gottes: Entwürfe zur Ekklesiologie* (Düsseldorf: Patmos-Verlag, 1969), 340, note 1.

being as the human being really is? ... Are not human beings as they really are that which is insufficient, that which needs to be overcome and exceeded? Does not the entire dynamic of history arise out of the yearning to transcend human beings as they really are? Is not the pivotal point of the faith of both Testaments that the human being is only made right through conversion, that is, in ceasing to be what he or she is? Will not Christianity be meaningless if it is brought back into that which is common to all precisely where we await the new, other, and saving transformation? Is it not the case with such a conception that makes essence into history but also history into essence that an enormous static exists despite the talk of self-transcendence as the content of the human being? A Christianity that is only the reflection of that which is common to all might be inoffensive, but is it not also unnecessary?[89]

Here we see a criticism of what Ratzinger considers the foundation of Rahner's theory of an anonymous Christianity in which, in contrast to Küng, the concern is not with the taking seriously of members of other religions but in which the anthropo-optimism of Rahner, discussed in chapter three of our study, is rejected.

In a similar vein Rahner has been criticized on this point by the French theologian Henri de Lubac, who concedes that the existence of individual 'anonymous Christians' when this is rightly understood, is possible - indeed, even likely - but rejects the idea of an anonymous Christianity in which a whole group are seen to already possess, of their human nature alone, that which is essential for salvation, and need only be informed of this to turn their implicit faith into explicit faith. Such a view entails a too optimistic view of the 'natural person' which cannot be accepted by a Christian theology oriented toward a more 'traditional' and realistic anthropology. Lubac explains:

> No Christian would deny that there are 'anonymous Christians' in the various cultures and societies who have accepted in one way or another the insights that arise from the Gospel. That such insights can be found elsewhere, through the secret workings of the Holy Spirit, is also to be conceded. But only by drawing a false conclusion could one deduce that there is spread throughout all humanity an 'anonymous Christianity' [*anonymes Christentum*], a so-to-speak 'implicit Christianity,' over against which preaching has only the task of bringing it to a state of being explicit - as if Christ in his revelation has done nothing other than to bring that to light what was already everywhere present.[90]

Rahner himself, however, in a response to Lubac's criticism, seems to miss the radicalness of the critique and suggests that the problem between himself and Lubac is largely semantic, based upon some ambiguity in the German word "Christentum." Hence he concludes that in Lubac's case, "anyone who concludes

---
[89] Ratzinger, *Theologische Prinzipienlehre: Bausteine zur Fundamentaltheologie* (Munich: Erich Wewel, 1982), 173f.
[90] Henri de Lubac, *Geheimnis aus dem wir leben*, trans. Karlheinz Bergner and Hans Urs von Balthasar (Einsiedeln: Johannes Verlag, 1967), 151.

that there are anonymous Christians should not raise any objections against the point that in that case there is an anonymous *Christentum* (Christendom) in this sense as well." So it is that, in the question of the use of the terminology 'anonymous Christian' and 'anonymous Christianity' one must either accept or reject both terms, according to Rahner, if one wishes to be consistent.[91]

From the Protestant perspective - which tends to build its anthropology largely upon the theology of Augustine - there is a natural tendency to approach Rahner's theory with a certain amount of skepticism, seeing in it what is for Rahner a typical anthropo-optimism which, while consistent with his own formulation of the doctrine of humanity found already in *Spirit in the World*[92] and his emphasis upon the universal significance of the Christ event, creates serious theological problems.[93] Pannenberg, between whose own thought and Rahner's we have found so many parallels, chooses here to follow a somewhat different path. Although using different language, Pannenberg admits the existence of something very similar to Rahner's anonymous Christians. Like Lubac, however, his own anthropology does not allow him to take up the theory of an anonymous Christianity as such. The recognition of 'anonymous Christians' is based for Pannenberg upon an implicit relationship or response to Christ determined by what light 'non-Christians' have and not by anything inherent within the human being as such. Hence Pannenberg writes:

> When it is taken into consideration that the significance of Jesus in the final judgment is, first of all, the criterion for a person's - indeed every person's - relationship with God, then this means that God views and judges not only Christians but all people from the perspective of their explicit or implicit relationship to the life and teaching of Jesus. But this occurs especially with a view toward the merciful love that found expression in the mission of Jesus. Therefore those people who have not become confessing members of the Christian church can participate in the destiny of that humanity that has the new life which has appeared in Jesus Christ when their hearts are open to the nearness of God and his kingdom which Jesus preached.[94]

Hence the universality of the significance of the Christ-event and the salvation offered through it, just as in the thought of Rahner, cannot be restricted

---

[91] Rahner, "Anonymous Christianity and the Missionary Task of the Church," 162. [*Schriften* 9:499f.]

[92] So, for example, Francis Fiorenza, "Karl Rahner and the Kantian Problematic," xliv.

[93] Similar ideas have, of course, been expressed by Protestant theologians. The tendency, however, has not been to construct an ecclesiology upon them. Karl Barth, for instance, wrote already in his book, *The Teaching of the Church Regarding Baptism*, trans. Ernest Payne (London: SCM Press, 1948), 32, that "there are of course secret members of the Church of Jesus Christ, not recognised as such by themselves, making no profession, and not acknowledged as such by others. But the Church is not built up by such, either internally or externally. She does not shine in such persons, nor can she in them realise the purpose of her existence, the glorifying of God."

[94] *ST* 3:686,

to 'explicit' Christians. Pannenberg's doctrine of humanity, however, which we have previously examined in comparison with that of Rahner, makes impossible a participation of human beings in salvation based upon any inherent qualities and separate from a redeeming relationship with Jesus Christ.

## 5.2 Wolfhart Pannenberg: Theology as the Science of Religion

Pannenberg has argued that theology, properly understood and in its most fundamental form, should be conceived of as the science of religion. The importance of any single religion, e.g., the Christian religion, and its particular stage of development can only be fully seen, according to Pannenberg, within the framework of a history of world religions. This means, therefore, that the sciences of religion "form the appropriate framework for the practice of Christian theology and all its disciplines." Hence the science of religion, according to Pannenberg, is (or at the very least should be) the fundamental theological discipline.[95] In the following section we shall examine the context of Pannenberg's proposal within the context of Protestant thought as well as the specific form that it takes as applied not only to the study of the Christian religion but of the other religions as well.

### 5.2.1 The theology of religions in Protestant thought

The Roman Catholic theologian Paul Knitter is certainly correct in his assessment that, "the lack of a formed and integrated theology of the non-Christian religions among Protestant thinkers is painfully evident, still today."[96] Unlike Roman Catholic theologians there is no series of Council documents which serves to direct and unify (some might suggest 'restrain') Protestant thought on the question of the world's religions. And there is no one who has carried as much weight on the subject as Karl Rahner on the Catholic side whose views have served to focus the debate.[97] Yet nevertheless there are certain discernible strands of thought within recent Protestant thought, from Schleiermacher to the present, which have exerted significant influence on the wider Protestant tradition and which merit further examination. We shall focus here especially on those thinkers who have particular significance for understanding Pannenberg's own contributions to the development of a 'Protestant' theology of religions.

---

[95] *TPS*, 361f. [*WtT*, 364.]
[96] Paul Knitter, "What is German Protestant Theology Saying About the Non-Christian Religions?" in: *Neue Zeitschrift für systematische Theologie und Religionsphilosophie* 15 (1973), 38.
[97] So similarly Peter Beyerhaus, "Zur Theologie der Religionen im Protestantismus," in: *Kerygma und Dogma* 15 (1969), 100, who observes: In contrast to the "Aufnahme dieser Herausforderung durch die katholische Theologie seit Karl Rahner mit ihrer beachtlichen inneren Geschlossenheit erscheint - von rühmlichen Ausnahmen abgesehen - die Reaktion der protestantischen Theologie zögernd und uneinheitlich, gedanklich oft vage oder spekulativ."

### 5.2.1.1 Liberal theology and the world's religions (Schleiermacher, Harnack, Troeltsch)

If the background to Rahner's approach to the question of non-Christian religions is the pre-Vatican II discussion of the "no salvation outside the church" axiom, then for Pannenberg it is the heritage of liberal theology's treatment of the question of the absoluteness of Christianity in light of the world religions. At a time when the Roman Catholic Church was still inclined to interpret the *extra ecclesiam nulla salus* axiom as applying to the Roman Church, Protestantism was in the midst of a sort of self-proclaimed 'enlightenment' which came to classic expression in the liberal theology of the nineteenth century. Among Protestant theologians it was Schleiermacher, the 'father' of liberal theology himself, who first reflected seriously and in a new way about the nature of religion and who left his mark on the entire development of the theology of religion which followed after him.[98]

For Schleiermacher, religion was understood in his 1799 *On Religion: Speeches to its Cultured Despisers* as "not knowledge or science, either of the world or of God . . . [but] in itself it is an affection."[99] And later in his *Christian Faith*, religion is defined more precisely as the feeling or consciousness "of being absolutely dependent, or, which is the same thing, of being in relation with God."[100] Rather than judging a religion to be true or false,[101] as had been the case in Protestant theology from Luther and Calvin to his own time, with non-Christian religions being designated simply as *religio falsa*,[102] Schleiermacher classified religions according to their "stage of development" in which Christianity, as the "religion of religions," held the highest place or level. After comparing

---

[98] So George Augustin, *Gott eint - Trennt Christus? Die Einmaligkeit und Universalität Jesu Christi als Grundlage einer christlichen Theologie der Religionen ausgehend vom Ansatz Wolfhart Pannenbergs*, 37.

[99] Friedrich Schleiermacher, *On Religion: Speeches to its Cultured Despisers* [1799], tr. John Owen (New York: Harper & Row, 1958), 36. In his *Speeches*, as Barth summarizes, Schleiermacher was concerned to draw his readers' attention "to the fact that among the religions that are commended the only one for them in practice is the Christian religion, which is relatively, though not absolutely, the highest and noblest and purest. (Barth, *The Theology of Schleiermacher: Lectures at Göttingen, Winter Semester of 1923/34*, ed. Dietrich Ritschl, trans. Geoffrey Bromily (Grand Rapids: Eerdmans, 1982), 245).

[100] Schleiermacher, *The Christian Faith* [1830], trans. H. Mackintosh, J. Steward, et al. (Edinburgh: T. & T. Clark, 1986), 12.

[101] Cf. *ibid*. 33, where Schleiermacher writes that "our proposition excludes ... the idea ... that the Christian religion (piety) should adopt towards at least most other forms of piety the attitude of the true towards the false. For if the religions belonging to the same stage as Christianity were entirely false, how could they have so much similarity to Christianity ...? And if the religions which belong to the lower stages contained nothing but error, how would it be possible for a man to pass from them to Christianity?" This view of Schleiermacher was later rejected by Barth as a "dazzling bit of sophistry," questioning the apparent assumption in Schleiermacher's argument that "non-Christian religion *as such* ... [is] receptivity to Christianity." (Barth, *The Theology of Schleiermacher*, 225.)

[102] Cf. Beyerhaus, "Zur Theologie der Religionen im Protestantismus," 87.

Christianity with the other religions, therefore, Schleiermacher felt warranted in concluding that "Christianity is, in fact, the most perfect of the most highly developed forms of religion."[103] Yet even as the religion of religions Schleiermacher did not assign permanence to Christianity as a religion, which would never "reign within humanity as the only form of religion," but rather to its essential worldview so that each new "epoch of humanity will be the palingenesis of Christianity and will awaken its spirit in a new, more beautiful form."[104]

The effect of all this on the concept of religion was to give it a new and independent status by basing it not upon divine revelation or even metaphysics but upon anthropology in that religion came to be seen as a human feeling of dependence. Religion was no longer simply the awareness or knowledge of God but this awareness or knowledge of God now became the product of religion. As Pannenberg explains: "Schleiermacher's *Speeches on Religion* gave the independence of religion a new foundation. Religion no longer owed its freedom from metaphysics and moral philosophy to the authority of the truth of God. It now had a basis of independence in anthropology with its claim to be a separate province in the mind. The concept of God was now a product of religion ..."[105] Yet Pannenberg does not follow Schleiermacher in his approach to religion, noting that the main limitation of his position is that "he studies religion or piety only as an organisation of subjective experience, not as the self-manifestation of divine reality" - which for Pannenberg is precisely the main focus in the study of religions.[106]

The view of non-Christian religions which arose among liberal theology, contrary to what one might expect, was often more colored by the European imperialism of the time than by the concepts of the fatherhood of God and the brotherhood of man. This is especially to be seen in one of the last of the great liberal theologians of the last century, Adolf von Harnack. In his famous rectoral address at the University of Berlin in 1901 Harnack argued against the establishment of chairs for the study of world religions (*Religionswissenschaft*) fearing that the theological faculties would be thereby transformed into faculties for the study of religion in general.[107] In the process he argued that the study of one religion alone, namely the Christian religion, was sufficient to understand all

---

[103] Cf. *ibid.*, 34ff., and esp. 38ff.
[104] *Über die Religionen*, 188ff.
[105] *ST* 1:125f. [140.]
[106] *TPS*, 371. [*WtT*, 374.] An additional problem with Schleiermacher's view has been pointed out by Paul Tillich, *A History of Christian Thought*, ed. Carl Braaten (New York: Simon & Schuster, 1967), 402, who writes that Schleiermacher "subjects Christianity to a concept of religion which at least by intent was not derived from Christianity but from the whole panorama of the world's religions." Additionally, Friedrich Heiler, *Erscheinungsformen und Wesen der Religion* [1961], 2ed. (Stuttgart: Kohlhammer, 1979), 13, has contended that the main weaknesses of Schleiermacher's position are: "Eine Neigung zum Immanentismus und Psychologismus wie zur ästhetischen Betrachtung des Religiösen."
[107] Harnack, *Die Aufgabe der theologischen Facultäten*, 16.

others. In this manner Harnack never seriously dealt with other religions as such. Proclaimed Harnack: "Whoever knows this religion, including its history, knows all religions." Similarly, Harnack, in whose comments an unmistakable Christian chauvinism is to be recognized, asked rhetorically: "What meaning does Homer, the Vedas, the Koran have alongside of the Bible?"[108] Indeed, for Harnack, as we saw in chapter one, the question of the study of non-Christian religions was fast becoming a moot-point, since Christianity, following in the wave of European colonialization, was replacing systematically the other religions. For Pannenberg the critical weakness of Harnack's argument was that it "presupposed not only a claim for the absoluteness of Christianity in advance of any discussion, but in addition the claim that Christianity possessed a monopoly of political validity. It is this latter claim which shows how far Harnack was from regarding the absoluteness of Christianity as something requiring examination within a framework of investigation into the history of religions." The need for theology today, however, Pannenberg is convinced, is to engage in dialogue with other religions, "which is impossible if the premise that the Christian religion possesses sole validity is declared in advance to be not open to discussion."[109]

Harnack's voice was not the only one coming out of liberal theology at the turn of the century, however. Another view of non-Christian religions, and one which Pannenberg found greatly preferable to Harnack's, was that of Ernst Troeltsch. Like Harnack Troeltsch was also a student of Ritschl, but his wrestling with the problem of the absoluteness of Christianity led him in a different direction than Harnack.[110] Just a year after Harnack's rectoral address, Troeltsch proclaimed the superiority of Christianity over the other world religions an open question.[111] In the preface to the first edition of his 1902 book, *The Absoluteness of Christianity and the History of Religions*, Troeltsch made clear the difference between his own view and that of Harnack when he wrote:

> The scholars who belong to theological faculties are by nature committed to some definite point of view that has to be acquired before they begin their educational work. However, the process of thought that leads to this point of view and the theological theories that develop it are not thus bound. Such thought must ... begin by treating this viewpoint as something that is hypothetically to be called into question. On the basis of general considerations, it infers as result that which was once seriously doubted and which was first permanently

---

[108] *Ibid.*, 11. Indeed, for all areas in which other disciplines would have an interdisciplinary interest in religion, Harnack contends that the Christian religion and its history provides more than enough material so that one would hardly have time or need to turn to the other religions. (p. 14).

[109] *TPS*, 360f. [*WtT*, 362f.]

[110] So Rosenkranz, 177.

[111] Indeed, Troeltsch had already said as much in his October 1901 lecture, "Die Absolutheit des Christentums und die Religionsgeschichte," which itself was a topic assigned to him and "bezieht sich bereits auf die durch eine Reihe vorhergehender Veröffentlichungen von Troeltsch ausgelöste Debatte." So Trutz Rendtorff, *Theologie in der Moderne: Über Religion im Prozeß der Aufklärung*, vol. 5 in the series: *Troeltsch-Studien* (Gütersloh: Gerd Mohn, 1991), 73.

adopted because of comprehensive reflections based on principle. ... All this relates, however, only to the basic question of the normative validity of Christianity. Questions of a more specific nature are ... not disposed of at so basic a level but must remain open problems for the work of a theological faculty.[112]

For Troeltsch, in contrast to Harnack, theology could not survive as an academic discipline unless it broadened its base to include the study of religion and religions. "Hence theology is dependent upon the philosophy of religion. Only on the basis of this discipline will theology be able to construct the essence and meaning of Christianity in such a way that the modern spirit of a freedom from presuppositions will be satisfied."[113] Hence Troeltsch, in reference to the formulation of a theological theory of the place of Christianity among the world religions, writes that "such a theory must, in my opinion, go into the general history of religion more thoroughly than Harnack appears inclined to allow."[114] For Troeltsch, therefore, the question of the absoluteness of Christianity could not be maintained as presupposition and the study of the general history of religions consequently bypassed as no longer being of any particular relevance - all vital questions in regard to the place of Christianity already having been settled. Troeltsch's conclusion, then, was that "it is impossible to construct a theory of Christianity as the absolute religion on the basis of a historical way of thinking or by the use of historical means. Much that looks weak, shadowy, and unstable in the theology of our day is rooted in the impossibility of putting such a construction on Christianity."[115] Yet although Troeltsch was unwilling to proclaim Christianity the absolute religion he was nonetheless, like Harnack, convinced of its superiority to other religions. Troeltsch confessed:

> Christianity remains *the* great revelation of God to men, though the other religions, with all the power they possess for lifting men above guilt, grief, and earthly life, are likewise revelations of God, and though no theory can rule out the abstract possibility of further revelations. Christianity remains *the* deliverance, even though the power over the natural man and his cravings which is at work in every religion is also genuine deliverance. ... Above all, Christianity remains the work of Jesus, ... even though we discern the power and activity of God in other heroes and prophets of religion, it is in Christianity, more profoundly than anywhere else, that faith in God is bound up with the vision of the life and passion of him who reveals and guarantees that faith.

Hence, in Troeltsch's view, the Christian,

---

[112] Ernst Troeltsch, *The Absoluteness of Christianity and the History of Religions* [1902], tr. David Reid (London: SCM Press, 1972), 27.
[113] Troeltsch, "Voraussetzungslose Wissenschaft," [1897] in: *Gesammelte Schriften*, vol. 2, 192.
[114] *The Absoluteness of Christianity*, 27.
[115] *Ibid.*, 63.

need not be alarmed if he discovers elements related to Christianity in Buddhism or Zoroastrianism; if he finds in Plato, Epictetus, or Plotinus religious ideas and powers that are actually or apparently parallels and anticipations of Christianity. God is alive and manifest in them, too. ... The religious man need not shrink back if he finds Christianity living on earlier religious developments that form part of its present environment .... These too are all, in their own right, living religious movements in which God is at work, and Christianity has been nourished by all these elements that it encounters and to which it is related. Indeed, it has become Christianity's distinctive task to make itself the crystallization point for the highest and best that has been discovered in the human spiritual world, its fitness for this task of attracting and sustaining such values being due to its superior power.[116]

Troeltsch's view of Christianity as the highest stage of development among all the various expressions of religion, as well as his general theory of religions, is nowhere more clearly or succinctly expressed than in the opening paragraphs of his *Glaubenslehre*, based upon lectures given in 1911 and 1912. He wrote:

... Christianity is the final, comprehensive breakthrough ... toward the formation of a religion of redemption that is in principle universal, ethical, pure spiritual, and personality developing. Inasmuch as this religion includes the deepest and most comprehensive, and at the same time the most inner and personal communion with God *in Christo* that most strongly overcomes suffering and sin, it is the highest revelation. As such it has incorporated the highest developments of classical societies into itself.[117]

Although Pannenberg could not follow Troeltsch's psychological, anthropological centered conception of religion nor his conception of history,[118] Troeltsch's conviction that the question of Christianity's absoluteness must not become a presupposition no longer open to discussion, his argument that theology needs a broader base in the study of religions, and his willingness to see God's

---

[116] *Ibid.*, 126f.
[117] Troeltsch, *Glaubenslehre, nach Heidelberger Vorlesungen aus den Jahren 1911 und 1912*, [1925] ed. Gertrud von le Fort (Aalen: Scientia Verlag, 1981), 1f.
[118] The distinction between Troeltsch and Pannenberg on this crucial point is especially clear in Troeltsch's lecture, "The Place of Christianity among the World Religions," written for delivery at the University of Oxford in 1923, albeit Troeltsch died before it could be delivered. Summarizing the position he took in *The Absoluteness of Christianity* he wrote: "History cannot be regarded as a process in which a universal and everywhere similar principle is confined and obscured. ... [Rather,] the universal law of history consists precisely in this, that the Divine Reason, or the Divine Life, within history, constantly manifests itself in always-new and always-peculiar individualizations - and hence that its tendency is not towards unity or universality at all, but rather towards the fulfilment of the highest potentialities of each separate department of life. It is this law which, beyond all else, makes it impossible to characterize Christianity as the reconciliation and goal of all the forces of history, or indeed to regard it as anything else than a historical individuality." Troeltsch, "The Place of Christianity among the World Religions" [1923], in: John Hick and Brian Hebblethwaite, eds., *Christianity and Other Religions: Selected Readings* (Philadelphia: Fortress Press, 1980), 17.

presence in other religious traditions, all anticipate, as we shall see, many important elements in Pannenberg's own theology of religions. Indeed Pannenberg, who saw the primary issue at stake between Harnack and Troeltsch as being whether theology could be restricted to Christianity alone and still be a positive science or whether it needed a broader base in the study of comparative religion, sided clearly with Troeltsch, recognizing a certain affinity with his own thought. For Pannenberg, theology's claim to universality does not imply an imperialistic claim that the other religions have nothing to say and are not worth studying or that the superiority of Christianity is or ever can be a closed question. Hence Pannenberg writes: "No basic objections can be made against the fact that theology within the Christian tradition concentrates on a theology of Christianity, provided that the assumption of the superiority of the Christian revelation to other religious traditions remains in principle open to discussion and is not isolated from criticism."[119]

### 5.2.1.2 Dialectical theology and religion (Barth)

Karl Barth, drawing the consequences from his newfound emphasis on revelation, broke away from the relativizing tendency of liberal theology in regard to religions and their truth claims.[120] Rather than classify Christianity within the field of world religions as the highest or true religion Barth launched a vehement attack against religion in general, which he saw as human effort, and sought to remove from Christianity the stigma of 'religion' by contending that it was not a religion since it is based upon the word and actions of God and not humans, that is to say, Christianity is not a human religion but the witness to God's revelation. The opposition that exists between religion and revelation in Barth's thought comes to clear expression when he contends that "revelation does not link up with a human religion which is already present and practised. It contradicts it, just as religion previously contradicted revelation. It displaces it, just as religion previously displaced revelation; just as faith cannot link up with a mistaken faith, but must contradict and displace it as unbelief, as an act of contradiction."[121]

For Barth, therefore, "the real catastrophe of modern Protestant theology," and he understood thereby liberal Protestant theology,[122] was that it had "lost its

---

[119] *TPS*, 323. [*WtT*, 326.]

[120] As Pannenberg, *TPS*, 317f. [*WtT*, 320f.], explains, both Harnack and Troeltsch assumed Christianity's status as a religion. This assumption was attacked by Barth "on the ground that the matter of theology was not human religion but God's revelation. In Karl Barth's eyes, 'the attempt to reconstitute theology as the "science of religion"' was 'a disloyal act which provokes revulsion and wrath.'" Hence "Barth's charge against neo-Protestantism was that it had reversed the relation between religion and revelation."

[121] Cf. Barth, *CD* I.2, 303.

[122] Heiler, *Erscheinungsformen und Wesen der Religion*, 4ff., interprets the Barthian protest against religion not so much as a reaction against liberal theology as an extreme reaction against the modern science of religion (*Religionswissenschaft*). Michael von Brück, *Möglichkeiten und Grenzen einer Theologie der Religionen* (Berlin: Evangelische Verlagsanstalt, 1979), 27, on the

object, revelation in all its uniqueness. And losing that, it lost the seed of faith with which it could remove mountains, even the mountain of modern humanistic culture. That it really lost revelation is shown by the very fact that it could exchange it, and with it its own birthright, for the concept of 'religion.'"[123] In what George Augustin has characterized as an apologetic attempt to rescue Christianity[124] Barth maintained dogmatically that "religion is unbelief. It is a concern, indeed, we must say that it is the one great concern, of godless man." For Barth, the fact that religion is something produced by humans, particularly humans without God, is the judgment of revelation against all religion and religions.[125]

Yet Barth also seems to hold his conception of religion in dialectical tension, distinguishing between religion as unbelief and true religion.[126] He can state, for instance, that religion stands not only in opposition to revelation but it is also the unavoidable 'human face' of revelation. Hence Barth, while opposing divine revelation and human religion to one another, does not wish to deny the fact that there is a human element of revelation since revelation presupposes an encounter between God and humanity. He writes: "If we are going to know and acknowledge the revelation of God as revelation, then there is this general human element which we cannot avoid or call by any other name." This, in turn, implies that "God's revelation has to be regarded as a religion among other religions ... [if] the Church and faith are able and willing to take themselves, or their basis, seriously." To deny, therefore, that revelation is also in some sense "man's religion, and therefore ... a religion among other religions ... would be to deny the human aspect of revelation, and this would be to deny revelation as such."[127] Indeed Barth even contended, with specific reference to Christianity, that "the abolishing of religion by revelation need not mean only its negation: the judgment that religion is unbelief. Religion can just as well be exalted in revelation, even though the judgment still stands. It can be upheld by it and concealed in it. It can be justified by it, and - we must at once add - sanctified. Revelation can adopt religion and mark it off as true religion."[128]

---

[123] other hand, has stressed in his interpretation of Barth's critique of religion, "daß es Barth nie und nirgends um eine phänomenologische oder religionsgeschichtliche Bestimmung der Religion geht. Er steht immer in konkreter Auseinandersetzung mit dem Protestantismus seiner Zeit, der seine Wurzeln weitgehend in der Theologie Schleiermachers hat."
Barth, *CD* I.2, 294. And vice versa, revelation becomes a threat (or crisis) for human religion since its origin is in the divine. As Schwarz, *The Search for God*, 31f., observes, "according to Barth the real crisis of religion is revelation, since there the whole religious process is reversed. God comes down to man and man no longer ventures to come to terms with God on his own."

[124] Augustin, 38.

[125] Barth, *CD* I.2, 299f. The proposition that religion is unbelief, contends Barth, "is not in any sense a negative value-judgment ... [but] the judgment of divine revelation upon all religion."

[126] Cf. *CD* I.2, 325ff. For a detailed study of Barth's positive statements about religion see Michael von Brück, *Möglichkeiten und Grenzen einer Theologie der Religionen*, 45ff.

[127] *CD* I.2, 281, 283f.

[128] *Ibid.*, 326.

Also, Barth considers religions as "constants of human existence and history," which, however deformed and confused, must still be understood as part of God's good creation.[129] It is even possible for Barth to recognize that the religions of the world are genuinely seeking God who is unknown to them. Each religion, according to Barth, is indeed a work of the world - but it is also "a work with which the world tries to deal with ... God ... in a much more thoughtful and reflective way than by trying to deny him." The rise of religions, therefore,

> may be traced to the fact that the world objectively finds itself confronted with the true and living God and adapts itself positively to its inability to escape his self-declaration, in which, of course, it does not know him. It meets this God who makes himself known by attempting in its own way to make itself acquainted with him, that is, by doing justice to him who is his own 'datum.' ... The various religions are the various attempts of the world to make something out of the presence and revelation of God which is known to it but not recognized by it.[130]

True religion in Barth's perspective, therefore, as von Brück has pointed out, "points toward God; the point of religion is to say to the human being that the reality in which he or she lives is a condition of forlornness. Then the unbroken relationship with God which religion, also when negatively, still points to, will be comprehended as that which has been lost. Religion points humans thereby to their own essence which can only be restored in Redemption."[131] And although he identifies Christianity exclusively as the "true religion"[132] he also seems to leave open the possibility that the religions of the world, even as human efforts, can be said to witness to the reality of God without knowing it, that is, in an implicit way. These elements in Barth's view of religion, therefore, would seem to suggest a reexamination of his harsh criticism of religion.[133]

---

[129] CD IV.3.2, 743. Even here, however, Barth wants to maintain the distinction between Christianity and other religions since Christianity is not of this world and the people of God does not have its origin in creation but in the election of Jesus Christ.

[130] CD IV.4, Lecture Fragments, 129f.

[131] Michael von Brück, Möglichkeiten und Grenzen einer Theologie der Religionen, 47.

[132] CD I.2, 326. Barth writes: "There is a true religion: just as there are justified sinners. If we abide by that analogy - and we are dealing not merely with an analogy, but in a comprehensive sense with the thing itself - we need have no hesitation in saying that the Christian religion is the true religion." Here again, then, we note the dialectical tension in Barth's thought in which Christianity is said not to be a religion - in the sense that religion is understood to be unbelief, but inasmuch as there can be a true religion, then that true religion is Christianity.

[133] One such alternate reading of Barth's judgment on religion which takes this dialectic into account, it would seem, is to be found in von Brück, Möglichkeiten und Grenzen, 27f. A 'defence' of Barth's position is possible, he suggests, if we understand religion from Barth's perspective and recognize that his attack upon religion as 'unbelief' is directed primarily against Christianity itself. Hence von Brück, coming from the perspective of the science of religions, is able to suggest that the essence of Barth's critique need not be understood as a judgment against the individual, living religions as such. Von Brück, however, recognizes that this is not the only possible interpretation of Barth, and that a determinative judgment on Barth's concept of religion is difficult owing to the fact that Barth's comments on religion are often vague and seemingly contradictory. (p. 61).

Yet it is precisely Barth's apparent rejection of religion, however, which seems to be the domininant theme in his treatment of religion. It is also the aspect of his thought on religion that most interpreters have focused upon or reacted to, including Pannenberg. We turn our attention, therefore, once again to this aspect of his thought. The criticism has been raised that by attacking religion in general the risk is run that in the end one would not be able to 'exonerate' Christianity from the charge of also being a religion and the rhetoric of the dialectical theologians would be turned against Christianity itself.[134]

Barth's approach also had the effect, that by taking theology outside the realm of religion, it isolated theology from the dialogue with the world religions and from all academic studies of comparative religion.[135] Hence not only did Barth not consider theology a science on the level with the other sciences, so that they might potentially enter into dialogue with one another, but Christianity was not a religion either, so there was very little to be gained from inter-religious dialogue.[136] Apologetically, in Barth's attempt to 'rescue' Christianity, he had built an impenetrable fortress around it that stifled virtually all opportunity for fruitful dialogue and effective apologetics. As Pannenberg has observed: "Theological claims that Christianity is not a religion but rather the 'annulment' and 'overcoming' of the religions ... are unable to pull Christianity out of the reach of general critiques of religion. And in relation to the non-Christian religions, such sovereign gestures already give decisive indication of a controversy that is to be carried on precisely by theology itself, namely, the controversy about the true faith."[137]

It would be a mistake, however, to assume that Pannenberg rejects Barth's insights regarding religion completely, for he finds his emphasis on the importance of God over religion and religions to be correct. Hence he writes that it is understandable that "Barth should passionately protest in opposition to this whole

---

[134] Cf. also Pannenberg, "Reden von Gott angesichts atheistischer Kritik," in: *Gottesgedanke und menschlicher Freiheit*, 30f., and Augustin, 39.

[135] Cf. Knitter, "What is German Protestant Theology Saying About the Non-Christian?" 39, who writes that Barth's "critique of religions as basically opposed to revelation ... casts a very suspicious shadow over all religious phenomena." And, although this condemnation of religion is directed primarily to the understanding of Christianity as a religion, "when such a concept is part of a study of the 'other religions' it obstructs any real encounter with them and colors them as, essentially, irrelevant for theology."

[136] For Barth, *CD* I.2, 356f., the absoluteness of Christianity is assumed from the very beginning and the only thing Christianity has to say to the other religions or their adherents is the proclamation of its own truth and absoluteness.

[137] Pannenberg, "Toward a Theology of the History of Religions," in: *BQ* 2:67, note 4. ["Erwägungen zu einer Theologie der Religionsgeschichte," in: *Grundfragen*, 253, note 5] Rahner, like Pannenberg, is unable to accept Barth's conception of religion. He writes: "The history of religion, even outside explicit, verbalized, and institutionalized Christianity ... is not merely the vain attempt of *man* with the aid of his natural transcendentality to establish from below a relationship to God, but is also always and everywhere from the outset a history of revelation and salvation coming from above, even though this history of grace is *really* history: that is, a slowly increasing articulation of this grace in man's consciousness which can take on a variety of forms and even be terribly debased." (Rahner, "Foundations of Christian Faith," 9f.)

procedure [prevalent in the modern study of religions] that in methodologically subjecting the reality of God to the reality of religion it abandons the reality of God beyond repair." The self-understanding not only of the Christian faith but of all other religions as well, agrees Pannenberg, "begins with the primacy of divine reality and its self-declaration over all human worship of God."[138] Braaten, noting as well Pannenberg's indebtedness to Schleiermacher, concludes rightly that Pannenberg "unites the thesis of Schleiermacher that religion is an essential dimension of human life with the antithesis of Barth that upholds the primacy of God over against all religion, in a synthesis in which the primacy of the reality of God appears in the medium of religious experience as its fundamental orientation." Hence, in Braaten's judgment, Pannenberg's quarrel with Barth on this point "has less to do with dogmatic content than with method of procedure."[139] Although there is certainly much to consider in this observation one must finally ask, however, especially in the disagreement between Barth and Pannenberg, whether method can ultimately be separated from content.

### 5.2.1.3 *Attempt to overcome impasse of liberal and dialectical theology (Tillich)*

In the swirl and confusion of approaches to other religions among modern Protestant thought no thinker has drawn Pannenberg's attention and formed the immediate background for the formation of his own position more than Paul Tillich. It is to his contribution to the development of a theology of religions that we now turn our attention.

Paul Tillich, in wrestling with the problem of Christianity among the world's religions, could not accept what he found in liberal theologians from Schleiermacher to Harnack, who made Christianity the highest or absolute religion, nor what he found in Barth's rejection of non-Christian religions as human religions in contrast to Christianity as revealed 'religion.'[140] In distinction to Barth, Tillich did not place religion and revelation in opposition to one another but contended that humans experience revelation and the name we give to this experience of revelation is simply religion. Barth and those who follow him, according to Tillich, "forget that revelation must be received and that the name for the reception of revelation is 'religion.'" Tillich explains: "Revelation is never

---

[138] *ST* 1:127. [141.]
[139] Braaten, 299.
[140] Tillich, *A History of Christian Thought*, 404. The early Tillich, however, was much closer to Barth's view, developing a line of thought parallel to that of Barthian dialectical theology in which religion was seen as a human product which sought to emower and thereby falsify the "Unbedingten." Before the revelation of the "Unbedingten," i.e., of God, all religion was seen to be nothing. This is especially clear in his 1922 article, "Die Überwindung des Religionsbegriffs in der Religionsphilosophie," in: *Gesammelte Werke*, vol. 1 (Stuttgart: Evang. Verlagswerk, 1959), 388. He wrote: the philosophy of religion can only realize its true nature when it recognizes, "daß nicht die Religion der Anfang und das Ende und die Mitte in allem ist, sondern Gott, und daß jede Religion und jede Religionsphilosophie Gott verlieren, wenn sie nicht auf den Boden des Wortes stehen: Impossible est, sine deo discere. Gott wird nur erkannt aus Gott."

revelation in general, however universal its claim may be. It is always revelation for someone and for a group in a definite environment, under unique circumstances. Therefore, he who receives revelation witnesses to it in terms of his individuality and in terms of the social and spiritual conditions in which the revelation has been manifested to him. In other words, he does it in terms of his religion." Hence, "he who gives an account of divine revelation simultaneously gives an account of his own religion."[141]

If Christianity denies that it is a religion then it ultimately denies its own revelatory experience. As Tillich elsewhere contended: "If Christianity rejects the idea that it is a religion, it must fight in itself everything by which it becomes a religion. ... If Christianity fights against itself as a religion it must fight against myth and cult, and this it has done. ... But the forces ... fighting to preserve Christianity as a religion were ultimately stronger, in defense and counterattack. The main argument used in the counterattacks is the observation that the loss of cult and myth is the loss of the revelatory experience on which every religion is based."[142] Yet at the same time Tillich was also able to contend that "if Christianity denies itself as a religion" it may be able to understand secularism in a new and more positive way; and that no religion, including Christianity, will be lasting unless it negates itself as a religion.[143] Yet it would be a mistake to interpret this as a rejection of religion in a Barthian sense,[144] for Tillich, by speaking of Christianity or any other religion denying itself as a religion is referring not to a choice between divine revelation and human ritual or effort but to a religion's breaking through its own particularity.[145] The implication of this view for the study of other religions, according to Pannenberg, is that,

> it is impossible to look at divine revelation in advance on its own, in some way before all human religion, and compare it with religion. It follows that religious traditions, with the variety of their assertions about divine reality and divine activity, must first be allowed to appear as religions and therefore as an

---

[141] So Tillich, "Biblical Religion and the Search for Ultimate Reality," in: Paul Tillich, *Main Works/Hauptwerke*, ed. Carl Heinz Ratschow, vol. 4 (Berlin: De Gruyter, 1987), 358f. Cf. also Tillich, "The Significance of the History of Religions for the Systematic Theologian," in: Tillich, *Main Works/Hauptwerke*, vol. 6, (1992), 432f. where he writes: "Revelatory experiences are universally human. Religions are based on something that is given to a man wherever he lives. He is given a revelation, a particular kind of experience which always implies saving powers. One never can separate revelation and salvation. There are revealing and saving powers in all religions. God has not left himself unwitnessed."

[142] Tillich, "Christianity and the Encounter of the World Religions," in: Paul Tillich, *Main Works/Hauptwerke*, vol. 5 (1988), 322f.

[143] *Ibid.*, 324f.

[144] So similarly James Adams, *Paul Tillich's Philosophy of Culture, Science, and Religion* (Washington, D.C.: University of America Press), 1982, 185f.

[145] "Christianity and the Encounter of the World Religions," 325.

expression of human experience and its processing. Only then can they be tested for reliability and truth.[146]

In Tillich's last public lecture he choose to break new ground and challenge concepts that he and others had long held.[147] In his lecture, titled "The Significance of the History of Religions for Systematic Theology," Tillich noted that in taking up this topic with seriousness he has already, at least implicitly, made two fundamental decisions. In the first place, he has separated himself from a theology which rejects all religions with the exception of his own. And second, he has rejected "the paradox of a religion of non-religion or theology without theos, also called a theology of the secular."[148] That is to say, Tillich is calling for a theology of religion that not only rejects the tradition of Christian exclusivism of theology but also the secular attitude of skepticism and rejection of religion in general. Hence, as Tillich explained: "We have to break through two barriers against a free approach to the history of religions: the orthodox-exclusive one and the secular-rejective one. The mere term 'religion' still produces a flood of problems for the systematic theologian, and this is increased by the fact that the two fronts of resistance, though coming from opposite sides, involve an alliance."[149] What is needed, according to Tillich, is a theology of the history of religions which, in its positive evaluation of universal revelation, must hold both of these tendencies in tension for both have something necessary to offer. Such a "theology of the history of religions can help systematic theologians to understand the present moment and the nature of our own historical place, both in the particular character of Christianity and in its universal claim."[150]

Tillich thus sought to find a middle way between various extremes in contemporary Protestant approaches to a theology of religion. He wanted to steer a course between the exclusivity of the Barthian rejection of religion and the radical secularity of the death of God theologians. In his own approach he was open to other religions and their truth claims but rejected syncretistic attempts to bring these together. And while he was open to the "possibility" of the Christ event having universal significance, he did not advocate the triumph of the Christian faith over non-Christian religions. As Tillich wrote:

> Does our analysis demand either a mixture of religions or the victory of one religion, or the end of the religious age altogether? We answer: None of these alternatives! A mixture of religions destroys in each of them the concreteness

---

[146] *TPS*, 319. [*WtT*, 321f.]
[147] As George Augustin, 40, explains; "kurz vor seinem Tode erkannte ... [Tillich] die Bedeutung der Religionsgeschichte für die Systematische Theologie an und eröffnete damit den Horizont einer neuen Theologie der Religionen. So forderte er bei seinem letzten öffentlichen Vortrag eine neue Hinwendung der christlichen Theologie zur Religionsgeschichte und deren positive Bewertung."
[148] Tillich, "The Significance of the History of Religions for the Systematic Theologian," 432.
[149] *Ibid.*, 434.
[150] *Ibid.*, 435.

which gives it its dynamic power. The victory of *one* religion would impose a particular religious answer on all other particular answers. The end of the religious age ... is an impossible concept. The religious principle cannot come to an end. For the question of the ultimate meaning of life cannot be silenced as long as men are men.[151]

If Tillich's analysis, however, does not suggest one of these approaches where, then, does it lead? For Tillich the present encounter of the world religions shows Christianity that "it will be a better bearer of the religious answer as long as it breaks through its own particularity." It achieves this, however, not by abandoning its own tradition for some universal concept but by penetrating the depth of its own religion through devotion, thought and action since, "in the depth of every living religion there is a point at which the religion itself loses its importance, and that to which it points breaks through its particularity, elevating it to spiritual freedom and ... to a vision of the spiritual presence in other expressions in the ultimate meaning of man's existence."[152]

Although Pannenberg, as we shall see, had a great appreciation for Tillich's contribution and indeed found much useful within it, he regarded it ultimately as deficient. As Braaten notes: "Pannenberg finds Tillich's approach deficient on two counts. First, it falls short of being a *theology* of the history of religions, focusing more on the human response than on the divine reality to which religious experience is directed. Second, it neglects the dimension of history, and thus can hardly do justice to the function of Christianity within the world of the religions."[153]

### 5.2.2 Toward a theology of the history of religions

#### 5.2.2.1 *The anthropological starting point of a theology of religion*
In common with Rahner Pannenberg shares an anthropological foundation for his theology of religion.[154] Pannenberg thus contends that "the study of religion presupposes as its basis a general anthropology to provide a frame of reference for all discussions about the status of religious concepts in the weft of the human world, and in particular for meeting the arguments of modern atheism."[155] For Pannenberg the turn toward anthropology in philosophy has significance, as we have already seen, for human reflection about the divine.

---

[151] "Christianity and the Encounter of the World Religions," 324f.
[152] *Ibid.*, 325.
[153] Braaten, 295.
[154] As Pannenberg notes, he accords intentionally "fundamental theological rank to anthropology as the basis of a theology of religion" (*ST* 1:157f., note 111, [173f., note 120.]). And also, he contends that a philosophy of religion which is able to construct a general concept of religion and introduce within this context the idea of God as all-determining reality "would require a general anthropology as a basis" (*TPS*, 367f. [*WtT*, 370f.])
[155] *TPS*, 422. [*WtT*, 424.]

Hence, the turn to anthropology in philosophy finds its counterpart in theology in which "the development of theology's self-understanding can ... be regarded as an independent, and originally much more far-reaching, counterpart to the development of an anthropocentric concept of God in post-Renaissance philosophical theology."[156] And because theology itself, as we shall see, has its foundations in the study of comparative religion, a philosophy or theology of religion itself takes its starting point with anthropology. For Rahner this was clear since a metaphysical anthropology based upon the fact of human transcendence was the presupposition of a philosophy of religion which has to do ultimately with the transcendental human person's asking the question about God.

For Pannenberg, similarly, inasmuch as religion is humanity's asking the question about God, a theology of religion must take as its starting point the anthropological context of the world-openness which leads to the openness toward God. And a philosophy or theology of religion so founded upon anthropology is of vital significance for the truth claims of Christian theology. According to Pannenberg, without "a public consciousness of the constitutive and essential meaning of the theme of religion for being human, the specific Christian statements about humans remain restricted to a cultural obscurity and can thank the number of Christianity's followers for their influence, but not the wieght of their truth claims."[157] Or, as Pannenberg has elsewhere maintained, if religious assertions are to be able to claim universal relevance they must have a foundation, or starting point, which demonstrates their relationship to the rest of human experience.

Pannenberg suggests that anthropology alone could be able to provide this foundation if it could be shown that the idea of God, or at least of a mysterious ground of being, is implied in the movement of human existence beyond all that is finite and that persons find themselves referred to this transcendent mystery. Yet this does not go deep enough for it deals only with the structure of human existence, leaving the question about the independent existence of the reality of God or divine powers unaddressed. Pannenberg suggests that the abstractness of statements about the anthropological structures must be overcome in order to ground the claim to universal relevance of religious statements anthropologically. When we do this we can contend that, "if it belongs to the structure of human existence to presuppose a mystery of reality transcending its finitude and to relate oneself to this as the fulfillment of one's own being, then in actuality man always exists in association with this reality."[158] Hence the conclusion of the matter, as Pannenberg explains, is that the reality of religious experiences cannot "be decided yet on the basis of the formal structure of human existence, but rather only in men's association with the transcendent mystery that is always

---

[156] *Ibid.*, 308. [310.]
[157] *Anthropologie in theologischer Perspektive*, 8. [From the forward to the German edition, not included in the English translation.]
[158] "Toward a Theology of the History of Religions," 102f. [*Grundfragen*, 282f.]

presupposed in the structure of human existence and which proves in the actual course of life whether it is sustaining or not, ... reality or nonentity."[159]

Pannenberg further believes to have found empirical indication that religion is indeed a constitutive part of our human nature in "its universal occurrence from the very beginnings of humanity, and especially its basic importance for all cultures and probably also for the origin of speech."[160] In Pannenberg's 1986 article, "Religion und menschliche Natur," he explores more fully the empirical evidence for the inherent religiosity of human beings. For Pannenberg it is clear that religion belongs to the characteristics of humans that separate them from animals just as much as speech and the use of tools.[161] Pannenberg suggests three specific findings from the realm of cultural anthropology which support his claim that the religiosity of humans is empirically demonstrable. First is the antiquity of the practice of the burial of the dead which is an indication of some sort of belief in a life beyond death. Pannenberg points out that in modern anthropology the practice of the burial of the dead has been seen as a criterion for determining the end of the transition phase of animal to human and thus also for the determination of the beginning of humanity. This means, according to Pannenberg, "that from the very beginning religion belonged to humans as a decisive criterion for the distinction of the human from the prehuman."[162]

As a second evidence Pannenberg mentions the religious foundation of all ancient cultures, which is generally undisputed within the field of cultural anthropology. And third, and what Pannenberg holds to be the most controversial evidence, is the origin of language, in which some researchers believe religion played a decisive role.[163] Additionally to be noted in this regard is Pannenberg's argument, which he has elsewhere brought forward, that the failure of modern secular cultures to repress their dependence upon religion as well as the universal presence of religious themes corresponds "to the feature of human behavior that is described as openness to the world, ec-centricity, or self-transcendence."[164]

Moving away from Pannenberg's attempt to empirically demonstrate that religion belongs to the essence and structure of human nature we look now at his grounding of religious statements. In Pannenberg the validity of religious statements finds its grounding in a fashion similar to Rahner's approach. In

---

[159] *Ibid.*, 110. [289.]
[160] *ST* 1:155. [171.]
[161] Pannenberg, "Religion und menschliche Natur," in: *Sind wir von Natur aus religiös?*, ed. W. Pannenberg, et al., 9. Cf. also Pannenberg, "Macht der Mensch die Religion oder macht die Religion den Menschen?" in: *Religion als Problem der Aufklärung: Eine Bilanz aus der religionstheoretischen Forschung*, ed. Trutz Rendtorff (Göttingen: Vandenhoeck & Ruprecht, 1980), 153.
[162] *Ibid.*, 12. Pannenberg bases his arguments especially upon the work of Karl J. Narr, "Beiträge der Urgeschichte zur Kenntnis der Menschennatur," in: Hans-Georg Gadamer and P. Vogler, eds., *Kulturanthropologie*, vol. 4 (Munich, 1973): 3-62.
[163] Cf. *ibid.*, 12ff.
[164] *ST* 1:155. [171.]

language reminiscent of Rahner's argument of transcendence from creaturliness Pannenberg contends that; "if the one God is to be the Creator of the human race, then as self-conscious beings we must have some awareness, however inadequate, of this origin of ours. Our human existence necessarily bears the mark of creaturehood, and this cannot be totally hidden from our awareness of ourselves."[165] Yet Pannenberg wishes also at the same time to distinguish his anthropological grounding of religious statements from that found in Rahner's *Hearers of the Word*, contending that he goes beyond Rahner's statements according to which the human person is always a potential hearer of a possible word or revelation of God in a decisive way since Rahner's analysis of the anthropological structures focuses only on the one true Christian revelation[166] and does not set human religious experience within the proper context of the process of history - which as we will see in the following section is decisive for Pannenberg's development of a theology of the history of religions.[167]

At stake ultimately for Pannenberg in the anthropological grounding of religious experience and statements are the truth claims of Christianity itself in the context of modern, Western society. "If religion is not a constitutive human theme ... then the Christian assertion of divine reality has lost the basis of its plausibility." Hence, whether we like it or not, within the context of modern Western culture, "anthropology has become the basis of certainty about the reality of God."[168] This does not, however, mean that humanity, rather than God becomes the focus of religion or that religion can be reduced to anthropology.[169] Rather, the anthropological starting point for a theology of religions presupposes the universality of God as creator of all things. Precisely because God has created all things his creatures respond inevitably to his reality through religion. Hence religion, for Pannenberg, is understood as "the primary form of perceiving the reality of God," and, as such, "the issue of religion also belongs to anthropology." As Pannenberg further explains, "this is in itself a witness to the reality of God, the creator of everything; to argue that the human being is by nature the religious

---

[165] *Ibid.*, 157. [173.]

[166] In this connection Pannenberg has also suggested that Rahner's theology of religions falls short of the goal of a *critical* theology of religions inasmuch as it does not approach other religions with open criticalness but is more a dogmatic theology of religions that produces an interpretation of religions on the basis of a previous religious position. (So Pannenberg, *TPS*, 365, [*WtT*, 368.])

[167] "Toward a Theology of the History of Religions," 103, note 51. [*Grundfragen*, 283, note 47.] Pannenberg explains: "Since Rahner ... projects his analysis of anthropological structures only toward the occurrence of the one Christian revelation in its true form, conceiving this not within the context of a historical process but rather as something that is supposed to 'intersect human history in its spatio-temporal extension in a pointlike manner', the history of men's actual associations with this mystery ... is always passed over, so that the revelation envisaged as something pointlike always retains the appearance of something extraordinary and without continuity with the process of history."

[168] *ST* 1:157. [173.]

[169] While Pannenberg argues for an anthropological starting point for a theology of religions it must be noted that he rejects modern attempts to reduce religion to anthropology. So Braaten, 300.

animal is certainly not enough to demonstrate the reality of God, but is indispensable in any affirmation of that reality."[170]

### 5.2.2.2 Pannenberg's proposal for a theology of the history of religions

In Pannenberg's decisive 1962 article, "Toward a Theology of the History of Religions," he seeks to answer Paul Tillich's call for Christian theology to adopt a new approach to the history of religions.[171] Tillich sought, as we have seen, to evaluate positively other religious traditions but also to give proper attention to the Christian message's claim to universal relevance. Tillich is even open to the possibility, which Pannenberg would certainly locate in the resurrection of Jesus, that "there may be ... a central event in the history of religions which unites the positive results of those critical developments in the history of religion in and under which revelatory experiences are going on - an event which, therefore, makes possible a concrete theology that has universalistic significance."[172] Not unexpectedly, Pannenberg, with his concern for universality and for the grounding of theology upon the broader base of the study of religion, responded to Tillich's challenge. Behind Tillich's concern Pannenberg sees the prevailing of the thought of Ernst Troeltsch who left, as we have seen, the question of the absoluteness of Christianity open and developed a theology on the basis of the history of religions which did not and could not "ascribe any 'absolute' or ultimate truth to the Christian revelation." Yet, although Pannenberg is convinced that Protestant theology must once again go beyond the limitations of dialectical theology and face openly and without dogmatic restrictions the fact that the Christian religion is one among many he believes that a return to the impasse of the subjectivism of Troeltsch's position is also not an answer.[173]

Pannenberg begins with the assumption, which he also finds in Tillich's challenge, that "a theology of the history of religions can be taken seriously outside its own community of faith only to the extent that it appeals to ... the 'facts of the sciences of religion' and is able to argue from these."[174] Hence Pannenberg presents a methodology for the study of religions which is "in no way obligated to derive its statements from the Christian revelation."[175] This approach is pursued by Pannenberg over against the so-called kerygmatically grounded approach as proposed by Althaus in which the legitimacy of the Christian religion within the context of world religions cannot be demonstrated historically but can only be based on the decision of faith.[176] Thus for Pannenberg the theologian's arguments

---

[170] "A Response to My American Friends," in: *The Theology of Wolfhart Pannenberg*, ed. Braaten and Clayton, 313f.
[171] Cf. "Toward a Theology of the History of Religions," 65. [*Grundfragen*, 252.]
[172] Tillich, "The Significance of the History of Religions for the Systematic Theologian," 433.
[173] "Toward a Theology of the History of Religions," 67f. [*Grundfragen*, 254.]
[174] For this and the following see *ibid.*, 68f. [255f.]
[175] *Ibid.*, 116. [293.]
[176] Cf. Paul Althaus, "Mission und Religionsgeschichte," in: *Zeitschrift für systematische Theologie* 5 (1928):550-590, esp. 588.

cannot presuppose specifically Christian beliefs as their point of departure for a theology of the history of religions but should instead rely on "observable states of affairs." This leads Pannenberg to reject a primarily phenomenological approach, as suggested by Tillich, in favor of an historical approach, based upon his conviction that "the religious particularity of Christianity would itself first come into view through its function in the process of the history of religions."[177]

Entirely consistent with his theological method, therefore, Pannenberg insists upon allowing the truth claims of the Christian religion and its place among the world religions to be established by the results of the impartial study of comparative religions.[178] As Braaten explains, "Pannenberg is striving for a method of a *theology* of religion and religions that can claim intersubjective validity in the midst of all the scientific approaches to religion, psychology, sociology, phenomenology, and history." In doing so, however, Pannenberg consciously "takes the risk of placing all his theological principles on the open market of public accountability, holding nothing back on a private Christian reservation."[179] Of course, this is precisely what Pannenberg intends and what he believes is the precondition to a 'Christian' theology of the history of religions being taken seriously outside the realm of the Christian community. For Pannenberg, Christian theology, in light of the increasing contact today with the competing truth claims of other religions, has essentially two choices:

> It may hold on to its positivist position with an appeal to divine revelation. If it does, however, it will lose any hope of intellectual legitimation for its claim to general validity, since it will be assuming this claim rather than proving it in a situation in which it has been challenged by the claims of other religions and beliefs. Alternatively, the theology practised within the Christian tradition may see its role as Christian theology as to make the superiority of Christianity to other systems of belief the explicit object of investigation and proof in a theology of religions. Since the Renaissance ... this has been regarded as the work of Christian apologetics and later of fundamental theology and has been pursued with varying energy and success.[180]

---

[177] "Toward a Theology of the History of Religions," 70f. [*Grundfragen*, 255f.] One sees here as well the distinction between Pannenberg and other attempts to ground a theology of the history of religions. Prominent among modern efforts is Hendrick Kraemer's work, *The Christian Message in a Non-Christian World* (London: Edinburgh House Press, 1947). As Braaten, "The Place of Christianity among the World Religions," 306, has noted: "The difference between Kraemer and Pannenberg is that what for Kraemer is a premise of faith ... is for Pannenberg a conclusion of reason."

[178] Hence, as Knitter, 49, observes, "Pannenberg insists that he is not asserting this divine reality and man's search for it as a theological or philosophical principle or a 'religious apriori' which he applies to the religions. Rather, he finds this reality and search within the *history* of the various religions and *therefore* asserts it."

[179] Braaten, "The Place of Christianity among the World Religions," 294.

[180] *TPS*, 323. [*WtT*, 325f.]

As Pannenberg brings the Christian religion into the open market place, however, to be examined on equal footing with the other religions by the various sciences of religion, it is - consistent with his theological method - the science of the history of religions which he holds to be decisive for determining the place of Christianity among the other religions. The popular approach of the phenomenology of religion is helpful, contends Pannenberg, for establishing certain facets of the human religious condition and experience, but it is "only through historical portrayal that one comes as close as possible to the actual course of the concrete life of man." Pannenberg rejects the view of the history of religions proposed by Hegel as inadequate since it "treats the individual religions as self-enclosed, more or less unalterable types, and allows them to be linked only by means of historical succession."[181] In order to attain a basis for an appropriate comparison between the different religions in their totality, according to Pannenberg, the interconnectedness and unity of the history of religions must be recognized. Only then can we attribute to Christianity its proper place among the other religions of the world.

Pannenberg rejects as inadequate the attempt to explain "the whole history of religions on the basis of a hypothesis about its beginning" as is usually done, especially on the basis of evolutionary models for the understanding of the development of human religions.[182] Pannenberg's unique contribution to the attempt at a unitary view of the history of religions is, taking the cue from the philosophical insight that has formed his view of history and revelation, that "the unity of the history of religions is ... not to be found in their beginnings, but rather in their end." According to Pannenberg:

> The struggle of religious traditions with each other points beyond the present to another form of religious unity which is trying to take shape in such struggles. Such a unity has always attained a merely particularistic form in the history of religions up to now. But it would seem to be the most distinguished task of religious-historical research to investigate the occasions and motives that have from time to time contributed to such developments, since the unity of the history of religions is not simply to be presupposed as given - ... but to be inquired after in its growth within the processes of history.[183]

This move allowed Pannenberg to answer two questions. First, what is the place of Christianity in the history of religions? And second, what is the worth of non-Christian religions? We turn our attention here to the first of these questions and will take up the second in the following section.

Pannenberg assigns to Christianity an historically important role in bringing into contact the various religious traditions of the world and creating a secular understanding of human existence which has lead to an homogenization of various

---
[181] "Toward a Theology of the History of Religions," 78. [*Grundfragen*, 262.]
[182] *Ibid.*, 83. [266.]
[183] *Ibid.*, 94. [275.]

cultures. The religious traditions of the world are seen to have a multiplicity of starting points. A common history of religions is first possible when "suitable conditions bring about a competition between the different religions stemming from a collision between their competing intentions of universal meaning." Beginning with this assumption Pannenberg suggests that "one can begin to speak of a global process of integration for the first time in relation to the history of Christian missions." As Pannenberg explains:

> Christian missionary activity ... drew together the different, more or less isolated religious traditions into a world history of religion. The unification of the religious traditions of mankind taking place in this process does not appear for the first time with the displacement of other religions by Christianity. Rather, the simple fact of the different religions moving into relationship with each other mainly through the impact of the Christian missions brought to the fore a unity in the religious world situation, albeit one filled with tension. ... Thus, by means of its thrust toward a universal mission, Christianity has become the ferment for the rise of a common religious situation of the whole of mankind.[184]

Only in this connection can one speak of a single religious history of humanity. And Christianity, as the decisive catalyst in this situation, demonstrates its universal relevance through the impact of its universal mission. In this way, explains Pannenberg, "the history of Christianity is of special interest in the history of religions on account of its specific contribution to the rise of a worldwide religious situation."

Christianity distinguishes itself not just in the historical role it played because of its universal mission but also because of its unique content. It is no accident, in Pannenberg's view, that Christianity has played the role that it has in bringing the religions of the world together into a common history for Christianity is uniquely open to the eschatological future and thus to the end toward which all religions in some sense point. This perspective Pannenberg traces back to Israel, who, in light of their particular experience of God, learned, "in contradistinction to other peoples and their religions, ... to understand the reality of human experience as a

---

[184] *Ibid.*, 93f. [274f.], for this and the following quote. For Pannenberg, therefore, the history of the process of religious integration is essentially the history of Christian missionary expansion. He writes: "The process of religious integration ... advanced ... in the outreach of the Christian missionary movement beyond the Hellenistic realm, especially by the conversion of the Slavic and Germanic peoples to the Christian faith, and then by the colonization of America, and finally by encountering the religions of the Far East and the illiterate cultures of Africa and Australia, which at that time along with their histories entered the stream of the world history of religion which the Christian mission had mediated." (p. 95 [276]). One might rightly ask, however, whether such conclusions are really the result of an unbiased examination of the history of religions and not to be explained, at least in part, by the author's own commitment to the Christian tradition? Also, is it really appropriate to speak of the histories of other religions, regardless of how primitive they may appear to us, as having no universal historical significance until the point at which they come into contact with (and thus become important for) Christianity?

history moving toward a goal which had not yet appeared."[185] According to Pannenberg, decisive for the history and understanding of Christianity is the fact that for Israel, "the history which it experienced, along with its unfinished future, which included the future of the world and humanity, was seen as the manifestation of God."[186] Hence the future-oriented, universal perspective decisive for the role Christianity has played and is playing in unifying the history of religions is rooted in the faith of Israel. As Braaten has written, in Pannenberg's view, "the sustaining power of Christianity to endure in world history lies in its openness to the future, a feature rooted in Israel's interpretation of divine revelation as promise.

A religion that lives by promise toward the future can cope with the vicissitudes of the historical process better than religions related to the past-oriented myth of primordial time."[187] The unique and special role of Christianity among the religions of the world, therefore, is to be found not just in the role Christianity has played historically in bringing the religions together into a common history but also and more significantly in its eschatological orientation.[188] And here also is to be located Christianity's claim to 'absoluteness' for its God, who is the power of the future, cannot be superseded by any other future or any new experience of God. Hence Pannenberg can contend that "in the God of the coming reign, who was proclaimed by Jesus, the divine mystery is revealed in its inexhaustibility."[189]

On the basis of Christianity's eschatological outlook and role played in enabling a historical understanding of reality which made possible the study of its own history and that of other religions Pannenberg believes to be able to draw an empirical and unprejudiced assessment of the place of Christianity. He contends:

> It is ... true that the Israelite-Christian tradition has in fact shown an unusual degree of assimilating and accommodating power, and its historical sense and openness to the future have enabled it not to expel from consciousness the historic changes which have taken place in its religious awareness, but to take account of it to a much greater degree than, for example, mythical religions can. These, however, are not dogmatic but empirical statements about the uniqueness of the Judeo-Christian tradition as compared with other systems of religious tradition. It was of course this particular religious tradition which first made possible a historical understanding of reality in general, and through it the historical study of itself and other religious traditions, but it is hardly possible now to regard this by itself as a dogmatic prejudice which might interfere with the unprejudiced evaluation of phenomena.[190]

---

[185] Ibid., 113. [291.]
[186] ST 1:169. [186.]
[187] Braaten, "Christianity among the World Religions," 304.
[188] Cf. Augustin's treatment of eschatology as the key to a Christian theology of religions in *Gott eint - Trennt Christus?* 339ff.
[189] "Toward a Theology of the History of Religions," 114. [*Grundfragen*, 292.]
[190] TPS, 366f. [*WtT*, 370.]

Despite the logical force of argumentation, however, the suspicion lingers that Pannenberg arrives at this assessment not just because of his methodology but also because of his basic commitment to the Christian religion.[191] Indeed, Pannenberg himself is aware of the difficulty, noting that it is inevitable "that every investigator should bring a subjective position to his work, nor would it be desirable to eliminate this, since the different interests and approaches can open up different aspects of the subject. The science of religion is no different from any other discipline in this respect."[192] Rather than using this as justification for unavoidable prejudice, however, he has nevertheless elsewhere cautioned that a "direct application of the actual but only subsequently discovered ... relationship of a religion to Christianity would not do justice to the specific situation of that other religion and to its relationship with the divine mystery." Hence Pannenberg believes that theology's contribution to the history of religions should consist not in "some sort of construction developed from the standpoint of Christian dogmatics, but ...in working with an unprejudiced openness to create space in the history of religions for the appearing of the divine mystery *and* for its debatability."[193] To what extent, however, adherents of other religions can accept Pannenberg's program or any of its conclusions as "unprejudiced" and "open" within the context of inter-religious dialogue remains itself a question open to discussion.[194]

### 5.2.2.3 Non-Christian religions as witnesses to an all-determining reality

In the first volume of his *Systematic Theology* Pannenberg observed that the one-sided exposition of Rm. 1:19-20 solely in terms of a philosophical natural theology has led to an unduly negative assessment of non-Christian religions. Over against this assessment Pannenberg contends that, "today we have to correct this false development and arrive at a more nuanced judgment on the world

---

[191] Pannenberg, of course, recognizes that no researcher of religion approaches the subject without certain preconceived ideas. He writes: "Just as in other scientific disciplines, the student does not approach such investigations [of religion] with a mind which is *tabula rasa*. He brings ... an interest in the object of his study, and has preconceptions about it .... He may also be a Christian. His Christian faith ... may enable him to form questions and conjectures which prove productive for his investigation. On the other hand, they may also in one way or another deprive him of an impartial appreciation of his object .... In either case, however, the theologian's private religious affiliation belongs to the heuristic, not the probative, context of theological statements. Confusion between the two is most likely where a personal religious conviction is used as the basis for an argument for which intersubjective validity is simultaneously claimed."(*Ibid.*, 320f.[323f.]). What is not so easy, however, is determining when such confusion has taken place within a particular researcher's evaluative judgment of his or her own or another religious tradition. Even in the case of a critical rationalist like Pannenberg the recognition of the danger is no guarantee that personal faith commitments will not color the interpretation of the results of scientific investigation.
[192] *Ibid.*, 366. [369.]
[193] "Toward a Theology of the History of Religions," 117. [*Grundfragen*, 294f.]
[194] Braaten (307f.), for instance, questions whether an argument for Christianity from reason alone is either possible or desirable. He writes: "I have frequently had the impression that, after a long and detailed argument, Pannenberg reaches a conclusion, which he claims to have demonstrated *sola ratione*, but somehow the ordinary layperson already holds the same conclusion *sola fide*."

religions."[195] Already in his 1962 article on a theology of the history of religions Pannenberg sought to do precisely that. As indicated in the preceding section Pannenberg's location of the unity of the history of religions at their end rather than their beginnings allows him to evaluate the non-Christian religions in light not of where they are or where they have been but of where they are going and toward that which they point. Thus God as the power of the future is not only the end of the history of the Christian religion but of the unified history of all religions as has already been manifested in Jesus Christ. Pannenberg writes: "As the power of the future, the God of the coming reign of God proclaimed by Jesus already anticipates all later epochs of the history of the church and of the non-Christian religions. From this standpoint, the history of religions even beyond the time of the public ministry of Jesus presents itself as a history of the appearance of the God who revealed himself through Jesus." From this viewpoint, "the alien religions cannot be adequately interpreted as mere fabrications of man's strivings after the true God. Ultimately, they have to do with the same divine reality as the message of Jesus." And in this sense, although they perceive "the appearance of the divine mystery only in a fragmentary way," they are genuine witnesses to God as all-determining reality.[196]

Yet all religions are not for this reason on an equal footing with Christianity. As Braaten writes: "Although all the religions are striving after the same divine mystery as revealed in Jesus, something unique and definitive happened in the message and history of Jesus." Hence, although the God revealed in Jesus Christ is the same God witnessed to in various ways in other religions there is a decisive difference - a difference which has to do, not unsurprisingly, with eschatology. As Braaten succinctly summarizes Pannenberg's argument:

> The eschatological kingdom proleptically present in Jesus can be seen retrospectively to be active in all epochs prior to Christ and in all religions as the power of their end. Christianity can be assimilative of the elements of truth in other religious traditions, because they too function as witnesses ... to the coming of the fullness of truth beyond their own limitations. Since the God of the future was present in Jesus as the eschatological power of salvation, demonstrated by God's raising of Jesus from the dead, ... Jesus holds a place of unique significance as the key to the future of the world and its salvation.[197]

That the non-Christian religions also witness to God's reality is also to be seen in the very unity of the history of religions to which Pannenberg has given so much weight. The fact that there is an increasing unity of religions, at least in the formation of a common history of religions, is for Pannenberg nothing less than a reflection of the unity and universality of the one creator God. For Pannenberg the unity of the concept of religion also implies the "presupposition of the unity of

---
[195] *ST* 1:118. [132.]
[196] *Ibid.*, 115.
[197] Braaten, 306.

humanity." Thus all the religions conceal within them the divine mystery which is the mystery of the one God. Therefore "the claims of the gods and the concrete conflicts between them are finally referred to the unity of a divine reality" that is manifested within them. Hence Pannenberg can also contend that "the increasing unity of religion in religious history, in spite of the plurality, corresponds to the unity of the divine reality which is coming to light in this history through all the changes and upheavals." And for Pannenberg, the manifestation of this reality, whose form is still a matter of debate among the various religions, is called revelation - within and as the history of religions.[198]

In this light it is the task of theology to examine "the historical religions to determine how far the all-determining reality of God makes itself known in them as the unifying unity of all reality distinct from itself."[199] The assumption that the non-Christian religions are also witnesses to the all-determining reality not only implies the *task* of theology but also its *method* of examining other religions. If non-Christian religions to some extent witness to the divine reality then they must be tested by the standard of their own understanding of this reality to determine to what extent their understanding of this reality enables them to understand and interpret their experience of reality in general. The application of this methodology, Pannenberg explains;

> is not the reduction of traditional statements of faith to anthropology which has been rightly objected to in the mere psychology, sociology or phenomenology of religion. Testing by the standard of the particular tradition's own understanding of divine reality does more than see how far the rest of the contents of the tradition agree with its understanding of God. In addition it tackles the more important question of whether the particular tradition has fulfilled in one historical situation, or now fulfils, the claim implicit in its talk of a God with power over reality. Does it, in other words, provide an interpretive approach to reality which gives insights into the way it is experienced in practice?[200]

The very task and method of a theology of religions which Pannenberg proposes, therefore, presuppose the claims of the world's religions to witness to a divine reality and take these claims seriously It judges each against the standard of its own understanding and experience of the divine reality to which it bears witness.

### 5.2.3 **Pannenberg's doctrine of election and non-Christian religions**

#### 5.2.3.1 *The place of election in Pannenberg's theology*
Frequently overlooked in examinations of Pannenberg's thought is the place he gives to the doctrine of election. Ignored or brushed aside with a few strokes of the pen by many contemporary theologians, Pannenberg has wrestled with the

---
[198] *ST* 1:170f. [187f.]
[199] *TPS*, 327. [*WtT*, 330.]
[200] *Ibid.*, 320. [322f.]

doctrine of election and its implications for the corpus of theology since the beginning of his theological career. Already in his 1953 doctoral dissertation at the university of Heidelberg, *Die Prädestinationslehre des Duns Skotus im Zusammenhang der scholastischen Lehrentwicklung*,[201] Pannenberg had engaged the problem of election. It was a question he would continue to come back to throughout the course of his theological career. In 1957 he took up the question briefly again in his article, "Der Einfluß der Anfechtungserfahrung auf den Prädestinationsbegriff Luthers," in which he already made the connection between election and history which would become a central theme in his development of the doctrine of election.[202] It was, however, first with the appearance of his 1977 book *Human Nature, Election, and History* (which appeared the following year in German as *Die Bestimmung des Menschen*) that one could really begin to gain a view of Pannenberg's own view of election and its place in the structure of his theology. His previous examinations of 'classical' views of election are significant, however, in that his own conception of the doctrine of election arises directly out of his critique of the classic doctrine of election.[203] Pannenberg lists three aspects of this classical view which are characteristic for it and which he finds problematic. First, "the timelessness of the divine decision in regard to its subject, [second,] the restriction of its objects to individuals (in most cases to unrelated individuals), and finally the predominance of a transcendent salvation as constituting the purpose decided upon in the act of election."[204]

In two significant articles included in this work, "Election and the People of God" and "Election and History" several crucial insights into Pannenberg's doctrine of election are to be gleaned. First, rather than understanding election as relating primarily to the individual, or even to Christ, Pannenberg relates election to the people of God, that is to say, the central point of the doctrine of election is that God chooses to himself a people. In the classical doctrine of election the object of election is the individual person who is "presented in abstraction from any social and temporal context. ... In contrast to it, the early Old Testament notion of election was primarily related to the people of God." And it is to this conception that Pannenberg seeks to return.[205] The elect individual, then, is

---

[201] Cf. Pannenberg, *Die Prädestinationslehre des Duns Skotus im Zusammenhang der scholastischen Lehrentwicklung* (Göttingen: Vandenhoeck & Ruprecht, 1954).
[202] Pannenberg, "Der Einfluß der Anfechtungserfahrung auf den Prädestinationsbegriff Luthers," in: *Kerygma und Dogma* 3 (1957): 109-139. Also to be noted are two short articles on the subject which appeared in the period immediately following his Luther article, namely, "Erwählung III. Dogmatisch," in: *Die Religion in Geschichte und Gegenwart* (*RGG*) II (1958): 614-621; and "Prädestination IV. Dogmatisch," in: *RGG* V (1961): 487-489.
[203] So Greiner, *Die Theologie Wolfhart Pannenbergs*, 172f.
[204] Pannenberg, "Election and the People of God," in: *Human Nature, Election, and History*, 46. [Cf. "Erwählung und Volk Gottes," in: *Die Bestimmung des Menschen*, 43]
[205] *Ibid.*, 47. [Cf. 43f.] The term 'people of God,' however, presents certain ambiguities. While it is often used to refer to the whole of the Christian church it cannot be so easily assumed that only the church is implied, overlooking the continuing role of Israel as God's people. But even this

primarily understood as being elect within the social and historical context of the people of God and in this manner his or her election is not abstract. Corresponding to this concept is another important point in Pannenberg's doctrine of election which he develops later more fully and which we will examine in our next section, namely, the elect individual is accountable for his or her "mission" which takes on a universal scope which implies a significance of God's election not just for the people of God but for all humanity. This is especially to be seen in the early Christian interpretation of the universal significance of Jesus' mission.[206]

Another important insight into Pannenberg's doctrine of election is already hinted at in his article on election and the people of God when he suggests that "the sense of God's action in history has been lost in consequence of a one-sided development in the doctrine of election" and regrets the fact that the classical doctrine as found in Thomas Aquinas and Calvin "offers little reference to history."[207] It is in his article "Election and History," however, that the significance of the doctrine of election for a theology of history is first thematically explored. Noting that every serious theology of history refers to God as "the determinative power active in historical reality," Pannenberg points to the importance of Israel's understanding of its election and of the related category of promise for its conception of history.[208] Indeed, Pannenberg contends that "the most fundamental category ... in a theological description of history within the context of the Jewish-Christian tradition is the category of *election* in referring to the definitive intention in the corporate experience of the vocation of a people."[209] The concept of election means that it was God himself and not merely human initiative which constituted the social and religious identity of a people. The most basic contribution of the concept of election to a theology of history, therefore, is that "it provides some intelligible interpretation of statements affirming actions of God in history." Moreover, the concept of election gave Israel an understanding of history as progressing toward a goal, i.e., as future-oriented, which was distinct from the conceptions of history of other ancient peoples.[210]

It is to these basic themes that Pannenberg returns in his comprehensive treatment of the doctrine of election in the third volume of his *Systematic Theology*. The location of the treatment the doctrine of election within the plan of his systematic theology is significant. Unlike many Protestant thinkers who have taken up the doctrine under soteriology, or Thomas Aquinas who dealt with it within the context of the doctrine of God, Pannenberg follows Schleiermacher in

---

[206] difficulty, according to Pannenberg, points to the promise and breadth of the term 'people of God' (pp. 60f.).
*Ibid.*, 50. [Cf. 47.]
[207] *Ibid.*, 46. [Cf. 42.] For a discussion of the loss of history in the classical doctrine of predestination and Pannenberg's response to it see Koch, *Der Gott der Geschichte*, 217ff.
[208] Pannenberg, "Election and History," in: *Human Nature, Election, and History*, 87. [Cf. "Erwählung und Geschichte," 90.]
[209] *Ibid.*, 89. [Cf. 92f.]
[210] *Ibid.*, 91f. and 100ff. [Cf. 95f. and 106ff.]

treating the doctrine of election within ecclesiology - although unlike Schleiermacher he takes up the topic at the end rather than at the beginning of his treatment of the doctrine of the church. And for Pannenberg, given his contention that election relates primarily to the people of God, this is precisely where one would expect to find it within the corpus of his theology. By titling the chapter dealing with election "Election and History" Pannenberg indicates that the ultimate focus of his treatment will be on the implications of the doctrine for an understanding of history, although this is preceded by a thorough discussion of its implications for the individual and for the people of God. It is, however, within the treatment of election and history that the implications of the doctrine for Pannenberg's understanding of non-Christian religions become manifest. It is to this question, then, that we now turn our attention.

5.2.3.2 *Election, universality and non-Christian religions*
When one examines the doctrine of election in light of the theme of universality one is immediately confronted by an apparent conflict between God's universal salvific will and the particularity of the election of a certain people or certain individuals by God. Rather than abandon the doctrine of election or push it into a safe corner as something not easily fitting into his overall program of universality, Pannenberg wrestles with the questions raised by the doctrine of election, asking specifically what the implications are for the world's religions. In doing so the discussion is placed firmly within the framework of his understanding of history in which the doctrine of election becomes a "*Verbindungsmoment*" connecting the divine will or intention with the course of human history and the history of human religions.

In the third and final volume of his *Systematic Theology* the most thorough treatment of the question of election by Pannenberg to date is to be found. Within the context of his discussion of election and history the question of the non-Christian religions is addressed. For Israel, its conception of election was fundamental to its understanding and experience of history as well as its relation to God. "In the case of Israel the special relation of the people to God is not cosmologically grounded. It rests on divine election, on choice from among many peoples, all of which also derive from God's creation of humanity."[211] Not only this but even the social and political systems of Israel are grounded upon election rather than upon cosmology, as was the case among other cultures. As Pannenberg explains: "The high cultures of the ancient Orient understood their political-legal systems as being grounded religiously just as did ancient Israel. The foundation of these systems, however, though traced to a divine act, was not traced to an act of election. Instead they bound the origin of the social and

---
[211] *ST* 1:150. [166.]

political order with that of the cosmic order."²¹² Hence the entire understanding and perception of history in Israel is to be distinguished from that of other ancient developed cultures. Contends Pannenberg: "If in Israel the origin and development of a consciousness of history in the sense of a history of divine action was closely bound to the concepts of divine promise and election, which assume a certain wholenss of divine actions, then there was also to be found alongside of this other origins of historical consciousness in the high cultures of the ancient orient."²¹³

One of the critical differences that Israel's election-based understanding of history made was that for it history was moving progressively toward a goal - a concept lacking in the other ancient cultures.²¹⁴ Rather than a concept of the flow of history based upon God's election and promise the other ancient cultures normally based their understanding of history upon the experience of crisis periods or of some crucial events in the life of the people. Concepts of election in these cultures, in contrast, appear to occur only seldom and then only in relation to isolated individuals such as a king chosen for his position. The people as such were never seen in these cultures nor in their religions as the object of divine election. Thus Israel had from its very beginnings a concept of history which gave it a decisive openness to the future lacking in neighboring cultures and religions. Because, therefore, election was related to the entire people in Israel it "became there the starting point for a consciousness of historical processes that was wide-ranging and always open to new attempts at elaboration."²¹⁵

For the historical understanding of Israel the connection of the concept of election to the entire people is decisive since it is not the idea of election itself but its relation to the entire people rather than simply the king or royal family which determines the point at which Israel in its history of the covenant obtains its unique salvation-historical conception over against the surrounding peoples. Also, it is only through the connection of the idea of election to the whole people that it was possible for Israel to ground historically its cultural order upon the concept of divine election and promise rather than founding these cosmologically.²¹⁶

How, however, are other peoples and their religions to be viewed in light of Israel's understanding of its election and unique relationship and covenant with God? Could Israel's self-understanding as elect people of God be generalized to include other peoples? The concept of election in the Old Testament with its

---

212 *ST* 3:524, As Pannenberg, *ST* 1:261, [285.], has also indicated, even Israel's "description of God as Father has its basis in an act of election" so that it is to be seen that Israel's entire view of itself in distinction to that of other peoples is determined by divine election.

213 *Ibid.*, 525.

214 Cf. *ibid.*, 525f., where Pannenberg notes, for instance, that "die Erinnerung an vergangene Zeitalter, Könige, Dynastien war in Summer und im alten Ägypten allerdings nicht verknüpft mit dem Gedanken eines Fortschritts der Geschichte auf ein Ziel hin, wie er durch den Verheißungs- und Erwählungsglauben Israels für das jüdische Geschichtsbewußtsein kennzeichnend wurde."

215 *Ibid.*, 526. (translation my own)

216 *Ibid.*, 526f.

specific focus on the people of Israel in distinction from all other peoples would appear to speak against this. One cannot, however, on this basis argue that God has no plan for other peoples. Pannenberg writes:

> In contrast to the other nations Israel is elected by God as own people (Dt. 7:6f.). That excluded the possibility that God's relationship to other peoples could be of the same nature as his relationship to Israel. It did not, however, exclude the possibility that the creator of the world might enter into special relationships with other nations and cultures which could be described in a general sense under the concept of election. This is suggested through the word given to the prophet Amos: 'Have I not led Israel out of Egypt just as I led the Philistines out of Caphtor and Aram out of Kir?'[217]

This insight also has significance for the application of the concept of election as a descriptive category for a theology of history. Commenting in his article "Election and History" upon this same text from Amos Pannenberg notes that it establishes "an important perspective for the understanding of the descriptive character of the concept of election in its application in the portrayal and interpretation of history. This concept has to do with the distinguishing features of an experience of liberation which has constitutive significance for the entire subsequent history of a people. It this sense election is not restricted to the people of Israel."[218]

More intriguing and fruitful, however, than the idea that the election of Israel does not exclude God's special working with other peoples is Pannenberg's suggestion that through the particular election of Israel a basis is provided for a universal meaning of God's election for all peoples within the context of a general theology of religions. Especially for the Christian religion this understanding can provide the basis for universal mission.[219] Pannenberg contends in this regard that

> in a general theology of religions the concept of election in a general sense could find application in the relationship between the divine government of the world and the history of the various religious cultures of humanity. The history of Christianity, which like the people of Israel is called to a community of faith with

---

[217] *Ibid.*, 527.
[218] Pannenberg, "Erwählung und Geschichte," in: *Die Bestimmung des Menschen*, 94. The English original does not contain several of the most significant statements of this passage and the crucial last sentence has been added, thus the German revision has here been quoted in my own translation. The original reads: "This is important for the understanding of the descriptive character of the category of election. That category is related to the experience of a redemptive and foundational event that constitutes the further history of a people." "Election and History," in: *Human Nature, Election, and History*, (Philadelphia: Westminster Press, 1977), 90.
[219] As Koch, *Der Gott der Geschichte*, 224, notes: "Der entscheidende Fortschritt, den Pannenberg aus der kritischen Durchsicht der klassischen Gestalt der christlichen Erwählungsgedanken ... gewinnt, besteht im Gedanken der *geschichtlichen* und *korporativen* Erwählung, mithin in der Interpretation der göttlichen Erwählung als verantwortlicher *Sendung des Volkes Gottes* für den weiteren Kontext der gesamten Menschheit."

the electing God, can and must first be portrayed theologically from the perspective of a history of election. In connection with the aspects of the covenant obligations associated with this election the mission to the rest of humanity and God's dealings with his people can and must also be portrayed.[220]

The universal mission is thus seen to be the reverse side of the particularity of election. This is especially to be seen, according to Pannenberg, inasmuch as "God's righteous will to renew human society on the basis of its relationship with him ... is directed toward the whole of humanity." Here Pannenberg finds the basis for the universal Christian mission precisely in the particularity of the church's election so that the election of God's people has universal significance for all peoples of all religions. Pannenberg writes:

> The insight into the general link between election as a setting apart from the peoples of the world and the mission of the elect to be witnesses in the world establishes the framework for an understanding for the unique nature of the Christian task of mission: To proclaim the Gospel to all peoples and make disciples of them through baptism in the name of the triune God (Mt. 28:19) means to bring in people of every nation into the symbolically mediated presence of the coming Kingdom of God which has already begun in Jesus Christ, and thereby to serve God's purpose of reconciling humans to himself and with one another.[221]

Thus the doctrine of election, understood as directed primarily toward the people of God, is not only crucial for this people's understanding of their experience of history, but it is also decisive for the development of a theology of history. Rather than leading to a theology of history, however, which focuses abstractly on the isolated history of an individual elect people, the particularity of election in Pannenberg's thought becomes bound with the universality of mission and with the unity of the history of religions which are all moving toward a common goal of history. The doctrine of election, understood in this manner, is therefore seen not only to be consistent with Pannenberg's conception of universal history and the universal relevance of the Christ event, but it is also seen to be constitutive for these propositions.

### 5.2.3.3 Israel, the Church, and the elect 'people of God'

As we have already seen, Pannenberg has found the application of the term 'people of God' as the object of God's election to the church alone as problematic in regard to the relationship between the church and the Jewish people.[222] The role of Israel in determining the Christian church's view of history and of its own identity as the object of God's election has significant implications for the

---
[220] *ST* 3:528,
[221] *Ibid.*, 534.
[222] "Election and the People of God," 60f. [Cf. "Erwählung und Volk Gottes," 59f.]

treatment of contemporary Judaism in Pannenberg's thought.[223] Judaism, although recognized as a non-Christian religion, is not dealt with in the same manner as the other non-Christian religions. In the first place, Pannenberg's statements on Judaism are marked by the problematic history of Christianity with the Jews and are focused on the need for reconciliation and strong condemnations of anti-Semitism and the theological errors which have historically contributed to it. Hence Pannenberg writes that "the appalling history of Christian enmity towards the Jews was encouraged in the first place by an error; for the Gentile Christian church laid responsibility for the death of Jesus on the Jewish people alone, in contrast to the rest of mankind, instead of seeing the Jewish people as representatives of mankind in general, even in its participation in the trial of Jesus. By vindicating the non-Jewish section of mankind through the accusation of the Jewish people - in a highly un-Christian attitude of mind - the solidarity between Christians and God's chosen people, on which Paul still laid such stress, disintegrated."[224]

Pannenberg thus rejects the idea that the Jews have been rejected by God in order to transfer their election to the Christian church. This perspective is decisive for his dialogue with Judaism as a non-Christian religion for the Jews are not just non-Christians in the same sense as members of other non-Christian religions but they also continue to be an elect people of God with a religious history of God's promise and election shared with the Christian church.[225] Hence the dialogue with Judaism in Pannenberg is also distinct from that carried on with other religious traditions because of the continuity Pannenberg emphasizes between the old and the new covenant - between Israel as people of God and the Christian community as people of God.[226] There is indeed a new covenant in Christ's blood but this does not mean, and the New Testament nowhere implies, that there is a "new" people of God which replaces the "old." For Pannenberg this means that: "Contemporary Christian theology should deal openly with the relationship of the church to the concept of the elect people of God that is suggested by Paul's statements on this topic. Undoubtedly the church may understand itself as the people of the new covenant with God that is established in

---

[223] Pannenberg is indebted here, in part, to the contemporary dialogue between Jews and Christians which has brought out the many similarities in Jewish and Christian faith and their common roots. This is especially significant for the context of German Protestantism in which these common roots "waren vergessen oder verdrängt, seit die evangelische Theologie der Aufklärung das Alte Testament zum Buch der jüdischen Religion erklärt hat, demgegenüber die christliche Religion sich allein auf das Neue Testament zu gründen habe." So Pannenberg, "Das christliche Gottesverständnis im Spannungsfeld seiner jüdischen und griechischen Wurzeln," in: H. Friedlander and W. Pannenberg, *Der christliche Glaube und seine jüdisch-griechische Herkunft*, EKD Texte 15 (Hannover: Kirchenamt der EKD, 1986), 13.

[224] *The Apostles' Creed*, 82.

[225] Cf. also Koch, *Der Gott der Geschichte*, 224f.

[226] Cf. *ST* 3:509ff. It might be questioned, however, whether in Pannenberg's emphasis upon continuity between the old and new covenants there is still place for the recognition of the Old Testament as a history of failure and disappointment within the history of salvation?

the blood of Christ and renewed in each celebration of the eucharist. But this does not mean that for this reason the church may set itself as the 'new' people of God over against the old, Jewish people of God as if this people, along with the old covenat, were now no longer valid."[227] And similarly, Pannenberg contended in dialogue with the Jewish theologian Pinchas Lapide, that: "Christianity may not, in relation to Judaism, understand itself as a new religion, the origins of which are only by coincidence of history to be found within the Jewish people. Instead, the preaching of Jesus had to do with nothing other than the true meaning of the Jewish faith in God, and Christianity remains bound to this starting-point."[228]

Israel's continuing status as people of God, therefore, has implications for dialogue with and mission toward Judaism. There cannot be, contends Pannenberg, a mission to Jews which is of the same type as the mission to other peoples and members of other non-Christian religions. Christianity must recognize Israel's special position as God's people and that this people preceded us in the faith in the one true God. The church must renounce all forms of pressure to convert (*Bekehrungszwang*), but it cannot abandon its responsibility to challenge the Jewish self-understanding in relation to Jesus and the identity of Jesus as son of the Father with the God of Israel.[229] This is especially necessary inasmuch as Israel's self-understanding is also decisive for the origin of the Christian church and for our own self-understanding as people of God. Hence,

> In relation to the Jewish people the witness of the Christian is centered upon the fact that the God of Israel has revealed himself ultimately in Jesus of Nazareth and therefore first to the Jews. ... This includes, however, the idea that Jesus as the 'Son' of the Father belongs inseparably to the identity of the God of Israel, since Jesus' message of the Kingdom of God ... was concentrated on the first commandment of the decalogue and, as the interpretation of this commandment, is also the criterion for the exclusivity of the trust in God that is demanded by this God. Here there is found a challenge to the self-understanding of Israel which, in connection with the events of the history of Jesus, ... has become the basis for the establishment of early Christianity. The clarification of this relationship from that time until the present day has been indispensable as a central theme of the Christian-Jewish dialogue.[230]

---

[227] *Ibid.*, 516.
[228] Pannenberg, "Das Besondere des Christentums: Gegenwart und Zukunft der Versöhnung," in: Pinchas Lapide and Wolfhart Pannenberg, *Judentum und Christentum, Einheit und Unterschied: Ein Gespräch* (Munich: Chr. Kaiser, 1981), 19.
[229] Jesus is thus not to be understood only as the Messiah for the Gentiles but not for the Jews. As Pannenberg points out: "Dabei ist nach Paulus nicht nur für die Christen, sondern auch für das jüdische Volk der neue Bund auf Jesus gegründet, der sich bei seiner Wiederkehr seinem Volk als der von ihm erwartete Messias erweisen wird" (*ST* 3:513). To maintain otherwise would constitute an abandonment of the claim to Jesus' universal validity.
[230] *Ibid.*, 514f.

But finally, what is then the relationship between Israel and the church? Are they two distinct peoples of God? For Pannenberg this is impossible since the implication of God's universality and unity (and the unity of his kingdom) in his work of election is that there must be a single people of God which is the object and goal of his election. Hence "the category of the people of God has no plural. But is offers room for all to participate in the reign of God over a transformed and renewed humanity. The Christian church is not exclusively identical with the eschatological people of God. It is only a provisional form of this people and a sign of the future completion of this people that will include not only members of the church but also the Jewish people and the righteous from all cultures of the world who are coming to the feast of the reign of God."[231] Thus the scope of God's election is seen to be truly universal in that the 'people of God' who are the objects of this electing activity include ultimately - seen from the perspective of the eschatological end of history - both the church and Israel as one elect people and, indeed, persons out of all cultures and races. As Pannenberg has poignantly contended: "The election of Israel was aimed at the blessing of all mankind, and this vocation continues. ... The church is not the 'new Israel' as if the old one were no longer God's elected people. The church is an extension of the election of Israel, including within its community members from all nations. In this way, the election of Israel is continued; the Christian church symbolizes the eschatological universality of the Kingdom of God."[232] Hence, as Pannenberg writes: "God's act of election has as its ultimate goal the community of a renewed humanity in the kingdom of God."[233]

### 5.3 Excursus: The Universality of God and the Atheistic Critique

*5.3.1 Pannenberg: Atheism and the metaphysics of subjectivity (Feuerbach and Nietzsche)*

One of the most unique and fruitful features of Pannenberg's dialogue with atheistic worldviews is his 'acceptance' of the atheistic critique of God. We have already seen in regard to the thought of Ernst Bloch how the atheistic critique becomes the starting point for Pannenberg's development of a concept of God which avoids the pitfalls of more traditional conceptions.[234] More fundamental is his acceptance of Feuerbach's atheistic critique. As William Hill has noted: "Pannenberg has established himself as a Christian theologian who argues powerfully for the reality of God against the various forms of atheism issuing from the Enlightenment. He does this, however, by accepting the critique of God

---

[231] *Ibid.*, 517.
[232] Pannenberg, "The Social Predicament and Human Responsibility," in: *Human Nature, Election, and History*, 30. [Cf. "Die Gesellschaftliche Bestimmung des Menschen und die Kirche," in: *Die Bestimmung des Menschen*, 26.]
[233] *ST* 3:565,
[234] Cf. section 4.1.2.1.

begun by Feuerbach rather than fleeing from it into 'biblical supernaturalism ... or into an existential decision of faith."[235] Pannenberg is able to do this, in part, because of his recognition of the fact that modern atheism is essentially an outgrowth of the Western Christian tradition.[236] For this reason, his long-running dialogue with atheism has a strikingly different character than his dialogue with and discussion of the world's non-Christian religions. One has the sense that one is witnessing an internal dispute, as if Pannenberg were addressing a Christian heresy rather than a non-Christian or even anti-Christian worldview. And if modern Western atheism is a Christian heresy then Pannenberg would say that its error - or point of divergence from the orthodox faith - is in its attributing too much weight to the human subject and developing around this human subject a metaphysics of subjectivity.

Already in a 1960 lecture on the types of atheism and their theological significance Pannenberg identifies the modern metaphysics of subjectivity, especially as found in the thought of Feuerbach and Nietzsche, as underlying and leading to modern atheism.[237] Feuerbach's emphasis upon the human subject allowed him to advance "the first form of mature atheism" in his science of religion in which he defined religion as the distinguishing of man from himself through the setting up of God before him as the antithesis of himself. Thus the infinity of the human essence, as seen in the human powers of reason, will, and love, is assumed.[238] After Feuerbach, according to Pannenberg, "theology has to learn that ... it can no longer mouth the word 'God' without offering any explanation; that it can no longer speak as if the meaning of this word were self-evident; that it cannot pursue theology 'from above,' as Barth says, if it does not want to fall into the hopeless and, what is more, self-inflicted isolation of a higher glossolalia, and lead the whole church into this blind alley." Hence theology, in its debate with atheism, is referred to the open market place of ideas to which Pannenberg so often refers, with no special privileges or advantages. Rather than simply surrender the field to the Feuerbachian critique of religion - and thereby endangering the truth of Christian speech about God, Pannenberg argues that "the struggle over the concept of God has to be conducted ... in the fields of philosophy, the sciences of religion, and anthropology. If Feuerbach should prove right in these fields, then the proof of atheism for which he strove would in fact be accomplished."[239]

---

[235] Hill, *The Three-Personed God*, 155f.
[236] For a discussion of modern atheism's roots within the Judeo-Christian tradition see Schwarz, *The Search for God*, 16ff.
[237] Cf. Pannenberg, "Types of Atheism and their Theological Significance," in: *BQ* 2:193ff. ["Typen des Atheismus und ihre theologische Bedeutung," in: *Grundfragen*, 354ff.]
[238] *Ibid.*, 188f. [350f.]
[239] *Ibid.*, 189f. [351f.] As Pannenberg has elsewhere noted: "If the human being could do as well without relating his or her understanding of human existence and of the world of human experience to God, that in itself would be strong evidence against religious belief of any sort, even though it might not amount to a conclusive proof against the existence of God. For this reason,

Pannenberg's own response to Feuerbach is to accept the basic premise, at least provisionally, of God as the essence of humanity which he borrowed from Hegel and to take this not as the human's immanent essence, as Feuerbach, but following Hegel to understand essence as that which transcends appearance in which God is the essence of the human person precisely as the person's transcendent destination.[240] By conceding this point in this manner Pannenberg is able to identify human subjectivity with what has been called openness to the world and connect this to his argument, elsewhere developed, for openness toward God so that the modern metaphysics of subjectivity can be said itself to be built implicitly upon the presupposition of God. Pannenberg argues:

> The fact that human subjectivity in its infinite self-transcendence, which modern anthropology somewhat misleadingly designates as 'openness to the world' or 'ec-centricity', always presupposes an infinity transcending itself which is to be described not as a mere psychological datum, as in Troeltsch, but as an ontological structure of man's being. This brings out the point that ... the modern metaphysics of man's subjectivity is conceivable only on the presupposition of a God. Against Feuerbach, this means that man is essentially referred to infinity, but is never already infinite himself. Theology may not take the religious-psychological atheism of Feuerbach as an occasion to retreat into a supranaturalistic wildlife sanctuary. Rather, what is called for is to carry the struggle about the truth of the idea of God into the area of the understanding of man.[241]

The same basic approach is applied to Nietzsche's atheistic critique as well. Pannenberg agrees with Heidegger's analysis that Nietzsche's comment on the death of God is the consequence of his metaphysics of subjectivity. Because of his presupposition of subjectivity - to which the idea of God belongs in modern metaphysics - Nietzsche was compelled to subject all truth - including any truth about God - to the valuation of the human will. This means, as Pannenberg explains, that within Nietzsche's thought "God could only appear as a value, and it is already at this point - and not primarily in the atheistic transvaluation of religious values, especially those of the Christian tradition - that the root of Nietzsche's atheism is to be seen. God as the *highest value* is already a posit of the human will, and a departure from the deity of God."[242]

For Pannenberg this means that Heidegger, in his analysis of Nietzsche from the perspective of an inquiry into being, has essentially provided theology with the right direction in responding to Nietzsche's form of atheism. As was the case with Feuerbach this means theology must take into account in a serious way the

---

anthropology has become the most prominent battleground in the contest between theists and atheists." ("Response to My American Friends," 314.)

[240] As Pannenberg notes later in his argumentation, Feuerbach's conception cannot simply be labeled as false for it "shares in the truth of the modern metaphysics of subjectivity." *Ibid.*, 197. [358.]

[241] *Ibid.*, 191f. [353.]

[242] *Ibid.*, 193f. [354f.]

modern metaphysics of subjectivity and confront the atheistic challenge squarely on its own ground. As Pannenberg explains, the implication for theology is that "its concept of God must be thought out in connection with the philosophical question about being if it is to be a match for the atheism of Nietzsche." Specifically, this means:

> Any type of speech about God that fails to take into account the subjectivity of modern man, his sovereignty over nature, his self-transcendence ..., necessarily lacks convincing power today, especially against a form of atheism which on its part is grounded in the subjectivity of modern man. The question about the being of God can only be stated in the form of the question about the being that must always be presupposed by man precisely with respect to his subjectivity; the question about being to which he is referred for the actual ground of the possibility of his freedom in relation to the world.[243]

In regard to the ground of human freedom, indeed, of human subjectivity, it would seem that only God can come into question. But here there is precisely a problem when God is understood, as Ernst Bloch pointed out, as a being presently at hand who is almighty and all-knowing, for this contradicts the possibility of genuine human freedom.[244] Bloch's critique of God presents a somewhat different challenge to theology in that it diverges from Feuerbach inasmuch as Bloch does not clothe humanity in infinity but recognizes the finiteness of human existence.[245] Yet Bloch is unable to recognize any kind of divine being who transcends human finitude. His critique focuses rather on the problem of human freedom, contending that the idea of an omniscient, omnipotent God who is "presently at hand" is inconsistent with human freedom. At this point Pannenberg, rather than trying to rescue the 'traditional' theological view of God as an almighty, all-knowing being presently at hand accepts the atheistic criticism as correct. He concedes: "A being presently at hand who acts omnipotently and omnisciently would make freedom impossible." Pannenberg suggests, then, that such a being could not be God and that our understanding of God must be transformed. He explains: "Such a being would not be God, because he could not be the all-determining reality, since at the very least the reality of the freedom and subjectivity of human beings would be denied him." Hence, according to Pannenberg:

> If Christian theology today wishes to conceive of God as the source of human freedom, then it can no longer think of God as a being presently at hand. The time of metaphysical innocence in this question has passed. What separates us from this time is modern atheism. In this regard the atheistic critique can be given credit for helping theology to achieve greater clarity over its own theme,

---

[243] *Ibid.*, 195f. [356.]
[244] Bloch, *Das Prinzip Hoffnung*, 2:1413.
[245] So Pannenberg, "The God of Hope," 240f. [*Grundfragen*, 392.]

that is, over the reality of God who is no longer to be confused with a being presently at hand.[246]

This new clarity which the modern atheistic critique has heped theology to achieve has forced us to take a new look at the biblical view of God. There, according to Pannenberg, we find the conception of the deity as a being who is irreconcilably different from a presently at hand, almighty God. When we return to this conception of God then "God would be thought of by theology precisely as the reality who is the source of freedom and who makes the subjectivity of human beings possible." That is to say, with Pannenberg's proposed reconceptualization of God[247] based upon the acceptance of this aspect of the atheistic critique, there is seen to be a ground of human freedom and subjectivity upon which modern atheism founds its arguments which lies outside of humans.[248] And this, in turn, at least indirectly, witnesses to the possible existence of God as ground of human existence.[249]

Pannenberg's approach to the dialogue with modern atheism is thus seen to be consistent with the whole of his theological program. Rather than advocating any sort of retreat into a pre-modern worldview or claiming any sort of special privileges for the Christian truth claims[250] he approaches the atheistic challenge on the intellectual territory of philosophy, anthropology and the sciences of religions.[251] As was also the case in his approach to the non-Christian religions Pannenberg takes the root of the discussion back to anthropology where he finds a universal common ground upon which the Christian truth claims can confront the atheistic critique upon the very anthropological ground from which it springs.[252] Hence Pannenberg has contended that "theologians will be able to defend the truth

---

[246] Pannenberg, "Reden von Gott angesichts atheistischer Kritik," 40f., and for the following quote.
[247] Cf. our discussion of the futurity of God in chapter four for Pannenberg's specific conception of God as the power of the future who is real but not a power presently at hand. Hence God does stand in contradiction to the idea of human freedom.
[248] A similar critique of modern atheism can be deduced from the various writings of Rahner on atheism according to Weger, *Karl Rahner: An Introduction*, 64f.
[249] Cf. "Reden von Gott angesichts atheistischer Kritik," 44ff.
[250] Pannenberg, *ST* 1:47f., [57.], warns a "'retreat to commitment' hands the Christian faith over to an atheistic psychology of religion which traces the irrational need to believe back to secular roots."
[251] Pannenberg, "Types of Atheism," 20 [*Grundfragen*, 360], explains that the theological controversy with atheism "on its own grounds" cannot go any further than the explication of the question of what God might be beyond the traditional concept which atheism rejects in its encounter with what remains for it an 'empty transcendence.' For Pannenberg, the possibility that this empty transcendence can be (indeed is) "encountered as person, as God, is something that has to be carried out in the field of the history of religions; and the test of its truth is reserved for investigation of the particular form of the individual religions."
[252] Pannenberg, "Reden von Gott angesichts atheistischer Kritik," 35, writes that it is "kein Zufall, daß der neuzeitliche Atheismus spätestens seit Feuerbach seine Argumentation auf die Anthropologie konzentriert hat, wie es bei Marx, Nietzsche, Freud, Sartre deutlich ist. Die atheistische Argumentation entspricht damit der anthropologischen Konzentration, die sich in der neuzeitlichen Geschichte der philosophischen Theologie, speziell der Gottesbeweise, vollzogen hat."

precisely of their talk about God only if they first respond to the atheistic critique of religion on the terrain of anthropology. Otherwise all their assertions, however impressive, about the primacy of the Godness of God will remain purely subjective assurances without any serious claim to universal validity."[253] In this manner Pannenberg has sought to put the Christian message's claim to universality into apologetic practice precisely where many of his contemporaries have held their distance or opted for some form of retreatism for it is also and especially here that theology's claim to universal relevance, if it is to be taken at all seriously, must be tested in confrontation and dialogue with that very worldview which seeks to interpret God, the ultimate foundation of theology's universality, as an anthropological projection.

### 5.3.2 *Rahner: Atheism and implicit Christianity*

For Rahner, in distinction to Pannenberg, today's atheism is not the atheism of Feuerbach and Nietzsche nor even that of Marx. Even if there appears to be a great diversity among the various forms of atheism to be found today, they all share, according to Rahner, common assumptions and characteristics that allow one to speak of contemporary atheism in the singular. Namely, "everywhere it is an atheism conditioned by today's rationalistic and technological society."[254] The question which we must here address, however, is not whether Rahner is correct in distinguishing contemporary atheism from that of Feuerbach and Marx, but how he enters into dialogue with this modern, rationalistic atheism on the basis of his conviction of the universal implications and truth claims of the Christian message.

As we have seen at the beginning of this chapter the Second Vatican Council developed a layered view of religions corresponding with their nearness to Christian faith as confessed by the Catholic Church. In this schema after the Roman Church follow the other Christian churches, then the non-Christian monotheistic religions, beginning with Judaism and then Islam, next the other world religions followed by the animistic or primitive religions and finally by atheism.[255] In this light the question which must be asked of Rahner as a Catholic theologian is to what extent and in what ways his theory of an anonymous Christianity also applies to those who confess themselves to be atheists?

For Rahner the position of the Council concerning God's salvific will toward atheists is clear. As he points out, "the Second Vatican Council explicitly states that God does not refuse salvation to a man who, through no fault of his own, has still not attained to any explicit acknowledgment of God, who, in other words, so far as the level of his conscious awareness is concerned, must be called an 'atheist.'"[256] Yet over against misunderstandings of this and similar statements,

---

[253] *ATP*, 16. [16.]
[254] Rahner, "The Church and Atheism," in: *TI* 21:137. ["Kirche und Atheismus," *Schriften* 15: 139.]
[255] Cf., for instance, the encyclical of Paul VI, "*Ecclesiam suam*," (1964); *Lumen gentium* 13; "*Nostra aetate*;" and the Pastoral Constitution "*Gaudium et spes.*"
[256] "Church, Churches and Religions," 48. [*Schriften* 8: 372f.]

that some have taken to imply that it really makes no difference whether one confesses Christ or is an atheist, Rahner has cautioned that although not even an active Christian can be existentially absolutely sure of salvation an atheist is especially endangered along his or her possible way to salvation.

> The *offer* of salvation is indeed open to the atheist, but this does not yet mean that salvation has in reality been effected, for this 'realization' follows much hiddenness, ambivalence and hence actual uncertainty. ... The absolute demands of the conscience are in truth able to be heard by the atheist without ... [an] explicit connection to God, but in the context of this ungrounded and very deficiently motivated form they are most often overlooked, not followed, and misunderstood.[257]

Nevertheless, Rahner contends that the church, also for the atheist, is a universal sign of salvation. Yet he qualifies that this statement "has validity in any case for those atheists who are atheists not due to any fault of their own, that is, who have not been disobedient to the dictates of their own conscience."[258] No criteria, however, are given for how one might determine whether one is an atheist due to one's 'own fault.'[259] It is merely assumed that such persons exist, and for these atheists the church is "the historically tangible, sacramental sign, that in them this mysterious, salvific grace of faith is nonetheless at work above and beyond their explicit atheism."[260] Thus the question which confronts us in modern atheism is the possibility of implicit Christians among explicit atheists, which is the theme of Rahner's 1967 article, *"Atheismus und implizites Christentum"* in which he seeks to interpret the significance of his theologoumenon of anonymous Christianity for the phenomenon of modern atheism in light of the pronouncements of the Second Vatican Council.

In this article Rahner sets forth the thesis that also in atheists it is possible for an implicit Christianity to be found. This foundational thesis consists of two parts, supported by the pronouncements of the Council. First, because the Council does not affirm the scholastic thesis that there cannot be a positive atheism over a long period of time without the individual bringing guilt upon him or herself, Rahner contends that the opposite thesis is assumed. Namely, the fact that an explicit atheism may exist in normal adults even to the end of one's life does not constitute an evidence of moral guilt.[261] The second part of Rahner's

---

[257] Rahner, "Die Atheisten und die Religion," a 1968 interview with the Yugoslavian Roman Catholic journal *Druzina*, in: Karl Rahner, *Kritisches Wort: Aktuelle Probleme in Kirche und Welt* (Freiburg: Herder, 1970), 141f.

[258] Rahner, "The Church and Atheism," 142f. [*Schriften* 15:144f.]

[259] Indeed, for Rahner, which form or mixture of forms of atheism are to be found in a particular person and to what extent, therefore, they are atheists 'through no fault of their own' "ist *letztlich das Geheimnis des allein richtenden Gottes.*" Rahner, "Atheism," in: *HtT* 1:216.

[260] "The Church and Atheism," 144. [*Schriften* 15:145.]

[261] Cf. "Atheism and Implicit Christianity," 146ff. [*Schriften* 8:188ff.]

thesis, which he contends is confirmed also by the Council, is that even atheists are not excluded from the attainment of salvation - under the condition that they have not acted against their moral conscience. Hence even atheists are included within the salvation-optimism of the Council.[262] This does not mean, as Rahner points out, that the good will or good intentions of the atheist simply replace knowledge of and faith in God for the assumption is that an atheist acting in good conscience is seeking the truth but has not been able to find or understand it fully. In this way the requirements of his or her moral conscience are fulfilled without equated or replacing faith in God with acting in good faith.[263]

Rahner, in this manner, believes to have demonstrated that a "guiltless" atheism can be understood as an implicit Christianity inasmuch as "a blameless categorial atheism can be a freely accepted, transcendental theism."[264] And such a freely accepted transcendental theism can also, according to Rahner, in the categorical atheist, be revelation, potential faith, and salvific belief. Hence the salvation-optimism of the Council, which truly has universal implications, is seen to be a justified optimism. Therefore Rahner can conclude that "a theism which is elevated through grace and which is freely accepted ... is a justifying theism and hence an implicit Christianity. And this kind of existential transcendental theism (although not necessarily the object of reflection) is also possible in the case of a (categorial) blameless atheist, whose actions are good and arise from an absolute commitment; therefore *this* kind of atheist can be an implicit Christian."[265]

We have seen, therefore, that for Rahner as for Pannenberg the implications of the universality of the Christian faith have led to ground-breaking and fruitful treatment of the question of contemporary atheism. In contrast to Pannenberg, however, Rahner has seldom engaged atheism or its arguments directly in dialogue but has instead focused on establishing, on the basis of a dogmatic *a priori*, a perspective of atheism which he hopes will lay the foundation for necessary further dialogue. At this point the methodological differences between the two thinkers reveal themselves in the forms of response to the atheistic challenge. The shared assumption of the universal validity of theology, however, remains the driving force behind the endeavors of both theologians in their respective treatments of the question.

## 5.4 Summary and Conclusions

### 5.4.1 *Jesus as universal criterion of salvation*

Rahner contends that also for the non-Christian religions the light which is to be found within them is based upon the person of Jesus Christ and that Jesus

---

[262] *Ibid.*, 149 and 150. [192 and 194.] Cf. also "*Lumen gentium*" 16.
[263] *Ibid.*, 152f. [196f.]
[264] *Ibid.*, 160. [207.]
[265] *Ibid.*, 163. [211.]

Christ is thus to be found in the non-Christian religions as well.[266] In arriving at this conclusion, however, Rahner does not follow the approach of the phenomenology of religion or any other science of religion but rather approaches the question dogmatically.[267] And in this approach we see a distinction to Pannenberg who, though sympathetic to the conclusions reached, finds problematic the tendency in Rahner and other Roman Catholic theologians to arrive at them dogmatically, bypassing the sciences of religion.[268] Rahner contends:

> A dogmatic theologian has to think *a priori* here, unlike the religious historian, whose task is to discover Christ as far as possible *a posteriori* in the non-Christian religions. This means that the dogmatic theologian's reflections can provide only something like a provisional indication for the religious historian. ... The question here is ... simply this: what dogmatic principles and reflection have we to postulate prior to a historical investigation, with regard to the question to be formulated and the probable result, when we are considering whether Christ can be present in the non-Christian religions? Whether the religious historian can then himself fulfil this expectation *a posteriori*, whether he falls short of it in the facts he discovers, or whether he perhaps goes even further - that must remain an entirely open question here.[269]

This 'a priori' dogmatic consideration is prompted by Rahner's understanding of the universal salvific relevance of Jesus Christ. Hence "a 'presence' of Jesus Christ throughout the whole history of salvation and in relation to all people cannot be denied or overlooked by Christians if they believe in Jesus Christ as the salvation of *all* people."[270] In support of this position Rahner goes on to suggest two dogmatic presuppositions appropriate to the question at hand. First, he suggests that there is a general supernatural divine will to salvation which is really efficacious and which implies a universal opportunity of faith. And second, when a non-Christian obtains salvation through faith, hope and love, the non-Christian religions cannot be thought to have played no positive role.[271] Given these assumptions the question which must be asked is how Jesus can be understood as being present and efficacious in the non-Christian religions.[272] In asking the question itself, however, we see that for Rahner it is not conceivable that there

---

[266] Rahner, "The One Christ and the Universality of Salvation," 216f. [*Schriften* 12:272f.], contends that "all men only achieve salvation through Christ," but recognizes as well that "this is not self-evident and is sometimes not given sufficient consideration in contemporary theory when the question of non-Christian religions and the universality of salvation is being discussed."
[267] So Rahner, "Jesus Christ in the Non-Christian Religions," in: *TI* 17:39ff. [*Schriften* 12:370ff.] Cf. also *FCF*, 311ff. [*Grundkurs*, 303ff.]
[268] Cf. *TPS*, 365. [*WtT*, 368.]
[269] "Jesus Christ in the Non-Christian Religions," 40. [*Schriften* 12:370ff.]
[270] *FCF*, 312. [*Grundkurs*, 304.]
[271] "Jesus Christ in the Non-Christian Religions," 40f. [*Schriften* 12:371f.] Cf. also *FCF*, 313f. [*Grundkurs*, 305f.]
[272] And this question, arising as a result of the two presuppositions stated by Rahner, is itself "prior to an a posteriori investigation ... and an a posteriori description." (*FCF*, 315. [*Grundkurs*, 307.])

could be salvation outside of or apart from Christ, that is to say, Christ is assumed *a priori* to be the criterion of salvation. In regard to so-called anonymous Christians, therefore, Rahner insists that it is important "that the heathen in his polytheism, the atheist in good faith, the theist outside the revelation of the Old and New Testaments, all possess not only a relationship of faith to God's self-revelation, but also a genuine relationship to Jesus Christ and his saving action."[273] Yet how, one might ask, is this possible when one as an 'anonymous Christian' has little if any explicit knowledge of either Jesus or his saving action?

If members of non-Christian religions can be saved without an explicit knowledge of the Christian religion, then it must be explained how it is that Christ can be in these non-Christian religions. For Rahner the answer is that "Christ is present and operative in non-Christian believers and hence in non-Christian religions in and through his Spirit.[274] After showing that Jesus can and must be identified with the Spirit at work in the non-Christian believer[275] Rahner concludes that "Jesus Christ is always and everywhere present in justifying faith, because this is always and everywhere the seeking *memoria* of the absolute bringer of salvation, who is by definition the God-man, who arrives at his consummation through death and resurrection."[276] Or, elsewhere, "Jesus Christ is the historically concrete presence of God's promise of himself to all humankind at all times and in all places."[277] Thus even in the non-Christian religions there is only one absolute bringer and criterion of salvation - even when he is not consciously confessed or known - namely Jesus Christ.

For Pannenberg as for Rahner Jesus is the only possible universal criterion of salvation. Important, however, is how this criterion is understood. Pannenberg resists the tendency of some Protestant groups, especially of so-called "evangelicals" to make a personal encounter with Jesus the basis of this universal salvation criterion. Hence he writes: "It is right that the occurrence of a personal encounter with Jesus through the Christian message and the response of faith to it is cannot be the *universal* criterion for participation in salvation or for the exclusion from salvation." Pannenberg contends instead that the universal criterion for salvation is to be found in "the factual correspondence or non-correspondence of the individual's behavior with the will of God as proclaimed by Jesus." Specifically, this means that those who Jesus never knew (or who never knew Jesus), but have nevertheless done the works of love which correspond to his message, participate factually in the salvation of the kingdom of God and will

---

[273] "The One Christ and the Universality of Salvation," 220. [*Schriften* 12:276f.]
[274] *FCF*, 316. [308.]
[275] Rahner argues, here, that "insofar as the event of Christ is the final cause of the communication of the Spirit to the world, it can truly be said that this Spirit is everywhere and from the outset the Spirit of *Jesus* Christ, the Logos of God who became man." (*Ibid.*, 318. [309.])
[276] "Jesus Christ in the Non-Christian Religions," 46f. [*Schriften* 12:378.]
[277] "The Church and Atheism," 143. [*Schriften* 15:144.]

be shown mercy at the final judgment.[278] In taking this position Pannenberg makes a clear break with the theology of Augustine, who considered even the virtues of the pagans to be glaring vices.[279]

From this starting point of Jesus as universal criterion of salvation Pannenberg is also able to express a salvation-optimism in regard to those who do not explicitly confess Christ which bears, as we have seen, some resemblance to Rahner's theory of an anonymous Christianity, without using that actual terminology.[280] For Pannenberg the possibility of salvation outside the church is most clear in the account of Jesus' descent into hell in I Peter 3:19f. which we examined in chapter three. On the basis of this passage Pannenberg is able to contend that Jesus' descent into hell expresses the extent to which all those persons "who lived before Jesus' activity and those who did not know him have a share in the salvation that has appeared in him." Hence the descent into hell definitively demonstrates for Pannenberg that those "outside the visible church are not automatically excluded from salvation."[281]

Also, it is precisely in Jesus as the universal criterion of salvation that Christians recognize their advantage in being explicit Christians rather than having only an implicit faith. The advantage, according to Pannenberg, "consists in the fact that in the person of Jesus they *know* the model of the participation in eternal life, and moreover, in the fact that through the binding of their life with Jesus Christ in baptism and in faith they can already now be certain of their future participation in eternal life."[282] In other words, there is still advantage in being explicitly Christian and thus still ground for Christian mission for only in explicit faith in Christ do we know the actual person who is the criterion of our salvation and only in connection to him through baptism and explicit faith can we possess assurance of our salvation.

### 5.4.2 *Theology's claim to universality and the truth claims of the world's religions*

Both Rahner and Pannenberg have done considerable service to their respective traditions by providing a positive assessment of the value of non-Christian religions without sacrificing Christianity's claim to universality. Indeed, the distinct and innovative approaches of both theologians arise out of their commitment to the universal relevance of Christianity's truth claims. Although the methodological differences, with Rahner's dogmatically oriented *a priori*

---

[278] *ST* 3:661f. Also for those who are alienated from the church there remains the possibility of participation in God's salvation but, as Pannenberg stresses, "auch für solche allerdings bleibt der von der Kirche verkündigte Christus Jesus das Kriterium der Teilhabe am Heil Gottes" (p. 567).

[279] Cf. Augustine, *The City of God*, trans. Marcus Dods (New York: Random House, 1950), 158ff. [V, 12] and 706f. [XIX, 25].

[280] Cf. *ST* 3:686.

[281] *Jesus - God and Man*, 272. [*Grundzüge*, 280.]

[282] *ST* 3:663.

approach and Pannenberg's reliance upon the sciences of religion and the *a posteriori* approach which they entail, distinguish the programs of the two theologians also in their theologies of religion, the similarity in their conclusions is once again striking.

In both theologians one finds an apologetic based on the underlying conviction of theology's - and Christianity's - universality. In contrast to some advocates of religious pluralism who find no basis for Christianity's claim to absoluteness and propose merely an inter-religious exchange of ideas, both Pannenberg and Rahner approach non-Christian religions with the conviction that Christianity, precisely in its claim to universality, is relevant for them too and has something concrete to say. In this one finds a basis for mission that goes beyond the mere dialogical exchange of ideas that some would today define as 'mission.'

Similarly, not only does the recognition of theology's universality provide the basis for non-Christian religions to be approached with the truth claims of the Christian message, but it also allows both Pannenberg and to give a positive evaluation to non-Christian religions and see God at work and witnessed to in them in such a way that they too have something to say to the Christian theologian. Hence the apologetic implication of theology's universality is twofold in relation to the non-Christian religions. Christianity finds the basis for constructive dialogue and indeed mission in the conviction that the universal validity of the message of the gospel means it has something concrete to say to adherents of all other religions. At the same time, however, the crass imperialism and arrogance of Christianity's claims to absoluteness found in many previous theologies of religion is avoided inasmuch as the recognition of theology's universality also means the recognition that God is everywhere at work - even in non-Christian religions - and that they too are not left wholly without God's grace and that what they have to say cannot be irrelevant for Christian theology.[283]

---

[283] Even though it has been observed that, "Rahner's theologoumenon of the anonymous Christian was never intended to be an apologetic instrument, nor can it be used as such." (Weger, *Karl Rahner: An Introduction*, 118), one must recognize that this theologoumenon, or at least its theological foundations, is nevertheless foundational for Rahner's apologetic in regard to the non-Christian religions. As an 'instrument' of apologetics we would agree that it has no function. Who, after all, would begin a dialogue with a non-Christian by insisting that they consider the possibility that they may very well be an anonymous Christian? Yet on the basis of this view Rahner is able to approach the non-Christian with the message of the gospel and its truth claims, recognizing the need for explicit faith, and yet also recognize that the non-Christian religion is not devoid of truth and is not irrelevant for Christian theology.

# Chapter Six

## THE UNIVERSALITY OF THEOLOGICAL SCIENCE AND THE NATURAL SCIENCES

### 6.1 Rahner: Theology and the Regional Sciences

#### 6.1.1 Foundations of the dialogue between theology and the natural sciences

##### 6.1.1.1 *Historical context of theology/science dialogue in Roman Catholic thought*

As a Roman Catholic theologian Rahner's view of and dialogue with the natural sciences must be understood within the context the history of the relationship between the Roman Catholic Church and the natural sciences. This history, rightly or wrongly, continues to be dominated by the shadow cast over it by the so-called Galileo affair. The incident sheds light not only upon the self-consciousness of contemporary Roman Catholic thought in regard to the scientific community, but also into the political workings of the church's hierarchy which to the present day has continued to play a decisive role in the science/theology dialogue within Roman Catholic theology.

A series of rather complicated events seems to have made Copernicanism and its chief defender, Galileo Galilei (1564-1642), the subject of a controversy that extended to Rome itself. Galileo, against the advice of his supporters, decided to go to Rome personally in late 1615 to defend the Copernican theory, as well as his own reputation, before Pope Paul V. There he was confronted by Cardinal Bellarmine in the so-called 'first trial' of Galileo. Galileo argued that Scripture is not a science text and that statements such as those concerning the motion (or lack thereof) of the earth, sun and planets should not be interpreted literally. He also was convinced of the correctness of the Copernican theory and seemed to want it recognized, perhaps too quickly, as more than just a theory. Bellarmine, on the other hand, adopted an exegetical method that required a literal interpretation of the biblical passages in question and demanded that the Copernican theory be considered as just that, unless it could be proven.[1]

Pope Paul V seems to have pressed the Congregation of the Index for a quick decision. The result was that Copernicus' *de revolutionibus* was placed on the Index "until corrected." One could still read Copernicus' book with

---

[1] Cf. Jerome J. Langford, Galileo, *Science and the Church* (Ann Arbor: University of Michigan Press, 1966), 78.

permission, however, and his theory could still be discussed, but only as an hypothesis "false and contrary to Scripture" and not as fact.² Galileo himself was not forced to abjure his opinion at this hearing and even sought and procured a letter to that effect from Cardinal Bellarmine.

When Maffeo Barberini, an old friend and defender of Galileo, became Pope Urban VIII in 1623 Galileo wasted little time in returning to Rome and seeking permission to publish his long anticipated book on the system of the world.³ After several discussions with the Pope, Galileo obtained permission to discuss his theories hypothetically and impartially. Urban was unwilling, however, to revoke the decree of 1616, although Galileo, in long argumentation, attempted to persuade him to do so.⁴ In conversation with Galileo, as Alfred North Whitehead relates the story, the Pope,

> ... made use of the irrefutable argument that, God being omnipotent, it was as easy for him to send the sun and the planets round the earth as to send the earth and the planets round the sun. ... Galileo was annoyed - and very naturally so, for it was an irritating sort of argument with which to counter a great and saving formulation of scientific ideas. Unfortunately he went away and put the pope's argument into the mouth of Simplicius, the man in the *Dialogues* who always advances the foolish objections.⁵

The perceived personal insult, combined with the challenges against the authority of the papacy from the Reformation and pressure from Spain to follow a political agenda favorable to its dynastic ambitions, put tremendous pressure on Urban to act so that the condemnation of Galileo, which finally took place on June 22, 1633, took on the character of a "genuine political necessity" for Pope Urban VIII.⁶ The original, harsh sentence of life imprisonment was commuted to house arrest, which enabled Galileo, even though his writings were now forbidden, to continue writing and to publish his works clandestinely. Galileo died on January 8, 1642, almost 78 years of age and still under house arrest. It was not until 1992, 350 years after his death, that Galileo was officially 'rehabilitated' by the Roman Catholic Church.⁷

While the Roman hierarchy's involvement in questions concerning natural science has caused considerable difficulty and tension in the relationship between the natural sciences and Roman Catholic theology it also arose out of the

---

2   For this and the following see *ibid.*, 97ff.
3   *Ibid.*, 111.
4   Stillman Drake, "A Biographical Sketch," in: *Galileo: Man of Science*, ed. Ernan McMullin (Princeton Junction: NJ: The Scholar's Bookshelf, 1967), 62.
5   Alfred North Whitehead, "The First Physical Synthesis," in: Whitehead, *The Interpretation of Science*, ed. A.H. Johnson (New York: Bobbs-Merrill, 1961), 5.
6   Ludovico Geymonat, Galileo Galilei: *A Biography and Inquiry into His Philosophy of Science*, trans. Stillman Drake (New York: McGraw Hill, 1965), 139.
7   Cf. "Galilei: Mißverständnis ausgeräumt," and "Schmerzliches Mißverständnis im 'Fall Galileo' überwunden," in: *L'Osservatore Romano* 22, nos. 45 and 46 (Nov. 6 and 13, 1992), both page 1.

essentially correct conviction that theological knowledge and the knowledge gained from the natural sciences are not unrelated or irrelevant for one another - a view which dominated, as we shall see, much of Protestant thought during the last four centuries. Of particular significance is the Roman Catholic view of the relationship between faith and reason which took expression in the midst of the turmoil between theology and the natural sciences in the middle of the nineteenth century. In Pius IX's encyclical "*Qui pluribus*" (1846) he criticized those who attack the Christian faith on the basis of "philosophy, which is completely engaged in investigating the truth of nature" and contended that even if faith is above reason there can never be a real conflict between the two for both arise out of the same source in the eternal and unchanging truth of God. Reason and faith, therefore, help one another and faith has the special function of being able to "liberate reason from all errors."[8]

Expanding upon this statement the First Vatican Council, in its Dogmatic Constitution "*Dei Filius*" (1870), reiterated that a real disagreement cannot arise between faith and reason since the same God who revealed himself and provided the ground for faith also gave humans the light of reason (*rationis lumen*). Once again it is affirmed that a mutual relationship between faith and reason exists and that "*fides vero rationem ab erroribus liberet ac tueatur eamque multiplici cognitione instruat.*" The church, therefore, does not resist the sciences but promotes them since true science witnesses to the fact that it has it origin in God who is "lord of the sciences." Hence "*Dei Filius*" proclaims boldly:

> *Quapropter tantum abest, ut Ecclesia humanarum artium et disciplinarum culturae obsistat, ut hanc multis modis juvet atque promoveat. Non enim commoda ab iis ad hominum vitam dimanantia aut ignorat aut despicit; fatetur immo, eas, quemadmodum a Deo scientiarum Domino profectae sunt, ita, si rite pertractentur, ad Deum iuvante eius gratia perducere.*[9]

The wall of separation between faith and natural science (reason) reflected in the Baconian concept of the "two books" or the two-language theory was thus clearly rejected by the First Vatican Council. Yet the idea, reiterated also by the Council, that faith can and should correct reason of its errors, when interpreted as applying also and perhaps especially to the natural sciences, has often fostered more distance than dialogue.

---

[8] Pius IX, "*Qui pluribus*" (Nov. 9, 1846), in: Denzinger, 2775f.
[9] Dogmatic Constitution "*Dei Filius*," (April 24, 1870), caput 4., in: Denzinger, 3017ff. Cf. also the statement of Leo XIII in his encyclical "Providentissimus Deus," (Nov. 18, 1893) - (found only in early editions of Denziger, no. 1947) where he writes concerning the study of scripture: "*Scripturae sacrae doctori cognitio naturalium rerum bono erit subsidio, quo huius quoque modi captiones in divinos libros instructas facilius detegat et refellat. - Nulla quidem theologum inter et physicum vera dissensio intercesserit, dum suis uterque finibus se contineant, id caventes secundum S. Augustini monitum, 'ne aliquid temere et incognitum pro cognito asserant.'*"

The conviction that the church, specifically the magisterium of the Roman Catholic Church, had the final say over the natural sciences has continued from the time of Galileo into the modern period. That the contention that faith should correct reason of its errors was in fact interpreted as meaning that the church (i.e., the Roman magisterium) should 'supervise' the natural sciences is to be seen in the 1864 Syllabus of Errors issued under Pope Pius IX less than two decades after his encyclical "*Qui pluribus.*" Here it is contended that it is an error to think that the science of philosophy and morality can or must withdraw from the supervision of the authority of the church (57), or that human reason has the same rank as religion and that the theological sciences should be placed on the same level as the philosophical sciences (8).[10]

This approach also led to the initial rejection of the theory of evolution. As Rahner noted, "the first explicit ecclesiastical pronouncement of an official kind [regarding the theory of evolution] was made at the local synod of Cologne in 1860. Here even the moderate theory of descent was rejected. ... In 1895, M. D. Leroy, O.P., had to retract the view he had expressed on moderate transformism ... [and] in 1899, P. Zahn for the same reason had to withdraw from commerce his book *Dogma and Evolution* at the command of the Holy Office."[11] Only with Pius XII's Allocution to the Papal Academy of Sciences in 1941[12] and more poignantly in his encyclical *Humani generis* did it become 'officially' permissible for Roman Catholic theologians (and biologists!) to consider the possibility that the theory of evolution may be correct. As *Humani generis* states: "*Ecclesiae Magisterium non prohibet quominus 'evolutionismi' doctrina, ... pro hodierno humanarum disciplinarum et sacrae theologiae statu, investigationibus ac disputationibus peritorum in utroque campo hominum pertractetur,* ..."[13]

That this attitude has continued into our own century - with somewhat of an unusual twist - is to be seen in Pius XII's judgment on the Big Bang theory of the origin of the universe. The apparent close parallels of the theory of the Big Bang to the idea of a *creatio originans* led Pope Pius XII to take the virtually unprecedented step in 1951 of declaring the theory to be compatible with the Christian doctrine of creation.[14] For Pius XII this meant that the 'Big Bang' represented a point beyond which human reason and science could not extend, a point beyond which one could only keep silent in face of the inscrutable mystery of God and his creative act. Yet, although in this instance the magisterium appeared to be deciding in favor of natural science rather than opposing it - as in the Galileo affair - essentially very little had changed in regard to the attitude of

---

10 Pius IX, "*Syllabus*," (Dec. 8, 1864), in: Denzinger, 2957 and 2908. (Cf. also 2909-2914).
11 Rahner, "Hominisation (Evolution II. B)," in: *Sacramentum Mundi* 2:295f. ["Hominisation" in: *SM* 2:758f.]
12 Cf. earlier editions of Denziger, 2286.
13 "*Humani generis*," in: Denzinger 3896.
14 See Pius XII, "Modern Science and the Existence of God," in: *The Catholic Mind* (March 1952), 182-192.

the magisterium concerning natural science and its relationship to theology since the time of Galileo.[15] Not only did it appear that theology was being bound with a particular scientific cosmology, but once again the pope was found to be making a pronouncement, albeit a positive one, in regard to the accuracy of a scientific theory. Nevertheless, the effect upon Roman Catholic theologians was to encourage more dialogue and openness toward the natural sciences.[16] Indeed, Rahner's own engagement with the natural sciences must also be seen within the context of what has been perceived as a new openness and support of the value and validity of the natural sciences.

Although the attitude of the Roman magisterium played a dominant role in the relationship between theology and the natural sciences from Galileo to our own time other factors also come into play which are relevant for understanding the context of the relationship between theology and the natural sciences in the Roman Catholic Church. Of particular significance for Rahner is the long history of achievements in the natural sciences by his own order, the Society of Jesus. Through a certain amount of intellectual freedom which predominated within its ranks the Order proved to be fertile ground for a number of natural scientists. From the earliest days mathematics - which is the fundament and language of so many of the natural sciences - was highly valued. The Jesuits also carried on remarkable astronomical studies, especially in light of the difficulties associated with Copernicus and Galileo, and operated observatories from Parma to Peking.[17] Additionally, the thought of a number of individual thinkers on the relationship between natural theology and science has helped to form the context of the science/theology dialogue within the Roman Catholic tradition. Especially significant is the impact of the Jesuit priest and natural scientist Pierre Teilhard de

---

[15] Rahner's disagreement with this traditional approach to the natural sciences by the Roman magisterium is expressed cautiously in one of his last writings, "'Paul VII. an Peppino' - Ein Papstbrief aus dem 21. Jahrhundert," in: *Das Papsttum: Epochen und Gestalten*, ed. Bruno Moser (Munich: Südwest Verlag, 1983), 288. Rahner, speaking as he wishes future popes would speak to this issue, writes: "Sowenig die Wahrheit des Christentums dem richterlichen Spruch des profanen Selbstverständnisses des Menschen und seiner Wissenschaften unterworfen ist, so notwendig ist - um sich diese christliche Wahrheit wirklich aneignen zu können - ein dauernder Dialog zwischen den Trägern der christlichen Botschaft und den Trägern des profanen Selbstverständnisses des Menschen notwendig, ein Dialog, der nie abgeschlossen ist. Gott hat nun einmal nicht gewollt, daß dieses zweifache Wissen adäquat in Personalunion in einem einzigen Menschen existiere, und auch nicht in einem Papst. Und darum muß auch ein Papst, auch wenn er ... seine ... Lehrautorität in Anspruch nimmt und reden muß wie einer, der Macht hat ..., dennoch immer auch in einem offenen Dialog seine Botschaft ausrichten."

[16] Even with this impetus, however, there has been very little dialogue from the side of theology which actually took place. As Rahner was well aware: "In recent decades theology has not occupied itself very intensively with borderline questions between the natural sciences and itself." So Rahner, "Natural Science and Reasonable Faith: Theological Perspectives for Dialogue with the Natural Sciences," in: *TI* 21:16. [*Schriften* 15:24.]

[17] Cf. Hubert Becher, *Die Jesuiten: Geschichte und Gestalt des Ordens* (Munich: Kösel, 1951), 220ff., and esp. 238f.

Chardin who has had significant influence upon a whole generation of theologians, including Rahner, and whose thought we will take up later in this chapter.[18]

### 6.1.1.2 The regional character of the individual sciences

Rahner, like Pannenberg, was convinced that theology had universal relevance and that this meant, also in relation to the natural sciences, that theology not only can learn from the special sciences but also has something to say to them. In a passage which typifies Rahner's approach to the natural sciences he contends that for theology,

> it is utterly unacceptable ... to regard some object (or the inquiry into it) as dogmatically or theologically irrelevant just because it is also to be found in the field of the profane sciences or has such a scientific aspect or consequence. One cannot allot their respective competencies to theology and the sciences simply by telling them to 'part and be friends'. One cannot begin by timidly banishing the objects of theology to an 'existential' beyond, the sphere of 'the events of faith', with the result that they are no longer even capable of disturbing the profane sciences or being disturbed by them.[19]

That theology and the natural sciences must have the possibility to 'disturb' and 'be disturbed' by one another is clear. This implies, of course, a dialogue (or at least the possibility of dialogue) between theology and the natural sciences. Before we turn our attention, however, to the form and tone of this dialogue as it manifests itself in Rahner's own theology we must ask how Rahner perceives the natural sciences in relation to theology. That is to say, we must inquire as to which conceptual model of the natural sciences and theology serves as the basis in Rahner's thought for a possible dialogue between the two.

Throughout Rahner's writings one conceptual model of the natural sciences recurs, namely, the conception of the natural sciences - and of the special sciences in general - as regional sciences. In approaching the question of the relationship between theology and the natural sciences Rahner presupposes, "that every science is *per definitionem* a particular branch of human knowledge [*eine regionale Erkenntnis*], but that this does not apply to divine revelation and theology, ... and finally that this fundamental difference must have a decisive influence upon the relationship between theology and the sciences." Each of the special sciences, according to Rahner, implies a regional, categorical knowledge because they have to do with the examination and comparison of individual phenomena.[20] As regional sciences the natural sciences are limited

---

[18] On the influence of Teilhard upon Roman Catholic theology see Leo O'Donovan, "Der Dialog mit dem Darwinismus," in: *Wagnis Theologie*, ed. Herbert Vorgrimler, 216.
[19] "Theological Reflections on Monogenism," 274. [*Schriften* 1:300.]
[20] "On the Relationship between Theology and the Contemporary Sciences," in: *TI* 13:95. ["Zum Verhältnis zwischen Theologie und heutigen Wissenschaften," in: *Schriften* 10:105.]

epistemologically - both individually and taken together - since their knowledge is necessarily a knowledge of the parts. Hence,

> Natural science as one element within the single whole of man's knowledge knows a great deal 'about' matter, that is, it determines ever more exact relationships of a functional kind among the phenomena of nature. But since it abstracts from man ... it can know a great deal 'about' matter, but it cannot know *matter itself*, although its knowledge does lead back to man himself in an a posteriori way. This is really self-evident: the field or the whole cannot be determined by the means by which the parts are determined.[21]

Through this model Rahner is able to distinguish theology and the natural sciences in their nature and tasks. Because the natural sciences are regional sciences they investigate "in a posteriori experience individual experience which human beings ... encounter in their world." Theology, on the other hand, "has to do with the totality of reality as such, and with the ground of this reality, and its method is ultimately one of a priori questioning."[22] Theological statements, Rahner contends, are located properly in the transcendence of the human person and in the person's transcendental experience, which is "orientated towards that absolute Mystery ... which we call 'God', and which constitutes the true 'subject' of theological statements."[23] Thus Rahner contends, seen from this perspective, that there is a clear distinction between natural science and theology. He writes:

> The natural sciences investigate concrete individual phenomena which people encounter in their objective experience. ... With the methods of natural science it is not possible at all for human beings to let themselves be confronted all at once with all possible phenomena of reality. ... These sciences as such offer no possibility of doing this. They necessarily proceed from an individual phenomenon within a larger spectrum of realities and experiences which are possible but which have not yet been realized. Theology, on the other hand, makes an affirmation about God as the one and absolute ground of all realities. It grounds the multiplicity of all realities which can be experiences as individual realities in an absolute reality, which is not one individual element *within* this

---

[21] FCF, 182. [*Grundkurs*, 184.] This view of Rahner's has found some favorable response among natural scientists, at least to the extent that there seems to be an emerging agreement that the natural sciences are not able to explain the whole of reality. Physicist Wolfgang Wild, "Vom Weltverständnis der heutigen Naturwissenschaften und seinen Konsequenzen für den Umgang mit der Welt: Ein Beitrag zum Dialog zwischen Karl Rahner und den Naturwissenschaften," in: *Vor dem Geheimnis Gottes den Menschen verstehen: Karl Rahner zum 80. Geburtstag*, ed. Karl Lehmen (Freiburg: Katholische Akadamie, 1984), 37, notes that concerning Rahner's contention that while the natural sciences have to do with individual phenomenon, theology is concerned with the whole of reality and its ground: "Dieser Aussage wird heute die große Mehrheit der Naturwissenschaftler zustimmen; die lange vorherrschende Überzeugung, daß auch die Naturwissenschaft das Ganze der Wirklichkeit erfassen und den diesen Ganzen zugrunde liegenden Sinn erkennen könne, ist dahingeschwunden."

[22] "Natural Science and Reasonable Faith," 19. [*Schriften* 15:26f.]

[23] "On the Relationship between Theology and the Contemporary Sciences," 96. [*Schriften* 10:106.]

manifold world, but rather its ground, which ... establishes it and holds it together.[24]

Since it is the task of theology, which deals with God, that is, with the whole of reality, to address questions of the original unity of all realities and not the natural sciences, Rahner contends that "natural science may and should be methodologically atheistic." There is no need, according to Rahner, in linking one individual phenomenon to another to "bring God into the picture."[25] This does not imply, however, that Rahner believes that God has nothing to do with the individual processes and phenomena studied by the natural sciences for these are parts of the greater whole of reality of which God is the ground. Indeed, Rahner contends that in dialogue with the natural sciences theology must insist that "from the point of view of their inception and in their end result the things that natural scientists themselves personally pursue in their science reach beyond the immediate object of these sciences, ... and this it is which compels them to be something more than natural scientists."[26] Rahner, instead, is addressing the question of competencies. The special sciences, as regional sciences, cannot be expected to examine the whole in its original unity. This, rather, is the function of theology. Hence, as Rahner explains, "the whole, when viewed as a sum which has been added up, requires a whole which is originally one single whole. But this step is not the task of the natural sciences, but of metaphysics and theology."[27]

Theology, therefore, is seen to have a unique and special status over against the various regional sciences. This does not, however, imply a return to the idea of theology as "queen of the sciences" in the sense in which this was understood in medieval thought when theology dominated over the other sciences. Theology, rather, is seen to have a special role in relation to all the regional sciences but remains only one science among many. As Rahner confesses: "Theology, ... known as the supreme science, is not a kind of sovereign ruler reducing the other sciences to acting as its instruments and carrying out its plans; it is *one* science among others, with the special task of providing a living example of the fact that the pluralism of the sciences does not permit any dominion that could be exercised by man in a kind of theological totalitarianism."[28]

### 6.1.1.3 *Epistemological-theological foundations of the science/theology dialogue*

For Rahner the question of epistemology lies at the heart of the dialogue between natural science and theology. From the standpoint of theology, Rahner has contended that it is desirable that both sides in the dialogue "treat in general

---

[24] "Natural Science and Reasonable Faith," 19ff. [*Schriften* 15:26ff.]
[25] *Ibid.*, 21. [29.]
[26] "Theology Today," in: *TI* 21:66. ["Theologie Heute," in: *Schriften* 15:72.]
[27] "Natural Science and Reasonable Faith," 21. [*Schriften* 15:29.]
[28] Rahner, "On the Relationship between Natural Science and Theology," in: *TI* 19:19. ["Zum Verhältnis von Naturwissenschaft und Theologie," in: *Schriften* 14:67.]

some epistemological questions and some questions of the philosophy of science regarding the essence, autonomy, points of tangency, lines of demarcation, and possible areas of conflict" between theology and the natural sciences.[29] Theology, given the nature of its task and because it is almost always carried out in dialogue with philosophy, has a more natural interest in epistemological questions than the natural sciences. Indeed, "fundamental theology cannot do without ongoing dialogue with traditional epistemology." This natural and necessary interest of theology in issues of epistemology, however, does not, according to Rahner, "alleviate the extreme difficulty of dialogue between the natural sciences and theology starting right from problems of epistemology." One problem is that neither natural scientists nor theologians are agreed among themselves on epistemological questions.[30] More significantly, however, the approaches to 'knowing' within the theological and scientific camps are very different from one another, which makes dialogue between the two difficult.

At this point Rahner proposes a unique solution to the problem of epistemology in the natural science/theology dialogue, namely the possibility of an "existentiell epistemology" which allows for the coexistence of varying convictions within theology and the natural sciences. An existentiell epistemology, as understood by Rahner, would entail "a basic justification ... for a permissible and sustained coexistence of simultaneous convictions in the same subject, wherein a *positive* and intelligible synthesis has not, or, at least, has not yet been achieved." Such an existentiell epistemology would, according to Rahner, allow for "a peaceful relationship between theology and natural science" even in those areas where significant disagreement is to be found. What his proposal does not mean, however, is an acceptance of a two-language or 'two books' view of reality in which theology and the natural sciences each go their own way and have nothing to say to one another. Rather, ongoing dialogue can and must take place precisely in the broad area between "a positive synthetization of elements of knowledge from diverse disciplines and the determination of an absolute contradiction positively recognized as such."[31] Hence, as long as an absolute determination of a contradiction has not been achieved - which is very difficult when all the facts are not yet in or have not yet been properly evaluated - then there is still the room for and necessity of dialogue.

This dialogue - and indeed the relationship between theology and the natural sciences in general - is characterized by the very plurality which Rahner has sought to give expression to in his proposal of an existentiell epistemology. From the standpoint of theology Rahner has proposed the unique - and by his own admission unusual - proposition that "the relationship between theology and natural science can be defined theologically perhaps most clearly in the light of

---

[29] "Natural Science and Reasonable Faith," 16. [*Schriften* 15:24.]
[30] Ibid., 17. [24f.]
[31] Ibid., 18. [25f.]

the theological notion of concupiscence." Rahner assumes that the concept of concupiscence applies as well to the realm of knowledge as to that of human will and freedom. By concupiscence Rahner does not, however, simply understand sinfulness. Rather, in this context, concupiscence means that "despite an original unity of man there is a pluralism of his faculties and impulses which in practice can never be integrated into an absolute unity surveyable and controllable from a single point." This non-integrated pluralism of faculties within the human as knower means there will necessarily be "an irreversible pluralism of sciences."[32]

What implications, however, does this proposal of understanding the relationship between theology and the natural sciences as one characterized by concupiscence have upon the actual functional relationship between these two respective fields? The conclusions Rahner draws from this insight are two. First, the plurality of sciences is unavoidable and thus the autonomy and worth of the individual natural sciences must be recognized by theology.[33] The Christian teaching on concupiscence means, according to Rahner, "that there is an insuperable pluralism of the sciences which cannot be completely reduced to a humanly comprehensible system, but must be endured with a prudent restraint and the humility befitting the creature." Hence the unease which the natural sciences often create today for theology cannot be allowed to mislead theology into a denial of their autonomy and meaningfulness.[34] And certainly not because theology feels that they are a threat to its own theological knowledge based upon revelation, for "the genuine results of the sciences cannot ... contradict the teachings of Revelation, because truths which ultimately derive from the same fount of all reality and truth cannot mutually cancel one another."[35] And this point brings us to the question of the potential unity of the plurality of knowledge.

The second conclusion which Rahner draws from the theological conception of concupiscence is that because the human being was originally created as a unity theology, which deals with the unified and unifying ground of all reality, must work toward integrating these various sciences into a unity while at the same time realizing that achieving such a unity is not possible because of concupiscence which is imbedded into our human nature. As Rahner explains:

---

[32] "On the Relationship between Natural Science and Theology," 18. [*Schriften* 14:65f.]
[33] For Rahner, this means more than simply overcoming historical areas of conflict as in the case of Galileo or the conflict over the theory of evolution. For although these conflicts have today largely been resolved, "this does not mean that the task of theology in relation to the natural sciences has been fulfilled, the task, namely, of allowing itself to be instructed by them on their own terms." So Rahner, "Theology as Engaged in an Interdisciplinary Dialogue with the Sciences," 92. [*Schriften* 10:101.]
[34] "On the Relationship between Natural Science and Theology," 19. [*Schriften* 14:66f.]
[35] Rahner, *Hominisation: The Evolutionary Origin of Man as a Theological Problem*, trans. W. O'Hara (New York: Herder and Herder, 1965), 11f. [*Die Hominisation als theologische Frage*, *QD* 12 (Freiburg: Herder, 1961), 16.]

Theology deals with the one all-embracing and sustaining source of all reality and with the one all-integrating and reconciling goal of all history that we call God. But, insofar as theology acknowledges this God precisely as the incomprehensible mystery and declares man to be eternally distinct from this God of original unity, the singular uniqueness and dignity of theology in principle simply does *not* provide the means and the way to overcome this pluralism of the sciences.[36]

Nevertheless, the pursuit of the unity of the individual, regional sciences is an essential task of theology that is not without fruit. He contends, therefore, that theology's function of integrating the individual sciences into a unity "will continually achieve positive results; people will continually perceive ... how things hitherto merely juxtaposed in consciousness fit in with each other." This is the case even in spite of the fact that there will never be "universal formula" within the history of knowledge. The only unity that is possible - within the context of our pluralistic pursuit of knowledge "is the surrender of all knowledge in a *docta ignorantia* to the eternally abiding mystery of God and his underivable will." Hence even the recognition, epistemologically and theologically, of the inevitable plurality of human pursuits of knowledge is able to point ultimately to the unity of God - and by implication is able to lend a certain unity to the plurality of sciences. Therefore the unity to be found in the surrender of our knowledge to the eternal mystery of God is something which is not produced but is granted to us in our act of entrusting the plurality of knowledge to the "only radically one God." And this unity is then also seen to be "part of the task of integrating the pluralism of our knowledge into a unity."[37]

For Rahner, the conclusion of the matter as pertains to the natural science/theology dialogue is that theology must abandon its traditional role of passing judgment over the natural sciences or of determining their legitimacy.[38] Theology cannot, therefore, call the right of existence of the natural sciences into question. Instead, it must learn to live with these in an open and mutual dialogue which recognizes the irreversible plurality of knowledge but which nevertheless, in humble recognition of the unity of the divine mystery, seeks to integrate human knowledge. Hence, according to Rahner, "faith and theology do not really give the natural sciences their right to exist, but find them already existing and thus see that their validity must be recognized even in the light of the very nature of the understanding of man produced by faith; they see that they must live together with

---

[36] "On the Relationship between Natural Science and Theology," 19. [*Schriften* 14:66f.]
[37] *Ibid.*, 21. [69.]
[38] As Rahner, *ibid.*, 19f. [67.], has written: "Theology is accustomed to declare that in a case of conflict it possesses ultimately the competence to decide between true and false, since it can appeal to divine revelation. This traditional statement of its claims by theology may in principle and formally be completely correct. But fundamentally and in the light of historical experience, in such cases of conflict between theology and natural science, theology is equally and frequently compelled to reexamine itself, to understand itself better, to give way to natural science."

these sciences in an open dialogue the concrete outcome of which cannot exactly be foreseen by either side."[39]

### 6.1.2 Rahner's evaluation and use of evolutionary theory

#### 6.1.2.1 *Rahner's assessment of evolutionary theory's significance for theology*

We have already seen in Rahner's conception of the natural sciences as regional sciences that not only can the natural sciences not be expected to take God into account in their methodologies but they should not do this because they would be overstepping their competence as regional sciences. In doing this Rahner is staking out the ground of the whole of reality and of God, who underlies this whole, as the territory of theology and metaphysics. Yet Rahner also recognizes that the regional sciences have their own special competencies and that theology has no special competence to pass judgment upon their results. This is nowhere to be seen more clearly than in Rahner's attitude toward the theory of evolution. Rahner, in his treatment of the implications of the theory of evolution and of the evolutionary view of the world for theology[40] does not evaluate or pass judgment upon the theory itself but rather assumes it. In his treatment of the question of evolution in his article "Natural Science and Christian Faith" Rahner begins by stating that he is "proceeding from the assumption that it is correct that there is a development which determines the entire cosmic reality and continues on through it."[41] Similarly, he has elsewhere contended that theological reflection "proceeds on the assumption that the fact of evolution is established by natural science ... [since] with the resources of theology or philosophy this can neither be proved or rejected as impossible."[42]

This does not mean that Rahner does not recognize that there are problems with evolutionary theory or that it has its opponents. He opens his article on Christology in light of the evolutionary worldview, for instance, by stating boldly that he intends not to question this view but simply to "presuppose that there is such a thing as an evolutionary view of the world, even though this is neither self-evident objectively nor unobjectionable from a methodological point of view."[43] Indeed, Rahner suggests that the more radical question for the theologian would be not to inquire how Christian faith can be understood in light of the evolutionary theory but to ask "how an evolutionary view of the world can be justified before

---

[39] *Ibid.*, 23.
[40] The scope of influence of evolutionary theory upon Rahner's thought is broad. O'Donovan, "Der Dialog mit dem Darwinismus," 217, points out that Rahner has discussed the implications of the evolutionary worldview for theological loci ranging from the doctrine of creation to anthro-pology, from Christology to the theology of history, and from eschatology to Christian ethics.
[41] "Natural Science and Reasonable Faith," 33. [*Schriften* 15:40f.]
[42] Rahner, "Evolution II. Theological," in: *Sacramentum Mundi* 2:289. ["Evolution II. Theologisch," in: *SM* 1:1251.]
[43] Rahner, "Christology within an Evolutionary View of the World," in: *TI* 5:157. ["Die Christologie innerhalb einer evolutiven Weltanschauung," in: *Schriften* 5:183.]

Christian faith."[44] Why, then, does Rahner treat evolutionary theory and the evolutionary view of the world as something that he as a theologian should simply presuppose instead of critically engaging the theory itself? For Rahner the answer is simple. Because this is beyond the competence of theology and belongs instead to the competence of the natural sciences - just as the question of God is beyond the competence of the natural sciences. It is hence not surprising, as Eicher observes, that it is not "the structures of a phenomeno-logical history of the evolution of species ... that has captured Rahner's imagina-tion; Rahner's philosophical efforts are much more based upon the working out of the onto-logical condition for the possibility of evolutionary development."[45]

The focus of Rahner's treatment of the implications of the theory of evolution, therefore, is upon the metaphysical and theological implications of the evolutionary *worldview* and seldom touches upon details of the scientific theory (or better theories) underlying this worldview. Hence, whether the assumption of evolution "is really correct; whether it has to be restricted; for what areas of universal development ... natural science can offer solid arguments and for what areas it cannot; what more precise kinds of 'mechanisms' must be presumed and can be demonstrated for the individual stages of development: all these are questions primarily for the natural scientist and ... lie beyond the competence of the theologian."[46] Theologians, then, are not in the position nor is it their task to defend or denounce specific scientific theories. Rahner's approach to the theory of evolution exemplifies his approach to the conclusions of the natural sciences in general. The theologian must deal with the scientific theories which present themselves and command attention due either to the force or implications of their conclusions or because of the place they hold in formulating the worldview of modern persons. Hence, in regard to the method of approach to the question of evolution, Rahner contends:

> Theologians have the right to presume the most extreme positions of evolutionary thinking (provided these make some degree of sense and do not actually constitute manifest metaphysical disregard for the boundaries on the part of the natural sciences). Then they ask themselves whether they can live with these positions. Theologians do not have to defend these positions themselves, since that is the business of natural scientists. ... The theologians' position, then, is always a hypothetical one: *if* the exponents of the natural sciences maintain this or that, then ...[47]

Yet Rahner's view of evolutionary theory would seem to go beyond a simple *if - then* pragmatism which necessitates our taking the theory seriously whether we wish to or not on the basis of its status in the scientific community. The

---
[44] *FCF*, 178. [*Grundkurs*, 180.]
[45] Peter Eicher, *Die anthropologische Wende*, 373.
[46] "Natural Science and Reasonable Faith," 33. [*Schriften* 15:41.]
[47] *Ibid.*, 33f. [41.]

number of writings Rahner has devoted to the topic as well as the theological interpretations of evolution which he has developed - which we will explore in the following sections - suggests an overall positive, personal evaluation of the evolutionary worldview. Indeed, Rahner has contended that inasmuch as Christian theology holds that all creaturely being is in a process of becoming and change because of its finitude, and that the world in its unity is headed toward a single goal of completion, "the concept of evolution can be employed to describe, in a general and comprehensive way, what characterizes all the reality, distinct from God, which lies within the horizon of our experience."[48] Therefore, as Donald Gelpi has observed, "Rahner himself feels that the theologian must not merely demonstrate the absence of any contradiction between evolutionary theory and revelation. He must also explore their similarities and show possible points of contact between them."[49]

### 6.1.2.2 *Evolution and hominisation*

For Rahner there was no doubt that the question of the appearance of humanity in its scientific, empirical form is also a theological question.[50] Given the importance of anthropology within Rahner's theological program as a whole, therefore, it is not surprising that he has turned so often to the question of *hominisation*. The term hominisation was brought into theological vocabulary by Teilhard de Chardin who held, as Schwarz has summarized, that through the process of hominisation "humanity became human and emerged from the animal world to the noosphere."[51] Rahner, who adopts much of the terminology of Teilhard, draws an important conclusion from the very process of the human's evolving from the cosmosphere to the biosphere and finally into the noosphere - the realm of the human. This process, according to Rahner, implies theologically the connection of humanity and of each individual human to the world as a whole.[52] That is to say, in correspondence with the thematic of universality, the

---

[48] "Evolution II. Theological," 289. [*SM* 1:1252.]
[49] Donald Gelpi, *Life and Light: A Guide to the Theology of Karl Rahner* (New York: Sheed and Ward, 1966), 40.
[50] So Rahner, "Die Frage nach dem Erscheinungsbild des Menschen als Quaestio disputata der Theologie," in: *QD* 7, 11.
[51] Hans Schwarz, *On the Way to the Future: A Christian View of Eschatology in the Light of Current Trends in Religion, Philosophy, and Science*, rev. ed. (Minneapolis: Augsburg, 1979), 118. The term hominisation, as used in the biological sciences, describes or indicates the "stammesgeschichtlichen (phylogenetischen) Vorgang, durch den der Mensch in seinem leiblichen Erscheinungsbild (aufrechter Gang, frei gewordene vordere Gliedmaßen, hohe Schädelkapazität, mächtig gesteigerte Gehirnmasse, reduzierter Gesichtsschädel) und in seiner Psyche (geistgeprägtes Verhalten mit Denken, Sprache, Entscheidungsfreiheit, sozialen Institutionen und Kultur) in kontinuierlicher Transformation aus einer angenommenen Primatengruppe des Tertiärs geworden ist." So Paul Overhage, "Hominisation I. Naturwissenschaftlich," in: *Herders theologisches Taschenlexikon* 3:310.
[52] Rahner, *Hominisation: The Evolutionary Origin of man as a Theological Problem*, *QD* 12, trans. W. J. O'Hara (New York: Herder and Herder, 1965), 24, noting the new freedom in Roman

evolutionary process - especially as conceived by Teilhard - witnesses to our connectedness as individuals (as parts) to the whole of the world. As Rahner explains:

> If man as a spiritual person derives from the biosphere by evolution, then he still belongs to it, if only as the term into which the material world and the biosphere rise above and beyond themselves. Man's derivation from the material and biological world is an enduring one. And in that respect in every human being the entire cosmos attains anew a unique self-possession. Every human being is in dialectical unity both a portion of the cosmos, rooted in the cosmos, and a unique appropriation of the whole cosmos.[53]

The implication of this insight that we have evolved from the biosphere and have our roots within it raises, according to Rahner, two theological questions. First, "does the origin of man from the biosphere signify that in him, the biosphere principles which determine its spatio-temporal unities ..., are still present?" That is to say, does the human 'soul' contain subordinated elements or "forms" out of the biosphere? The formal concept of self-transcendence allows neither a definitely positive or negative answer to this question. If, however, it is possible to conceive of a plurality of forms within the human person as some sort of inheritance form the biosphere then, according to Rahner, the old question of the plurality of forms in the human is raised anew and in an urgent manner, "because through biochemistry and genetics, ... we are now slowly arriving at the possibility of forming a concrete idea of these 'forms' and their manifestations."[54]

The second question implied by humanity's origin from within the biosphere looks not back into our past and the potential inheritance we may have brought with us from our evolutionary past but looks rather to the future of the human race. The question, then, is whether "the history of the biosphere in teleological relation to man is still continuing *within* man as he at present exists?" For Rahner the incarnation of Christ, rather than confirming that in our present form and mode we have already attained to the fullness of humanness, suggests rather - and one notes here the similarity with Teilhard, that the history of the evolution of humans is continuing, or at the very least that one cannot reject the idea that this history of development will continue on theological grounds - for Christ has shown us through his humanness how far we yet have to go.[55]

---

Catholic theology to explore such questions raised by the theory of evolution, writes: "As regards the way man is connected with the whole of material reality, the Church's teaching permits us ... to think of man's original connection between the animal kingdom and man's corporeal nature."

[53] "Evolution II. Theological," 293. [*SM* 1:1260.]
[54] *Ibid.* [1260f.]
[55] *Ibid.* [1261.] Rahner writes: "If it is firmly held that the proper nature of man as a personal spirit open to infinity, cannot *per definitionem* be further exceeded and has already reached its absolute culmination in grace and the Incarnation, nothing in principle can be objected to the idea of a further history of man in his biosphere."

Although Rahner presupposes the origin of the human race from the biosphere humans are "not simply and solely the product of the 'biosphere'" but are also and more fundamentally a creation of God. This is in the first place to be seen from metaphysical anthropology which establishes that there exists a radical difference between human beings and the animal world. This means, then, that "a causal origin of man from the world around him, even if it is thought of as active self-transcendence, within the requisite dynamism of the divine concursus, has at the same time quite definitely the character of a new, direct creation by God." And secondly, the origin of humans as the creation of God and not simply a product of the biosphere can be seen in the theological consideration that 'soul' and 'matter' "signify substantial principles of an individual being, not two complete beings subsequently combined." Because soul and matter form a substantial unity it is therefore inappropriate to speak of the soul as being created by God and to attribute the formation of the body to evolution alone. Hence for Rahner the theological understanding of the unity of body and soul can only mean that "the whole man is directly created by God."[56]

This connection between body and soul implies at the same time, however, that the "evolution of the body can only mean that the whole man takes his origin from the world around him." These two conclusions, drawn from the fact of the unity of body and soul, would seem to contradict one another. Rahner contends, however, that both statements made simultaneously about the same humanity are possible "because the concepts of becoming and causal dependence do not exclude but rather ... include a 'qualitative leap.'" Or, as Rahner also explains, the causal dependence of the creature upon God is not incompatible with evolution when seen within the context of "the divine dynamism which supports from within ... [the creature's] becoming."[57]

In evolutionary theory all being is in dynamic evolution toward fullness of perfection. As Gelpi indicates, the significant point here for Rahner's thought is that "in an evolutionary context fullness of perfection comes to mean self-transcendence, even at the level of substance." Therefore once we take the step - as does Rahner - of grounding "the self-transcendence of created being in the absolute being of God, there is no fundamental philosophical or theological difficulty in admitting evolution, even the evolution of man."[58] Hence Rahner's solution to the tension between evolution and direct creation is the supposition that "God supports most intimately, from within the creature as a mutual being in its becoming, in its movement of self-development and self-transcendence. Becoming ultimately means active rising beyond self, in which God so moves the mover that it receives its own self-movement and is directed toward him." The universe, including human life, is seen in its evolving to have a "a single goal, its

---

[56] Rahner, "Hominisation (Evolution II. B)," 294. [*SM* 2:754f.] Cf. similarly "Die Frage nach dem Erscheinungsbild des Menschen als Quaestio disputata der Theologie," 18.
[57] *Ibid.* [755.]
[58] Gelpi, 40f.

salvation, transfiguration and accomplishment in the kingdom of God" and it is "directed and impelled by God from the start towards that goal." And this goal, according to Rahner, is to be found in humanity itself as pinnacle of God's creation.[59]

Hence Rahner contends that "the becoming of the material world can ... be regarded as oriented from within by God, in dynamic self-transcendence towards man, in whom the world achieves immanence, subjectivity, freedom, history and personal fulfilment." Only at this point, that is, in light of the end of his theological and philosophical considerations, does Rahner define what he means by hominisation. Namely, "hominisation designates that occurrence in nature in which the universe finds itself in man and is consciously confronted with its origin and goal."[60]

With his reflections on hominisation Rahner has sought to affirm both the evolution and the direct divine creation of the human being, overcoming the either/or choice between the two which has characterized much of modern thought within both the theological and scientific communities. Yet Rahner is not naive regarding the actual tension between the biblical-theological view of human origins and that of evolutionary theory arising out of the natural sciences.[61] He does not intend, therefore, to imply that "the two sets of statements of natural science and of theology regarding the beginnings of mankind, can be made directly and positively to coincide in a concrete picture, so that it can be stated just how things happened." Yet at the same time "it cannot be said ... that the two sets of statements contradict one another."[62]

### 6.1.2.3 Christology within an evolutionary worldview (Teilhard de Chardin)

The work of Teilhard de Chardin has left its mark upon modern Roman Catholic theology. This is perhaps nowhere to be more clearly seen than in the thought of Karl Rahner. As O'Donovan has observed: "Theologians in the generation following Teilhard have strived to take up similar themes in their own work. None of them, however, has given the question a more central or thorough treatment within his own work than ... [Karl Rahner]."[63] Similarly, the Protestant theologian George Lindbeck has also noted that "Rahner has developed views resembling Teilhard de Chardin's (though theologically and philosophically much

---

[59] "Hominisation (Evolution B)," 296. [*SM* 2:759.]
[60] *Ibid.*
[61] Rahner, *Hominisation*, 101f., has summarized the basic difference between the biblical and scientific-evolutionary view of human origins as follows: "The beginning of mankind according to scientific anthropology is a beginning in indigence and vacuity as the lowest point of a rising curve, whereas the biblical and ecclesiastical curve has a beginning in plenitude and the line of 'development' descends from it. ... For the natural sciences, Paradise in a way stands at the end of evolutionary development, for the Bible, at the beginning of a history."
[62] *Hominisation*, 107f.
[63] O'Donovan, "Der Dialog mit dem Darwinismus," 217.

more subtle and sophisticated) by attempting to interpret the modern evolutionary world outlook in terms of a biblical, realistic eschatology."[64]

In the preceding section we have already briefly examined the influence of Teilhard upon Rahner's conception of hominisation. For Teilhard, however, the process of hominisation is just one stage in the overall evolutionary process. In the next and final stage the world experiences 'christification' through which all things will achieve their culmination in the 'Omega Point.' We will examine here briefly Teilhard's conception of christification and then turn our attention to the impact of this christological interpretation of the evolutionary process upon Rahner's own thought.

Teilhard, like Rahner a Jesuit priest, dedicated most of his energies as a thinker to the espousal of an emerging "Christian evolutionism."[65] Teilhard divided the evolutionary process into four distinct, ascending phases. First, there is the *cosmosphere* of the inanimate world in which there is not yet life. Then comes the *biosphere* in which life appears. Through a process of hominisation there then appears the *noosphere* in which human beings are the pinnacle of the evolutionary process to that point.[66] It is primarily in this sphere that we now find ourselves. The process of evolution, however, in Teilhard's view, has not yet reached its culmination. Already through the appearance of Christ and the process of christification we are on our way to the *christosphere* which itself will culminate in the Omega Point where all things will be taken up into Christ.

Hence for Teilhard the figure of Christ (and Christology) plays a central role in his evolutionary view of the world - and vice versa. Indeed, the concepts of evolution and Christ are inseparably related in his thought. He contends that: "A Christ whose features do not adapt themselves to the requirements of a world that is evolutive in structure will tend more and more to be eliminated out of hand. ... And correspondingly, if a Christ is to be completely acceptable as an object of worship, he must be presented as the saviour of the idea and reality of evolution."[67] As in the later Rahner, the incarnation of Christ is central for understanding Christ's role within the evolution of the world - specifically the world of humans. In bringing Christ and evolution together - which means bringing Christ and the universe together - Teilhard postulates a *Christus-Universalis*, or universal Christ, who is a synthesis of Christ and the universe. This, however, is by no means "a new godhead - but an inevitable deployment of the mystery in which Christianity is summed up, the mystery of the Incarnation."[68]

---

[64] So George Lindbeck, "The Thought of Karl Rahner, S.J.," 213.
[65] Cf. Pierre Teilhard de Chardin, "Christianity and Evolution," in: *Christianity and Evolution* (New York: Harcourt, Brace, Jovanovich, 1969), 173ff.
[66] For Teilhard's discussion of the character of the biosphere and the formation of the noosphere, especially through the processes of socialization and individuation, see Teilhard de Chardin, *Man's Place in Nature*, trans. R. Hague (London: Collins, 1966.)
[67] Teilhard de Chardin, "Christology and Evolution," in: *Christianity and Evolution*, 78.
[68] Teilhard de Chardin, "How I Believe," in: *Christianity and Evolution*, 126.

The evolutionary process, according to Teilhard, reveals a universal cosmic center, in which everything arrives at a goal, in which everything finds its explanation, and through which everything is steered. And in this universal cosmic center we must recognize the *Christus-Universalis* in his fullness. The process of evolution and Christ are then closely identified and interdependent so that "by disclosing a world-peak, evolution makes Christ possible, just as Christ, by giving meaning and direction to the world, makes evolution possible."[69] This bond between Christ and universe continues until the eschaton. The *Christus-Universalis* is then revealed as the Omega-Point - the true end of the evolutionary process in which all things are brought together and find their fulfillment.

Rahner, in his crucial article "Christology within an Evolutionary View of the World," reveals his indebtedness to Teilhard in connecting Christology and evolution but also departs from Teilhard's thought in several significant ways.[70] In the first place, Rahner makes clear that he is approaching the topic not armed with the theorems and language of the natural scientist as did Teilhard, but as a theologian. As he has similarly written in his *Foundations of Christian Faith*: "We are trying to avoid the theories which Teilhard de Chardin has made current. If we reach the same conclusions, so much the better, and we do not have to avoid that deliberately. We ourselves only want to reflect here upon what every theologian could say if he brought his theology to bear upon those questions which are raised by an evolutionary view of the world."[71] Rahner begins, therefore, not with the scientific data, but with his view of "man as the being in whom the basic tendency of matter to find itself in the spirit by self-transcendence arrives at the point where it definitely breaks through."[72] Hence Rahner, in raising the question about Christology within an evolutionary view of the world, is essentially asking a "transcendental question, but it has a historical concreteness in the hearer" - a concreteness which Rahner characterizes as "the situation of an evolutionary view of the world."[73] This means that the being of the human person must be seen within a conception of the world as a whole - a world which by most modern persons its understood as an evolving world. It is then this being of the human person, in the context of the world as a whole, which "'awaits' its own consummation and that of the world." That this self-transcendence will ultimately succeed and has already begun is witnessed to definitively by the hypostatic union. Seen from this perspective, Rahner contends, "the Incarnation appears as the necessary and permanent beginning of the divinization of the world as a

---

[69] *Ibid.*, 128.
[70] Yet Gelpi, *Life and Light*, 39, observes that although "Rahner has taken pains to distinguish his own approach to the problem of evolution from that of Teilhard ... there remains a certain kinship of spirit between them."
[71] *FCF*, 180. [*Grundkurs*, 182.]
[72] "Christology within an Evolutionary View of the World," 159f. [*Schriften* 5:185f.]
[73] *FCF*, 178. [*Grundkurs*, 180.]

whole."⁷⁴ In this manner Rahner, from his theological *a priori* considerations, arrives like Teilhard at the importance of the incarnation as a, if not the, pivotal point in human evolution (or becoming).

But how does Rahner move from his *a priori* theological considerations to correlating the evolving cosmos and the Incarnation? As Gelpi rightly observes, Rahner's attempt to understand the place of the incarnation within an evolving cosmos, and vice versa, the role of an evolving within the context of the divine plan for the Incarnation, rests upon two fundamental assumptions: "First, that the ultimate goal of creation is indeed the gracious and gratuitous self-communication of God to his creature; second, that the evolutionary self-transcendence of the world is intended by God with a view to this divine self-communication."⁷⁵

Rahner takes as his starting point, therefore, the supposition that the goal of the world consists in God's communication of himself to it and that this self-communication of God to the world culminates in the historical appearance of a Savior. As Rahner explains, the title of 'Savior' is then given to "that historical person who, coming in space and time, signifies that beginning of God's absolute communication of himself which inaugurates this self-communication for all men as something happening irrevocably." Hence the whole movement and history of God's communication of himself in the cosmos - even before the appearance of this Savior - are based upon his appearance. With echoes of Teilhard, Rahner understands Christ, especially in his becoming flesh and entering into the history or process of the world, as the goal of its history - of its development. "The whole movement of this history lives only for the moment of arrival at its goal and climax - it lives only for its entry into the event which makes it irreversible - in short, it lives for the one whom we call Savior."⁷⁶ Hence, as Rahner has elsewhere written, "the God-man is the initial beginning and the definitive triumph of the movement of the world's self-transcendence into absolute closeness to the mystery of God."⁷⁷

Within the framework of this understanding Rahner seeks to understand how the hypostatic union and the Incarnation fit into "an evolutionist view of the world." Rahner's conclusion - and in contrast to Teilhard his arguments are almost entirely theological and barely touch upon the scientific aspects of the theory of evolution - is that the Incarnation is to be regarded as "an absolutely proper and new rung in the hierarchy of world-realities which quite simply surpasses all the world-realities given so far or to be given in the future yet without being itself necessary for these lower stages themselves." Such a view, then, would imply, in Rahner's view, that the Incarnation, from the point of view of theology, can be seen as "the climax surpassing all the other world-realities arranged in ascending layers" and that it can be therefore "positively fitted into an

---

[74] "Christology within an Evolutionary View of the World," 160f. [*Schriften* 5:186f.]
[75] Gelpi, 42.
[76] "Christology within an Evolutionary View of the World," 173ff. [*Schriften* 5:201f.]
[77] *FCF*, 181. [*Grundkurs*, 183.]

evolutionary world-view."[78] In this manner Rahner believes to have provided a model in which he has "fit Christology into the framework of an evolutionary world-view of a cosmos which evolves towards that spirit who attains absolute self-transcendence and perfection through and in an absolute self-communication given by God in grace and glory."[79]

At first reading it may appear difficult to distinguish Rahner's position at this point from that of Teilhard. Indeed, as Rahner himself admitted, the conclusions they reached are in many regards the same. One distinction between the two is that Rahner speaks of the goal toward which the cosmos is heading as the kingdom of God.[80] What he refers to as the kingdom is essentially the same as what Teilhard intends with his concept of Omega Point. Rahner writes, for instance, that "the 'Omega Point', as Teilhard de Chardin called it ..., towards which the world moves in its spirit is what is theologically termed the kingdom of God." Yet for Teilhard the individual seems to become lost in the evolutionary cosmic march toward the future Omega Point.[81] Rahner, however, by means of his transcendental method, stresses the fulfilment of the individual in the reaching of the Omega Point, or kingdom as he prefers. Hence the kingdom of God (Omega Point) comes in its fullness "in the vision of God, which is imparted to every spirit in its fulfilment." And for Rahner, this is precisely what is explained by a transcendental understanding of the nature of man."[82] Hence Rahner's emphasis, even in the eschatological fulfilment in the Omega Point, is not upon the cosmos as such but rather individual human persons.

The most fundamental and important distinction between Rahner and Teilhard, however, is a methodological one. Teilhard remains very much the natural scientist, convinced of the correctness of the theory of evolution and eager to show how it fits into God's plan for the salvation of the world. Rahner, on the other hand, never regards evolution methodologically as more than a theory -

---

[78] "Christology within an Evolutionary View of the World," 176 and 180. [*Schriften* 5:203f., 208.]

[79] *Ibid.*, 184. Rahner has here emphasized the Incarnation as the culmination of creation rather than as a restoration needed due to human sin. In this point he follows Teilhard who encountered difficulty with the magisterium over this precise issue. Rather than parting company here with Teilhard, Rahner seeks, first of all, to point out that the reproaches against Teilhard that accuse him of rendering sin harmless have not understood him correctly, and second, that Teilhard (and Rahner) stand in a tradition within Roman Catholic theology going back to the Christology of Duns Scotus and the so-called "Scotist school" and which has never been objected to by the magisterium. This tradition views the "Incarnation first of all, in God's primary intention, as the summit and height of the divine plan of creation, and not primarily and in the first place as the act of a mere restoration of a divine world-order destroyed by the sins of mankind." Hence the question is not an either/or choice between the traditional view of original sin and the Teilhardian view of evolution, but rather one of emphasis. Given the anthropo-optimism we have found to characterize Rahner's anthropology, the appeal of Teilhard's thought at this point is not surprising - given that Rahner's own thought, quite independent of Teilhard, has run in this direction.

[80] Cf. "Hominisation (Evolution B)," 296. [*SM* 2:759.]

[81] So also the critique of Teilhard by Schwarz, *On the Way to the Future*, 122.

[82] See "Transcendental Theology," 289, [*SM* 4:991.], for this and the above.

albeit one which he regards quite favorably. Inasmuch, therefore, as the theory does not contradict revelation Rahner seeks to explore its implications for Christian faith. He does not, however, seek to "deduce the Christian doctrine of Incarnation from an evolutionary view of the world as a necessary consequence and a logical development."[83] His view of the Incarnation and its importance for the world, therefore, would be just as true and pertinent if the world were static and not evolving.[84] Unlike Teilhard neither Rahner's Christology nor his anthropology are dependent upon the evolutionary view of the world but are founded upon theological considerations that the theologian brings into the dialogue with the natural sciences as presuppositions of faith.

## 6.2 Pannenberg: Theology as "Queen of the Sciences"

### 6.2.1 Foundations of the dialogue between theology and the natural sciences

#### 6.2.1.1 *The science/theology dialogue in the history of Protestant thought*

Pannenberg has been leading a campaign to reunite theological and other types of knowledge, especially knowledge gained through the natural sciences, long held by most natural scientists and theologians alike to have little if anything to do with one another. To set Pannenberg's program in context one must view the relationship between theological and natural-scientific knowledge within the history of Protestant thought. As Harold Nebelsick, in his excellent study, *Circles of God*, has demonstrated, theological knowledge and the knowledge gained from investigations of the physical world were not separated in the ancient world. Indeed, "the main motivating force behind the pursuit of natural knowledge from the time of Babylon and Greece in the East to the time of the Renaissance in the West was *theological* rather than *scientific*."[85] The intellectual world of the ancients was not divided into neatly separated categories such as physics, ethics, mathematics, theology, astronomy and metaphysics. Rather, in antiquity the world was viewed as a "relatively unified and coherent whole."[86] By the time of the Reformation, however, this situation had already began to change. Whether the Protestant Reformation helped to accelerate the separation of theological and natural-scientific knowledge or whether it simply experienced a change in intellectual climate that would have occurred in much the same way if there had

---

[83] *FCF*, 179. [*Grundkurs*, 181.]

[84] As Gelpi, 44, observes, the centrality Rahner assigns to "the incarnation in history remains true whether one ... conceive[s] of natural and human history as evolving ... or not. With or without evolution, Christ is the definitive and irrevocable insertion of grace into the progress of human events. He is the definitive promise of grace...and...the ultimate motive for the divine creation."

[85] Harold P. Nebelsick, *Circles of God: Theology and Science from the Greeks to Copernicus* (Edinburgh: Scottish Academic Press, 1985), xiii.

[86] So David Lindberg, "Science and the Early Church," in: *God and Nature: Historical Essays on the Encounter between Christianity and Science*, ed. David Lindberg and Ronald Numbers (Berkeley: University of California Press, 1986), 21.

been no Reformation at all is disputed. What is not disputed is that already in the Reformers one finds an emerging awareness of the independent status and value of the natural sciences - and along with it the beginnings of the separation of the spheres of theological and scientific knowledge within Protestant thought.

That Luther had a relatively positive evaluation of the pursuit of natural knowledge can be gleaned from several of the Reformer's comments. In his Epiphany sermon from the *Wartburg Postil* (1521-1522) we glimpse something of Luther's view of natural science as he bemoans the pitiful state of knowledge in the universities of his day: "The knowledge of nature, formerly known as magic and now referred to as physiology, is the knowledge which discovers the powers and processes in nature. ... But this knowledge is no longer pursued in the universities, and the peasants are better versed in it than the magi of today, the masters of natural knowledge ... who, with eyes closed to the world, pursue their learning with great expense."[87] That the so-called masters of natural knowledge ought to open their eyes to the world around them, that the study of the physical world is in itself good, can be seen in Luther's comment in a lecture on Ecclesiastes that "it is not an evil thing to investigate the nature and the qualities of things" since "the causes and the objects of the world are the most evident of all, [and] far from difficult to know."[88]

Yet if Luther seems to leave a legitimate place for the natural sciences, he remains skeptical of their ultimate value, and readily place theology before them in terms of importance. In his commentary on Romans, for instance, we read:

> The philosophers so direct their gaze at the present state of things that they speculate only about what things are and what quality they have, but the apostle calls our attention away from a consideration of the present and from the essence and accidents of things and directs us to their future state. ... Therefore I warn you all as earnestly as I can that you finish these studies quickly and let it be your only concern not to establish and defend them but to treat them as we do when we learn worthless skills. ... For ... the study of the nature of things, their accidents and their differences, will quickly grow worthless. ... So also the creation of God, which is skillfully prepared for future glory, is gazed upon by stupid people who look at its mechanics but never see its final goal.[89]

While Luther's apparent diminishing of science and the present world in order to emphasize a theological concern for the future may be seen by some as a negative view toward the natural sciences, it actually had a liberating affect on them. While Luther clearly prefers theology to the natural sciences, he

---

[87] Martin Luther, "The Gospel for the Festival of the Epiphany," in: *Luther's Works*, vol. 52, ed. Helmut Lehman (Philadelphia: Fortress Press, 1974), 162.
[88] Luther, "Notes on Ecclesiastes," in: *LW*, vol. 15, ed. and trans. Jaroslav Pelikan (St. Louis: Concordia, 1952), 18.
[89] Luther, "Lectures on Romans," in: *LW*, vol.25, ed, H Oswald, (St.Louis:Concordia, 1972), 362ff.

significantly distinguishes and separates the two. This is especially apparent in Brenz's report of the Marburg Colloquy in which Luther is recorded as saying:

> The universe is ... the greatest of all bodies and yet, even according to the view of science, it is not in a place because outside of the universe there is neither place nor time. Even the Aristotelians declare that the most distant planet is not in a place. ... The debate concerning space and its nature belongs to the realm of mathematics; theology, however, deals, rather, with the omnipotence of God which is above all mathematics.[90]

We see, therefore, in Luther a distinguishing of the natural sciences from theology and a valuation of scientific disciplines that, in the context of his own time, must be seen as a positive development for the pursuit of knowledge of the physical world. A similar attitude is to be found in John Calvin, the other great Reformer of the sixteenth century.

In regard to the natural sciences and their role in revealing God's glory Calvin wrote: "There are innumerable evidences both in heaven and on earth that declare his wonderful wisdom; not only those more recondite matters for the closer observation of which astronomy, medicine, and all natural science are intended, but also those which thrust themselves upon the sight of even the most untutored and ignorant persons."[91] If the pursuit of science, therefore, can truly witness to the glory of God, then scientific ability must be seen as a gift from God - even when such gifts are possessed by the 'ungodly.' Calvin asks, in this regard: "Shall we say that they are insane who developed medicine, devoting their labor to our benefit? What shall we say of all the mathematical sciences? Shall we consider them the ravings of madmen? No, we cannot read the writings of the ancients on these subjects without great admiration. ... But shall we count anything praiseworthy or noble without recognizing at the same time that it comes from God?" And furthermore, "... if the Lord has willed that we be helped in physics, dialectic, mathematics, and other like disciplines, by the work and the ministry of the ungodly, let us use this assistance. For if we neglect God's gift freely offered in these arts, we ought to suffer just punishment for our sloths."[92]

There is also in the Reformers a flexibility in biblical interpretation that allowed scriptural statements to be accommodated to current scientific viewpoints. As we see, however, in Luther's offhand rejection of 'Copernicanism' on the basis of a biblical passage,[93] this was not always readily put into practice -

---

[90] Luther, "The Marburg Colloquy" [1529], in: *LW*, vol. 38, ed. Martin Lehmann (Philadelphia: Fortress Press, 1971), 75.

[91] John Calvin, *Institutes of the Christian Religion*, 2 vols., trans. Ford Lewis Battles (Philadelphia: Westminster Press, 1960), 53 (1.5.2).

[92] Ibid., 274f (2.2.15 and 16).

[93] Cf. Luther, *Table Talk*, in: *LW*, vol. 54, trans. and ed. Th. Tappert (Philadelphia: Fortress, 1967), 358f., where Luther, referring, as Tappert suggests (358, note 401) "undoubtedly to Nicholaus Copernicus," says: "There was mention of a certain new astrologer who wanted to prove that the

yet the principle was there. Calvin, who seems to have been more unequivocal on this point than Luther, wrote in his commentary on Genesis:

> ...Astronomers investigate with great labour whatever the sagacity of the human mind can comprehend. Nevertheless, this study is not to be reprobated, nor this science to be condemned, because some frantic persons are wont boldly to reject whatever is unknown to them. For astronomy is not only pleasant, but also very useful to be known. ... Nor did Moses truly wish to withdraw us from this pursuit in omitting such things as are peculiar to the art; but because he was ordained a teacher as well of the unlearned and rude as of the learned, he could not otherwise fulfil his office than by descending to this grosser method of instruction. ... Moses, therefore, rather adapts his discourse to common usage.[94]

This foundation, along with an emphasis on the radical sovereignty of God - which has been linked to the rise of "the passivity of matter in the mechanical philosophy" of the seventeenth century[95] - created, according to some, an atmosphere in which the pursuit of the natural sciences flourished.[96] The Protestant Reformation certainly had an impact on the development of science in the critical sixteenth and seventeenth centuries. Just what that impact may have been, however, is probably impossible to ascertain with any degree of certainty.

A further decisive step in the separation of scientific and theological knowledge which has had immense impact not only upon Protestant thought but upon the understanding of the relationship between theology and the natural sciences in general was taken by the Anglican layman and scientist Sir Francis Bacon (1561-1626). Bacon developed a methodology and philosophy of science which helped determine the course of scientific development and its relationship with religion - especially Christianity - for almost four centuries. Bacon is most significant for the history of the relationship between scientific inquiry and religious faith for his doctrine of the "two books," also known as the "Baconian

---

[94] earth moves and not the sky, the sun, and the moon. ... that fellow ... wishes to turn the whole of astronomy upside down. Even in these things that are thrown into disorder I believe the Holy Scriptures, for Joshua commanded the sun to stand still and not the earth. [Joshua 10:12]."
Calvin, *Commentaries on the First Book of Moses*, vol. 1, trans. J. King (Edinburgh: Calvin Translation Society, 1847), 86f.

[95] Gary B. Deason, "Reformation Theology and the Mechanistic Conception of Nature," in: *God and Nature*, 170.

[96] Robert K. Merton and, more recently, Christopher Hill and Charles Webster have argued, for example, that the scientific interest and achievements of Puritan England were spawned by Puritan theology. Cf. Robert K. Merton, *Science, Technology, and Society in 17th Century England* (1938); Christopher Hill, *The Intellectual Origins of the English Revolution* (Oxford: Claredon Press, 1965); and Charles Webster, *The Great Instauration: Science, Medicine and Reform 1626-1660* (London: Duckworth, 1975). What one must not forget, however, is that while the much heralded *Royal Society of London* (founded 1660) is remembered for its Puritan influence, it was the *Lincean Academy* (founded in 1603 by Italian Catholics) that merits the title of "the first true scientific society." (Drake, "A Biographical Sketch," 59). And also, while the scientific achievements of the English Puritans are indisputable, they are at least equaled by the advances made by the Counter-Reformation Jesuit Order during approximately the same period.

compromise."[97] Bacon suggested that two 'books' existed; the book of God's word, i.e., the Bible, and the book of God's works, i.e., the physical world. By sharply distinguishing between the knowledge gained by the study of scripture and that gained through the study of the natural world Bacon was able to establish the independence of science as an academic discipline while preserving the integrity of theology. In *The Advancement of Learning* Bacon wrote:

> Let no man upon a weak conceit of sobriety or an ill-applied moderation think or maintain, that a man can search too far, or be too well studied in the book of God's word, or in the book of God's works; divinity or philosophy: but rather let men endeavour an endless progress or proficiency in both; only let men beware that they apply both to charity, and not to swelling; to use, and not to ostentation; and again, that they do not unwisely mingle or confound these learnings together.[98]

Not only did Bacon argue against the unwise mixing of scientific and theological studies, but he also was insistent that the respective sources of the two books not be mixed with or forced to conform to theories and presuppositions of our own invention. That is to say, the words of scripture and the works of nature must be allowed to speak for themselves and not be forced to fit the preconceived molds of those pretending to objectively study either of these two respective books. Against the practice of the medieval scholastics Bacon wrote: "Their pride inclined [them] to leave the oracle of God's word, and to vanish in the mixture of their own inventions; so in the inquisition of nature, they ever left the oracle of God's works, and adored the deceiving and deformed images which the unequal mirror of their own minds, or a few received authors and principles did represent unto them."[99]

While the Baconian compromise provided "for the freedom of students of nature from harassment by interpreters of biblical texts"[100] it also provided theology 'freedom from harassment' by interpreters of nature. Bacon made this clear when he wrote:

> We conclude that sacred theology is grounded only upon the word and oracle of God, and not upon the light of nature. ... This holdeth not only in those points of

---

[97] The concept of two books, however, did not originate with Bacon but appears first in the 15th century physician and philosopher Raymundus de Sabunde's *Theologia naturalis; sive liber creaturarum* (ca. 1436). In this, his only published work, he argued that two books have been put at human disposal; created nature and the Bible, which latter was given to humanity after the first book could no longer be understood because of the fall. Since both books, however, come from God, they cannot contradict. Cf. Schaarschmidt, "Raimund von Sibinde," in: *Realencyklo-pädie für protestantische Theologie und Kirche*, vol. 16 (Erlangen, 1905), 415ff.; and "Raymond of Sabunde" in: *The New Catholic Encyclopedia*, vol. 12 (New York: MacGraw-Hill, 1967).

[98] Francis Bacon, *The Advancement of Learning* (1605), (London: Dent, 1965), 8. (1.1.3).

[99] *Ibid.*, 27f. (1.4.7).

[100] J. Moore, "Geologists and Interpreters of Genesis in the 19th Century," *God and Nature*, 323.

faith which concern the mysteries of the Deity, of the Creation, of the Redemption, but likewise those which concern the moral law truly interpreted. ...it is a voice beyond the light of nature. ... So then the doctrine of religion, as well moral as mystical, is not to be attained but by inspiration and revelation from God.[101]

The most important effect of Bacon's concept of the two books, for our study, however, is not the proclaimed 'freedom of harassment' that natural scientists and theologians obtained but the epistemological separation of theological knowledge and the knowledge of the physical world. The distinguishing of the natural sciences from the theological and philosophical sciences found in the Reformers, while giving significant and needed independence to the budding natural sciences, did not imply that theological knowledge and the knowledge gained from the study of the natural world had nothing to do with one another and should never be mixed. Thus the Baconian compromise represented a radical epistemological division between theology and the other sciences which has had an impact not only on the self-understanding of the natural sciences but upon theological thought as well into our own century.

Reinforcing the influence of the thought behind the 'two books' theory in Protestant thought - especially among German Protestants - was the Kantian division between moral and theoretical knowledge which has led to the idea that theology's only real or possible contribution to knowledge in modern society is in the realm of ethics, while natural science, on the other hand, belongs to theoretical knowledge. Pannenberg has observed that "the purely mechanical description of the origin of the planetary system in the pioneering work of Kant" led to the independence of the scientific worldview from any relationship with God - and this despite the fact that Kant himself "was still motivated by a strictly Calvinistic understanding of God in transcendent majesty."[102]

The influence of the 'two books' concept among modern Protestant theologians is most clearly to be seen in the thought of Karl Barth, who believed that theology and science operate in "two fundamentally distinct spheres," by which he meant "heaven and earth," or the realms of the transcendent and the empirical.[103] For Barth this meant in practice that "exact science can furnish no means of an approach to an ontology of the cosmos," and that "dogmatics has no business to broaden out into cosmology."[104] Hence for Barth, theology "is fundamentally free in regard to all world-pictures, that is, to all attempts to regard what exists by the measure and with the means of the dominant science of the time."[105] With such a viewpoint, one should not be surprised to find that, although

---

[101] Bacon, *Advancement of Learning*, 209f. (2.25.3).
[102] Pannenberg, "God and Nature: On the History of the Debates Between Theology and Natural Science," in: Pannenberg, *Toward a Theology of Nature*, 50f. ["Gott und Natur," in: *Theologie und Philosophie* 58 (1983), 481f.]
[103] Karl Barth, *CD* III.2, 13.
[104] Ibid.
[105] Barth, *Dogmatics in Outline* (New York: Harper & Row, 1959), 59.

Barth devotes over two hundred pages to the nature and doctrine of time within the context of his treatment of the doctrine of creation, he makes no reference to either Einstein or relativity theory.[106] Neither should it surprise us that in the entirety of Barth's *Church Dogmatics*, "there are references to Shakespeare, but none to Schrödinger; references to Hölderlin, but not to Heisenberg; references to Bach, but not to Bohr."[107] As Pannenberg noted:

> The intellectual mind-set of the twentieth century has become accustomed to assuming that no relationship or connection can be validly affirmed between the God of the Christian faith and the understanding of the world in the natural sciences. The majority of European theologians of our century appear actually to have considered this situation as an advantage, as an opportunity to concentrate theology on biblical revelation. This is exemplified by Karl Barth's decision to refrain from any reference to scientific insights and methods in the doctrine of creation of his *Church Dogmatics*.[108]

In the so-called left wing of dialectical theology much the same problem is to be found. As Pannenberg has noted, a related phenomenon is to be seen in Bultmann's program of demythologization in which myth is classified as essentially allegorical and as belonging to a pre-scientific age. Bultmann suggests, indeed, that Mythos itself "can be described as primitive scientific thought" to the extent that it seeks to explain the world.[109] Myth, however, seeks to speak about a reality, "that lays beyond the objectifiable, observed and controllable reality." Instead, it speaks of a reality that is especially important for the human being, a reality, "that for the individual demands salvation or damnation, grace or wrath, respect and obedience."[110] Although Bultmann, as Pannenberg observes, ascribed a hermeneutical and not a polemical function to his efforts[111] the effect was something other than simply hermeneutical. By classifying myth, including biblical myth, in this way, modern scientific persons were freed from the burden of having to think that the Bible and its message had anything to do with them or their world. Pannenberg writes:

> Despite his emphatic assurance that his concern was not to eliminate myth but rather to interpret it, we find in Bultmann an interpretation that removes the 'mythical' form inasmuch as it understands it as the expression of a self-evidency

---

[106] Cf. Barth, *CD* III.2, 437-640.
[107] John Honner, "Not Meddling with Divinity: Theological Worldviews and Contemporary Physics," in: *Pacifica* 1 (1988), 256.
[108] "God and Nature," 50. ["Gott und Natur," 481.]
[109] Rudolf Bultmann, "Zum Problem der Entmythologisierung," in: *Glauben und Verstehen*, vol. 4 (Tübingen: J.C.B. Mohr, 1993), 134.
[110] *Ibid.* 133.
[111] Cf., for instance, *ibid.*, 128, where Bultmann writes: "Unter *Entmythologisierung* verstehe ich ein hermeneutisches Versuch, das mythische Aussagen bzw. Texte nach ihrem Wirklichkeit befragt. Vorausgesetzt ist dabei, daß der Mythos zwar von einer Wirklichkeit redet, aber in einer nicht adäquaten Weise."

that is also to be portrayed in a non-mythological way. The concept of myth here serves to free the Christian tradition from those elements that appear to be incompatible with an understanding of the world and of the self that is orientated to modern science.[112]

Hence a sort of two books or two languages theory is assumed but with a twist. All that belongs to the category of pre-scientific myth and has no meaning for the modern person can - indeed should - be reinterpreted (or eliminated). The suspicion arises, therefore, in regard to Bultmann's program of demythologization, "that under the label of 'mythical' certain fundamental elements of the religious thematic in general are written off as being irreconcilable with modern science."[113] Thus Pannenberg rejects also Bultmann's approach, which shares certain fundamental assumptions with that of Barth.

More recently Langdon Gilkey has advocated a similar dichotomy between the realms of theology and natural science. The verdict of the scientific community following the Darwinian controversy has, in Gilkey's opinion, "effectively removed religious truth from the area of matters of fact" in such a radical sense that from this time on "no serious theologian ... has claimed that ... he could establish anything relevant to the data or conclusions of scientific inquiry." That is to say, theology must now be understood "to possess no legitimate ground to interfere with either scientific inquiry or scientific conclusions" since, "theological truth no longer contains the sort of knowledge which entails particular factual propositions." The only legitimate aspects of theological language, then, in Gilkey's view, are "its transcending aspects pointing to ultimacy and sacrality." Theology, then, speaks appropriately of "symbol" and "myth," and natural science of facts, since the language of theology is "symbolic" and not "directly applicable to reality 'out there.'"[114]

It is against this background that Pannenberg's efforts to stake claim to the universal relevance of theology, also in regard to the natural sciences, must be

---

[112] Pannenberg, *Christentum und Mythos: Späthorizonte des Mythos in biblischer und christlicher Überlieferung* (Gütersloh: Gerd Mohn, 1972), 17f.

[113] *Ibid.*, 19. Hence Pannenberg, pointing to the problems entailed in Bultmann's approach, asks: "Wenn aber die religiöse Thematik nicht schlechthin im Namen moderner Wissenschaft als antiquiert abgewiesen werden kann, erhält dann nicht vielleicht auch der echte Mythos aufs neue Anrecht und Chance, auf sein Eigengewicht geprüft statt zusammen mit vielerlei heterogenen Sachverhalten pauschal für erledigt erklärt zu werden?"

[114] Langdon Gilkey, *Religion and the Scientific Future* (London: SCM Press, 1970), 18ff. The thought expressed in Gilkey's writing has been dubbed the 'two language' theory and rests upon the basic concepts of the 'two books' theory. Namely, if there are two different and distinct books then it follows that there are two different languages employed by natural scientists and theologians - which in modern times has had the effect of excusing both sides from talking with one another. For a colorful description of the impact of the two language theory upon the science/theology dialogue (or lack thereof) see Ted Peters, "Pannenberg on Theology and Natural Science," in: W. Pannenberg, *Toward a Theology of Nature: Essays on Science and Faith*, ed. Ted Peters (Louisville: Westminster/John Knox Press, 1993), 4.

understood.[115] After generations of Protestant thinkers who, whether seeing natural science as the friend or enemy of faith, have essentially been agreed that theological and 'scientific' knowledge and concerns have little or nothing to do with one another, Pannenberg's contention that there is ultimately only one book, that is to say, that what the natural sciences have to say is relevant for theology and what theology has to say is relevant for the natural sciences, must be understood as a radical break with the majority opinion within Protestant thought since the time of Bacon. And the apologetic implication of this break must also not be overlooked. When theology begins by confessing that there are two distinct books that have little or nothing to do with one another or that it speaks only of symbol and myth and has nothing concrete to say about 'reality out there,' then it has abandoned its apologetic task in relation to the natural sciences. In this light, Pannenberg's assertion of theology's universality in relation also to the natural sciences is fundamental to the establishment of a viable apologetic in the modern, scientific world.

Yet Pannenberg is neither the first nor is he alone in efforts to overcome this impasse. Already in the early part of the century Karl Beth[116] and Arthur Titius[117] sought to make progress in breaking down the barrier between theological and scientific knowledge. Especially insightful was the thought of Beth who saw a working knowledge of the natural sciences as an apologetic necessity for Christianity. He argued that "only a genuine insight into the work of natural science itself can put theology in the position to come to terms with the objections against Christianity based on the theses of natural history as well as to put itself in

---

[115] Also belonging to this background is the present reality that the division which Pannenberg seeks to overcome does not just exist between theology and the natural sciences but extends at a broader and more fundamental level to a growing division between the human sciences (*Geisteswissenschaften*) and the natural sciences. This problem was particularly brought to attention by the British novelist and intellectual C. P. Snow when he suggested in his 1959 Rede Lecture at Cambridge that 'two cultures' have developed in the Western world pitting the natural sciences against the human or intellectual sciences. Snow contended that: "The intellectual life of the whole of western society is increasingly being split into two polar groups. ... Literary intellectuals at the one pole - at the other scientists. ... Between the two a gulf of mutual incomprehension - sometimes hostility and dislike, but most of all a lack of understanding." Charles P. Snow, *The Two Cultures* (Cambridge: Cambridge University Press, 1965), 3f.

[116] Cf. Karl Beth, *Die Moderne und die Prinzipien der Theologie* (Berlin: Trowitzsch & Sohn, 1907), esp. 302-330; and *Der Entwicklungsgedanke und das Christentum* (Berlin: Runge, 1909).

[117] Cf. especially Arthur Titius, *Religion und Naturwissenschaft: Eine Antwort an Professor Ladenburg* (Tübingen: J.C.B. Mohr, 1904); and *Natur und Gott: Ein Versuch zur Verständigung zwischen Naturwissenschaft und Theologie* (Göttingen: Vandenhoeck & Ruprecht, 1926). In the former work Titius rejects the idea either that religion (particularily the Christian religion) and natural science inevitably contradict one another or that they have nothing to do with one another. He contends that an "innere Beziehung" exists between religion and natural science in those areas where their areas of interest come into contact: Indeed, the findings of natural science are not without relevance to theology. He even suggests (echoeing the physico-theology of the 17th and 18th centuries) that "die Vorstellung von der Notwendigkeit des Naturgeschehens ... ist ... ein abgeblasster Rest des Glaubens an Gottes Walten!" (pp. 66 and 71).

the proper state of mind for these situations."[118] And although Beth proposed a "two kingdoms" understanding of the realm of nature and the realm of the spirit (where theology is located) he resisted those who would absolutely divide natural science and theology so that they could not possibly come into conflict[119] or that theology could have nothing to say pertinent to the natural world. Hence he suggested that even though theology and natural science operate in essentially different realms theology is also able to relate to the natural realm (though in a different way than the natural sciences). Epistemologically, therefore, the two sciences cannot be completely separated. "Theological knowledge," contended Beth, "stands together with that of the natural sciences on one line, both are scientific ways of knowing."[120] Indeed, in an argument which in many ways anticipates Pannenberg's thought, Beth contended that our belief in God as creator and preserver of the entirety of the natural world implies that theology can ignore neither the created order nor what the natural sciences are saying about it: "The Christian faith contains the conviction that all the parts of the whole natural world are dependent upon God as creator and caregiver, and theology seeks to express the truth of this statement in a scientifically acceptable manner."[121]

These early efforts were followed shortly thereafter by the groundbreaking work of Karl Heim who had a significant, albeit limited impact upon Protestant thought, especially in Germany, on the attitude toward the natural sciences.[122] In Heim we find a definitive break with the then dominant theological conceptions of the relevance of the natural sciences for theology. "In Heim the theme of faith and natural science stands in a comprehensive theological framework which shows the question of natural science to be not only legitimate but also irrefutable. This conviction separates Heim from the theology of the Ritschlian and Barthian schools."[123]

Apart from his new openness to the natural sciences Heim's most significant contribution to the science/theology dialogue was his development of a bi-polar view of reality. Heim was motivated by the desire to make the idea of God comprehensible to the modern, scientific worldview.[124] To achieve this Heim proposed that the physical world and the experience of it be understood as "the

---

[118] Beth, *Die Moderne und die Prinzipien der Theologie*, 303.
[119] Indeed, the natural sciences were recognized as being able to force theology to reevaluate its own position - something which theology should not fear but should be thankful for. As an example of this possibility Beth points to the historical fact, "daß Naturwissenschaft uns in der Theologie dazu verholfen hat, einem alten Schöpfungsbegriff für immer den Abschied zu geben, und dies dürfen wir ihr nicht vergessen." (*Ibid.*, 308.)
[120] *Ibid.*, 306.
[121] *Ibid.*, 308.
[122] Cf. Hans Schwarz, *On the Way to the Future*, 122. who notes that "Heim is the only Protestant theologian of stature [of his generation] who chose as his own the task of bridging the chasm between theology and natural science."
[123] So Hermann Timm, *Glaube und Naturwissenschaft in der Theologie Karl Heims* (Berlin: Eckart-Verlag, 1968), 109.
[124] Cf. Karl Heim, *Christian Faith and Natural Science* (New York: Harper, 1957), 151ff.

space of polarity or the *polar space"* which encompasses the relationships of the world of space-time objects, including time itself.[125] The question which must be asked, however, is whether there is not something beyond this polar realm? That is to say, "Is the polar world-form the only form of existence there is?" When such a possibility exists then there must be a different 'being' from that of the polar realm of existence "in which the whole world-form of polarity is transcended, yet not by the blotting out of the entire contents of the world but by the recasting of them in a new form." When such a 'second form' of being exists then the polar realm would not be negated by it but would taken up into it positively.[126] Thus Heim postulates a bi-polar realm connected by the unity of time and in which a distinction remains between the two 'dimensions,' which, however, share in the same reality and are therefore not unrelated. Heim does not, therefore, as some have thought, postulate the existence of an additional dimension to encompass the reality of God.[127] Rather, it is in the suprapolar realm (*überpolare Raum*) - which takes up into it the reality of the polar realm - that Heim locates God, contending that "the suprapolar realm is indeed ... the realm in which God is present for us."[128] In this way the transcendence of God is maintained but a connection is also maintained with the natural realm. Thus, as Timm has noted, Heim's proposal of a bi-polar understanding of reality made communication between natural science and and theology possible.[129]

Yet it was the thought of Heim's contemporary Karl Barth that dominated theological thinking in regard to the natural sciences. In these early efforts, however, deficiencies are also to be noted. Pannenberg, for instance, while commending the work and contributions of Heim as pioneering, notes that "Heim

---

[125] *Ibid.*, 156.
[126] *Ibid.*, 160ff.
[127] Pannenberg, *ST* 2:90, note 232 [110f., note 232], however, following the critique of W.H. Austin, seems to understand Heim also in this way. He contends: "The problem with Heim's form of the thesis is that in keeping with contemporary discussions of multidimensional spaces, he tried to arrive at suprapolar space by introducing a new dimension, as in the transition from line to depth." Heim, it is true, spoke of the mathematical possibility with Euclidean geometry of conceiving of multiple spaces, including those which are beyond sensory perception (Heim, *Die christliche Gottesglaube*, 56ff.) and suggested the possible appearance of a new 'space' in which "etwas möglich ist, was im anschaulicher Raum unmöglich wäre" (69). This new, unseen 'space,' however, was not considered by Heim as a part of the physical world or as an added dimension to it. Heim had in mind, rather, a space in the sense of the Kantian theory of space which is "eben gerade nicht ein ens, ein Seiendes, eine Wirklichkeit, ein 'Ding an sich,'" but which is rather to be thought of as "eine Beziehung, in die einer Wirklichkeit zur mir, den anschauenden Subjekt, tritt" (183f.). Heim understood the suprapolar space in which God is present for us not as a phys-ical 'space' and not as something which encompassed or contained God in his ultimate reality. He wrote: "Wenn wir von überpolaren Raum sprechen, kann damit nicht die ewige Wirklichkeit Gottes selbst gemeint sein, sondern nur ein Aspekt, eine uns zugekehrte Seite, von der Gott für uns ... zugänglich sein kann." The suprapolar space means also that God is not outside or beyond the world, that is, God is not in some additional dimension separate from our own (184ff.).
[128] Heim, 183.
[129] Timm, 111f.

often connected the two realms [theology and natural science] only by a figurative transfer of scientifically defined concepts to theological problems. Even the concept of dimension is probably used only figuratively when Heim related the realm of theological statements as a new dimension, as the dimension of the 'suprapolar,' to the dimension of the scientific space-time world."[130] Indeed, Pannenberg suggests that although Heim made great strides, in contrast to Barth, in recognizing that theological talk about God as creator is empty unless it can relate to the description of nature in the natural sciences, his thought nevertheless still bore remnants of a sort of two-language or two books perspective. In Pannenberg's view "even Heim, for all his competence in conversations with scientists, was more concerned to relativize the level of scientific conceptualizing and description of nature in toto by presenting it as a form of thought, over against which theology represents a quite different form of thought. The two forms of thought are not 'polarized' but, as Heim said, 'superpolar.' Therefore, even Heim did not really enter into a theological appropriation and critique of the conceptual foundations of natural science."[131] It is then precisely the challenge to break with the tradition of Barth and to enter into a full "theological appropriation and critique of the conceptual foundations of natural science" that Pannenberg takes up as a central task of his own theology.

### 6.2.1.2 *Implications of theology's universality for the natural sciences*

In an article directed toward natural scientists Pannenberg stakes theology's claim to universality and reveals how radically he has broken with the Baconian theory of the 'two books' and similar ideas which have tended to isolate (and "protect") theology and the natural sciences from one another. Pannenberg contends: "If the God of the Bible is creator of the universe, then it is not possible to understand fully or even appropriately the processes of nature without any reference to that God. If, on the contrary, nature can be appropriately understood without reference to the God of the Bible, then that God cannot be the creator of the universe, and consequently he could not be truly God and could not be trusted as a source of moral teaching either." Hence, according to Pannenberg, the abstract knowledge of the physical processes gained through the natural sciences should not "claim full and exclusive competence regarding the explanation of nature and, if it does so, the reality of God is thereby denied by implication."[132]

---

[130] "Contingency and Natural Law," in: *Toward a Theology of Nature*, ed. Ted Peters, 75f. ["Kontingenz und Naturgesetz," in: A.M. Klaus Müller und Wolfhart Pannenberg, *Erwägungen zu einer Theologie der Natur* (Gütersloh: Gerd Mohn, 1970), 37.]

[131] Pannenberg, "The Doctrine of Creation and Natural Science," in: *Toward a Theology of Nature*, 32. [Originally published in English.]

[132] Pannenberg, "Theological Questions to Scientists," in: W. Pannenberg, *Toward a Theology of Nature*, ed. Ted Peters, 16. Peters, "Pannenberg on Theology and Natural Science," 1f., writes that "it may seem as though Pannenberg is violating something sacred. Since the rise of the so-called 'two cultures,' the Western mind has tacitly dubbed the scientific to be 'holy' and the religious to be 'profane.' ... Now, however, Pannenberg seems to be profaning what Western

The implications of theology's universality in Pannenberg's thought are therefore seen to be primarily twofold. First, theology must be open to and can learn something of value from all the various special sciences inasmuch as these have to do inevitably with some aspect of God's creation. Second, theology has something to say to each of the special sciences and is in a unique position to order them and provide them a frame of reference since, if God does indeed exist, then theology is the only science which has as its object that which is of decisive relevance to all the other sciences.[133] This latter point is especially significant in an age when theologians seem often to exhibit a timidness in regard to the special sciences.[134] Indeed, Pannenberg contends that, "without the critical collaboration of theology and philosophy the unity of knowledge, which prevents the sciences from totally disintegrating into a set of completely separate disciplines and ossifying, would no longer be appreciated."[135]

The universality of theology also implies that faith and reason cannot be separated from one another, moving faith into a protected and impenetrable sphere where it is safe from the assaults of the natural sciences. Pannenberg not only rejects Barth's efforts to construct a fideistic theology but also the very idea that theological knowledge based upon "revelation" and rational knowledge based upon empirical investigation are two separate things. In this way he also separates himself from his former teacher Karl Jaspers who shared many of the same assumptions about the epistemological division between theological and empirical knowledge as his Basel colleague Karl Barth. Jaspers wrote: "If revealed faith in its theology makes claims about empirical and universally applicable and ascertainable facts, then it is always in the wrong over against

---

[133] Enlightenment culture has held sacred. He is brashly reentering the epistemological holy of holies and contending that loss of an awareness of God actually constricts what we learn about the nature of nature."
This role of theology over against the other sciences was indicated already by Martin Kähler, *Die Wissenschaft der christlichen Lehre* [1883], reprinted from the 3rd ed. of 1905 (Neukirchen-Vluyn: Neukirchener Verlag, 1966), 38f. Kähler wrote: "Theology, in its historical development, has approached the move toward the unity of science. The academic standing of theology is testimony to the fact that it does not seek isolation, and that its fundamental importance for the whole of knowledge has been recognized. Many lines can be drawn, of course, which indicate clearly theology's special field. Yet it would be a denial of theology's unique nature if at the same time its effective addition to the total scientific effort is not affirmed and the contributions which can and should flow from its enterprise to the other sciences are not pointed out."

[134] As Pannenberg has observed: "The chain of defeats of theological apologetics by the natural sciences makes it understandable that the caution of theologians, who no longer want to burn their fingers, has been increasing in the last decades." Pannenberg, "Contingency and Natural Law," 73f. ["Kontingenz und Naturgesetz," 35.]

[135] Pannenberg, *TPS*, 13. [*WtT*, 17.] Ted Peters, "Pannenberg on Theology and Natural Science," 1, notes that "whereas most of the religious community timidly seeks ways to incorporate the worldview of twentieth-century physics and biology by adjusting the religious vision accordingly, Pannenberg has reversed the process. ... [H]e proceeds to challenge scientists to consider incorporating the idea of God into the picture they paint. Unless God is properly considered, he argues, a scientific theory cannot fully comprehend the reality of the world it seeks to explain."

methodically compelling science. Where science stands in opposition and the scientifically minded person must, through the appropriation of the methods of its knowing, be in agreement, there remains only this choice: to follow science or to consummate the *sacrificium intellectus*." For Jaspers this means that theology has no chance against natural science. "If the knowledge of science stands against statements of faith, then faith has lost."[136] Yet theology, according to Jaspers, has nothing to fear from the natural sciences for it can never come to a real confrontation between the two since faith based upon revelation "is not able to be reached by scientific knowledge, but also remains untouched by it."[137]

Theology's status as universal science makes precisely this sort of epistemological division between faith and reason impossible since the unitary character of all knowledge is presupposed by theology's claim to universality. Theology cannot avoid the special sciences but is obligated to engage them in dialogue and to open its assertions, at least in principle, to "verification" from them. Only when it takes this risk can theology begin to reclaim its role among the special sciences as that science which, having God as its subject matter, is the only truly "universal" science.

Yet this must be clearly qualified by pointing out that for Pannenberg, theology's status as universal science does not mean that it is the queen of the sciences in the medieval sense of dominating the other sciences. Don Olive summarized Pannenberg's position well in this regard when he wrote:

> As a universal science, theology is reevaluated to the place of 'queen of the sciences,' although certainly not in the earlier sense of dictator. Theology is not to impose either subject matter or methodology upon the other sciences. ... Theology's proper task is to provide the ground upon which all other disciplines can become fully what they can be. The sciences all benefit as individual disciplines precisely because each is provided with the valid ontological ground - the creator, sustainer God. Theology serves as the comprehensive discipline because its subject matter is God.[138]

### 6.2.1.3 *The possibility and need of a theology of nature*

By affirming the universality of God and the relevance of theology for the natural sciences (and vice versa), Pannenberg, as has been noted, "is challenging us to develop a theology of nature that relies on both modern science and classical Christian commitments regarding creation, conservation, and governance."[139] Pannenberg, however, has himself taken up the challenge implied by his own commitment to the universality of theology and has sought to develop the foundations for a theology of nature. Decisive for this effort is his 1970 article,

---

[136] Karl Jaspers, *Der philosophische Glaube angesichts der Offenbarung* (Munich:Piper,1962), 100.
[137] *Ibid.*
[138] Don H. Olive, *Wolfhart Pannenberg*, 36.
[139] Peters, "Pannenberg on Theology and Natural Science," 2.

"Contingency and Natural Law" which he opened with the question: "Can there be at all something like a theology of nature?"[140]

One task of a theology of nature, in Pannenberg's view, is to overcome the Cartesian dualism of spirit and matter. To accomplish this, suggests Pannenberg, contemporary theology needs to go beyond Newton's theological conception of the physical universe which was markedly non-Trinitarian.[141] Hence, according to Pannenberg, "a theology of nature must go back behind Newton's thought on the presence of God with his creatures through space and time if theology is to avoid the spell of a powerless dualism of spirit and matter." A contemporary theology of creation (or nature), in distinction from Newton, will make use of "the possibilities of the doctrine of the Trinity in order to describe the relationship of God's transcendence and immanence in creation and in the history of salvation." Specifically, Pannenberg suggests that "a renewed doctrine of the Trinity would combine the Logos doctrine of the ancient church with contemporary information theory and recognize the activity of the divine spirit in the self-transcendence of life and its evolution."[142]

Additionally, a theology of nature, in Pannenberg's thought, must be distinguished from natural theology.[143] It must also be separated from a dependence upon the term 'creation' which leads to a misleading focus upon only the beginning of the world rather than the entire natural process. According to Pannenberg, a theology of nature must provide a "theological interpretation of natural reality." This means, especially with reference to Pannenberg's commitment to the universality of theology, that a theology of nature "would have to address nature in its entire process and in its present circumstance, including its beginning history. It would have to relate all of nature to the reality that is the true theme of theology - the reality of God."[144] A theology of nature, therefore, cannot concern itself with only certain aspects of the natural realm or its processes, but must be concerned with the whole of natural reality - indeed, with the whole of reality in general. Pannenberg proposes that this is only possible through an

---

[140] "Contingency and Natural Law," 72. ["Kontingenz und Naturgesetz," 34.]

[141] On Newton's largely unknown anti-Trinitarian writings see Richard Popkin, "Newton's Biblical Theology and his Theological Physics," in: *Newton's Scientific and Philosophical Legacy*, ed. P. Scheurer and G. Debrock (Dordrecht: Kluwer, 1988), 81ff.; and Frank Manuel, *The Religion of Isaac Newton* (Oxford: Clarendon Press, 1974), 57ff.

[142] "God and Nature," 65f. ["Gott und Natur," 499f.] Pannenberg took up this latter proposal already in his 1972 article, "The Doctrine of the Spirit and the Task of a Theology of Nature," in: *Towards a Theology of Nature*, where, examining the thought of Pierre Teilhard de Chardin and Paul Tillich on 'spirit,' he explores the question of whether modern theologians, in an effort to overcome Cartesian dualism through trinitarian thought, can "in any intellectually serious way attribute a function in the explanation of nature to the Holy Spirit" (128). He suggests that this is possible when we understand spirit as applying to the total sphere of life and especially to the self-transcending tendency of organic life as seen in the evolutionary process (135f.).

[143] Cf. *ST* 1:107ff. [121ff.], and our discussion in section 1.5.4.

[144] "Contingency and Natural Law," 72f. ["Kontingenz und Naturgesetz," 34.]

understanding of nature as history - a proposal which allows him to connect the natural processes of the world to his concept of universal history.

Given the challenge of this task, the cornerstone of Pannenberg's theology of nature is to be found in the role he attributes to contingency. For Pannenberg, "the first preparatory task of a theology of nature" is to take up the question of whether the order of occurrences describable as regularity in the natural sciences can be understood as a form of contingency, "that is, as founded on contingent occurrences."[145] The importance of contingency for Pannenberg is to be traced to the biblical perception of God and reality.[146] "On the basis of the Israelite understanding of God ... the experience of reality is characterized primarily by contingency, particularly contingency of occurrences." For Pannenberg, this biblical contingency is understood as a contingency of all events upon God who is responsible for each new and unforeseen thing which happens. This sort of contingency, however, "stands apparently in fundamental contrast to the question of an unbreakable order in the natural events ... as well as to the understanding of classical modern science regarding the thoroughgoing regularity of nature."[147] Because of this apparent incompatibility of the biblical conception of contingency and the natural-scientific view of regularity, "the understanding of all events as contingent occurrences with all variation in details which agrees essentially with the biblical concept of God ... had to be considered as unbelievable and abolished" within modern thought. The deterministic worldview which lay behind this rejection, however, began to unravel with the arrival of quantum physics - which has provided a new context for the discussion of the question of the relationship of contingency and regularity in the processes of the world.[148]

From the postulate of the biblical conception of contingency and its relation to the view of regularity found in the natural sciences Pannenberg moves to a second decisive point, namely, the question of whether "the understanding of the contingency of occurrences as actions of the biblical God throws light on the conceivability of order and regularity in the horizon of the contingency of occurrences." For Pannenberg the answer is affirmative and he proposes that there thus exists a special structure of the understanding of reality based upon contingency from which he draws three relevant points for our understanding of history and the processes and occurrences of the world of which history consists. First, Pannenberg recalls that the contingency of occurrences means that "again

---

[145] *Ibid.*, 81f. [42.] For Pannenberg, contingency is understood as "that which is not necessary *on the basis of what is past*. In distinction from other contingencies which refer negatively to other concepts of necessity and thus are determined in their particularity ... I designate ... contingency as *historical* contingency" (116, note 11, [75, note 11.]).

[146] As Hefner, "The Role of Science in Pannenberg's Theological Thinking," 271, notes, Pannenberg "believes that contingency is a basic consideration for the Christian outlook, because the understanding of God which was bequeathed to the Christian church from Israel was one in which 'the experience of reality was primarily through contingency.'"

[147] "Contingency and Natural Law," 76. ["Kontingenz und Naturgesetz," 37f.]

[148] *Ibid.*, 77f. [38f.]

and again something new happens, without precedence. And exactly in this, Israel experienced ever anew the power of its God. History presents itself in a series of ever-new occurrences, which despite many similarities are unforeseen. Their course is irreversible."[149]

A second crucial point to be made on the basis of the structure of reality implied by the understanding of the contingency of events is that despite the emphasis upon the newness and unprecedentedness of occurrences, connections between occurrences are nevertheless to be seen. "However, these connections become visible only from each end of a process. ... Every event throws new light on earlier occurrences; this now appears in new connections." For the Israelites this meant that their thinking implied what Pannenberg has named an "eschatological ontology" which meant that future events can cast light on past events showing what their significance was so that the "essence" of an event "is never really completely finished in the present. Hence the eschatological perspective of Israel, which was decisive for the formulation of a Christian eschatology, arises out of Israel's perception of the contingency of events.[150] As Hefner explains: "Lawful regularities were recognized, as well, [by the Israelites] but they are also contingent upon the action of God. The reality of the future also arose out of this context, because the Israelites were aware that they were a part of a continuum that was not yet complete."[151]

Upon this second point Pannenberg draws a third conclusion about the structure of reality based upon the contingency of events, namely, that the "true phenomenon of historical continuity backward raises the question of the reality which reveals itself in it." For Pannenberg, this means that contingent events already always enter a context of human experience and throw light back upon those occurrences that are already part of our experience or tradition. Hence, "each event is something new that happens to us from the future which is until then still unrealized. It establishes anew the connection with that which happened earlier by altering the context of experience previously found in our historical experience."[152] Upon this basis Pannenberg moves on in his article to address the question of whether the totality of reality, including what we call nature, can be characterized as history in the sense which he has suggested. Further, Pannenberg believes the question must be raised "whether in nature also the element of connection, of continuity, can be understood, as in the history of humanity, in the contingent occurrences themselves as a continuity 'backward.'"[153]

For Pannenberg, therefore, one might conclude that his theology of nature is essentially a theology of contingency which is applied not just to the contingency of historical actions but also the contingency of natural processes which, as he

---
[149] Ibid., 82f. [43.]
[150] Ibid., 83f. [43ff.]
[151] Hefner, "The Role of Science in Pannenberg's Theological Thinking," 272.
[152] "Contingency and Natural Law," 84f. ["Kontingenz und Naturgesetz," 45f.]
[153] Ibid., 86. [47.]

argues, must also be understood historically. Does this imply, however, a subordination of nature to history - and consequently of the natural sciences to the science of history? And if so, can such a subordination be justified epistemologically?

### 6.2.1.4 *The natural sciences and the primacy of history*

In Pannenberg's treatment of the special sciences we encounter a subordination of the natural sciences to the science of history. In his treatment of anthropology this is especially evident. Thus Pannenberg has written that "it is only through historical portrayal that one comes as close as possible to the actual course of the concrete life of man. In contrast to this, all general forms of anthropology, be they biologically, psychologically, or sociologically oriented, remain preliminary abstractions."[154] Nearly two decades later he expressed essentially the same view in *Anthropology in Theological Perspective*. There we read that,

> Human life, whether it is the life span of the individual or the larger story of peoples and states, takes concrete form in history. When compared with this concreteness, the approaches taken in human biology, sociology, and psychology show themselves to be only abstract approximations to human reality. History is the *principium individuationis* ... in the life both of individuals and of peoples and cultures. ... Of all the disciplines that have the human being for their subject, the science of history and historiography come closest to grasping human reality as it is experienced.[155]

In a similar manner Pannenberg, in his discussion of the eschatological end of history in volume three of his *Systematic Theology*, despite his use of the findings of the natural sciences to support the view that the world will have an end,[156] contends that "the claim that belongs properly to Christianity that there will be a future end of the world cannot be built upon the knowledge of the physical world gained from the natural sciences." The most that can be said on the basis of the findings of the natural sciences, especially physics, in this regard, is that they do not contradict this view.[157] The fact that we are living in a world and participating in a history that will come to an end, according to Pannenberg, is best demonstrated not by the natural sciences, which can play only a supporting role in this regard, but by history. He writes: "The fact that we are confronted

---

[154] "Toward a Theology of the History of Religions," in: *BQ* 2:78. [*Grundfragen*, 262.]
[155] *ATP*, 485. [472.]
[156] Cf., for instance, *ST* 2:151ff., [177ff.], esp. 157ff. [184ff.] On the transition toward abandoning the idea of the eternity of the universe and accepting its finitude Pannenberg writes: "The change came with the theory of relativity, which taught us to see space and time as dependent on the mass and velocity of bodies and thus permitted us to think of the world as spatially unlimited yet finite." (154, [180]). Pannenberg argues that even before the theory of relativity, the Second Law of Thermodynamics brought the conception of an end of the world back into the consideration of physics and of modern thinking as well. (157f., [184f.])
[157] *ST* 3:634f.,

with an end of the world and of human history in general is pointed to by another ground apart from the eschatological perspective of physical cosmology and ecological problems. It is the inner logic of the historicalness of our consciousness."[158] Because every occurrence and experience must be understood within the context of the totality of all occurrences and because the totality of reality, as well as the experience of this reality, is to be thought of as an uncompleted process within time, Pannenberg reaches the conclusion, based upon the presuppositions of his philosophy of history, that the world will have an end. Hence, "*that* the world is heading toward an end can only be brought to awareness as the implication of the view of the whole of reality as a single process, as history."[159]

The subordination of the natural sciences to the science and philosophy of history in Pannenberg's thought is grounded upon his theology of nature in which, as we have already seen, nature itself is understood as historical. Crucial for Pannenberg is the fact that time is irreversible and that all natural processes flow in one temporal direction only. In his 1981 article, "Theological Questions to Scientists," Pannenberg asks whether the "reality of nature [is] to be understood as contingent, and are natural processes to be understood as irreversible?"[160] By posing this question Pannenberg is suggesting that irreversibility and contingency are related and that irreversibility may even be rooted in contingency so that the two principles would be inseparable.[161]

For Pannenberg, therefore, as Peters has rightly indicated, "the reality of nature is first and foremost a historical reality."[162] Hence for Pannenberg the category of history provides a more appropriate description of natural processes than do natural laws and the regularities which they describe. Arguing on the basis of contingency Pannenberg contends that whereas the description(s) of the regularities of natural processes in the form of natural laws are essentially abstractions from the contingent conditions under which they occur, historical continuity is able to bring together "the contingency of events ... with the emergence of regularities. Thus the category of history provides a more

---

[158] *Ibid.*, 635f.

[159] *Ibid.*, 636. Hefner, "The Role of Science in Pannenberg's Theological Thinking," 281, hints that for Pannenberg the evolution of the world is also the triumph of history over the physical and biological levels of development. Hence "history becomes at a higher, more complex, and (in the epoch in which humanity is the dominant species) more critical level, what the physical and biological processes were for preceding levels."

[160] Pannenberg, "Theological Questions to Scientists," in: *Toward a Theology of Nature*, 21. On the question of the irreversibility of time see also *ST* 2:107f., [130f.]

[161] Cf. *ibid.*, 22, where Pannenberg notes that although the irreversibility of natural processes is often demonstrated on the basis of entropy - which in turn has been "applied to cosmology and has contributed to relativistic models of the universe such as the big bang theory ... the ultimate basis of irreversibility may rather be looked for, as Carl F. von Weizsäcker suggests, in the irreversibility of time. Here, then, contingency and irreversibility may have their common root."

[162] Peters, "Pannenberg on Theology and Natural Science," 10.

comprehensive description of the continuous process of nature" than do natural laws.[163]

Given the priority which Pannenberg gives to history in relation to the natural sciences, making history a sort of universal science, one might ask what is the relation between history and theology. Is theology's universality and status as the universal science in Pannenberg's thought infringed upon by the place he gives to history? For Pannenberg the answer to the question would clearly have to be no since history derives its apparent universality from theology upon which it is grounded. Indeed, Pannenberg questions whether the unity of history, which is so important for his own thought, can have any other than a theological foundation. The dependence of both the philosophy of history and the science of history upon theology in Pannenberg's thought is put succinctly when he writes that the "ancient theological foundation to the understanding of history has remained effective not only in the Christian theology of history; but it remains in the modern West for philosophy of history and historical methodology in general an open question as to whether the unity of history as such can be based on anything else but theology." And further, given that the ancient Israelites found the unity of all occurrences in the unity of God's acting in history and Christianity was able to think of history as a unity "because for Christians the end of history has already become a previous event ... it may be doubted whether the idea of the unity of history can at all be separated from these theological roots."[164]

Given this dependence of the philosophy and methodology of history - as well as the idea of its unity - upon theology, and the seeming subordination of the natural sciences to history in Pannenberg's thought, the question which must be asked is what implication this perspective has for the dialogue with the natural sciences that he seeks to pursue? One could easily imagine that physicists and cosmologists, for instance, might find difficulty with the findings arising out of their disciplines being given the role of only supporting material to demonstrate a conclusion, for instance that the world will have an end, that seems to have been already decided upon the basis of historical considerations - especially when these are based upon a philosophy of history built upon theological roots. Yet despite the potential for such difficulties this is not Pannenberg's intention. Indeed, since theology - given his understanding of revelation as history - is based upon history, if the natural sciences are also found to examine a natural world that is also first and foremost historical, then common ground has been found and a potential bridge built between the two worlds that will further dialogue between them. Ted Peters has summarized Pannenberg's intention well at this point.

> What Pannenberg capitalizes on is ... [his] recognition that nature has an essential historical dimension, because history may provide the open gate that will permit increased traffic between the scientific side and the theological side of

---

[163] "Theological Questions to Scientists," 22.
[164] "Contingency and Natural Law," 86. ["Kontingenz und Naturgesetz," 46f.]

the fence. Theologians are at home in history. God acts. And God's acts have historical effects, and such effects can be apprehended only as contingently and temporally unique. Theology can be understood as the study of the history of God's activity. So, what Pannenberg is trying to do is to move the scientist from a focus on the abstracted uniformities of nature to the pre-supposed background of nature's contingent course of events; and this should open up the possibility of dialogue with the theologian on common ground.[165]

Whether of course this approach will actually have the effect of establishing common ground and fostering greater dialogue remains an open question. Not only must natural scientists be convinced of the essentially historical nature of all physical reality but they must also be convinced that this implies that the science and philosophy of history have a certain priority over the other special sciences. They must also be convinced that time is irreversible (which today, especially after Hawking's reversal of his opinion on this question,[166] is seldom disputed) and that nature is therefore an historical reality that provides genuine common ground with theology, which deals with a God who acts in history. An additional difficulty is that not all theologians are willing to attribute as much weight to history as Pannenberg, especially, for instance, in regard to his thesis concerning revelation as history or his particular philosophy of history. Pannenberg's attempt to base the dialogue between natural science and theology upon a presupposition of the priority of history would seem to have much potential. At the same time, however, it would seem that both natural scientists and theologians would need to be convinced of the correctness of some fundamental assumptions which Pannenberg makes before the fruitfulness of his proposal could be fully explored.

Pannenberg, however, is aware that much work remains to be done in this regard, especially as pertains to the compatibility of the understanding of nature as history with the biblical conception of history. It is not just the task of natural science, however, to examine this question, but also poses a challenge for theology. Hence, as Pannenberg writes, "it is no longer strictly a scientific question as to whether nature can be understood, in the sense of the foundation to the biblical thinking of history, from the contingency of divine actions." Hence, "the theological question as to whether the connection of the events of nature can

---

[165] Peters, 10.
[166] Cf. Hawking, *A Brief History of Time: From the Big Bang to Black Holes* (New York: Bantam Books, 1988), 143ff. Hawking, assuming a closed universe, wrote: "At first, I believed that disorder would decrease when the universe recollapsed. This was because I thought that the universe had to return to a smooth state when it became small again. ... [But] I had made a mistake: the no boundary condition implied that disorder would in fact continue to increase during the contraction. The thermodynamic and psychological arrows of time would not reverse when the universe begins to recontract or inside black holes" (p. 150). Because the debate has raged over the irreversibility of time through most of the present century with a consensus only recently seeming to have taken shape. Pannenberg's thesis, therefore, about the historical reality of nature, would seem dependent upon what some would consider an emerging and not yet universally held consensus about the irreversibility of time.

be understood in the sense of the biblical conception of history on the basis of the contingency of divine actions ... retains a special status relative to the scientific way of thinking." Theology, then, cannot just compare the results of scientific investigations but must refer to what natural science has determined in regard to the relationship between contingency (which underlies the biblical view of history) and the regularity of events (which underlies the scientific conception). Theology, then, will have to "find in these circumstances the counterinstances and the proofs by which a theology of nature is tied to the reality of nature."[167]

For Pannenberg, therefore, the 'primacy of history' together with the significance of the biblical understanding of contingency is not simply the proposal of one of several possible approaches to dialogue with the natural sciences but is seen by Pannenberg as fundamental and essential to any possible natural science/theology dialogue. Hence, as he has contended:

> The discussion between theology and natural science becomes relevant only when it can be shown that the motif of contingency, which is central for the Jewish/Christian comprehension of events as divine action, open up an aspect of events that scientific investigation ... tended to cover up and that, nevertheless, is indispensable as a correlative for the central concept of natural science, regularity. ... Thus it is clear that the characteristic of reality founded on divine action has its home as contingent already in the horizon of a confrontation of theology with scientific thinking.[168]

### 6.2.2 Pannenberg's appropriation of metaphors from physics

*6.2.2.1 The concept of 'field' within philosophy, physics and theology*
The seminal form of modern field theories can be traced back to the Stoic doctrine of the divine *pneuma* (spirit) which has been identified as the "direct predecessor of the field concept" in modern physics.[169] For Pannenberg this is of fundamental importance for it is the roots of the field theory in philosophy which allows it, in the form taken in modern physics, to seen also as a metaphysical category with implications for theology. As Pannenberg has written: "The field concept, which Einstein put in the place of a system of inertia of space-time ... has, strictly speaking, not only a function within the frame of physical theory but is at the same time, on the basis of its origins, also a metaphysical category of the conception of nature."[170]

Within the natural sciences, the history of the modern concept of field theory begins with the experimental and theoretical work of the nineteenth-century British chemist Michael Faraday on electricity and magnetism. Faraday, unhappy

---
[167] "Contingency and Natural Law," 97. ["Kontingenz und Naturgesetz," 57f.]
[168] *Ibid.*, 115, note 10. [74f., note 10.]
[169] Max Jammer, "Feldtheorie," in: *Historisches Wörterbuch der Philosophie* (Darmstadt: Wissenschaftliche Buchgesellschaft, 1972), 923.
[170] "God and Nature," 65. ["Gott und Natur," 499f.]

with the concept of 'action at a distance' in which force was seen simply to leap across space, developed a concept of force in which forces themselves were "the sole physical substance"[171] and were all interconnected to such an extent that the "mutual relation and conversion of forces would surpass the human intellect."[172] The concepts of force and fields of force were known long before Faraday, "but the prevailing viewpoint was not to regard such 'fields' as constituting, in themselves, actual physical substance. ... However, Faraday's profound experimental findings led him to believe that electric and magnetic fields are *real physical 'stuff.'*"[173]

Although considered the founder of modern field theory, Faraday himself never spoke of fields of force but used the phrase "physical lines of force" to describe his concept of field theory. Although there has been some controversy as to what precisely Faraday's field concept was, its essential features would seem to be, "that force is a substance, that it is the only substance and that all forces are interconvertible through various motions of the lines of force."[174] Although most of these features were not adopted in successive concepts of field theory the essential idea of a field theory itself was developed further by James Clerk Maxwell and Heinrich Hertz and, within classical physics, culminated in the relativity theory of Albert Einstein. Also, since Dirac's pioneering work, the concept of field theory has been carried over into quantum theory.

Quantum field theories, which arise from the combination of concepts taken from special relativity and quantum mechanics, have been helpful in overcoming the tension of the wave-particle dualism.[175] To assume, however, that quantum field theories are a complete and final description of the nature of quantum 'reality' is a mistake. Such theories may very well turn out to be nothing more than provisional descriptions of quantum relationships. Even if this does not prove to be the case, the analogical character of the 'field' concept, especially within quantum physics, must not be overlooked.[176]

In quantum theory the concept of force, and of fields of force, takes on a sort of double analogical character. First, the concept of force in classical physics is essentially "a device for the economy of thought, based upon analogy with human

---

[171] William Berkson, *Fields of Force: The Development of a World View from Faraday to Einstein* (London: Routledge and Kegan Paul, 1974), 50.
[172] Michael Faraday, *Lectures on the Various Forces of Matter and Their Relations to Each Other* (London: Richard Griffen, 1861), 131.
[173] Roger Penrose, *The Emperor's New Mind: Concerning Computers, Minds, and the Laws of Physics* (Oxford: Oxford University Press, 1989), 185.
[174] Cf. Nancy Nessian, "Faraday's Field Concept," in: *Faraday Rediscovered: Essays on the Life and Work of Michael Faraday, 1791-1867*, ed. D. Gooding and F. James (London: Macmillan Press, 1985), 183 and 175ff. Nessian discusses five different views regarding what Farady's field concept actually was.
[175] Cf. John Polkinghorne, *The Quantum World* (London: Longman, 1984), 7ff.
[176] Cf. Penrose, *The Emperor's New Mind*, 289.

experience."[177] In quantum mechanics the concept of force and fields of force become a sort of double analogy since they rely upon analogy with classical physics. As Jammer has written, in quantum mechanics "the concept of force ... is introduced in complete analogy to macroscopic dynamics and is consequently, strictly speaking, an analogy of an analogy." The analogical character of the concepts of force and fields of force is significant for the discussion of the implications of such concepts for theology. Words such as 'field' and 'force' are analogies which help us comprehend physical reality - they are not themselves reality - unless perhaps they be understood as mathematical reality. Hence caution should be exercised in drawing philosophical and theological conclusions from such ideas - especially in light of the theoretical and practical problems which continue to plague many field theories.

Nevertheless, despite the essentially analogical nature and sometimes provisional character of field theories they hold a rich possibility for metaphors which can be explored by theology. Indeed, Pannenberg operates with a tri-level appropriation of meaning in regard to the concept of field. First is the original and for theology especially significant philosophical conception. Second is the concept arising out of the natural sciences, especially physics, which we have briefly examined. And finally, Pannenberg postulates a theological meaning of the field concept. Although there is an inter-relatedness within the three levels which can potentially foster fruitful interdisciplinary dialogue, they are not identical. The scientific understanding of field, therefore, is not necessarily determinative for the theological conception and application of the field concept. Hence the concept of field theory can, for example, be employed by theologians as a model for understanding God's sustenance of the creation through the Holy Spirit - although physicists may have difficulty with such applications given their own specific conceptions of field.

Among theologians T. F. Torrance seems to have first made use of field theory in this capacity in his 1969 book, *Space, Time and Incarnation*. Torrance suggested that we must allow the incarnation to create a field of 'organic connections' within which we can speak and think about the incarnation. This 'field,' contended Torrance, "is surely the interaction of God with history understood from the axis of Creation-Incarnation. ... Our understanding of this field will be determined by the force or energy that constitutes it, the Holy and Creator Spirit of God."[178] Pannenberg himself has demonstrated how the theological understanding of field, while remaining related to the concept in the natural sciences and thus not closing off avenues of dialogue, can go beyond the understanding of field in physics and take on new and potent theological meaning. An example of this is to be found in Pannenberg's understanding of the future as

---

[177] Max Jammer, *Concepts of Force: A Study in the Foundations of Dynamics* (Cambridge, MA: Harvard University Press, 1957), 250, for this and the following quotation.

[178] T. F. Torrance, *Space, Time and Incarnation* (London: Oxford University Press, 1969), 70f.

determining the present. In modern physics Pannenberg suggests that if the appearance of micro-occurrences in their respective moments of manifestation can be understood as the "field of possibilities of future occurrences" then this would have significant consequences for natural philosophy and theology. That this field of future possibilities can have a determinative impact on the present and can be described as a "possibility field of future events" means that the concept of field, in this instance,

> the field concept undoubtedly takes a new turn vis-à-vis the field theories of physics. This is true at any rate as regards its prior use in physics. Even though field concepts in physics may speak of a force field as the origin of what is possible in the future, we have here an extension of such usage. We are thinking not only of the priority of the future over the present and the past but also of the basic creative dynamic of the field in relation to the phenomena that take place in it.[179]

Theologian Ted Peters, commenting on Pannenberg's work on the concept of field theory, has suggested that the field concept, revitalized in modern physics, is theologically significant for three reasons.

> First, the problem with the post-Newtonian reduction of forces to mass in motion is that the resulting picture of the universe precludes any divine force. If God does not have a body, and if all forces require a prior body, then God cannot have force. This problem is eliminated with contemporary field theory. ... [Second,] dynamic field theories ... claim a priority for the whole over the parts. The value of this is that God and the whole are correlate categories. ... This brings us to the third reason that field theory in physics is theologically significant: it provides a possible means for conceiving of the divine Spirit as active in the natural world.[180]

It is toward this later possibility that Pannenberg has directed most of his attention in regard to the theological implications and understanding of the field concept. It has proven to be one of the most intriguing as well as one of the most controversial aspects of his thought.

### 6.2.2.2 *Field theory and the Holy Spirit*

Wolfhart Pannenberg has given a great deal of attention to the relationship between field theory and the doctrine of the Holy Spirit. He contends that, "since the field concept as such corresponds to the old concept of *pneuma* and was derived from it in the history of thought, theologians should consider it obvious to relate the field concept of modern physics to the Christian doctrine of the dynamic presence of the divine Spirit in all of creation."[181] As the leading advocate of the

---
[179] *ST* 2:100f., [122f.]
[180] Peters, "Pannenberg on Theology and Natural Science," 13.
[181] "The Doctrine of Creation and Modern Science," in: *Toward a Theology of Nature*, 40.

use of field theory models for understanding the sustaining work of God's Spirit in the creation Pannenberg takes as his starting point the fact that "the theological affirmation that the world of nature proceeds from an act of divine creation implies the claim that the existence of the world as a whole and of all its parts is contingent."[182] How, however, is such contingency to be understood as a continuing activity of the Creator under the category of a *creatio conservata*, i.e., God's continued sustaining of the physical universe? Pannenberg suggests that the field theories of modern physics provide insight into how this is to be understood. He writes:

> The turn toward the field concept in the development of modern physics has theological significance. This is suggested not only by its opposition to the tendency to reduce the concept of force to bodies or masses but also because field theories from Faraday to Albert Einstein claim a priority for the whole over the parts. This is of theological significance because God has to be conceived as the unifying ground of the whole universe if God is to be conceived as creator and redeemer of the world. The field concept could be used in theology to make the effective presence of God in every single phenomenon intelligible.[183]

We also see here that the concept of field holds an additional appeal for Pannenberg in its apparent usefulness for conceptualizing God's universality. Inasmuch as the concept of field portrays the contingency of all matter and all occurrences, the biblical view of all things as contingent upon God finds a fruitful conceptual model in the field theories of modern physics. And when theology can think of the Holy Spirit as field then this model becomes even more significant.

Pannenberg cautions, however, that he is proposing only a model and does not intend to equate the activity of the Holy Spirit with the field theories of physics. He writes: "To be sure, even a cosmic field conceived along the lines of Faraday's thought as a field of force would not be identified immediately with the dynamic activity of the divine Spirit in creation. In every case the different models of science remain approximations. ... Therefore, theological assertions of field structure of the cosmic activity of the divine Spirit will remain different from field theories in physics."[184] This is where Pannenberg's program becomes difficult for many to follow in that he seems to do precisely what he has cautioned against, namely, to develop new conceptual models for the Trinity, the Holy Spirit, and angels in light of the concept of field theory. And in the case of his doctrine of angels, at least, there seems to be an identification of these messengers of God with specific physical forces and fields. Yet for Pannenberg the fact that scientific models of field are only approximations and that the use of the concept of field will be necessarily different in physics and theology provides the

---

[182] *Ibid.*, 34.
[183] *Ibid.*, 38f.
[184] *Ibid.*, 40f.

justification for theology breaking out of the conceptual mode of physics and exploring new, theologically-based, applications of the field model. Pannenberg, for instance, justifies the introduction of the concept of field theory into our understanding of the doctrine of God on the ground that God is spoken of biblically as "spirit," i.e., the Greek word *pneuma* which eventually became associated with the concept of fields of force in physics.[185] In regard to the relation of the Holy Spirit to the Father and the Son Pannenberg develops his own 'theological' field theory. Pannenberg writes:

> Criticism of [the] traditional way of speaking about God as though the reference were to subjectivity (*nous*) led to the insight that it is more in keeping with what the Bible says about God as Spirit, or about the Spirit of God, to view what is meant as a dynamic field that is structured in trinitarian fashion, so that the person of the Holy Spirit is one of the personal concretions of the essence of God as Spirit in distinction from the Father and the Son. The person of the Holy Spirit is not himself to be understood as the field but as a unique manifestation (singularity) of the field of the divine essentiality. But because the personal being of the Holy Spirit is manifest only in distinction from the Son (and therefore also from the Father), his working in creation has more the character of dynamic field operations.[186]

An intriguing part of Pannenberg's larger understanding of God's continuing sustenance of the physical cosmos is the place he assigns to angels - which he also integrates into his understanding of 'field.' Pannenberg suggests that, "from the point of view of the field structure of spiritual dynamics one could consider identifying the subject matter intended in the conception of angels with the emergence of relatively independent parts of the cosmic field."[187] And if one keeps in mind that the idea that angels are personal spirits can be explained by "the fact that the concept of person in phenomenology of religion is related to the impact of more or less incomprehensible 'powers,'" the problem of person in the doctrine of angels can be overcome. Thus, "if one considers this background of the biblical language about angels as personal realities, they may very well be related to fields of forces or dynamic spheres, the activity of which may be experienced as good or bad."[188] In his *Systematic Theology* he goes so far as to contend that, "if we define forces like wind or fire or stars as angels of God, then we are relating them to God their Creator and to the human experience of being affected by them as servants of God or as demonic powers that oppose his will." Why, then, asks Pannenberg, should not the forces of nature in the forms that they

---

[185] *ST* 2:83, [104.]
[186] *Ibid.*, 83f., [104.]
[187] "The Doctrine of Creation," 41.
[188] *Ibid.*

are known to modern persons, be described as servants and messengers of God, that is to say, as angels?[189]

From the viewpoint of the natural sciences Pannenberg's work with the field concept understandably presents special difficulties. In the first place, as we have already indicated, it would seem that for Pannenberg field theory becomes more than simply a model or paradigm for theological reflection inasmuch as an actual identification seems to be made between various physical fields of force and angels. Is there ultimately a qualitative distinction, one might ask, between Pannenberg's proposal to understand angels as physical force fields and identifying God with the sum total of physical laws or forces in the universe? That is to say, is there a danger in Pannenberg's program that angels, the Holy Spirit, and ultimately 'God' could be reduced to metaphors for physical realities?

Additionally, there are a number of field theories in the natural sciences - biological as well as physical. Within physics alone there are classical and quantum field theories of different types. Pannenberg does not distinguish between any of these. What he does do is use the general idea of 'fields of force' and build his theological field model upon this general notion, borrowing ideas from various and sometimes unrelated field theories. But which field theory (or theories) does Pannenberg rely upon most in formulating this general concept. The essential idea of lines of force (or fields of force) developed by Faraday in the middle of the nineteenth century seems to provide Pannenberg with his basic paradigm. This itself, however, leads to other problems. First, Faraday's ideas concerning fields of force have been greatly altered, diversified, and advanced in the last 130 years. Some of his concepts regarding fields of force have never been verified or have been proven inaccurate, e.g., the idea of the conservation of force in which force depleted in one field must be replaced in another and the connection between gravity and electromagnetism. Pannenberg seems particularly reliant upon Faraday's vision "to reduce all the different forces to a single field of force that determines all the changes in the natural universe."[190] Modern physics, however, while seeking a unified field *theory* that would combine classical and quantum field theories, has long ago abandoned the idea that a single unified *field* exists. By relying extensively upon pre-Einsteinian, pre-quantum theory concepts of field, Pannenberg would seem to neglect his goal of relating "the field concept of modern physics to the Christian doctrine of the dynamic presence of the divine Spirit."[191]

This would seem to account, perhaps, for some of the strong criticism Pannenberg has received from contemporary scientists, by whom he has been accused of misunderstanding and/or misusing the concept of field theory. Jeffrey Wicken, for instance, commenting on Pannenberg's use of field theory, writes:

---

[189] *ST* 2:106f., [129.]
[190] "The Doctrine of Creation," 38.
[191] *Ibid.*, 40.

> If we want to use the word *energy* or *field* in science-theology discourse, let us do so in some way commensurate with their understandings in physics. Talking about 'spirit' as 'energy' and granting it by implication the status of physical law runs dangerously close to usurping the hard-won denotative language of science for physicalizing theology. This serves neither enterprise. ... *Field* has been used in a spectrum of senses in science ranging from the specifically denotative to the connotative to the metaphorical. Pannenberg uses them all in pursuing a theology of wholeness in evolutionary process.[192]

Wicken concludes that, "although as metaphor this notion [of field] is rich for theology, taken literally it binds God needlessly to physics. Is God conceived here as a *field in physics*? If so, why the need for God at all?"[193]

Pannenberg's use of the field concept has attracted similar criticism, albeit generally more cautious, from fellow theologians. Typical of the assessment of many theologians is the judgment of Peters:

> Pannenberg rushes in where two-language angels have feared to tread. He does not say that spirit *is like* a force field. He says spirit *is* a force field. There is a directness and a literalness here that seems to throw caution to the wind. One can admire his scholarly courage, but perhaps this assertion should retain its hypothetical status for a period to await confirmation or disconfirmation. ... New discoveries and new theories have repeatedly whipped up the winds of change, and new waves of thought have again and again swamped and sunk previously held scientific ideas. How long will field theory stay afloat? If someday it should sink, will Pannenberg's theology of the spirit sink with it?[194]

Pannenberg, however, has anticipated this criticism, asking already in his "Doctrine of Creation and Modern Science," whether the concept of field as he makes use of it amounts "to more than equivocal language which ... [has] little in common with the meaning of the word in physics?" His answer to this question is that theology is justified in using the field concept, and particularly in giving theological and metaphysical meaning to it which my not be rooted in any specific field theory in modern science, since "the field concept was originally a metaphysical concept."[195] This brings the discussion, then, back to Pannenberg's justification of separate philosophical, theological, and scientific understandings and uses of the field concept. While he is quite correct concerning the historical origin of the concept in Greek philosophy and theology's right to give the term its own interpretation(s), we must ask whether this approach is the most prudent in view of pursuing a dialogue with the modern sciences.

---

[192] Jeffrey Wicken, "Theology and Science in the Evolving Cosmos: A Need for Dialogue," in: *Zygon* 23:1 (March 1988), 48 and 51.
[193] *Ibid.*, 52.
[194] Peters, 14.
[195] "The Doctrine of Creation," 39.

As the numerous criticisms and misunderstandings that have arisen in connection with Pannenberg's conception of field theory would seem to suggest, the concept has taken on rather specific meanings and applications in the natural sciences - and thereby in modern thought in general - and supplementing, amending or replacing these with specifically theological understandings - particularly when one attempts simultaneously to relate these theological uses to those in modern physic - leads inevitably to misunderstanding and confusion.

The field concept certainly plays a crucial role in Pannenberg's development of a theology of nature (especially as a model for understanding contingency on the level of natural processes) as well as in the overall framework of his emphasis upon universality. Field theory also has value as a metaphor for God's continuing sustenance of the universe and may very well influence the way in which theology confesses this continuing, 'creative' presence of God not only in its own 'in house' reflections - but also in dialogue with natural science.[196] If it is not to become a bone of contention, however, between theology and the natural sciences, perhaps theology should not exercise its right to develop its own under-standings of the concept specific to theology and limit itself to working with those that have become part of the common vocabulary of modern, educated persons.

### 6.2.2.3 *Contingency and natural law*

As we have already seen in our discussion of Pannenberg's theology of nature the concept of contingency plays a central role in his understanding of nature. Indeed, the role of contingency, together with the concept of field, play such an important role in Pannenberg's thought that Philip Hefner has characterized his overall program as "a theology of contingency and field."[197] In reference to the title of this section Pannenberg would certainly want to qualify that his use of the concept of contingency is not, in a strict sense, a "utilization of a metaphor from physics" since the idea has biblical roots and because he assigns the concept unique theological meaning.[198] Yet because the term is also used in modern physics we must inquire as to its meaning there as compared to its application by Pannenberg as well as to the response of natural scientists to Pannenberg's use of the term contingency.

---

[196] Hefner, "The Role of Science in Pannenberg's Theological Thinking," 273, recognizes this potential when, regarding the insight of modern field theories that causes do not originate in them-selves nor operate in isolation only upon individual entities, he suggests "that the biblical imagery of all things being rooted in the source of nature and history, God, not only has a point of contact with the scientific understandings of reality, but also has something to contribute to those understandings: the insight that the largest field of all, which embraces all of reality, is God."

[197] *Ibid.*, 266.

[198] As Pannenberg explains: "The issue of contingency in historical experience - as a mark of God's action - impressed itself upon my mind early in the course of my studies, in connection with the medieval doctrine of God's prescience and predestination. Later on I found it useful in dialogue with scientists." So Pannenberg, "Theological Appropriation of Scientific Understandings: Response to Hefner, Wicken, Eaves, and Tipler," in: *Zygon* 24:2 (June 1989), 256.

We turn first to Pannenberg's use of the concept of contingency in his dialogue with the natural sciences. The contingency of the physical universe, for Pannenberg, is implied already in the Christian doctrine of creation - which forms the starting point for his discussion with scientists. Specifically, Pannenberg contends that,

> the theological affirmation that the world of nature proceeds from an act of divine creation implies the claim that the existence of the world as a whole and of all its parts is contingent. The existence of the world is contingent in the sense that it need not be at all. It owes its existence to the free activity of divine creation. So does every single part of the world. [Also] ..., there is a close tie between this contingency and time insofar as the possibility of existence is tied to the future. The structural modes of reality are rooted in temporality.[199]

Hence Pannenberg's understanding of contingency, as we have previously indicated, is rooted in his understanding of the universality of God's creative activity. This is true not only for the beginning - in a *creatio originans* but also in God's activity of conservation (*creatio continua*), both of which must be seen as the unified creative activity of the one true God. Hence for Pannenberg, creation did not take place only at some initial beginning point of time but continues to occur in each and every moment of the world's continuing existence. Every creature and every activity or event, therefore, "is dependent on divine cooperation, a *concursus divinus*. There is no activity and no product of creative activity in the world without divine cooperation."[200]

Hence contingency, understood theologically, points to the dependence of all persons and all things in each and every moment of their existence upon God. This can also be seen in the appearance in Pannenberg's thought - entirely consistent with his overall program - of a contingency of the past and present upon the future. The fact that God is the power of the future and stands at the end of history is further witness to the contingency of all created 'things,' including time, upon the one God.

This understanding of contingency, however, was challenged, according to Pannenberg, by the concept of inertia arising out of seventeenth-century natural science. "The principle of inertia as formulated by Descartes means that no longer is the continuous existence of any given state of affairs in need of explanation but only the occurrence of any changes in this status." Within theological and philosophical thought this concept led to the deistic conception of God as a clockmaker who wound the universe up and left it to run on its own - which idea constitutes a fundamental denial of the contingency of the world in all its parts and

---

[199] "The Doctrine of Creation and Modern Science," 34.
[200] *Ibid.*, 34f.

at all times upon God.²⁰¹ Deism, therefore, is seen by Pannenberg to be the "consequence of the introduction of the principle of inertia in modern physics."²⁰² Indeed, the seriousness with which Pannenberg takes the challenge of inertia to contingency is reflected in his article "Theological Questions to Scientists," in which his first question is whether it is "conceivable, in view of the importance of contingency in natural processes, to revise the principle of inertia or at least its interpretation?"²⁰³

Given Pannenberg's theological understanding of contingency and the challenge arising out of the 'modern' principle of inertia, it is of special importance to Pannenberg what contemporary physics are saying about contingency that might contribute to the ongoing theological effort to understand God's relationship to the whole of his creation. Therefore Pannenberg insists that "any contemporary discussion between theology and science should focus in the first place on the question of what modern science, and especially modern physics, can say about the contingency of the universe as a whole and of every part in it."²⁰⁴

Physicist and theologian Robert John Russell has found much of value in Pannenberg's perspective, pointing out that he is "moving to recover the tradition of continuous creation within the doctrine of creation, to identify contingency as a *common* element in both forms of creation theology, and to reappropriate a cosmological and scientific context for theological hermeneutics." Yet precisely because Pannenberg is seeking to regain a scientific context for his theological interpretation of the doctrine of creation the natural scientist, according to Russell, must ask certain questions. Specifically: "How fruitful is Pannenberg's particular choice of scientific language in his discussion of the contingency of the world as a whole (global contingency) and the contingency of each part of the world (local contingency)? And how do these relate to the contingency of the laws of nature (nomological contingency)?"²⁰⁵ After a detailed examination of Pannenberg's proposals Russell remains uneasy with the fact that Pannenberg, while having demonstrated the fruitfulness of the topic, has given little or no attention "to the meaning of contingency in quantum physics, relativity theory, or thermodynamics" or even of genetics or evolutionary biology, if one takes the discussion outside the bounds of physics. Russell is also puzzled over Pannenberg's focus upon inertia

---

²⁰¹ Pannenberg, "Theological Questions to Scientists," 19f., notes that this has been highlighted in recent times by the German philosopher Hans Blumenberg who, in Pannenberg's view, has "demonstrated in some detail that the introduction of the principle of inertia in seventeenth-century physics was to replace the dependence of physical reality on God's activity of continuous creation with the idea of self-preservation." Pannenberg's reference is to Blumenberg's article "Selbsterhaltung und Beharrung: Zur Konstitution der neuzeitlichen Rationalität," in: *Subjektivität und Selbsterhaltung*, ed. Hans Ebeling (Frankfurt/M: Suhrkamp, 1976): 144-207.
²⁰² "The Doctrine of Creation," 35.
²⁰³ "Questions to Scientists," 19.
²⁰⁴ Ibid.
²⁰⁵ Robert John Russell, "Contingency in Physics and Cosmology: A Critique of the Theology of Wolfhart Pannenberg," in: *Zygon* 23:1 (March 1988), 26.

as the main challenge to contingency - something he considers, in light of the present state of discussions within physics, to be an "anachronistic target."[206]

The biochemist Jeffrey Wicken has also found much good in Pannenberg's use of contingency, but, like Russell, questions how attentive Pannenberg is to the current state of discussion in the natural sciences. He contends that Pannenberg seems to put "too many metaphysical eggs in the basket of physics, and a misconceived physics as well." And suggests that his theological reflections on contingency continue "theology's long tradition of making itself vulnerable to scientific erosion by anchoring itself to physical cosmology."[207] These criticisms would seem to a certain extent justified and point to real weaknesses in Pannenberg's thoughts on contingency which we have also seen in his treatment of the field concept.

Wicken's criticism, however, that Pannenberg's observations on natural laws are all physics and no theology and that Pannenberg fails to draw the line between "where science ends and theology begins" represents a fundamental misunderstanding of Pannenberg's program. What Wicken seems to miss is that Pannenberg is seeking precisely to show that a clear line cannot be drawn between theology and the natural sciences when God is confessed as Creator of the world and that reflection upon the data of natural science is also, in some sense, "theology." Indeed, Wicken seems to reveal in many ways the persistence of the very "two books" perception of reality among natural scientists which Pannenberg is striving to overcome.

Also in Russell's question asking how fruitful is Pannenberg's "choice of scientific topics and language in his discussion of contingency" we see a difference in perspective. For Russell and others trained in the natural sciences "contingency" is first and foremost a term arising out of modern physics. What Russell does not seem to take fully into account is that for Pannenberg contingency is first of all a term descriptive of the biblical relationship of God to the events of history, and that the insights of modern physics into contingency are essentially secondary to its basic meaning. That is to say, for Pannenberg contingency is a theological concept and its use by the theologian must not be determined by its use in physics. Neither should the theologian have to justify the use of the concept before the natural sciences as if it were their exclusive possession. Yet we notice here in these two examples of field theory and contingency that Pannenberg's insistence upon theological definitions of terms now common in the natural sciences based upon their origins (either etymologically or conceptually) in philosophy or biblical thought has led to misunderstandings and difficulties in the dialogue with natural scientists - even with those who are relatively attuned to theological language and concerns.

---

[206] *Ibid.*, 40f.
[207] Wicken, "Theology and Science in the Evolving Cosmos," 49f.

Pannenberg, in responding to these and similar criticisms by scientists in regard to his use of both the concept of field and that of contingency admits that he has taken a risk in employing these concepts in theology. Specifically, he admits that, when brought into theology, "the field concept gets slightly transformed." Hence Pannenberg is well aware that his field concept "is no longer the field concept of classical electrodynamics and gravitational theory." The legitimacy of such a transformation of the field concept - or of any concept from the natural sciences - is justified, however, according to Pannenberg, if two conditions are met. First of all, this transformation or "reshaping" must be deliberate and must be "done in continuity with the profound implications of its conceptual history." In regard to this requirement Pannenberg would seem to be on fairly firm ground with his application of the field and contingency concepts, at least from the perspective of the development of his own theology. The second condition - and we will focus our attention on this requirement since is has direct and more obvious implications for the dialogue with the natural sciences - is that such theological reshaping and use of a concept from the natural sciences is justified only "when it sheds new light on current scientific problems."[208]

In regard to the second condition for justification of such "reshaping" of concepts from the natural sciences the question which must be asked is, who it is that determines whether a particular theological reinterpretation or reshaping of a scientific concept actually "sheds new light on current scientific problems." This condition points to the fact that while Pannenberg argues for a distinctive theological understanding of such concepts as field and contingency he wants at the same time to continue to recognize these theological understandings as having meaning for the natural sciences. Do theologians themselves, however, determine whether their reshaped concepts shed new light on problems of natural science?[209] And if so, how would the competency to do this be demonstrated or justified? Additionally, would this also imply that natural scientists could reshape theological terminology (and this has already occurred, as for instance in the case of the concept of *creatio ex nihilo*[210]) and then tell theologians what new light this sheds on theology? Or does one expect that natural scientists should or would

---

[208] Pannenberg, "Theological Appropriation of Scientific Understandings: Response to Hefner, Wicken, Eaves, and Tipler," 256.

[209] Pannenberg, indeed, suggests what new light his use of the field concept might shed on problems in quantum mechanics and thermodynamics, using the example of his understanding of the future as a field which has power in the present. He writes: "The philosophical interpretation of quantum mechanics is still very controversial; indeed, it has proven impossible to account for all sides of the experimental situation in terms of either field or particle. ... A reformulation of the field concept in connection with the assumption of a priority of the future over the present and past might create new possibilities of interpretation, particularly so because it allows us to consider contingency as a manifestation of a field (and perhaps also by overcoming the dualism of object/observer). For the same reason there might be applications to the task of comprehensively accounting for the processes studied by non-equilibrium thermodynamics." (*Ibid.*, 256.)

[210] Cf. Mark Worthing,, *God, Creation and Contemporay Physics* (Minneapolis: Fortress Press, 1996), 93ff., for a discussion of this phenomenon.

actually seek to verify whether theological reshaping of terminology specific to their own respective disciplines sheds new light on problems they are seeking to solve or on their understanding of natural phenomena. Or, if one were to propose that natural scientists and theologians evaluate the validity of such concepts together the objection would have to be dealt with that the present state of the theology/science dialogue has not yet achieved a level that would potentially allow for such a program - even if its legitimacy could be agreed upon.

Not only would such attempts seem to lead to confusion in the dialogue between theology and the natural sciences, but theological reshaping of scientific concepts itself, as for example Pannenberg's use of field theory and contingency, would seem to take on the character of quasi-scientific theories if one makes their ability to shed new light on problems in the natural sciences a condition for their validity. Would it not be sufficient, one might ask, that such reformulations, if they are to be pursued at all, are required simply to shed light on theological problems? By restricting this requirement in this way the epistemological barrier between natural science and theology, which Pannenberg is seeking to remove, would not be re-established. This would occur only if it were insisted *a priori* that no theological insights into or reshaping of scientific concepts could possibly shed any light on actual problems connected with the natural sciences. This, however, is something entirely different from the apparent suggestion that such reshaping of concepts from the natural sciences by theology *must* shed light on current scientific problems.

## 6.3 **Summary and conclusions**

### 6.3.1 *Theology, natural science, and apologetic common ground*

As was the case in their approach to non-Christian religions, significant similarities between the apologetic praxis of Pannenberg and Rahner in regard to the natural sciences are to be noted despite methodological differences. Both authors reveal a commitment to the dialogue with the natural sciences that aims at taking theology out of its twentieth-century ghetto and overcoming its epistemological isolation in relation to the special sciences that has prevailed through much of the century. For both theologians we have seen, in this chapter as well as in chapters one and two, a commitment to the unity of knowledge which - albeit in varying forms - is grounded ultimately both in the unity and universality of God. Both Rahner and Pannenberg have also developed conceptual models for understanding the natural sciences which, although differing in significant ways from one another, are founded upon the commitment to the universality of theology. Rahner, as we have seen, understands the natural sciences as regional sciences while theology is more than a 'science' for its object is the incomprehensible mystery of God. Hence theology, according to Rahner, is more than a regional science but must "speak of the unfathomable primordial ground of all reality," that is to say, God.[211] Theology, therefore, must extend its interests to all areas dealt with by the various special sciences whereas the interests and competencies of the special sciences are restricted to their specific, limited objects. Thus Rahner's conceptual model of the natural sciences as they relate to theology is grounded upon his understanding of the universality of theology.

Pannenberg similarly founds his conceptual model of the natural sciences as they relate to theology upon his conception of theology's universality. His concept of history, a concept itself grounded upon theology, forms the basis for his understanding of nature as historical and thus establishes common ground between the natural sciences and theology, which latter deals with God's contingent activity within history. Hence the universal contingency of all historical acts and all 'historical' processes of nature upon God forms the basis for the dialogue between theology and natural science.

It is also of significance that, although Rahner and Pannenberg have concentrated in very different areas of the natural sciences, both have dealt with issues raised by the natural sciences which correspond to themes of unity and universality. Although the number of potential points of contact or common ground for dialogue between natural science and theology has expanded dramatically in recent decades both theologians have focused their energies upon areas which imply overarching worldviews and which point to the unity and interconnectedness of all things. For Rahner, evolutionary theory provided the format for his investigations; for Pannenberg, modern physics has provided the opportunity to take up again themes which he finds already in Greek philosophy and the Old Testament, namely field theory and contingency. Rahner, in his emphasis upon the implications of the evolutionary worldview does not miss the fact, as Gelpi observes, that "fundamental to all evolutionary theory is the idea of the unity of the cosmos ... [which] appears most clearly in man himself."[212] And Pannenberg, as we have seen, is also well aware of the implications of the concepts of field and contingency for understanding the relation of the parts to the whole and for conceptualizing a universal history contingent upon God which also includes the realm of nature.

Rahner, starting from an essentially *a priori* methodology, and Pannenberg, opting for an intentionally *a posteriori* approach, find themselves arriving at similar positions in their dialogue with the natural sciences. The common thread and commitment to theology's universality, we would suggest, has played a decisive role in bringing these two theologians from two different traditions and with two very different, and in part conflicting methodologies to what is a very similar apologetic approach to the natural sciences.

Yet much work remains to be done in dialogue and in developing the specific programs of Rahner and Pannenberg. Both theologians have been criticized, and

---

[211] "Theology Today," 60. [*Schriften* 15:67.]
[212] Gelpi, *Life and Light*, 40.

not without some justification, for not really engaging in dialogue with the natural sciences but with merely borrowing concepts from them without paying sufficient attention to the meaning of these concepts within the context of the natural sciences. Yet the fact remains that it is precisely Pannenberg and Rahner who have drawn more attention from natural scientists in recent years and stirred more debate between theology and the natural sciences than most other contemporary theological thinkers - many of whom have been more attentive to the details and interpretation of specific scientific theories.

The claim of the universality of the Christian message and thus of theology's own field of interest, we would suggest, accounts at least in part for the attention given Pannenberg and Rahner by natural scientists and those engaged in dialogue with the natural sciences. A theologian who is attentive to the details of contemporary scientific theories (unlike Rahner) and/or who is careful to employ terms with special meaning in the natural sciences in a corresponding fashion in theology (unlike Pannenberg) - but who essentially maintains that theology and the natural sciences operate in two separate epistemological spheres - may be politely applauded by natural scientists but seldom engaged in dialogue. Where would the common ground be found in such cases - other than perhaps in an agreement that the two fields of reflection have little or nothing of a concrete nature to say to one another? The claim of theological universality, on the other hand, is at the same time a claim to apologetic common ground. It is the insistence that the results of the natural sciences are relevant to theology and that theology, whose object is the one Creator of all physical reality, is not irrelevant to the natural sciences.

When this claim can be intellectually justified within the context of the theology/science dialogue - and Pannenberg and Rahner, beginning from two very different methodological approaches, have made much progress in this direction - then real dialogue becomes not only possible but unavoidable. Early exchanges may indeed be faltering and reveal just how different are many of our perceptions and presuppositions. But the foundations for dialogue - and indeed for the *apologetic* justification of Christian belief within the context of the modern scientific worldview - have been laid in the work of Karl Rahner and Wolfhart Pannenberg. This, I would suggest, and not the specifics of either of their own respective efforts in this dialogue, will prove to be their most important and lasting contribution to the ongoing conversation between the science of theology and the natural sciences.

# SUMMARY AND CONCLUDING OBSERVATIONS

## 7.1 Contrasting Methodologies, Converging Apologetic

We have attempted in this study to draw connecting lines between the programs of Pannenberg and Rahner, giving attention to both contrasts and similarities with a view toward elucidating their respective commitments to theology's universal character. The question that gave rise to this study and that has occupied us throughout is: How is it that two theologians with such different starting points and from such diverse theological and philosophical traditions come not only to share so many common concerns but also to arrive so often at similar conclusions? Whereas Pannenberg advocates an *a posteriori* approach to doing theology, arising out of his pervasive critical-rationalism, Rahner employed an *a priori*, transcendental method rooted in Thomistic theology, Kantian philosophy, and Christian mysticism.[1] Yet our examination of their respective methodologies revealed unexpected parallels which hint at a deeper unity between the two thinkers. Both emphasize the importance of metaphysics for theological reflection, although what Pannenberg terms 'metaphysical' is usually called by Rahner 'transcendental.' Likewise, the human experience plays a critical role for both. Hence, on the level of praxis, anthropology becomes an important starting point for their theological reflections. Both accept the possibility of a natural knowledge of God; Pannenberg on the basis of a universal revelation open to "all who have eyes to see," and Rahner on the basis of human transcendental experience. Yet for Rahner, too, the possibility of a natural knowledge of God exists only because of the universality of God's self-disclosure within human history - a self-disclosure that for both theologians reaches its pinnacle in Jesus Christ.

Yet despite these several intriguing parallels, the methodologies of Pannenberg and Rahner remain fundamentally different and in many respects even contradictory, so that any attempt to bring them together under a single unifying concept is impossible. The question, therefore, of what accounts for their common concerns and similar conclusions at so many points cannot be answered satisfactorily on the level of methodology.[2] Instead, it is only when the theological foundations of theology's universality in both systems are examined that the convergence between the two thinkers becomes explicable.[3] This

---

[1] Cf. our treatments in 1.7.1, 2.2.1 and 2.6.5 and the comparison of methodologies in 2.7.1.

[2] The fact that many points of convergence appear explicable in light of their doctrines of God and humanity rather than their respective methodologies raises the question of to what extent the particular methodologies of both theologians are essential to their conclusions. Does methodology precede, in good 'scientific' fashion, the conclusions arrived at, or are their particular methodologies themselves merely the result of reflection upon prior and more fundamental (*a priori*) theological commitments? The question is especially pertinent because both theologians (to some extent) have become associated with the advocacy of a particular theological method.

[3] Cf. 3.4.1 and 4.3.1 where this point is more thoroughly discussed.

foundation is for both theologians twofold, building on the unity of humanity on the one hand, and on the universality of God on the other.

The unity of the human race and the universality of the experience of freedom, sin, and death - themes both Pannenberg and Rahner have developed extensively in dialogue with the profane sciences - become the preconditions for their apologetics. Only when humanity is one and this one humanity shares the common experiences of freedom, sin and confrontation with death can the Christian message lay claim to universal relevance. Hence even Rahner, with his *a priori*, transcendental approach, develops a theology "from below" that begins intentionally with the concrete data of human existence.

Yet despite the common anthropological starting point it is ultimately the doctrine of God which holds the key to the claim of theological universality for both theologians. There exist intriguing similarities in their emphasis upon the futurity of God[4] - although this is more thoroughly developed by Pannenberg than Rahner - that merit further examination. It is, however, the derivation of theology's universality from God as its true object that is most crucial to the programs of both thinkers. Although, as is often the case, both make use of different terminology, the point they make is essentially the same. Pannenberg, speaking of God as *creator* of the entire universe (and thereby as *all-determining reality*), and Rahner, speaking of God as the *ground of all being*, both seek to establish the necessary contingency of all things upon God. What unites both approaches and distinguishes them from much of contemporary theology is the consistency and radicality with which God's universality is applied. If God is the ground of all being and the creator of all that exists, then it follows that God must be relevant for all persons and all things. Likewise, the knowledge of God and the speech about God (theology) must also be relevant for all persons and for all other disciplines. At the same time the knowledge gained from other disciplines is necessarily relevant for theology.

Upon this basis Pannenberg and Rahner build their apologetic approach not only to the modern, scientific worldview, but also to the world's religions and atheism. A theology - when it is what it ought to be - that speaks *of* a God who is universal and upon whom all things are contingent, and speaks *to* a humanity that is one and that shares the common experiences of freedom and sin - has not only the right but also the obligation to engage all worldviews and all disciplines (indeed all persons) in apologetically-oriented dialogue.

*7.2 Theological Method as Foundation for Apologetics*

Pannenberg put the apologetic challenge of theology today succinctly when he wrote: "How can theology make the primacy of God and his revelation in Jesus Christ intelligible, and validate its truth claim, in an age when all talk about God is reduced to subjectivity, as may be seen from the social history of the time

---
[4] Cf. 4.2.4.4.

and the modern fate of the proofs of God and philosophical theology?"[5] If we agree with Pannenberg that the main apologetic task of theology is to make the message of God's revelation in Christ *intelligible* and to *validate* its truth claims - and we can find no convincing reasons to reject this understanding - then it is clear that for Pannenberg the answer lay not with any mere reformulation of the presentation of assertions of dialectical or liberal theology, but with a new and rigorous look at theology's methodological foundations.[6] If the message of the Christian faith is to be made intelligible and its truth claims validated in the modern world, then the methods of Christian theology must be made intelligible and validated as well. If this is not done, all attempts at a credible apologetic in the modern world must be abandoned. We would then be left either with a Barthian positivism of revelation, that is, a series of pious assertions which are subject neither to verification nor to human reason; or with a neo-liberal subjectivism in which we are left with no assertions at all but merely with pious sentiments whose relative worth and usefulness must constantly be reassessed. Because Pannenberg could accept neither of these alternatives he devoted his efforts to building a credible theological method. This, we would suggest, is his major contribution to Christian apologetics.

Karl Rahner, coming from the Roman Catholic tradition, was faced with a somewhat different apologetic context. Yet for Rahner, too, the apologetic effort begins with questions of theological method. If Rahner's theological method can be rightly described as transcendental, then so can his apologetic. The *a priori* assumption is that all persons, whether explicitly aware of it or not, have a fundamental orientation to that transcendental ground of their being which Christian theology knows as God. The apologetic task, then, for Rahner, as James Bacik describes it, involves a 'maieutic' process "of bringing latent ideas into explicit consciousness." Thus what Rahner seeks to achieve apologetically is not the initiation into a completely new experience or that which is foreign,

> but ... the disclosure of an experience that is already present, although in a hidden way. The maieutic process is one of awakening and activating a sense of the mystery which already rules our lives, of educating people toward a spontaneous realization of the significance of the ever-present deeper dimensions of life.[7]

Rahner's *a priori* assumption that a transcendental experience of the mystery that we call God is at least implicit in all persons does not itself suggest a specific apologetic method so much as it lays the foundation for all apologetic efforts.

---

[5] *ST* 1:128.

[6] Ted Peters, "Truth in History: Gadamer's Hermeneutics and Pannenberg's Apologetic Method," 56, is correct when he observes that for Pannenberg, "apologetic and methodology are not separate departments of Christian theology ... [for] through his honest quest for truth, Pannenberg is constructing a single framework which encompasses both tasks."

[7] James Bacik, *Apologetics and the Eclipse of Mystery: Mystagogy According to Karl Rahner* (Notre Dame: University of Notre Dame Press, 1980), 17.

This is the case inasmuch as the Christian, when confronted with 'non-Christian' persons (and worldviews) must be aware that these persons already stand in relationship to God's revelation since as human beings they are in their creatureliness potential hearers of a possible revelation from God. For Rahner, therefore, the apologetic implication of the fact that God is the ground of all being, is that there are no persons, cultures, worldviews, or ideologies for which this God is not relevant - indeed, in whom/which God is not already present in at least an implicit way. And it is this insight, coupled with the fact of God's universal salvific will, which led to his theory of an anonymous Christianity - a theory which is itself not an apologetic tool for Rahner but rather a foundational presupposition for all apologetic efforts.[8]

## 7.3 *Universality as Leitmotif in Rahner and Pannenberg: Summary and Critique*

We have put forward the thesis in this study that the motif of universality is the key not only to the interpretation of the thought of both Karl Rahner and Wolfhart Pannenberg, but is also the key to comprehending the similarities in their programs. For both theologians the emphasis upon universality in its several inter-related and inter-dependent forms, e.g. universality of God, universality of theology, and universality of human experience, has been consistently emphasized and suggests itself as a natural starting point in a comparison of their systems.

"Without a sound claim to universal validity," Pannenberg has written, "Christians cannot maintain a conviction of the truth of their faith and message. For a 'truth' that would be simply my truth and would not at least claim to be universal and valid for every human being could not remain true even for me."[9] With this conviction of the importance of the universality of the Christian message, Pannenberg has set out to develop a comprehensive methodogical and apologetic program that supports and builds upon this claim. For Rahner, too, the Christian message is universal and cannot be seen merely as one truth claim among others.[10] What is of special significance, however, for both Pannenberg and Rahner, is not that they make reference to the universal relevance of the Christian message or to God's universality on occasion, but that the theme of universality runs consistently through their respective writings from questions of methodology and anthropology to Christology and the doctrine of God and finally to their respective theologies of religion and dialogue with the natural sciences.

The *Leitmotif* of universality plays a determinative role in the thought of both Pannenberg and Rahner and is pursued by both not just in their theological reflections, but in their approach to dialogue with non-Christian religions and the special sciences. Indeed, it is precisely this concern for and commitment to theology's universality that has led to some of the most innovative aspects of their

---

[8] So similarly Weger, *Karl Rahner: An Introduction to His Theology*, 118.
[9] *ATP*, 15. [15.]
[10] Cf., for example, *FCF*, 312. [*Grundkurs*, 304.]

respective programs. Without the commitment to universality, for instance, Pannenberg's defence of the scientific status of theology, his interpretation of history, his understanding of contingency, etc. would not be possible - at least not in their present forms. For these are all dependent upon and contribute to an overall conception of universality - of history, of God, of human experience - and of the relation between the whole and the parts and an emphasis upon unity (e.g., unity of God, of knowledge, of humanity) that stands at the center of Pannenberg's theological program.

Karl Rahner is less explicit in his concern for universality than Pannenberg. Yet he, too, is dependent in his thought upon a network of inter-related concerns for wholeness and universality without which his program would lose its fundamental coherence. His conception of the unity of knowledge, for instance, developed already in *Hearers of the Word*, forms the basis of his epistemological system. And without an understanding of God as the ground of all being *and* of the fundamental solidarity of humanity - seen even in the need for a monogenistic origin of the human race - his transcendental method would not be viable.

We live in an age characterized intellectually by the so-called two-language theory separating epistemologically theological knowledge from the knowledge pursued by the other sciences, and moreover in an age which has been characterized as having succumb to two cultures[11] in which a growing division and even alienation exists between the human and the physical sciences. In this context and in light of the programs of Pannenberg and Rahner, we would suggest that commitment to theology's universality and to the themes of universality arising from it is necessary to prevent theology becoming (or perhaps better, remaining) irrelevant to most modern persons. It is no longer possible, we would contend, to conceive of a fruitful apologetic in the modern world that does not begin with the assumption of the universal relevance of the Christian message and of the universal relevance of that discipline whose task it is to understand and to make understandable this message, namely theology.

The question, however, that inevitably must be asked, is how consistently Pannenberg and Rahner themselves have applied the motifs of universality, developed thoroughly in their theoretical treatments, in the actual context and praxis of apologetics. Universality, understood in the context of the thought of Pannenberg and Rahner, has a twofold emphasis or implication. In the first place, it means theological knowledge is relevant to all other areas of knowledge, that is to say, Christian theology has something concrete and specific to say to the other sciences and to the non-Christian religions. In this regard both Rahner and Pannenberg have exhibited a great deal more boldness in putting forth theology's claims to universal relevance than many of their theological colleagues.

The second implication of theological universality, however, is that theology must not only speak to all but must also *listen* to all. As Pannenberg and Rahner

---
[11] So the analysis of C. P. Snow, *The Two Cultures*, 2ff.

have both made clear, the very concept of universality implies that even the non-Christian religions and the natural sciences have something to say to theology and that it is part of theology's task to listen - and that with just as much earnestness and conviction as with which it speaks.[12] Here, however, both have encountered criticism. Even Pannenberg, who seeks to build his theology of religions upon an *a posteriori* examination of the phenomena of religions, finds himself accused of reaching precisely the conclusion one would expect of one committed to the Christian tradition. And Rahner, with his theory of anonymous Christianity, has frequently been accused of making non-Christians into implicit or anonymous Christians, regardless of how explicitly and *un*anonymously they may wish not to be Christians. In the area of the dialogue with the natural sciences the same problem is encountered. Rahner, by "assuming" the theories of modern science (e.g., the theory of evolution) never really engages natural science as such but seeks conceptual models from the sciences that he applies to traditional Christian themes - an approach which of itself is not problematic so long as it does not become a substitute for actually listening to what the other has to say.

Pannenberg, who has given much more attention to engaging the natural sciences as such, especially modern physics, has similarly encountered difficulties. By giving his own theological meaning to such concepts as 'field' and 'contingency' he has been accused of not listening to the words as natural scientists themselves apply them, hearing instead only that which fits his own program.[13] Of course, Pannenberg's dialogue with the natural sciences is still in process and a definitive judgment on it is not yet possible. Nevertheless, one has to ask in the case of both Rahner and Pannenberg whether, in the praxis of dialogue, they have taking the implications of their own programs with the radical seriousness that these demand. This question, still being asked by those too few theologians and even fewer natural scientists (to remain with the example of the science/theology relationship) who are seriously engaged in the dialogue between theology and the natural sciences, requires further treatment.

Even, however, if the actual apologetic praxis of Rahner and Pannenberg is not pursued by Christian apologists this does not necessarily imply that the foundation they have laid is false. Our study has shown that the programs of universal theology, especially the foundations of this theology as developed by Pannenberg and Rahner, have much to commend themselves to all those committed to a reasoned and *reason*able defence of the Christian faith, indeed, to all those committed to dialogue. These foundations, we would suggest, have a validity independent of the actual praxis of theological universality found in Pannenberg and Rahner themselves, and merit more careful examination.

---

[12] Hence Rahner, "Theology as Engaged in an Interdisciplinary Dialogue with the Sciences," 92. [*Schriften* 10:101.], holds it a vital part of theology's task to "be instructed by ... [natural science] on its own terms" and not simply to be content with a cordial relationship with the sciences.

[13] Cf. especially 6.2.2.2 and 6.2.2.3 for an analysis of these criticisms.

# BIBLIOGRAPHY

## A. Works by Wolfhart Pannenberg

Pannenberg, Wolfhart. "Analogy and Doxology," in: *Basic Questions* 1.

_____. *Anthropology in Theological Perspective*, trans. Matthew J. O'Connell. Philadelphia: Westminster Press, 1985.

_____. "Anthropologie in theologischer Perspektive: Philosophisch-theologische Grundlinien," in: *Sind wir von Natur aus religiös?*, ed. W. Pannenberg. Düsseldorf: Patmos, 1986.

_____. "Antwort auf G. Sauters Überlegungen," in: *Evangelische Theologie* 40 (March/April, 1980): 168-181.

_____. *The Apostles' Creed in the Light of Today's Questions*, trans. Margaret Kohl. London: SCM Press, 1972.

_____. "The Appropriation of the Philosophical Concept of God as a Dogmatic Problem of Early Christian Theology", in: *Basic Questions* 2.

_____. "Atomism, Duration, Form: Difficulties with Process Philosophy," in: *Metaphysics and the Idea of God*.

_____. *Die Auferstehung Jesu und die Zukunft des Menschen*, Eichstätter Hochschulreden, vol. 10. Munich: Minerva Publikation, 1978.

_____. "An Autobiographical Sketch," in: *The Theology of Wolfhart Pannenberg*, ed. C. Braaten and P. Clayton, 1988.

_____. *Basic Questions in Theology*, 2 vols., trans. George Kehm. Philadelphia: Fortress Press, 1970/1971.

_____. "Das Besondere des Christentums: Gegenwart und Zukunft der Versöhnung," in: Pinchas Lapide and Wolfhart Pannenberg, *Judentum und Christentum, Einheit und Unterschied: Eine Gespräch*. Munich: Chr. Kaiser, 1981.

_____. *Christentum und Mythos: Späthorizonte des Mythos in biblischer und christlicher Überlieferung*. Gütersloh: Gerd Mohn, 1972.

_____. "Das christliche Gottesverständnis im Spannungsfeld seiner jüdischen und griechischen Wurzeln," in: H.Friedlander and W. Pannenberg, *Der christliche Glaube und seine jüdisch-griechische Herkunft, EKD Texte* 15. Hannover: Kirchenamt der EKD, 1986.

_____. "Christlicher Glaube und menschliche Freiheit," in: *Kerygma und Dogma* 4 (1958): 251-80.

_____. "Constructive and Critical Functions of Christian Eschatology," (Ingersoll Lecture) *Harvard Theological Review* 77:2 (1984): 119-139.

_____. "Contingency and Natural Law," in: Pannenberg, *Toward a Theology of Nature*.

_____. "The Crisis of the Scripture Principle," in: *Basic Questions* 1.

_____. "The Doctrine of Creation and Natural Science," in: *Toward a Theology of Nature*.

_____. "The Doctrine of the Spirit and the Task of a Theology of Nature," in: *Toward a Theology of Nature*.

_____. "Dogmatic Theses on the Doctrine of Revelation," in: *Revelation as History*, ed. W. Pannenberg, trans. David Granskou.

_____. "Der Einfluß der Anfechtungserfahrung auf den Prädestinationsbegriff Luthers," in: *Kerygma und Dogma* 3 (1957): 109-139.

_____. "Einsicht und Glaube: Antwort an Paul Althaus," in: *Theologische Literaturzeitung* 88:2 (February 1963): 81-92.

_____. "Election and History," in: *Human Nature, Election, and History*.

_____. "Election and the People of God," in: *Human Nature, Election, and History*.

_____. "Erwählung III. Dogmatisch," in: *Die Religion in Geschichte und Gegenwart: Handwörterbuch für Theologie und Religionswissenschaft*, 3rd. ed. Tübingen: J.C.B. Mohr, 1958, vol. 2:614-621.

_____. *Faith and Reality*, trans. John Maxwell. Philadelphia: Westminster Press, 1977.

_____. "Father, Son, Spirit: Problems of a Trinitarian Doctrine of God," trans. Philip Clayton, in: *Dialog* 26:4 (fall 1987): 250-257.

_____. "The Future and the Unity of Mankind," in: *Ethics*, trans. Keith Crim. Philadelphia: Westminster Press, 1981.

_____. "God and Nature: On the History of the Debates Between Theology and Natural Science," in: Pannenberg, *Toward a Theology of Nature*.

_____. "The God of History," in: *Cumberland Seminarian* 19 (winter/spring 1981): 34ff.

_____. "The God of Hope," in: *Basic Questions* 2.

_____. *Gottesgedanke und menschliche Freiheit*. Göttingen:Vandenhoeck & Ruprecht, 1972.

_____. *Grundfragen systematischer Theologie: Gesammelte Aufsätze*, vol. 2. Göttingen: Vandenhoeck & Ruprecht, 1980.

_____. "Hermeneutic and Universal History," in: *Basic Questions* 1.

_____. *Human Nature, Election, and History*. Philadelphia: The Westminster Press, 1977.

_____. *Jesus - God and Man*. trans. Lewis Wilkens and Duane Priebe. London: SCM,1968.

_____. "Macht der Mensch die Religion oder macht die Religion den Menschen? Ein Rückblick auf die Diskussionen des religionstheoretischen Arbeitskreises," in: *Religion als Problem der Aufklärung*, ed. Trutz Rendtorff.

_____. *Metaphysics and the Idea of God*, trans. P.Clayton. Grand Rapids: Eerdmans, 1990.

_____. "Der Mensch - Ebenbild Gottes?" in: *Glaube und Wirklichkeit: Kleine Beiträge zum christlichen Denken*. Munich: Christian Kaiser, 1975.

_____. "Nachwort von Wolfhart Pannenberg," in: Ignace Berten, *Geschichte, Offenbarung, Glaube*. Munich: Claudius Verlag, 1970.

_____. "Der neue Mensch," Sermon from Easter Sunday, 1970, in: *Gegenwart Gottes: Predigten*. Munich: Claudius Verlag, 1973.

_____. "Eine philosophisch-historische Hermeneutik des Christentums," in: *Theologie und Philosophie* 66:4 (1991): 481-492.

_____. "Prädestination IV. Dogmatisch," in: *Die Religion in Geschichte und Gegenwart: Handwörterbuch für Theologie und Religionswissenschaft*, 3rd. ed. Tübingen: J.C.B. Mohr, 1961, vol. 5:487-489.

_____. *Die Prädestinationslehre des Duns Skotus im Zusammenhang der scholastischen Lehrentwicklung*. Göttingen: Vandenhoeck & Ruprecht, 1954.

_____. "Problems of a Christian Doctrine of God," in: Pannenberg, *An Introduction to Systematic Theology*. Grand Rapids: Eerdmans, 1991.

_____. "Redemptive Event and History," in: *Basic Questions* 1.

_____. "Reden von Gott angesichts atheistischer Kritik," in: *Gottesgedanke und menschliche Freiheit*.

_____. "Religion und menschliche Natur," in: *Sind wir von Natur aus religiös?*, ed. W. Pannenberg. Düsseldorf: Patmos, 1986.

_____. "A Response to My American Friends," in: *The Theology of Wolfhart Pannenberg*, ed. C. Braaten and P. Clayton.

_____. "Response to the Discussion," in: *Theology as History*, ed. James M. Robinson and John B. Cobb Jr. New York: Harper & Row, 1967

_____, ed. *Revelation as History*, (including an introductory essay by Pannenberg) trans. David Granskou. New York: Macmillan, 1968.

_____. "The Social Predicament and Human Responsibility," in: *Human Nature, Election, and History*.

_____. "Die Subjektivität Gottes und die Trinitätslehre," in: *Kerygma und Dogma* 23 (1977): 25-40.

_____. *Systematic Theology*, vols. 1 and 2., trans. Geoffrey Bromiley. Grand Rapids: Eerdmans, 1991, 1994.

_____. *Systematische Theologie*, vol 3. Göttingen: Vandenhoeck & Ruprecht, 1993.

_____. "Theological Appropriation of Scientific Understandings: Response to Hefner, Wicken, Eaves, and Tipler," in: *Zygon* 24:2 (June 1989): 255-271.

_____. "A Theological Conversation with Wolfhart Pannenberg," *Dialog* 11 (1972): 286ff.

_____. "Theological Questions to Scientists," in: *Toward a Theology of Nature*.

_____. *Theology and the Kingdom of God*. Philadelphia: Westminster Press, 1969.

_____. *Theology and the Philosophy of Science*, trans. Francis McDonagh. Philadelphia: Westminster Press, 1976.

_____. "Theta Phi Discussion with Wolfhart Pannenberg," in: *The Asbury Theological Journal*, 46:2 (Fall 1991): 17-25.

_____. "Theta Phi Talkback Session with W. Pannenberg," in: *The Asbury Theological Journal* 46:2 (fall 1991): 37-41.

_____. *Toward a Theology of Nature: Essays on Science and Faith*, ed. Ted Peters. Louisville: Westminster/John Knox Press, 1993.

_____. "Toward a Theology of the History of Religions," in: *Basic Questions* 2.

_____. "Types of Atheism and their Theological Significance," in: *Basic Questions* 2.

_____. "Weltgeschichte und Heilsgeschichte," in: *Probleme biblischer Theologie: Gerhard von Rad zum 70. Geburtstag*, ed. Hans Walter Wolff. Munich: Chr. Kaiser, 1971.

_____. *What is Man?*, trans. Duane Priebe. Philadelphi: Fortress Press, 1970.

_____. "What is a Dogmatic Statement?," in: *Basic Questions* 1.

_____. "Wie wahr ist das Reden von Gott? Die wissenschaftstheoretische Problematik theologischer Aussagen," in: *Grundlagen der Theologie - Ein Diskurs*, W. Pannenberg, G. Sauter et al. Stuttgart: Kohlhammer, 1974.

_____. "Wie wird Gott uns offenbar?" in: *Glaube und Wirklichkeit: Kleine Beiträge zum christlichen Denken*. Munich: Chr. Kaiser, 1975.

_____ and Lewis Ford. "A Dialog about Process Philosophy," in: *Encounter* 38 (1977).

_____ and Pinchas Lapide. *Judentum und Christentum, Einheit und Unterschied: Eine Gespräch*. Munich: Chr. Kaiser, 1981.

_____ and Rodulf Schnackenburg. *Ostern und der neue Mensch*. Freiburg: Herder, 1981.

_____,G.Sauter, et al.*Grundlagen der Theologie-Ein Diskurs*. Stuttgart:Kohlhammer,1974.

## B. Works by Karl Rahner

Rahner, Karl. "The Abiding Significance of the Second Vatican Council," in: *TI* 20.

_____. "Anonymous Christianity and the Missionary Task of the Church," in: *TI* 12.

_____. "Anonymous Christians," in: *TI* 6.

_____. "Anonymous and Explicit Faith," in: *TI* 16.

_____. "Atheism and Implicit Christianity," in: *TI* 9.

_____. "Atheismus," in: *Herders theologisches Taschenlexikon*, 1:210-218.

_____. "Die Atheisten und die Religion," in: Karl Rahner, *Kritisches Wort: Aktuelle Probleme in Kirche und Welt*. Freiburg: Herder, 1970.

_____. "Christianity and the Non-Christian Religions," in: *TI* 5.

_____. "Christology within an Evolutionary View of the World," in: *TI* 5.

_____. *The Church and the Sacraments*. New York: Herder and Herder, 1963.

_____. "Church, Churches and Religions," in: *TI* 10.

_____. "The Concept of Mystery in Catholic Theology," in: *TI* 4.

_____. "Current Problems in Christology," in: *TI* 1.

_____. "Death as Fulfillment," in: *Karl Rahner in Dialogue*," ed. P.Imhof and H.Biallowons.

_____. "The Dignity and Freedom of Man," in: *TI* 2.

_____. "Eternity from Time," *TI* 19.

_____. "Evolution II. Theological," in: *Sacramentum Mundi* 2:289-294.

_____. "Exkurs: Erbsünde und Monogenismus," in: Karl-Heinz Weger, *Theologie der Erbsünde*, Quaestiones disputatae 44. Freiburg: Herder, 1969.

_____. "Experience of Transcendence from the Standpoint of Christian Dogmatics," *TI* 18.

_____. "The Foundation of Belief Today," in: *TI* 16.

_____. *Foundations of Christian Faith: An Introduction to the Idea of Christianity*, trans. William Dych. New York: Seabury Press, 1978

_____. "Die Frage nach dem Erscheinungsbild des Menschen als Quaestio disputata der Theologie," Introduction to Paul Overhage, *Um das Erscheinungsbild der ersten Menschen*, Quaestiones disputatae 7. Freiburg: Herder, 1959.

_____. *Gnade als Mitte menschlicher Existenz: Ein Gespräch mit und über Karl Rahner aus Anlaß seines 70. Geburtstages*. Freiburg: Herder, 1974.

_____. "Grundsätzliche Überlegungen zur Anthropologie und Protologie im Rahmen der Theologie," in: *Mysterium Salutis: Grundriss Heilsgeschichtlicher Dogmatik*, vol. II, ed. Johannes Feiner and Magnus Löhrer. Zürich: Benziger, 1967, 406-420.

_____. "Grundzüge einer katholisch-dogmatischen Interpretation der nichtchristlichen Religionen," in: *Pluralismus, Toleranz und Christenheit*. Nuremburg, 1961.

_____. *Hearers of the Word*, trans. Michael Richards. New York: Herder and Herder, 1968.

_____. ed. *Herders theologisches Taschenlexikon*, 8 vols. Freiburg: Herder, 1972/1973.

_____. "The Hermeneutics of Eschatological Assertions," in: *TI* 4.

_____. *Hominisation: The Evolutionary Origin of Man as a Theological Problem*, trans. W. O'Hara. New York: Herder and Herder, 1965.

_____. "Hominisation (Evolution B)," in: *Sacramentum Mundi* 2:294-297.

_____. "Immanent and Transcendent Consummation of the World," in: *TI* 10.

_____. "Intellectual Honesty and Christian Faith," in: *TI* 7:63.

_____. "Jesus Christ in the Non-Christian Religions," in: *TI* 17.

_____. "Karl Rahner antwortet Eberhard Simons. Zur Lage der Theologie: Probleme nach dem Konzil," Das theologische Interview 1. Düsseldorf, 1969.

_____. *Karl Rahner: Erinnerungen im Gespräch mit Meinhold Krauss*, ed. Meinhold Krauss. Freiburg: Herder, 1984.

_____. *Karl Rahner in Dialogue: Conversations and Interviews, 1965 - 1982*, ed. Paul Imhof and Hubert Biallowons, trans. Harvey Egan (New York: Crossroad, 1986).

_____. *Kritisches Wort: Aktuelle Probleme in Kirche und Welt*. Freiburg: Herder, 1970.

_____. "On the Relationship between Theology and the Contemporary Sciences," in: *TI* 13.

_____. "The Language of Science and the Language of Theology," in: *Karl Rahner in Dialogue*, ed. P. Imhof and H. Biallowons.

_____. "Die Logik der existentiellen Erkenntnis bei Ignatius v. Loyola," in: Rahner, *Das Dynamische in der Kirche, Quaestiones disputatae* 5: 74-148. Freiburg: Herder, 1959.

_____. "Membership of the Church According to the Teaching of Pius XII's Encyclical '*Mystici corporis Christi*,'" in: *TI* 2.

_____. "Mensch III. Zum theologischen Begriff des Menschen," in: *Herders theologisches Taschenlexikon*, 5:29-37.

_____. "Monogenism," in: *Sacramentum Mundi* 4:105-107.

_____. "Natural Science and Reasonable Faith," in: *TI* 21.

_____. "Observations on the Concept of Revelation," in: Rahner and J. Ratzinger, *Revelation and Tradition, Quaestiones disputatae* 17.

_____. "On the Current Relationship between Philosophy and Theology," in: *TI* 13.

_____. "On the Relationship between Natural Science and Theology," in: *TI* 19.

_____. *On the Theology of Death, Quaestiones disputatae* 2. New York: Herder and Herder, 1965.

_____. "On the Theology of the Incarnation," *TI* 4.

_____. "The One Christ and the Universality of Salvation," in: *TI* 16.

_____. "Original Sin," in: *Sacramentum Mundi* 4:328-334.

_____. "'Paul VII. an Peppino' - Ein Papstbrief aus dem 21. Jahrhundert," in: *Das Papsttum: Epochen und Gestalten*, ed. Bruno Moser. Munich: Südwest Verlag, 1983.

_____. "Philosophy and Philosophizing in Theology," in: *TI* 9.

_____. "Philosophy and Theology," in: *TI* 6.

_____. "Potentia oboedientialis," in: *Sacramentum Mundi* 5:65-67.

_____. "Reflections on the Contemporary Intellectual Formation of Future Priests," in: *TI* 6.

_____. "Reflections on Methodology in Theology," in: *TI* 11.

_____. "Reflections on the Unity of the Love of Neighbor and the Love of God," in: *TI* 6.

_____. "Religion III. Der theologische (-normative) Begriff der Religion," in: *Herders theologisches Taschenlexikon* 6:212-213.

_____. "Religious Feeling Inside and Outside the Church," in: *TI* 17.

_____. "Revelation II. God's Self-Communication," in: *Sacramentum Mundi* 5:353-355.

_____. et al., eds. *Sacramentum Mundi*, 6 volumes. New York: Herder and Herder, 1968.

_____. "A Scheme for a Treatise of Dogmatic Theology," in: *TI* 1.

_____. "The Sin of Adam," in: *TI* 11.

_____. "Some Clarifying Remarks about My Own Work," in: *TI* 17.

_____. "The Specific Character of the Christian Concept of God," in: *TI* 21.

_____. *Spirit in the World*. London: Sheed and Ward, 1968.

_____. "Sündenlehre," in: *Herders theologisches Taschenlexikon*, 7:168-170.

_____. "Theological Considerations on the Moment of Death," in: *TI* 11.

_____. "The Theological Dimension of the Question about Man," in: *TI* 17.

_____. *Theological Investigations*, 23 vols. New York: Crossroad, 1961-1992.

_____. "The Theological Problems Entailed in the Idea of the 'New Earth,'" in: *TI* 10.

_____. "Theological Reflections on Monogenism," in: *TI* 1. [English translation of "Theologisches zum Monogenismus," in: *Schriften*, 1.]

_____. "Theologische Anthropologie," in: *Lexikon für Theologie und Kirche*, ed. Josef Höfer and Karl Rahner. Freiburg: Herder, 1957.

_____. "Theologische Erkenntnis- und Methodenlehre," in: *Herders theologisches Taschenlexikon* 7:256-262.

_____. "Theology and Anthropology," in: T. Patrick Burke, ed., *The Word in History: The St. Xavier Symposium*. New York: Sheed and Ward, 1966.

_____. "Theology as Engaged in an Interdisciplinary Dialogue with the Sciences," in: *TI* 13.

_____. "The Theology of the Symbol." in: *TI* 4.

_____. "Theology Today," in: *TI* 21.

_____. "Transcendental Theology," in: *Sacramentum Mundi* 6:287-289.

_____. *The Trinity*, trans. J. Donceel. New York: Herder and Herder, 1970.

_____. "The Unity of Spirit and Matter in the Christian Understanding of Faith," in: *TI* 6.

_____. "What is a Dogmatic Statement," in: *TI* 5.

_____. "Ideas for a Theology of Death," in: *TI* 13.

_____. *Zur Reform des Theologiestudiums*, Quaestiones disputatae 41. Freiburg: Herder,1969.

_____. *Zur Theologie der Zukunft*. Zürich: Benziger, 1971.

_____ and Pinchas Lapide. *Encountering Jesus - Encountering Judaism: A Dialogue*, trans. Davis Perkins. New York: Crossroads, 1987.

_____ and Wilhelm Dantine. *Intellektuelle Redlichkeit und Christlicher Glaube, Glaube und Wissenschaft: Ihre Kritische Funktion*. Freiburg: Herder, 1966.

_____ and Josef Höfer, eds. *Lexikon für Theologie und Kirche*. Freiburg: Herder, 1957.

_____ and Joseph Ratzinger. *Revelation and Tradition*, trans. W.J. O'Hara. Quaestiones disputatae 17. London: Burns & Oates, 1966. [English translation of *Offenbarung und Überlieferung*, QD 25. Freiburg: Herder, 1965.]

_____ and Karl-Heinz Weger. *Was sollen wir noch glauben? Theologen stellen sich den Glaubensfragen einer neuen Generation*. Freiburg: Herder, 1979.

## C. Secondary Sources

Albert, Hans.. *Traktat über kritische Vernunft*. Tübingen: J.C.B Mohr, 1968.

Alcalá, Manuel. "Das Spannungsverhältnis von Theologie und kirchlichem Lehramt im Leben und im Werk Karl Rahners," in: *Wagnis Theologie*, ed. Herbert Vorgrimler.

Althaus, Paul. "Mission und Religionsgeschichte," in: *Zeitschrift für systematische Theologie* 5 (1928): 550-590.

_____. "Offenbarung als Geschichte und Glaube: Bemerkungen zu Wolfhart Pannenbergs Begriff der Offenbarung," in: *Theologische Literaturzeitung* 87:5 (May 1962): 321-330.

Altmann, Walter. *Der Begriff der Tradition bei Karl Rahner*. Frankfurt/M: Peter Lang, 1974.

Andresen, Carl, ed. *Handbuch der Dogmen- und Theologiegeschichte*, 3 vols. Göttingen: Vandenhoeck & Ruprecht, 1980-1984.

Aquinas, Thomas. *Summa Theologica*, in: *Basic Writings of Thomas Aquinas*, 2 vols., ed. Anton C. Pegis. New York: Random House, 1945.

Augustin, George. *Gott eint - trennt Christus? Die Einmaligkeit und Universalität Jesus Christi als Grundlage einer christlichen Theologie der Religionen ausgehend vom Ansatz Wolfhart Pannenbergs*. Paderborn: Bonifatius, 1993.

Augustinus, Aurelius. *The City of God*, trans. Marcus Dods. New York: Random House, 1950.

_____. *De catechizandis rudibus*, ed. Gustav Krüger. Tübingen: J.C.B. Mohr, 1968.

Bacik, James J. *Apologetics and the Eclipse of Mystery. Mystagogy according to Karl Rahner*. Notre Dame, London: University of Notre Dame Press, 1980.

Balthasar, Hans Urs von. *Cordula oder der Ernstfall*. Einsiedeln: Johannes Verlag, 1967.

_____. *Rechenschaft 1965*. Einsiedeln: Johannes Verlag, 1965.

Bantle, F. "Person und Personbegriff in der Trinitätslehre Karl Rahners," in: *Münchner Theologische Zeitschrift* 30 (1979):11-24.

Barth, Karl. *Church Dogmatics*, 4 vols., trans. and ed. Geoffrey Bromiley and T. F. Torrance. Edinburgh: T. & T. Clark, 1936-1969.

_____. *Dogmatics in Outline*. New York: Harper & Row, 1959.

_____. "Fünfzehn Antworten an Herrn Professor von Harnack," in: *Anfänge der dialektischen Theologie*, ed. J. Moltmann.

_____. "Theology," in: Karl Barth, *God in Action*, trans. E. Homrighausen and K. Ernst. New York: Round Table Press, 1936.

_____. *The Theology of Schleiermacher: Lectures at Göttingen, Winter Semester of 1923/34*, ed. Dietrich Ritschl, trans. Geoffrey Bromily. Grand Rapids: Eerdmans, 1982.

Bartley, William. *Flucht ins Engagement*. Tübingen: J.C.B. Mohr, 1987.

Beinert, Wolfhart. "Universitätstheologie und Kirche," in: *Stimmen der Zeit* 211:11 (November 1993): 723-740.

Berten, Ignace. *Geschichte, Offenbarung, Glaube: Eine Einleitung in die Theologie Wolfhart Pannenbergs*, trans. Sigrid Martin. Munich: Claudius, 1970.

Beth, Karl. *Die Moderne und die Prinzipien der Theologie*. Berlin: Trowitzsch & Sohn, 1907.

Beyerhaus, Peter. "Zur Theologie der Religionen im Protestantismus," in: *Kerygma und Dogma* 15 (1969): 87-104.

Bloch, Ernst. *Das Prinzip Hoffnung*, vol. 2. Frankfurt/M: Suhrkamp, 1959.

Bloesch, Donald G. *Essentials of Evangelical Theology*, v.1. New York: Harper & Row, 1978.

Bokwa, Ignacy. *Christologie als Anfang und Ende der Anthropologie: Über das gegenseitige Verhältnis zwischen Christologie und Anthropologie bei Karl Rahner*. Frankfurt/M: Peter Lang, 1990.

Braaten, Carl. "The Current Controversy on Revelation: Pannenberg and his Critics," in: *Journal of Religion* 45 (1965): 225-237.

_____. "The Place of Christianity among the World Religions: Wolfhart Pannenberg's Theology of Religion and the History of Religions," in: *The Theology of Wolfhart Pannenberg*, ed. C. Braaten and P. Clayton.

_____. "Toward a Theology of Hope," *Theology Today* 24 (July 1967): 208-226.

_____ and Philip Clayton, eds. *The Theology of Wolfhart Pannenberg: Twelve American Critiques, with an Autobiographical Essay and Response*. Minneapolis: Augsburg, 1988.

Bridges, James. *Human Destiny and Resurrection in Pannenberg and Rahner*. Rice University Dissertation, 1986.

Brück, Michael von. *Möglichkeiten und Grenzen einer Theologie der Religionen*. Berlin: Evangelische Verlagsanstalt, 1979.

Buckley, Michael. "Within the Holy Mystery," in: *A World of Grace*, ed. L. O'Donovan.

Bultmann, Rudolf. *History and Eschatology*. Edinburgh: The University Press, 1957.

_____. "New Testament and Mythology," in: *Kerygma and Myth*, trans. Reginald Fuller. London: SPCK, 1953.

_____. "Zum Problem der Entmythologisierung," in: *Glauben und Verstehen*, vol. 4. Tübingen: J.C.B. Mohr, 1993.

_____. "Theologie als Wissenschaft," [1947], in: *Zeitschrift für Theologie und Kirche* 81 (1984): 447-469.

_____. *Theologische Enzyklopädie*, ed. E. Jüngel and K. Müller. Tübingen:J.C.B.Mohr, 1984.

Cabada-Castro, Manuel. "Ort und Bedeutung des philosophischen Gottesbegriffs in Denken Karl Rahners," trans. Evelin Höhne, in: *Wagnis Theologie*, ed. Herbert Vorgrimler.

Calvin, John. *Commentaries on the First Book of Moses*, vol. 1, trans. J. King. Edinburgh: Calvin Translation Society, 1847.

_____. *Institutes of the Christian Religion*, 2 vols., trans. Ford Lewis Battles. Philadelphia: Westminster Press, 1960.

Campenhausen, Hans von. *Der Ablauf der Osterereignisse und das leere Grab* [1952]. Heidelberg: Carl Winter, 1966.

Camps, Arnulf. "Die heutige Stellung der Römisch-Katholischen Kirche zu den nichtchristlichen Religionen," *Jesus Christus und die Religionen*, ed. A. Paus. Vienna:Verlag Styria,1980.

Carr, Anne. "Starting with the Human," in: *A World of Grace*, ed. Leo O'Donovan.

_____. *The Theological Method of Karl Rahner*. Missoula, Montana: Scholars Press, 1977.

Clayton, Philip. "Anticipation and Theological Method," in: *The Theology of Wolfhart Pannenberg*, ed. C. Braaten and P. Clayton, 1988.

_____. "The God of History and the Presence of the Future," in: *Journal of Religion* 65 (January 1985): 98-108.

Cobb, John Jr. "Pannenberg and Process Theology," in: *The Theology of Wolfhart Pannenberg*, ed. C. Braaten and P. Clayton.

_____. "Wolfhart Pannenberg's 'Jesus: God and Man,'" in: *Journal of Religion* 49 (1969): 192-201.

_____ and David Griffin. *Process Theology: An Introductory Exposition*. Philadelphia: Westminster Press, 1976.

Colpe, Carsten. "Bemerkungen zu Adolf von Harnacks Einschätzung der Disziplin 'Allgemeine Religionsgeschichte,'" in: *Neue Zeitschrift für systematische Theologie und Religionsphilosophie* 6 (1964): 51-69.

Conway, Eamonn. *The Anonymous Christian - A Realitivised Christianity? An Evaluation of Hans Urs von Balthasar's Criticisms of Karl Rahner's Theory of the Anonymous Christian*. Frankfurt/M: Peter Lang, 1993.

Cullmann, Oscar. *Salvation in History*, trans. S. G. Sowers. London: SCM, 1967.

Daecke, Sigurd Martin. "Soll die Theologie an der Universität bleiben? Zur Auseinandersetzung um eine Begründung der Theologie als Wissenschaft," in: W. Pannenberg, G. Sauter, et al., *Grundlagen der Theologie - Ein Diskurs*. Stuttgart: Kohlhammer, 1974.

Denzinger, H. and A. Schönmetzer, *Enchiridion Symbolorum, Definitionum et Declarationum De Rebeus Fidei Et Morum*. Freiburg: Herder, 1976.

Devereux, Anne Rogers. *Der Vorgriff (The Pre-Apprehension of Being) and the Religious Act in Karl Rahner*. Ph.D. diss., Georgetown University, 1973.

Dilthey, Wilhelm. *Der Aufbau der geschichtlichen Welt in den Geisteswissenschaften*, in: *Gesammelte Schriften*, vol. 7. Göttingen: Vandenhoeck & Ruprecht, 1965.

DiNoia, J. A. "Karl Rahner," in: *The Modern Theologians*, vol. 1, ed. David Ford.

Drewermann, Eugen. *Glauben in Freiheit oder Tiefenpsychologie und Dogmatik: Dogma, Angst und Symbolismus*. Düsseldorf: Walter-Verlag, 1993.

Dulles, Avery. "Pannenberg on Revelation and Faith," in: *The Theology of Wolfhart Pannenberg*, ed. C. Braaten and P. Clayton, 1988.

_____. *Revelation Theology: A History*. New York: Herder and Herder, 1969.

Dych, William. "Method in Theology According to Karl Rahner," in: *Theology and Discovery*, ed. William Kelly.

———. "Theology in a New Key," in: *A World of Grace*, ed. Leo O'Donovan.

Eicher, Peter. *Die Anthropologische Wende: Karl Rahners philosophischer Weg vom Wesen des Menschen zur personalen Existenz*. Freiburg, Switzerland: Universitätsverlag Freiburg, 1970.

Evers, Georg. "Die 'anonymen Christen' und der Dialog mit den Juden," in: *Wagnis Theologie*, ed. Herbert Vorgrimler.

Fichte, Johann Gottlieb. *Grundlage der gesamten Wissenschaftslehre* [1794]. Hamburg: Felix Meiner, 1970.

———. "Über den Grund unsers Glaubens an eine göttliche Weltregierung," [1798] in: *Die Schriften zu J. G. Fichtes Atheismusstreit*, ed. Frank Böckelmann. Munich: Rogner & Bernhard, 1969.

Fiorenza, Francis "Karl Rahner and the Kantian Problematic," in: Rahner, *Spirit in the World*.

Fischer, Hermann. "Fundamentaltheologische Prolegomena zur theologischen Anthropologie: Anfragen an Pannenbergs Anthropologie," *Theologische Rundschau* 50:1 (1985): 41-61.

Fischer, Klaus. *Der Mensch als Geheimnis: Die Anthropologie Karl Rahners*. Freiburg: Herder, 1974.

Ford, Lewis. "An Alternative to *creatio ex nihilo*," *Religious Studies* 19 (1983): 205-213.

———. "The Nature of the Power of the Future," in: *The Theology of Wolfhart Pannenberg*, ed. C. Braaten and P. Clayton.

Fries, Heinrich. "Fides quaerens intellectum," in: *Vernunft des Glaubens*, ed. Jan Rohls and Gunther Wenz.

Füssel, Kuno. Der Wahrheitsanspruch dogmatischer Aussagen: Ein Beitrag Karl Rahners zur theologischen Wissenschaftstheorie," in: *Wagnis Theologie*, ed. Herbert Vorgrimler.

Gadamer, Hans-Georg. *Truth and Method*, trans. Wm. Glen-Doepel. London: Sheed and Ward, 1975.

———. "Die Universalität des hermeneutischen Problems," in: Gadamer, *Kleine Schriften*, vol. 1. Tübingen: J.C.B. Mohr, 1967.

Gelpi, Donald. *Life and Light: A Guide to the Theology of Karl Rahner*. New York: Sheed and Ward, 1966.

Gensichen, H. W. "Tendenzen der Religionswissenschaft," in: *Theologie als Wissenschaft in der Gesellschaft*, ed. H. Siemers and H. Reuter (1970).

Gilkey, Langdon. *Reaping the Whirlwind*. New York: Seabury, 1976.

———. *Religion and the Scientific Future*. London: SCM Press, 1970.

Gläßer, Alfred. *Verweigerte Partnerschaft? Anthropologische, konfessionelle und ökumenische Aspekte der Theologie Wolfhart Pannenbergs*. Regensburg: Friedrich Pustet, 1991.

Greiner, Friedemann. *Die Menschlichkeit der Offenbarung: Die transzendentale Grundlegung der Theologie bei Karl Rahner*. Munich: Chr. Kaiser, 1978.

Greiner, Sebastian. *Die Theologie Wolfhart Pannenbergs*. Würzburg: Echter Verlag, 1988.

Grenz, Stanley. "The Appraisal of Pannenberg: A Survey of the Literature," in: *The Theology of Wolfhart Pannenberg*, ed. C. Braaten and P. Clayton.

———. *Reason for Hope: The Systematic Theology of Wolfhart Pannenberg*. Oxford: Oxford University Press, 1990.

Habermas, Jürgen. *Zur Logik der Sozialwissenschaften*, 5th. ed. Frankfurt/M: Suhrkamp, 1982.

Hamilton, William. "The Character of Pannenberg's Theology," in: *New Frontiers in Theology: Discussions among Continental and American Theologians*, vol. 3, *Theology as History*, ed. James Robinson and John Cobb. New York: Harper & Row, 1967.

Harnack, Adolf von. *Die Aufgabe der theologischen Facultäten*. Giessen: J. Ricker'sche Verlagsbuchhandlung, 1901.

---. "Fünfzehn Fragen an die Verächter der wissenschaftlichen Theologie unter den Theologen," [1923] in: *Anfänge der dialektischen Theologie*, vol. 1, ed. J. Moltmann.

---. "Offener Brief an Herrn Professor K. Barth," and "Nachwort zu meinen offenen Brief an Herrn Professor Karl Barth," in: *Anfänge der dialektischen Theologie*, vol. 1.

Hefner, Philip. "The Concreteness of God's Kingdom: A Problem for Christian Life," in: *Journal of Religion* 51 (1971): 188-205.

---. "The Role of Science in Pannenberg's Theological Thinking," in: *The Theology of Wolfhart Pannenberg*, ed. Braaten and Clayton.

Hegel, Georg Wilhelm Friedrich. *Enzyklopädie der philosophischen Wissenschaften im Grundrisse* [1830], in: *Gesammelte Werke*, vol. 20. Hamburg: Felix Meiner Verlag, 1992.

---. *Lectures on the Philosophy of History*, vol. 3., trans. E. Haldane and F. Simson. London: Routledge and Kegan Paul, 1968.

---. *The Philosophy of History*, trans. J. Sibree. New York: Dover Publications, 1956.

Heidegger, Martin. *Sein und Zeit* [1926]. Tübingen: Max Niemeyer, 1967.

Heijden, Bert van der. *Karl Rahner: Darstellung und Kritik seiner Grundpositionen*. Einsiedeln: Johannes Verlag, 1973.

Heiler, Friedrich. *Erscheinungsformen und Wesen der Religion*, 2nd. ed. Stuttgart: Kohlhammer, 1979.

Heim, Karl. *Christian Faith and Natural Science: The Creative Encounter between 20$^{th}$ Century Physics and Christian Existentialism*. New York: Harper & Brothers, 1957.

Herder, Johann Gottfried. *Outlines of a Philosophy of the History of Man*, trans. T. Churchhill. New York, 1966.

Hick, John. *Faith and Knowledge*. Ithaca, NY: Cornell University Press, 1966.

Hill, William. *The Three-Personed God: The Trinity as a Mystery of Salvation*. Washington, D.C.: Catholic University of America Press, 1982.

Hodgson, Peter. "Pannenberg on Jesus," in: *Journal of the American Academy of Religion* 36 (1968): 373ff.

Holwerda, D. "Faith, Reason and the Resurrection in the Theology of Wolfhart Pannenberg," in: *Faith and Rationality: Reason and Belief in God*, ed. Alvin Plantinga and Nicholas Wolterstorff. Notre Dame, IN: Univerisity of Notre Dame Press, 1983.

Holz, Harald. *Transzendentalphilosophie und Metaphysik: Studie über Tendenzen in der heutigen philosophischen Grundlagenproblematik*. Mainz: Matthias-Grünewald-Verlag, 1966.

Huyssteen, Wentzel van. *Theology and the Justification of Faith: Constructing Theories in Systematic Theology*, trans. H. F. Snijders. Grand Rapids: Eerdmans, 1989.

Imhof, Paul and H.Biallowons, eds. *Karl Rahner: Bilder eines Lebens*. Zürich: Benziger, 1985.

Jammer, Max. *Concepts of Force: A Study in the Foundations of Dynamics*. Cambridge, MA: Harvard University Press, 1957.

---. "Feldtheorie," in: *Historisches Wörterbuch der Philosophie*. Darmstadt: Wissenschaftliche Buchgesellschaft, 1972.

Jaspers, Karl. *Der philosophische Glaube angesichts der Offenbarung*. Munich: Piper, 1962.

Jenson, Robert. *God after God: The God of the Past and the God of the Future, Seen in the Work of Karl Barth*. Indianapolis: Bobbs-Merrill, 1969.

---. "Jesus in the Trinity: Wolfhart Pannenberg's Christology and Doctrine of the Trinity," in: *The Theology of Wolfhart Pannenberg*, ed. C. Braaten and P. Clayton.

Joest, Wilfried. *Fundamentaltheologie: Theologische Grundlagen- und Mehodenprobleme*. Stuttgart: Kohlhammer, 1988.

Kant, Immanuel. *The Critique of Pure Reason*. Chicago: William Benton, 1952.

Kasper, Walter. "Christologie von unten? Kritik und Neuansatz gegenwärtiger Christologie," in: *Grundfragen der Christologie heute*, ed. Leo Scheffczyk. Freiburg: Herder, 1975.

_____. *Der Gott Jesu Christi*. Mainz: Matthias-Grünewald, 1982.

Kelly, William J., ed. *Theology and Discovery: Essays in honor of Karl Rahner, S.J.* Milwaukee: Marquette University Press, 1980.

Kern, Walter. "Erste philosophische Studien 1924-1927," in: *Karl Rahner: Bilder eines Lebens*, ed. P. Imhof and H. Biallowons.

Kim, Yung-Han. "Die universal-heilsgeschichtliche These der Rahnerschule und Pannenbergs universal-geschichtliche Konzeption," in: *Glaube und Geschichte: Heilsgeschichte als Thema der Theologie*, ed. Helge Stadelmann. Wuppertal: Brockhaus, 1986.

Knitter, Paul. "What is German Protestant Theology Saying About the Non-Christian Religions?" in: *Neue Zeitschrift für systematische Theologie und Religionsphilosophie* 15 (1973): 38-64.

Koch, Kurt. *Der Gott der Geschichte: Theologie der Geschichte bei Wolfhart Pannenberg als Paradigma einer Philosophischen Theologie in ökumenischer Perspektive*. Mainz: Mattias-Grünewald-Verlag, 1988.

_____. "Gottes Handeln in der Geschichte und die Bestimmung des Menschen: Zur geschichtstheologischen Neuinterpretation des christlichen Erwählungsglaubens bei Wolfhart Pannenberg," in: *Catholica* 33 (1979): 220-239.

Kolden, Marc. *Pannenberg's Attempt to Base Theology on History*. Ph.D. dissertation, University of Chicago, 1976.

Kraemer, Hendrick. *The Christian Message in a Non-Christian World*. London: Edinburgh House Press, 1947.

Kuhn, Thomas S. *The Structure of Scientific Revolutions*. Chicago: University of Chicago Press, 1970.

Küng, Hans. "Anonyme Christen - wozu?" in: *Orientierung* 39 (1975): 214-216.

_____. *Does God Exist?* New York: Doubleday, 1980.

_____. *On Being a Christian*, trans. Edward Quinn. New York: Doubleday, 1984.

Lang, Albert. *Die theologische Prinzipienlehre der mittelalterlichen Scholastik*. Freiburg: Herder, 1964.

Lehmen, Karl, ed. *Vor dem Geheimnis Gottes den Menschen verstehen: Karl Rahner zum 80. Geburtstag*. Freiburg: Katholische Akadamie, 1984.

Lindbeck, George. "The Thought of Karl Rahner, S.J.," in: *Christianity and Crisis* 25 (18 October 1965): 211-215.

Lonergan, Bernard. *Method in Theology*. London: Darton, Longman & Todd, 1972.

_____. "Response to Fr. Dych," in: *Theology and Discovery*, ed. Wm. Kelly.

Losinger, Anton. *Der anthropologische Ansatz in der Theologie Karl Rahners*. Ottilien: Erzabtei St. Ottilien, 1991.

Luther, Martin. "The Gospel for the Festival of the Epiphany," in: *Luther's Works*, vol. 52, ed. Helmut Lehman. Philadelphia: Fortress Press, 1974.

_____. "Lectures on Romans," in: *LW*, vol. 25, ed. H. Oswald. St. Louis: Concordia, 1972.

_____. "The Marburg Colloquy" [1529], in: *LW*, vol. 38, ed. Martin Lehmann. Philadelphia: Fortress Press, 1971.

_____. *Table Talk*, in: *LW*, vol. 54, trans. and ed. Th. Tappert. Philadelphia: Fortress, 1967.

Macquarrie, John. "Theologians of our Time V. Karl Rahner, S.J.," in: *The Expository Times* 74 (April 1963): 194-197.

_____. "What Is a Human Being?" A review of W. Pannenberg's *Anthropology in Theological Perspective*, in: *The Expository Times*, vol. 97 (April 1986): 202-203.

Maréchal, Joseph. *Le point de départ de la métaphysique, Leçons sur le développement historique et théorique du problème de la connaissance*, vols. 1-5. Louvain, 1922-26.

Mayr, Franz. "Vermutungen zu Karl Rahners Sprachstil," *Wagnis Theologie*, ed. H.Vorgrimler.

McCool, Gerald A., "Introduction: Rahner's Philosophical Theology" in: *A Rahner Reader*, ed. G. McCool. New York: Seabury, 1975.

_____. "Karl Rahner and the Christian Philosophy of Saint Thomas Aquinas," in: *Theology and Discovery*, ed. Wm. Kelly.

McCoy Jr., John. *Soteriology and the Doctrine of God: A Historical Typology and an Analysis of the Theologies of Karl Rahner and Wolfhart Pannenberg*. Ph.D. dissertation, Princeton Seminary, 1979.

McDermott, Brian. "The Bonds of Freedom," in: *A World of Grace*, ed. Leo O'Donovan.

McKenzie, David. *Wolfhart Pannenberg's Religious Philosophy*. Washington: University of America Press, 1980.

Metz, Johann Baptist. *Faith in History and Society: Toward a Pactical Fundamental Theology*, trans. David Smith. London: Burns & Oates, 1980.

_____. "An Identity Crisis in Christianity? Transcendental and Political Responses," in: *Theology and Discovery*, ed. Wm. Kelly.

Möhler, Johann Adam. *Symbolism or Exposition of the Doctrinal Differences between Catholics and Protestants as Evidenced by their Symbolical Writings*, trans. James Robertson. London: Gibbings & Company, 1894.

Molnar, Paul. "Can We Know God Directly? Rahner's Solution from Experience," in: *Theological Studies* 46 (1985): 228-261.

Moltmann, Jürgen, ed., *Anfänge der dialektischen Theologie*, v. 1. Munich: Chr. Kaiser, 1966.

_____. "Der 'eschatologische Augenblick': Gedanken zu Zeit und Ewigkeit in eschatologischer Hinsicht," in: *Vernunft des Glaubens*, ed. J. Rohls and G. Wenz.

_____. *Theology of Hope*, trans. James Leitch. New York: Harper & Row, 1975.

_____. "Trends in Eschatology," in: *The Future of Creation: Collected Essays*, trans. Margaret Kohl. Philadelphia: Fortress, 1979.

_____. *Trinität und Reich Gottes: Zur Gotteslehre*. Munich: Chr. Kaiser, 1980.

Motzko, Maria. *Karl Rahner's Theology: A Theology of the Symbol*. Ph.D. diss., Fordham University, 1976.

Muck, Otto. *The Transcendental Method*, trans. Wm. Seidensticker. New York: Herder and Herder, 1968.

Müller, Klaus A. M. and W. Pannenberg. *Erwägungen zu einer Theologie der Natur*. Gütersloh: Gerd Mohn, 1970.

Neuhaus, Gerd. *Transzendentale Erfahrung als Geschichtsverlust? Der Vorwurf der Subjektlosigkeit an Rahners Begriff geschichtlicher Existenz und eine weiterführende Perspektive transzendentaler Theologie*. Düsseldorf: Patmos, 1982.

O'Callaghan, Michael. "Rahner and Lonergan on Foundational Theology," in: *Creativity and Method: Essays in Honor of Bernard Lonergan, S.J.*" ed. Matthew Lamb. Milwaukee: Marquette University Press, 1981.

O'Donovan, Leo J., ed. *A World of Grace: An Introduction to the Themes and Foundations of Karl Rahner's Theology*. New York: Crossroad, 1981.

_____. "Der Dialog mit dem Darwinismus," in: *Wagnis Theologie*, ed. Herbert Vorgrimler.

_____. "Karl Rahner, S.J., 1904-1984," in: *Journal of the American Academy of Religion* 53:1 (March 1985): 129-131.

Olive, Don. *Wolfhart Pannenberg*, in: *Makers of the Modern Theological Mind* series, ed. Bob Patterson. Waco, TX: Word Books, 1973.

Overhage, Paul. "Hominisation I. Naturwissenschaftlich," in: *Herders theologisches Taschenlexikon* 3:310-315.

———. *Das Problem der Hominisation: Über den biologischen Ursprung des Menschen*, Quaestiones disputatae 13. Freiburg: Herder, 1961.

Parker, Thomas. "Faith and History: A Review of Wolfhart Pannenberg's *Jesus - God and Man*," in: *McCormick Theological Quarterly* 22 (1968): 74ff.

Pesch, Otto. *Frei sein aus Glaube: Theologische Anthropologie*. Freiburg: Herder, 1983.

———. "'Frei sein aus Gnade:' Hinweise zu einer theologischen Anthropologie," in: *Sind wir von Natur aus religiös?*, ed. W. Pannenberg.

Peters, Ted. "Pannenberg on Theology and Natural Science," in: W. Pannenberg, *Toward a Theology of Nature*, ed. Ted Peters. Louisville: Westminster/John Knox Press, 1993.

———. "Truth in History: Gadamer's Hermeneutics and Pannenberg's Apologetic Method," in: *Journal of Religion* 55 (1975): 36-56.

Petri, Heinrich. "Die Entdeckung der Fundamentaltheologie in der evangelischen Theologie," in: *Catholica* 33:4 (1979): 241-261.

Pfüller, Wolfgang. *Zum Problem der Wissenschaftlichkeit der Theologie: Kritische Erörterung der theologisch-wissenschaftstheoretischen Positionen Gerhard Sauters und Wolfhart Pannenbergs*. Dissertation, Martin-Luther-Universität, Halle-Wittenberg, 1979.

Phan, Peter C. *Eternity in Time: A Study of Karl Rahner's Eschatology*. London: Associated University Press, 1988.

Plessner, Helmuth. *Die Stufen des Organischen und der Mensch: Einleitung in die philosophische Anthropologie* [1928]. Berlin: Walter de Gruyter, 1965.

Pöhlmann, Horst Georg. *Abriß der Dogmatik: Ein Kompendium*, 5th. ed. Gütersloh: Gerd Mohn, 1990.

Polk, David. "The All-Determining God and the Peril of Determinism," in: *The Theology of Wolfhart Pannenberg*, ed. C. Braaten and P. Clayton.

Popper, Karl. *The Logic of Scientific Discovery*. London: Hutchenson, 1968.

Puntel, Lourencino B. *Analogie und Geschichtlichkeit*. Freiburg: Herder, 1969.

———. Review of Holz' book, *Transzendentalphilosophie und Metaphysik*, in: *Philosophisches Jahrbuch* 75 (1967): 217-227.

Ratzinger, Joseph. *Das neue Volk Gottes: Entwürfe zur Ekklesiologie*. Düsseldorf: Patmos-Verlag, 1969.

———. *Theologische Prinzipienlehre: Bausteine zur Fundamentaltheologie*. Munich: Erich Wewel, 1982.

Rendtorff, Trutz, ed., *Religion als Problem der Aufklärung: Eine Bilanz aus der religionstheoretischen Forschung*. Göttingen: Vandenhoeck & Ruprecht, 1980.

———. *Theologie in der Moderne: Über Religion im Prozeß der Aufklärung*, vol. 5 in the series: *Troeltsch-Studien*. Gütersloh: Gerd Mohn, 1991.

Roberts, Louis. *The Achievement of Karl Rahner*. New York: Herder and Herder, 1967.

Rohls, Jan. "Credo ut intelligam: Karl Barths theologisches Programm und sein Kontext," in: *Vernunft des Glaubens*, ed. J. Rohls and G. Wenz.

———. *Theologie und Metaphysik: Der Ontologische Gottesbeweis und seine Kritiker*. Gütersloh: Gerd Mohn, 1987.

——— and Günther Wenz, eds. *Vernunft des Glaubens: Wissenschaftliche Theologie und kirchliche Lehre, Festschrift zum 60. Geburtstag von Wolfhart Pannenberg*. Göttingen: Vandenhoeck & Ruprecht, 1988.

Russell, Robert John. "Contingency in Physics and Cosmology: A Critique of the Theology of Wolfhart Pannenberg," in: *Zygon* 23: 1 (March 1988): 23-43.

Sauter, Gerhard. "Grundzüge einer Wissenschaftstheorie der Theologie," in: *Wissenschaftstheoretische Kritik der Theologie*, ed. G. Sauter. Munich: Chr. Kaiser, 1973.

———. "Theologie als Wissenschaft: Historisch-systematische Einleitung," in: *Theologie als Wissenschaft*, ed. G. Sauter. Munich: Chr. Kaiser, 1971.

———, ed. *Wissenschaftstheoretische Kritik der Theologie*. Munich: Chr. Kaiser, 1973.

———. "Überlegungen zu einen weiteren Gesprächsgang über 'Theologie und Wissenschaftstheorie,'" in: *Evangelische Theologie* 40 (March/April 1980): 161-168.

———. *Vor einem neuen Methodenstreit in der Theologie?* Munich: Chr. Kaiser, 1970.

Scheffczyk, Leo. *Die Theologie und die Wissenschaften*. Aschaffenburg: Pattloch Verlag, 1979.

Schleiermacher, Friedrich. *The Christian Faith* [1830], trans. H. Mackintosh, J. Steward, et al. Edinburgh: T. & T. Clark, 1986.

———. *Hermeneutik und Kritik* [1838], ed. Manfred Frank. Frankfurt/M: Suhrkamp, 1977.

———. *On Religion: Speeches to its Cultured Despisers* [1799], trans. John Oman. New York: Harper & Row, 1958.

Scholz, Heinrich. "Was ist unter einer theologischen Aussage zu verstehen?" in: *Theologie als Wissenschaft*, ed. G. Sauter.

———. "Wie ist eine evangelische Theologie als Wissenschaft möglich?" [1931] in: *Theologie als Wissenschaft*, ed. G. Sauter.

Schoonenberg, Piet. "Der Mensch in der Sünde," in: *Mysterium Salutis* II, ed. J. Feiner and M. Lohrer. 845-938.

———. *Original Sin*, trans. J.Donceel. Notre Dame: University of Notre Dame Press, 1965.

Schreiner, Peter. "Roman Catholic Theology and Non-Christian Religion," in: *Journal of Ecumenical Studies* 6 (1969): 376-399.

Schwarz, Hans. *Evil: A Historical and Theological Perspective*, trans. Mark Worthing. Minneapolis: Fortress Press, 1995.

———. *Method and Context as Problems for Contemporary Theology: Doing Theology in an Alien World*. Lewiston, NY: Edwin Mellen Press, 1991.

———. *On the Way to the Future: A Christian View of Eschatology in the Light of Current Trends in Religion, Philosophy, and Science*. Minneapolis: Augsburg, 1972.

———. *The Search for God: Christianity - Atheism - Secularism - World Religions*. Minneapolis: Augsburg, 1975.

Sheehan, Thomas. *Subjectivity and Transcendental Method as the Fundamental Groundwork of Karl Rahner's Theological Anthropology*. Ph.D. diss., Fordham University, 1971.

Solte, Ernst-Lüder. *Theologie an der Universität: Staats- und kirchenrechtliche Probleme der theologischen Fakultäten*, in: *Jus Ecclesiasticum*, v. 13. Munich: Claudius Verlag, 1971.

Stroble, Paul. "Review of Pannenberg's Systematic Theology, vol. 1," *Journal of the American Academy of Religion* 61:2 (summer 1993): 375-377.

Teilhard de Chardin, Pierre. *Man's Place in Nature: The Human Zoological Group*, trans. R. Hague. London: Collins.

———. *Mein Glaube*. Freiburg: Walter-Verlag, 1972.

Tillich, Paul. "Biblical Religion and the Search for Ultimate Reality," in: *Paul Tillich, Main Works/Hauptwerke*, ed. Carl Heinz Ratschow, vol. 4. Berlin: De Gruyter, 1987.

———. "Christianity and the Encounter of the World Religions," in: *Paul Tillich, Main Works/Hauptwerke*, vol. 5, 1988.

———. *A History of Christian Thought: From Its Judaic and Hellenistic Origins to Existentialism*, ed. Carl Braaten. New York: Simon & Schuster, 1968.

———. "The Significance of the History of Religions for the Systematic Theologian," in: *Paul Tillich, Main Works/Hauptwerke*, vol. 6, 1992.

_____. *Systematic Theology*, vol. 1. Chicago: University of Chicago Press, 1951.

_____. "Die Überwindung des Religionsbegriffs in der Religionsphilosophie," in: *Gesammelte Werke*, vol. 1. Stuttgart: Evangelisches Verlagswerk, 1959.

Timm, Hermann. *Glaube und Naturwissenschaft in der Theologie Karl Heims*. Berlin: Eckart-Verlag, 1968.

Titius, Arthur. *Natur und Gott: Ein Versuch zur Verständigung zwischen Naturwissenschaft und Theologie*. Göttingen: Vandenhoeck & Ruprecht, 1926.

Torrance, Thomas F. *Reality and Scientific Theology*. Edinburgh: Scottish Academic Press, 1985.

_____. *Space, Time and Incarnation*. London: Oxford University Press, 1969.

_____. *Theological Science*. London: Oxford University Press, 1969.

Tracy, David. *Blessed Rage for Order: The New Pluralism in Theology*. New York: Seabury, 1978.

Tripole, Martin. "Philosophy and Theology - Are They Compatible? A Comparison of Barth, Moltmann, and Pannenberg with Rahner," in: *Thought* 53:208 (March 1978): 27-54.

Troeltsch, Ernst. *Die Absolutheit des Christentums und die Religionsgeschichte* [1902]. Tübingen: J.C.B. Mohr, 1929.

_____. *Glaubenslehre, nach Heidelberger Vorlesungen aus den Jahren 1911 und 1912*, [1925] ed. Gertrud von le Fort. Aalen: Scientia Verlag, 1981.

_____. "The Place of Christianity among the World Religions" [1923], in: John Hick and Brian Hebblethwaite, eds. *Christianity and Other Religions*. Philadelphia: Fortress, 1980.

_____. "Rückblick auf ein halbes Jahrhundert der theologischen Wissenschaft," [1908] in: *Gesammelte Schriften*, vol. 2, *Zur religiösen Lage, Religionsphilosophie und Ethik*. Aalen: Scientia Verlag, 1962.

_____. "Voraussetzungslose Wissenschaft," [1897] in: *Gesammelte Schriften*, vol. 2, Aalen: Scientia Verlag, 1962.

Tupper, Frank. *The Theology of Wolfhart Pannenberg*. Philadelphia: Westminster Press, 1973.

Vorgrimler, Herbert. *Wagnis Theologie: Erfahrungen mit der Theologie Karl Rahners*. Freiburg: Herder, 1979.

Weger, Karl-Heinz. "Überlegungen zum 'anonymen Christentum," in: *Wagnis Theologie*, ed. Herbert Vorgrimler.

_____. *Karl Rahner: An Introduction to His Theology*, tr. D. Smith. New York:Seabury,1980.

Weischedel, Wilhelm. *Der Gott der Philosophen: Grundlegung einer philosophischen Theologie im Zeitalter des Nihilismus*, vol. 2. Darmstadt: Wissenschaftliche Buchgesellschaft, 1972.

Wess, Paul. *Wie von Gott sprechen?* Vienna: Verlag Styria, 1970.

White, Harvey W. "A Critique of Pannenberg's *Theology and the Philosophy of Science*," in: *Studies in Religion/Sciences Religieuses* 11:4 (fall 1982): 419-436.

Whitehead, Alfred North. "The First Physical Synthesis," in: Whitehead, *The Interpretation of Science*, ed. A.H. Johnson. New York: Bobbs-Merrill, 1961.

Wild, Wolfgang. "Vom Weltverständnis der heutigen Naturwissenschaften und seinen Konsequenzen für den Umgang mit der Welt: Ein Beitrag zum Dialog zwischen Karl Rahner und den Naturwissenschaften," in: *Vor dem Geheimnis Gottes den Menschen verstehen*, ed. Karl Lehmen. Freiburg: Katholische Akadamie, 1984.

Willems, Bonifac. *Erlösung in Kirche und Welt, Quaestiones. disp.* 35. Freiburg:Herder, 1968.

Williams, Daniel. "Response to Pannenberg," in: *Hope and the Future of Man*, ed. Ewert Cousins. Philadelphia: Fortress, 1972.

Wittgenstein, Ludwig. *Tractatus logico-philosophicus*, trans. D. Pears and B. McGuinness. London: Routledge & Kegan Paul, 1961.

Frank M. Hasel

# Scripture in the Theologies of W. Pannenberg and D. G. Bloesch
## An Investigation and Assessment of its Origin, Nature and Use

Frankfurt/M., Berlin, Bern, New York, Paris, Wien, 1996. 337 p.
European University Studies: Series 23, Theology. Vol. 555
ISBN 3-631-49264-2    pb. DM 89.--*

Scripture has always played an important role in Christian theology. This study provides an issue-oriented overview of the concepts of Scripture in Protestant theology from the 16th century Reformation onward. It then sets forth the concepts of Scripture in the theologies of two contemporary systematic theologians: W. Pannenberg and D. G. Bloesch. It analyzes, compares and evaluates the theological and anthropological presuppositions that have influenced their concept of Scripture. Despite fundamentally different starting points and other significant distinctions Pannenberg and Bloesch reveal surprising similarities. This seems to suggest that for both the concept of Scripture is determined ultimately by presuppositions that are derived and shaped *extra scripturam*.

**Contents:** Scripture in theology – a typological overview · Scripture in Pannenberg's systematic theology · Scripture in Bloesch's systematic theology · Analysis of their theological and anthropological presuppositions · Assessment and suggestions

*"Perhaps the most impressive feature of his dissertation is the thoroughness of the research, both with respect to the writings of Pannenberg and Bloesch and in terms of the broad range of theological responses to their positions as a whole as well as their views on Scripture. The author has consulted virtually every piece of writing in all the pertinent languages. The dissertation is well constructed and its arguments clearly developed. It is reader-friendly – clearly written in a style quite easy to read, ..."*
**Prof. Dr. Carl E. Braaten, Professor of Systematic Theology, Lutheran School of Theology at Chicago**

*"... Hasel's dissertation is especially noteworthy ... for its clear, balanced, accurate, and thorough going portrayal. It is the definite work on its topic ..."*
**Prof. Dr. Kenneth A. Strand, Professor Emeritus of Church History and Co-director of the Ph.D./Th.D. Programs, Andrews University, Berrien Springs**

Peter Lang ≡ Europäischer Verlag der Wissenschaften
Frankfurt a.M. • Berlin • Bern • New York • Paris • Wien
Auslieferung: Verlag Peter Lang AG, Jupiterstr. 15, CH-3000 Bern 15
Telefon (004131) 9402121, Telefax (004131) 9402131
- Preisänderungen vorbehalten - *inklusive Mehrwertsteuer